LISTENING
TO STONE

HAYDEN HERRERA

FARRAR, STRAUS AND GIROUX   NEW YORK

LISTENING TO STONE

THE ART AND LIFE OF
ISAMU NOGUCHI

Farrar, Straus and Giroux
18 West 18th Street, New York 10011

All photographs courtesy of the Isamu Noguchi Foundation and
Garden Museum, New York, unless otherwise noted.

Owing to limitations of space, illustration credits can be found on page 577.

Library of Congress Cataloging-in-Publication Data
Herrera, Hayden.
    Listening to stone : the art and life of Isamu Noguchi / Hayden Herrera.
      pages   cm
    Includes bibliographical references and index.
    ISBN 978-0-374-28116-8 (hardback) — ISBN 978-0-374-71296-9 (e-book)
    1. Noguchi, Isamu, 1904–1988.   2. Sculptors—United States—Biography.
3. Japanese American sculptors—Biography.   I. Title.

NB237.N6 H47 2015
730.92—dc23
[B]
                                                                 2014031274

Designed by Jonathan D. Lippincott

Farrar, Straus and Giroux books may be purchased for educational, business, or
promotional use. For information on bulk purchases, please contact the Macmillan
Corporate and Premium Sales Department at 1-800-221-7945, extension 5442, or
write to specialmarkets@macmillan.com.

www.fsgbooks.com
www.twitter.com/fsgbooks • www.facebook.com/fsgbooks

1   3   5   7   9   10   8   6   4   2

Frontispiece: Noguchi carving one of the marble elements for his sunken garden
at the Beinecke Rare Book and Manuscript Library at Yale, 1964

For Margot and John

CONTENTS

LISTENING TO STONE

INTRODUCTION

In the fall of 1955 Marcel Breuer, chief architect of the new UNESCO headquarters in Paris, asked Isamu Noguchi if he would design a patio for delegates. Noguchi, as was his wont, expanded the job to include an adjacent garden. The so-called Japanese Garden was a turning point in his career. Before this commission, he had, in the 1930s, been a successful portraitist, and in the 1940s his sculptures assembled out of carved and slotted stone slabs garnered the attention of critics, dealers, and museums. Early in the 1950s exhibitions and commissions in Japan made him a celebrity in his father's country. But his UNESCO garden not only brought him the renown that would lead to major public projects in the following decades, it also taught him about the kind of sculpture he wanted to make. In his autobiography Noguchi wrote: "I like to think of gardens as sculpturing of space: a beginning, and a groping to another level of sculptural experience and use: a total sculpture space experience beyond individual sculptures. A man may enter such a space: it is in scale with him; it is real."[1]

But designing this Paris garden was more than a new way of thinking about sculptural space. The two years it took Noguchi to create it were important, he said, because they had led him "deeper into Japan and into working with stone."[2] As his design progressed, he realized that with rocks he could connect the world above with the world below. He called stone "the direct link to the heart of the matter—a molecular link. When I tap it, I get an echo of that which we are. Then, the whole universe has resonance."[3] From his childhood in Japan, he knew that the rocks in gardens were more important than the plants. Rocks were a garden's bones. Emerging from the raked sand in Zen gardens, rocks were like islands rising from the sea. "The Japanese have learned that peace is established in a garden by rocks," he told an interviewer a few months before his UNESCO garden opened. "There is a lesson in humility for me as a sculptor; if the rock is better before I touch it, what is there for me to do?"[4] It was this attitude that, in the last two decades of his life, inspired Noguchi to spend just as much time listening to stone as carving it.

In April 1957 Noguchi traveled to Japan to look for stones for his garden in Paris. In Kyoto he met the master gardener Mirei Shigemori, who took him to a mountain area on the island of Shikoku on the Inland Sea. During two days of steady rain Noguchi clambered over wet boulders whose shining tops emerged from the current of a small brook deep in a ravine. When he found one that spoke to him, he let out a cheer from beneath his paper umbrella. He chose eighty rocks—altogether weighing some eighty-eight tons. They were, Noguchi said, "very bright blue, almost too beautiful . . . the ones I picked looked flat and light, so that perhaps you get the feeling that they [are] jumping about or happily enjoying themselves or dancing."[5] The stonecutters who worked with him were amazed at his avidity. He was electrified by the search. What the Japanese call "stone-fishing" became one of Noguchi's passions.

The blue stones were moved to the coast at Tokushima, where Noguchi and Shigemori spent four days moving them into an arrangement that, to Shigemori's disapproval, followed Noguchi's preconceived plan. The stones would serve to punctuate space, to direct a stroller's footsteps, and to offer surprise. From this time on, stone became his central passion. "To search the final reality of stone beyond the accident of time, I seek the love of matter. The materiality of stone, its essence, to reveal its identity—not what might be imposed but something closer to its being. Beneath the skin is the brilliance of matter."[6] Because stone is ancient and endures, it offered Noguchi a way of dealing with time's passage.

As Noguchi's enthusiasm for rock grew, he became increasingly sensitive to each stone's individuality. "Stones are like people. Some are more alive than others . . . They seem to be going, you know, at another clip."[7] Photographs of Noguchi carving or placing stones show a man immersed in an impassioned dialogue. In an essay about his work at UNESCO, he said: "My effort was to find a way to link that ritual of rocks which comes down to us through the Japanese from the dawn of history to our modern times and needs. In Japan, the worship of the stones changed into an appreciation of nature. The search for the essence of sculpture seems to carry me to the same end."[8]

1

PARENTS

When Isamu Noguchi was a boy of ten roaming the hills above the sea in Chigasaki, Japan, he searched for wild azaleas and rare blue mountain flowers to add to the primroses, violets, and daisies that already bloomed in his garden. He persuaded a local horticulturalist to give him clippings. Soon he had about fifty rosebushes irrigated by a ditch of his own devising. And, in the Japanese fashion, he placed a rock in the garden to give a feeling of weight and permanence. When he returned home from one of his plant-searching forays with muddy feet and his mother complained, he responded, "There's such fine mud on that mountain, so rich and black and slippery. I wish we had our garden full of it."[1]

Noguchi decided that when he grew up he would become a landscape gardener or a horticulturalist. Years later, looking back on his childhood, he attributed his passion to embed himself and his sculpture in nature to his early years in Japan. "Primarily," he said, "what we carry around with us is a memory of our childhood, back when each day held the magic of discovering the world. I was very fortunate to have spent my early childhood in Japan . . . one is much more aware of nature in Japan—not a vast panorama of nature but its details: an insect, a flower. Nature is very close, a foot away."[2]

Noguchi's love of gardens with moving water and carefully placed boulders would reemerge in the many gardens that he designed beginning with his 1951 Reader's Digest garden in Tokyo and ending in the 1980s with *California Scenario*, in Costa Mesa. Driven by his feeling of placelessness, Noguchi learned to invent oases for himself and others to inhabit, places where he could calm his restless energy.

Although Noguchi maintained that it was through his gardens that he came to a reverence for stone, it is clear that his love affair with rocks began when he was a child. "Stone is the fundament of the earth, of the universe," he said.[3] "We come from stone and we return to it, it is the earth itself."[4] Torn between East and West, Noguchi never felt that he belonged anywhere. He called himself a "waif," a "wanderer," a "loner." He was a person for whom fierce personal attachments were rare. Rocks, on the other hand, were something he could rely on. Cutting into them with chisel and hammer was a way of merging with the earth, making it his "place."

Noguchi's childhood in Japan formed what he called "the private side" of his being.[5] His American mother, Leonie Gilmour, was, he said, his strongest influence, and it was from her that he developed an interest in art. He described his mother as shy, reserved, and sensitive.

Leonie Gilmour

"I think I'm the product of my mother's imagination."[6] His father, Yone-jiro (Yone) Noguchi, was mostly absent. But the fact that his father was a well-known poet was something that Noguchi mentioned often with pride. In his own work Noguchi hoped to "take the essence of nature and distill it—just as a poet does."[7]

Yone Noguchi never formally married Leonie Gilmour, and lived with her and Isamu only briefly. Nevertheless, Leonie thought that her son was more like his father than he was like her. In the introductory paragraph of his autobiography, published in 1968, Isamu wrote: "With my double nationality and double upbringing where was my home? Where my affections? Where my identity? Japan or America, either, both—or the world?"[8] Twenty years later he posed the same question: "After all, for one with a background like myself the question of identity is very uncertain. And I think it's only in art that it was ever possible for me to find any identity at all."[9] But, unlike the paintings of his contemporaries, the Abstract Expressionists, Noguchi's sculptures did not explore his own identity, nor did they delve into the tumult of his subconscious. Rather, he sought to connect with the earth.

Leonie Gilmour was an extraordinarily unconventional and self-reliant woman. She was five feet three and slender with light brown, wavy hair and soft gray eyes. In photographs, wearing spectacles, she looks delicate, schoolmarmish, and charmingly Irish. Her father, Andrew Gilmour, was, according to Noguchi, an Irish Protestant who emigrated from the village of Coleraine in the far north of Ireland to America sometime in the nineteenth century. Possibly he was part of the influx of Irish immigrants fleeing the potato famine of the 1840s, although there is some evidence that he left home to escape family problems.[10] Noguchi, who knew Andrew Gilmour only through a photograph, said that he was "quite handsome, with a beard," though what impressed him most was his grandfather's intrepidness.[11] "My mother told me that he went swimming, one day in Sheepshead Bay on New Year's day." Perhaps it was his grandfather's example that prompted the adult Noguchi to terrify friends by swimming far out beyond breaking waves.

It was probably in the early 1870s that Andrew Gilmour married Noguchi's grandmother, a nurse named Albiana Smith. She was the daughter of Aaron Smith, a fairly prosperous man of Irish descent, and a mother who was descended from a French fur trader and a Cherokee woman. Leonie, the first of Albiana's two daughters, was born in New York City on June 17, 1874. Her younger sister Florence was born a few years later. Andrew and Albiana never divorced, but they did not live together for long. Andrew had two daughters about the same ages as Leonie and Florence by another woman, while Albiana brought up her daughters alone.

Leonie and Florence attended the progressive Ethical Culture School (then called the Working Man's School) founded in 1876 by the New York Society for Ethical Culture. The school emphasized the integration of manual and academic training and children were taught how to use tools, an experience that proved formative. Years later Leonie would apprentice her son to a carpenter, and, when he was thirteen, she sent him to a progressive boarding school that taught boys not just academics but also manual skills.

After Ethical Culture, Leonie went to the Bryn Mawr School, a boarding school in Baltimore founded in 1884 by five young women who believed that girls should be offered as rigorous an education as boys. The school was preparatory for Bryn Mawr College and its curriculum included modern and classical languages, science, and athletics. A superior student with a keen interest in literature, the seventeen-year-old Leonie entered Bryn Mawr College outside Philadelphia in 1891 on a full scholarship. After an early focus on chemistry, she majored in history and philosophy, and in her sophomore year she won a scholarship to the Sorbonne, where she spent a year studying French literature. Noguchi maintained that his mother translated the work of the nineteenth-century French Romantic novelist George Sand, a writer whose bold novels promulgated freedom for women.

After graduating from Bryn Mawr, Leonie lived with her mother in New York and looked unsuccessfully for editorial work. She finally took a job at Saint Aloysius Academy, a Catholic girls' school in Jersey City, where she taught Latin and French. In the evenings she struggled with her own writing. Her letters to her great friend and fellow Bryn Mawr graduate Catherine Bunnell speak of books that she was reading—works by Schiller and the poet William Young, and George Du Maurier's *Trilby*, and they hint at her own literary ambitions: "I've been thinking up the plot of a problem story this afternoon. I want to write it down tomorrow if my energies don't evaporate overnight."[12] In a joking tone, she said she hoped to get it published. Changing the subject, she said, "I got a new hat. That is, I took an old black straw hat, somewhat dingy, and with a watercolor brush and bottle of ink improved it into a suitable crowning achievement for a lady of literary and artistic tastes. A whole big bunch of cabbage roses stuck on." Other letters allude to her loneliness and to a disappointing romance.

To supplement her income Leonie sought freelance editorial jobs. Early in 1901 she answered an advertisement placed in a newspaper by Yone Noguchi, who needed someone to help him with his English writings and to type his manuscripts. Yone wrote Leonie back, giving his address as 80 Riverside Drive on Manhattan's Upper West Side:

> Miss Leonie Gilmour:
> Dear Madam: Permit me! I am a young Japanese who advertised in the Herald and received your letter. I called on your place but not finding even a person.
> I don't need any English teacher—yes, I do! I want one who can correct my English composition. Can you take such a task? I suppose that you are able, with good English and literary ability. About three pages a week. How much you charge? Pray answer me!
> Yours
> Yone Noguchi
>
> P.S. Tell me when you can see me, then we will talk about— that's better, I suppose.[13]

Leonie took the job, and within a few weeks Yone wrote to her saying how grateful he was for the work she had done. He apologized for paying her so little and asked her to work on four different manuscripts. "Am I not asking you to do too much? I am afraid I do! . . . And one more thing. I think that I will come to see you on next Sunday night. Say, about 8 o'clock. Doesn't it suit you?"[14] Despite Yone's awkward English, Leonie, a lover of poetry, was happy to participate in its creation. Though Yone's poems tended to be rhapsodic and trite, she was clearly drawn to their romanticism. A few years later she told a mutual friend: "I confess the sort of poetry I like best is that which makes me

Yonejiro Noguchi

slightly drunk—and I find ideas to be not a necessary ingredient in producing the divine intoxicant—in fact they have a sobering affect [*sic*]."[15] As the letters and manuscripts went back and forth and as their meetings became more frequent, the tone of Yone and Leonie's exchanges became less formal. Within a few weeks, he would sign a letter "Yours Jap friend, Y. N."

Yonejiro Noguchi was born in the town of Tsushima in rural central Japan on February 8, 1875, the youngest son of Denbee Noguchi, who, though he claimed Samurai descent, was a shopkeeper selling such items as geta (wooden sandals), umbrellas, and paper.[16] Upon graduating from the First Prefectural Middle School, Yone moved to Tokyo, where he attended a preparatory school for Keio Academy (later to become the prestigious Keio University). Japan, after being isolated from the world for so many years, was eager to catch up with the West, and when Yone entered Keio the curriculum emphasized Western culture. Yone practiced his English and, like many students at the time, dreamed of going to America. On November 13, 1893, the eighteen-year-old Yone left school and, with only one hundred dollars in his pocket, sailed steerage class from Yokohama to San Francisco on the steamship *Belgic*. In his autobiography Yone Noguchi recalled: "My friends saw me off at Shimbashi Station [in Tokyo]. I felt most ambitious when they wished me godspeed; but my heart soon broke down when my oldest brother, who came to Yokohama to bid me a final farewell, left me alone on the Belgic."[17]

Upon his arrival in San Francisco, Yone and a group of fellow passengers found lodging at the Cosmopolitan Hotel, where he marveled at the pleasure of the sheets and soft pillow—Japanese pillows were made of wood. He was amazed also by the splendor of Californian women: "What lovely complexions, what delightfully quick steps." American women were, to his eyes, a "revelation of freedom and new beauty." They looked, he said, like "perfectly-raised California poppies."[18]

The day after his arrival he presented a letter of introduction to a member of the Patriotic League (*Aikoku domei*), a radical group of political activists who had fled Japan and aimed to reform their country's government.[19] The league published a daily paper, *The San Francisco News* (*Soko shinbun*), and Yone was hired without pay to deliver the paper to its two hundred subscribers. Along with several other young league members he lived at the paper's O'Farrell Street office, sleeping on a table covered with newspaper. Yone found this life tough, but he was pleased to have time for reading, especially Lord Byron, his favorite author.

Before long, Yone realized that by associating with his Japanese co-workers he was not learning English. He therefore attended elementary school to improve his English and took various jobs cleaning, dishwashing, waiting on tables, and translating newspaper articles for *The San Francisco News*. After about a year he decided that he needed to resume his literary studies. A friend told him about Joaquin Miller, a well-known poet, essayist, and bohemian guru who lived in the Oakland Hills overlooking the bay. Yone climbed the hill to a small white house set in the midst of fruit trees and rosebushes. "I fell in love with the place at once . . . More than the place itself, I fell in love with Mr. Miller, whose almost archaic simplicity in the way of living and speech was indeed prophet-like."[20] To the young Yone Noguchi, the septuagenarian Miller was "the very symbol of romance and poetry." Miller had long white hair and an even longer white beard. He wore a cowboy hat and boots, a red sash for a belt, and a diamond ring, and he sometimes threw a bearskin over his shoulders. Occasionally he dressed more formally in a dark double-breasted vest and a dark felt hat. He had worked as a mining-camp cook, a lawyer, a judge, a newspaper writer, a Pony Express rider, and a horse thief (for which he was briefly incarcerated). During the Gold Rush years he moved to Northern California, lived in a Native American village, and married a Native American woman. He had a number of wives but when Yone met him he was single.

Called the "Poet of the Sierras" and the "Byron of the Rockies," Miller was the author of several books of poetry, the most famous of which was *Songs of the Sierras*, published in 1870. One of his poems, "Columbus," was memorized by schoolchildren and ended with "Sail on! Sail on! Sail on!! And on!," a line that Yone Noguchi remembered Miller reciting in a voice that "leapt like a leaping sword."[21] From 1886 until his death, in 1913, Miller lived at "The Hights" (the name he gave to his Oakland Hills home). He wrote poetry in the morning, planted trees and shrubs in the afternoon, and built monuments to General John C. Frémont, Robert Browning, and Moses. To the north of his house he built his own funeral pyre.

When Yone appeared at his door, Miller must have been charmed by the young man's handsome face with its chiseled jawline, sensuous mouth, and large, dark, sensitive-looking eyes. He invited Yone to stay in a cabin attached to his own. Instead of paying for his keep, Yone cooked breakfast and dinner and performed various odd jobs. Finally having found a home that made him happy, Yone made the decision of his life: "I secretly decided that I would become a poet."[22] He spent his mornings writing poetry and reading. Edgar Allan Poe and Walt Whitman were his favorite Americans, but he also read the great seventeenth-century haiku poet Bashō and a book about Zen Buddhism. In the afternoons he helped Miller garden and clear land. He took to heart Miller's advice to be intimate with nature and to value silence. During the four years that Yone spent at The Hights, the two men spoke very little.

In June 1896 Yone published five poems in *The Lark*, a San Francisco journal to which Joaquin Miller was also a contributor. This first entry into the world of print was for Yone "the greatest of joys, and I never felt anything like it again."[23] The following year he published his first book, *Seen and Unseen, or Monologue of a Homeless Snail.* After a period of embedding himself in nature at Yosemite, in 1897 he published a second book of poems, *The Voice of the Valley.*[24] In spite of his clumsy English and rather maudlin, hyberbolic rhetoric, his poems were well received in San Francisco literary circles. Readers were impressed that a young Japanese man was writing in English about his passionate response to nature. His work seemed delightfully exotic, a bridge between East and West.

Prompted by what he called his "mad desire to ally my soul to the heart of Nature as nakedly as possible" and "to heed the calling voice of trees, hills, waters, and skies in the distance," Yone embarked on what he called "tramp-journeys."[25] His models were Bashō, who wrote poetry while traveling by foot in northern Japan, and the eighteenth-century Anglo-Irish writer and poet Oliver Goldsmith, who liked to go "vagabondising" in Europe. Yone set out for the Yosemite Valley. After a night under the stars he wrote a poem, the first lines of which read, "Oh Repose, whose bosom harbors the heavenly dream-ships, welcome me, an exiled soul! / Thou, Forest, where Peace and Liberty divide their wealth with even a homeless convict."[26]

At the outset of his next tramp journey to Southern California, he wrote in his diary: "Silence is eloquent; the universe talks much. Solitude does not simply mean loneliness, but warm familiarity. I love the solitary life. I decided to walk along the shore all night. I wrote a poem."[27] Yone tramped to Los Angeles again in 1899. This time he seems to have left The Hights without informing friends of his plans, and one friend, Kosen Takahashi, wrote to a mutual acquaintance that Yone was his "eloping lover." He had wooed Yone "as a boy do so for a girl," Takahashi said.[28]

When Yone returned to Miller's cabin in early April 1899, he resumed work on *O'cho-san's Diary,* a book inspired by the publication of John Luther Long's *Madame Butterfly.* (Titled *The American Diary of a Japanese Girl,* it would be published two years later in three installments in *Leslie's Monthly,* and as a book in 1902.) The diary is the story of the visit to America of Miss Morning Glory, a feisty and independent girl, quite different from the stereotype of the self-abnegating Japanese woman. For help with his English prose, Yone often called upon

Blanche Partington, a cultural reporter for *The San Francisco Call*. On July 12, 1898, he had written Blanche: "I am writing on O'cho-san's Diary more and more. I wish therefore, you will work on with it when you got back to your home, for the preparation to make it appear in some newspaper."[29] But his relationship with Partington was fraught. Yone could be demanding and childish if he did not get his way, and as Partington tired of his whining, she tried to extricate herself from his demands.

Though he enjoyed California, Yone knew that to establish a literary reputation, acceptance in Manhattan counted for more than success in San Francisco. In May 1900 he headed east, traveling by train first to Chicago, where he stayed for about a month, working on essays about his impressions of the city commissioned by *The Evening Post*. He then moved on to New York, which he described to Partington as a "monster with the head of Goddess and the four legs of animal . . . New York is the warmest heart like a mother, and is the coldest like a razer [*sic*]."[30] This seems to have been his last letter to Partington until four years later, when he passed through San Francisco on his way home to Japan. Within six months of his arrival in New York, he had found Leonie Gilmour, who could take over Partington's editorial role.

A few days after Yone arrived in Manhattan he was pickpocketed and wrote a friend of Joaquin Miller's for a loan. Charles Warren Stoddard, once part of California's literary bohemia, was a gay poet best known for his collections of homoerotic stories recalling his sojourns in the South Sea Islands, *South-Sea Idyls* (1874), and for *The Island of Tranquil Delights* (1904). He liked to befriend very young men and was always in search of what he called a "Kid."[31] "I am so much downhearted," Yone wrote, "Help me! Will you? Help me!"[32] Stoddard sent ten dollars and in August Yone went to Washington, D.C., to meet Stoddard for the first time. Although the forty-seven-year-old Stoddard wrote in his diary that he had been disappointed that Yone had not turned up wearing a kimono, he was smitten.[33] When Yone returned to New York after a stay of several weeks in Stoddard's "Bungalow," he wrote to his host: "My dear Charlie. How rare your sweet magnetism! Your breath so soft and impressive like Autumn rain! Your love—thank God! so heavenly!"[34] Turn-of-the-century letters often suggest a sexual intimacy between same-sex correspondents when in fact the writer is merely expressing fondness. Yone did, however, avow in an article about

Stoddard's "Bungalow" published in *The National Magazine* that he sometimes slept with Stoddard. In New York, Yone took a room at 80 Riverside Drive and then moved to a Japanese boardinghouse at 41 East Nineteenth Street. He spent the next year finishing his *Diary of a Japanese Girl*, which would be published as a book by Frederick A. Stokes. A year and a half after his first visit to Washington, D.C., Yone sent Stoddard a photograph of himself, to which Stoddard waxed euphoric, calling him his baby. "I must nurse you well, and take such very, very good care of you."[35] Another of Stoddard's letters said he wanted to hold Yone in his lap and fondle him and at night he would embrace him, "the two of us upon the one pillow . . . Now come, place your lips to mine in one long rapturous kiss!"

Yone Noguchi's apparently amorous relationships with men did not preclude heterosexual interests. It was probably late in 1901, a few months after Leonie began working for him, that he met and fell in love with the twenty-five-year-old Ethel Armes, a cultural reporter for *The Washington Post*. Although he could have asked Ethel to edit his work, he continued sending it to Leonie. His letters to her comment (most often favorably) on his own writing, but he insisted that she be frank in her evaluations of his efforts: "Say, Leonie, cut it short if you want! Change words if they don't fit properly . . . Don't be afraid."[36]

Leonie, it appears, also took to asking Yone for advice on her own work. When in 1901 she sent him one of her stories, he told her it was too realistic. "Your story . . . has not much value, I declare."[37] He also objected to her story's moral position; it had defended a divorced woman who planned to remarry: "I don't think that people can change husband or wife as if with socks or underwear."

Around this time he told Leonie of a story he had written about the misery of an American woman married to a Japanese man. "Crow should be in comradeship with crow," he wrote. Perhaps Yone was trying to warn Leonie not to become infatuated with him. But Leonie was more and more drawn to Yone, whom she admired as a poetic creature whose physical beauty, boyish charm, and evident need for her were no doubt seductive. Nonetheless, they continued to quarrel. In a letter of September 10, 1901, Yone wrote, "Dear Leonie. Please don't! Let us laugh!" Three weeks later they have had yet another contretemps. Apparently he had lost his temper with her—like his son Isamu, Yone was prone to flashes of rage. Perhaps to placate Leonie and to keep her working on his manuscripts, he encouraged her to send one of her stories to *Red Book*.[38] Probably the chief cause for her pique was that he had told her that their relationship was no different from his relationship with his male companions—an ungallant assertion, to be sure.

Yone had been in Rochester, New York, for several months when he wrote to Leonie in September 1902 saying that he planned to return to New York City in October and then to go on to London. There he took up lodgings with Yoshio Makino, a Japanese artist friend who lived in southwest London, and, having failed to find a publisher for his poetry, he decided to self-publish *From the Eastern Sea*, a sixteen-page pamphlet of eight poems. Makino designed the cover and Yone sent his slim volume to people such as William Butler Yeats, Laurence Binyon, and William Michael Rossetti. Rossetti made some minor revisions to Yone's text and wrote him that the poems were "full of a rich sense of beauty, and of ideal sentiment."[39] Binyon wrote that the book had "an atmosphere of beauty and suggestion which is peculiar to itself and unlike anything we have already."[40] Thanks to the favorable critical response, the University Press published an expanded version of the book, which Yone dedicated to Stoddard. Just before Christmas he received a letter from Ethel Armes telling him that she was engaged and that Yone should not have abandoned her. Meanwhile Stoddard continued to write, discouraging Yone from marrying Ethel and applauding his literary success. With people like Algernon Charles Swinburne and Rossetti praising him, Stoddard said, Yone's fame was certain to be instant, like Lord Byron's.

Back in the United States, Yone's relationship to Leonie remained businesslike, but there were signs of increasing intimacy. "Are you deadly tired of me?" he asked in a teasing letter. "I am something like a jellyfish which has no head and tail. I don't know what I am going to do . . . (Anyhow, what's the matter with you?) You are quite blue, aren't you? Come, now, it's awfully foolish to be blue."[41] He was, he said, planning to go to Japan. Most likely this was the cause of Leonie's sadness. Instead of departing, he made a promise of a permanent bond with Leonie. On November 18, 1903, he wrote one line on a page from a notebook: "I declare that, Leonie Gilmour is my lawful wife."[42] Perhaps she required such a vow before they became lovers.

After this marriage delaration, Leonie appears to have moved in with him at his apartment at 121 West Sixty-fourth Street. Their cohabitation probably lasted about half a year. (There are no letters from him to her during this period.) In February she became pregnant, but neither this nor his "marriage" to Leonie prompted Yone to end his relationship with Ethel. Indeed in June 1904, when Leonie was four months pregnant, he wrote to Stoddard that he was still planning to marry Ethel. On August 3, 1904, Yone left New York, traveling by train first to Birmingham, Alabama, where he stayed with Ethel's family for four days, and from there to San Francisco, where he boarded the *Manchuria* bound for Japan. He appears to have had little regret at leaving the six-months-pregnant Leonie behind.

From the Japanese point of view, Yone, having conquered the literary worlds of the West, could come home in triumph. In January 1905 he wrote to Stoddard that he was being feted with numerous receptions and that Ethel would soon join him. "We—I and Ethel—will work together and hard as possible, and build an ideal home, and then you will come. What a dream!"[43] Still, Yone did not earn much money. He discovered that it was not possible for him to write and publish in Japanese. The Japanese saw Yone as too Westernized both in his writing and in his person. "With blue eyes and features like those of a foreigner it is hard to think of him as being Japanese at all," wrote the well-known poet Sakutaro Hagiwara.[44] "I have no confidence in either language," Yone admitted years later in a poem. "In other words, I guess I am a dual citizen."[45] Similarly, Isamu Noguchi would say that he belonged nowhere and was a citizen of the world.

2

DEAR BABY

W hen Leonie's pregnancy became visible, her mother, Albiana, moved to Los Angeles to find a place for Leonie to live until the baby was born. Leonie soon followed, and in time her sister Florence joined them. At first Leonie and Albiana lived on East First Street in downtown Los Angeles. From there the eight-months-pregnant Leonie wrote to Catherine Bunnell on October 30, 1904, that she was busy sewing and reading and that their home had a garden with roses and vegetables and a view of a green cemetery and of "hills and cottages and gardens set off against the far away mountains like a picture hung on the wall before you."[1] Of Yone she wrote: "It may be I shall not see him again. I have a fancy as if he were a bird that flew through my room and is vanished."

Her abandonment pained Leonie more than she would admit. Years later, in a letter to her daughter Ailes, who was in despair over a failed love affair, Leonie revealed how much she had suffered at the loss of a love: "One of the strangest phenomena of life is a sudden violent love affair . . . they come and go—leaving the poor victim powerless to keep themselves . . . Then too—one idealizes the beloved beyond all semblance of fact—& when disappointment & disillusion come, life is too terrible—one hardly has the strength to go on. I know only too well. What an ecstasy of joy—being in love brings—but it is as unstable and evanescent as the froth of champagne."[2]

Isamu Noguchi was born on November 17, 1904, at the Los Angeles County Hospital, a charity hospital, which was all Leonie could

afford. When she registered she gave her name as "Mrs. Yone Noguchi." Ten days later the headline of an article in the *Los Angeles Herald*
ran: "Yone Noguchi's Babe Pride of Hospital. White Wife of Author
Presents Husband With Son."[3] A photograph showed the infant Isamu
swaddled in the arms of a hospital nurse. His eyes seem to look out at
the world with wonder. The text read:

> "Kawaii Kota [*sic*]," meaning dear baby, are the words which Yone
> Noguchi, the author of "The American Diary of a Japanese Girl,"
> begins his book, and out at the county hospital the story of an-
> other little life has begun, and the little son which has been
> born to the wife of the author and poet, is just such another
> baby as the one described by him in the first page of his book.
>   The young man gives promise of being in every way a fine
> specimen of the kind that is holding the attention of the whole
> civilized world. [The Russo-Japanese War of 1904–05 was
> making headlines at this time.] In spite of the fact that baby was
> born under the flag of Uncle Sam and that his mother is an
> American woman, of the blue eyed type, he has not a single trace
> of anything but Japanese and the hair and eyes are as black as
> his father's ever were. Out at the hospital he is quite the center
> of attraction and the nurses have endowed him with the name of
> "Bobbie" for lack of a better one. He is exhibited on all occasions
> and there is no treat the son of the illustrious poet can not have
> for the asking.[4]

After Isamu was born, Leonie and her mother moved to a tent village
outside of Pasadena where, with money from Florence's savings from
her salary at the *Encyclopedia Britannica*, they purchased a plot of land
and lived in a tent. For Albiana, Leonie arranged for the construction
of a one-bedroom shack. Leaving Isamu in the care of her mother,
Leonie found work first as a typist at the Los Angeles Chamber of
Commerce and then as a stenographer and assistant bookkeeper at an
iron foundry.[5] Years later Noguchi mused about his birth: "I suspect
that I was an accident, unexpected and inconvenient."[6] But in her letters to Catherine Bunnell, Leonie spoke adoringly of the child she
called "baby" while waiting for Yone to give him a Japanese name. On
New Year's Day 1905 she wrote to thank Catherine for her Christmas

presents: "Baby has tried on his shoes and he thinks they will fit nicely about the time he gets ready to wear shoes. At present he keeps his feet tucked away in his petticoat. They are very pretty (feet and shoes) Wish I had a decent picture to send. That newspaper picture [in the *Los Angeles Herald*] is rank injustice. He's a sweet pretty boy. Don't know just who he looks like. At first he had a decided resemblance to his daddy, but it's wearing off. He has a funny little Irish-Japanese smile that would do your heart good to see."[7]

In April 1905 Leonie received the first (extant) letter from Yone since he had returned to Japan, indeed, the first letter since his declaration of marriage. He began: "I received your letter of March 10th and I am glad Baby is all right." He then launched into the one subject that seemed to matter to him: her work on his manuscripts and her efforts to sell his writings. Yone sent Leonie articles to be edited and she sent them on to be published by their friend Frank Putnam. "And you take some money out, and send me the rest," he instructed.[8] Often in his correspondence with Leonie, he complained about being poor.

Yone's April letter to Leonie does not mention his personal travails. He had hoped that Ethel would arrive in Japan in March and that they would be married. But a female reporter for the *Los Angeles Herald* told Ethel about Yone's affair with Leonie and Isamu's birth. Ethel was outraged. In an undated letter to Stoddard, she wrote: "I haven't been able—literally to write a sane line since it all happened. Her name is Leonie Gilmour or Gilman and I believe she goes as Mrs. Noguchi . . . She says—you know—that Yone lived with her the year—all that year he was writing to me & we were engaged—she says he was married to her all that time. I heard from him a few weeks ago & he says he lived with her one week only & that she lies. I do not think she lies . . . You can give me your impression at least. But it makes no difference—there is the child—his treatment of that woman."[9]

No sooner had Ethel broken off their engagement than Yone turned to Leonie and asked her to come to Japan. His April letter said: "Of course, you know, Leonie, you are wiser. You do what you think right and good. I cannot pursuade [*sic*] you, this matter especially you know." Leonie's reaction to the news of Yone's involvement with Ethel was forgiving. Meanwhile, Yone wrote to Stoddard as if the crisis caused by the women finding out about each other was trivial: "Did Ethel write to you about the Los Angel's [*sic*] woman? It is not so black with me as you may fancy. Don't trouble yourself with that matter, pray. I will settle it myself. And in fact it was all settled—a long time ago."[10] He begged Stoddard to come to Japan, assuring him that all he would have to pay for was his steamship passage. His house at 81 Hisakata, Koishikawa, was, he said, about a mile from the center of Tokyo. It was surrounded by trees and flowers and had two servants. "Will you come over? I will treat you like a Lord . . . no money is necessary, after your arrival in Japan I make money enough for myself, and besides for somebody else . . . come over here, and live with me—can't you?"

Leonie's letters to Catherine suggest that her longing for Yone was counterbalanced by her delight in motherhood. "First Baby is growing fast and fair. I named him Yosemite, but his papa has not condescended to set the seal of his august approval thereon. He says: 'I will send some good name soon. I am pondering upon it.' And he still continues to allude to his lordship as IT." The baby, she told Catherine, could walk and "say whole lots of things. He has a lively temper. When he gets mad he jumps up and down so hard I'm afraid he'll injure his feet."[11]

 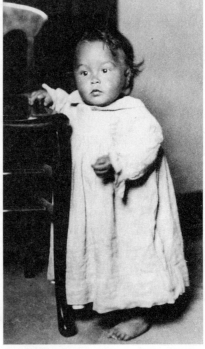

Isamu, aged about nine months, in his native California

That fall, Leonie planted a vegetable garden. A photograph of Isamu at about age one shows him standing near a tomato plant and wearing a dress that reaches his ankles but exposes his bare feet.[12] The fourteen-month-old Isamu was, Leonie wrote to Catherine, a "wonderful conversationalist, singer, actor, storyteller, climber, dancer, jumper, and general stirrer-up of things."[13] Time spent at her desk, she said, had been productive. "The *National Magazine* printed the third of the series of my Mirabel and Dousabel stories this month. I wrote another a few days ago which I like better than the others." Meanwhile the correspondence between Yone and Leonie grew more heated as Yone alternated between urging her to join him in Japan and dissuading her from coming, usually because of his lack of money. In February 1906, Leonie came to a decision: she and "Baby" would be better off staying in California.

> Listen! America is a good country, California in particular. Baby is well. He is happy. Tho' we be poor, he does not suffer from it. Maybe our way of living is not quite civilized—We live in a tent, where rains and wind come in at will—Baby has no shoes on his feet. He runs free as a squirrel on the hillside. Does it matter, our way of life? Roses are glowing on his cheeks. We built a little California house of one room beside the tent. There my mother lives. And there I took Baby in on the day it was finished. He was like a caged bird eagerly looking to door and windows for a way to escape . . . And education. Education is free here. I do not think much of "school" myself. I could myself teach him everything he would learn in school.[14]

Leonie acknowledged that as far as the aesthetic side of life Japan might have more to offer, but insisted that Isamu would do just as well in an American art school. She was concerned that if she and Isamu lived in Japan, Yone's work would suffer:

> But how about your poetry? Where will you find it? In business? In the crowding cares and responsibilities? In the companionship of a wife you *do not love*? You shut love out of your life— human love, which is also divine. Why? Because Frank Putnam thinks you should? Because of awakened thoughts of responsibility toward your boy? Maybe you think you will make amends

for the past. Past is past. You cannot *amend* it. Maybe you think we, Baby and I, need you. We do not.

Therefore I think it better we live apart. If I have chance to have work in Southern Japan someday I will come. And you can see Baby all you like. And we will have proper separation when you get ready—and you will remarry according to your better and riper judgment. Baby and I have each other to love. Yes, that's better.[15]

Despite her decision, Leonie was ambivalent. She wrote to Frank Putnam: "Honestly I do love Yone . . . simply I wish to do what is the very best thing and for once in my life I believe I have decided wisely. It is a relief to have a thing definitely decided anyway. Really I am not 'good enough' for him."[16]

Yone's letters to Leonie in the following months reveal his diminishing enthusiasm for her coming to Tokyo. "Is your decision firm like a rock?" he wrote on April 2. "I know that you are wise always. And Baby is too little, and I am afraid that he will soon turn to be a little Jap boy. I really think that California is a better place to educate one and raise aprightly [*sic*] . . . I am glad Baby is doing nicely. He will be a great boy, I am sure." Undisclosed in these letters is Yone's new affair with one of his servants, the seventeen-year-old Matsuko Takeda, whom he would marry six years later after they already had several children together. Nonetheless, Yone continued to expect Leonie to serve as his American editor and agent.

In the meantime, Leonie continued to write and submit her own stories to Putnam. To supplement her income she was "picking flowers for the market," typing and revising a manuscript for a young Greek playwright, and "cudgeling my brain for thoughts upon the subject of 'Engaged Girls' in answer to a most polite request from 'Good House-keeping.'" The thirty-one-year-old Leonie concluded her letter to Putnam on a wistful note: "The days are flying away—carrying my youth, alas! Some gray hairs are shining among my brown."[17]

Despite Yone's dissuasion and Leonie's April letter declaring that she would remain in California, Leonie reversed her decision that fall, and decided to go to Japan. She wrote to Stoddard on December 6 that she was going as soon as they had enough money. "I am going to make a little Japanese boy out of my son."[18] Yet she knew that Yone could not be counted on as a husband or father: "I quite agree with you," she wrote to Putnam, "that poets—at least some of them—were not made for domestic uses. So I shall open the door of the cage as soon as I get over there."[19]

Leonie's decision to go to Japan may have been prompted by California's change in attitude toward Japanese immigrants. Americans had been pro-Japanese during the Russo-Japanese war, but Japan's postwar expansionism in China met with American disapproval, especially in California. Already in 1905 a law prohibiting marriage between Caucasians and "negroes" or "mulattoes" had been amended to include "Mongolians." The influx of Japanese laborers incited angry protests in some San Francisco labor unions, and the press was full of alarmist talk of the "Yellow Peril." In 1906 the San Francisco school board ordered the children of Japanese immigrants to attend segregated schools. California farmers established the Asiatic Exclusion League and orange growers around Pasadena set up signs saying that no Japanese or Chinese would be hired.[20] For a mother with fierce pride in her son, who wanted to protect him from the sting of racial prejudice, these changes were surely disheartening.

The last letter to Putnam that Leonie posted in the United States was written on January 23, 1907. She said she planned to leave soon, but she was still "pegging away" at her typewriter, writing the sequel to what she called her "tent story," which had been published in the December issue of *West Coast Magazine* and was titled "A Little California House."[21] Isamu, she said, "talks wisely about going on a big ship on the great wa-wa to see Papa. If you ask him what is a ship he smiles knowingly or points to a shadowy corner, saying 'see, cunning little ship!' He has the art of never being surprised or taken unawares. The funniest thing about telling a funny story before him is that he always laughs loudly before you get to the point of the story." About joining Yone in Tokyo, she said: "Am I glad or sorry? Really, I don't know. Call no man happy until he is dead . . . Yone's letters are ominous, to say the least. He warns me not to bring any 'dreams' with me. Oh, well, I am tired of trying to do anything with him. I guess Baby Bob and I will take care of each other."

3

TOKYO

Leonie booked steerage-class passage on the *Mongolia*, a Pacific Mail Steamship Company vessel, and on March 9, 1907, she and Isamu left Los Angeles bound for Japan via San Francisco. There were 1,400 third-class passengers, mostly Chinese laborers, crammed into the lower decks. Leonie and Isamu had a small cabin under the boiler room.[1] For most of the seventeen-day trip, Isamu lay seasick in his baby carriage. When the ship docked at Yokohama, not far from Tokyo, on March 26, Yone was there to meet them. "The arrival of my two-year-old boy, Isamu, from America was anticipated as it is said here, with crane-neck-long longing. This Mr. Courageous [the Japanese ideograph for Isamu means "brave"] landed in Yokohama on a certain Sunday afternoon of early March . . ."[2] Hitherto called Baby, Bob, or Yo, Noguchi was finally given the name Isamu.

Yone boarded the ship and found his way to Leonie and the baby's cabin. In his autobiography, published in London in 1914, he described the calm, yellow sunlight that lit the carriage in which lay the "little handful of a body" of his half-asleep son. "Now and then he opened a pair of large brown eyes. 'See papa'; Léonie tried to make Isamu's face turn to me; however, he shut his eyes immediately without looking at me, as if he were born with no thought of a father . . . I thought, however, that I could not blame him after all for his indifference to father, as I did not feel, I confess, any fatherly feeling till, half an hour ago."[3]

As Yone and Leonie pushed Isamu's carriage toward the train and then home, Yone realized how everything must seem strange to Isamu, the street sounds, the language, the way people looked, and the melancholy clacking of wooden geta on the pavement. Leonie was cold and exhausted. Isamu was pale and thin, and Yone wondered what had happened to the plump baby that Leonie had described. Isamu was quiet but not peaceful: "Now and then he opened his big eyes, and silently questioned the nature of the crowd which, though it was dark, gathered round us here and there." A white woman pushing a baby carriage containing a not-quite Japanese-looking child was a curious sight. "In no more than the dying voice of an autumn insect, Baby suddenly asked mother where was his home."

For the next several days Isamu kept crying. "It tried my patience very much," Yone recalled, "and I did not know really what to do with him. He cried on seeing the new faces of the Japanese servant girls, and cried more when he was spoken to by them." He kept on crying when Yone gave him a present of a Japanese toy dog made of cotton. "My earliest memories are not happy," Noguchi wrote years later, "nor do I think back on my later childhood as being particularly so in spite of Japan being a child's paradise."[4]

On his fifth day in Tokyo, Isamu told his mother that he wanted to go home to his grandmother in Pasadena. "Where's Nanna?" he asked. "Far, far," said Leonie. Isamu repeated her words several times and then turned white and silent. To cheer him up Leonie said, "Baby, go and see papa." Isamu moved toward Yone's room and slid the *shoji* open a crack, but when his father turned to look at him he shut it quickly and ran to Leonie crying, "No, no!" Yone heard Isamu tell Leonie that his father was not there. "I must have appeared to his eye as some curiosity, to look at once in a while, but never to come close to. However, I was not hopeless; and I thought that I must win him over, and then he would look at me as he did his mother."

No matter how hard Leonie tried to create a bond between Isamu and Yone, Isamu was his mother's child. His father remained a distant figure, probably more so as the months went on and Yone's double life became more embroiled. His common-law wife Matsuko became pregnant the month that Leonie and Isamu arrived. The demands of two households must have been anathema to a man as self-absorbed as Yone, a man who longed for solitude and to "live in poetry."

In the beginning Yone did try to fulfill his promise to Leonie to be a good father. He was amused that when he clapped his hands for the servants, Isamu would come running and kneel before him just like the housemaids. "I was much pleased to see that he was growing familiar with me. And he even attempted to call me 'Danna-Sama' (Mr. Lord), catching the word which the servants respectfully addressed to me. It was too much, I thought; however, I could not help smiling delightedly at it." Leonie and Yone may have exacerbated Isamu's cultural confusion. "You Japanese baby?" Leonie asked, and Isamu turned to his father and said yes. When Yone asked him if he would like to remain an American, he turned to his mother and said yes.

Soon after arriving in Tokyo, Leonie wrote to Putnam about what it was like joining the "husband" whom she had not seen in almost three years. "Yone and I don't fight, but as far as happiness with a capital H, why I fear we are both too selfish as you say. Yone changed so much I would hardly have known him—especially in the shape of his nose and the acquisition of a moustache. Yone seems to like the Boy tho' he doesn't approve of his manners which have suddenly flowered into a sort of wild Indian Savagery amazing and dismaying. (For much attention has turned his little head.) Everybody calls him 'Bo-chan' which is Baby-Lord, and I tell you he lords it over them." She was lonely, she said, especially because she did not speak Japanese, and her usual independence was thwarted by the difficulty of finding her way around Tokyo's tangled unpaved streets."[5]

Noguchi's memories of his childhood were vague: "It's difficult to piece together what was my childhood," he told an interviewer in 1988.[6] "My clearest recollection is of riding on somebody's back and being fondled and enjoying myself immensely. There was a bamboo fence, I remember, and I would peer across it, and this was, you might say, my one clear recollection, of, you might say, happiness—of having finally found a situation of security. I think my feeling towards Japan comes from this very initial sort of relief that I felt of being safe and on 'terra firma,' coming across the ocean on a shaky boat must have been unpleasant for me." Yet he recalled that insecurity was "a fixed part" of his childhood. The open space of a playground on a hill near his father's house, for example, filled him with foreboding. When cherry blossoms fell and scattered soon after he arrived in Tokyo he was saddened.[7] "Things which are so far back are not like a part of myself, more like the life of somebody else," he wrote in his autobiography. "To me it all seemed like chance. Choice, if any, came much later."[8]

As the weeks went by the scrawny toddler that Yone had welcomed in Yokohama turned into a plump, healthy boy. He came to love Japanese food. After eating breakfast with his parents he would go into the kitchen and share a second breakfast of rice with the servants. He also liked wheat gluten candy made in the shapes of animals. Every morning the candy salesman would walk along the street beating a drum to advertise his wares. "Donko, don, donko, don, don," Isamu would cry in imitation of the drumbeat. He would then insist that one of the servant girls carry him on her back with his bottom perched on her obi (a wide sash worn with a kimono), as is customary for Japanese children.

Isamu quickly picked up Japanese words and customs: when a guest departed he would call *"Sayonara,"* and when an uncle gave him an American and a Japanese flag he shouted *"Banzai!"* Soon he ventured out beyond the garden to play blindman's buff with the neighborhood children who at first had looked at him as an oddity. When children

 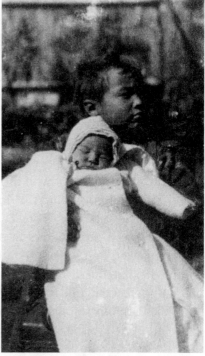

Isamu in Tokyo, aged about five (*left*); holding his half-sister, Ailes, 1912 (*right*)

passed the house they would shout "Baby san," thinking that was Isamu's name.

Isamu played with any household object that he could move. He kept on sliding the *shoji* open and shut and Yone had to hide the clocks because Isamu would wind them so tight that they no longer functioned. In the evenings as he sat with his parents, he enjoyed chasing their shadows. When his own shadow vanished behind another shadow he looked downcast. "Go to papa!" Leonie would then say. "He will give it to you." Isamu would poke and prod his father's kimono in search of his shadow until Yone would say, "There it is, Baby," and would move aside to let his son's shadow reappear on the wall.[9]

Although Isamu often tried his father's patience, Yone indulged him. Whenever Yone passed a store he would look to see if there was something that he could buy for Isamu. If Isamu delayed his bedtime by insisting on seeing the moon, Yone would hang a lamp with a blue globe on the other side of a *shoji* screen and Isamu would soon be contentedly asleep. "Any child," Yone noted, "appears wonderful to his father; so is Isamu to me. I confess that I made many new discoveries of life and beauty since the day of his arrival in Japan."[10]

By the time these memories of Isamu's early Tokyo days were published, Isamu was ten and had been living apart from his father for many years. Yone's visits were rare. Noguchi told an interviewer, "Our family really had no cohesion. I should hardly say 'our family' because I did not belong to his family."[11] Not only did Yone have another family he was attending, but also he took weekly sojourns in Kamakura, a seaside town about an hour southeast of Tokyo that was once Japan's capital city and is famous for its many Buddhist temples. Yone would repair to one of the largest, Engaku-ji, a beautiful Zen Buddhist monastery founded in the thirteenth century that is spread over a vast area and comprises many subsidiary temples. Yone's routine was to teach at Keio University two days a week and then spend the rest of the time in Kamakura, away from the mundane demands of his two families. In 1910 he published a compilation of his poetry and essays called *Kamakura*, in which he wrote about his pleasure in the monastery's gift of solitude and in the calming Buddhist rituals.[12] On May 19, 1907, less than two months after Leonie and Isamu's arrival in Tokyo, Yone wrote to Charles Stoddard from his temple retreat: "Yesterday, my boy Isamu and Mrs. Noguchi were here, making some noise; and last night, they returned home in Tokyo, leaving me in my beloved Silence without which I cannot exist."[13]

With Yone's help, Leonie found pupils who wanted to learn English. In July 1907 she wrote to Catherine Bunnel thanking her for sending a sponge cake recipe and telling her a little about her students—a lieutenant, a professor of electrical engineering, and a banker. Leonie also planned, starting in September, to teach two mornings a week in a small girls' school run by a Mrs. Sakurai. About Isamu, she reported that he was picking up Japanese quickly but that she herself was not.[14]

The winter of 1907–08 was difficult for Leonie. When Yone and Matsuko's daughter Hifumi was born that December, Yone registered her birth. But he never registered Isamu, and when he had a son in 1909 he listed him in the household register as his firstborn son. Presumably Leonie was ignorant of these births, but Yone was less and less attentive to her and to Isamu. On February 26, 1908, Leonie wrote to Putnam: "I felt generally miserable in my innards this winter—too cold."[15] Japanese houses had no central heating—a brazier was the only source of heat, and the paper *shoji* panels did little to keep out the cold. "I'm homesick for the country—Japanese country, American country, any country where there are fields and blossoms and breezes and unscented by city odors. And a garden. I'm just crazy to dig. But we are shut up in Tokyo, and likely to remain so for the rest of our natural lives, unless we happily die young . . . And poor Baby! 'What are you doing baby?' I called out, seeing him holding his wooden geta, with trowel in hand. 'Nothing, mama, nothing,' he answers. 'Nothing to dig.'"

On March 13, 1908, Leonie wrote to Catherine: "I have had only one week's vacation from teaching since I came here. That was last summer. And in spite of my best endeavors I can earn only some 85 yen a month, with which it is not easy to keep house, keep a girl to take Isamu to school, keep us all in clothes and shoes, and send 20 to mama every month. It takes as hard work to earn that 85 yen as to earn as many dollars in America, but it doesn't go nearly as far since most of the staples, bread, butter, sugar, chocolate, oatmeal etc are imported from America." Yone contributed part of his salary to help with household expenses, but in general, Leonie said, she was "footing it alone here. Yone in his temple in Kamakura is happily oblivious of the cares and worries of this sordid world. There he spends his time sleeping, smoking, writing divine *poetry*, emerging twice a week to lecture at Keio College."[16]

In spring 1908 Leonie and Isamu moved to 90 Myogadani Street in the Koishikawa district, "a tiny little house on a hilltop close by a grove of tall trees where a Ho Ho! Kikyo! (nightingale) sings to me daily."[17] She also reported to Catherine that Yone was back in Kamakura. "He has engaged a room in a temple where he can write in peace, far from the madding crows of Baby and me. Incidentally this leaves me in something like your idea of earthly bliss—a little house, one pretty little maid servant, and nobody to bother. Isamu thrown in for good measure. I'm quite enjoying it. Chance to get some work done. That means typing Yone's new book chiefly, with teaching, housework etc—thrown in. Really awfully busy."

In July Leonie and Isamu spent two weeks at the seashore at Yaidzu in Shizuoka, where they were invited by Leonie's friend Setsu Koizumi, the widow of Lafcadio Hearn, an American Japanophile writer who had taught English literature at Tokyo Imperial University. Hearn and Koizumi's two older sons had been Leonie's pupils since the previous autumn. Their two younger children were eight and five, young enough to be Isamu's playmates. Yone, who had just finished writing a book about Hearn, was impressed that Leonie was staying in a house where Hearn had spent his summers.[18] Noguchi remembered: "My mother used to take me along with her to call on people. Among them was the family of Lafcadio Hearn, whose children she taught for a while. The Hearn family lived in Okubo and had a beautiful garden. Thus cautiously did I come to know the world."[19]

On June 13, 1909, Leonie wrote to Catherine about how independent and full of curiosity four-and-a-half-year-old Isamu was. "He is everything to me," she said.[20] She noted her son's attraction to mechanical things and to nature, two interests that would persist in his adult life and that would greatly affect his art. Testifying to his interest in nature and in working the earth, a neighbor reported, "One day Isamu-san covered the whole front gate of the house with gobs of mud. I didn't actually see him do that but I did see the gate completely covered with mud when I passed by. His mother did not scold him at all. Without fussing she simply had the maid clean the gate off with water."[21]

The following April Leonie took a part-time job teaching English at the Kanagawa Prefecture Girls' Higher School in Yokohama.[22] She wrote to Catherine on November 3, 1910, that at his school Isamu had made a sketch of the sea that he called "Ibariken by Moonlight." It was so subtle that "you had to look hard to see anything on the paper—and then you perceived some faint blue lines representing the waves of the sea, with a few pale yellow sails on it."[23] He had, she said, decided to become an artist instead of a soldier. "'Why?' said I. 'Because' said he 'all the soldiers got to die, and I don't want to die. Even a general has to die.'" She told Catherine that because the commute to her teaching job was too long, she was thinking of moving once again and had found for Isamu a private kindergarten that had just been opened by a man named Morimura. It had "Goats, chickens, monkey, peacock, sea-saws, swings etc. Very small, very high-toned, a trifle expensive . . . Isamu says he likes it 'because it is such a beauty garden.'"

When she next wrote Catherine on December 23 Leonie and Isamu had moved to a small house surrounded by fields in Omori on the southern edge of Tokyo. Omori was on the water, but their hilltop house looked inland toward Mount Fuji. Of her life with six-year-old Isamu, she reported that they had been to the Russian Circus: "Isamu was in ecstasies. There was one man Mr. B—famous horse trainer. Isamu whispered to me: 'He is a _Great Man!_' Poor little Isamu. His hero worship is strangely placed. He told his papa the other day that he hoped to become a great man some day, but that he could not become so great as mama. Tonight he is busy making a book. His cheeks are red red roses. I think the country air does him good."[24]

Isamu's year at the Morimura School was happy. Compared to most Japanese schools it was progressive. It valued individualism and the students did not wear uniforms. A photograph taken in 1911 of Isamu's graduating class shows six boys and four girls. Behind them stand the staff of nine women and one man, who may be Mr. Morimura. Isamu is the smallest boy and the only child who holds his rolled-up diploma to his mouth as if it were a flute. On the first page of his autobiography Noguchi wrote: "My first recollection of joy was going to a newly opened experimental kindergarten where there was a zoo, and where children were taught to do things with their hands. My first sculpture was made there in the form of a wave, in clay and with a blue glaze."[25] His wave sculpture was, he recalled, "much talked about in kindergarten and my mother never forgot it. She kept hoping I would eventually become an artist."[26] Looking back near the end of his life, Noguchi remembered his attendance at the Morimura School as pivotal: "My awakening to consciousness out of this dark and uncertain time came with my being taken to Morimura Gakuen . . . I was finally among people who seemed to take me as one of them, or rather, as somebody of interest to them, somebody that they related to as a student, appropriate, I imagine, to my being there . . . and a half-breed person such as myself was a welcome addition, I believe."[27] The feeling of being accepted, of not being treated as a *gaijin*, was to Isamu a great relief. Even if at that young age he would not have known the meaning of prejudice, he surely felt it. He came to realize that "the Japanese do not accept foreigners as another person equal to themselves"[28] and he continued to be touchy about his mixed blood, his being foreign, and his illegitimate birth for the rest of his life.

On May 3, 1911, Leonie wrote Catherine that in Omori she knew only one of her neighbors, but that Isamu had friends. She described Noguchi's cleverness in circumventing discipline. When she told him it was time for bed, he countered, "I can't go now, because I told the neighbor's boy I would not go to bed so early, and I *have to* tell the truth."[29] Perhaps that neighbor's boy was the teenage Tomio Iwata, who did in fact live next door and who recalled that Isamu, for all his resistance to bedtime, "never behaved like a spoiled child or acted petulantly toward his mother. Rather, he treated his mother like a teacher—with respect."[30] Iwata delighted in teasing Isamu: "Isamu was always too proud to admit defeat or give in, and he was greedy about food, so he was an easy target to teasing and torment." Once Tomio hoisted Isamu up onto an exercise bar and left him dangling with his feet too far from the ground for him to jump. "Isamu began to scream his lungs out . . . I just pretended I didn't hear or care. Then suddenly the gate swung open, and Mrs. Leonie came bounding into the yard as fast as a rabbit. Without a word she grabbed Isamu, hugged him to her body, and immediately fled back to her house." Noguchi said that he and his mother were "very close and in fact I had nobody excepting for her. She was, you know, my total link to life, and I'm sure that this was not good for me, but that was the case."[31]

4

CHIGASAKI

By September 1911 Leonie and Isamu had moved again, this time to a seaside village called Chigasaki, about two hours from Tokyo but close to Kamakura. It is possible that Leonie left Omori because her landlord no longer wanted to rent to her. He had apologized to her neighbors about renting to a foreign woman, explaining that it had seemed wasteful to leave the cottage empty. Another reason for the move may have been that she was pregnant. She had conceived a child in late April. By moving to Chigasaki she could avoid the stigma of being a pregnant and unmarried woman. Leonie may have felt uncomfortable but she was not ashamed. She felt that marriage was constricting for artists and that marital possessiveness led to divorce.[1]

Noguchi often described the seven years that he and his mother lived in Chigasaki (during part of which he went to boarding school) as idyllic. But his anxiety never left him. With Leonie teaching at the girls' school, he was on his own for much of the day. Compared to the protective and nurturing Morimura kindergarten, the local elementary school was tough. His description of his childhood in Chigasaki is full of nostalgic poetry:

> There the land is a dark sand, covered with the small pines of the seashore . . . Through the village runs the Tokaido road with its magnificent pines of Hiroshige. At first we lived in the house of a farmer whose wife raised silkworms on trays of mulberry

leaves in the house. It was there that I attended two years of the local schools.

I had by then become a typical Japanese boy, knowledgeable in the ways of nature; such as how to skin the young willow twigs to make whistles, or where to find eels. There were all the festivals I delighted in, the obon dancing in the streets, the kites in the wind, the many-colored, *mochi* "rice cakes" roasted on forked branches over autumn bonfires. There was a travelling Kabuki troupe. There were sunsets to which we sang "Yu yake ko yake."[2]

In a letter to Catherine written on January 15, 1912, little more than two weeks before she gave birth, Leonie said nothing about being pregnant. She spoke mainly about Isamu: "Mr. Bear," the teddy bear that Catherine had given him before he left America, was, she wrote, his favorite toy. The bear was "wildly trying to climb the <u>dango</u> tree on the bureau. The <u>dango</u> are rice cakes stuck on the bare twigs of a wintry branch, with tiny oranges similarly stuck here and there." As usual, Leonie spoke proudly of her son's intellectual development. "Isamu's young mind is now intent on the problem of the first firstest man. I gave him three theories for a choice, Adam and Eve and the garden, the Norse legend about the cow licking the stones, and the monkey's clever child. He promptly rejected the latter, saying, 'Nowadays no monkeys turn into men, and even the most clever monkey child is only a foolish monkey.' He said he liked the one about God and Adam and Eve the best."[3]

Noguchi remembered his mother's love of literature: "My fondest recollection is of Mother reading to me. She read to me according to her taste. As a result I believed in Apollo and all the gods of Olympus long before I knew of any other . . ."[4] "Beyond that, Chaucer, Uncle Remus, and Lady Gregory are about equally mixed. It was she who instilled in me a love of the artistic."[5] Leonie absorbed everything she could about Japanese art and shared this passion with her son, reading Japanese fairy tales to Isamu and taking him to see temples and gardens. When she took archery lessons at a nearby temple, Isamu was given a small bow. When he was six or seven she gave him a samurai outfit complete with a mask.

Isamu's attachment to his mother was almost too intense: "My mother seemed always to be calling me. Frail and small, with grey-blue eyes, she would come home at evening to my infinite relief. How I lived in fear of losing her!"[6] Leonie loved to swim and the sea became for him "a dangerous place of dark winds and typhoons . . . my mother would swim far out, farther than I could see, and I was in constant dread that she might never come back . . . I would say I was relatively happy in Chigasaki, though most often alone while my mother was away working."

Isamu coped well with the long hours of solitude between his arrival home from school and his catching sight of his mother as she walked home from the train station. On January 27 Leonie did not come home at all, and she was gone for a number of days. She went into labor while teaching at the girls' school in Yokohama, and returned home with a daughter, Ailes, named for a line from an Irish poem: "Ailes was a girl that stepped on two bare feet." Noguchi was seven, and as he recalled, Ailes' birth "threw my whole life off course, into another turbulence of doubt and dismay. For, whereas I had been the total center of [my mother's] attention, now it was distracted, and my world was not the same."[7]

Although Ailes' arrival caused him distress, there was the compensation that Leonie was now home most of the time. They also moved from the rented room in the farmhouse where the owner kept silk-worms to a little cottage on the estate of a viscount who only occupied his house in the summer. Leonie encouraged Isamu to plant a garden, which helped him to deal with the misery of having to share her with Ailes. "I believe," he recalled, "that I managed to retain my equilibrium in the house in Chigasaki. I built a garden, under my mother's urging. I spent a lot of time there, working on the garden, and growing various plants. There were a great variety of roses that I grew there in the following years. There were peach trees in the garden which grew and bore fruit. The cycle of the seasons was clearly a part of my conscious-ness . . ."[8] Isamu turned the overflow from a pump into a brook. "To this was attached my earliest feeling of guilt, for I stole a rock from a neighbor's wood to place there. Each time Haruhiko san came to call, I expected him to recognize his rock. He never did."[9]

Leonie never divulged the name of Ailes' father, and the mystery became for Noguchi and Ailes a source of tension. "I never asked my mother," Noguchi said. "She never told me. She's never told my sister, for that matter, that I know of."[10] Some people believe that Ailes' father could have been Yone, for he continued to need Leonie's editorial help and he was often at nearby Kamakura. But his paternity seems unlikely: it is said that Yone felt "betrayed" when Leonie gave birth to Ailes and that he used it to rationalize his further distancing of himself from her.[11] Most likely Ailes' father was one of Leonie's students—Noguchi remembered that some pupils were close to his mother. In a 1988 interview he said: "I suspect that among her pupils . . . intimate relationships might have developed, older pupils. There are letters in my sister's possession that indicate that sort of thing. Certain offers to adopt me, for instance . . . I remember one Englishman who wanted to adopt me. This Englishman, as I remember, was named Paget."[12]

Ailes' son, Jody Spinden, discovered a letter to Leonie inserted into an old notebook that she had used to teach penmanship. It was dated December 19, 1912, when Ailes was almost one. The signature at the bottom of the page was torn off. The return address the writer gave is thought to have once been a student boardinghouse near Tokyo Imperial University. "Dear Madame," he wrote. "I will be busy now because of school examination. Suddenly last night I have dreamed about you and baby. I am anxious about baby as something happed [sic] in her fortune. But I wonder [indecipherable] I have something that never go out of my mind . . . in the morning and at night, especially every Sunday, and now. You understand . . ."[13]

Perhaps the man who fathered her daughter was Leonie's old friend Matsuo Miyake. After he left California for Japan in 1905, Miyake wrote Leonie frequent letters. "How is our dear baby?" he wrote on September 28, 1905. "I would pray thee be not mindless when thou feelith his tender cheeks." Miyake's eagerness for Leonie to come to Japan suggests a highly intimate relationship: "Will it not be delightful," he asked, "to live in a Niphon no Iye, a Japanese residing house, together, you and I?!"[14]

In October, eight months after Leonie had arrived in Tokyo, Miyake wrote, ". . . is your babe healthy and dancing on his papa's arms?"[15] In a February 1910 letter that he probably wrote after Leonie had discovered that Yone had a second family, he said, "You say you have a big sorrow in your heart. Don't you think your brother does not know of his sister's sorrow. I am always thinking of you and of your circumstance."[16] The following October he inquired about her separation from

Yone—would Yone support her? Would she be able to keep custody of Isamu? Would she stay in Japan? He invited her to come to Osaka and live with him. He offered to help her financially as much as possible. He signed, "Your <u>brother for ever</u>, Matsuo."[17]

Noguchi did not have many friends in Chigasaki. He lost one, the grandson of the viscount's caretaker, when the boy cut down the viscount's favorite bamboo. Leonie wrote about the incident to Catherine:

> Did I tell you the disastrous outcome of the cherry-tree legend: you see Isamu told that story to his chum, Sho Morita. Sho-chan, being fired with emulation and desirous of taking the first steps to becoming a great man, promptly chopped down Danna's (that's his lord and master viscount Fukuoka) most precious bamboo. He promptly owned up, and was given the thrashing of his life by his grandfather. Furthermore, his grandmother told Isamu that before he came to the neighborhood Sho taro had been a good boy, but owing to Isamu's pernicious influence he was becoming the worst kind of boy. Isamu was so depressed he stayed in the house a whole day, occasionally muttering "am I a bad boy? Am I the worst boy in the world?" etc.[18]

The loss of this friend must have been especially painful because the village children in Chigasaki, mostly the offspring of fishermen, treated Isamu as an outcast. With his curly hair, pale eyes, and Western clothes, he clearly was different. "So in a sense I was brought up in a house alone and separate from the kind of common interests of children."[19] Often the children teased and tormented him, especially when he was on his way home from school. They yelled names at him and threw stones or pushed him into rice paddies when he couldn't outrun them. "After all," Noguchi recalled, "I was something of a freak, without any doubt, and children don't hide their feelings." Because he lacked friends, his mother was all the more central to his life. But he liked to test her love. He remembered the "childhood trauma, of running away, of feeling abandoned, and wanting to go away and 'they'll be sorry later on.' My mother was dragging me back all the time."[20] But she could not always protect him.

When Noguchi was eight, Catherine Bunnell sent him Charles Kingsley's classic children's book about Greek mythology, *The Heroes*. Leonie thanked her, saying that Isamu was a "worshiper of Apollo."[21] In March she reported to Catherine that she and Isamu had read all the labors of Hercules and the story of Perseus. They were halfway through the story of the Argonauts. "Isamu is an admirer of Hercules, especially, though that hero has not ousted his beloved Apollo. And if you please, he prefers in future to be called 'George Apollo' a combination of George Washington and the sun-God."[22]

In March Isamu was in bed with the measles. On April 5, 1913, Yone wrote to Leonie: "So sorry to hear Isamu is ill. I hope he is well by this time."[23] He enclosed an article about his poetry for her to type and a check. His book of poems *The Pilgrimage* had, he said, received numerous complimentary letters from England's literati—people such as Arthur Ransome, Ezra Pound, and Katherine Mansfield. He was, however, in "heavy debt" because he had built a new house.

Noguchi said that one of his few memories of his father, whom he seldom saw after his first months in Japan, was Yone's appearance when he had the measles: "I was sick and he came to call on me and I felt very puzzled and good about this. But so far as I can remember, this may have been the last time I saw him . . . [until] I took off for America at the age of thirteen."[24] "I never felt sorry for myself abandoned by my father, [or] for my mother's misfortunes, for the fact that I was very poor. It probably did color my attitude, give me the drive to try to rectify things a bit for myself. I consider whatever incentive drives you to do something is good."[25] Indeed, Noguchi's difficult childhood prompted him to excel. "Is fortune or misfortune the better teacher?"[26] he asked in his autobiography. Clearly he felt that adversity had forced him to cope. Yet his solitary upbringing and his feeling of being a misfit surely contributed to Noguchi's becoming, for all his wit, charm, and sophistication, a very defended person.

After the April 5 note, there is only one more letter from Yone to Leonie while she was still in Japan. It was written on January 17, 1914, while Yone was in London being lionized. He had given a lecture at the Japan Society and was, he said, to be the guest of honor at the Poets' Club dinner. "Yesterday I was invited by Bernard Shaw and tonight am going to take a dinner together with Yeats. And so on—you see, I am splendid in condition, but not financially . . . How are Isamu and baby? I promised Isamu that he shall have picture-cards occasionally; please tell him: 'His papa is tremendously busy, but tomorrow, no, the day after tomorrow, he will go to some shops and buy something for him.'"[27]

5

ST. JOSEPH COLLEGE

In September 1913 the eight-year-old Noguchi was sent to St. Joseph College, a school for both day students and boarders in the large port city of Yokohama, just south of Tokyo. The campus comprised several large European-style buildings set on the bluff overlooking the harbor. Isamu's distress over his new sibling must have been exacerbated by this decision on Leonie's part—a decision she probably made because she saw her son's unhappiness at the local school in Chigasaki. Founded in 1901 by the Roman Catholic Marianist Society, the purpose of St. Joseph was to educate the sons of foreigners of any creed or race. The teachers were Catholic brothers from many different countries, and instruction was in English. The children came, Noguchi recalled, "from all parts of the Orient and I think there were others like me of half-parentage . . . Mixed Japanese such as myself was probably the exception. There may have been other mixed people, from China or someplace, so that it was not entirely that I was so exceptional."[1] Even though at St. Joseph he was no longer thrown in a classroom full of the children of fishermen, his feelings of being different increased.

Leonie registered Isamu at the school as Isamu Gilmour, not Isamu Noguchi, and she herself reverted to her maiden name. Most likely she took back Gilmour because Yone married Matsuko Takeda. In a September 1913 letter to Catherine, Leonie wrote that Yone had "followed the line of least resistance and married his maid servant, a homely and ignorant little wench who cooked his meals. He might have gone further and found better. In Japan marriage is chiefly a matter of

convenience. And she was right there. But somehow I feel sorry—
awfully sorry. He's a very good fellow . . ."[2] In discussing Yone's "Oriental doctrine of no-resistance," Leonie was parroting Yone's thoughts
about the value of nonassertiveness, ideas that Noguchi would come to
share. In an essay about haiku poetry, Yone wrote that haiku express
the spirit of nature, not the will of man. Americans, he said, should
"live more of the passive side of Life and Nature," for there was beauty
in inaction.[3] Quoting Lao-tzu, he urged, "Assert non-assertion." Years
later the nonassertiveness of his son's sculpture (as compared with the
muscular dynamism felt in the work of other artists of his generation
such as David Smith) made Noguchi's work seem to some viewers more
Asian than American.

To get to St. Joseph's school Isamu walked a mile to the Chigasaki
station and caught the 5:52 a.m. train. When he arrived at Yokohama
an hour later he had to walk two and a half miles up to the Bluff, a
section of Yokohama with Victorian-style mansions, many of which
were inhabited by foreigners. Noguchi enjoyed the commute. "The
first times were very exciting and I remember very well commuting to
Yokohama—the railroad station, the run through town, running through
Chinatown, going to the Bluff where the school was, and the experience of school . . . coming back again on the train and then to the little
house . . . this must have gone on for several years."[4] Perhaps because
the commute was exhausting, during one period Noguchi became a
boarder.

Since Chigasaki was a summer place, and during the fall and
winter his friends moved back to the city, Isamu felt, looking back, that
it made sense for him to go to St. Joseph, even though he did not immediately make friends there. "I felt always a little bit outside the general
community. It was a Catholic school; I was not Catholic . . . I wished
I could be a Catholic; I didn't know how to. My mother was not reli-
giously oriented. You might say she was a real skeptic about such matters."[5] Noguchi envied the Catholic children: "I would surreptitiously
join them in early Mass. Mr. Griffin, the Scoutmaster, was the only
person in Yokohama whom I felt really cared about me." Mr. Griffin
"tried to make me into a good boy scout. I took it very seriously of
course." There was also a minister who gave Isamu a Bible, which he
kept all his life. As he was a loner, what other students talked about
among themselves did not, he said, concern him. But sometimes his

separateness got him into trouble: "I remember an occasion when we had gone off someplace to play outside and I felt myself being put upon and I remember I had practiced about what I had learned of 'jujitsu' on one of them, his name was Young, and [I] threw him over my head, and I thought I had hurt him. I was terribly worried."

At one point during his years at St. Joseph College, probably early in 1914, "there came a reprieve . . . Mother decided to build a house, and insisted that we do it together. She selected a spot close to the sea on the edge of a pine grove overlooking potato fields. It must have been spring, for soon I was there constantly, following every detail. It was a semi-Japanese house with a round window on the second floor, which on a clear day would frame Mount Fuji off to the west."[6]

Like Yone, Leonie had great admiration for Japanese domestic architecture, and she wanted her son to learn how to build a Japanese house. In later years Noguchi would share this admiration and he would choose to live part of the year in a traditional Japanese house with almost no furniture and with tatami mats on the floor. The spareness and the structural straightforwardness of Japanese houses would also be a major influence on his sculpture.

Perhaps because it was awkward for a woman, especially one not fluent in Japanese, to order contractors around, Leonie put Isamu in charge. "She wanted me to watch the carpenters, to have a position you might say, in relation to the building of the house, a supervisor or something: somebody to look after and be with the carpenters, who she admired. And the design of the house was mostly Japanese with a few flourishes, you might say, which were foreign or oriented more to her comfort."[7] Constructing the Chigasaki house was a tremendous boost to Isamu's self-confidence: "And that was my big experience, which started me off into consciousness and a part of my life ever since."

On the first of March, 1914, Leonie wrote Catherine to say how "bumptious" she felt about her new house.[8] Catherine had sent her four hundred yen, half of which she paid to the carpenters. The other half she deposited in the bank. She hoped to return two hundred after six months with interest paid by the bank. The other two hundred she would repay when she could. Leonie drew for Catherine a plan of her triangular house showing the parlor, the adjacent living room, and Isamu's room and veranda opposite the entryway. The kitchen and bath were in the triangle's apex. On the south were glass doors looking out onto pine trees. Upstairs was Leonie's twelve-foot-square room with its view of Mount Fuji and the sea. On two sides of the house, barley fields waved in the wind.

The day after the May 5 Japanese holiday called Tango no Sekku (Boys' Day), Leonie wrote to Catherine that this was the day that families with male children hang paper carp on tall poles.[9] She noted that she was living in poverty but was considered to be rich, hence her house had been burglarized three times. Two nights ago a burglar had made off with four coats, a box of letters, a box of "machine fixings," an English songbook, a parasol, a tin of cornstarch, and Isamu's bundle of schoolbooks. As he fled through the neighbor's pine forest he dropped everything except Isamu's coat and Leonie's parasol.

On August 23 Leonie described for her friend the late summer sound of insects and the voices of farmers passing by with their harvest hung at either end of a pole that rested on their shoulders. "This is the land of sweet potatoes and watermelons and peaches. We've been reveling in the last two fruits all summer."[10] She described Isamu sitting cross-legged: to see "his startling green eyes reflecting the watermelon rind, is to get a glimpse of the poetry of savagery."

Noguchi recalled that the year of house building was the year in which he made friends "for the first time."[11] During the summer months vacationers from Tokyo came to Chigasaki. Two law professors at Tokyo Imperial University had villas nearby and Isamu and Ailes befriended their children. One of the children, Kazuko Makino, recalled that Ailes spent much of the day at the Makino house and that Isamu came along. "He must have played with my older brother but somehow I remember him as always alone."[12] Isamu was, she observed, wary and untrusting. "What I remember about Isamu now is that he never walked across the beautiful lawn in the front of the house but always went through the dark grove of pines at the end of the back garden." She also remembered the way Noguchi would sit by the round window in his mother's bedroom and watch for the arrival of the train that brought Leonie home from Yokohama.

Isamu's closest friend that summer was fifteen-year-old Haruhiko Fujii. Together with the Makino children, Isamu and Haruhiko spent afternoons at the beach. Leonie would sometimes join them. As Kazuko recalled, she would throw the children that didn't know how to swim into the deep water to teach them to stay afloat. Then she would swim to a small island some two miles offshore, terrifying the children that she might drown.

Leonie's August 23 letter to Catherine lamented the coming of fall for Isamu: "Alas, on the 15th of September he will give up his liberty, don clothes ('foreign' clothes) even shoes, and catch the early train— 5:52 a.m.—for school, and every day and every day and every day, as he says, it will be the same old thing." Two and a half months later, Leonie told Catherine that Isamu continued to insist that he was an American. She had been typing Yone's new book on "Blessed England," and she noted that in Japan children sang "God Save King George," but that Isamu and Ailes sang "Hail Columbia, Happy Land!" Isamu, she said, teased his sister mercilessly: "You don't know what is Columbia, you little foolish ignorant thing!" "I do," Ailes would say. "Then what is it?" Ailes met her brother's challenge: "Over there," she said, pointing.[13]

That autumn Catherine wrote with the news that she was engaged. Isamu, who had developed a fantasy love for his godmother, was not pleased. Leonie passed along a message to Catherine dictated by Isamu. "Please wait!" he implored. "A man shouldn't marry till he's 20. That's about ten-'leven years. I'm growing pretty tall, and I might just suit her, you know." Isamu's marriage proposal was announced with "a comical smirk of masculine conceit, and twirling an imaginary moustache." A year later, after Catherine wrote that she had married, Leonie reported that Isamu was outraged. "Make plants grow?" he said of his rival's talents. "Why that's just like me, and I'm fond of animals, too, especially puppies . . . I like Shakespeare too."[14] Leonie said that she was glad Catherine had not married a writer. "No offense to the order of the plume, but you know they're apt to dawdle around the house and get in the way."

In spring 1915 Leonie wrote to Catherine about her garden with cabbage, lettuce, and a strawberry patch. "Isamu's garden is brighter with pansies, yellow primroses, violets, English daisies and so on. And there is one white wisteria in full bloom, and a small magnolia tree with large purple flowers. Isamu is taken with 'wander-lust' every Sunday lately, and tramps over the hills and far away, ten or twelve miles at a jaunt in quest of rare blue flowers that grow 'only at the tip top of the mountain,' or wild azaleas or the like, which he laboriously carries home."[15]

Leonie and Isamu continued to commute to Yokohama. She taught school from eight in the morning until two in the afternoon, after which she had a number of private students. One was the daughter of Yokohama's mayor. She wryly noted that while the mayor rode about in a horse and carriage, she and Isamu rode in a *jinrikisha*, a small two-wheeled rickshaw carriage drawn by one or two people. She told Catherine that while teaching she had had a "sort of a stroke" and she had lain down with her head packed in ice while her students fanned her. After this she was plagued with headaches. Leonie was now a forty-one-year-old single mother of two. "I don't think she had very much joy in life," Noguchi said.[16]

During her vacation that summer of 1915, Leonie relaxed and occupied herself with "swimming, eating, and sewing."[17] She told Catherine that Isamu had reached a critical point in his education: "He objects strenuously to going to school and is begging me to teach him at home this winter. Of course the long train journey every day is a strain upon him. On the other hand, education at home with a busy mother for teacher is apt to be desultory. He has decided to be a landscape gardener or horticulturalist, and is quite an enthusiast on this his chosen specialty, but he don't [*sic*] see the use of arithmetic, spelling and all that [illegible word] for a gardener. He thinks a man should begin his life work young."

Noguchi had his way. His mother became his teacher. "She taught me botany, as she thought I might become a forester, and semi-apprenticed me to a local cabinet-maker in Chigasaki. There I learned the basic uses of wood tools; to sharpen them, to plane, to saw, pulling in the Japanese way. Of the joining and interlocking of beams, I learned the simpler kinds. I also carved wood panels for above the sliding doors (*fusama*), some of which were antiqued by burning and rubbing with straw and wet sand. And I made carvings in cherry wood of such traditional themes as rabbits in waves and dragons in clouds."[18] For Noguchi the clay wave that he had made in kindergarten, these decorative wooden pieces, and especially his learning how to use tools, were steps toward his becoming a sculptor.

Noguchi also credited his preference for simplicity and his insistence on honesty of structure to his childhood in Japan. "The Japanese tradition has a great respect for materials and how things are made. It's a culture closer to the tactile sense of things, which is very important to me. For me it comes through a childhood experience of knowing that things aren't just painted over, that the structure is part of the design."[19] Besides carpentry and gardening, there was another craft that Isamu enjoyed at this time and that he also saw as early preparation for becoming an artist. While he was being home-schooled he "became involved with making hats; that is, hierarchic affairs such as that winged one of Perseus . . . The hats I made were my first expression as an artist."[20] Remembering these months of living at home years later, Noguchi said, "This was a period of pleasant memory to me. My mother was more around and had time to spend with me and teach me things. Of course, there was always Ailes, and that probably kept her around the house, too . . ."[21]

On February 24, 1916, Leonie repaid Catherine the last twelve dollars that she owed and went on to discuss Isamu's restlessness: "He is begging me to let him go to America next winter, spend two or three years, perhaps returning when he is old enough to enter an art school here. He has 3 reasons for going. 1. Curiosity to see the unknown. 2. A desire to play baseball. 3. Admiration of Christopher Columbus. (also 4. A wish to get letters from mama)." She said that Isamu had written to a Japanese steamship company and discovered that he could get passage from Yokohama, to Honolulu, to San Francisco, and finally to Los Angeles. The cost of a second-class ticket for someone under twelve was about thirty-nine dollars. Leonie asked Catherine for advice. "How is Florence situated in regard to schools? And would she perchance welcome him as a cheap boarder?" Leonie worried that the itinerary that Isamu had planned would keep him at sea for a month, which was dangerous in wartime. "And think of the German submarines prowling around!" Isamu was undeterred. "He has already made a plan for a trunk which he intends to make himself and is making a list (daily lengthening) of things to take; it includes a silver spoon, chopsticks, gold cup, tools, Teddy bear, favorite book, and other appurtenances to an ideal bachelor den."[22]

In an undated letter from the summer of 1916, Leonie told Catherine that she was learning shorthand in order to get a better-paying job.[23] (Her current salary was 150 yen a month.) She was still considering the possibility of the eleven-and-a-half-year-old Isamu going to America: "If I could only find someplace where Isamu could earn part of his expenses—I am sure there are such schools, but it is hard to find them from this end of the line. He is really clever with tools—does a sort of wood carving—makes boats and aeroplanes after Art Smith's models and the like. Splendidly strong and healthy—but blissfully void of aspirations, quixotic standards, democratic ideas and all that sort of thing that are supposed to be in the atmosphere of America (and I believe they truly are)."

On July 31, 1916, Leonie wrote that she was "putting in time" in Tokyo as secretary to Robertson Scott, editor of *The New East* magazine.[24] During the week she lived in Tokyo. On Sundays she returned to Chigasaki. The children were being looked after by a "very competent little country maid" who cooked their meals, and Isamu had returned to St. Joseph. According to the neighbor's daughter, Kazuko Makino, when Leonie took the job at *The New East* and had to be in Tokyo for three or four weeks, Ailes moved into the Makino house, but Noguchi refused to move. A neighbor's housekeeper prepared his meals.[25]

Not only did Leonie have her suspicions about the "immorality" of the other boys at St. Joseph, but also the commute was exhausting, and she felt "a weariness to the flesh."[26] "And still my bank account is at ebb tide (never a balance of more than 2 or 3 yen at the end of the month). As the boy grows so do his needs—so do his father's financial delinquencies. I keep the sewing machine merrily humming all summer." The following year, to avoid the commute, Leonie and her children moved to Yokohama. They returned to Chigasaki on Sundays. She was still feeling poor—she had lost some of her jobs because of the economy and wartime inflation. A job she had taken at Miss Mander's girls' school was now part time at half pay. Nevertheless she managed to send ten dollars to her father, who was ill, and she planned to do so every month. "I've taken a little two room house at the foot of the bluff. The Bluff is where the swell foreigners live. At the foot are the poor Japanese. But this house is quite new and cozy."[27] She was, she said, sitting on the floor. She hoped to acquire a chair at the next auction. Her letter ended with "Isamu very well, his American ambitions soaring."

Isamu never felt at home in Yokohama. In his autobiography he wrote: "Living in a foreign-style house, attending a foreign school, I became a foreigner to myself, a stranger in the land."[28] Perhaps also living in the poor section of Yokohama below the rich houses on the Bluff made him uneasy: "I was becoming aware of the various social classes and goings-on in Yokohama . . ."[29] Noguchi did remember having some fun "playing hooky from school to go to a movie, let's say, that sort of thing. So there was a life in Yokohama that I was gradually becoming accustomed to when my mother suddenly decided to send me off to America."

As Noguchi told it, his mother was the one who forced him to go to America. He later surmised that Leonie believed that the stigma of being of mixed blood would be less in America. Also she was worried that he had become too friendly with an English boy named Jeffrey Faron, whose family lived in Yokohama. "I'd started spending time, more and more time there, even at night, and I don't think my mother approved of this—that I'd finally made a friend, and that it should be a foreigner may have been sort of distressing to her, I don't know why . . . maybe she felt that if I was going to be with foreigners, like a foreigner, I might as well go to America . . ."[30] In addition, Noguchi suspected that his mother was upset about his newfound interest in girls: "There were these girls—one of them in particular—that I quite fancied. In fact that was during the time of my, a sort of awakening sexuality, you might say."[31]

In 1916, Leonie had written to the Interlaken School in Indiana for a prospectus. She had learned about the school from a recent article titled "The Daniel Boone Idea in Education," published in *Scientific American*, and she thought it would be perfect for Isamu.[32] Interlaken was founded by Edward Aloysius Rumely (1882–1964), a physician, industrialist, educator, newspaperman, and heir to a tractor and farm equipment manufacturing company in La Porte, Indiana. While studying medicine in Europe, Rumely had much admired the progressive schools he had seen in Germany and Switzerland and he longed to start a similar school. The Interlaken college preparatory school for boys was in the country, near the small village of Rolling Prairie on the outskirts of the manufacturing town of La Porte. The school's motto was "Knowledge through Experience." The hope was that boys should learn by doing—and especially by doing things with their hands, for muscles and minds were interconnected. It aimed to foster individualism, self-reliance, and honesty, and to turn the "sons of the directing class of our civilization" into "sympathetic, understanding, resourceful, clean living, clean thinking American gentlemen . . . fit leaders of men in this industrial Republic."[33]

The school buildings were set beside a lake on an 800-acre farm. Some of the buildings were log cabins built by the students themselves. The boys worked at many chores—including carpentry and farm work, as well as cleaning their own rooms, setting the table for meals, serving food, and washing dishes. Sports were important, but academic work was rigorous. Classes were conducted using the Socratic method. The students sat in a circle and asked and answered questions.

The first extant letter from Leonie to Interlaken is addressed to the school's superintendent and dated April 5, 1918. She enclosed a photograph of Isamu and said that Interlaken would be the ideal school for him, but that the expense was a problem, even at the reduced rate of $400, which she had been offered. Would it be possible, she asked, "for the boy to earn a small part of his expense at school, say 50 to $100 a year, and also to earn his keep during holidays."

About Isamu, she wrote:

He has a very strong inclination for manual work, in fact rather a surplus of motor energy . . . Regarding the character and temperament of the boy. He has a tendency to be very absorbed in the thing he is interested in for the moment, to the exclusion of all else; to ignore other people and their claims; to be domineering and self-willed. Is very impressionable. Will imitate those whom he admires. Very sensitive to beauty. He is the son of Yone Noguchi a Japanese author and poet, who is somewhat known in America, especially in California, where he spent some years with Joaquin Miller. Since my separation from him, I have taken my own name, and the boy also has taken my name. He inclines to admire all things American, and to slight his Japanese ancestry."[34]

Interlaken offered to reduce the tuition to $350 payable in installments and notified Leonie that there was also a summer school for $165, of which Isamu could likely earn $70. Leonie bought passage for Isamu on the *Amerika-maru*, which left Yokohama on June 27, 1918, bound for Seattle. From Seattle, Isamu would make his way by train to Rolling Prairie.

In his autobiography, Noguchi recalled that Leonie had "decided that I had better become completely American, and took me to the American consul, who performed a ritual, mumbling over a Bible, which I believe was my renunciation of Japanese citizenship."[35] The photograph of "Isamu Gilmour" in the U.S. passport that Leonie obtained for him from the American consul shows a beautiful thirteen-year-old boy with intelligent, somewhat wistful eyes and an almost too sensitive mouth, very like his father's.

Nonetheless, Isamu had misgivings at the prospect of going to America. He had finally begun to make friends at St. Joseph College, and separating from his mother was painful. "I felt abandoned," he recalled.[36] "For my part," Noguchi wrote in his autobiography, "there wasn't much choice. I was to be an American banished as my mother had decided. No more Japan and the sands of Chigasaki."[37] In his late sixties he put it this way: "I was a waif from the age of thirteen and home was where I made it. We make our life what we dream about."[38] What he perhaps did not know was that his mother had wanted to

Isamu's passport
photograph, 1918

return to America but she was unable to raise the money for her and Ailes' passage.

When Leonie took Isamu to board the *Amerika-maru*, his father, whom he had not seen in five years, appeared unexpectedly and tried to prevent his departure. Noguchi recalled that Yone, whose eldest son by Matsuko Takeda had died two years before, offered to adopt him and to enter his name in the household register. Leonie refused.[39] As Leonie and Yone argued, Isamu, urged on by his mother, moved up the gangplank. "You are to stay in Japan!" Yone commanded. Isamu stood paralyzed until Leonie said, "No!" Isamu looked at his father and echoed his mother's "No!"[40] With this, he and Leonie boarded the ship and went to find his berth.

"The fact that my mother sent me away was a shock," Noguchi recalled. "It took me a while to get used to being alone and then being independent. And then becoming over-independent perhaps . . . I have trouble with galleries for instance . . . But this sense of independence from my mother was already developing before she sent me away. As a matter of fact, I preferred to stay away from the house. It was already a revolt against parental control."[41]

6

INTERLAKEN

The trip across the Pacific was, Noguchi said, "fabulous . . . with two Fourth-of-Julys at the international-date-line. My first view of America was the pine-spired coastline of the North West and the passage past Victoria to Seattle. There was a man from the YMCA on the pier who took me into town and put me on a train."[1] The man made sure that Isamu had a nametag inscribed with his destination attached to his shirt. He gave Isamu a stick of Juicy Fruit chewing gum: "What a wonderful country to have such a wonderful thing like that. So I felt very happy about America . . ."[2] On the three-day trip the train was packed with soldiers (World War I would not be over for another four months). The soldiers were amused by Isamu and gave him food and drink. In Chicago Isamu changed trains and two hours later changed again to a local intercity line. When he finally arrived at Rolling Prairie, the journey had taken three weeks. "How I had gotten there from Japan is due to the luck that attends little boys. This also accounts for my quickly finding friends and being introduced to America in the ideal setting of the Indiana countryside, during the best possible time of year, in a summer camp. My mother had judged well in selecting this school where boys 'learned to know by doing.'"[3]

At Rolling Prairie station Isamu was met by someone from Interlaken. The two-mile walk to the school passed through cornfields blanketing low, undulant hills. Isamu was amazed at the openness of the land and the dry heat. "I got the feeling of America superimposed on the old Japanese. It was a view of nature which was quite different. Here nature is appreciated for its vastness, its sweep . . ."[4]

On July 25 C. A. Lewis, the director of the summer school, wrote to Dr. Rumely about Isamu's arrival: "I have a little Jap in camp—half Japanese, half English. He's a peach. He was muchly interested in wood-work, wanted to go to the wood-shop. I sent him, with flying colors. He came back to me almost in tears. 'I wanted to make something that I've planned for a long time, and Mr. Hedrain [the rigid Swedish shop teacher] set me to planing a block of wood, just to plane it.'" Mr. Lewis arranged a space with a bench and storage shelves where Isamu could work. He was amazed by what Isamu produced with the Japanese tools he had brought with him: "He can carve a Jap cod a heap better than Hedrain could in a year of Sundays, and he can make a spoon more quickly and artistically than Hedrain can in his—So I have him at it, and the boys are already weaving a path to his door."[5] Among the pieces that Isamu carved that summer was a frieze of seaweed, fish, and shells on a headboard.

In a 1946 *Art News* article on Noguchi, the critic and editor Thomas B. Hess told a similar, but partly apocryphal story. Isamu, he said, "appeared at the door of Dr. Edward Allen Rumely, Director of Interlaken, with a prospectus in his hand, demanding tools. Later that day, Rumely remembers, one of the boys came to him saying: 'Sir, there's the strangest kid outside, he pulls the chisel and pushes the saw.' Rumely went out and saw there, squatting under a tree, his newest pupil carving on a wooden plate a fish and flowers of Japan."[6] The problem with this version of events is that Rumely was not at Interlaken when Isamu arrived. Thanks to drought, crop failure, and overextended finances, his tractor company was sold in 1915, and he and his family moved to New York City. In July 1918, the month in which Isamu arrived at Interlaken, Rumely was arrested and convicted of perjury. He was perceived to be pro-German because of certain views expressed in *The Evening Mail*, the New York newspaper for which he served as publisher and editor in chief. The case dragged on until 1924. Noguchi recalled that Rumely was "a remarkable man, who out of idealism made this school . . . He is a great influence on me, although for almost a year, I was out of touch."[7]

Noguchi was happy living in a tent at summer camp; perhaps it reminded him of the tent he and his mother had lived in when he was a toddler in California. The campers swam in Silver Lake before breakfast. At 6:00 a.m. they ate eggs and milk from the school's own dairy. After breakfast there were various chores to be performed and then another swim at noon. In the afternoon they studied and engaged in sports. Lights out was at nine. Isamu's roommate, an older Filipino boy named Agapoan, taught Isamu how to ride a horse.[8] Noguchi recalled that Agapoan had been sent to an exposition in San Francisco to be put on display as "a sample of a wild man . . . He was a wild boy from the Igarat, you know. Lived in trees."[9]

Because of the war, communication with Japan was difficult. Although Isamu missed his mother, he had spent so much time alone during the last decade that he had learned not to need the people he loved. Asked if he thought about his mother while in Indiana, Noguchi said: "I thought of her always, with thinking how what a tough time she had. Financially and so forth . . . I'm sure my father never helped her."[10]

In a September 14, 1918, letter from Leonie to Rumely's daughter, who had given her news of Isamu, Leonie asked to be kept informed, for Isamu's letters were too brief, and those from the school's superintendent, too businesslike.[11] By the time Leonie wrote this letter, Isamu's life had been transformed. The school had closed due to the anti-German backlash and probably also because of Rumely's arrest. In late August the campus was taken over by army recruits who were to establish an army motor pool. "That fall the school did not open," Noguchi recalled. "Instead, the place was turned into a motor truck training camp, and while all the other children went home, I was left alone to watch soldiers, trucks, mess halls and barracks take over the grounds. I became a sort of mascot."[12] "Even the Igarat boy had a place to go to. I didn't . . . But then . . . the soldiers were coming in so it was very exciting . . . I liked it even better. I was alone then. I was boss."[13]

Noguchi camped out with two caretakers in a deserted faculty building. "I had the use of a horse upon which I rode out like a cowboy at four in the morning to fetch the mail and the victuals, getting back in time to make breakfast."[14] In early October the school's superintendent sent Leonie a cable: "School Closed Send Money Advice." Leonie wrote back: "In the emergency I wish Isamu to go to public High School in La Porte and will be obliged if you will consult with the secretary of the Y.M.C.A. about finding a home for him. If there is a Boy Scouts organization the scout master might be interested in helping to place him."[15] In mid-October she received three letters from Isamu and one from the school asking for tuition—Leonie's checks seemed to have gone astray in the mail. On October 14 Leonie responded: "My first thought on hearing of the closing of the school, was that I must take the first opportunity to go to America myself, and I am now trying to make an engagement over there. If you hear of an opening I should be glad to know of it." There was, she said, the possibility of secretarial work for a member of the Bryn Mawr faculty, but the salary of one hundred dollars did not seem sufficient for the journey to America and living expenses. She thought the cost of living might be cheaper on the West Coast.[16]

That autumn many of the soldiers came down with the influenza, a worldwide epidemic that killed some twenty million people in 1918. Noguchi recalled that some of the soldiers died and that he, too, was stricken with a high fever. While recovering in bed he read Arthurian legends in *Morte d'Arthur* and perused the Bible.[17] After the Armistice on November 11, the soldiers left and the caretakers tried to keep the place going. "Winter came, and I had no place to go, since my mother could not afford to send me elsewhere. Nobody seemed to be in charge of me."[18] As usual, he managed. "I felt like Daniel Boone . . . I would get in a canoe and paddle across the lake there and look for food and this and that. And there was a dog I liked."[19] The period of being alone at Interlaken lasted only about a month, but Noguchi said that it had felt much longer. In December the wife of the school's treasurer, Mrs. C. A. Lewis, took Isamu home with her to Rolling Prairie, where she enrolled him in public school and found him work in a garage. The school placed Isamu in a class with children younger than himself, which must have been humiliating. "I had my birth certificate . . . I had no school diploma, no nothing. So they put me backwards."[20] Even worse, unlike the liberal atmosphere of Interlaken, the Rolling Prairie public school children looked askance at this foreigner. He was small for his age and there was a Japanese cast to his features. Once again he felt like a misfit. "Yeah, in Rolling Prairie they ganged up on me. They were gonna beat me up. And I remembered enough jiu-jitsu, so I threw one over my head. And then they became very quiet, very quiet. Very respectful . . . you have to prove yourself."[21]

7

LA PORTE

Isamu was rescued again the following year when Rumely, out on bail, came to Indiana to arrange the sale of Interlaken. He brought Isamu back to his home in La Porte, Indiana, and put him up with the family of Dr. Charles S. Mack, a sixty-two-year-old former professor of homeopathy at the University of Wisconsin and the pastor of a local Swedenborgian church. The New Church, of which Rumely's wife Fanny was also a member, was based on the ideas of the eighteenth-century theologian and mystic Emanuel Swedenborg and taught that all things are connected by universal analogy, that there is one God and he is the Lord Jesus Christ, and that salvation comes not through faith alone but also through charity, which meant being good and useful to others. Charles Mack and his wife, a former schoolteacher, had six children, four of whom were grown while the two younger boys lived at home. Julian Mack was a year older than Isamu, and Isamu looked up to him. For the next three years Isamu lived comfortably with the Macks while he completed high school, earning his keep by tending furnaces, mowing lawns, and delivering newspapers. For all his feeling of security in his new home, Noguchi's underlying anxiety remained: "I constantly worried about my mother in Japan and developed a moral loathing for my father."[1]

The Macks treated Isamu as a family member. He attended church with them and, though Dr. Mack did not try to influence his religious beliefs, Isamu did absorb some aspects of Swedenborgian thinking. His friend the art critic Dore Ashton wrote that Noguchi believed that his preoccupation with myth derived in part from his exposure to Swedenborgianism, and she quoted Noguchi saying: "They believe the Bible is a myth which had to be interpreted. They reveal the artistic merit of the Bible."[2] Ashton noted the influence on Noguchi of the Swedenborgian concept of a universal rhyme scheme in which all aspects of nature are related.

After Rumely returned to New York, he kept in touch, writing Noguchi letters full of avuncular advice. Soon he became the first of Noguchi's substitute fathers. In a 1988 letter to Dr. Rumely's daughter Mary, who was seven years younger than Isamu, Noguchi reminisced about his relationship to her family: "And I think back on all those years and the friendship with your family which permitted me to survive in a strange land. You were my family inasmuch as I had one . . ."[3] In his letters to Isamu, Rumely guided his reading. He sent him books, for example, by Theodore Dreiser and Frank Norris. He also instructed him to keep an account book, and he gave him fifteen dollars to open a bank account. In September 1919 he wrote: "First, I wish to know how you are using your money and to guide you by suggestion. Second: You can practice economy better if you know what you are spending for. Third: The habit of careful accounting is an essential for many lines of work and you must learn it now. Let me know how your school work is getting on."[4]

What is probably the first of Isamu's undated letters to Dr. Rumely from La Porte reported on his reading, including *The Three Musketeers, The Count of Monte Cristo, My Three Years in America* by Count Bernstorff, and a number of books on physics, agriculture, and chemistry.[5] In what must be his next letter he informed Rumely that he had opened a savings account and that he had ten dollars left. He enclosed his report card for the first semester and told of his plans to build a wooden model hydroplane. Isamu did not have to pay for room and board, but he had to earn his spending money. To this end, besides his various odd jobs, he cleaned the fireplace, chopped wood, and mowed the lawn for Emmet Scott, Mrs. Rumely's father and a former mayor of La Porte. Rumely often said to him that he was giving him "the best advantage anybody has, and that was no advantage."[6] Noguchi came to see himself as a "typical American Horatio Alger story."[7] He told the *New Yorker* writer Calvin Tomkins: "So, you see, I'm a Hoosier. I had a Japanese childhood but an American boyhood, with a paper route and all those things."[8]

The following spring he found work at a laboratory. With much improved penmanship Isamu wrote to Rumely: "It is two weeks since I started working at the laboratory, so I asked Dr. Martin for my pay. He asked 'How much do you want?' I replied $5. He said the laboratory could not aford [sic] it and that as the training would be very valuable to me, I ought not to ask for any. I have enjoyed the work very much but I guess I will have to look for another job . . ." In a postscript he added, "I hope your trial ends speedily."

Another of Isamu's letters to Rumely reported: "The bysycle [sic] frame busted so I had to get another and the tire is about to go on the blink otherwise the byclycle [sic] is all right as I got another frame from the Great Western.

"All these tough lucks however are counteracted by the fact that I have aquired [sic] a dandy coat from Mrs. Voth on Maple Ave, which she gave to me because her son had outgrown it. This coat is just about new being thick and kind of greenish black. Mrs. Mack said it could not be got for $30."

During his first winter in La Porte, Isamu learned from a January 18, 1920, *New York Times Magazine* interview with Yone that his father was in the United States for a three-month lecture tour. In the article, titled "America as Fountain of Youth to the Japanese," Yone spoke of his youthful days in America, but, not surprisingly, made no mention of having fathered a half-American son. Although in late November he was in Chicago, a two-hour train ride from La Porte, and although Leonie had asked him to contact Isamu, he did not bother to get in touch. In a September 9, 1919, letter to Leonie, Yone had written: "I lost interest in you and even in Isamu."[9]

Leonie left Japan with Ailes in 1920. She managed to get as far as San Francisco, where she supported herself and Ailes by selling Japanese woodblock prints and various Japanese curios, an occupation that she would continue after moving to New York in 1922. If she did not immediately make efforts to retrieve her son, she no doubt knew that he was in good hands and was receiving a proper American education thanks to Edward Rumely and the Macks.

That summer, when Isamu and Julian Mack visited the Rumelys' house on Lake Michigan, Fanny Rumely reported to her husband that Isamu was a wonderful swimmer and was going to teach seven-year-old Isabella how to swim. "Isamu is very nice indeed. When I see him lokin [sic] a little [illegible word] faced I jolly him up and he immediately

Julian Mack, Isabel Rumely, and Isamu at Duneland Beach, Indiana, 1920 (Courtesy of the Edward A. Rumely Papers, Lilly Library, Indiana University)

responds and is so lightning quick at everything he does. He considers M[a]ry's every wish the law. He really spoils her and she enjoys queening it."[10] To Isamu, Julian Mack was like an older brother. They loved to box until they were "all in."

Isamu made toys—a wooden sleigh, a dollhouse, and a Cinderella carriage—for Isabel, her older sister Mary (nine), and for Scott, age two. In a letter thanking Edward Rumely for sending him the *New York Times Magazine* article about his father, he wrote a postscript: "I have made a sled much larger than the one I made before for my boss he furnishing all the material. He gave me extra pay and a 8-6-2 in box of candy for making it. It is going to be used to carry papers in from the depot." As at Chigasaki, Isamu worked on a garden. "I think it's going to be dandy," he told Rumely. "I have some carnations, Daisies, sweet alyssiums, and Forget-me-nots coming up. Also Marigolds, cornflowers and nasturtiums which are to be planted later. I have the garden dug and a bed made."

In a long undated letter, from July 1920 or 1921, Isamu told Rumely about a camping trip he had made on his own. "Last Saturday, it was the third, I decided to go to Logansport. So I started out at two o'clock with my camp outfit and the bysicle [sic]. About thirty miles south of here I had a flat tire and had to walk about three miles till I came to Knox where I got a new tire."[11] Isamu camped for the night on the bank of the Tippecanoe River, a spot where he had camped two years earlier with a "bunch of Interlaken boys." About ten miles south of Knox, Isamu came upon a lake, which he called "one of the prettiest sights I ever saw the moon was shining and lights were twinkling on the oposite [sic] shore." On the fourth day he got lost, but finally found his way home at six o'clock. "That is how I enjoyed the 'glorious 4th.'"

Isamu did well at La Porte High School, where he was known as Sam Gilmour. He graduated at the top of his class in 1922. Because he had a reputation as a draftsman, he was chosen to draw the illustrations for his class yearbook. The senior class, with typically fond ribbing, elected Isamu the "Biggest Bull-Head" in the class. Next to his yearbook photograph, Isamu wrote his motto, a quotation from Henry Clay: "Sir, I would rather be right than be president."[12] For all his feelings of being a misfit, Isamu seems to have been well liked. Yet one classmate, a Wilbur Flickinger, recalled that Isamu was a loner. "He was kind of a quiet type of individual. We peddled papers together."[13] Another schoolmate, R. K. McLean, remembered Isamu as "a curly headed, bright quick speaking boy, very private . . . His only manifestation of being a sculptor was a carved pair of skis—in an intricate oriental design."[14]

When Isamu finished high school, Rumely asked him what he would like to do with his life. "I said promptly, artist. It was an odd choice, considering that art had become altogether foreign to me since coming to America. I did not show any particular aptitude. On the contrary, I had acquired what is known as a healthy skepticism, and perhaps even a prejudice against art, since my father was an artist— that is, a poet. Apart from William Blake, whom I had rediscovered through Swedenborg, it was a time of negation and disbelief. Yet now my first instinctual decision was to become an artist."[15]

Rumely warned Isamu that he would not be able to make a living as an artist. "He said, you'd better be a doctor, like he was . . . And so even before, while [I was still] going to high school he got a job for me at one point working in a laboratory."[16] Isamu had done brilliantly in chemistry, biology, physics, and math—an aptitude for science that would stand him in good stead years later when he designed technologically complex public monuments. But Rumely was broadminded enough to let Isamu try his hand at art, so that first summer after Isamu's graduation, Rumely organized an apprenticeship for him with his friend the academic sculptor Gutzon Borglum, who had not yet carved the heads of presidents on Mount Rushmore.

When Isamu arrived at Borglum's estate in Stamford, Connecticut, in the summer of 1922, Borglum was working on the first of his gigantic sculptural projects, a memorial to the heroes of the Confederate Army to be carved on the face of Stone Mountain in Georgia. It was to be a high-relief frieze of a group of equestrian figures, including Robert E. Lee, Stonewall Jackson, and Jefferson Davis, followed by a column of soldiers. That summer Borglum was busy with the sculpture's clay and plaster models. (Borglum had only finished Lee's head when, thanks to his irascible, authoritarian personality, he fought with the project's commissioner and, in a rage, smashed his models and abandoned the project.)[17]

A large, powerful-looking man with a mustache and a prominent chin, Borglum is said to have had little time for anyone who was not a millionaire or a congressman. Even worse, he was a bigot who believed that to be an American you had to have been born of American parents. "I didn't get along with Borglum," Noguchi said.[18] "He was a very irascible fellow who enjoyed having people feel badly."[19] To earn his keep, Isamu did odd jobs:

> It was my job to tutor his son, to get the horses to pose, to pose myself on a horse as General Sherman [actually Lee], and to cut down all the dead chestnut trees for firewood as winter approached. My only chance at sculpture turned out to be a head of Lincoln, a subject in which Borglum specialized. But I enjoyed the company of some wonderful Italian plaster casters, who taught me casting. In the end Borglum told me I would never be a sculptor, so I decided to follow Dr. Rumely's advice and become a doctor.[20]

Although Noguchi claimed that Borglum did not teach him and only had him doing chores, the Noguchi scholar Bonnie Rychlak, who worked for Noguchi for many years, claimed Isamu did learn carving, molding, and casting methods from Borglum and, while in Borglum's employ, he made a number of reliefs and sculptures of birds, cows, and other animals in plaster and terra-cotta.[21] The art dealer Julien Levy, who in 1933 wrote one of the earliest and most insightful articles about Noguchi, reproduced a photograph of what he identified as Noguchi's first sculpture, a bust of a man with a hood.[22]

After his summer apprenticeship, Isamu went to live with the Rumelys in their Riverside Drive apartment. "I felt liberated coming from the country to a big city like New York."[23] Although he spent much of his life in other places, New York City remained Noguchi's principal home for the rest of his life.

8

I BECAME A SCULPTOR

Abandoning, for the time being, his ambition to become a sculptor, Isamu followed Rumely's advice and applied to Columbia University. A letter of recommendation from Rumely called Isamu a "most promising student of much more than ordinary ability."[1] Isamu began medical studies in January 1923. "At night I worked in a restaurant, and Dr. Rumely kindly raised the money to pay for my tuition."[2]

During his premed studies at Columbia, Isamu met Dr. Hideo Noguchi, a distinguished bacteriologist and a graduate of Tokyo Medical College who had joined the Rockefeller Institute for Medical Research when he was twenty-eight, in 1904.[3] Having met Isamu's father during Yone's 1920 visit to New York, he took it upon himself to look after Isamu, taking him to dinner at Japanese restaurants and introducing him to his colleagues at the Rockefeller Institute. Even though Isamu was still an undergraduate, Hideo Noguchi arranged for him to work as an assistant in the laboratory of Dr. Simon Flexner, the doctor with whom he himself had worked when he first arrived in America in 1900.

For Isamu, life as a medical student was miserable. He was "totally isolated, no friends . . . Attending class, that's all . . . And hating it."[4] The only professor he remembered well was Raymond Weaver, who taught a course on Dante. "He gave me a passing grade no matter what I did. He thought I deserved it."[5] When Isamu asked Hideo for advice, the doctor said it would be better, and more honest, for him to become an artist like his father. "He himself was an amateur painter—painted fish on his vacations—and he was very enthusiastic about my becoming a sculptor and really tried to promote it. In fact, he tried to get me to do a head of him; he offered me three hundred dollars. But I thought there wasn't enough dignity in his head."[6]

Sometime in the autumn or early winter of 1922, Isamu's mother and half sister arrived in New York. "She was stuck in San Francisco," Noguchi recalled, "probably because of finances . . . So it took her two years to get her breath and get her finances straightened out a bit."[7] During the summer of 1923, after his first term at Columbia, Isamu worked as a chauffeur for Emmet Scott in La Porte. On September 6 he wrote to Rumely, who was still embroiled in his court case, that he would return to New York by the seventeenth and that he wanted to live with his mother, who had taken an apartment at 39 East Tenth Street.[8] Leonie secured a scholarship for Ailes to go to the Ethical Culture School. Once again she tried to make a living by importing and selling Japanese curios: netsuke, jewelry, and woodblock prints.

Living with his mother and half sister soon got on nineteen-year-old Isamu's nerves. He had not seen them for six years, and he could not adjust to being under his mother's wing. "If she had thought to break my dependence in sending me away, my own reaction had been to feel deserted. My extreme attachment never returned, and now the more motherly she became, the more I resented her."[9] The rebellious streak that had begun in the months before he left Japan returned in full force: "I didn't want her to tell me what to do, you see. I was very independent-minded. I got this studio finally when I was nineteen . . . that's the price you pay for being alone—you get used to being alone ."[10]

When Leonie discovered that Isamu was preparing for a career in medicine, she was upset. Years later, in a letter to Catherine, she described confronting Rumely about this. She had, she said, "turned up one day at Dr. Rumely's office and hotly denounced him for turning a boy of artistic temperament toward a career for which he was entirely unsuited. It is quite true, that Dr. Rumely and I had an awful row on that score, and the Doctor, then Isamu's best friend and advisor, persisted in his opinion, so that Isamu, as you know, took a year and a half at Columbia at a pre-medical course. I have just found a notebook of Isamu's, neatly labeled 'chemistry and biology.' Inside is nothing but sketches of vagaries, fishes, rabbits, nude ladies etc. Not one word of any science."[11]

One spring evening in 1924 Isamu returned to his mother's Tenth Street apartment and found her eager to tell him about an art school that she had noticed in the neighborhood. The Leonardo da Vinci Art School, recently founded by two sculptors, was housed in a red-brick converted church building at 288 East Tenth Street on the corner of Tompkins Square Park. The school's purpose was to offer art education to the neighborhood's mostly Italian immigrant community. Tuition was six dollars a month or, if needed, free. "It was a night school, a settlement school, for people who didn't have the means to go to school . . . So I went by there and took a look."[12]

Onorio Ruotolo, the school's director, had come to the United States from Italy in 1908. When Noguchi met him he was a successful academic portraitist who did busts of such luminaries as Arturo Toscanini, Thomas Edison, Enrico Caruso, Theodore Dreiser, and Helen Keller. He was also a poet, cartoonist, and book illustrator, and was said to have been an anarchist.[13] Heavy-set with a mop of curly black hair, Ruotolo in his mid-thirties was a welcome contrast to the mean-looking Borglum. In Noguchi's memory he was "very handsome with flashing eyes," a "passionate man" who followed his instincts.[14] Ruotolo's instinct told him that Isamu had a talent that must be fostered. As Noguchi recalls, the director spotted him when he visited and asked, "'Wouldn't you like to study here?' I said I wasn't interested in sculpture." Isamu explained that he had stopped by because his mother had told him to.

Although Isamu at first rejected Ruotolo's offer to enroll, the director persisted, saying, "Oh, come on, do something," and Isamu reluctantly agreed to copy a plaster cast of a foot. Ruotolo was impressed. "You must become a sculptor," he said. "Well, I can't afford it," said Isamu. "I'm working in a restaurant. I haven't got time."[15] Ruotolo offered him a scholarship. "I began attending evening school but then announced that I couldn't go on because I had a job and also went to college. Ruotolo suggested that I should work for him and give up the restaurant job, and he would pay me the equivalent. How could I resist? I became a sculptor, even against my will."[16] Ruotolo's teaching involved levitations and séances. "He claimed that he taught me psychically. I worked as in a trance, with each new sculpture hailed and promoted by him." As Ruotolo's studio assistant, Isamu's job was to clean up the studio and help with various chores. "I remember the first summer I was with him I helped him illustrate John Macy's book on *The History of Man*. He made some sort of pseudo woodcuts."[17] As his engagement with sculpture deepened, Isamu gave up medical school.

To affirm his new role as an artist, Isamu took back his father's name. Noguchi was, he thought, a better name for an artist than the more prosaic Gilmour. And in terms of the visual arts, Japanese culture had more cachet than Irish culture. Also, it was a way of putting distance between himself and his mother. "Perhaps [the name change] was an effort at righting something that was wrong in myself, in my work, a lack of identity between what I was and what I could or should be. I hated my father, yet here adopted his name."[18]

To make ends meet, Isamu found jobs as a sculptor, with Ruotolo's help. The first was to make a candy mold, but portrait commissions soon followed. Various young women he met at art school sat for portrait busts, and the Rumely family commissioned a bust of Emmet Scott, who had recently died. A 1924 photograph shows Isamu beside

Isamu working on the bust of Emmet Hoyt Scott, 1924

Scott's bust and holding a sculptor's tool. The sculpture is, like Isamu's other early works, academic, but it does convey something of Scott's intelligence and kindness. Isamu also made a bust of Rumely's mother-in-law and reliefs of the Rumely children. Each portrait plaque cost five dollars in plaster, thirty-five dollars to cast in bronze, fifteen for the wooden frame, and three for a photograph. The total for two bas-reliefs that he delivered was $116.00. On March 26 Isamu wrote to thank Rumely for sending a check, which "came in mighty handy."[19] In an undated letter he asked Rumely to send fifteen dollars so that he could pay his rent.[20] He also asked permission to send Isabel Rumely's portrait to the National Academy exhibition.

In late March Isamu wrote to Rumely, who was serving a sentence of thirty days at the Tarrytown, New York, jail: "It is 11:30 P.M. as I write this letter. I have just come in from a walk with Mr. Onorio Ruotolo, the sculptor . . . He reiterated that you were one of the most magnificent of men—a victim of this 'system.' We talked of other things besides—of sculpture and education. His educational theories are quite sound. He believes in encouragement . . . He like you inspires! . . . I wish you good luck."[21] And Rumely was lucky: according to Fanny Scott Rumely's memoir of her husband, various eminent citizens came to his defense, among them his friend Henry Ford, who told President Coolidge that he would sit outside the White House door until Coolidge pardoned Rumely."[22] Coolidge was persuaded.

Though Isamu had decided not to pursue medicine, Rumely remained affectionate and encouraging. "My dear Isamu, you have the real stuff in you!" he wrote on June 2, 1924. "I admire that quality which enables you to stick through the night to get out a job. It is that quality which will carry you far in life, and which is so valuable in combination with your sensitiveness and artistic abilities."[23] In another letter, Rumely said watching Isamu grow up had been "one of the worthwhile experiences of my life."[24]

Isamu moved quickly from copying plaster casts to the life class. He later recalled that his first sculpture was of Oscar Wilde's Salome. "Then I did Jesus Christ. I would say I was extremely facile."[25] Two other early sculptures mentioned in a letter from Isabel Rumely to Noguchi are an allegorical heart made of thorns and a bronze flying fish that was a study for a fountain.[26] Isabel also remembered a line drawing of God with a sad face and a heavy burden on his shoulders that the nineteen-year-old Isamu had made for a little magazine and had given to Dr. Rumely. It was an illustration for a poem called "The Great Captive" by the Indian English poet Harindranath Chattopadhyay (brother of the poet, freedom fighter, and stateswoman Sarojini Naidu, who knew Isamu's parents). Mary Rumely, who owned the drawing in 1970, copied the words of the poem that Isamu had written on the back of his drawing and sent them to Isamu in a letter. Part of it reads: "God is as much a prisoner, dear friend, as you and I . . . God is a mighty captive in the sky's enameled tower."[27]

After only three months Isamu held his first one-man exhibition at the school. The show included twenty-two plaster and terra-cotta sculptures. Eager to publicize the genius of his young protégé, Ruotolo proclaimed him to be the "new Michelangelo."[28] "He would call up the newspapers and all these reporters would come traipsing in and we would have a news conference."[29] One reviewer for *The World and Word* waxed ecstatic over Isamu's show. The headline ran "19-Year-Old Japanese American Born Shows Marked Ability as a Sculptor." The piece was illustrated by a photograph of Isamu and four of his sculptures: *Fountain Study*, *Christ-Head*, *The Archer*, and *Salome*. The text compared Isamu to a Donatello faun, and said that his head of Christ had "the mature feeling for a person that is more than human, a sorrow more than divine."[30]

Isamu was soon honored by his election to various prestigious groups such as the National Academy of Design and the Architectural League. Both institutions exhibited his work regularly. One of Isamu's heads was shown in Paris, and he exhibited frequently at the Pennsylvania Academy and in the National Sculpture Association exhibitions. He had been invited to join the National Sculpture Association and the Grand Central Galleries. Twice he participated in Prix de Rome shows and both times he won honorable mention. "Because of Ruotolo's beating the drum . . . I became a kind of celebrity at the National Sculpture Society and the Architectural League. In those days the Architectural League was very, very academic."[31]

Within a few months, Isamu's rebellious spirit forced him to move on. "I seldom went to school, and Mr. Ruotolo even moved himself to another studio to allow me the full use of his own."[32] The studio he borrowed from Ruotolo was on Fourteenth Street, just south of Union Square. After incurring Ruotolo's displeasure by refusing to welcome some of Ruotolo's friends to his studio on the grounds that he was too busy working, Isamu was "thrown out." He took a new studio at 127 University Place on the corner of Fourteenth Street, and Rumely agreed to help him with his rent. Isamu relished having his own studio. "I became a sculptor on my own."[33]

In New York, Isamu came to know several of his father's friends, one of whom was the avant-garde dancer and choreographer Michio Ito, who, around 1915, had been part of William Butler Yeats and Ezra Pound's London circle. In 1916 Ito moved to New York, where he choreographed Broadway reviews. Three years later he opened his own dance studio. The experimental "dance poems" he invented influenced a younger generation of choreographers including Martha Graham. Like Yone and Isamu, Ito was seen as a cultural link between East and West. When Isamu met him in 1925, Ito was a handsome thirty-three-year-old ladykiller married to one of his dance students. Isamu must have been attracted to Ito's milieu—beautiful dancers, sophisticated literary friends. He loved to watch dance performances. Years later Noguchi recalled how much he had learned from Ito as well as from Ito's younger brother Yuji, a set and costume designer.[34]

When Ito posed for Isamu in 1925, Isamu produced his first unconventional sculpture. The portrait looks like a Noh mask—in his early twenties Ito had performed in Yeats's Noh play *At the Hawk's Well,* and he was now preparing to put on the play in New York. Isamu molded the head in papier-mâché and later had it cast in bronze. He transformed a long lock of Ito's hair into a handle. Although the piece is severe and stylized, it does convey the dancer's dynamic presence. Ito liked the work so much, he asked the young portraitist to make similar masks for his production of Yeats's play.

In the mid-1920s Isamu continued to sculpt heads and figures: "I was doing a figure of a Russian girl named Nadia Nikolaiova—a head. She was a girl with a nice figure who danced in the Serpent and in a club."[35] Nadia was a ballet dancer who, in 1926, posed for free so long as Isamu would give her a percentage of the selling price. In eight months Isamu created the best known of his early academic sculptures, a full-length serpentine nude figure of Nadia called *Undine (Nadja).* The water nymph from the popular ballet *Ondine* is imagined as if she were underwater, so that her mass of wavy hair floats upward. Her clasped hands are raised above her head in that position of vulnerability

Isamu working on *Undine* (*Nadja*), 1926

and exposure so popular in depictions of the female nude. Her sensuous body with its exaggerated swing of the hip is highly erotic. The way light moves over her skin seems to echo the artist's excitement.

On February 2, 1927, perhaps in order to sell this sculpture, Isamu wrote a one-page essay about *Undine*:

> Tortuous as a flame or as the spray from a sea wave she stands— dynamic action thrills in every part of her, from the curve of her foot to her flying hair—and yet an eternal serenity seems to preside over her. Have you noticed when watching a flame or when watching a storm at sea that Nature never appears to overexert herself?—an infinite reserve seems to linger in even its ultimate thrust . . .
>
> As to her spirit, why, I should say that she moves us all, each probably in a different way, or in several different ways. To me she represents a wonderful awakening; and what a marvellous vista of subtle connotations does that not imply![36]

The figure sculptures that Isamu made in the 1920s were first modeled in clay and fired, then a mold was made, and finally plasters and bronzes were cast by the Roman Bronze Foundry in Queens, New York. Since casting was expensive, he sometimes had buyers finance the process.

Having finished *Undine* in 1926 and garnering great praise, Isamu had confidence in his mastery of the techniques of academic sculpture. With success came an expansion of his world. "I was befriended by several people. I mean being young and sort of wanting to be an artist, people would befriend you somehow or other."[37] In his downtown neighborhood he met an increasing number of artists and art dealers. "I liked the life around there."[38] But the satisfaction was short-lived. Although Isamu was, as he recalled, "the hope of the academy," he was restless. "By twenty-one I had run the gamut and was disillusioned."[39] Needing to find a way to move beyond his academic work, he began to visit galleries that showed modern art. "In 1926 when I was twenty-one, the horizons of art rapidly opened for me. I was a frequenter of Alfred Stieglitz's gallery, An American Place and the New Art Circle of J. B. Neumann, who became my counselor and friend. I began going to all the not-too-frequent exhibitions of modern art."[40] Isamu was enthralled.

The catalytic event for Isamu's transformation into a modernist sculptor was his 1926 visit to the Brummer Gallery's Brancusi show, organized by the Dada artist Marcel Duchamp, who shepherded the young Isamu around the exhibition. "The exhibition of Brancusi that year on the beautiful top floor of the Brummer Gallery completely crystallized my uncertainties. I was transfixed by his vision."[41] Years later, asked how, given his academic training, he could respond to Brancusi, Noguchi said that while Neumann and Stieglitz had probably recommended that he see the Brancusi show, he had come to appreciate Brancusi's work "purely on my own . . . I mean it was not something through any conversation or introduction other than just that I happened to see it."[42] He did acknowledge that "there must have been conversations with Stieglitz and Neumann which disposed me that way." Isamu's familiarity with the Japanese emphasis on simplicity and reverence for materials also triggered his immediate enthusiasm for Brancusi's work.

Like Rumely and Ruotolo, Neumann and Stieglitz were among those people who saw something in Isamu that made them want to help him. Born in a village in Austria-Hungary in 1887, Neumann opened a gallery in London in 1910, immigrated to the United States in 1923, and opened the New Art Circle. He not only showed European artists like Munch, Kandinsky, and Rouault, but he also had a few Americans such as Oscar Bluemner, Max Weber, and Walt Kuhn. "Neumann showed those [artists] of his own taste, which were somewhat expressionist . . . some of the German Expressionists and things like that. But we were friends. He was one of my early backers." It was probably in the early 1930s, when Noguchi sculpted his portrait, that Neumann wrote a profile called "Reflections About Isamu Noguchi": "For Noguchi, so it seems to me, a background deeply rooted in American psychology is immensely important. Anyone familiar with his past sculpture will readily recognize a typically American approach in his direct, decisive grasp of each subject."[43]

Stieglitz told a story about Isamu's first visit to the recently opened Intimate Gallery in February 1926. When asked where he came from, Isamu replied, "From all over the world."[44] He spoke admiringly of an O'Keeffe painting of deep blue petunias: "That is nature expressed as nature would do it," Isamu reputedly said. "If there were a living petunia, a third one next to the two painted ones, they would recognize each other."

"The boy spoke of the 'professional' attitude," Stieglitz recalled, "as against the 'play' spirit of workmanship and things made not for exhibition but to satisfy the worker, such work alone being real . . . The young man said that nature was like a huge keyboard of a musical instrument and that the man who could pick out chords, could see relationships, was the artist."

If this story is accurate, Isamu already harbored certain ideas—art as play, nature as the basis of art—that would continue to characterize his approach. Isamu was drawn to the older man's outpouring of controversial opinions. People like Stieglitz, Noguchi said, have "their own authority. They did not have to ask other people."[45]

In 1926 a chance conversation changed the course of Isamu's life. "One day when I was out at the Roman Bronze Works, the director, Mr. Bertelli, told me that Mr. Harry Guggenheim had seen a piece of mine and suggested that I try for the newly founded Guggenheim fellowship."[46] Isamu wasted no time in finding people in the art world— Neumann, Stieglitz, and the prominent academic sculptor James Earle Fraser—to recommend him for the grant. Fraser, he said, "represented my academic past." The other two stood for his desire for change. Isamu asked Rumely for a letter of recommendation as well, and Rumely gave a picture of Isamu's youthful strength of character, intelligence, and talent: "He could carve wood; he could work with all tools; he could hammer metal designs; draw as almost no student in the school . . . If he can secure for himself the requisite preparation that will include training, travel and contact with the artistic treasures of Europe and broadening experience in productive work, he should rank as one of America's great artists ten years hence."[47]

Isamu's 1926 essay for his Guggenheim application reveals how dramatically his thoughts and feelings were inspired by his modern art awakening. The essay also reflects his early absorption of Japanese culture, his knowledge of Rumely's philosophy of education, and the Swedenborgian concepts he learned about as an adolescent while living with the Mack family. A crucial statement of Isamu's outlook, the Guggenheim essay contains many ideas that would guide him for the rest of his life: "It is my desire to view nature through nature's eyes, and to ignore man as an object for special veneration. There must be unthought-of heights of beauty to which sculpture may be raised by this reversal of attitude. An unlimited field for abstract sculptural expression would then be realized in which flowers and trees, rivers and mountains as well as birds, beasts and man would be given their due place." He said he wanted to "become once more a part of nature—a part of the very earth, thus to view the inner surfaces and the life elements." The materials out of which his sculptures would be made would, he said, be part of their content. "As yet, I have never executed any of those ideas. I have rather been saving them as sacred until such time as I should have attained technical confidence and skill . . . My proposal, therefore, should I be so honored as to receive your fellowship, would include a travel study and production period of three years—the first year to be spent in Paris, where I should endeavor to acquire proficiency in stone and wood cutting, as well as in a better understanding of the human figure."

During the fellowship's second year he would travel to India, China, and Japan. "I have selected the Orient as the location for my productive activities for the reason that I feel a great attachment for it, having spent half my life there. My father, Yone Noguchi, is Japanese and has long been known as an interpreter of the East to the West, through poetry. I wish to do the same with sculpture . . . May I, therefore, request your assistance in enabling me to fulfill my heritage."[48]

The Guggenheim Fellowship was awarded, and Isamu received a grant of $2,500 for one year. It seemed a fortune. He would have to reapply each year for a maximum of three years. On the day before he sailed, his mother helped him pack and then accompanied him to dinner at a little Armenian restaurant where they met his Bulgarian friend Boris Majdrakoff, whose portrait Isamu had recently made. On March 19, 1927, Rumely hosted a going-away party with fifteen guests at a Japanese restaurant where they ate raw fish and drank sake. Leonie later wrote to Catherine that among the many speeches, Ruotolo warned Isamu against the seductions of women, saying that though they were the source of much inspiration, they could also be "a source of danger." At this Isamu winked at a pretty young woman named Nita and she threw him a kiss.[49] Leonie's speech advised her son to "keep his head," but Isamu answered, "What's the use of putting water in the soup?" When Isamu was asked to say something, "all he did was to get up and grin all around and say that he hadn't a thing that he wished to say but that he felt fine and hoped that they all did the same and he drank their health in sake."

After this festive meal, many of the guests accompanied Isamu to his ship, due to sail at midnight. Nita was clearly sad to see him go, and,

as Leonie reported to Catherine, kissed him before he set off. "I suspect there's a romance there and wonder how long it will take to cure
the ache of parting, and perhaps, probably, find other loves. She is a
Russian girl and deaf, so she speaks with a slow drawl, not so very dis-
tinctly. She posed for several of his studies, but not for Undine. That
was Nadia."

Two days after Isamu's departure, Leonie wrote telling him that after
seeing him off Nita had kept assuring her that Isamu was "the nicest
boy she ever knew."[50] Ailes, Leonie reported, had been disappointed
that her brother had left without her saying goodbye. Isamu had given
his sister the wrong date, and she had come into the city one day too
late.

In her son's absence, Leonie took charge of some of his business
affairs. In late March she wrote Catherine that *Undine* had been cast
in bronze and was on exhibition at the Grand Central Art Galleries.
"The price marked on it is $4500. The art gallery gets 20% of the sell-
ing price, $1500 goes to Mr. Albee, who put up the money for the cast-
ing, and Isamu promised 10% to his model, Nadia, who heroically
posed for over a period to 8 months without accepting any return."[51]
Leonie had asked Mr. Albee to either buy *Undine* or grant an extension to the loan.

Leonie told Catherine that Isamu had offered to send her a part of
the fellowship money every month. She refused it knowing that the
cost of material for sculpture was high. "But he says I may retire after
four years."[52] She was, she said, "camping" in Isamu's studio for the week:
"No heat but gas, which makes me sick, so I have to turn it off. Cold
as a barn . . . Ice cold running water outside the room. Smells of the
toilet in the hall. Noisy, dusty—rats running about." In spite of his
early success, Isamu's finances remained precarious.

On March 27, the Cunard Line's RMS *Aquitania* left Isamu in England where he stopped for a few days before proceeding to Paris.

On his first night in London Isamu met the artist Nina Hamnett in
the lobby of his hotel. She introduced herself to him as a painter and
took him for a ride around Hyde Park and then to the glamorous
Café Royale. "She was," he later recalled, "the first person to tell me
about Henri Gaudier [Brzeska], saying that she had posed for him a

few times."[53] Indeed, Hamnett had once been the modernist sculptor Gaudier-Brzeska's lover. She was also a friend of Brancusi's, and possibly sent Isamu off to Paris with a letter of introduction to him.

On Easter Sunday, just before he left London, Isamu wrote Rumely thanking him for a telegram that he had received on the second day of his transatlantic voyage. "While you have burdened me with your expectations you give me renewed courage. As always you steel me to my best efforts."[54]

9

I WILL RIVAL THE IMMORTALS

Noguchi always spoke of his first days in Paris as being guided by fate. "I was at a café sitting next to a man and he said, 'What do you want to do?' And I said, 'I would like to meet Brancusi.' 'Come with me,' he said, and he introduced me to Brancusi, and with that I started working for Brancusi, the great Rumanian sculptor."[1] The stranger he met at the café, however, was the American poet Robert McAlmon, who knew everyone, including Nina Hamnett. Most likely Hamnett had given Isamu a letter of introduction to McAlmon. Isamu (whom I shall hereafter call Noguchi because Paris was where he came into his own) gave different versions of this story throughout his life, but it is undeniable that roughly a month after arriving in Paris on March 30, 1927, Noguchi became Brancusi's assistant.

By April 16, Noguchi had moved into a studio found for him by the Japanese painter Tsuguharu Foujita, a popular figure in the Paris art world whom he had met through a letter of introduction from Michio Ito. He wrote to Rumely that the 7 rue Belloni studio was well located and had good proportions, and that he had been lucky to find it because studios for rent in Paris were scarce.[2] "I visited the École des Beaux-Arts accompanied by Mr. Krans of the American University Union—to the class of stone carving in particular. I was rather disappointed and have therefore decided to cut stone privately under the direction of a sculptor stone cutter." Noguchi's lack of enthusiasm for the École des Beaux-Arts is not surprising: "I was trying to find a way to get away from the academic . . . I really wanted to find another way."[3] In order to improve his understanding of the human figure he enrolled in drawing classes at the Académie de la Grande Chaumière and the Académie Collarosi.

Even at a distance, Rumely remained a mentor for Noguchi. He sent him books, words of wisdom, and, to maintain his health, jars of a yeast extract called Vegex.[4] Noguchi read widely during this time, especially in French, in an effort to learn the language. He preferred technical books to novels—to him their language was less challenging. "I spend ideal evenings reading geometrical theorems and Bergson's philosophy."[5] In later years, when he was working on complex public sculptures, Noguchi's grasp of mathematics and technology always astonished his colleagues. The philosopher Henri Bergson's ideas about intuition, duration, and the élan vital, or vital impetus that drives evolution and human creativity, were very much in vogue with the intelligentsia in these years, and some of them would remain part of Noguchi's thinking.

That March Rumely advised Noguchi to make contacts and choose his friends carefully. He should plan his time, keep fit, read, be receptive in order to learn from others, and, finally, he should keep his individuality but not be overly assertive about his opinions. "You have the possibility of becoming a master," Rumely said. "Be confident about your future . . . You have a destiny to fulfill, be ready to learn, and believe in yourself!"[6] That Noguchi took this last bit of advice to heart can be seen in an extraordinary letter he wrote to Rumely thanking him for two books, one of which was about Napoleon:

> The Napoleon I have already started and find it well writen [sic] and intensely interesting. Indeed I am inclined to credit my reading of this book at this time with far reaching psychological significance. I am already finding many of my actions justified by him and feel that here is a man whom I can admire and understand. He has much to teach me much that I have already felt as evil but necessary—such for instance as the taking of every possible advantage. This I have considered unworthy but as I read the histories of great men I find it invariably true that they have always cajoled and grabed [sic] every opportunity by the neck and have done that which nature and circumstance made it easiest for them to do . . .

I have only now realized how really important and how specialized and competitive is the study of art. It is the most exacting of taskmistresses and the practice of it the most sacred of obligations since by it is elevated not the mind only but the imagination and emotions as well. I hereby solemnly dedicate my life to its pursuite [sic] and will avoid all other objectives as I would the pest. Time! Give me but uninterupted [sic] time and I will rival the immortals.[7]

Paris was ebullient with café life taken up by expatriates from all over the world. Michio Ito had given Noguchi letters of introduction to a number of artists and intellectuals, among them the painters Foujita and Jules Pascin and the writer Ezra Pound. Because his French was limited (he did attend a few classes at the Alliance Française), most of Noguchi's friends were American. "However," he told Rumely, "I am trying to widen my French acquaintanceship." Noguchi the misfit was put somewhat to rest; in the Parisian Bohemia, the more exotic a person's background the better. "Whereas previously I had very few friends, in France I suddenly came upon, you might say, people who were either like me or that I could accept, or who could accept me. After all, this business of . . . discrimination didn't exist there . . ."[8]

In Paris Noguchi found a sexual freedom that did not exist in New York. With his charm, intelligence, and good looks, he was soon caught up in the life that revolved around the Montparnasse cafés. "In Paris in those days," he recalled, "the café was the center of meeting and so forth; it was a very easy way of meeting people and of striking up a conversation. I mean the best way, in fact, the life of Paris was the life of the street."[9] Legend has it that Noguchi had a love affair with the famous artist's model and nightclub singer Kiki de Montparnasse— a wildly liberated creature whose lovers over the years included many artists but most important the American photographer and painter Man Ray.

In his autobiography Noguchi recalled, "And for the American group, of which I became a part, there was an enclave on the rue Vercingétorix, with Andrée Ruellan, Stuart Davis, Morris Kantor, and Beno. I saw a good deal of Alexander Calder, often helping him with his wire circus, and then going dancing. There was Lajos Tihanyé, my mute Hungarian friend, and Arno Brecher, the German sculptor who became my neighbor."[10] Other friends were the American painter Adolf Dehn and the Russian-born French sculptor Ossip Zadkine, who took him to the Russian Christmas celebration at the Hôtel Lutetia. At his afternoon drawing classes Noguchi met a number of American art students, among them Marion Greenwood, whose portrait he would sculpt two years later in New York and with whom he had a love affair.

In November 1927 Noguchi wrote to both his mother and to Rumely to tell them that his friend the American painter Andrée Ruellen, whom he had met at the Académie de la Grande Chaumière, was coming to New York to organize an exhibition of her paintings. To Leonie he wrote: "You know I have a prejudice about mixing female friends and mothers—however I am giving this case a special dispensation. She is a nice girl, inteligent [sic] etc—judge for yourself."[11] To Rumely he described Ruellen as "a good friend" and "an extremely tallented [sic] young American artist."[12] After classes at the Grande Chaumière, Noguchi and Ruellen would explore the city: "Everyday," Ruellen recalled, "we visited art galleries and museums together and went to cafés to talk about art. Isamu didn't know much about Paris so I took him on walks through the city. We didn't take the bus to go anywhere. Mostly we just walked. He seemed to be attached to everything about Brancusi. He even wore Romanian wooden shoes like Brancusi did. And he talked over and over about how Brancusi lived for nothing but work. I can't say that in our circle Isamu attracted special attention for his talent. But I thought that he had a wonderful sense of beauty."[13]

Although Ruellen saw Noguchi simply as a friend, he fell in love with her. When she was in New York in late November he wrote to her that when he received her letter, he "was transcendent—happiness had become joy—I jumped up and clutched the air and would have shouted, but that again would never do, so I dashed out to your old studio . . ." He went on to tell her,

Love to me is actual but at that moment I am also a tyrant . . . Only the unatained [sic] holds for me the glamour of infinite possibilities and while a love may last for ages it is only a static condition, and ever present now, fixed like a landmark in the passage of time. All that is past may never have been and is only held fixed by the ice of our memories. The creative impulse is entirely dependent upon a perfect realization and a harmony with the present. Neither the past nor the future has anything to do with love or art.

Alas—we are not escargots . . . [14]

He was, indeed, a tyrant. Ruellen remembered Noguchi becoming miserably jealous when he found other guests in her studio. Once he was so belligerent that Ruellen's mother ordered him to leave. Noticing how Noguchi's face would sometimes darken, Ruellen surmised that something in his childhood had injured him deeply. "He was part of our group of American artists but he never really showed his feelings to anyone."[15] He told Ruellen about his bitterness toward his abandoning father, but he also gave her a book of Yone's poems and expressed pride in his father's accomplishments. Noguchi's single-minded ambition impressed Ruellen: "Isamu paid no attention to what he wore or what he ate. The only thing that seemed to possess him was pursuing his dream to become a 'great sculptor.'" Noguchi was, Ruellen said, "too handsome for his own good," and his strong ego sometimes made him "astonishingly selfish." At some point during his Paris sojourn Ruellen and other friends of Noguchi's were upset because of his "woman trouble." Perhaps she was referring to his love affair with an older woman, an art dealer, soon after he arrived in Paris. Things got complicated when a former girlfriend, possibly Nita, arrived from New York. For a while Noguchi and this girlfriend lived together and Noguchi pretended she was his wife. But when she became pregnant, Noguchi insisted that she have an abortion. The operation was botched and she became critically ill.[16]

From April to August 1927, Noguchi spent the mornings at Brancusi's studio in the impasse Ronsin, a cul-de-sac of studios to the west of the Gare Montparnasse and just off the rue de Vaugirard. In the afternoons he studied drawing. Brancusi, at fifty-one, was, Noguchi recalled, "at the height of his powers."[17] "He was very assured . . . very pleasant then, very sort of open, very happy."[18] For all his admiration, Noguchi felt that Brancusi was no longer forging new ground: "He'd done practically everything he's famous for—that is to say, rather than creating new forms, he was trying to perfect those he'd already done . . . I'm a perfectionist too, of course, but not that much and in a different way . . . I'm always looking for a new solution. I'm not interested in producing things I've done before."[19]

Like Noguchi, Brancusi had learned wood carving as a boy, when he worked as a shepherd in the Carpathian Mountains. Later, when he carved a violin while working as a servant, his talent was recognized and he was sent to the local arts and crafts school. After some academic training in Bucharest and Munich, he walked to Paris in 1904 to attend the École des Beaux-Arts. But his memory of Romanian folk art would eventually turn him against academic art. He came to scorn realistic representation of the figure as "*biftek.*" Although he admired Rodin, he chose not to study with him: "Nothing grows in the shadow of big trees," he said.[20]

Brancusi was patient and generous with his new apprentice. His eyes, Noguchi observed, were "brilliant," always shining. "So, too, were Picasso's, but Picasso's were like bullets coming at you while Brancusi's always smiled. He made me a convert. It was my last conversion."[21] What Brancusi communicated through his gaze was especially important because he and Noguchi had no language in common. As Noguchi began to pick up a little French, he understood snippets of what his new mentor said. "I remember vaguely a story of a crocodile on the beach at Deauville with attendant adventures. Once he told me of his breaking a leg and being taken to a hut in a forest at night, from which predicament he had been saved by his knowledge as a sculptor by casting his leg in plaster! I was convinced he was filled with all kinds of mystic lore . . ."[22]

Noguchi called Brancusi's studio "a laboratory for distilling basic shapes."[23] The rugged simplicity of the space and furnishings seemed a reflection of the purity and vigor of the man. "Wherever he was, everything had to be all white. He wore white, his beard was then already white. He had two white dogs that he fed [in a white basin] with lettuce floating in milk." His sculptures were covered with white cloths. Noguchi's friend Dore Ashton said that Noguchi often talked about Brancusi's studio's "almost sacred atmosphere."[24] Brancusi had made a kind of oasis, a place where his sculpture and his life were one. Noguchi, too, would make spaces that were havens where visitors could be transported outside of time.

Brancusi started his new apprentice off by showing him how to carve a flat plane in order to cut a base out of limestone. "First he taught me how to correctly cut and true the edges and then by cutting grooves to level the space between, then on to squaring the cube. He was insistent on the right way to handle each tool for the job and material, and on the respect to be accorded to each."[25] The Romanian was tremendously disciplined: in his studio "everything was always proper," Noguchi recalled. Although there were "a lot of stones all over the place," Brancusi was "a very neat person."[26] In time, Noguchi, too, became almost obsessive about the placement of tools in his studio, and like Brancusi he was greatly concerned with how his sculptures were displayed.

Noguchi learned to use Brancusi's primitive tools such as his frame saw, which was about four feet long. The apprentice pulled from one end and the master from the other. The saw had to cut with its own weight. It should not be forced.[27] Noguchi also did studio chores such as sweeping the floor after the chips flew, and sharpening the tools, which "was a ritual before all others." "I was his helper, his sort of right hand. He would give me things to do that he thought I could do. He was very kind to me. After all, I didn't ask him for anything. He didn't have to pay me . . . I was useful."[28] At other times Noguchi felt that he was of little help to Brancusi, in part because it was difficult for Brancusi to delegate work. "He was entirely oriented to craft," Noguchi said. "And everything he did had to go through his hand in a very vigorous way."

Brancusi was adamant about sculpture being true to the material: "To give matter another role than the one nature intended it to have is to kill it," he said.[29] He passed along this reverence for materials and his deep respect for tools to Noguchi, who observed that Brancusi's "work came from the creativity of the hand, how you hold a saw, what kind of saw you hold . . . It was not a question merely of the result but of the process."[30] Another time Noguchi put it this way: "It was the wood itself and its contact with the chisel that he liked—not something faked up, painted, or ill-treated. With metal it wasn't some sort of patina he was after, or something applied with acids. He wanted to scrape away all the excrescences on the surface and get back to the original nudity of the metal itself—which for him was polished metal, of course. I too have a distaste of pictorial qualities in sculpture, of those eroded, decayed surfaces one associates with painting."[31]

Brancusi allowed Noguchi to work on one of his *Birds in Space* and on one of the marble sculptures. "He gave me that tool called 'the

Chemin de Fer,' which makes a terrible noise . . . like zzzztttt."[32] The *Chemin de Fer* consisted of a series of saw blades fixed in wood. While Noguchi worked on the surface of the marble, "Brancusi would file away at a pale alloy bronze casting of another of his *Birds*. The long file had to go its full length, curving over the roundness . . . always there was this striving after perfection that could only be had through his own hard labor."[33] From Brancusi Noguchi learned about seeking exact contours and polishing a sculpture's skin until it felt just right. Every few weeks Brancusi would send Noguchi off to the Salon des Tuileries to polish and repolish his bronze *Leda* (1925), which was on exhibition there. Brancusi also taught Noguchi the need for focus. "Concentrate and stop looking out of the window!" Brancusi would shout.[34]

Noguchi made no sculptures of his own during this period. He did make one painting in the studio of his new friend, the American modernist Morris Kantor. In response to his mother's pressuring him to do his own work, he wrote her: "Really both of you and Mr. Boris are hard on me in pumping me with questions as to what I am sculpting for the very simple reason that I am not. All I do during the day is cut marble for somebody else. Have not made a thing for myself. Anyway I am sending Mr. Boris a copy of my quarterly report to the foundation which you may get—but it is really uninteresting. I will not do any creative work for a long time until I am completely oriented to my new medium and method of thought. Ahem. Lovingly Isamu."[35] Leonie's letters to Noguchi continued to be full of maternal advice: "Be careful not to breathe any marble dust as it injures the lungs." She told him to wear woolen shirts to combat Paris's autumn chill and to burn charcoal sparingly because it was dangerous to his health.[36]

What Noguchi was doing during his months with Brancusi was preparing himself for modernism by absorbing Brancusi's methods and ideas. The process of relinquishing his academic training was a struggle. Stone carving was new to him and was "the opposite of whatever I had so quickly learned of the tricks and easy effects of clay."[37] "And the process of unlearning is sometimes more difficult than the process of learning."[38] But Brancusi was an uncompromising mentor. He impressed upon Noguchi the "immediate value of the moment," that is, the work you are producing now. Brancusi would tell Noguchi, and Noguchi repeated this idea many times, that he should "never make things as studies to be thrown away. Never think you're going to be further along than you *are*—because you're as good as you ever will be at the *moment*. That which you *do* is the thing."[39]

The way Brancusi distilled nature to find its essence was a revelation to his young apprentice. "What Brancusi does with a bird or the Japanese do with a garden is to take the essence of nature and distill it—just as a poet does. And that's what I'm interested in—the poetic translation . . . to get to the kernel, to touch most poignantly the key forms."[40] For Noguchi nature remained the keystone and pure abstraction was suspect. "Brancusi used to say how lucky were the young people of the new generation such as myself, who could look forward to uninhibited and true abstraction, not like himself who always started out from some recognizable image in nature. I remember listening with some skepticism, and wondering whether he was bequeathing a blessing or a curse."[41]

For both Noguchi and Brancusi, sculpture meant a return to origins, a search for primordial forms. Brancusi, Noguchi said, "really wanted to go back to the origins of sculpture, the origins of how it was conceived and made."[42] Noguchi could have been talking about himself when he wrote of Brancusi: "The memory of childhood, of things observed not taught, of closeness to the earth, of wet stones and grass, of stone buildings and wood churches, hand-hewn logs and tools, stone markers, walls, and gravestones. This is the inheritance he was able to call upon when the notion came to him that his art, sculpture, could not go forward to be born without first going back to beginnings."[43]

In August the floor of Brancusi's studio collapsed under the weight of his sculptures and his heavy plaster display tables. Noguchi spent several weeks helping Brancusi transport his tools and furnishings and helping him to fix up his new studio. "Immediately Brancusi began to build the skylight for his new place."[44] But by this time Noguchi wanted to do his own work. In one of his quarterly reports he told the Guggenheim Foundation's secretary, Henry Allen Moe, "I have busied myself in purchasing equipment, in making drawings and in studying the history of French art."[45] Noguchi heeded Brancusi's advice and moved out from the shadow of the big tree.

10

OUT FROM THE SHADOW
OF A BIG TREE

In his Guggenheim application, Noguchi wrote that after a year in Paris he intended to travel to India and to the Far East. But in November 1927 he changed his mind, explaining to Rumely that he believed Paris was the place where he could advance in his art.[1] He asked Rumely for a loan; his patron obliged by purchasing a sculpture. A month later he wrote that his current plan was to go to Italy after a January visit to England. He hoped also to visit the Junkers plant at Dessau when Rumely was in Germany, "both because I am interested in aeroplanes and because I wish to make several things in plate aluminum. I have had this project in mind for a long time and am intensely interested."[2] Noguchi's admiration for airplanes paralleled Brancusi's admiration for the shape of propeller blades. Both men's attraction to certain forms of modern technology revealed itself in the streamlined simplicity of some of their works.

Noguchi felt ready to begin incorporating all that he had learned from Brancusi into his own work and, at the same time, to move into a direction of his own. Although he had still not produced a sculpture in Paris, he was thinking about carving hard stone and working with metal. Full of enthusiasm about the prospect of setting up his own studio, Noguchi went on a tool-buying and tool-making spree. He created what he called a "perfect traveling laboratory" with demountable sculpture stands, benches, grind-wheel and forge; "all have been packed and are now in storage ready to be shipped wherever I may wish."[3] To prepare himself for making sculpture, he had been drawing what he called "Studies in sculptural outline." In these sixty-five highly finished black-and-white abstractions executed in gouache, Noguchi explored various aspects of modernist form as a means of finding his own sculptural language—one that retained Brancusi's perfectionism and clarity but that also showed his awareness of other vanguard trends such as Purism and Constructivism. Although he had been attending sketch classes to improve his grasp of the figure, the drawings were not made at the art academies but in his studio, and they are the farthest thing from academic studies. Wire-thin black lines and precisely contoured flat shapes, made by stenciling, masking, and using a ruler, are set against a uniform background. Graphic boldness makes the compositions read as emblems, and gives them a freshness that seems up-to-date even today. Some drawings show Noguchi distilling abstract shapes from natural forms. "I craved a certain morphologic quality. I developed a deep interest at the time in cellular structure and col-

Paris Abstraction,
1927–28. Gouache on
paper, 25¾×19¾ in.

lected books on paleontology, botany, and zoology."[4] Already at this early date, Noguchi was drawn to the contrast between geometric and organic shapes. This dialectic would continue for the rest of his life.

To invent his own formal vocabulary he looked in many directions at once. Some of his drawings recall sculptors like Naum Gabo in the way that lines and shapes suggest three-dimensional structures in open space. The Noguchi scholar Bruce Altshuler noted the influence of the semiabstract, clean-cut shapes in Stuart Davis's *Eggbeater* series (1927–28), some of which Noguchi most likely saw after Davis arrived in Paris in 1928.[5] Noguchi's gouaches also show his awareness of Jean Arp's biomorphism, and of the simplified, flat, somewhat mechanical shapes seen in the Purist canvases of Fernand Léger, Amédée Ozenfant, and Le Corbusier. Perhaps he also knew the Purist paintings of the American expatriate Gerald Murphy, who was then living at Cap d'Antibes. Noguchi's drawings have a similar graphic vivacity, which, in the case of Murphy, came in part from an appreciation of French advertising design. About his search for his own language, Noguchi said, "If you're looking for yourself, and you haven't got the foggiest idea, isn't it natural that you try everything?"[6] Finally Noguchi felt he had learned enough about himself and about the possibilities of abstract form that he was ready to try out his ideas in three dimensions. The drawings were, he said, studies for sculptures or "going along side of it."[7] Of the approximately twenty-two sculptures that Noguchi would make during the second year of his fellowship, about half were conceived in these drawings.

But before he started sculpting he embarked on another kind of formal research—the study of Oriental art. "I had gotten the Guggenheim Fellowship with the proposal that I would go to India. I got stuck in Paris and I was very ashamed of this, you see. I thought, 'Oh, I'll never get it [the fellowship] the second year.'"[8] In his December report to the Guggenheim Foundation he mentioned that he had just read *L'Art Chinois Classique* by D'Ardenne and that he had been studying Oriental art objects at the Louvre, the Musée Guimet, and at the Cernuschi Museum. "I wanted the Guggenheim for another year so I decided to go to England and study up on India at the British Museum. And I went there, spending a whole month at

Noguchi in his Gentilly studio, 1928

the British Museum Library . . ."[9] Noguchi arrived in London toward the end of December, and on January 12, 1928, he wrote to Mr. Moe enclosing his application for a fellowship renewal. He noted that though his year of training had been useful, he was ready to begin sculpting again. He expressed chagrin that he had not created anything of his own.[10]

He also wrote to Rumely telling him that his plans were now "completely organized, indeed my whole outlook has gone through a happy metamorphosis since coming to England. There is no doubt that Paris has a very disintegrating effect upon certain natures but this also was, I think in my case, quite beneficial for I believe I have thereby gained a firmer control over my inclinations."[11] Noguchi was steeling himself for a year focused on actually producing sculpture, and he planned to avoid Paris's "disintegrating effect," which almost certainly meant involvement with café life and women.

Despite his concerns, the second year of the fellowship was awarded that spring and Noguchi returned to Paris, where he began to sculpt. "Needless to say, all my good intentions of going on to India vanished again the moment my fellowship was renewed. All I wanted to do was to make sculpture . . ."[12]

Noguchi moved to a new studio at 11 rue Dedouvre in Gentilly, a southern suburb of Paris. Although he wanted to get away from Brancusi, he set up his studio to look just like Brancusi's. "I had exactly the same kind of wood, the same table."[13] He made wooden bases for his sculptures like those of Brancusi, and he bought antique tools and hung them neatly on a whitewashed wall, as did Brancusi. He even acquired an enormous wooden winepress like Brancusi's. "I was completely Brancusi," Noguchi mused late in his life.[14] "Brancusi was very strong and in this case, how to get away from him? My struggle has always been to be free from other artists and maybe even from yourself ultimately, because you have to keep running not to be stuck." When Noguchi finally began to sculpt, he made a few figures to exorcise Brancusi.

The first abstract sculpture Noguchi made in his Gentilly studio was *Sphere Section*, which consisted of a sphere of marble sixteen inches in diameter with one quarter removed. The simplicity was inspired by Brancusi, but *Sphere Section* was not distilled from nature. It is a pure geometric abstraction. In his autobiography Noguchi said that

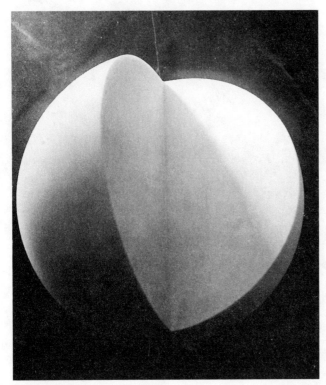

Sphere Section, 1928.
Marble, ht. 16 in.
Lost

this sculpture was "in the nature of an exercise."[15] He told the drawings expert Paul Cummings, who did a number of interviews with him
in 1973, "You have to make a cube; and from a cube you make the
corners. Otherwise you'll never get a sphere . . . I mean it was not trying to be art; I was merely trying to learn how to make a sphere."[16]
Noguchi saved both parts of this object and later he added a piece of
metal to the quarter section he had extracted from the sphere, thereby
creating a new sculpture.

Noguchi's gouaches gave him many options to explore. He carved
solid volumes out of wood and stone and he constructed sculptures out
of sheet metal. Soon he saw that his sheet metal sculptures were more
than just a way to distance himself from his mentor: "By bending or
juxtaposing the two dimensions of one plate to another a plausible three
dimensions was possible. This struck me as the means to circumvent
all the intermediate steps that plagued sculpture; all the castings of
plaster and bronzes that removed sculpture from whatever was fresh

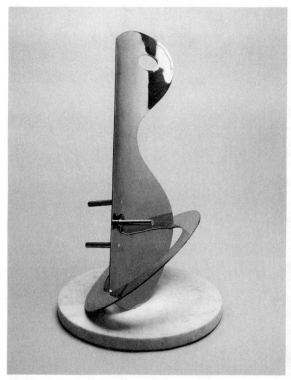

Leda, 1928. Brass,
ht. 28 in.

and original in its inception. I felt I had entered into that stream of opening awareness which is the art of our time."[17] Inspiration came from many sources: "What were my influences? The Russian constructivists; and Picasso, of course, who had by then made some compositions of metal rod and wire. Behind may have been childhood memories of paper use in Japan."[18]

Only six of the abstract sculptures that Noguchi made in 1928 have survived. Most of the extant works are made of sheets of shiny brass. Noguchi bent the brass sheet to create volume but he also aimed for lightness, not only in the reflective surfaces, but also in the way the shapes seem to float. The sculptures have a certain gestural energy. In *Leda*, a subject that had also inspired Brancusi, a biomorphic figure (highly abstracted in a way that recalls Arp and Picasso) reels backward in shock at her ravishment by an invisible swan. The metal rods penetrating the sheet metal, and indeed the way the whole "figure" penetrates a tilted sheet metal ring, might also allude to the sexual encounter tak-

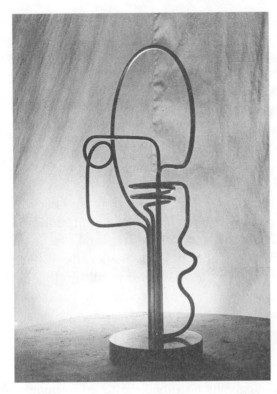

Power House, **study for a neon tube sculpture, 1928. Zinc, ht. 14 in. Lost**

ing place. Closer to Brancusi's contained volumes are Noguchi's solid volumetric polished brass sculptures. *Foot-tree,* for example, brings to mind Brancusi's 1924 *The Cock.* The wire-and-brass *Abstraction in Almost Discontinuous Tension (Tensegrity)* shows Noguchi suspending forms in space three years before Calder's first kinetic abstraction: "Two pieces floating in air, not touching, but balanced in tension. A concept I had not heard of and so considered as an invention."[19] Another radical idea, seen in *Power House,* was the use of neon tubes.

Of his 1928 sculptures Noguchi wrote: "With the work I was doing in sheet metals (ship-brass), I was interested in getting a certain plasticity of form, like something alive—and I wanted it to imply a certain imminent motion. Joints, if possible, were never fixed (no welding) but grooved, held by gravity or tension."[20] But Noguchi was not satisfied. The sheet metal sculptures seemed too calculating and not sufficiently sculptural: "Not to seek the intrinsic form and content of a material, but to impose its effect, was somehow wrong."

In a letter to Rumely of January 28, 1929, Noguchi enclosed his application for a renewal of his Guggenheim fellowship for the third year.[21] The application explained what aspects of sculpture he would explore in the coming year and expressed optimism that he would get the grant "purely on the merit and interest of the work accomplished." He enclosed as well what he called "a rather dithrambic [sic]" treatise on his work. This text contained ideas that would continue to inform his art, for example, art's relationship to "time and place" and the idea that all art past and present shares the same principles. He said that he was a "lover of nature" and that "trees and flowers were my early companions and sea and mountain were ever to the front and back of me . . . These works are preferably intended as images of moods— moods of flowers, of the vegetative and purely structural aspects of nature." He saw his sculptures as "simple chords—others but a song. Beautiful in themselves, I believe that they will recall to all some memory." For all this note of modesty, he was convinced that his art had a noble future: "It became self evident to me that in so called abstraction lay the expression of the age and that I was particularly fitted to be one of its prophets."

Noguchi's fellowship was not renewed, possibly because the abstract sculptures shown in the photographs he submitted failed to impress the Guggenheim authorities, or because the plan to travel to India and the Far East set forth in his original proposal had not been fulfilled. "Just as I had feared, and due, I thought, to my perverse inconstancy, I did not get a third fellowship. I had to return from the magic land of France to the grim necessities of New York. The pursuit of art based on reflective leisure had now to be superseded by application to a job."[22] Early in 1929 Noguchi sublet his Gentilly studio and left for America. "I just locked the studio when I went to New York, expecting to come back."[23]

11

HEAD BUSTER

Although Noguchi found the move from Paris, "the heart of all that mattered," to the "cold world" of New York difficult, he was soon taking pleasure in conquering Manhattan's café society, looking for patrons, and arranging for exhibitions.[1] With help from Rumely, he rented a studio at the top of the Carnegie Building on West Fifty-seventh Street.

On March 31, 1929, *The New York Times* ran an article about American artists showing in Paris, among them Noguchi and Calder. Of Noguchi, the reviewer said his work creates "a mood, vigorous and sturdy, to which one makes a physical rather than an emotional response."[2] In April, at the little-known Eugene Schoen Gallery on East Sixty-first Street, Noguchi had a solo show of the abstract works he had brought back from Paris. Critical response was positive, but, Noguchi said, "I didn't sell anything. And I needed money badly."[3] Besides feeding and housing himself, Noguchi wanted to help support his mother. Anxious that he would not have enough to eat, he would gorge when someone asked him to dinner.[4]

Economic stress together with his disappointment that his abstract sculptures had not found wide appreciation, and perhaps also his continuing wish to distance himself from Brancusi, prompted Noguchi to change course—one of the many abrupt changes in artistic direction for which he would later be famous. Having recently declared himself "particularly fitted" to be a prophet of abstraction, he now abandoned abstraction and turned to portraiture, a mode at which he had been adept before his Parisian sojourn. Although most of his busts are so lively that it is clear that making them was not just a chore, Noguchi always maintained that he had made heads in order to survive. His autobiography describes his return to figuration as a loss of heart: "There was never a denial of making abstractions[,] only a recognition of inadequacy on my part, I was poor and could not afford it. On the other hand, I was too poor inside to insist upon it. How [does one] presume to express something from within when it is empty there? I felt myself too young and inexperienced for abstraction: I would have to live first . . ."[5]

One positive aspect of "head busting" was that Noguchi met all kinds of people. He did not hesitate to ask new acquaintances and especially beautiful women to pose for him. "I asked George Gershwin to sit for me and I asked a black girl who sang in the Methodist Church in Harlem. I used to go there with e.e. cummings and his wife, Marion Morehouse."[6] Noguchi realized that many people sat for him out of kindness, "because of the friendship they felt towards me; because they wanted to help me."[7]

Many of his sitters were luminaries—or soon-to-be celebrities—in the Manhattan intelligentsia as well as society people, some of whom were persuaded to pose for him by Rumely. Noguchi usually worked on five clay busts at a time, covering the unfinished heads with a damp cloth between sittings. Most portraits required about seven sittings. When the bust was complete, he would make a plaster mold of it and then sometimes he had it cast in metal. Even after he switched from metal casting to direct carving in wood or stone in 1932, he continued to make a preliminary sketch in clay. Among his more than two dozen portraits from 1929 are those of Buckminster Fuller, Martha Graham, George Gershwin, Julien Levy, Marion Greenwood, Marion Morehouse, Berenice Abbott, and Lincoln Kirstein. Noguchi did not only portray artists and socially prominent people. He also sculpted people whose beauty caught his attention, such as the waitress Ruth Parks, whose 1929 portrait with her hair tied on top of her perfectly oval head has all the elegance of fifteenth-century Italian portrait busts of women by Francesco da Laurana or Desiderio da Settignano—and, of course, some of the simplicity of Brancusi. Noguchi considered these 1929 portraits to be his most impressive because he had felt free when he was working on them. Making portraits was, he said, "like exercises in a fixed form, as a sonnet is to poetry."[8]

Noguchi told Katharine Kuh that he kept making heads longer than he should have. By the early 1940s he had lost interest in portraiture and only occasionally worked in the mode. "I don't think portrait heads are a complete sculptural expression. It's difficult to express what you want when you are mixed up with another personality—the sitter."[9] His last portrait, done in 1950, was of President Sukarno of Indonesia. A September 18, 1951, letter from Noguchi to Sukarno said, "I hope you will find merit in the head and that it expresses those parts of your character which are deeper and more expressive for historians of the future."[10]

By the time he made Sukarno's head, Noguchi had produced over one hundred portraits, a group of sculptures amazing for its variety and vigor, its sensitivity to abstract qualities of shape, silhouette, texture, and light, as well as for its catching of a likeness. Most of the portraits, especially the earlier ones, show Noguchi's ability to penetrate into the sitter's being. "Humanity is an interesting thing, after all," Noguchi said. And humanity revealed itself "in nuances of character and bone structure and flesh as it flows and ages."[11] Portraiture was to him "more than just a willful gouging and changing. One tries to find what it is in those eyes, that brow, and behind it."

He must have been particularly fascinated by Marion Greenwood's face. His cast iron portrait of Greenwood shows a handsome, large-eyed woman with a powerfully determined look about her mouth and chin. He was in love. A letter from Noguchi to Greenwood of August 8, 1929, says: "I have been finishing your head and now it's perfect—looking at me—and as I worked I saw you, and even now I feel you in the room. It seems as though I have stolen some essence— calling you back—I wonder whether you felt me kiss you on your brow?"[12]

What gives his 1929 portraits a special intensity was Noguchi's need to connect. Trying to catch the essence of a person in seven sittings allowed him a kind of structured intimacy.

Noguchi's sleek bronze head of Gershwin combines Art Deco–like stylization with a streamlining of form familiar from Raymond Duchamp-Villon's bust of Baudelaire. Gershwin's solemn face with downcast eyes suggests that the composer is listening to some inner music. In a brief essay about Gershwin, written in 1938, Noguchi said, "The problem is indeed one of trying to avoid having any opinion whatsoever of the sitter so as to let the image emerge which is as complex

Marion Greenwood, 1929.
Iron, 16×9×10⅛ in.

Noguchi and Marion Greenwood,
c. 1930s

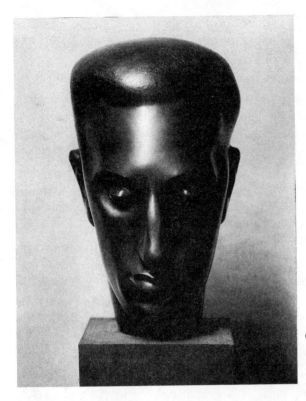

George Gershwin,
1929. Bronze,
15¾×8½×10½ in.

and simple as life . . . Such an ideal situation existed when George Gershwin posed for me in 1929. I had barely met him. I neither liked him, nor did I dislike him . . . This head remains. An exterior of self assurance verging on conceit does not hide the thoughtfulness of a rich and sensitive nature."[13]

Another of Noguchi's portrait subjects was Kay Murphy Halle, a beautiful journalist whose likeness Noguchi sculpted in 1934 and who remained a good friend for many years. It was Kay Halle who had introduced Noguchi to Gershwin, and she liked to tell the story of the time when Gershwin, who had not yet met Noguchi, stopped by her New York apartment and fell in love with a sculpture that she had borrowed from Noguchi in the hopes of selling it for him. "I'll take it," Gershwin said, and he asked the price. "Now George, the artist is a very famous fellow and it's going to cost a lot," Halle warned. Gershwin wanted the sculpture at any price and is said to have bought it for five thousand dollars.[14] Halle helped Noguchi in other ways as well. During the Depression years she tried to make sure that he ate: "Sometimes when I had a rich beau coming for dinner, I would ask Bucky [Buckminster Fuller] and Isamu to drop in beforehand. Then, when my beau came, I would take him aside and say, 'I've done the most awful thing. I forgot I promised to have dinner with these young fellows. They are very poor so we'll have to eat at some dreadful place, but I can't turn them down.' Usually the beau would say, 'Let's all have dinner together on me.' We would go to a swell restaurant and they would have a good eat."[15] A 1966 letter from Halle to Noguchi told him how much she admired a sculpture in marble recently acquired by the Cleveland Museum: "How it took me back to your 'lean' days in the middle 30s when we were together so much and introducing you to George Gershwin and watching you being honored and sought out and the purity and taste and genius of your work never varying from its high excellence."[16]

Noguchi's portraits are excellent likenesses in spite of the liberties he took as he transformed the sitter's features according to what he felt about their essence. As the art dealer Julien Levy, who met Noguchi in Paris in 1927 and whose portrait Noguchi sculpted in 1929, observed, "Noguchi was discovering a means of applying the formal elements of sculpture to enhance the psychological implications of a portrait. Everything from the general outline to the most minute details of texture, was significant of his estimate of his subject. The choice of material, determination of scale, even the shape of the base, all were part of the general consideration, so that, if the portrait were featureless, there should still remain a sort of impression of the subject."[17]

During this time, Noguchi began to frequent Romany Marie's tavern in Greenwich Village, which he had heard about from Brancusi. Romany Marie's had various venues, but in 1929, when Noguchi began to eat there, it was on Minetta Street. The bohemian, Brooklyn-born Romany Marie dressed like a Gypsy, and created a place that drew artists, dancers, and writers because of its warm atmosphere and because Romany Marie sometimes let artists pay for meals with artworks. Among the artists who "hung out" at her tavern were Arshile Gorky,

Reuben Nakian, David Smith, John Graham, Willem de Kooning, and Stuart Davis. Buckminster Fuller came there almost every night, and in exchange for meals he designed the bar, painted the walls with aluminum paint, and arranged the lighting. It was at Romany Marie's that Noguchi met him. "Bucky got me to help him with painting the place up solar, you see."[18] Late in 1929, both at Romany Marie's and at Noguchi's studio, Fuller gave lectures about his Dymaxion House, a six-sided, self-sufficient, mass-producible dwelling suspended by guy wires from a central mast. Fuller was famous for talking for hours on end in what he himself called his "congenital comprehensivist's outpourings which, unchecked often employ 300 word sentences."[19] Many listeners' eyes glazed over. Noguchi was enthralled.

Buckminster Fuller was eight years older than Noguchi and he followed Rumely and Brancusi in becoming the younger man's mentor. Even though they were close, for some twenty years Noguchi, out of respect, called his friend "Mr. Fuller." "He was," Noguchi recalled in 1986, "also a great influence on me, because he represented America and the new technology of space and structures. He was, you might say, a messiah—a man who dreamed and who tried to teach people about the world as he saw it; the structural world and his idea of the future which he thought could come from proper application of engineering."[20] At this stage, Noguchi was still rebelling against Brancusi's "too-idealizing" influence. "Bucky was for me the truth of structure which circumvented questions of art. He taught me, but left me free to seek my own ways."[21]

In 1929 Noguchi moved from the Carnegie Building to a top-floor space on Madison Avenue and Twenty-ninth Street. It had formerly been a laundry and had high windows all the way around. "By then under Bucky's sway I painted the whole place silver, top, bottom, and sides, to the effect that one was almost blinded by the lack of shadows. There I made his portrait head in chromeplated bronze, also form without shadow."[22] Fuller's mental alacrity, his ever-changing vision of the world, is captured in the constant flicker of light over the polished metal. The materiality of Fuller's head is almost invisible. As Fuller noted in his insightful but dense 1960 essay on Noguchi, "what Noguchi saw that others did not see, was that completely reflective surfaces provided a fundamental invisibility of the surface . . . Isamu saw here an invisible sculpture, hidden in and communicating

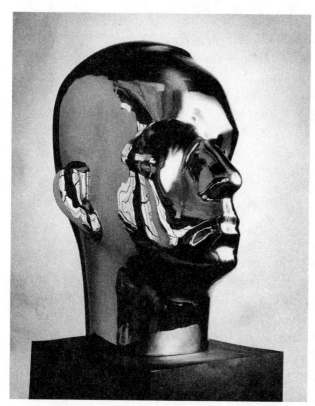

Buckminster Fuller,
1929. Chrome plate
bronze, ht. 13 in.

through a succession of live reflections of images surrounding the invisible sculpture."[23]

Fuller's head, with its firm chin, determined mouth, and bold forehead, looks masterful. The smooth concavities of his eyes—the exact
shapes are difficult to read because of reflections—seem to gaze into
the future and into himself at the same time. "He's a visionary," Noguchi said. "He liked to go one step further than anyone else."[24] The
sculpture's pared-down form brings to mind Fuller's fondness for
streamlined design and his familiarity with fluid mechanics. Fuller,
Noguchi said, "thought all our ills stemmed from an accumulation of
bad habits and weighty possessions—and that the good things had to
be distilled back to essences. I think this corresponds to my own artistic outlook, and to my Japanese background. Talk of doing more with
less—that's precisely what Bucky is after . . . what he's trying to do is
nail down one fundamental truth."[25]

Noguchi and Fuller were both short—Noguchi was five feet six and a half and Fuller was about five feet five. Both were driven by immense energy. Speaking of Fuller, Noguchi told an interviewer: "He used to drink like a fish. He had become a God-possessed man, like a messiah of ideas . . . Bucky didn't take care of himself, but he had amazing strength. He often went without sleep for several days, and he didn't always eat either."[26] Fuller recognized his own extreme vitality when he noted, "I seem to be a verb." Of Noguchi's strength, Fuller wrote, "he always went to work at daylight. Everywhere he worked with the swift and almost ferocious vigor and total bodily coordination of a tiger." Both men valued imagination and both were fascinated by science. Noguchi called Fuller "a poet of our times."[27] Fuller called Noguchi a "scientist-artist."[28]

Noguchi loved the fact that Fuller was an upper-class New Englander whose ancestry went back to a decade after the Mayflower, and included the transcendentalist Margaret Fuller. Fuller recalled that when he first met Noguchi, he saw in his new friend a "stated envy of the natives of various lands who seemed to him to 'belong to their respective lands.'"[29]

Another key player and portrait subject in Noguchi's life at this time was the modern dancer and choreographer Martha Graham. He met Graham through Michio Ito, who had danced with Graham in the vaudeville venue Greenwich Village Follies, in 1923, and who two years later directed Graham's sixth Follies performance. Graham recalled another way they may have met: "Isamu's mother had helped with the costumes for my company then, soon his sister Ailes came to study at my school and to enter my company . . . It was through that association that Isamu entered my life. Young and vibrant, with masses of curly hair, he was like an Italian boy, for which he was often mistaken."[30]

"I made a head of the great dancer Martha Graham soon after I got back to America," Noguchi said. "At that time she was not known, but she lived around the corner from Carnegie Hall, nearby where I had a studio, so I used to go and watch her classes. There were many pretty girls there, and I would draw them."[31] Actually, Noguchi made two portraits of Graham in 1929. The first head was twelve inches high and depicted her as gaunt, almost skull-like, with pronounced cheek-bones. Her eyes are downcast and inward looking: perhaps Noguchi picked up on the earnest, sorrowful mood of many of Graham's dances. The rough, animated surface of the bronze, so different from Fuller's smooth glistening chrome, bears the marks of the sculptor's fingers working the original clay model. The second head, three inches taller, was more flattering, less emaciated, and less sad. Now Graham's eyes are open and her appearance is more conventionally feminine. "One of these heads," Noguchi told Paul Cummings, "the first one, was rather tragic. And Martha didn't like it, she didn't want to be tragic. She wanted to be forward-looking and full of expectations, hope. So I did another head representing the other Martha."[32]

In February 1930 Noguchi exhibited fifteen portrait heads at the Marie Sterner Gallery at 11 East Fifty-seventh Street. The show drew rave reviews. The *New York Times* critic Edward Alden Jewell wrote: "As a portraitist, while still true to the fundamental principles of abstraction, Noguchi can rank with the best . . . Isamu Noguchi is decidedly a young man with a future, unless the present have [sic] nothing to do with the case."[33] Jerome Klein of *The Chicago Evening Post* said Noguchi's heads caught both anatomy and psychology, and they were "quivering with life." Noguchi's talent, he said, might "lead modern sculpture into a new road."[34] Late in February 1930 Noguchi and Buckminster Fuller drove to Cambridge, Massachusetts, for Fuller to promote his Dymaxion House and for Noguchi to install an exhibition of his work at the Harvard Society for Contemporary Art.[35] Noguchi packed Fuller's station wagon with sixteen bronze portrait heads, two figure sculptures (a standing nude and *Sun Worshiper*), plus a group of drawings and the model of Dymaxion House. When they arrived, Noguchi installed his portraits on lengths of shiny new, galvanized furnace pipe—a radical substitute for conventional pedestals. From Cambridge, the pair moved on to Chicago, where Noguchi showed the same group of works at the Arts Club, again garnering favorable reviews.[36]

By spring 1930, Noguchi wrote in his autobiography, "I had finally managed to acquire the means to pursue my repeatedly interrupted trip to the Orient, and self discovery."[37] He planned to go to Paris to pick up his sculpting tools from his Gentilly studio, and then proceed to India, Japan, and China. Late in March Noguchi wrote to Rumely from Chicago's Hotel Knickerbocker: "Tomorrow morning I leave for Cincinnati, then on to New York to arrive there around the eighth and from there, the gods willing, on to Europe again. I am taking this course fully apreciative [sic] of all that you have advised me to the contrary—and my only wish is that you may in time be convinced of its necessity."[38] Despite Noguchi's financial success with portraiture, he had to borrow five hundred dollars from the actress Aline Mac-Mahon to finance his trip. He repaid her by sculpting her portrait in marble in 1937.

12

TO FIND NATURE'S REASONS

On April 16, 1930, Noguchi sailed to France aboard the steamship *Aquitania*. Two telegrams were sent to him on the ship, one from Dr. Rumely and one from Fuller, though only Rumely's arrived before the ship set sail: "Discipline yourself. Keep your best energies for your work. Live intensely, taste all experience that life holds. Produce more . . . I have loved you more than you know."[1] Fuller's telegram, which Noguchi did finally receive, was in typical Bucky-speak:

> Ducy self sorry not newyork wish you bonvoyage but hope there greet your return from new inevitably expansive phase your already significantly universal development stop . . . ideal being art which is progressive individual radionic synchronization of time with eternal now through revelations nonwarpable triangle intelligence faith love
> Buckminster Fuller.[2]

On April 17 Fuller wrote Noguchi a more comprehensible letter: "Quite sad today at thought of your leaving—But really too glad at your good fortune to pull a very long face about it."[3] Noguchi kept Fuller's letter and telegram with him during his travels. He also kept Fuller's book about his plan for industrially produced housing. It was one of two hundred copies of *4-D Time Lock* mimeographed in 1928 and distributed to friends.

In leaving Manhattan, Noguchi left behind not only his success as a portraitist but also his triumphs in high society. Extricating himself from the need to court the rich and privileged must have been a relief. In traveling east he was looking for a way to get back to himself, so that he could make art that was his own. Noguchi's desire to go to Japan was motivated also by a yearning for reconciliation with his father. He realized that in becoming an artist he was following in his father's footsteps. He had, in his 1927 Guggenheim application, said that he wanted to go to the Orient because his poet father was known as an interpreter of the East to the West, something he himself wanted to do through sculpture.

Noguchi returned to his studio in Gentilly determined that this time his voyage to the East would not be sidetracked. Sticking to his plan, he said in his autobiography, was "no easy task, considering the fascination of Paris. It took me over two months to get a transit visa for Siberia, through which I had decided to travel to Japan."[4] He wanted to stop in Russia on his way east, but the visitor's visa was never granted. Instead he secured a transit visa to traverse Russia. On May 6 his mother wrote to him that she had attended to his commissions as best she could, and that she had written to his father and to her old friend Mr. Paget, who lived near Chigasaki. "When you go to Japan I hope you learn the special technique of Japanese wood carving! Take all your wood carving tools."[5] Her letter from the following month exhorted, "Now be wise, foresighted, careful of your health, be your own god and your own star."[6]

During the spring and early summer months in Gentilly, Noguchi made one sculpture, a twelve-inch-high male figure with a large head, a short neck, and a powerful chest. With outstretched arms and legs spread wide, the posture resembles that of Leonardo da Vinci's *Vitruvian Man*. It was based on a model named Sarach, but it seems to represent Everyman. Noguchi called it *Glad Day*, after a poem by William Blake. With his overlarge head, strong jaw, and immense vitality, it might be a spiritual portrait of Buckminster Fuller, to whom it once belonged. In the months before his trip to the East Noguchi also drew from the model at the Académie de la Grande Chaumière. The art dealer John Becker bought a group of these drawings, and while Noguchi was in Japan he showed them at his gallery at 520 Madison Avenue in early March 1931. Reviews were positive. Edward Alden Jewell wrote in *The New York Times* of Noguchi's increasing renown. He found in the drawings "something universal and eternal. Noguchi's line is as pure as Ingres's and as evocative as Picasso's. The drawings are manifestly those of a sculptor . . . but they represent in every instance finished work, with all the sculptural implications realized, rather than notations flung off 'on the wing' like Rodin's."[7]

In Paris Noguchi looked up old friends from his Guggenheim days. "One day I called on Sandy Calder, who told me that he had himself started to do abstractions and no longer thought of me as crazy. He said he had been influenced by Mondrian. I wondered why Mondrian."[8]

In preparation for his departure, Noguchi constructed a large box in which to place his tools and sculptures, and which he would eventually ship to New York. In July he locked up his studio and left Paris, "expecting to come back, and I never came back."[9] He traveled first to Berlin and then took the Trans-Siberian Railroad to Moscow. "But a shock had come to me before leaving, in the form of a letter from my father, suggesting that I should not come to Japan using his name. How could I stop? I decided to go to Peking instead."[10] This paternal rejection would pain Noguchi for years to come. But resilience was a quality he came by early. He would try to rediscover his Asian roots in China rather than in Japan.

Soon after arriving in Moscow, Noguchi went to the Tourist Bureau to see if he could extend his stay. He was hoping, among other things, to see Constructivist artist Vladimir Tatlin's *Monument to the Third International*, a tower of steel, glass, and iron in the form of a double helix spiraling four hundred meters high. Tatlin had made a model for the tower in 1919, but, as Noguchi discovered, the tower had never been built. The tower's openwork structure would remain in Noguchi's mind when, three years later, he designed his *Bolt of Lightning . . . Memorial to Ben Franklin* (actually built in 1984). Noguchi's various pylons that twist according to the double helix and even the openwork metal spiral of his *Challenger* monument (1988) may refer back to Tatlin as well.

The officials at the Tourist Bureau told Noguchi that he had to take the next train out of Moscow because his visa was only for transit. But Noguchi was lucky: "There was a very tall man standing around there and he overheard this conversation. He came up and said, 'Permit me, but aren't you an artist?' I said, 'Yes.' So he said, 'Permit me,' and he went and talked to this lady there. And she said, 'I'm terribly sorry, but there aren't any trains out for several days, so you can stay because there are no trains.'"[11]

A man he had met on the train to Moscow introduced Noguchi to a ballerina whose husband was teaching in Siberia. "So she took me around. It was wonderful . . . I saw the theater and had a look around and met her friends and so forth . . . I was only there three days, but it didn't seem to me three days."[12] From Moscow Noguchi wrote to Ailes: "Last night I saw a troop of native dancers and musicians from Uskas Turkestan. Beautiful and entirely exotic. Here the theater is the only amusement and everybody goes. Moscow is more and less than I had imagined. The churches and things of the past extremely colorful, the present hard and industriously grey. The people of the old regime are more beautiful than the present."[13]

On his way to Peking he traveled through Manchuria, and on July 30 he wrote to his mother from the Grand Hotel Chinese Eastern Railway in the city of Harbin, where he was stranded waiting for his luggage. He was headed for Peking first, he said, and possibly Kyoto from there. "It would be a splendid idea to return by way of India and model Gandi's [sic] head if it can be arranged."[14] That October Leonie wrote him one of her motherly letters, advising him to avoid trachoma by wearing white cotton gloves and washing his hands frequently.[15] Should there be any violence in Peking, she told him to pretend he was French. On November 21, four days after his twenty-sixth birthday, Noguchi wrote a Christmas note to Leonie and Ailes.[16] He said he had sent them presents including a toy—"a little fellow who is my friend of the last few months"—and an old-fashioned hat and some paper lanterns.

Noguchi was happy in Peking. "If my father did not want me, Peking had heart and warmth to spare. There must be a habit of welcome to a stranger. Friends appeared: Nadine Hwang beautiful lieutenant in the army of the young marshal Chan Hsueh-liang (who wanted me to become a general), Carl Schuster, Jean Pierre De Bosc at the French Legation and Wu Taitai."[17] He wrote to his mother in December that he had a very good Japanese friend, a businessman and art collector named Sotokichi Katsuizumi, with whom he took long walks, ate Japanese food, and once a week enjoyed a soak at a Japanese bathhouse.

Over the five months he spent in Peking he grew to love and admire the Chinese and their culture. Noguchi told Cummings that Peking was like Paris. "It's a city of great antiquity, you know, a thousand years. I mean you find Yuan walls there. It's a culture that is so embedded in the place that it had a life of its own."[18]

Because prices in Peking were low, Noguchi was able to rent a house that came with a cook who spoke French and who could manage French as well as Chinese cuisine. The staff also included a houseboy and a rickshaw boy, plus their families. The rickshaw boy would "go out and bring back girls off the street to pose for me. Drawing them, I came to know the people as well as I did the life of the city on all levels. I felt confident that I could maintain myself as such an artist. My cook was my chief critic—the only one, I believed."[19] Before long, Noguchi noted, he was "a householder" studying Chinese in the mornings, overseeing his staff, and "receiving merchants."[20] He relished this gracious life. He acquired a flock of Chinese pigeons that had small flutes made of gourds attached to them. When the pigeons flew the flutes made a *hoo* sound. "Fifty pigeons flying through the air with a hoo!"[21] The memory of these pigeons was still with him when, three years later, back in America, he designed a musical weathervane.

While in Peking, and inspired by Tang dynasty ceramic figures, Noguchi made a rather primitive-looking sculpture of a half-crouching, half-recumbent female. Since materials were hard to find, he modeled *Chinese Girl* out of dental plaster. He also made a sculpture of a bird, probably the bird now called *Peking Duck*. The duck's head with its open beak seems to be hatching out of a roundish egg, an early instance of that favorite Noguchi theme, emergence, or coming into being. Noguchi's honesty about processes and materials is already evident: the ceramic duck shows the seam where the plaster mold opened. The duck has the simplicity of Tang figurines seen through the eyes of a Brancusi devotee. Like Brancusi's *Bird in Space*, *Peking Duck* is distilled to an avian essence, but Noguchi's duck seems earthbound, whereas Brancusi's bird, pure spirit, soars.

Most of the work he produced in Peking was ink brush drawing. He drew nubile young women found for him by his rickshaw boy, nude couples in relaxed unself-conscious poses, and mothers with babies in their arms. "Then, shifting to materials more natural to the place, I made enormous drawings with fantastic brushes and expressionistic flourishes upon their incredibly beautiful paper. I did figure drawings, because that was what I knew how to do."[22]

Katsuizumi introduced Noguchi to the painter Ch'i Pai-shih (also spelled Qi Baishi). The sixty-seven-year-old Ch'i was a charismatic teacher at the Peking Institute of Art and a highly respected painter who had adopted the spontaneous, broad-brushed style of the Literati Painters of the Sung dynasty. He believed that "painting must be something between likeness and unlikeness," and he told Noguchi that a painting is incomplete without a poem and a seal. He gave Noguchi a painting of narcissi inscribed "Who says that flowers have no passion."[23] He was an accomplished seal maker; Noguchi began to sign his drawings with the seal that Ch'i made for him. Ch'i taught Noguchi to control the flow of ink and to keep his line fluid. The contours that define volumes look as if Noguchi made them by moving his arm in free, sweeping gestures that accord with the shapes he observed in the models. The "expressionistic flourishes"—Noguchi's attempt to

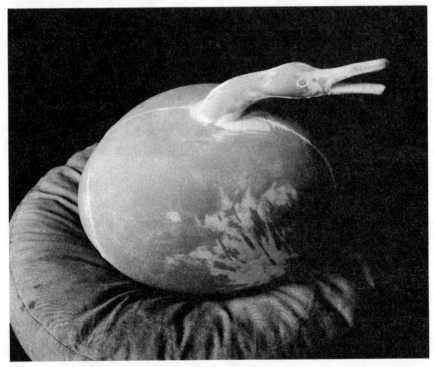

Peking Duck, 1930. Terra-cotta, ht. 12 in. Lost

imitate the bold strokes of the Chinese eccentric painters—often seem a clumsy overlay to Noguchi's linear grace. His deft capturing of posture and anatomy owed much to his hours of sketching from the model at the Parisian academies.

During his months in Peking, Noguchi devoured everything he could of Chinese art. He was enthralled with the fifteenth-century Temple or Altar of Heaven, whose forms, he said, stood for a cosmology expressing a view of earth's relation to the universe. Within a vast temple complex, the structure that most impressed him was a tiered wooden temple that combined circular and square shapes. In Chinese thought, the square symbolized the earth and the circle the heavens. The square and the circle would, in Noguchi's public sculptures starting in the 1960s, have similarly symbolic meanings. When Noguchi searched for the source of the numerous forgeries of ancient ceramic pieces that he encountered in Chinese antiques shops, the antiques dealers would invariably say the fakes came from Japan. "Because," Noguchi quipped, "everything bad came from Japan. So all the imitations are Japanese, all the real ones are Chinese, of course!"[24] Seven years later, when the conflict between China and Japan had become a crisis, Noguchi expressed his gratitude for what he had learned about life and art in China, and he noted that "virtually all Japanese art springs from Chinese roots . . . The essential Japanese attitude toward life—the love of contemplation, the affection for nature—comes from China, too."[25]

On December 28, after five months in Peking, he wrote to his mother thanking her for sending addresses of people for him to look up in Japan. He felt that he had to leave Peking because "my splendid living had reduced my resources precariously . . . I wanted to see something of Japan before my money ran out completely and I didn't see why I should have this hesitancy I did, or why my arrival should ever be known. I resolved that it would only be a temporary absence from Peking after which I would return to learn the art of the brush, learn how to be with nature, how to live."[26]

Shortly before departing for Japan he wrote to Ailes, "Although my memories of it are my happiest, I go there loaded with doubts the reasons for which are within myself . . . but I'm by no means averse to find myself to have been mistaken in which case I would of course stay for a while—my talent of spending money drives me faster and faster to little old New York."[27]

13

A CLOSE EMBRACE
OF THE EARTH

Noguchi sailed to Kobe on the SS *Marei-Maru*. On January 24, 1931, he wrote to Marion Greenwood that his ship was passing through Japan's Inland Sea: "A perfect morning the water like glass—the innumerable islands look fantastic."[1] The boat stopped for a few hours at Moji on the southwest coast of Japan, where, Noguchi wrote to Ailes, the "girls are good to look at. A reporter took me for a long walk and showed me the sights."[2] Before traveling northeast to Tokyo on the Fuji Special Express, he briefly visited Kyoto and "fell promptly in love with the place."[3] "I was greeted by the people here as if I were somebody who belonged here."[4] When he stepped off the train at the Tokyo railroad station on January 28, a crowd of reporters was there to meet him. He discovered that the inquisitive reporter he had befriended on the boat from China had written a story about him for the major Tokyo newspaper, the *Mainichi shinbun*. The headline ran "Yearning for His Father the Poet." The article quoted—or misquoted—Noguchi saying: "I remember my father's face very well. I never forgot him for a moment and I always talked about him with my mother. I never got out of my head the idea of going to Japan, where my father was, and now I am finally realizing my hopes."[5] Another newspaper reported: "He has returned to Japan to visit his father whom he had not seen for 20 years. It is his intension to continue his study of sculpturing while staying with his father."[6] Noguchi disabused the reporters: "I have come to Japan not as the son of the poet Yone Noguchi. I have come as the American Isamu Noguchi to see Japan for my own sculpture . . . I want to see how Japanese culture has progressed, I want to look at the splendid sculpture of ancient Japan in Kyoto and Nara, and I want to work here under their inspiration . . . I will not meet my father."[7]

Yone Noguchi learned about Isamu's arrival from the newspaper. When reporters came to his house, he told them: "I really want to see my son. I want to do what I can for him. I did not know that he was coming to Japan . . . I do not deny that he is my son."[8] Early in February Noguchi and Yone met at the Marunouchi Hotel opposite the Tokyo railroad station where Noguchi was staying. Noguchi described the meeting (and subsequent meetings) as "trying." He said he felt more pity and resentment than anger toward this man who could not look him in the eye. "It was his wife, as she was about to have a child, who had been difficult, he said—my being the eldest."[9] His stepmother Matsuko felt that her husband's having sired a half-American child would bring shame on her family, which now consisted of five children, plus the one in her belly. Three of her children had died in infancy. No doubt Yone shared his wife's misgivings, for, as the political mood in Japan turned more and more nationalistic, he had embraced nativist, right-wing views.

Noguchi soon moved from the Marunouchi Hotel to a new house in the Nihonbashi section of downtown Tokyo, an area that had recently been rebuilt after being destroyed by the horrific earthquake of 1923. The house was loaned to Noguchi by his father's older brother, Totaro Takagi, who had been adopted into his wife's wealthy family and who was now a widower. Most nights Takagi spent with his mistress, so Noguchi had the run of the house plus the luxury of a maid. His uncle Takagi replenished Noguchi's dwindling finances and he "showered me with kindness, as did other relatives who gave me to understand that they favored my mother."[10]

"My father would come to call on me, and we would hold long silent conversations. Then he would take me around to introduce me to various artists he thought I should meet, such as Takamura Kotaro and his father Koun."[11] Takamura was a Rodin-inspired sculptor and poet who had studied in New York, London, and Paris. After returning to Japan in 1909 he had written a manifesto in favor of modern art and artistic freedom. But in the late 1920s he, like Yone Noguchi, became stridently nationalistic and anti-Western. Noguchi wasn't interested: "I wanted, on the contrary, the Orient."

Noguchi became friends with Ikuma Arishima, head of the Nikkaten artists' association, and Arishima included one of Noguchi's Peking brush paintings and a recent sculpture of a crouching wrestler
in the Eighteenth Nikkaten Art Association Exhibition. The French
critic Élie Faure saw the show and, Noguchi recalled, admired Noguchi's brush drawing of a reclining Chinese girl with her head resting on
her elbow. Noguchi was "the one genuine eastern artist," Faure said.[12]

While in Tokyo, Noguchi went to Karuizawa, a mountain resort in
Nagano Prefecture, to see Inazo Nitobe, author of the well-known
Bushido: The Soul of Japan. He and his American wife, Mary, were
friends of his father's and Noguchi had met them as a child. A prominent educator and diplomat, Nitobe had served as an undersecretary
of the League of Nations and then as a member of the Japanese Imperial Parliament. When Noguchi visited him he was known for his distaste for Japan's increasing militarism. Both Inazo Nitobe and his wife
were Quakers and, Noguchi recalled, they addressed each other as
"thee" and "thou." Their adopted son, Yukio, the editor of *The Japan
Times*, befriended Noguchi, and it was probably through Yukio that
Noguchi managed to have a photograph of Buckminster Fuller's Dymaxion House published on the front page of that newspaper.

On one visit to the Nitobes, Noguchi recalled, "[Charles] Lindbergh
showed up in the woods in back. He had flown across the Aleutian
Islands . . . he was very chased up by the press. So he came from the
woods in back, with Mrs. Lindbergh."[13] Thanks to Noguchi, the Lind-
berghs escaped the newspaperman Upton Close, who was at the front
door trying to get in. "And he was the man who was to announce the
start of the war with Japan on the radio in 1941." Through the Nitobes
Noguchi met members of Tokyo's elite and a year or so later, when
Nitobe was in the United States, Noguchi sculpted his portrait.

Noguchi immersed himself in ancient Japanese art that he saw in
museums and temples. He attended Noh theater and no doubt Kabuki, too. Years later he wrote that what he liked about Kabuki was the
stylized gestures, the "rich cadence of the dialogue," the grotesque
makeup, and the masks. He also liked the *hanamichi*, the so-called
flowery road, which is a ramp or bridge that runs from the back of the
theater to the proscenium and that is used for the actors' entrances
and exits.[14] "I used to think that coming to the Orient was walking
backwards, to look backwards so you can see where you're going. Then

you know where you are going, or at least you have some notion of what you are looking for."[15]

During his two months in Tokyo, Noguchi made two portraits in plaster. *Tsuneko San* is a portrait of the maid who served him at his uncle Takagi's house. With her parted lips and soft cheeks, she looks youthful, gentle, and innocent. The other portrait was of his uncle Takagi—bald, wrinkled, and kindly with eyes downcast as if in meditation. For all Takagi's calm, you feel the life of the mind pulsing within. The portrait brings to mind sculptured portraits of Zen priests of the Kamakura period as well as the Chinese portraits of priests upon which those Japanese likenesses were based. Noguchi recalled that he did his uncle's portrait "by way of thanks."[16] A third sculpture from the Tokyo months was of the famous sumo wrestler Tamanishiki, whom Noguchi met and sketched when an acquaintance took him to a sumo wrestling stable. Noguchi said that he made this sculpture and the portraits of Tsuneko and Takagi in clay, then made plaster casts, and from those casts he made molds from which he made terra-cottas.[17]

In Noguchi's recollection, he was restless and tormented by "conflicting emotions during his time in Tokyo."[18] Japan was also in a state of crisis. Looking back on this period, he recalled, "The preparations for war had already begun . . ."[19] He told Dore Ashton: "The police were after you all the time, wanting to know where are you, who are you, what are you doing over here. All right, I was an American. I was visiting there. I was taking it all in. And all the ancient Japanese virtues and ancient Japanese art, songs and so forth, were pre-empted by the military."[20]

When Noguchi told his father that he wanted to work with a forger of Tang figurines, Yone introduced him to Jiro Harada, head of the Tokyo Imperial Art Museum (now the Tokyo National Art Museum). Harada suggested that Noguchi might work with Jinmatsu Uno, a Kyoto potter famous for his reproductions of Chinese-style celadon ware. Indeed, Uno's celadon reproductions were so authentic-looking that, as Noguchi recalled, in London they were sold as Chinese antiques to Japanese buyers who brought them back to Japan.[21]

Noguchi went to Kyoto to work with Uno, who welcomed him into his large family, served as a new mentor, and lent Noguchi a small zinc-roofed kiln worker's cottage in Kyoto's Higashiyama district. Noguchi described the four or five months he lived in Kyoto as a "period of great introspection and silence," a period when, "seeking after identity with some primal matter," he enjoyed a "close embrace of the earth." Kyoto, he said, was a "dusty city of unpaved streets of indescribable charm. I felt a refuge from the vicissitudes of my emotional life at the time and thus I feel very grateful to it."[22]

He told Dore Ashton: "I was all alone. I had a pottery I went to, I did things in ceramics. But I was also exposed to all these gardens and a way of life which was then very somnolent. Nobody ever went there. Everything was full of dust. But there I perceived an art which was beyond art objects. It's the way of life, you might say . . ."[23] Noguchi's rediscovery of Buddhist gardens, to which his mother had introduced him as a child, prompted a new way of thinking about the sculptural enterprise. A sculpture did not have to be a self-defined object. It could also be a space or a garden and earth could be a material for art.

While in Kyoto Noguchi got to know the American scholar of Oriental art Langdon Warner, who, Noguchi recalled, was "on a shopping trip" for the Kansas City Museum.[24] Warner took him to Nara to see Horyuji Temple, a magnificent and huge Buddhist complex with vast grounds and numerous subtemples. On the way to Nara they passed ancient grave mounds, which Noguchi later compared to mounds built by the Hopewell and Adena Indians in Ohio. The idea of raising the earth to make a marker or a monument would stay in his mind two years later when he designed the immense earth pyramid titled *Monument to the Plow*.

A few blocks from Noguchi's cottage at 36 Senyuji Monzen cho was the Kyoto Museum, where he discovered haniwa, a form of sculpture that would influence him for the rest of his life. Starting in the third century, these mostly hollow and basically cylindrical unglazed ceramic figures, animals, and houses were placed around grave mounds. "Simpler, more primitive than Tang figurines, they were in a sense modern, they spoke to me and were closer to my feeling for earth."[25] Haniwa had the same pared-down purity as Brancusi's sculpture. Until then, like Brancusi, Noguchi had spurned clay because it was associated with the tradition of Rodin. Haniwa made clay seem an appropriate material for modern sculpture.

The most impressive of Noguchi's Kyoto sculptures, and the most haniwalike, was *The Queen*, now in the Whitney Museum of American Art. It is forty-five inches high and consists of five stacked cylindrical or

The Queen, 1931. Terra-cotta, ht. 45½ in. (Courtesy of the Whitney Museum of American Art, New York; gift of the artist. Photograph by John Tsantes)

rounded shapes. The lower two flared cylinders (one with a pair of arms attached) form the queen's body. The third cylinder up is the head on top of which two rounded shapes form a headdress. The effect is both majestic and, thanks to the queen's akimbo arms and huge headgear, funny. *The Queen* could be seen as an outsize chess piece. She also recalls Brancusi's segmented columns; her rough wooden base was surely inspired by Brancusi as well.

Using Uno's climbing kiln, Noguchi fired numerous terra-cotta sculptures and vases that amazed and baffled his host. When Julien Levy saw this group of Kyoto sculptures exhibited at the John Becker gallery in 1932, he wrote that Noguchi "executed some of his finest work to date, including a group of vase forms that were merely turned on the wheel but are so direct and at once subtle and monumental, that one sometimes wishes he would forego some of his more ambitious projects and give us more of these comparative 'trifles.'"[26]

Noguchi's June 1 letter to his mother said he would be back in New York early in September. "And then I have been feeling now that I want to stay put in one place for a long time—a sculptor you know can not travel and expect to do much work . . . as I said before I want to be where you and Ailes are—rather selfish on my part I guess."[27] On July 24 he wrote again: "Expect to leave Japan in about a month—before which time I will again be sending cases addressed to myself [care of] yourself 119 East 17th Street." There would, he said, be three cases from China, about three from Japan, and two from Paris. He asked Leonie to look for a studio, which, he said, should be "very large—high ceiling and sunlight."[28] He wanted an extra room and he said he'd like to be on Fifty-seventh Street "on top of a skyscraper—at least." The rent, he said, should be about $100 or $125 per month. For an impoverished artist, Noguchi had high standards.

Japanese troops invaded Manchuria on September 18, 1931. The "Manchurian Incident" was the first overt act of war by a country that had been gearing up for aggression for many years. Noguchi took "the last boat out," he said. Before the invasion, he left from Yokohama on the *Chichibu-maru*. His feelings about Japan remained ambivalent. The xenophobia and militarism that he had witnessed were anathema to him, yet his passion for Japanese culture remained. After he returned to New York he wrote to his father: "I wish to tell you that I have no regrets about my trip to Japan. I believe it to have been all for the best. I feel grateful for whatever you were able to do for me there. I feel great attachment to Japan. I love it as much as I would some person for its faults as well as its virtues." Japan was, he said, "the foundation of my earliest dreams."[29]

His ship sailed to San Francisco by way of Hawaii. Upon his arrival in San Francisco on the evening of September 24, 1931, he wrote to Ailes to announce his "arrival in the land of the free."[30] He was "taking in this town; now it's 3 am." Relieved to be far away from militaristic Japan, he did not tell his sister about an unpleasant incident that delayed his disembarking in San Francisco. Years later he told an interviewer: "But when I got back to America, I had with me Bucky's book called '4-D.' It was mimeographed. So they wouldn't let me into the country, they said it was Communist literature . . . So I was stuck on the boat, the Chi Chibu-maru, in San Francisco Bay . . . They said 'no, no, no, you can't come in. You're a Communist' . . . Would you believe it? This book was taken up entirely with correspondence between Bucky and Mr. Vanderbilt!"[31] Noguchi finally contacted a lawyer who succeeded in getting him released from the boat and onto his homeland.

14

LONELY TRAVELER, SOCIAL LION

I t was autumn when I returned to the excitements of New York and to the same old problem of making a living."[1] Patrons for portraits were less plentiful due to the worsening economy. There were breadlines, soup kitchens, shanty towns, and political unrest. "The depression is rampant," he wrote to his father on November 1. "These people seem so tired—having seen the futility of their mad scramble after wealth—they have nothing. The whole place seems an enormous mistake—mostly sham."[2]

As he had hoped, Noguchi found a studio on Fifty-seventh Street, and he started to make portraits to pay the rent. Two terra-cotta heads of the great Mexican muralist José Clemente Orozco, who was then painting murals at Manhattan's New School for Social Research, were cast from the same plaster mold. Noguchi may have met Orozco at one of various group shows in which Orozco participated in 1931, or he could have run into him at either the Delphic Studios or the Downtown Gallery, venues where Orozco showed his work. Like Diego Rivera, Orozco was greatly admired by left-leaning Americans. The Mexican muralists' belief in public art with political and historical content was a model for many American artists during the Depression years. Noguchi's vigorously modeled portrait with its intense, deep-set, shadowed eyes and tightly closed lips captures much of the painter's intelligence and intransigence, his bitter irony and his capacity for tenderness and hope.

In 1932 Noguchi made another terra-cotta head, this time a portrait of his fifty-eight-year-old mother. His approach was straightforward—no gimmicks, no stylization, just the aging face of a wise and persevering woman. Her expression seems wistful, yet there is about her full mouth the hint of a smile, a smile that makes one think of Leonie's habit of making light of hardships. Perhaps there is in this portrait a touch of pity, too—Noguchi's sadness when he considered his mother's life, which had on the whole been a disappointment. She continued to scratch out a living by selling Japanese objects and by publishing the occasional magazine article.[3] Noguchi's portrait of Leonie reveals his deep attachment to her in spite of the fact that he sometimes chafed under her motherly intrusions.

Two of Noguchi's 1932 portraits were of prominent men in the art world. One was of his old friend the art dealer J. B. Neumann and the other was of the *New Yorker* art critic Murdock Pemberton. Neumann, then forty-five years old, most likely commissioned his portrait to help Noguchi. The sitter's eyes appear to gaze upward like some saint transfixed by a celestial vision. When this portrait was shown in December 1932 at the Reinhardt Gallery, the *Art News* reviewer said that the "cherubic and puffy" Neumann looked "as if he had just swallowed a couple of dozen larks and was about to go coloratura on us."[4] Murdock Pemberton, on the other hand, looks downward, his mouth tensed in concentration, his large forehead suggesting intellectual authority.

Possibly in anticipation of his 1932 show at the Reinhardt Gallery, Noguchi decided to vary his approach to portraiture. He began to carve in wood, in a style more modern. Among his well-connected portrait subjects was Suzanne Ziegler, a writer and a copy editor for *Harper's Bazaar*, *Vogue*, and *House and Garden*. Noguchi first modeled Zeigler's face in clay and then carved two versions of the portrait in wood. The version that he sold to Ziegler is smoothly finished and whitewashed so that she looks ghostly. The version he kept is rougher and unpainted and the top of the head is cut off in a manner that departs radically from verisimilitude. Apparently she did not like either version and would have destroyed the portrait she owned had not her husband intervened.[5]

One of the beautiful women whom Noguchi encouraged to sit for him in 1932 was the socialite and aspiring actress Dorothy Hale, with whom he had a love affair early the following year. In a 1965 letter to Noguchi his friend Kay Halle recalled what might have been an act of courtship: after dining with Halle and Hale, Noguchi sculpted a "wonderful phallus" as a gift for Hale.[6] The two went on a Caribbean cruise, and she accompanied him to London and Paris in June 1933. "She was a very beautiful girl," Noguchi recalled. "All of my girls are beautiful." Though the romance seems to have petered out, they remained friends until her suicide in 1938. "Bucky and I were there the night before she did it. I remember very well, she said, 'Well, that's the end of the vodka. There isn't any more.' Just like that, you know. I wouldn't have thought of it much, except afterward I realized that that's what she was talking about. Dorothy was very pretty, and she traveled in this false world. She didn't want to be second to anybody, and she must have thought she was slipping."[7] That night Noguchi gave her a corsage of yellow roses. Unhappy in love and disappointed in her acting career, she jumped from a high window of Hampshire House on Central Park South, an event recorded in one of Frida Kahlo's most dramatic portraits. Pinned to the black evening gown she had worn that final evening was Noguchi's rose corsage.

Another lovely woman to sit for Noguchi in 1932 was the actress Agna Enters. Her almond-shaped eyes may have been influenced by Picasso's portrait of Gertrude Stein. When the bronze cast was acquired by the Metropolitan Museum in 1934, the museum's bulletin recorded the acquisition and commended Noguchi's "ability to achieve accurate and sympathetic characterizations in a simple and direct manner."[8] It was not Noguchi's first museum attention; in November 1932 he sold his 1929 portrait of the waitress Ruth Parks to the Whitney Museum, and that same year he exhibited his portrait of Uncle Takagi at the Museum of Modern Art.

Noguchi had four exhibitions in 1932, three in New York and one in Chicago. In February he had two shows at once on two floors of the spacious Demotte Galleries at 25 East Seventy-eighth Street. Upstairs were the life drawings of nudes done in Paris and downstairs were the scrolls made in Peking. The other show, at the John Becker Gallery, included sculptures in terra-cotta, plaster, and bronze, as well as a few portraits. Reviews mention a sculpture called *Bird*, which must be *Peking Duck*, originally made in plaster while Noguchi was in China.

Also in the Becker show was *Erai Yatcha Hoi (Kintaro)*, a ceramic figure that Noguchi made in Kyoto. One newspaper reviewer gave a

loose translation of the title: "What a great guy I am!"[9] Noguchi added
the name "Kintaro" to the sculpture's title when he reproduced it in his
autobiography. Kintaro was a miraculous child born out of a peach in
a famous Japanese fairy tale, and Noguchi's plump male figure standing in a ritualistic fight posture has the same delicate primitivism
(seemingly derived from Tang figurines) as *Peking Duck*. Perhaps he is
a sumo wrestler challenging an opponent before a match, or perhaps
the figure records the moment when Kintaro confronts and vanquishes
a legendary monster.

Although not much sold at these exhibitions, reviews were mostly
favorable. Many critics noted Noguchi's virtuosity, his range of modes,
his rising fame, and his Japaneseness. The exception was Henry Mc-
Bride, the highly respected critic for *The Sun* (New York), who wrote a
snide review that must have felt like a slap in the face to Noguchi.
McBride saw Noguchi as an Oriental with highly suspect aspirations
toward Western cosmopolitanism. (McBride had the misapprehension
that Noguchi had been born in Japan and had come to the United States
as a child.) Noguchi, he said, "prefers now to have his art regarded as
Occidental. It will be difficult to persuade the public to this opinion, however. Once an Oriental always an Oriental, it appears."[10] Many reviewers emphasized Noguchi's blending of East and West. *The New Yorker*,
for example, said: "Noguchi is torn between the classic forms of the
Orient and the modern tendencies of the New World . . . He is certainly one of the more brilliant of the younger men."[11] *The New York
Times* found Noguchi's sculpture "compellingly beautiful."[12]

Noguchi once said that his 1932 exhibitions received more attention than any of his future shows. The Chicago Arts Club show com-
prising fifteen of the Chinese brush drawings and twenty portraits
opened in late March and then toured some twenty West Coast museums and went on to Honolulu. *The Evening Post*'s critic was amazed at
Noguchi's power as a draftsman and his "remarkable sense of just where
to put his subject" on the sheet of paper. She saw in the drawings a
"quietude" and a "strength without insistence on strength."[13]

While in Chicago for his openings, Noguchi made two portraits,
one of composer John Alden Carpenter and one of novelist and playwright Thornton Wilder. In its simplicity and serenity Noguchi's portrait of Wilder recalls Japanese portraits of Buddhist priests. Noguchi
lingered in Chicago in part because he wanted to avoid his Manhattan

creditors (he wrote to his mother asking her to make sure his studio there had not been sublet), but also because he had fallen in love with a beautiful, dark-haired dancer and choreographer named Ruth Page whom he had met at an Arts Club concert. The daughter of a brain surgeon and a pianist and the wife of a prominent lawyer, Page was known for creating ballets with American themes and for combining classical ballet with movement from sports, popular dancing, and everyday gestures. Noguchi bombarded Page with love letters and asked her to pose for him. Although her marriage was not unhappy, she felt that Noguchi was a soul mate. "I was crazy about Noguchi," she recalled. "But in a funny kind of way. I don't know what kind of way it was . . . He was one of the most beautiful men you have ever seen . . . He had a sort of lost, faraway look that was irresistible; very penetrating eyes that looked right into your soul"[14] Page came close to divorcing her husband so that she could marry Noguchi: "He wanted me to but I don't know . . . he had so many women, you know. I would have been just one among many." The affair went on for about a year, after

Ruth Page in Noguchi's
first sack dress, 1932

which they remained friends. In the 1940s Noguchi designed costumes and a set for her dance *The Bells*.

Leonie's April letter to her son said that she had gone to his studio and found an eviction notice on the door. There was a claim for $210 in rent. When she gathered his mail to forward it to him, she found a number of telephone and electric bills, and soon his telephone service was cut off.

Upon his return to New York, Noguchi was indeed evicted from his studio. His work was seized by a sheriff who turned out to be an American Indian who empathized with Noguchi and suggested that Noguchi just hand over the drawings that he didn't particularly want. "I took refuge in a vacant store on East 76th Street and moved eventually to a fancier place, having acquired fancy friends, to the Hotel Des Artistes."[15] At one point, probably in late 1932, Noguchi shared an apartment with the entrepreneur Sidney Spivak and his friend Paul Nitze (who eventually became U.S. secretary of the navy). In lieu of paying rent, Noguchi made portraits of Spivak and Nitze as well as one of Spivak's girlfriends (and later wife) Dorothy Dillon. Looking at his portrait years later, Nitze remembered that Noguchi was "fed up with it, so he whacked it with a 2-by-4."[16]

In this period, Noguchi and Buckminster Fuller sometimes slept on sofas in various friends' apartments. Endowed with the aura of confidence of the wellborn, Fuller was able to convince the Carlyle Hotel to let him and Noguchi use rooms that were unoccupied thanks to the Depression. As Noguchi recalled: "We would move in with our air mattresses and a drawing board and that was it. The less the better was his credo."[17]

After Noguchi found a studio, he embarked on *Miss Expanding Universe*, a thirty-inch-long, semiabstract, floating female figure that was inspired by Ruth Page's dancing and was given its title by Fuller. Modeled in plaster and later cast in aluminum, *Miss Expanding Universe* was to be suspended from the ceiling and thus seen from below like some levitating vision. With her flowing curves and pneumatic volumes the sculpture brings to mind the free forms of Jean Arp. Her head is but a featureless round peg, very like the vestigial heads of women in so many contemporaneous Surrealist images. Indeed, her shape recalls the biomorphic shapes in Noguchi's friend Arshile Gorky's drawings from the early 1930s, especially Gorky's ink studies for his *Khorkom* series. Her outstretched arms and legs are encased in a close-fitting skirt. The costume must be Noguchi's response to watching Page dance in a sack made of flexible knit fabric that he designed for her to wear in her dance titled *Expanding Universe*.

When *Miss Expanding Universe* was hung in Noguchi's Reinhardt Gallery show, Julien Levy felt ambivalent about what he saw as a turn toward semiabstract form: "These new figures seem only half-realized, amorphous," he wrote.[18] He wondered if Noguchi's mixed parentage had contributed to "a certain 'bi-polarity' of attitude which characterizes his work. He is always attempting a nice balance between the abstract and the concrete, the relating of fact to meaning, while specifically he exercises a vigorous interpretation of oriental and western aims."[19]

Noguchi told a *Time* reporter that "to me, at least, *Miss Expanding*

Miss Expanding Universe, 1932. Plaster, 40⅞×34⅞ in.

Universe is full of hope." This, he said, was by contrast with the "bitter-ness [and] hopelessness of so much modern art."[20] *Time*'s reporter called *Miss Expanding Universe* "a great white plaster shape, something like a starfish and something like a woman." Edward Alden Jewell wrote in *The New York Times* that he admired Noguchi's more abstract sculp-tures, but that *Miss Expanding Universe* "might strike you as resembling a sublimated scarecrow going through setting-up exercises in conjunc-tion with one of the early morning radio health programs."[21] Jewell preferred *The Flutter*, Noguchi's eighteen-inch-high chromium-plated bronze abstraction symbolizing the "grace of femininity," which had recently been installed over the door of the women's lounge in the new RKO Roxy Theater in Radio City.

Henry McBride was kinder to the Reinhardt show than he had been to Noguchi's two February exhibitions. He said that Noguchi's talent for drawing "wins him credence among connoisseurs for his more sensational exploits . . . There is no artist among us at present whose works differ so much from each other as do those of Noguchi."[22] Noguchi would always refuse to settle into one mode. He did not want to be pigeonholed. "I don't think I have any style," he told art critic John Gruen in 1968. "I'm suspicious of the whole business of style because—again it's a form of inhibition—the more I change, the more I'm me, the new me of that new time."[23]

In 1933 Noguchi began to carve portraits in stone as well as in wood. His first was the highly refined, coolly classical white marble head of Clare Boothe Brokaw (later Clare Boothe Luce). The choice of white marble was just right. Brokaw, a slender, blond, blue-eyed beauty with chiseled features, was often compared to a Dresden doll. But a sharp intelligence and steely strength lay beneath the fragile, feminine exterior. With its bold, straight-on glance and its sensuous but firm mouth, Noguchi's portrait gave her just the right mixture of fortitude and delicacy.

Noguchi most likely met Clare Boothe Brokaw through Dorothy Hale or Buckminster Fuller. Before becoming *Vanity Fair*'s managing editor, Brokaw wrote the magazine's "Hall of Fame" column and thus knew everyone in the worlds of art and literature. She married Henry R. Luce, publisher of *Time*, *Fortune*, and later *Life*, in 1935. Noguchi remained friends with her for many years. Legend has it that when she had a nose job she called Noguchi and asked him to adjust the

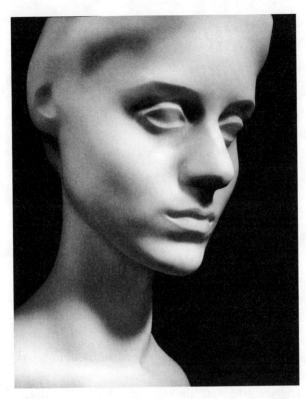

Clare Boothe Brokaw,
1933. Marble, 14×9 in.

nose of her 1933 portrait to make it resemble her new, improved nose. Noguchi maintained that he remembered the story of what Michelangelo did under similar circumstances: he pretended to chip away at the marble while letting a handful of marble dust trickle through his fingers.

15

TOWARD A SCULPTURE
OF SPACE

By 1933 Noguchi was a well-known portraitist with many friends in the worlds of art and privilege. "Portraits were a gregariousness," he wrote in his autobiography. "By now I was carving them directly in the hardest woods such as lignum vitae and ebony."[1] But, as in 1930 when he took off for Asia, Noguchi was restless. He wanted, he said, to break out of the "constricting category" of portraiture.[2]

Although Noguchi enjoyed the high life as he courted rich patrons, he also witnessed the misery and humiliation of breadlines and tent communities in Central Park. Like many other artists and writers in the 1930s, he became politicized: "These contrasts of poverty and relative luxury made me more and more conscious of social injustice, and I soon had friends on the Left. But Left or Right, it was a communion with people that I was interested in." He wanted to find a way to make abstract sculpture, "but I wanted other means of communication—to find a way of sculpture that was humanly meaningful without being realistic, at once abstract and socially relevant . . . My thoughts were born in despair, seeking stars in the night."[3]

Noguchi was determined to make sculpture part of lived experience, a shaping of a space: "In my efforts to go beyond what I then considered the entrapment of style in modern art and its isolation, I conceived of a *Monument to the Plow*."[4] This huge earthwork was to be "a triangular pyramid 12,000 feet at base—slopes 8 degrees to 10 degrees to horizontal—made of earth on one side, tilled in furrows radiating from base corner—one side planted to wheat and a third side

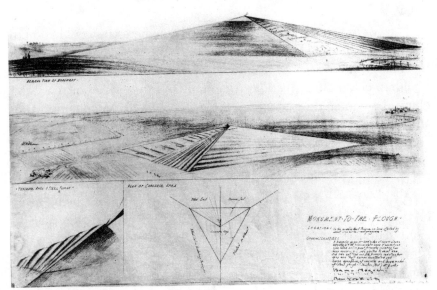

Monument to the Plow, 1933. Pencil drawing, dimensions unknown. Lost

half tilled soil with furrows radiating from apex and half barren, un-cultivated soil."[5] The plow at the top of the pyramid would be a "sym-bol of agriculture." Noguchi hoped that Edward Rumely, who had contacts with John Deere, might be able to persuade the company to build his monument. He proposed that it be built "in the middle of the West Prairie," or somewhere in Oklahoma. "But I was a little ahead of the time."[6]

Indeed he was. Four decades later Earthworks would be the most exciting new development in the field of sculpture. Artists like Mi-chael Heizer, Robert Smithson, and Walter de Maria moved tons of earth to create enormous sculptures in remote outdoor spaces in the West. Noguchi's impetus to make *Monument to the Plow* was in part motivated by his abiding need to be part of the earth. But he also felt an urge to connect with America's heritage. This emphasis on Ameri-can subject matter was widespread in the 1930s, especially after the Federal Art Project got under way in 1933.

Similarly, his 1933 proposal to build *Play Mountain* in New York City was impelled by his longing for connection. The playground, he said, was a metaphor for belonging and also a response to his childhood memory of being frightened by a "desolate" playground on a cliff near Tokyo.[7]

Play Mountain was to be a kind of "rook where you could go both inside and outside."[8] What he did not want was a playground enclosed by chain-link fencing, a "cage, with children in there like animals."[9] Children could climb his *Play Mountain* and then ride down a water chute. In winter the mountain could be used for sledding, and for summer there was a swimming pool and a bandstand for evening concerts.[10] Because it led to other environmental works, *Play Mountain* was, Noguchi said, "the kernel out of which have grown all my ideas relating sculpture to the earth."[11]

A third proposal for a large public sculpture was *Monument to Ben Franklin*, which was Noguchi's entry to a 1933 competition that invited sculptors to produce works "emblematical of the history of America." The tall metal structure resembled the telegraph towers that were beginning to appear on the country's horizons, and it revealed Noguchi's admiration for modern engineering feats such as suspension bridges and the airplane—an admiration that was fashionable among artists who liked to say that such inventions were more beautiful than most art. No doubt his friendship with Buckminster Fuller, with whose engineering inventions he was intimately familiar, also had

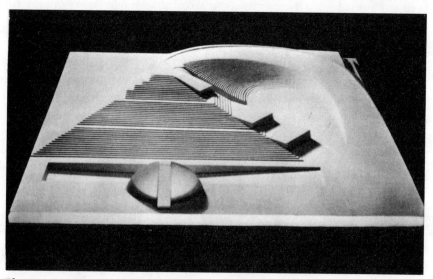

Play Mountain, 1933. Plaster model, 29¼×25¾×4½ in.

an impact on the design. At the bottom of the monument was a key, above which was an upward thrusting bolt of lightning. On the top was a kite. A model for the monument was shown in Philadelphia in 1934, but the piece was not built until 1984. Indeed, as Noguchi acknowledged, the technology to build such a monument was not available in the mid-1930s. In this fanciful frame of mind, and inspired by his memory of the Peking pigeons to which flutes made of gourds were attached, Noguchi designed *Musical Weathervane.* "This was to be made of metal, with flutings that would make sounds like those of an Aeolian harp. It was also to be wired so as to be luminous at night."[12]

In 1933 Noguchi was also involved with making a plaster model for Buckminster Fuller's Dymaxion Car, a streamlined vehicle with two wheels in front and one behind. Shaped like a blimp, it was a radical departure from the boxy sedans of the 1930s. The car was to be fuel-efficient and fast—it could go 120 miles per hour. Noguchi enjoyed his collaboration with Fuller: "Your ideas," he told Fuller, "were an abstraction which I could accept as being part of life and useful."[13]

Toward the end of June, accompanied by Dorothy Hale, Noguchi arrived in London, where he was to have a show at the Sydney Burney Gallery.[14] On July 9 he wrote to his mother that things were "still unsettled here," and that he planned to go to Paris the following week "to see how the stone cutting progresses."[15] When he returned to London, he would take a studio for a month and, if he could afford it, he would stay. If not, he would return to the United States. London, he said, "is not easy to get used to. It is expensive and inconvenient—yet undoubtedly there are a surplus of interesting people here once one can reach them . . . I am always full of expectations."

In Paris in mid-July Noguchi ordered white marble to make portraits. Back in London around July 25 he wrote to Leonie of his disappointment in Paris. He called it "that infernal place."[16] Indeed, Paris in 1933 was not the exuberant "moveable feast" that it had been in the 1920s. The Depression was as grueling there as it was in the United States, and, after the Nazi party won the election in January 1933, refugees fleeing Germany began to arrive.

It must have been during this Paris sojourn that Julien Levy took Noguchi and Clare Boothe Brokaw to the brothel Le Sphinx. Within minutes of arrival Brokaw turned on Levy in a fury, saying, "How dare

you bring us to such a disgusting spectacle?"[17] Levy was astonished—
Brokaw had asked to see such a place, thinking of it as one of the
sights of Paris. Levy retaliated a few months later when he gave a party
for the cast of Gertrude Stein and Virgil Thomson's *Four Saints in
Three Acts*. When Brokaw arrived, he welcomed her with "Why, Clare,
do come in. The last time I saw you was in a whorehouse in Paris." Noguchi must have arrived at Levy's party accompanied by Brokaw and
Dorothy Hale. With these two friends he traveled in February 1934
through Connecticut in Buckminster Fuller's Dymaxion Car. After
stopping to see Thornton Wilder in Hamden, they joined Fuller in
Hartford for the opening of *Four Saints in Three Acts*.

After some ten days in Paris, Noguchi returned to London and
rented Oak Cottage Studio, at Chiswick, a suburb west of London. A
transformed barn with no heat or electricity, the studio did offer excellent light. "I have had a great deal of difficulty getting to work over here,"
he wrote to Leonie on August 17, "but finally I am at it in this studio."[18]
At seven in the evening on Sunday, September 3, he had just stopped
working. It was "a beautiful day, and the church bells are ringing—
that is the only noise, otherwise utter quiet here by the river. I have
never had such relaxation in a long time. All my thoughts and energies
and attention are just now most taken up by this statue which I hope
to have finished for delivery in New York next month."[19] He said he felt
"out of touch with actuality," and he missed his mother and sister and
New York. He enclosed ten dollars, less than he had wanted to send,
but all he could afford.

By November, Noguchi was selling some drawings and making plans
to return to America, despite his concerns about New York creditors.
His letters to Leonie during this time brought no response, and he began to worry. Finally, he boarded the *Europa* on December 8 and when
he arrived in New York on December 17, he learned that his mother
had pneumonia and had been admitted to the understaffed and over-
crowded Bellevue Hospital on December 12. Leonie died two weeks
later at age fifty-nine. Losing his mother was wrenching for Noguchi.
He must have felt that he had neglected and in some ways rejected
her, in part because he was dependent on her love. In his notes for his
autobiography Noguchi wrote: "Mother's death 1933 added to my unhappiness & confusion—guilt."[20] Leonie left Noguchi a Japanese
woodblock print by the Edo-period artist Eizan Kikugawa. It depicted

the folktale hero Kintaro. To Ailes, Leonie left a print of a nursing mother by the same artist. Early in the new year Noguchi and Ailes met at a Japanese restaurant called Miyako to honor Leonie. She was buried near her mother Albiana in the family plot in Brooklyn's Cypress Hills Cemetery. Perhaps thinking of the way that haniwa figures provided company for the dead in ancient Japanese grave mounds, Noguchi put one of his terra-cotta sculptures from Kyoto in her grave. "I never asked my mother about her life. I have never known exactly when she separated from my father. All I know is that my mother loved my father all her life. She gave this love to me. It was my mother also who gave me a love of nature and of things Japanese—my mother and the fact of my being with her in Japan as a child."[21] Another time he said, "Everything I do is in a sense what she might have wished."[22]

16

ART WITH A SOCIAL PURPOSE

U pon his return to New York, Noguchi moved into an apartment in the Hotel des Artistes at 1 West Sixty-seventh Street—an elegant building, given his penury. Again, Rumely was instrumental in helping to secure and fund Noguchi's living quarters. In December 1933 the Public Works of Art Project (PWAP), the first of the federal art projects that were part of President Roosevelt's New Deal, got under way. Its aim was to employ visual artists whose possibility of selling art had nearly dried up in the four years of economic depression. The program lasted until June 1934 and was a precursor of the much larger and more influential federal relief program, the Works Progress Administration (WPA), which began in 1935 and lasted until 1943 and helped all kinds of artists as well as laborers secure a living. The Fine Arts Project (FAP), a section of the WPA, dealt with the visual arts.

Noguchi joined the PWAP early in 1934 and in February proposed his *Monument to Ben Franklin* and *Monument to the Plow*. Both proposals were rejected. A PWAP official noted that the Washington office "turned their thumbs down . . . so hard they almost broke their thumbnails."[1] That spring, when Noguchi sent the PWAP his design for *Play Mountain*, he was thrown off the project. The PWAP told him that he was removed from the rolls but could apply for reinstatement "provided he was willing to undertake work of a more purely sculptural character."[2]

In the politically charged atmosphere of the 1930s, Noguchi's urge to make art that expressed social values grew more intense. But once he was off the PWAP payroll he had to "fish" for portrait commissions. In 1934 he produced some ten portraits, one of them of A. Conger Goodyear, president of the Museum of Modern Art, who was a fan of Noguchi's work. Another project from this period was a proposal for a monument to the Battle of Appomattox Courthouse, the final engagement of the Confederate Army of Northern Virginia before General Robert E. Lee surrendered to General Ulysses S. Grant. Noguchi produced a model with forty-eight stone slabs inscribed with the names of the dead from forty-eight states in four rows. "In the middle of all this was a draped figure, very sad," Noguchi recalled. His friend the architect Ely Jacques Kahn, who had asked him to design the monument, was horrified. The military did not commission monuments against war, he said.[3]

Rejected by the PWAP, Noguchi tried to get the New York Parks Department to build *Play Mountain*. Noguchi ended up showing his playground design to Robert Moses, the man who, although never elected to public office, had major control over public projects in New York. Noguchi's autobiography places his meeting with Moses in 1933, but it almost certainly happened in 1934. He went accompanied by his friend and portrait subject the *New Yorker* art critic Murdock Pemberton, but when Noguchi showed Moses his plaster model, "Moses just laughed his head off and more or less threw us out," Noguchi recalled.[4] "I never had such a tough time. Mr. Moses took offense at me, thought I was trying to kill people, said a playground had to be tested equipment and that New York City could not afford to test my mountain."[5] Noguchi harbored the insult for decades. In 1980 he wrote in the catalogue for his Whitney Museum show, "Nothing could have been worse than this meeting—or more destructive of any self-confidence or more lasting in its effect."[6]

Fortunately, Marie Harriman, the lively wife of the businessman and statesman W. Averell Harriman, came to his rescue.[7] The Harrimans were among what he called his "fancy friends," people he courted for portrait commissions. Part of Noguchi detested the elite and part of him was enamored of it. Marie Harriman offered to host a show for him at her 61 East Fifty-seventh Street gallery in January 1935, and she gave Noguchi an advance of one thousand dollars to keep him going.

Fed up with the Federal Art Project, the Parks Department, and the position of the artist in capitalist society, Noguchi spent six months in the Woodstock artists' colony getting ready for his Harriman gallery show. In spite of Harriman's advance, he continued to struggle financially. A December 22, 1934, letter to a Mr. Howe asks him to intervene with a bank that for two years had owed him money for a "Ben Franklin Plaque." He also tried to make money by designing a swimming pool for the film director Josef von Sternberg, for whom the architect Richard Neutra was designing a Hollywood home. Noguchi gave the pool a biomorphic shape and at one end created a shallow area where Sternberg could loll in the sun. Nothing came of it.

At Marie Harriman's gallery Noguchi exhibited studies and models for his public art projects as well as fifteen sculptures and a group of his Peking brush drawings, plus two pen-and-ink drawings of birds in the zoo.[8] The portraits were done in marble, bronze, lignum vitae, chrome nickel steel, terra-cotta, and plaster. Other sculptures in the show were *Equestrian* (which must have been a nude sidesaddle rider that Noguchi made and had cast during his London sojourn), *Morning Exercises*, *Bird Swallowing a Stone*, and *Black Boy* (a figure carved in ebony). Harriman agreed to include the lynched figure of an African-American called *Death* in the show, but Noguchi's semiabstract travertine marble *Birth*, whose convoluted form may have been inspired by Henri Gaudier-Brzeska's 1914 *Crouching Figure*, was too much for her.

Death, a hanging nude man made of highly polished monel metal (a nickel alloy), created a scandal. Inspired by a photograph called *Lynched Figure* that he had seen in an article published in the left-wing journal *International Labor Defense*, it was, Noguchi told *The New York Times*, a protest against "man's inhumanity to man."[9] *Death*'s gleaming body, legs drawn up as if to escape the heat of flames, writhes in agony. To make the drama even more immediate, Noguchi hung the figure from a real rope attached to a metal gallows, thus implicating the viewer in the crime.

Reviews of the Marie Harriman show were mostly negative, but some critics lauded Noguchi's versatility and skill. The *New York Times* critic Edward Alden Jewell called Noguchi "a young sculptor of unusual artistic fertility and imagination with a sincere respect for craftsmanship." But he was put off by the show: "The last few seasons have witnessed an increasing absorption on Noguchi's part, in the bizarre and the experimental."[10] Jewell observed that although the somewhat

Death, 1934. Monel
metal, ht. 33 in.

abstract and stylized handling of the lynched man's anatomy did miti-
gate the horror of the subject matter, "to a disastrous extent, the por-
trayal is 'realistic.'"[11]

The review that most distressed Noguchi and that would continue
to smart for the rest of his life was written by Henry McBride, who
had already cut to the quick with his "Once an Oriental always an
Oriental" jibe. As if to retaliate, Noguchi would often bring up Mc-
Bride's insult, even quoting the nastiest part of McBride's review in his
autobiography. McBride called Noguchi a "wily" and "semi-oriental"
sculptor whose four public projects were insidious in their seductive-
ness: "All the time he has been over here [Noguchi] has been studying our weaknesses with a view of becoming irresistible to us." *Death*
appalled McBride: "The gruesome study of a lynching with a con-
torted figure dangling from an actual rope, may be like a photograph
from which it was made, but as a work of art it is just a little Japanese
mistake."[12]

Noguchi's response was: "That settled it! If what could be taken seriously as art precluded a search beyond the accepted purposes and dimensions, what was I to do? I wanted widening horizons and a way of art to seek for myself. I determined to have no further truck with either galleries or critics."[13] When the Harriman show closed in mid-February, Noguchi moved *Death* to the Arthur Newton Gallery, where the NAACP had organized a show called *An Art Commentary on Lynching*.[14] Among the thirty-eight artists included were Peggy Bacon and Thomas Hart Benton. Four days after the show opened, Noguchi, without explaining his motive, withdrew *Death*. Possibly he was angry at the omission of his name from the show's catalogue, or perhaps, for all his left-leaning values, he wanted to be a modernist and did not want his work associated with social realism.

In the 1930s abstract artists were fighting a difficult battle. Social realism and regionalism (so-called American Scene painting) were the dominant modes. Although Noguchi's work in the 1930s was mostly representational, he remained an advocate of abstraction. He later wondered if his having turned away from abstraction had to do with his "American background." The part of him that shared the puritan tradition of pragmatism and wariness of sensual pleasure made abstraction an indulgence. Even being an artist seemed an indulgence. "But this skepticism—which pervaded the atmosphere—after all there weren't many people to override it—my only way of overriding it was to find a reason for doing it other than that of art. It had to have a purpose."[15]

Noguchi's spirits were raised when his friend Martha Graham asked him to do a stage set for her dance *Frontier*. Noguchi had often attended Graham's rehearsals and when he could afford it he went to her performances. *Frontier* was one of a series of Graham dances whose theme was the American heritage. For Noguchi, who had returned from Japan full of enthusiasm for the United States and determined to find his American identity, it was the perfect subject. If Robert Moses had thwarted Noguchi's need for connection to his homeland, Martha Graham made this identification possible.

Accompanied by music by Louis Horst and originally titled "An American Perspective of the Plains," *Frontier* premiered at the Guild Theater in New York City on April 28, 1935. It was only six and a half

Martha Graham with Noguchi's stage set for *Frontier*, 1935

minutes long, but it conveyed the seemingly limitless expanses of the Midwest, which had so impressed Noguchi when he arrived at Rolling Prairie, Indiana, as a boy. Like Noguchi's *Monument to the Plow*, the dance honored the courage of pioneers conquering the West, but also evoked Martha Graham's childhood memory of train tracks seeming to stretch forever into the distance as she traveled with her family from Pittsburgh to Santa Barbara, California. Noguchi, who had watched the wake of the ship carrying him from Japan to America when he was thirteen, must have felt a kinship with Graham's experience.

Graham had always preferred an empty stage to the painted back-drops that were the standard scenery for dance. She recalled that Noguchi's design "came from our discussions of the hold, as an American, the frontier had always had for me as a symbol of a journey into the unknown."[16]

"This was the first time she had employed a set," Noguchi recalled.

"Through the use of rope I was able to create within the void of the stage a vastness of the frontier. That she asked me was no doubt due to our friendship and to my familiarity with the development of the modern dance."[17]

Noguchi's set consisted of rope tethered to the stage floor just behind a section of fence constructed out of poles on sawhorses and running to the two top corners of the proscenium. The rope, he said, "split the air of the stage," making a great V as it opened out toward the proscenium, pulling the spectator into a vast and heroic space.[18] The effect was to "throw the entire volume of air straight over the heads of the audience . . . The white ropes created a curious ennobling—of an outburst into space, and at the same time, of the public's inrushing toward infinity."[19]

Working with Graham allowed him to sculpt space and to make his set part of the dancers' movement. "With Martha, there is the wonder of her magic with props. She uses them as an extension of her own anatomy."[20] "It's not the rope that is the sculpture, but it is the space which it creates that is the sculpture."[21] The rapport between Graham's movements and Noguchi's set can be seen in the famous photograph of Graham standing in front of *Frontier*'s vestigial fence with one arm reaching to the sky and one leg raised in a diagonal that echoes the diagonal of the rope. Both her posture and Noguchi's rope are like immense compasses taking the measure of infinity. Graham's choreography, based on basic movements of contraction and release, seemed to embody some intense, primal emotion. For her and for Noguchi, breathing was an essential part of the dance. In the section of his autobiography devoted to dance and theater he wrote: "We breathe in, we breathe out, inward turning, alone, or outgoing, working with others, for an experience that is cumulative through collaboration."[22] Over the next decades Noguchi made some twenty sets for Graham and they remained beloved friends for the rest of his life.

Early in 1935 Noguchi tried to join the WPA Federal Art Project but was turned down. He claimed he was rejected because of an unflattering portrait he had done of Audrey McMahon, the director of the FAP for the New York region. "I mean she was sort of ugly as a mud fence and I guess I made her even more so."[23] The official reason for keeping

Noguchi off the rolls of the WPA was that he made a good living as a portraitist. Noguchi, always quick to feel aspersions, considered this "further proof of discrimination against me . . . In despair, I took off for Hollywood and there made some heads for money, with which to make an exploratory trip to Mexico."[24]

17

MEXICO

In June 1935 Noguchi borrowed Buckminster Fuller's Hudson and drove to California. He stayed long enough to make a few portraits and with the money he earned from these, together with six hundred dollars granted to him by the Guggenheim Foundation, he set off for Mexico City. Most likely he was encouraged by his friend and former lover Marion Greenwood, who had gone to Mexico in 1932 to study fresco painting and landed a mural commission in the city of Morelia.

Mexico in the 1930s was a mecca for artists and intellectuals drawn to the postrevolutionary ferment and to the cosmopolitan atmosphere of Mexico City. They were fascinated by the exoticism of a country that had kept its agrarian culture and where village life seemed not to have changed much since preconquest days. The "primitive" and the folkloric—pre-Columbian temples, open-air markets, traditional dances, folk songs, local crafts, native costumes—all had tremendous appeal. The fame of the Mexican Mural Movement launched in the mid-1920s by *Los Tres Grandes*, Diego Rivera, José Clemente Orozco, and David Alfaro Siqueiros, had spread to the United States and profoundly affected American muralists on the WPA.

When Noguchi arrived in Mexico City in mid-1935, he rented a small apartment for eight months and sought out Marion Greenwood and her sister Grace, who introduced him to the Mexican art world. The Greenwoods and their colleagues were working under the supervision of Diego Rivera painting the walls of a former convent that had been transformed into a market in a working-class neighborhood a few blocks north of the Zocalo, Mexico City's central square. They persuaded Rivera to get government permission for Noguchi to take over a hallway on the second floor of the market, a space that had been designated for the sisters to paint. Since Noguchi's proposal had all the standard leftist symbolism, Rivera gave him the go-ahead.

Noguchi worked on his relief mural during the last two months of 1935 and finished it early in 1936. His eight months in Mexico assuaged the anger and frustration of his recent time in New York. The Abelardo Rodríguez mural was, he said, a "social protest against the WPA."[1] "How different was Mexico!" Noguchi wrote in his autobiography. "Here I suddenly no longer felt estranged as an artist; artists were useful people, a part of the community."[2]

Perhaps inspired by Siqueiros's use of cement in his frescoes at the Chouinard School of Art in California, and enthused by Siqueiros's talk of using experimental materials and techniques for art, Noguchi decided to sculpt his mural in cement.[3] After the market's brick wall was built out to where volume was needed and carved away to give depth, cement was thrown onto the wall to give broad definition to shapes. A final coat of fine aggregate color and cement was mixed dry and then applied wet with a trowel and polished. In an article he contributed in 1936 to Art Front, the journal of the New York Artists' Union, Noguchi wrote that artists should abandon traditional techniques and materials and experiment with plastic, spray guns, and the pneumatic hammer. "Why not paper or rubber sculpture?" he asked. He extolled the idea of public art, art that had a use and was part of life. "Let us make sculpture that deals with today's problems. Draw on the form content so plentiful in science, micro- and macro-cosmic; life from dream-states to the aspirations, problems, sufferings and work of the people."[4]

A torn fragment of a 1936 newspaper clipping in Noguchi's archive has a photograph of the thirty-two-year-old Noguchi dressed in shirt, jacket, tie, and hat posing below his relief mural. As if in solidarity with his coworkers, he stands just below an image of a clenched fist—that favorite motif of the Mexican muralists. The quotes from him in the text reveal a newfound revolutionary fervor: "Capitalism everywhere struggles with inevitable death—all the machinery of war, coercion, and bigotry are as smoke from that fire." Labor, youth, and the

History Mexico, 1935–36. Colored cement on carved brick, l. 72 ft. Mexico City

red flag would, he proclaimed, create a world "with equal opportunity for all." Years later Noguchi looked back on his Mexican mural with its hackneyed leftist imagery as being propagandistic, but at the time, working alongside friends on a public mural that expressed shared political values was for him a great moral uplift.

History Mexico reads from right to left, the right section being the first thing you see as you come to the top of the stairs. The imagery is full of red flags, clenched fists, and proletarian figures battling oppression. As in Mexican muralism the heroes are the defiant worker and the peasant mother. The enemies are capitalists, fascists, the church, and war. One of the many clenched fists holds a pickax that beats down what appears to be a recumbent figure holding a swastika. A fat capitalist is murdered by a skeleton. On the far right is an abstracted depiction of the New York Stock Exchange and Trinity Church. Perhaps this juxtaposition was inspired by *My Dress Hangs There*, the tiny panel that Diego Rivera's wife Frida Kahlo painted in New York City in 1933 while Rivera was at work on his more obviously Communist Radio City mural. In her idiosyncratic protest against economic inequality under the capitalist system, Kahlo painted a red ribbon to link the

Stock Exchange (whose steps are a collaged graph saying "weekly sales in millions") and Trinity Church, which has a dollar sign in its stained glass window.

History Mexico has some gentler, more optimistic images: a recumbent mother suckles her baby, a boy confronts Einstein's $e=mc^2$. When Noguchi wrote to Buckminster Fuller to ask for an explanation of this formula, Fuller sent him a fifty-word telegram. Noguchi was amused when a man watching him working on his mural said that $e=mc^2$ meant *Estado=Muchos Cabrones*, meaning "the state equals many sons of bitches." Late in his life Noguchi said of his mural, "I went to Mexico and did a wall there that was more or less Communist . . . Not because I was a convinced Communist. But because I thought that this was the wave of the future. The inevitability of change . . ."[5]

The art world in Mexico was vibrant. Friendships were passionate, as were enmities. The latter were often political, given the conflicts between the various leftist ideologies, and muralists wielded not only brushes, but pistols. Diego Rivera and Frida Kahlo were at the center of this bohemian world. Their home in the San Angel district of Mexico City was alive with visitors—old friends and new ones from all parts of the world. Rivera was a well-known philanderer and female travelers were often the objects of his attentions. Kahlo entertained this mixture of artists, writers, composers, and globe-trotters with festive meals at a long table decorated with flowers and Mexican folk crockery. Sometimes her pet spider monkey added to the commotion by stealing fruit or her parrot, Bonito, waddled about the tabletop and pecked at the butter. In her habitual Tehuana costumes and with flowers and ribbons decking her hair, Kahlo was a colorful presence. With a few *copitas* (cocktails) her wit could become outrageous and she deployed swear words as freely as a mariachi.

One day, riding in a taxi with Noguchi, Rosa Covarrubias, wife of *Vanity Fair* illustrator Miguel Covarrubias, spotted Kahlo on the street and they stopped to say hello. "Rosa introduced us. And somehow or other, we went dancing."[6] Noguchi was enchanted. Kahlo, at twenty-eight, was at the height of her beauty, and the two soon struck up a love affair. With her voluptuous lips and her dark, penetrating eyes beneath joined eyebrows, she was far more alluring to Noguchi than women of more conventional prettiness. She was passionate, affectionate, and both strong and vulnerable. She had a mordant sense of

Frida Kahlo photographed by
Isamu Noguchi, 1936

humor and loved to laugh. In spite of being a partial invalid as a result
of a near-fatal bus accident in her youth, she was determined to fight
pain with joy. Noguchi recalled that Kahlo loved to sing and dance.
"That was her passion, you know, everything that she couldn't do she
loved to do. It made her absolutely furious to be unable to do things."[7]
Beyond the charm of her personality and beauty, Noguchi admired
Kahlo's work and recalled that she gave him a painting, but, years later,
he could not remember where it was.

    Kahlo and Rivera had separated briefly in 1934 (when he had an
affair with her younger sister Cristina), but by the time Noguchi came
to Mexico, Kahlo had forgiven both her husband and sister. Noguchi
recalled his affair with Kahlo: "I loved her very much. She was a lovely
person, absolutely marvelous person. Since Diego was well known to
be a lady chaser, she cannot be blamed if she saw some men . . . In those
days we all sort of, more or less, horsed around, and Diego did and so
did Frida. It wasn't quite acceptable to him, however. I used to have

assignations with her here and there. One of the places was her sister
Cristina's place, the blue house in Coyoacán."[8] As their attachment to
each other deepened, Noguchi and Kahlo decided to rent an apartment. One friend, the painter Marjorie Eaton, who went to Mexico at
the Riveras' invitation in 1934, recalled that the lovers ordered a set of
furniture for their rendezvous spot, but when they were expecting delivery, it never came. The truck driver assumed that the furniture was
for the Riveras' San Angel house, and he drove there and presented
Rivera with the bill. It was a fiasco, but it did little to discourage the
two lovers.

Noguchi had a twinkle in his eye when he recalled one of his "assignations." He was in bed with Kahlo at her family home in Coyoacán
when Chucho, the houseboy, warned them of Rivera's arrival. Noguchi
dressed as fast as he could, but one of Kahlo's hairless *escuincle* dogs
pounced on his sock and ran off with it. Noguchi scrambled up a tree
in the patio and fled over the roof, but Rivera discovered the sock. "Diego came by with a gun," Noguchi recalled. "He always carried a gun.
The second time he displayed his gun to me was in the [English] hospital. Frida was ill for some reason, and I went there, and he showed
me his gun and said: 'Next time I see you, I'm going to shoot you.'"[9]

In Frida Kahlo's personal archive in the blue house in Coyoacán are
several undated love letters from Noguchi. One of them was written
just before he left Mexico. Only the last page was saved, which begins
midsentence: "have given were not my heart so hardened and frozen
by distrust of this world. Forgive me dearest for not having been all I
should have been—Perhaps when we meet again (soon I hope) when
we love again I will have the courage and humility to be very real. But,
believe me I love you—you are to me every love thought—how I want
to be with you more and more your Isamu."[10]

By early summer in 1936, when he boarded a train bound for Orizaba,
Veracruz, where he would take a ship to New York, Noguchi was so
broke (having spent whatever he earned on materials for his mural)
that he had to sell Buckminster Fuller's Hudson and to produce portraits
of three well-heeled Americans in order to pay for his passage home.
The Mexican government paid him a fraction of what they owed him,
saying that he hadn't finished his mural by the deadline indicated in

his contract—a contract that he claimed never to have signed. "I only managed to collect half, or $88, of the money the government owed me for the work . . . but I have never regretted having had the opportunity of executing what was for me a real attempt at direct communication through sculpture, with no ulterior or money-making motive."[11]

The day after Noguchi left Mexico City he wrote to Kahlo from the Hotel Diligencias in Orizaba:

> I already feel cast adrift on a changing sea of Time, with no more familiar signs to make one forget how vast and strange this world is, how alone I am without you. Your beautiful flowers are in a glass here by my bed as fresh as yesterday.
>
> I think to call you up, then to take the next train back to try to explain something to you—I don't know what—the rain beats upon this tin roof and far away the insects are singing.
>
> Frida I have been so inarticulate with you and with myself also—please forgive me for being so dumb and selfish and blind. However, that I see light sometimes proves that I will come back to you one day grown up and more understanding and more worthy of you should you by then still care for Isamu.
>
> Good night my darling,—and when you hear the song of insects, and of rain and of wind, listen also for my voice.
>
> Isamu[12]

From on board the SS *Orizaba* of the New York and Cuba Mail Steamship Company, Noguchi wrote again. "Frida, I am such a poor letter writer being lazy and given too [sic] dreaming after each sentence—dreaming of things I wish I could have said to you while holding your hand—perhaps some day I may be able to—O, please give me the hope and the courage." Back in the United States in July 1936 he wrote Kahlo: "I dash from extremity to extremity—where is a job? It is all very pregnant with hope, wonderful things to do in a wonderfully vital land, if only they would give me half a chance! . . . there are the nights when I lie on top of the bed without a stitch on letting the sultry air gently cool my body wet and now tanned a deep color I often dream—you are near—we live together these nights!"

Noguchi and Frida remained lifelong friends. They saw each other in 1938 when she came to New York for an exhibition of her paintings at Julien Levy's gallery. In 1946, when Frida had a spinal fusion at New York's Hospital for Special Surgery, Noguchi visited her and gave her a glass-covered box with butterflies pinned to the back panel. In Kahlo's self-portraits butterflies are a symbol of transcendence. She hung the butterfly box over the door of her hospital room and later, back in Mexico, placed it on the underside of her four-poster bed's canopy. It was the last time Noguchi saw Frida. "She was there with Cristina," he recalled, "and we talked for a long while about things. She was older. She was so full of life, her spirit was so admirable."[13]

18

NEW YORK, 1936-39

After his exhilarating months in Mexico, Manhattan depressed No-guchi. "It was the time of civil war in Spain and the United Front. Meetings, resolutions and rallies followed each other."[1] He resumed his efforts to enroll in the WPA program, but was again rejected. This left him out of the camaraderie that developed among artists working for a pittance from the government. The artists met each week in paycheck lines, where they gossiped and held lively discussions about art and politics. Once again Noguchi turned to portraiture to make ends meet. He rented two carpenter's shacks at 211 East Forty-ninth Street, fixed them up as studios, and sublet one to his friend and fellow sculptor Ahron Ben-Shmuel. Besides making portraits Noguchi entered into every competition he knew of. "I even thought up projects, but all without success. I was willing to do almost anything to get out of my rut—to find the means to practice an art I did not have to sell."[2] Wishing to escape from his role as a fashionable portraitist, Noguchi acted on his growing conviction, first stated in his Marie Harriman exhibition brochure, that "sculpture can be a vital force in our everyday life if projected into communal usefulness."[3] He had made objects that were useful before. When he was twenty he had designed some sugar cake molds. In 1926 he designed a plastic clock called "Measured Time," and in 1933 he had invented his *Musical Weathervane*, a mass-producible sculpture.

In 1937 the Zenith Radio Corporation, responding to the anxiety that followed the 1932 kidnapping of Charles and Anne Morrow Lindbergh's baby, commissioned Noguchi to make an intercom device, which consisted of a boxlike receiver—the so-called Guardian Ear—to be placed in a child's or sick person's bedroom. The other half was the transmitter, a more or less oval, Art Deco–style abstract head made of walnut-colored Bakelite. This could be placed wherever the listening parent might be. Using Noguchi's "Radio Nurse," a parent could hear the sound of a baby's breathing even several rooms away. Looking back on his design, Noguchi wrote in his autobiography: "By a curious switch I thought of commercial art as less contaminated than one that appealed to vanity."[4]

His intercom received a lot of attention and its success led to other furniture designs. In 1939 Noguchi designed a coffee table for the new home of A. Conger Goodyear, whose portrait he had sculpted in 1934. The Goodyear table consisted of a free-form glass top supported by two biomorphic shapes. A year later Noguchi redesigned this table for the furniture designer T. H. Robsjohn-Gibbings. According to

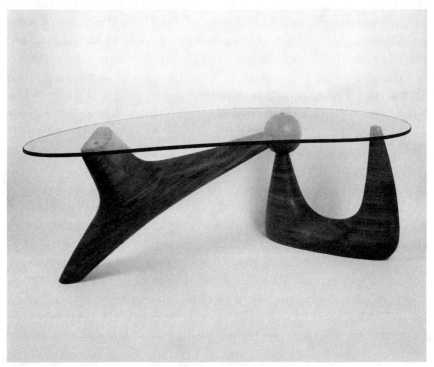

Table for A. Conger Goodyear, 1939. Rosewood, 30×84 in.

Noguchi, Robsjohn-Gibbings altered his design slightly and presented the table as his own design in 1942. Noguchi happened to see the Robsjohn-Gibbings variation in an advertisement. "When . . . I remonstrated, he said anybody could make a three-legged table. In revenge I made my own variant of my own table, articulated as the Goodyear table, but reduced to rudiments."[5] This table was illustrated in George Nelson's article "How to Make a Table," and in 1947 the Herman Miller furniture company (where George Nelson was design director) began to manufacture it. Noguchi considered this coffee table to be his most successful venture in the field of industrial design, and it continues to be popular today.

Perhaps inspired by Buckminster Fuller, and possibly also prompted by his involvement with industrial design, Noguchi became intrigued with the machine as a subject for art. His *1,000 h.p. Heart* (1938), a bulbous amalgam of organic and geometric shapes, is part human heart and part aeroengine. For this melding of the machine and human forms, Noguchi seems to have followed the example of the British modernist sculptor Jacob Epstein's *The Rock Drill* (1913) and perhaps also the French sculptor Raymond Duchamp-Villon's *Horse* (1914), a machine/animal hybrid. *1,000 h.p. Heart* conveys a feeling of burgeoning life that also recalls Noguchi's own 1934 sculpture, *Birth*.

After his return from Mexico, Noguchi saw a great deal of Arshile Gorky, whom he once said he had first met in 1932 at a gallery.[6] The two artists visited museums together and Noguchi listened attentively as Gorky held forth in front of his favorite paintings—paintings that Gorky felt so possessive about that if another visitor had the temerity to stand in front of them, Gorky would glower. "He was very, very well-versed in art history," Noguchi recalled. "I mean he was a great teacher, among other things, for me anyway." At the time, Gorky was well known in the art world but his occasional arrogance and frequent scene-stealing annoyed some of his fellow painters. Noguchi told Gorky's nephew Karlen Mooradian that he and Gorky had a special kinship because they both felt like exiles.[7] Both experienced discrimination and both felt a deep attachment to a foreign culture. In fact, although he pretended to be Russian, Gorky was Armenian. Gorky, Noguchi observed, liked to "put on a bit of mystification."[8] His role-playing was in part a way of distancing himself from his traumatic youth—the horrors of the Armenian genocide. Similarly, Noguchi tried to blot out his painful childhood by acting Japanese when the situation called for it and American if that seemed appropriate. Both artists were estranged from their fathers, whom they resented for abandoning their mothers and themselves.

In 1936 Noguchi joined the newly formed New York Artists' Union. "I associated myself with the laboring class; with the less fortunate people. And probably it comes from many different sources but I suppose my background of not belonging . . . had something to do with it."[9] The union, like the WPA, offered artists the camaraderie of penury and politics. Noguchi eventually dropped out of the artists' union, because, he said, "it was overrun by those interested more in the political angle of attacking the WPA than in art, or the furtherance of art as I saw it."[10] The Spanish Civil War and the rise of fascism brought artists together in support of leftist ideologies and the Spanish Loyalist cause. "I think it took the war really, and Stalin and his coming to terms with Hitler, to really sort of make us diverge from that very fixed and sort of convinced point of view."[11] Indeed, the 1939 Stalin-Hitler pact caused many artists and intellectuals to break with the Communist Party. There was a general feeling of disillusionment and ideological confusion.

On September 1, 1939, Noguchi, Gorky, and their friend the painter De Hirsh Margules were listening to the radio at Noguchi's studio when Germany's invasion of Poland was announced, precipitating the war in Europe. "We made several paintings together at that time," Noguchi recalled.[12] A semiabstract drawing upon which they collaborated reveals the intensity of their alarm. Noguchi apparently drew two large black planes in crayon and Gorky added bird's legs—a favorite Gorky motif in the late 1930s. By dipping the palms of his hands in red paste, Gorky also made the red handprints that speak of war's bloodiness. Noguchi used the seal that had been given to him by Ch'i Pai-shih to stamp the paper with the same red paste.[13]

During this period, Noguchi recalled, various factions sought his support. A Communist group invited him to go to Germany to make a portrait of Hitler and the Japanese consulate in New York asked him to make a statement in support of the Japanese war effort. Noguchi refused. "I avoided any kind of direct involvement," he said.[14] At about

Collaborative drawing by Noguchi, Arshile Gorky, and De Hirsh Margules on the eve of the German invasion of Poland, 1939. Mixed media on paper, 17½×22⅞ in.

the same time the American State Department asked him to send an open letter to his father. Noguchi hesitated and sought the advice of the Chinese ambassador, who said, "Don't do anything. Don't attack your father. You'll regret it."[15]

Early in December 1937 Noguchi had contributed one of his Peking brush drawings to an auction to raise money for China's defense held on December 5 at New York's Park Lane Hotel. Two days before the auction he was interviewed for an article titled "Japanese-American Artist Fears for Old Peiping," published in the *New York World-Telegram*. "Japan," he said, "overcome by a capitalist-militaristic group, has developed a frantic spirit of nationalism . . . It is tragic that instead of being grateful for all that Chinese culture had given Japan, Japan has set about the methodical business of maiming and slaughtering her people."[16] On December 13 the Japanese Imperial Army began a weeklong siege of China's capital city and massacred thousands of Nanking's inhabitants. The so-called Rape of Nanking horrified the

American public, and Noguchi was distraught. For years he had been wary of Japanese aggression. Now his fears were realized, and he felt that in some way he shared the Japanese guilt. *The New York Times* noted that at the auction, Noguchi's ink wash drawing of a Chinese woman nursing her child had drawn enormous interest and that K. C. Li, a Chinese merchant, had bid seventy dollars for it, and then offered to triple that price if Noguchi would explain publicly why he, as a Japanese-American, had chosen to help the Chinese cause. "I give this drawing as my way of showing the world that not all Japanese are militaristic," he responded.[17] Later in the evening during a raffle for an American-made automobile a little Chinese girl thrust her hand into a glass jar and pulled out a stub. The winning ticket was Noguchi's.

Noguchi's auctioned brush drawing has an inscription in Chinese characters that was added to the scroll three months later. It began: "I am a follower of great China and I have learned from its art. Today intruders are attacking the Asian continent, forgetting their cultural roots. I don't want to forget my art's teacher." Noguchi signed the inscription by stamping it with the seal that Ch'i Pai-shih had given him in 1930.[18]

Noguchi's sorrow over Japanese aggression was no doubt intensified by the knowledge that his father had become increasingly nationalistic. Yone's July 1938 letters to Mahatma Gandhi, whom he had met in the 1930s when on a lecture tour in India, and to his old friend the Indian poet Rabindranath Tagore defend Japan's invasion of China as a boon to the impoverished Chinese people and a battle to keep Asia for Asians. "No one can deny the truth in the survival of the fittest," he wrote to Gandhi. "When I say that the present war is a declaration towards the West to leave hands from Asia, I believe that there are many people in India, who will approve of us." To Tagore he wrote that "the war is not for conquest, but the correction of mistaken idea of China . . . Our enemy is only the Kuomintang Government, a miserable puppet of the West."[19]

In fall 1938 Noguchi presented Edsel Ford and the Ford designer Walter D. Teague with a model of his fountain design for the Ford Building at the upcoming New York World's Fair. He won the job and was paid $1,500 in three installments. Once again he combined machine forms with human anatomy. Just as Gorky in his WPA murals at the Newark airport had built his composition out of abstracted airplane parts, Noguchi created an abstraction based on automobile parts—wheel, chassis, and engine block. The only virtue of the resulting fountain, which Noguchi described as "an engine with chassis rampant!," was, he said, to teach him the use of magnesite.[20] However, after returning from the World's Fair, Noguchi wrote to Teague that he believed the fountain to be "an artistic success."[21] Noguchi went on to ask for more money—something that in the years to come he would do fairly often. When he felt that he had worked longer or had had greater expenses than stipulated in a contract, he would ask the commissioner for additional payment.

In 1938 Noguchi entered a national competition for a relief panel with imagery symbolic of the American press, to be placed above the door of the new Associated Press Building in Rockefeller Center. There were 188 entries from twenty-six states. The jury included Holger Cahill, the national director of the WPA's Federal Art Project, and the prominent architect Wallace K. Harrison, who had participated in the construction of Rockefeller Center and was a friend of Nelson Rockefeller. Noguchi submitted two sketch models, one that he had worked on for two months and one that he had dashed off in three days. Years later he said that both models were hangovers from what he called his social realist propagandistic relief mural in Mexico City.[22] Indeed, the AP design had much of the market mural's bombast.

The model that took three days was awarded the prize. "With a sudden surprise, my luck changed, or rather I got my just deserts," Noguchi recalled in his autobiography. "The real danger of a competition is that one might some day win one. Then there is the time-consuming job of execution—and one is stuck with its reputation."[23] Noguchi received $1,000 in prize money and was to be paid an additional $6,500 for completing the commission. The model had, in the lower right corner, a small figure of a nude man with bent legs and upraised arms. According to The New York Times, this figure symbolized "mankind in the focus of the news."[24] The diagonal lines crossing the plaque's background were, the Times said, "radiating wires indicating the worldwide network of Associated Press communications." To my eyes, the nude figure looks more like a shocked recipient of the news than the news's subject. Noguchi must have been aware of this figure's awkwardness, for he eliminated it when the plaque went into production.

Noguchi's ten-ton AP relief sculpture includes five muscular newsmen handling the tools of modern journalism—camera, telephone, wirephoto, teletype, and pad and pencil. Their superman bodies are typical of the heroic males seen in much public art of the Depression years when so many jobless men, unable to support their families, felt diminished. The figures are massed in a compact triangle with its apex thrusting diagonally downward, as if the press, like some angelic messenger, were bringing the news from on high. "The first characteristic of the press," Noguchi said in a press release, "is vitality. Next, is incisiveness injecting itself into all human activities in quest of truth. I must portray the gathering and disseminating of News, from a vantage point above the tumult."[25] In spite of the stylization of the figures, the plaque does convey the urgency of breaking news.

Although the competition had called for a bronze relief, Noguchi wanted to have his relief, which he first sculpted in plaster, cast in stainless steel, a material that was then used mainly by the automobile industry and for submarines and other military equipment. Noguchi chose it for his AP plaque because it was new and progressive and noncorrosive. It was the only metal other than gold or platinum that would not, the press release pointed out, "foul its own face." Casting the weighty 20-by-17-foot plaque in stainless steel turned out to be a huge job. "The grinding and welding, together with the plaster enlarging, took over a year of my energy," Noguchi recalled.[26] The relief was divided into nine sections, which were cast and then moved to a different plant where their edges were trimmed to an exact size so that the dividing lines between sections would be invisible, and where the surface was polished with high-speed grinding wheels. At one point Noguchi decided he wanted to reduce reflectivity, so he ground the surface in a variety of angles. An AP news story reported: "The sculptor, Noguchi, worked harder on the plaque than any workman, using the latest power tools, grinding wheels turning at 5000 to 25,000 R.P.M. He personally carved and contoured the finished metal plaque—just as sculptors of old personally finished their metal casts, not only becoming the first sculptor to learn this power tool technique, but studying light refraction and reflection first hand, and working out his contours by light wave measuring devices. Working 16 hours a day

Associated Press Plaque, 1938–40. Stainless steel casting, 20×17 ft. Rockefeller Plaza, New York

through two shifts—holding powerful grinders, Noguchi's hands were so calloused that he could not make a clenched fist when the job was completed."[27]

In order to move the AP plaque out of the foundry, one of the building's supporting pillars had to be cut away. Once outside, the piece was power-washed with two hundred gallons of nitric acid and two hundred gallons of ammonia to remove the marks of the iron tools and residual abrasive material. Then it was washed with three thousand gallons of boiling water. Two heavy-duty trucks carried the plaque's separate sections, each weighing about three tons, to Manhattan, where the pieces were unloaded and rejoined. The plaque, now titled *News*, was then hoisted by cranes into its place above the entrance to the Associated Press Building. When it was installed, Noguchi climbed the scaffolding and made some final touches with an electric buffing machine.

The unveiling of *News* at the end of April 1940 was presided over by Nelson Rockefeller, executive vice president of Rockefeller Center, and by Kent Cooper, general manager of the Associated Press. A photograph shows Rockefeller smiling at a smiling Noguchi, who wears pinstripes and carries his fedora. Cooper holds the rope that will remove the cloth that veils the plaque. In his speech Rockefeller said that the relief would "stand forever as a symbol of the freedom of the press."[28]

Not everybody was pleased by Noguchi's vision of American journalism. The *New York Herald Tribune* viewed the figures of the brawny newsmen as apelike: "There seems to be a suggestion here that news is a roaring, devouring monster—a brute force, unloosing a blitzkrieg at the reader down a stainless steel lightning flash, a naked giant, with a piece of copy paper swathed around his middle, bellowing through the world."[29] Another journalist said of the plaque: "It looks like the cerebellic convolutions of a diseased brain during an autopsy."[30]

While Noguchi was hard at work on his AP plaque, Brancusi came to New York for the May 10, 1939, opening of the new home of the Museum of Modern Art, the International Style building designed by Philip Goodwin and Edward Durrell Stone. Noguchi recalled that Brancusi was intrigued with the idea of making a sculpture in stainless steel: "We talked at that time of similarly casting his Endless Column. How unfortunate it was that he insisted on going back to Paris."[31]

•

After the unveiling of the AP plaque, Noguchi was whisked away and accompanied by a police escort to catch a flight from LaGuardia to San Francisco, where he would board a ship bound for Honolulu. He had been invited by the Hawaiian Pineapple Company to come to Hawaii to work on advertising and on two bas-reliefs incorporating Hawaiian people and subject matter. In addition, he had been offered an exhibition at the Honolulu Academy of Art, which already owned one of Noguchi's two bronze heads of Martha Graham and— according to the press—a bronze casting of *Tsuneko-san*. Among other works in the show were the portraits of Buckminster Fuller and George Gershwin; *Radio Nurse*; *Glad Day*, the nude equestrian he made in England; *Ebony Bird*, a sheet metal abstraction; and a model of the swimming pool he designed for Josef von Sternberg. There were also various drawings, models, and some studies for architecture (a column and a capital), which the press said showed "the possibilities for personalization of modern architecture to be developed perhaps in Hawaii."[32] Noguchi told the Honolulu press that people looking at his sculpture could interpret it as they wished. "One cannot express art in so many words or there would not be art . . . It can mean anything to the person who looks."[33] He concluded his remarks by saying, "To me, my art means a thousand things, and reactions are as many as there are people."

Before his trip to Hawaii Noguchi had discussed the possibility of designing a playground for Ala Moana Park with Harry Bent, a Hawaiian architect, and with Lester McCoy, Honolulu's parks commissioner. When he returned to New York in July, Noguchi made some models for playground equipment that were so beautifully designed they looked like sculptures. Nothing came from the designs in Hawaii, but in October 1940 *Architectural Forum* featured photographs of his playground designs and a statement from Noguchi: "A multiple length swing," Noguchi said, "teaches that the rate of swing is determined by the length of the pendulum not by its weight or width of arc . . . The spiral slide will develop instinct regarding the bank necessary to overcome the centrifugal force developed by the

Noguchi with plaster original of *Contoured Playground*, c. 1946

rate of slide."[34] Noguchi, fascinated by the technical aspects of different materials, went on to say that the slide could be made of steel or wood or cupric magnesium oxide covered with latex or cement with slip cement surfacing or possibly weather-resistant plastic. As with *Play Mountain*, when Noguchi later presented his playground designs to the New York Parks Department he was told that the equipment was too dangerous. (The designs for playground equipment were finally realized in *Playscapes*, 1976, in Piedmont Park in Atlanta.)

Noguchi responded with *Contoured Playground*, "which I conceived to be fail-proof for the simple reason that there was nothing to fall off."[35] It was, he said, "made up entirely of earth modulations. Exercise was to be derived automatically in running up and down the curved surfaces. There were crannies to hide in and mounds to slide down. In Summer water would flow and pool." The 1941 plaster model, with its soft undulations reminiscent of Miró's and Gorky's biomorphism, can be seen as the first of what Noguchi called his tabletop sculptures. Once again his playground proposal came to nothing, this time, he was told, because of the threat of war. "I felt the futility of anything ever happening. It was spring and I decided to move west." He would look for "new roots" in his native California.

19

CALIFORNIA

In spring 1941 the friendship among Noguchi; Gorky and his young fiancée, Agnes Magruder; and the art patron and mosaicist Jeanne Reynal was cemented by several country outings. One occasion was a luncheon at a Connecticut estate at which the four friends became bored and wandered off to swim in a pond and to smell the blossoming fruit trees. Noguchi picked a sprig of plumbago and wore it as a mustache. Gorky sang Armenian songs, whittled flutes, and talked about his childhood. Reynal decided that Gorky needed a change of scene and offered to arrange an exhibition for him in San Francisco. Soon a plan was hatched to head to California.

Early in July, the three friends left New York in Noguchi's new Ford station wagon (Reynal joined them later in San Francisco). Noguchi remembered the trip as an "epic trek." All three sat in the front because the back was packed with Noguchi's sculpting tools. Since Gorky did not know how to drive and Agnes did not have a license, Noguchi took and kept the wheel. They followed a southern route via Pennsylvania, Ohio, Indiana, and Oklahoma. Agnes recalled that they talked about gestalt theory, politics, and the role of the machine in society. Both Noguchi and Gorky were ardent and opinionated, and their discussions often turned to rants. "We argued all the way across," Noguchi recalled.[1] The fiercest arguments were about clouds. Gorky kept seeing old peasant women or Saint George slaying the dragon and other sorts of battles in the clouds. "Gorky, you turn everything into something else," Noguchi said. When Noguchi pointed out that a cloud was just a cloud, Gorky would counter: "Oh no, don't you see that old peasant woman up there?" Noguchi understood that "nature didn't look the same to him as it did to somebody else . . . Gorky always was sort of elaborating and weaving a lacework of Armenian imagery into whatever he saw, which is very beautiful."[2] Gorky constantly compared his view from the car window with his memories of what he called the Caucasus. "'Oh,'" he would say upon hearing Agnes or Noguchi praise the landscape, "'but we have bigger trees in Van and the hills are far more beautiful, and the grass is higher, and the fruit is redder and everything is better' . . . He drove me and Isamu crazy," Agnes recalled.[3]

The people they encountered along the way must have been curious about the two foreign-looking men—no doubt Noguchi and Gorky would have been subject to prejudice. When they stopped at roadside diners, Gorky behaved in a way that surely horrified the waitresses. "They fry everything but the ice cream!" he would exclaim.[4]

In the twenty-one years since his arrival in the United States Gorky hadn't been west of Philadelphia, and as the distance from Manhattan grew, he became more and more nervous. Noguchi would have understood that, as with Brancusi, Gorky's Union Square studio was part of his identity, a safe and beautiful world. "He panicked," Agnes recalled. It didn't help that during arguments Agnes sometimes sided with Noguchi. As they were crossing a bridge over the Mississippi, Gorky exploded: "Stop the car! I want to get out. I'm going to walk home!" He got out of the car and began to walk. Agnes raced after him. "He almost threw me into the Mississippi River!" she recalled.

Eventually, the travelers made it to Santa Fe, where Gorky's mood improved. Although they found Santa Fe overly precious, Gorky liked the surrounding countryside. He admired the Indian artifacts, the adobe houses and primitive ovens. They spent several days outside the city at the home of Oliver La Farge, the brother of their mutual friend (and Noguchi's portrait subject) Margaret Osborn. On Osborn's recommendation they visited the Painted Desert, where they were caught in a storm that blew sand into their faces. When the storm was over they couldn't find the road, and they wandered until they found a Hopi settlement. "We slept the night in a very fine hut. The rocks around there and various earth formations sent the sculptors and painters into fits . . . the works were labeled Modern Art and canyon beds were set aside as studios."[5] When they reached the Grand Canyon both men sat with their backs to the canyon and refused to express any awe. "Gorky and Isamu behaved like two clowns," Agnes recalled. "They felt the canyon was too big, that it looked like a picture postcard." They discussed what could be added to make the canyon more interesting: a clown on a bicycle crossing the chasm on a tightrope, perhaps.

When they arrived in Los Angeles and installed themselves in a hotel, Gorky's mood darkened. He wanted to find a cheaper hotel. Noguchi and Gorky went out to eat while Agnes, who was not feeling well, went to bed. She surmised that the two men had had another fight, because Noguchi came back without Gorky, knocked on her door, and came to her bedside to say good night. "Gorky suddenly burst into the room and dumped a whole bagful of lawn clippings on top of me. He must have gathered them from the hotel garden. He thought I was flirting with Isamu. But there was not a murmur of electricity between me and Isamu. Isamu would not have done that to Gorky. Isamu was just saying good night to me and asking whether I was feeling better. When Gorky dumped the grass cuttings on me, I said, 'Well, it's lucky it's not horse shit.' Isamu vanished promptly . . ."

In the days that followed, Gorky's disgruntlement increased and he threatened to take a bus back to New York. He was scornful of Noguchi's fishing for commissions in upper-echelon milieus and he took a dim view of the lavish portfolio that Noguchi brought out in order to make a sale. He and Agnes tagged along on Noguchi's social engagements, meeting Walt Disney, lunching with Anatole Litvak, the Ukrainian-born Hollywood film director, and dining with Litvak's former wife, the film star Miriam Hopkins.

Eventually, Gorky and Agnes made their way to San Francisco while Noguchi remained in Los Angeles. The tensions between Noguchi and Gorky heated up again during Noguchi's visits to San Francisco. At a Spanish nightclub, Agnes asked Gorky to dance. Although he loved to dominate parties by dancing Armenian dances and waving a white handkerchief, Gorky knew nothing about the fox trot. After a minute or two he walked off the dance floor, leaving Agnes stranded. "Then Isamu came and danced with me, and Gorky spent the whole time eyeing me with horror." Noguchi's friend the Chicago art dealer Katharine Kuh remembered running into Noguchi, Gorky, Agnes, and Jeanne Reynal in San Francisco that summer and accompanying them to parties and nightclubs, to Chinatown and the Noh theater. Noguchi was, she said, "as beautiful as the dawn because he was young then, had all his hair, and was really beautiful . . . During those days, I was repeatedly puzzled by Gorky's silence and his lethargic depression. Perhaps there had been a flirtation on Noguchi's part with Agnes Magruder, but I sensed something deeper between the two men. Gorky was hostile and hurt, Noguchi blithely untroubled. I think they were in competition not as artists but as personalities. Gorky felt altogether superfluous; Noguchi shone."[6]

While searching for portrait commissions in California, Noguchi moved in a circle that included successful writers, artists, filmmakers, actors, and wealthy citizens. One portrait commission came from Ginger Rogers, the movie star and dancing partner of Fred Astaire. Another came from the French painter Fernand Léger, who was teaching at Mills College in Oakland, and was preparing for a show at the San Francisco Museum of Art that would run concurrently with Gorky's exhibition. Noguchi also made a series of driftwood constructions, some of which incorporated rocks and bits of rope and resembled the fantastic objects that a number of Surrealist-inspired artists were concocting. "He was fascinated by the idea of erosion," Noguchi's friend the critic Thomas B. Hess recalled. "He was attracted to objects that had survived from another era and that had been formed by the process of destruction. He thought of them as 'time locks.'"[7]

If Noguchi had hoped to find his roots in his native city, he failed. His time in California became, he said, "more and more unsettled."[8] Something that must have upset him was the hostility toward the Japanese, which was much more palpable in California than on the East Coast. "The war in Europe," he recalled, "foreshadowed worse things to come, and I became personally very much aware of its spreading to the Pacific."[9] In Los Angeles Noguchi was invited to a birthday party for Peggy Guggenheim, who, with her lover, the Surrealist painter Max Ernst, had fled Europe earlier that year. When Noguchi arrived Guggenheim's sister Hazel refused to let him in. Although this episode took place before Pearl Harbor and before the United States had entered the war, Hazel told a collector friend, "We were shooting Japs at the time."[10]

On December 7, 1941, Noguchi was driving from Los Angeles to San Diego to look for some onyx for a sculpture. "I happened to turn on the radio and that's where I heard it." He heard Upton Close announce that in a sneak attack the Japanese had bombed the U.S. Navy's fleet in Pearl Harbor. In his autobiography Noguchi said, "Pearl Harbor was an unmitigated shock, forcing into the background all artistic activities."[11] "With a flash I realized I was no longer the sculptor alone. I was not just American but Nisei. A Japanese-American." Noguchi turned his car around and returned to Los Angeles. He wanted to get in touch with other Nisei and see what he could do to help.

Soon California was abuzz with talk that the Japanese navy might attack the United States. Noguchi felt the growing racial hysteria in California and the threat of mob violence. He realized that like other Japanese-Americans he might be seen as an enemy alien. He introduced himself to members of the Japanese American Citizens League (JACL) and began to work with them in an effort to convince the American public that Japanese-Americans were loyal citizens. In January the JACL's Anti-Axis Committee produced a radio broadcast: "The Japanese in America is on trial," it said. "WE ARE AMERICANS and we know that this is the American way . . . the democratic way. THIS AMERICA WE LOVE. This is the America for you and for me."[12]

At the many meetings he attended, Noguchi came to know his fellow Nisei, the majority of whom were much younger and came from a very different background. He even took Japanese lessons from his friend Shuji Fujii, editor of *Doho*, a progressive weekly Japanese-American newspaper. Most of the Nisei that Noguchi met didn't know what to make of him, and he in turn was dismayed by their timidity and conservatism. "I don't know whether they enjoyed my attention at all—I suspect probably not."[13]

At Jeanne Reynal's Montgomery Street apartment in San Francisco, Noguchi organized a group called Nisei Writers and Artists for Democracy. The group included his editor friend Shuji Fujii and Larry Tajiri, a leader of the JACL. Its purpose was, Noguchi recalled, to "counteract the bad press which we saw coming . . . to stop the hysteria that was developing."[14] A two-page typewritten text titled "Statement of Policy and Aims" set forth the group's concerns: "The anger we American citizens of Japanese extraction who are writers and artists felt on that historical December 7, 1941, when the fascist military of Japan attacked our country, has now crystallized into a cold determination that the Berlin-Tokyo-Rome Axis must be exterminated from the face of the earth . . . we stand ready to offer our individual and collective talents for the service of the land of our birth."[15]

Noguchi states in his autobiography that his involvement with the Nisei Writers and Artists group was "to no avail."[16] In a 1988 interview he said: "The Nisei don't want to have anything to do with liberals. They say, 'keep away! Leave us alone!'"[17]

On February 19, 1942, President Roosevelt signed Executive Order 9066, which decreed that West Coast residents of Japanese ancestry were now enemy aliens, and were to be evacuated from the Pacific Coast defense area. On February 21 the House Committee to Investigate National Defense Migration, chaired by Representative John H. Tolan, opened hearings in San Francisco to consider the advisability of the evacuation. In early March Noguchi represented the Nisei Writers and Artists group at the Tolan committee hearings. "I would go to these meetings . . . the Germans were represented by Thomas Mann and [German-born conductor] Bruno Walter. Thomas Mann made an impassioned plea and said it would be terrible 'if you lock us up again, who have just gotten away from Germany . . . and in San Francisco, Joe DiMaggio's mother spoke up for the Italians . . . that was a clincher! I mean that clearly fixed the Italians up. Who could they get to testify for the Japanese? For the Nisei? I remember saying a few words, but I was quite, not in my league."[18]

On March 18, 1942, Roosevelt established the War Relocation Authority, which was to cooperate with the War Department in evacuating, relocating, and, under the auspices of the War Relocation Corps, providing work for the evacuees placed in internment camps.[19] The evacuation of the Pacific Coast defense areas began on March 21. Some 119,000 people, two-thirds of them American citizens of Japanese descent and the rest Japanese immigrants, were ordered to leave their homes, their farms, and their jobs and to report to assembly centers such as the one at the Santa Anita Racetrack north of Los Angeles, where evacuees lived in stables until they were processed and moved to more permanent relocation centers. The War Relocation Authority published an upbeat circular for the evacuees that described the relocation centers as "pioneer" communities: "Within these areas you will have an opportunity to build new communities where you may live, work, worship, and educate your children. Life in these new communities will be as well-rounded and normal as possible under wartime conditions."[20] The opportunities for employment would be at factories producing clothing, wood products, ceramics, textiles, and building materials. There would also be clerical work, nursing, cooking, and work in construction, agriculture, and land reclamation. Pay was minimal—around twelve to nineteen dollars a month, depending on the type of labor. The War Relocation Authority chose ten sites in Colorado, Arizona, Wyoming, Utah, and Idaho in which to build internment camps. Since 45 percent of the evacuees had been engaged in agriculture, sparsely settled sites that could be developed for farming were favored.

On March 31, when the evacuation from the military area was under way, Shuji Fujii wrote on behalf of Noguchi, himself, and two other colleagues to Milton Eisenhower, director of the War Relocation Authority, and to Culbert L. Olson, governor of California. He asked for government support for a documentary film about the evacuation, for which they had already shot about one thousand feet of film. The film's purpose was to counter anti-Japanese hysteria by demonstrating to Americans the evacuees' "cooperative spirit," and also to show the evacuation in a favorable light to calm evacuees' fears. Years later Noguchi told an interviewer that he never saw the film and that the army had seized it.[21]

In late March, fearful that if he did not leave the West Coast he would be incarcerated, Noguchi left his car in Los Angeles and flew east from San Francisco to New York and Washington. He worried that his leaving California would be seen as cowardice. In Washington, he went to the State Department to ask if he could help. In his memory they said, "No, go away; there's nothing you can do . . . you're a half-breed; what do we want with you?"[22]

In Washington Noguchi met John Collier, the sympathetic and idealistic head of the Office of Indian Affairs, a man who for twenty years had fought for Native American interests. Collier had once visited the Interlaken School and he shared Rumely's progressive ideas about education and the importance of arts and crafts. The largest of the relocation camps, situated in Indian territory in Poston, Arizona, was under Collier's jurisdiction. Fired by his vision of an ideal community at Poston, Collier persuaded Noguchi that he could help build this community by joining it and designing a park and a recreation area. He also thought

Noguchi could boost the internees' morale by helping them to revive Japanese traditional arts and crafts about which the Issei (Japanese immigrants) knew something, but the Nisei (second-generation Japanese-Americans) almost nothing. Noguchi caught Collier's enthusiasm and volunteered to enter Poston. "Thus I willfully became a part of humanity uprooted."[23]

20

POSTON

Noguchi returned to Los Angeles to retrieve his car and headed for Arizona via San Francisco. He felt vulnerable being in the restricted zone, but, before he left the East Coast, he had armed himself with a letter from John A. Bird, assistant to the director of the War Relocation Authority in Washington. Bird wrote: "He is proceeding from Washington, D.C. to Barstow, California, to obtain his automobile and certain art materials, and thence to the Colorado River Indian Reservation. Any Courtesies extended Mr. Noguchi will be appreciated."[1] The letter explained that Noguchi was not an evacuee from a Pacific Coast defense area and that he had volunteered to work for the Bureau of Indian Affairs in order to develop a handicraft project. From San Francisco, Noguchi drove over the mountains into Nevada and then south to Poston. He arrived on May 8, 1942, shortly before the evacuees. "So I was sort of one of the people getting the place ready. I was friendly with some of the people there . . . except that when the internees arrived I became one of them, too, naturally. So I was stuck there and couldn't get out for seven months."[2]

At first Noguchi was enthralled with Poston's vast barren landscape. "The desert was magnificent—the fantastic heat, the cool nights, and the miraculous time before dawn. I became a leader of forays into the desert to find ironwood roots for sculpting."[3] But Noguchi soon found that he had almost nothing in common with the much younger Nisei. They saw him as a famous artist from Manhattan and did not feel at ease with him. As time passed, Noguchi became aware that because he was a volunteer and had access to the camp administration staff, he was suspected of being an informer.[4]

Circulars put out by the War Relocation Authority described Poston (then called Parker because its land could be irrigated by the nearby newly built Parker Dam) as a place with great agricultural potential.[5] "Here," said one of the circulars, "out of the sage brush and silt on the Colorado River Indian Reservation, evacuees from the Pacific Coast will develop a green irrigated valley for their own use during wartime and for the post-war use by the Indian tribes."[6] Photographs of Poston show countless identical barracks, all lined up symmetrically on straight and parallel paths. The camp looks almost as bleak as a concentration camp. The surrounding landscape is flat and featureless. Fenced in with barbed wire and with watchtowers with machine guns and searchlights moving across the terrain at night, it felt to some like a prison. But a Poston information bulletin listed with enthusiasm the government services provided—education, health, recreation, plus fire and police protection "which all Americans are privileged to enjoy and share . . . Poston is a part of democratic America, and so are its volunteer citizens."[7]

Among Noguchi's papers is an information bulletin with "General Instructions" for Poston's new arrivals. Evacuees were told to complete an admittance record at the registration office. They were examined by a doctor, fingerprinted, given a serial number, and asked to take a loyalty oath. They were also encouraged to enlist in the War Relocation Work Corps. After completing the registration process, they were assigned to living quarters in one of the camp's eight hundred one-story tarpaper-covered barracks. The camp was divided into rectangular blocks, each of which had twelve buildings, each with four apartments. There were also two barracks for single persons. Noguchi called the buildings "tarpaper shacks." In a draft of an article he wrote for *Reader's Digest* he said, "We live in unavoidable and intimate proximity. Each apartment of 20×30 is allotted to a minimum of five, very often with two families thrown together. Women and children must share a privacy identical to that of an army camp."[8] Should evacuees wish to make improvements to their apartments, lumber and tools were provided. In addition to the sleeping quarters, there were communal washrooms, a laundry, and a recreation hall in which there was a community store selling tobacco, candy, drug supplies, and "sundries."

Meals were taken in a dining hall. The allocation for food was thirty-seven cents a day, and Noguchi noted that the food was poorly cooked by inexperienced chefs. Many internees became sick. Life was regimented. A siren sounded at 7:00 a.m. and lights went out at 9:00 p.m.

Noguchi was assigned to apartment A, building 7, block 5. This was a bachelor quarters, but unlike other single men, Noguchi had a corner apartment to himself. He was put in charge of making adobe bricks with which to build a recreation and art center. Few of his Poston projects were carried out, however, as expenditures on Japanese evacuees were not a high priority and Noguchi was not given the tools or materials he needed. When he realized that no support was coming from the authorities, Noguchi decided that the internees would build the recreation and art center without the War Relocation Authority's help. The project would be constructed gradually by the internees, starting with a workshop to house equipment such as a sawmill and a planer. Future buildings would include rooms for ceramics, music, painting, sculpture, plus a small museum and a store. The recreation facility would provide space for sports from sumo to judo, baseball, football, and tennis. "This whole project is conceived to be owned and operated entirely by the evacuees," Noguchi told Poston's Community Council. "Already members of the athletic and art departments have contributed to getting timber preparatory to constructing the shelter where we will build the adobe bricks."[9] The project would, Noguchi said, boost the evacuees' morale, increase their self-reliance, and "strengthen a spirit of democratic participation."

One of Noguchi's jobs was to run a carpentry and wood carving shop. He did some teaching of ceramics as well. On May 31, in answer to a letter from John Collier, he said that he had finally been allowed to leave the camp in order to bring in clay. "It was my first trip outside the camp since coming in and sure was a thrill."[10] He informed Collier about the lack of materials for his projects, the dearth of skilled personnel, and the fact that there was still no newspaper for the evacuees. He apologized for complaining. It was, he said, "due probably to my inexperience in government red tape or the military mind—my lack of appreciation that we are war victims for whom even the minimum assistance for economic improvement may be subject to criticism . . . You see my usefulness here is terribly restricted." As Noguchi began to realize how helpless he was, his relationship to people in authority

underwent a subtle change. "How strange were my reactions on entering camp. Suddenly I became aware of a color line I had never known
before."[11] It was not long before he was treated as if he were just another internee. "There could have been some question of my position,
whether on the side of the administration or the internees, but with
the harshness of camp life came a feeling of mutuality, of identity with
those interned against the administration, in spite of personal friendships."[12] In a draft of the article for Reader's Digest Noguchi suggested
that part of the reason he had chosen to come to Poston was "a haunting
sense of unreality, of not quite belonging, which has always bothered
me [and] made me seek for an answer among the Nisei."[13]

A memorandum dictated on July 17 by Theodore H. Haas, an officer in Poston's legal department, said that Noguchi felt that the
best way to teach art to the camp's children was to give them examples of Japanese art that had no "war-like aspects."[14] Noguchi also
wanted to bring people like his friend Langdon Warner, a Harvard
professor of East Asian art, to Poston to lecture on Japanese art, and
he suggested that he invite some of his Japanese artist friends to lecture and to exhibit their work. None of these ideas came to fruition.
The authorities did not want to encourage evacuees to identify with
Japanese culture.

As the weeks of confinement went by, Noguchi's loneliness increased. Being at Poston, he said, "suddenly you become a member of
a minority group."[15] His morale must have temporarily improved when
John Collier visited Poston and gave impassioned speeches about the
creation of an ideal society. Collier was convinced that the Japanese
internees could turn desert into fertile ground: "Though democracy
perish outside, here would be kept its seeds," he told the internees.[16]
But if Collier proclaimed that democracy could be preserved at Poston,
Noguchi demurred: "As if you can save democracy by locking people
up."[17] Noguchi saw that the purposes of the War Relocation Authority
were "hopelessly at odds with that ideal cooperative community pic-
tured by Mr. Collier. They wanted nothing permanent nor pleasant.
My presence became pointless . . ."[18]

Noguchi did spend some of his time at Poston working on his own
sculpture. He finished the portrait of Ginger Rogers that he had started
in Los Angeles and made sculptures out of wood that he scavenged
from the desert. One inmate remembered a large, primitive wooden

carving that Noguchi had made and placed by his front door. This internee observed that Noguchi kept to himself. In the mess hall, he wore Japanese wooden geta clogs, ate alone, and then quickly returned to his room.[19] Noguchi scholar Robert J. Maeda, who was nine years old when he arrived with his family at Poston, remembers seeing Noguchi working on a sculpture outside of his barrack: "Was it because of his appearance, or was it his single-minded concentration on his work, which seemed to make irrelevant the world around him?"[20]

Noguchi expressed his discontent with life at Poston in an extraordinary May 30 letter to the Surrealist artist Man Ray:

> This is the weirdest, most unreal situation—like in a dream—I wish I were out. Outside, it seems from the inside, history is taking flight and passes forever. Here time has stopped and nothing is of any consequence, nothing of any value, neither our time or our skill. Our sphere of effective activity is cut to a minimum. Our preoccupations are the intense heat, the afternoon dust storms the food (35c a day) . . . O! for the sea!
> O! for an orange[21]

That same day, Noguchi wrote to the social realist artist George Biddle, who had helped to persuade President Roosevelt to establish the WPA Federal Art Project. "This must be one of the earth's cruelest spots," he told Biddle.[22] He explained that he had entered Poston to "help preserve self respect and belief in America."[23] The government, he said, "must think race hatred is good for the war spirit."

In July Noguchi was given an exhibition at the San Francisco Museum of Art (where Gorky had exhibited the year before). He was not allowed to leave Poston to see his show, which included abstractions from 1928, his bronze equestrian, models of his playground equipment for Honolulu, the model for *Contoured Playground*, and sculptures made in Los Angeles out of roots and branches. Alfred Frankenstein, critic for the *San Francisco Chronicle*, wrote that although Noguchi was "frighteningly versatile," he was "as much a master of the sculpturally abstract as Brancusi or Henry Moore, and he can also create a portrait head as startlingly life-like as anything by Houdon."[24] Also included were blueprints of his plans for Poston. As a result, the Farm Security Administration responded to the show by requesting sets of these prints. They were interested in using his ideas at other internment camps.[25]

Noguchi's attitude toward the camp administration and toward people in a position of authority outside of camp became increasingly deferential. In his article for *Reader's Digest*, probably written in late August or September, he described his growing awareness of differences in power: "The administration, some of whom I had known previously, seemed to change character. In my mind they seemed to have changed from the sensitive people I knew them to be into our keepers whose words was law. Nevermore could anything be done without first asking them. Along with my freedom I seemed to have lost any possibility of equal friendship. I became embarrassed in their presence."[26]

On July 27 he wrote again to Collier, his best link to people in Washington who might be capable of restoring his freedom:

Dear Mr. Collier,

After much hesitation and with deep regret I must finally ask you to do what is necessary to have me released . . . I am extremely despondent for lack of companionship. The Niseis here are not of my age and of an entirely different background and interest. Also I have become so out of touch with the administration that I do not know of what further use I can be in camp. I am sure they consider me more bother than help.

As you know I sought some place where I might fit into the fight for freedom. This might have been the place were I stronger or more adaptable. As it is I become embittered. I came here voluntarily, I trust that you will not have difficulty in securing this request.

With my sincere best wishes
I remain,
Isamu Noguchi

P.S I might add it's the heat that drives me frantic.[27]

The following day Noguchi wrote to E. R. Fryer of the War Relocation Authority asking to be given a job that would allow him to visit other camps. If no such job was possible, he asked to be released.

Noguchi's good looks and celebrity status didn't help his position at

Poston. Masayo Duus learned from former Poston internees that "young women often gathered in front of his room to get a look at him, and a few even made advances."[28] Some internees remembered a screaming fight between two married women, both infatuated with Noguchi. They tore at each other's hair as they wrestled each other to the ground. It was said that the husband of one of the combatants asked the administration to throw Noguchi out of the camp and that the husband of the other threatened to kill Noguchi.

Noguchi's pleas for release went unanswered. His misery was exacerbated by the failure of his liberal friends and acquaintances to fight against the incarceration of the Nisei: "Not one ever raised his voice. Because of their feelings about Russia, you see. So the only people who came to the rescue were the Quakers."[29]

On August 24 Noguchi went to see Wade Head, director of Poston. He had learned that internees with mixed blood or mixed marriages were to be released, but his name was not on the list. It seems that the military had received a secret file calling Noguchi a "suspicious person." What the Fourth Army Intelligence section found suspect was Noguchi's having moved back and forth between San Francisco and Los Angeles in the months before entering Poston. When he visited Santa Barbara to see an art collector they suspected him of investigating the local airport. When he went to see a sculptor friend in Carmel, they worried that his real purpose was to get information on a nearby naval facility.[30]

The military finally authorized Noguchi's release from Poston on November 2, 1942. A week later Noguchi wrote to Ailes: "It's taken me three months to get this permit to go out, so now I have a furlough and you will be seeing me for a while at least . . . We will have a lot to talk about and I will tell you what I have gone through . . . it's so indescribable, the life here, so removed from the reality of New York . . . I feel like Rip Van Winkle."[31]

The camp director issued Noguchi a thirty-day furlough on November 12. Noguchi never went back. That night he got in his station wagon and drove to Salt Lake City, where he stopped to see John Lafarge and Larry Tajiri, managing editor of *Pacific Citizen*, the official publication of the Japanese American Citizens League. He then moved on to Chicago and to Wisconsin to visit Taliesen, Frank Lloyd Wright's summer home near Spring Green. He had invited Wright to visit Poston and Wright had written a letter recommending Noguchi's release. "I went there to thank him. And his place was swarming with conscientious objectors. He read me excerpts from the books that he was writing. One of them was his esteem for this German philosopher called Heidegger, who was accused of being friendly to the Nazis. But he didn't care. Frank Lloyd Wright was a man who did not give a shit, because he felt that he was an American."[32]

In Washington, Noguchi met with Milton Eisenhower (director of the War Relocation Authority), with whom he talked about why people of Japanese ancestry had to be locked up and about the difference in aims between the War Relocation Authority and John Collier. What Noguchi learned was that "Collier was trying to make it pleasant, and they were trying to make it unpleasant."[33] Noguchi also met with Langdon Warner, who was an adviser to the U.S. government about Japan. They discussed the possibility of an exhibition and benefit for the Nisei to take place the following spring. He also looked up old friends in the hopes of finding some role for himself in the fight against fascism or at least a job that would allow him to extend his furlough. Through A. Conger Goodyear he tried to find work in the Intelligence Service. Nothing panned out. "I finally landed back in New York—it must have been late Fall of 1942 . . . I had about enough of all causes and everything else . . . I just chucked the whole works, I mean I wasn't going to have anything to do with it."[34] In his autobiography Noguchi described his feeling of relief after escaping from Poston: "Freedom earned has a quality of assurance. The deep depression that comes with living under a cloud of suspicion, which we as Nisei experienced, lifted, and was followed by tranquility . . . I resolved henceforth to be an artist only."[35]

Still, Noguchi was not able to completely disengage from social concerns. On February 1, 1943, he published an article in *The New Republic* in which he disavowed the press's opinion that recent riots at the relocation camps were fomented by pro-Axis groups.[36] The riots, he said, were to a great extent caused by frustration and by conflict between the Issei and the Nisei. Noguchi recommended that the internees should be self-governing and self-supporting. "How else than by establishing themselves productively can they hope to share in the peace?" Noguchi also organized the Arts Council of Japanese-Americans for Democracy, a New York City group of artists, writers, and musicians who wished to promote a better understanding of Japanese-Americans. Painter Yasuo Kunioshi was the chairman and Noguchi and the architect Minoru Yamazaki (who later designed the World Trade Center) were vice-chairmen.

Noguchi may have tried to abandon politics, but the government considered him to be politically suspect. He was under constant FBI surveillance from December 1942 to late in 1945. At one point he had to petition to be able to travel into the West Coast defense zone.[37] Being treated like an enemy alien intensified Noguchi's feeling of not belonging. In response, he hunkered down in his new "oasis, a studio with a garden at 33 MacDougal Alley," and focused on belonging to himself.

21

MACDOUGAL ALLEY

MacDougal Alley, where Noguchi lived from 1942 to 1949, was a charming cobblestone, gas-lit, dead-end lane just south of Eighth Street and a block north of Washington Square. Lined with old two-story houses and converted carriage houses and stables, many of them occupied by artists since the turn of the century, the alley seemed a world apart. Noguchi had the two brick buildings that once closed off the alley's end. Number 33 included not only his studio, but also a garden with a large tree and a flagstone path flanked by shrubbery and even a small fishpond. He called this haven "a sign of providence."[1] Here he returned to being a sculptor and also resumed an active social life, enjoying the company of artists who were part of the influx of Europeans escaping the war as well as the American artists who became part of this sophisticated milieu. An event that must have made him feel back in the swing of things was his inclusion in *20th Century Portraits*, curated by Monroe Wheeler at the Museum of Modern Art. The show, which opened shortly after he arrived in New York, included three of his portraits of prominent people: George Gershwin, A. Conger Goodyear, and Mrs. William A. M. Burden, Jr.

During his first summer of freedom, Noguchi carved stone. "My first piece, after emerging from camp, was *Leda*."[2] An erotic, softly curving, Arp-inspired alabaster shape, *Leda* has a hole that looks vaguely umbilical or vaginal and a lobe that suggests a woman's head flung back or perhaps a swan's neck. The sensuous mood of this sculpture continued in subsequent marbles such as *Time Lock* and *Noodle*.

Like *Leda*, these two are composed of organic forms with protuberances that convey Noguchi's fascination with germination and emerging life. "These straight carvings were to me the sure things of sculpture, long lasting (locked against time's erosion), sculptural sculpture." *Noodle*, Noguchi recalled, was carved directly: "This was for me an exorcism of all the byways I had traveled . . . there [at MacDougal Alley] I found my way back from the uncertainties of the 1930s to a more secure sense of my work as an artist."[3]

Part of Noguchi's sense of well-being came from his return to stone carving, a technique that he had learned as a youth from Brancusi. There was, Noguchi pointed out, a "reaction against Rodin," whose clay sculptures cast in bronze were considered to be too pictorial. "For a sculptor of my generation the bedrock of sculpture was a moral issue. Those of us in New York knew that *taille directe* [direct carving] was the ultimate virtue. Everything else was suspect if not dishonest."[4] There was a probity, he said, in trying to "find the basis of any given art or material . . . If we worked with stone, we wanted to find that stone . . . If it wasn't direct carved, you were just a son of a bitch."[5] Yet, wary of copying himself or settling comfortably into a particular style or technique, Noguchi changed course. He decided that "everything was sculpture. Any material, any idea without hindrance born into space, I considered sculpture."[6] Although he continued carving stone that summer, he also worked with all kinds of other materials— plastic, magnesium, string, fabric, metal, bones, shell, and driftwood. "I entered into a whole new series of quests. One was the key to the other."

Some of Noguchi's sculptures from the years after his escape from Poston express an angst that is clearly related to the war. *The World Is a Foxhole*, first called *I Am a Foxhole*, consists of a roundish bronze base (originally conceived as a wall plaque) with a crater (the foxhole) dug into its surface and a small peg protruding from the foxhole, suggesting, as Noguchi put it, the "thoughts of a soldier in a foxhole."[7] In the original piece that hung on the wall of Noguchi's MacDougal Alley studio, a wooden dowel with a red flag attached by string projected from the edge of the plaque straight out toward the viewer. The flag intimated hope, but it was also, Noguchi said, a signal of despair. "The war weighed heavily on my mind after my escape from that reality [Poston] to the safety and remoteness of New York," Noguchi said. "To

Noguchi in his
MacDougal
Alley studio,
1946 (Eliot
Elisofon / The LIFE
Picture Collection /
Getty Images)

Leda, 1942. Alabaster, 10¼×18¾×18¾ in.

Noodle, 1943–44. Botticino marble, ht. 26½ in.

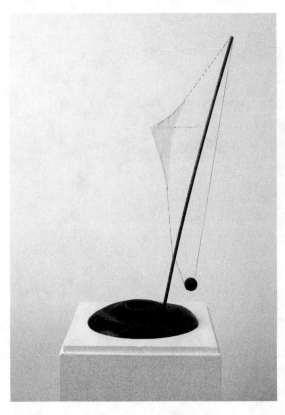

The World Is a Foxhole,
1942–43. Bronze, wood,
and string, ht. 32 in.

this haven came other refugees. Many artists from Europe became my
acquaintances. *The World Is a Foxhole* was among my works reflecting
this situation."

Another wall plaque, *My Arizona*, which refers to his experience at
Poston, is a square relief made of plastic and magnesite and divided
into four quarters. The upper left quadrant has a sheet of red plastic
with a round hole through which you see a round protrusion with a
stick in it. The red might allude to the red earth around Poston and to
the terrible heat of the desert sun. On the upper right is a mound with
a round crater that suggests a black hole of emptiness—that existential
anxiety so pervasive in the 1940s and 1950s. Thanks in part to his
knowledge of Zen, Noguchi was drawn to the idea of emptiness, but
this hole makes one think of the pointlessness and loneliness that Noguchi endured at Poston. It also brings to mind the fear of atomic annihilation, a subject that Noguchi talked about a great deal in the next

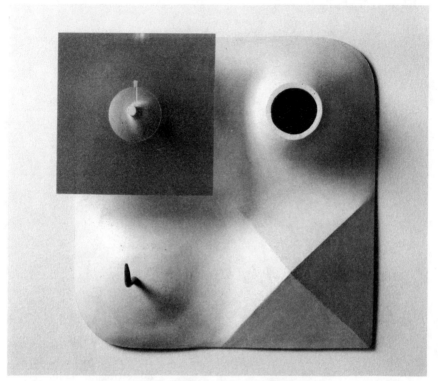

My Arizona, 1943. Magnesite and plastic, 18×18×4 in.

few years. On the lower left is a smooth round mound pierced by a piece of red plastic and on the lower right a four-sided pyramid, half dark and half light. These mounds, holes, and geometric shapes would recur in many of Noguchi's later sculptures.

This Tortured Earth was conceived to be viewed from above and is thus one of Noguchi's earliest tabletop sculptures. Noguchi thought of it as a model for a much larger antiwar sculpture to be made of earth. The swellings and hollows that flow like lava were inspired by a photograph of a bombed area in the African desert. The molten undulations look both cruel and eroticized, as in the contemporaneous paintings of his friend the Surrealist painter Roberto Matta Echaurren, in whose metamorphic landscapes the volcanic earth and the human body merge. Similarly, the elongated orifices in *This Tortured Earth* suggest female genitalia, but Noguchi's flesh/earth hybrid seems to writhe not in a combination of ecstasy and agony, as in Matta's paintings, but in

This Tortured Earth, 1943. Bronze model, 28×28×4 in.

agony alone. "*This Tortured Earth* was my concept for a large area to memorialize the tragedy of war. There is injury to the earth itself. The war machine, I thought, would be excellent equipment for sculpture, to bomb it into existence."[8]

The most despairing of Noguchi's wartime sculptures is *Monument to Heroes*. It consists of an upright black paper cylinder with holes cut out of it from which protrude wooden dowels, and actual human bones that Noguchi acquired from the attic of the American Museum of Natural History. In this sculpture, he said, he was "trying to get back to a sort of pre-art thing, trying to find something in the rubble . . . To go back is to go forward in a way, if you go back to bedrock, then you have something to stand upon."[9] The bones, he explained, are those of the heroes "who never return," and his monument to them was "a column for aviators who became heroes. The bones of the unknown—the residue of bravery, blown by winds."[10]

Monument to Heroes, 1943. Cardboard, wood, bones, and string, 28¼×15½×14 in.

In 1943–44 Noguchi made a series of biomorphic magnesite sculptures lit from inside. He called them "Lunars" and said that they were
an "attempt at a new art form." Using magnesite reinforced with bur-
lap, he created shell-like forms thin enough to transmit light from a
bulb placed inside. Such light sculptures made sense, he observed,
because human beings lived more and more indoors—"perhaps soon
in the atomic age, we will live in caves . . . I thought of a luminous
object as a source of delight in itself—like fire it attracts and protects
us from the beasts of the night."[11] Sometimes, as in *Lunar Landscape*,
Noguchi used colored lightbulbs, and the undulating surface cut with
erotic clefts again brings to mind Matta's contemporaneous *Psychological Morphologies*. But neither dealers nor critics were interested in
the Lunars, and Noguchi himself felt frustrated by their size limitation. He wanted sculpture to be part of space. "I thought of a room of
music and light, a porous room within a room—in the void of space."[12]

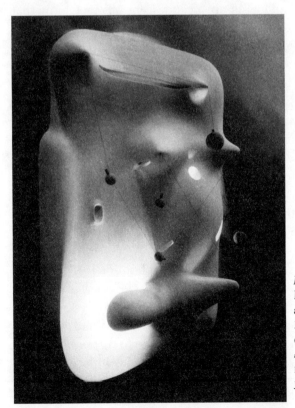

Lunar Landscape, 1944.
Magnesite, string, cork,
and electricity,
34½×24¾×7⅞ in.
(Courtesy of the Hirshhorn Museum
and Sculpture Garden, Smithsonian
Institution, Washington, D.C.; gift of
Joseph H. Hirshhorn, 1966)

He was able to expand his Lunars in several large commercial jobs, such as the undulating ceiling illuminated from within for Time Inc.'s Information Center or the Lunar wall in the stairwell of the SS *Argentina*.

Noguchi gave up making Lunars in part because the extreme malleability of magnesite conflicted with his interest in a more rigorous exploration of form in space. Also, Lunars didn't sell, and the Lunar walls were just decorations for the rich, whereas he wanted to make something that could be enjoyed by a wide range of people. With this in mind, in 1944, as a Christmas gift for Ailes, Noguchi made a lamp out of an aluminum cylinder with three wooden dowels for legs. That same year he designed what he called Lunar Lights, made out of plastic and metal. A year later Knoll Associates manufactured several versions of Ailes' three-legged lamp.

Lunar Infant packs a much higher emotional voltage than his other Lunars. Indeed, Noguchi felt it was his most successful sculpture in this mode. The magnesite "infant" is an incandescent abstract form that bears some resemblance to a human baby. Suspended from a wooden framework by a wire, it looks alarmingly vulnerable. A crack of light glows between what appear to be the "infant's" two heads. The suggestion that there are two heads touching each other brings to mind Noguchi's admiration for Brancusi's *The Kiss*. The particular tenderness expressed in *Lunar Infant*, the way the creature seems to have two heads, and the way it dangles helplessly makes one wonder if it had an immediate personal meaning to its maker. Possibly the strange poignancy of this sculpture and the sensuousness of several of his contemporaneous carvings might have something to do with Noguchi's romance at the time with Ann Matta Clark, Roberto Matta's wife, who had been abandoned by Matta soon after the birth of twin boys in June 1943.

Ann Clark had married the Chilean-born Matta in 1939 in Paris, where she had considerable success as a costume designer. She moved with him to New York the following year. But for all his abounding energy and cheerfulness, Matta was not one to accommodate crying infants. On August 17, 1944, Jeanne Reynal wrote to Agnes Magruder, who had married Gorky in 1941: "I believe [Isamu] is in love again, or so he writes, and from the general description I have a quaint feeling that it is the 'Parroqueeta.'" Ann Matta's nickname, said to have been

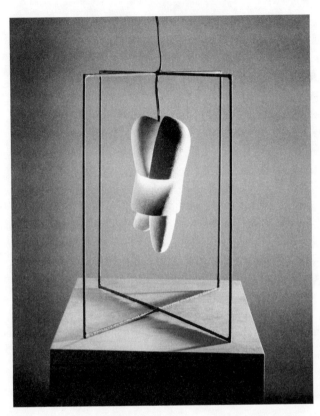

Lunar Infant, 1944.
Magnesite, electricity,
and wood,
22 × 16 × 16 in.

given to her by the poet and essayist André Breton, was Pajarito, or "Little Bird." She was gentle, calm, intelligent, and lovely. Everyone in the Surrealist circle was fond of her; she had an aura of purity and wisdom.

Although Matta's abandonment had left Ann in precarious economic straits, she had too much inner strength to play the role of jilted wife. When Matta was late in sending money for child support, and Ann was evicted from her New York apartment, Noguchi arranged for a friend (probably painter Robert Motherwell) to lend her a house in Amagansett, Long Island. A photograph of Noguchi, Ann, and her twin boys, together with a slightly older boy on a bay beach, may have been taken at this time. Slender and beautiful, the thirty-year-old Ann has, in the photograph, a mane of long brown hair, and Noguchi, with his lithe, strong, well-proportioned body, looks vigorous. The period when they became lovers was confusing and exhausting for Ann. She was used to leading a bohemian and often penurious life with Matta,

but now, with the responsibility for twin toddlers, she longed for security. Noguchi could help, but he had money worries of his own and
was not able to take on the support of a wife and children.

Several of Noguchi and Ann's friends recall that Ann was one of
the few women whom Noguchi really loved. He wrote to Jeanne Reynal in late November 1944 that he wanted to come west—no doubt to
Reno—so that Ann could get divorced and he could marry her. They
would, he said, spend some time camping in the mountains and he
would make some tables. He also told Reynal that Agnes and Gorky
approved of the match.[13] But Ann did not think that saddling Noguchi
with twins would be good for his art, and art, she knew, was the center
of his life. Friends say that although she was attracted to Noguchi's
separateness, and was grateful for his devotion, she was not in love
with him. Instead of marrying Noguchi, on March 8, 1945, she took
her twenty-month-old sons and went to visit their Chilean grandpar-
ents in Santiago.

22

LETTERS TO ANN

Immeditately upon Ann's arrival in Santiago, she began to receive impassioned letters from Noguchi that included everything from the details of his work and daily affairs to his hopes that she would marry him and return to New York with her children. He constantly asked her to call, to write, and referred frequently to the depression he felt without her. Everything he did, he said, reminded him of her. "I've been in such a deep blue funk since you went away, only your letters kept me going, now without a word from you for some time to come what'll I do? . . . I'm absolutely figety, don't know why. Maybe it's the spring, maybe its my work which simply wont come out the way I want it to, maybe its my giving up smoking—the main reason I guess is that you are gone away and I am lost."[1]

Noguchi's next letter to Ann (March 24, 1945) told her that he had just gone out into his MacDougal Alley garden "dressed in nothing" in order to till the soil and that he had finally started working but "got so depressed at your not being here that I quit. I'm planning to cut that large piece of stone [*Noodle*] in the garden starting next week." In one of her early letters from this time, Ann expressed a deep concern for her children. "I know that it is hard to make plans—dear—and carry them out. But I do think that we should both feel responsibility about our future. I know that when I get back I want to find a place and make a definite home—to make it as comfortable and beautiful as possible (naturally simple), and then to find some way to care for the children that I may be free enough to work at what I can do."

As the correspondence continued, Noguchi made frequent declarations of his love. "It's simply that I can not help it—you affect me that way even 6000 miles away—now that's something isn't it? It must be it!! O my dearest wire me telephone me <u>yes</u> meaning in case you didn't get my previous letter will you marry me?" Marriage became a theme for Noguchi, and he was constantly thinking of ways to lure Ann back and convince her that he could help her care for her twin boys. Indeed, he said that he would like to adopt them so that Ann could be free of her ties to Matta. In April he wrote: "You know what I want of marriage: a home, children, independence without obligations or attachments to anyone outside. To give and take completely is what I desire . . . If you feel that you've got to hold on to some part of Matta, I will never feel that you are completely my wife . . . If I am to assume total responsibility I'll have to make a lot of money—there's the rub. I think I could eventually do so, but it will take some time, and I will have to get organized and stop spending as much time as I do just

Noguchi, Ann Matta Clark, her twin sons, Gordon and Sebastian Matta, and an unidentified friend at a bay beach on Long Island, summer 1944

dreaming and 'experimenting.'" In the meantime he said that she should feel free to have a relationship with someone "more suitable," but he hoped that she would be as faithful to him as he was faithful to her. Ann's response was "I haven't found anyone who could compare with you—You know I love you—don't you?"

On April 23 Ann wrote: "You know that the thing I want the most in the world is to be with you—and to find a life together—or rather to make it together. However, maybe you are right. It is a lot to ask of an artist. It puts too much strain on both art and love—which I doubt if it could stand."

Remembering all the arguments they had had about why she was going, he wondered if it was his fault that she was gone. He trusted her opinion about his work and wrote that he was sometimes paralyzed with doubts. "You would be an enormous help in that direction; as well as in several others—that I can think of!!!" He told her of his wish to have a show. "I should have an agent or a gallery—I'm sure my bad luck in this respect is my own fault, but don't know how to correct it—you could help me if you were here." On May 19 he wrote: "I asked Julien [Levy] and he said no. And Pierre [Matisse] wont [sic] even bother to come down to see. And Peggy [Guggenheim] is not interested. And Kootz [Samuel Kootz] said no to Jean's suggestion. And I havnt [sic] bothered to see even lesser fry and I say to hell with them all."

By May Noguchi had begun to make his interlocking slab sculptures, works that were assembled out of several sections of carved stone or wood. On May 11 he wrote to Ann, "I just did a flat marble piece which I think you may like—I wish to god you were here to advise me about my work—I'm eager to get some more marble if I can find the mazuma." Perhaps a week later he made sketches of three wooden sculptures and a drawing of the stone sculpture (*Noodle*) that he had mentioned to Ann in earlier letters. Of love he said: "O baby you are so wonderfull!—who else but you could stand so beastly a temper as mine—you must admit though that I have been provoked by your running off down there."

Several of Noguchi's sculptures from 1944 and 1945, the voluptuous *Noodle* and *Time Lock*, for examples, seem to reflect his attachment to Ann. His alabaster *The Kiss*, an abstraction of the idea of an embrace, and his semiabstract *Mother and Child*, carved from onyx, are particularly tender images. In 1945 Noguchi also made two rather humorous and affectionate sculptures titled *The Bed*. One is carved out of African Wonder Stone, the other is cast in bronze. Surely these semiabstract images of a man and woman lying side by side on their backs reflect his initial happiness with Ann.

Yet his financial troubles persisted. "I've had $250 for those costumes I did, and I'm getting another $250 for doing something for 'Life' [magazine]. I seem to get $250 for everything I do—I must snap into a higher bracket—at my rate I seem to manage to get approximately that much per month these days. It would be not nearly enough for the 4 of us . . ." In another letter he pleaded, "O baby, please have the strength and the courage for me. Please be willing to stand poverty as well as riches, illness as well as wellness, sadness as well as happiness. And don't ever go away again." He apologized for "sliding down into my depression again." Often in the years to come Noguchi would refer to periods of misery. It seems likely that he suffered from severe clinical depressions.

Sometime in late May 1945, Noguchi wrote: "For the last two days I have been walking around looking at marbles out in Astoria—remember? . . . I walk the streets and can not settle down to work. O Lord why am I so miserable without you? . . . Must you go your way and I go mine, could we not work things out together?" He said that he had been in a room full of "belles but couldn't seem to cook up any interest . . . Without you I feel absolutely alone . . . Love surges over me like the salt sea—" He signed off: "Honey, bring love back to poor Isamu."

Ann wrote Noguchi on May 29 that her divorce papers with Matta would be signed on June 8. "And if you think I still have any yearnings in that direction, you couldn't be more wrong. I hope that I never have to see him again. So I wish you wouldn't keep harping on that particular subject—it irritates me." He responded: "I love you so much, I would give you the whole world and all the beauty it contains—for indeed I am enormously rich, the richest man in the world, capable of anything—or nothing. You are that way too, I know. Together how wonderful would be the world."

Noguchi's letters to Ann during the summer months are mostly about when she will return, how she will travel, and where they will live. He wrote of his fear that their long separation might damage their relationship. He spoke of a loneliness and "inertia" that was both physical and psychological. He reported on the films, plays, and concerts he had attended; his observations about these show a fine critical acumen. "I've been going to the movies a lot these days to kill the evenings," he wrote on July 18. "The evenings are my unhappy hours . . ." In the following months, Noguchi would continue to move from hope to despair as Ann's date for returning to New York was pushed back in letter after letter. He began to sound less insistent about her rejoining him in New York. He had no money and he had not found an apartment for Ann. On July 25 Noguchi warned her about how difficult life would be in New York. "I've been having the heebie-jeebies too, so I'm going off to the country." Upon his return he wrote: "I begin to see your point that we may both be just too haywire to be good for each other—there are of course mitigating circumstances, (very mitigating) that make us need each other desperately—I wonder how they balance each other, our needing each other and our being bad for each other. I suppose your going would indicate that you had such fears as this but alas we can not know how things are until we are together again and then it may be too late."

His August 11 letter was written five days after the Americans dropped the bomb on Hiroshima. Noguchi was horrified by the carnage in his father's country, but also relieved that "Wonderful Peace is here!!!" He told Ann that it might be unwise for her to give up the security of her situation in Chile for the "uncertainties" of life in New York and that she should perhaps postpone her return until spring, when he hoped to find a place in the country. "When the pain of parting has ground in sufficiently time does not seem to matter any more. I wouldn't be surprised if with the coming of peace I may be asked to help out in Japan. If there is any likelihood of its being soon I would suggest you wait there."

At the end of August his desire for Ann's return appears to have been rekindled, but misgivings and "a sort of nervous indecision" were getting in the way of work. He was impatient, and given to quarrels with friends such as Ruth Page. Even though Ann insisted that everything would be better with the war over, Noguchi maintained that things would only be right when Ann returned to New York.

In September he told Ann that his sets for Ruth Page's ballet *The Bells* had been postponed until mid-October, which pleased him: "I'm really only interested in doing sculpture, and sets are just another easy money pickup so far as I'm concerned." He concluded his letter: "I wonder how it will be when you get back—what about miracles and Magic? O darling dearest I wonder and I hope!!!!!!" There was another subject that began to dominate his correspondence: Ann's decision to see an analyst. "So your are being analized [sic]! I'm dreadfully sorry that you feel you need it—I think its awful. Its all in the mind, as they say, and once you decide that you're ill one becomes victimized by one doctor or another."

He was right to worry. Citing her analysis as part of the reason, Ann told him that she was not leaving Chile for a while. On September 20 Noguchi wrote: "My love—what can I say—the news that you are not coming back has knocked me out cold, in bed for the last two days, and I'm at a loss for words . . . time is that monster which is devouring us inch by inch and all the psychoanalysts and all the kings horses can not replace one wasted minute!"

When he wrote again on October 2 he had not heard from Ann in ten days. "Of course I am predisposed to be skeptical about this new-fangled 'psychoanalysis,' especially in this case. As you know I am very simple, and may not know of the depths of your depravity . . ." He was broke, he said, but he hoped to get some money in a few days:

> What a precarious existence! Maybe that's what you are frightened of. But really, what could be more transient than our life on earth, this vale of tears—and yet we all search after permanence, immortality or what have you. The best we can do is to have some sort of a philosophy to see us through—Can an analyst give you that? . . . Oh my darling, we have so short a time!!! It is what we have left of days that we have to live—each day that we do not live fully leaves us that much poorer . . . there simply does not seem anything I can do to evoke the touch of your hand, your breath upon my ear—how cruel this is.

He added in a postscript, "My dearest love is yours. However, it's silly of me I know, that I should be dubious about your actions when you say the sweetest things in your letters. By all means do whatever you think is best and stay as long as you want (not that I can boast of any influence)."

On the same day, Ann wrote that she was feeling "restless and homesick . . . Somehow, even from here I feel your disappointment, your resentment towards me for not being there. I feel your wordlessness—and exasperation. I, too, think it is inutile to try to explain—it is something you just feel—that's all. This real fact of separation has taken on shape and form and color so that I can see it sitting there between us gloating. How I hate it! What a horrible, ugly beast it is." Six days later she wrote again: "Darling, It was such a happy relief to have your letter today—including the scolding about psychoanalysis. It was really a masterpiece. Darling I see your point of view and of course neither analysis nor 'my new confidant' as you call him can take the place of you—or your love. God no! But it can make me a much more reasonable human being to live with. (I hope.)"

When Noguchi wrote Ann on October 13 he sounded as if the distance between them was insurmountable: "I cannot follow you any more where you have gone, much further now than Chile. I do not know the words, wordless, as you say—I do not know my way, a stranger . . . my mood is black as black, suicidal, the world frozen. But I know its no use breaking ones heart over 'wishful thoughts,' everything changes, the rocks and hills, only I wish you had not found it necessary to change yourself to the 'better' in any other persons [sic] immage [sic] than mine—Who sets the categories of love?"

On October 20 Ann wrote back: "My darling. I can't bear to think of your present state of mind. Your desperation and destructive thoughts. Somehow I can't imagine life without your love or my loving you." She acknowledged the difficulty of their making a life together. It would, she said, require "planning and work and sacrifice." She could cope with "black moments" if she knew that he was there. "Please don't ask me to give up." She then offered her perceptions of Noguchi's character:

I would like to talk about you, sweet—I think I know some of your weaknesses as well as your strength. You have a wonderful intuitive insight into life—and you live by a well-defined philosophy of your own—your own pattern as you call it. I don't think you need the help of psychoanalysis or anything like it.—of course everyone has a few quirks that could be ironed out by it—perhaps your attitude towards material success for instance—but the basic structure of you in front of life is strong, elastic, guided by your splendid intuition.

I can't help but feel that you are in a crucial moment of your life too—perhaps your falling in love with me was partly because it happened at the moment when you felt an inward need to tie the loose ends of your life together—to concentrate all your forces—your emotions . . .

Your art too has reached a culmination—a peak as to technical ability and conception which is rich and pure and honest. You thoroughly deserve success now. More still, I am certain that you are on the threshold of accomplishing the really great work of your whole life . . . Please darling—try actively to make our chance of happiness come true. Because I don't believe that happiness is something that is put in your mouth and all you have to do is let it melt there.

I love you and want you—

Ann

Noguchi answered Ann's letter a week later: "I've been in the deepest depression of my life . . . So I'll just keep working, my fingers to the bone—I mean it, my fingers are bleeding from being worn through—indeed I'm a mass of scars inside and out . . . I still haven't been able to arrange a show. I suppose that too is psychological, as well as my inability to make money. It seems I fight with whoever offers me a job, as though they were infringing on my privacy. So I live like a bum borrowing a little here and there . . . the memory image of you keeps me entranced ruining all my pleasure . . ."

On November 1 Ann wrote that although his letters were "heart-rending," the love he had expressed in his last letter gave her "fresh courage." Much of her letter was a kind of soul-searching—the anxious introspection of a young woman in an early stage of analysis. She spoke of her "infantile attitude towards life in general . . . You said that you think it may be the child in me that you love—but I am sure that you do not fully realize the meaning of that . . . I will never forget once when you talked to me when I was living in Macdougal Street. Remember? The room was almost dark—and you said that there was probably two people in me—the 'Pajarito'—and the Ann—and darling I will always love you for it that you instinctively chose the Ann which is the real me."

Noguchi's next letter to Ann was written in the first half of November: "By the time you get this I will be 41 years old; how awful!!!" His tone was less desperate, sometimes almost happy. His work was going well, and he was avoiding social life. Mostly his success came at the hands of Martha Graham, for whom he was regularly designing sets and costumes. But over the course of the month, as Ann remained in Chile, he seemed to grow more resigned to the idea that she might never return. "Even when you told me that you were not comming [sic] back till spring, it produced no shock, as though I had known that would be . . . By March it will have been a year since you went away— I wonder if you will ever come back, and what it will be like then." He ended his letter: "My love and a million kisses into the void!"

Although Noguchi's letters continue to profess his love for Ann, he seems more and more willing to relinquish her. Perhaps he was distracted. At a Surrealist party, he met the writer Anaïs Nin, a delicate, dark-haired Latin beauty with whom he had a brief affair in November 1945. In her diary she wrote of seeing Noguchi at a going-away party for André Breton: "Noguchi, with his startled, wistful air, tired from watching the moving of his big rose marble figure [Kouros] to the Museum of Modern Art . . ."[2] She called his MacDougal Alley studio "one of the lovliest places in New York . . . intimate and mysterious." When Noguchi showed her the miniature paper models for his current sculptures he spoke of the "tenderness" he felt for them. "They belong to me. They are human and possessable; they are near; they lie in the hollow of my hand." By contrast, he said, when his larger sculptures left the studio they no longer belonged to him.

A letter that was probably written in early December told Ann that he had "a frightful case of claustrophobia and stuckinthemud feeling," so he rented and fixed up a small, unheated space across the alley from his studio. After spending one frigid night in his new space he was in bed with a cold. "So I went back to my corner in the studio. Anyway the studio is considerably cleared out so I can get to work making the new sets for Martha Graham."

Noguchi's depression was worsened because his "haven," his Mac-Dougal Alley studio, was to be demolished in June to make way for apartment buildings. He told Ann that he hoped by then to have enough money to move to the country—"and if you were here that might even be pleasant." He had been Christmas shopping for Ann and the twins. "Everybody has money and is buying like mad so there is nothing left in the stores but for much money." He found a blouse for Ann and shorts for the boys. "Well I hope you will understand that my heart goes with these small gifts . . . How different it would be if you were here!"

He spent Christmas with Ailes and his intimate friend Luchita del Solar, and he must have telephoned Ann, because his December 30 letter said: "The telephone conversation as usual was quite unsatisfactory. What do you mean by saying you hoped to be able to come back in March? Is it the psychoanalisis [sic] that is going on ad infinitum?" He was, he wrote, "up to my ears in carpentry for Martha. Expect to leave for Chicago on the 10th of January. I'm disgusted to spend so much time away from my real work, but I want to recoup my finances a bit."

From Chicago, where he worked on sets and costumes for Ruth Page, he wrote of his despair that Ann might never return. "If you really want to come back I don't think anything would keep you away . . . but you have other loves besides—at least two very young men and who else besides I know not—So I guess you really don't need me at all. Love is a responsibility and a selfishness, and you may think me lucky to be so alone. But I don't, I would like to have a wife & children too—I may be getting too old for that now though, and I see no point in marriage without at least one child—do you? . . . It is not the atom bomb that will destroy the world, my world, in a couple of years, but time!"

On January 28, 1946, just after his return to Manhattan from Chicago, Noguchi wrote Ann about the premiere at Columbia University of Martha Graham's new dance, *Cave of the Heart*: "It went well—though the critics seem to have been generally shocked by it—I think its her best so far." He gave Ann news of various friends and art exhibitions, and of his work. He was fixing up his studio so that he could work inside with stone. He wished that he could concentrate on stone carving, but Martha Graham had a new dance for which she wanted him to design a set.

Two weeks later Noguchi wrote that he had had a cold for several weeks. "Also I've been blue and lonely and I couldn't get to work." In the weeks that followed he continued to bemoan his inability to work. In March he expressed his pointed suspicion that Ann's lack of letters might indicate that she had found another lover. He had heard in December that Ann was seeing a Chilean architect. In April he gave a big party for his Indian friend Gautam Sarabhai, whom he had met through the India League when Sarabhai was in New York working on the expansion of his family's cotton textile trade. He had also gone to various going-away parties for people bound for Europe, some of them Europeans who had found refuge in the United States during the war. "New York will be deserted excepting for the stick-in-the-muds [such] as I. I must say I get wanderlust too watching all these excited hopefuls." He went on to tell Ann about Gorky's operation for colorectal cancer. This was the second disaster for Gorky in 1946. A few months earlier his studio in Sherman, Connecticut, had burned down and he had lost much of his recent work. "They think they've gotten it all out. He will be out of the hospital in ten days . . . Now, if ever is the time for me to work, if only this goddamed lasitude [sic] would leave me!!"

As Ann's return date came closer, she became distressed. Noguchi was clearly disappointed: "I am very disturbed that you are unhappy, the accumulation of your indecisions and postponements . . . In any case your apartment is ready for you." He told her that he planned to see Merce Cunningham dance that evening. The following day he reported that the performance "was very pretty, suggestive and poetic but rather empty." He was about to have lunch with Jeanne Reynal, who was just back from California. "Everybody asks after you. You really have a load of friends here. All agree that you are the most Normal person they know . . . The Spring will be gone, and summer too if you don't decide to come back soon. O Christ what is it? That keeps you? My heart waits but time does not."

On May 17 he wrote one of his more poetic letters:

Darling, I was awakened this morning by the sweetest song of a thrush, singing a long composition such as they used to sing in Amagansett. And there are several Orioles here too flying arround [sic] in an eratic [sic] way as they must be very young. I'm waiting now for Jeanne Reynal who is driving Gorky out to Amaganset to look for a place. I'm to be their guide. I'm afraid its too late to find anything, but it will be nice to be in the country anyway, what with this incredibly beautiful singing which is like a refrain from a distant and lovely past. Is it altogether past and only to be remembered with the song of a thrush? I wonder.

A few days later he wrote that he and Gorky and Reynal had gone to Long Island and found no suitable rental for the Gorky family. As soon as he was home he set about planting things that he had dug up in the woods. "Theres a bright orange and black oriole drinking from the fishpond. A thrush fliters [sic] around in the wisteria . . . I felt so lonely out in Long Island with all those happy people—especially when we stoped [sic] one night at the Griffin House—everywhere so filled with memory for me, walking along the beach picking shells . . . Do please write oftener."

By the time Ann returned to New York in June, they had been apart for more than a year. "Dear Isamu, Here at last," Ann began an undated letter. In the following weeks she spent some weekends with Noguchi in the country. But their love affair was over. Not long after her arrival Noguchi introduced her to a beautiful young Indian girl, Jawaharlal Nehru's niece, Tara Pandit, with whom he had recently fallen in love. Over the years he continued to correspond with Ann sporadically and to concern himself with her and her twin sons' welfare, sending money when needed.[3] When in October 1988 he received the Order of the Sacred Treasure from the Japanese government for his contribution to understanding between Japan and the United States, he invited Ann to come to the ceremony at the Japanese consulate in New York. She could not make it. Afterward he wrote her: "You would have expanded my family attendance by about 30% I guess . . . Anyway you are someone I treasure from the past." He apologized for not being able to get out to Sag Harbor on Long Island to see her: "Time has got me by the neck! With ever love Isamu."

23

NOGUCHI AND MARTHA GRAHAM, PASSIONATE COLLABORATORS

Even when he insisted in his letters to Ann that he could not focus on work, Noguchi was producing some of his most beautiful sculptures, not only works like *Noodle*, but also sculptures that he assembled from carved elements. And he had other projects as well. For the Jefferson Memorial competition in St. Louis, Missouri, for example, he proposed an earthwork with geometric and biomorphic concavities and protrusions inspired by his recent visit to the prehistoric Great Serpent Mound in Ohio. Not surprisingly he did not win, but again, this didn't deter him.

During this time, Noguchi continued to work on sets for Martha Graham. Although his letters to Ann say that he designed for the stage in order to earn money, making sets that functioned as sculptures and that became part of the dancers' movements clearly fascinated him. His 1935 set for *Frontier*, in which he carved a large volume of space with two ropes, changed the way he thought about sculpture. In 1940 he designed the set for *El Penitente*, a dance about the rituals of Christian flagellation in the Southwest, and then in 1944, when the music patron Elizabeth Sprague Coolidge commissioned three dances from Graham and Noguchi designed the sets, he began a collaboration with Graham that lasted until the mid-1960s. *Appalachian Spring*, with music by Aaron Copland, *Hérodiade*, with music by Paul Hindemith, and *Imagined Wing*, with music by Darius Milhaud, were all performed in the fall of 1944 at the Coolidge Auditorium in Washington, D.C., a space designed for chamber music. Just as Japanese gardens are often designed to look larger than they actually are, Noguchi made the small stage appear large. "I tried to create a really new theater with hallucinatory space," he recalled.[1]

Appalachian Spring, the last of Graham's dances based on American themes, is about a young pioneering couple taking possession of a newly built house in the mountains of Pennsylvania. "New land, new house, new life; a testament to the American settler, a folk theater," was Noguchi's summary.[2] His set consisted of a spare structure of wooden poles that stood for the framework of a rudimentary house, a canvas panel painted to look like a clapboard wall, a tree stump, a log fence, and a semiabstract rocking chair placed on a raised area that stood for a porch. "I attempted through the elimination of all non-essentials to arrive at an essence of the stark pioneer spirit, that essence which

Noguchi's set for *Appalachian Spring*, 1944

flows out to permeate the stage. It is empty but full at the same time. It is like Shaker furniture." Graham recalled that to show Noguchi what she wanted for *Appalachian Spring* she took him to the Museum of Modern Art to see Giacometti's 1932 *Palace at Four a.m.* "He was not very happy about going, but we went. And he understood immediately the quality of space I was looking for."[3]

In *Hérodiade*, Graham turned from her cycle of dances on the theme of legendary America to dances inspired by Greek mythology and the Bible. This change had much to do with Graham's Jungian analysis, and her absorption in the writer Joseph Campbell's theories about myths in different cultures and in different times that shared the same elemental meanings and could potentially guide people to self-knowledge. Starting with *Hérodiade*, Graham's dances combined psychological exploration with mythic drama, a turn that suited Noguchi's mood as well: "I believed in Apollo—all the gods of Olympia long before I knew of any other," he once said.[4] "Everything I have done pertains to myth, from which the truth often emerges, too true to be comfortable."[5] Because Graham transformed classical myths and Bible stories by sending them through her own emotional experience, her dances, always intense, often earnest, and sometimes agonistic, were, Noguchi said, cathartic. "She goes through a kind of ritual each time."[6] Just as Graham's dances evoked an inner landscape, so Noguchi made the stage into a space of the imagination—a space that alluded to the primal feelings expressed by the dance.

Hérodiade's nominal subject was Herod and Herodias's daughter Salome's confrontation with herself. The dance is a soliloquy about a woman's journey into her unconscious. The set consisted primarily of painted wooden objects that look very like the biomorphic slotted slab sculptures made of interlocking forms that Noguchi began to make in 1944. These objects were clearly inspired by the free forms seen in the Surrealist paintings of Miró and Yves Tanguy, and in certain Miró-inspired Gorkys. The shapes are bonelike and suggest anatomy, yet in the dance they were also to function as furniture.

The dance itself, which Graham performed at the age of fifty, centers on a woman facing age and her own mortality. "Within a woman's private world," Noguchi recalled, "I was able to place a mirror, a chair, and a clothes rack. Salome dances before her mirror. What does she see? Her bones, the potential skeleton of her body. The chair is like

The dancer Mary O'Donnell on Noguchi's set for *Hérodiade*, 1944

an extension of her vertebrae; the clothes rack, the circumscribed bones on which is hung her skin. This is the desecration of beauty, the consciousness of time."[7]

Late in 1945 Noguchi designed two more sets for Graham, one for *Dark Meadow* and one for *Cave of the Heart*. When he wrote to Ann about *Dark Meadow* in November 1945, he said the dance concerned "the voyage of man (woman) in search of his soul. All the symbolisms are there ending up with the Grail (the womb) which renews life. I haven't got the faintest idea as to how I am to cope with such a grandiose subject matter." He coped by making four upright, mildly phallic, "primordial" shapes with Miróesque attachments. "They are not stones, but serve the same purpose of suggesting the continuity of time. They move and the world moves."[8]

In a December 1945 letter to Ann, Noguchi said Graham had asked him to do the sets for *Cave of the Heart*: "That's going to be the real one, the one both of us are really interested in on the theme of Media [*sic*, he meant Medea]." Medea was, he wrote in a subsequent letter, a victim of destiny. "Is destiny from without or within? A figment of the imagination too?" In *Cave of the Heart* Medea's fierce jealousy (prompted by Jason's abandonment) drives her to kill her and Jason's children as well as her female rival. The set Noguchi made was simple and dramatic—just a few rocklike forms. "I constructed a landscape like the islands of Greece. On the horizon (center rear) lies a volcanic shape like a black aorta of the heart; to this lead stepping stone islands."[9] These stone islands, inspired by the carefully placed rocks in Zen gardens, allude to Jason's voyage. Graham recalled that for this set she had made one request: "I said I would love to have a dress which shows the spiritual, the half-goddess quality of Medea, but I don't want to wear it all the time. I wanted to walk in and out of it."[10] At the end of the dance Medea donned Noguchi's exquisite construction made of brass wires that, wavering as she moved, suggested the wild flailing of her emotions. As she rose up to join her father, the setting sun, she vanished, but the shining wire dress was left behind like the sunset after the sun goes down.

Collaborating with Graham helped to dispel Noguchi's loneliness. He had not had an exhibition since 1935 and, while he had many friends among the Surrealists and the future Abstract Expressionists, he felt, as always, like an outsider. With Graham and her dances, on

Martha Graham with Noguchi's set for *Cave of the Heart*, 1946

the other hand, he had a passionate connection. In the section on theater and dance in his autobiography he wrote that dancers made his sets come to life: "Then the air becomes charged with meaning and emotion, and form plays its integral part in the re-enactment of a ritual. Theater is a ceremonial; the performance is a rite. Sculpture in daily life should or could be like this."[11]

Noguchi and Graham's work together over a period of thirty years was an extraordinary creative dialogue. They understood, respected, and deeply loved each other as artists and as human beings. They were passionate collaborators, not lovers. "Ours was purely, absolutely, a work relationship. I adored him, and I think he adored me. It never entered our minds to have anything except the best, and it never entered our minds to have a love affair. Never."[12] Their mutual empathy made it possible for Noguchi to invent sets that not only enhanced but also propelled Graham's choreographic invention. She said of working with Noguchi: "A curious intimacy exists between artists in a collaboration. A distant closeness. From the first, there was an unspoken language between Isamu Noguchi and me."[13] Noguchi put it this way: "I contribute to what Martha does. She claims that she has the idea but it is when I supply the setting that she becomes convinced. She says my objects are the things that give her the confidence."[14]

Noguchi and Graham both wanted their creations to be simple, poetic, and packed with meaning, but meaning expressed in formal and symbolic ways, never literal. Both were shapers of space, and both were interested in the idea of origins. Noguchi, sounding rather like Graham, wrote, "I thought of sculptures as transfigurations, archetypes, and magical distillations."[15] Graham loved Noguchi's spare aesthetic: "I realized," she said, "that everything was stripped to essentials rather than being decorative. Everything he does means something. It is not abstract except if you think of orange juice as the abstraction of an orange. Whatever he did in those sets he did as a Zen garden does it, back to a fundamental of life, of ritual. I forget who said it, but Noguchi illustrates the 'shock of recognition.'"[16]

Noguchi's love for the gardens and temples he had visited in Kyoto informed his dance sets' economy of form. An important element in both Japanese stroll gardens and Noguchi's sets was the experience of the body moving through space. The idea of defining space with rope in *Frontier* may have been inspired by the use of rope (often with fluttering strips of white paper attached) to indicate the sacredness of rocks or trees inhabited by deities (*kami*) at Shinto shrines. Noguchi's knowledge of Noh theater, a ritualistic form of drama developed in the fourteenth century, was another source for his spare aesthetic. Gestures and events in Noh theater were full of feeling, but they were always symbolic, referring not to a specific moment but to something universal. The bare stage with just a pine tree painted on the back wall became a landscape of the mind and the minimal props were simply triggers for the spectators' imagination. Speaking of Noh's influence on *Frontier*, Noguchi said that what he valued in Japanese art was that it belonged to "no time and place."[17]

Noguchi's autobiography describes how his and Graham's collaboration functioned: "In our work together, it is Martha who comes to me with the idea, the theme, the myth upon which the piece is to be based. There are some sections of music perhaps, but usually not. She will tell me if she has any special requirements—whether, for example, she wants a 'woman's place.' The form then is my projection of these ideas. I always work with a scale model of the stage space in my studio. Within it I feel at home and am in command."[18] Some nights he would receive a phone call from Graham: "Usually she called me up in the dead of night and said, 'Isamu I need your help and I have a wonderful idea and I want to tell you about it.' I'd go over there and she would go into a story about what she wanted to do . . . And then I'd go home and I'd give her the setting which would encompass such an emotional topic."[19]

Noguchi would appear at Graham's doorstep with the mockup stage set in a shoebox. Sometimes Graham would ask practical questions such as "Can we really lean on that?" or "What happens if you bump into it?"[20] Most often she was delighted. Sometimes she had her doubts. Then she would be gentle, not critical. "I have never said 'no' outright to Isamu, because one doesn't. If you know it won't work, you become very oriental. In other words I'd say, 'Well, that is extraordinary. Now I have to think about it overnight."[21] Mostly their collaboration was harmonious, but not surprisingly for two such intense and driven artists, there were disagreements. Takako Asakawa, one of Graham's dancers, recalled, "Sometimes I would get bumps on my arms because I would see Martha and Noguchi fighting each other, the two of them, because they were so much into what they were doing. 'Get out of here,' they would scream. Isamu would come the next day and they would make up. In art, they were like wife and husband."[22] In later years, during periods in which Graham was drinking heavily, she could become physically violent. In her memoir *Blood Memory*, Graham recalled that on one set, "there was a piece stage right that resembled a curiosity bone. What better symbol for sexuality or fear of it? But as beautiful as this set was, Isamu and I were not in agreement over something or other. This is the only time I can remember being angry with him . . . I slapped Isamu across the face during dress rehearsal . . . I suspect I was going through my violent period."[23] But Noguchi's and Graham's appreciation for each other was too deep for a permanent rift. Looking back, Noguchi wrote of the privilege of working with Graham: "And to hear her telephone me and say, 'Now, Isamu,' was the beginning of many, many happy occasions."[24]

24

THE ROCK AND
THE SPACE BETWEEN

Noguchi observed that his set for *Hérodiade* was closely related to the sculptures that he was beginning to make out of interlocking slotted biomorphic shapes carved from slabs of marble or balsa wood. Indeed, these sculptures, probably his best-loved works, developed right out of the plywood props that he made for *Hérodiade*. Another precursor was the biomorphic chess table and chess pieces that he designed for the December 1944 *Imagery of Chess* exhibition at Julien Levy's Surrealist-oriented gallery.

Noguchi once said that he always used materials that were available at the place where he happened to be working. In the mid-1940s, East Side marble yards were being closed to make way for urban renewal, and the slabs of marble used for surfacing buildings were plentiful and cheap. Noguchi found this marble beautiful. "The nature of its stability is crystalline, like its beauty. It must be approached in terms of absolutes; it can be broken, but not otherwise changed . . . I took particular satisfaction in its fragility, arguing the essential impermanence of life . . ."[1] In its fragility marble was, Noguchi said, like cherry blossoms. It was "hostage to time, permanent and impermanent. The attraction worried me, trapped in contradictions."[2]

In calculating weights and balances, what he called "the forces that conspire to hold up the figure," Noguchi used his knowledge of engineering: "Everything I do has an element of engineering in it— particularly since I dislike gluing parts together or taking advantage of something that is not inherent in the material. I'm leery of welding or

Noguchi in MacDougal Alley courtyard with *Strange Bird*, 1945.

pasting. It implies taking unfair advantage of nature."[3] Each interlocking slab sculpture was assembled from about eight separate pieces fitted together by slots cut into their edges. Like traditional Japanese houses, they were constructed without screws or nails. Noguchi recalled that when he made these sculptures he was "entranced by lightness and hanging." His carefully balanced shapes, his play with gravity, and the sculptures' feeling of suspension bring to mind the contemporaneous mobiles of his friend Sandy Calder, whose success always made Noguchi envious.

Noguchi's interlocking slab sculptures can be seen as a kind of "drawing in space," a phrase most often used to describe David Smith's openwork welded metal sculptures. Noguchi intended the spaces between his forms to be seen as positive shapes. He wrote in 1949: "If sculpture is the rock, it is also the space between rocks and between the rock and a man, and the communication and contemplation between."[4] That communication and contemplation, "the meaning of a thing," were all-important: "A purely cold abstraction doesn't interest me too much . . . Art has to have some kind of humanly touching and memorable quality. It has to recall something which moves a person— a recollection, a recognition of his loneliness, or tragedy, or whatever is at the root of his recollection."[5]

The infusion of humanity into Noguchi's sculptures was subtle and tender. It had none of the brash energy of the work of other sculptors associated with the New York School. Many of his sculptures were anthropomorphic, but in terms of feeling they were more contemplative than aggressive. Noguchi was not an Expressionist. He preferred calm and stillness, meanings that were timeless rather than immediate or passionately personal. His work's slow tempo alludes to emergence and growth. It is movement felt at the core of matter: "We see the exterior of the tree and inwardly we see the sap rising. The forms I try to create are not merely the appearance but the resonating energy inside . . . It is not movement going anywhere, but motion of a different sort. Inside matter there are atoms constantly in motion: if we could hear this action, we could probably hear a continuous sound. There is a roar created by mutual communication inside matter. What I wanted was that resonating energy inside."[6]

When Noguchi designed the interlocking sculptures, he first worked out the basic shapes in pencil on graph paper and then laminated the sheet of drawings onto black cardboard or craft paper. Next he cut out the contours of the drawn shapes with a razor blade without cutting into the black cardboard or craft paper. After peeling away the graph paper shape, he would examine the resulting silhouetted black shape. If a shape satisfied Noguchi he would then take the graph paper shape he had just peeled, paste it onto another sheet of black board, and cut the shape out of the board. The cut-out shapes could then be assembled to create miniature three-dimensional models for future slab sculptures by cutting slots or notches and then fitting the sections together. He would place these models on a miniature stage where he could move them around to see how his sculpture would look from all sides.

When it came time to translate his drawings into stone sculptures, the graph paper drawings helped Noguchi size up his shapes onto a large sheet of paper. He would cut the enlarged shape out of the paper to create a template whose contours he would trace onto a flat sheet of stone—usually marble—laid on sawhorses in his courtyard. Next he would cut the shape out of the stone using a circular saw with an eight-inch blade connected by a flexible shaft to a portable generator.[7] After a section of a sculpture was cut, he would cut out the peripheral notches that would make it possible to fit his interlocking shapes together.

The vitality of the voids between shapes gives Noguchi's interlocking slab sculptures a light and delicate poise. Some sculptures are noble and eloquent. The rather Picassoid *Figure*, the first slab sculpture he carved out of a marble in 1944, and *Kouros* have a definite hauteur. Others in the series, like *Fishface, Strange Bird, To the Sunflower*, and the priapic *Man*, are funny. *Humpty Dumpty*, a vaguely ovoid three-legged creature with a hole for an eye and various sproutlike shapes protruding from an opening in his chest, is both droll and sad. Indeed, its arch shape predicts the rather menacing anthropomorphic arch of his 1952 model for a memorial for the victims of the Hiroshima bombing. Noguchi told Katharine Kuh that *Humpty Dumpty* had to do with "things that happen at night, somber things . . . There are many sides of me I want to express—the loneliness, the sadness, and then something about me which you might call precise and dry which I want to express as well. I wouldn't want to express only my serious side—I'm also playful sometimes—and then again completely introspective."[8]

Remembrance, carved out of mahogany in 1944, brings to mind the

Man, 1945. Wood,
52⅝×19¾×12⅝ in. Private
collection, New York

Humpty Dumpty, 1946. Ribbon
slate, 59×20¾×17½ in.
(Courtesy of the Whitney Museum of
American Art, New York)

Remembrance, 1944.
Mahogany,
50½×24⅝×9 in.

mood of loss and longing in Gorky's 1933 drawing series titled *Night-time, Enigma, and Nostalgia*. The vertical elements on the left and right suggest two figures—a man and a woman, separated by a void. In this case, the boomerang shape—that favorite shape of Surrealist-inspired artists of the mid-1940s—could be the man's head and the palettelike shape that forms one of the sculpture's supports could be the female. The elements hooked over the boomerang seem to express helplessness and grief.

At nine feet, nine inches tall, *Kouros*, now in the Metropolitan Museum of Art, is the largest of the interlocking slab sculptures. In a November 1945 letter to Ann, Noguchi said that the sculpture expressed "an affirmation . . . I wanted something purposeful[,] bigger than our individual selves, classical and idealistic—representative of something that doesn't pass with the passage of time." *Kouros* was inspired by the formal simplicity of archaic Greek Apollonian figures. Indeed, Noguchi had a photograph of a kouros in the Louvre pinned to his studio wall.[9] The luminous pink marble from which Noguchi's *Kouros* is carved suggests youthful flesh. The figure's frontal stance, like that of an archaic kouros, has perfect equipoise. As in the Egyptian standing figures from which the Archaic Greek kouroses were derived, Noguchi's "effigy of man" is conceived with some of its forms facing forward and some facing sideways and at right angles to the frontal forms. Like *Man* from the previous year, *Kouros* has a small roundish head with a hole cut out of it through which projects what must be a nose. Like *Man* also, it has a protruding phallus, but here the sexual imagery is more subtle and, as in his friend Gorky's paintings, Noguchi's shapes are multivalent. With its perfect balance between solid and void, between verticals and horizontals, and between figuration and abstraction, *Kouros* manages to be at once powerful and poetic, majestic and tender. Noguchi observed that "the structure of *Kouros* defies gravity, defies time in a sense. The very fragility gives a thrill; the danger excites. It's like life—you can lose it at any moment . . ."[10]

Since his Associated Press plaque of 1938–39, Noguchi had received very little public attention, but the interlocking sculptures of the mid-1940s brought him back into view. Museums took an interest. Late in 1945 *Kouros* stood near the entrance desk at the Museum of Modern Art. In the spring of 1946 he contributed *Figure*, his earliest slab piece, to the Whitney's *Sculpture, Watercolor, and Drawing* annual exhibition. In the March issue of *Art News*, Thomas Hess wrote of the show: "First of all, and almost dominating the entire museum, is Noguchi's FIGURE. This monumental work is made of pink-blue Tennessee marble and has a splendid powdery-smooth surface. The grooved forms slide into each other like finely machined parts."[11] *Fourteen Americans*, one of a series of American shows that curator Dorothy Miller organized for MoMA over the years, opened on September 10, 1946, and included three sculptors—Noguchi, Theodore Roszak, and David Hare. Among the painters were Arshile Gorky, Robert Motherwell, Irene Rice Pereira, and Mark Tobey. Noguchi's work garnered a great deal of praise. He submitted *Lunar Infant*, the model for *Contoured Playground, My Pacific, Monument to Heroes*, and *Katchina*, all from the first half of the 1940s. Of his more recent work he contributed *Time Lock* and *Kouros*, as well as two interlocking slab sculptures from 1946, the black slate *Gregory* and the white marble *Metamorphosis*.

Noguchi with *Kouros* (ht. 117 in.) at the *Fourteen Americans* exhibition, 1946, Museum of Modern Art, New York (Eliot Elisofon / The LIFE Picture Collection / Getty Images)

Noguchi's statement printed in the exhibition's catalogue was his current sculptural credo:

> The essence of sculpture is for me the perception of space, the continuum of our existence . . . Since our experiences of space are, however, limited to momentary segments of time, growth must be the core of existence . . . growth can only be new, for awareness is the everchanging adjustment of the human psyche to chaos. If I say that growth is the constant transfusion of human meaning into the encroaching void, then how great is our need today when our knowledge of the universe has filled space with energy, driving us toward a greater chaos and new equilibriums.
>
> I say it is the sculptor who orders and animates space, gives it meaning."[12]

Over the years, Noguchi would place greater and greater emphasis on giving form to space. He also stressed growth and change, important not only for his art's formal development but also for the way his sculptures seem to be in the process of emerging and metamorphosing. His words about the adjustment of the human psyche to chaos and the void resound with that existential angst that was so pervasive (and fashionable) in the postwar years.

Thomas Hess's 1945 *Art News* article on Noguchi proclaimed (in that highfalutin tone typical of the late 1940s and 1950s and with a nod to James Joyce): "In the smithing of his soul he has forged the uncreated conscience of his race—humanity."[13] But, Hess noted, since 1938, Noguchi had been in a kind of exile, and that he "carried his exile inside him like a skeleton." What Noguchi had done was to fuse "in his art the East and West as they were fused in his body."[14] He concluded his essay with the prophesy that if Noguchi felt his art was turning into a formula he would "with the great courage which has characterized his whole career, return to exile, and with his tools of silence and cunning create sculpture in the dual reference of art and life."[15]

Noguchi's room of sculptures at the Museum of Modern Art delighted most reviewers, but New York's most powerful critic, Clement Greenberg, characterized Noguchi's sculptures as having "excessive taste, excessive polish, smoothness of surface, excessive clarity, and precision of drawing."[16] A review in *Art Digest* declared that Noguchi had reached "the intangible and superreality through the abstract," yet described the work as "a little cold."[17] Similarly, later critics would be put off by a coolness detected in Noguchi's work. Although his sculptures are certainly reticent, sometimes to the point of standoffishness, their coolness has, I think, to do with their contemplative quality. He was not communicating the tumult of his unconscious.

In November *Life* magazine published a three-page article on Noguchi that is smugly philistine. "At least a dozen top U.S. critics and museum heads believe that the puzzling objects shown at left and right . . . are first-rate art."[18] Noguchi, the author said, "patters happily about in his bare feet, cutting up marble slabs to fashion even more statues like those on the preceding pages." For all the condescension, the attention in such a mass-circulation magazine certainly increased Noguchi's fame.

25

TARA

The woman who accompanied Noguchi to the opening of *Fourteen Americans* was his new love, Nayantara Pandit, or Tara. The eighteen-year-old and her older sister, Lekha, had been sent to the United States because their parents were deeply involved in the struggle for Indian independence, whose leaders were constantly being harassed by the colonial authorities. Tara's mother, who was Nehru's younger sister, was jailed three times and Lekha had been arrested as well. Tara's father, an Oxford-trained lawyer, died in prison while Tara was in her freshman year at Wellesley College. Noguchi met the Pandit sisters at a dinner party given in their honor in 1943, but it was not until their second meeting, in 1946, that Noguchi was struck by Tara's youthful loveliness. By this time, he had probably realized that he and Ann would never marry, and in Tara he saw an intelligent tenderness and grace. He began to escort her to museums, art galleries, and art world parties. He gave her books to read, among them Kafka's *The Metamorphosis* and Lady Murasaki's *The Tale of Genji*. Tara felt close to Noguchi because, like her, he seemed to belong to both Asian and Western culture. (She had attended an American missionary school and had had Danish tutors.) She was pleased to find that, thanks to his weeks of reading about India in the British Museum Library in 1928, he knew an enormous amount about her country. The age difference of twenty-three years did not bother Tara. Noguchi was brilliant and handsome; he was attentive, gentle, and full of charm. His loneliness attracted her, too. "He swept me off my feet," she recalled.[1]

Nayantara (Tara) Pandit and Noguchi, 1946

However, when Noguchi proposed marriage, she refused, in part because of the age difference but also because his bohemian lifestyle,
though enchanting, was too different. She knew her family would
never consent to the marriage and did not want to go against their will.
She always knew that she would, after graduating from Wellesley, return to India, where in August 1947 her uncle Nehru became the
first prime minister of an independent India and that same fall her
mother was appointed to head the Indian delegation to the United
Nations.

In June 1947 Tara traveled to Mexico, a country that Noguchi
adored, and where he had many friends in the art world, among them
the artist and cartoonist Miguel Covarrubias and his wife, Rosa, who
invited Tara to stay in their Mexico City home. Noguchi made sure
that Tara also met his former lover Frida Kahlo. When she returned to
New York City in late August or early September, Noguchi asked her
to marry him once again. She declined and told him she planned to

return to India. During their last six weeks together, she posed for a portrait that suggested the pain they both felt. On October 5, in a hopeful mood, they jointly wrote three postcards to Kahlo. On the face of one card are the boldly printed words: "Don't Borrow Trouble GET MARRIED And Have Troubles of Your Own." On this postcard they wrote, "Darling—We plan to be with you within two years—so hold everything!" Another postcard said they missed her terribly, and the last one, written in Noguchi's hand but signed by both of them, said, "Tara goes to India on the 12th and I will join her next summer."[2]

On the evening of October 14, just before her departure from her room at Hampshire House on Central Park South, Tara wrote to Noguchi that she had finished knitting his sweater, her parting gift, but was apprehensive about going home: "The news from home today has been ghastly—no food in Delhi for days and my uncle's [Nehru's] position in the government grows more & more precarious. He will probably either resign or be thrown out very soon. I feel more strongly than ever the need to go back & be with him . . . The thought of you is the only sane, wholesome thing I have to hold on to in all this confusion. I know it will always be so. I can never tell you quite how much it has meant to me."[3]

From India, Tara continued to write to Noguchi, detailing the dramatic turns the country was taking and her place in them. The letters reveal her continuing love for Noguchi, even though she never regretted her decision to leave. "All my notions of happiness have been altered by you—and you have certainly shown me that human beings can be considerate, & courteous & civilized in close contact . . . Whatever happens—please don't ever forget all this. You can only mean more & more to me."

On February 2, 1948, she wrote to Noguchi about the assassination of Gandhi by a Hindu fanatic three days before. She was devastated. Gandhi had been a close friend of her paternal grandfather and had served as go-between for Tara's parents' marriage. Like many of her compatriots, Tara called Gandhi "Bapu," meaning "Father." "There is no way of describing to you the void that his death had created," she wrote, "how unbearably empty life is. He changed the entire history of so many millions of families in India, & ours was only one among them. He has meant something to every one of us, his love was a wonderful inspiring thing—almost like the love of God—so untiring, &

selfless, & wholeheartedly given." Tara felt what she called an "urgent need to be good." She must live up to the privilege of having been so close to Gandhi and Nehru. "I feel I will not be happy unless I serve India as fully & uncompromisingly as I am capable of doing." Unlike the hope-giving letters that Ann Matta had sent to Noguchi from Chile, the letters from Tara made clear that she would never return to be his wife.

Noguchi was so touched by Gandhi's work and his death that he designed a memorial for the leader and sent plans to Tara. She admired the "starkness & austerity" of the proposal and said it was in keeping with Gandhi's life and ideals. But the timing was wrong for such a project—India was in such flux and the "situation grows worse instead of better." Moreover, she said, Nehru was "anti-monument of any kind." More important, Tara's response included news that she had decided to marry an Indian man. Perhaps to cushion the pain, her letter waxed nostalgic about her and Noguchi's past love; but she remained firm in her decision and attempted to explain it fully.

Perhaps I shouldn't get married. There's you—& your outlook & opinions which I value above all others as far as my personal life is concerned. But you are always drawing me away from my sense of duty, & my feeling of having to fulfill myself as an Indian. You can't help that—& that's why I feel as close to you as I do. I've always felt that our relationship had nothing to do with time, or age, or country, or conventions. That's why it meant so much. But life isn't like that—not as I've seen it after I got home—it demands a great deal of one that one has no right to refuse. Being with you I would not care two straws about India or her fate. Alone, or among my own countrymen, it matters a lot.

Noguchi was bereft. He longed to go to India. Perhaps he felt he could change Tara's mind. But she wrote again in September that he should travel to India "for the sake of your work and your soul . . . But I don't think I would have the strength to see you there. The strength, perhaps, but not the heart."

A year later when Noguchi finally did travel to Bombay, he begged Tara to let him see her just once. They met for tea but the meeting must have been upsetting for Tara, for years later she did not remember it.

At the time, she was recently married and pregnant, but her relationship with her husband was fraught, in part because of his fierce jealousy of the feelings she continued to harbor for Noguchi. Her husband even insisted that she throw away Noguchi's letters as well as a ring and necklace he had made for her and all the books that were signed "from Isamu."[4]

26

1946-48

During the period of his attachment to Tara, Noguchi worked on sets for Martha Graham's *Night Journey* (1947), which was based on the theme of Oedipus and his mother, Jocasta, who, when she discovered that she had had intercourse with her son, committed suicide. For this dance, Graham asked Noguchi to produce a bed, and he made one whose tilted surface, shaped into bonelike forms that stood for a recumbent male and female, was, for the dancers, wildly uncomfortable. "Martha wanted a bed. I made a nonbed."[1] Another set that Noguchi designed for Graham in 1947 was the Miróesque *Errand into the Maze,* in which he used white rope to depict Ariadne's path into the Minotaur's labyrinth—what he called the "inner recesses of the mind."

Also in 1947 Noguchi designed the set and costumes for Merce Cunningham's *The Seasons.* Cunningham, who had once been a member of Martha Graham's company, had, along with the avant-garde composer John Cage, been commissioned by Lincoln Kirstein to do a piece for the recently founded Ballet Society. Immersed like Cage in Oriental philosophy, Cunningham wanted the dance to be cyclical, so he took the theme of the seasons. Noguchi described the dance as "a celebration of the passage of time."[2] Although he sometimes called time a "monster," his Japanese childhood gave him a special sensitivity to time's cycle. Noguchi designed a very simple set—a few mounds articulated with stripes to create a landscape, plus, at one moment, a spare web of rope spanning the proscenium, and at another a structure made of rods. He also designed striped costumes and masks that

Cunningham said were beautiful but difficult to use because "you had to hold them in your mouth in the Japanese way. If you opened your mouth to breathe the mask fell out."[3] The striped costumes were, Noguchi said, "comic and sad—like the human condition."[4] Cunningham recalled that the female dancers were unhappy with their tufted leotards: the stripes were stuffed so that they puffed out and the dancers felt this made them look fat. Tanaquil Le Clercq, who danced a pas de deux with Cunningham for "Summer," recalled that "for spring the girls tied on little tails. This always got a terrific laugh, which made Merce angry."[5]

Cunningham and Noguchi's collaboration was not always easy. Cunningham frequently had to adjust his dance to Noguchi's ideas, while Noguchi felt that some of his props were misinterpreted and used for the wrong seasons. But both men respected each other enough to resolve their differences. After only one full rehearsal of *The Seasons*, there was a crisis when suddenly they had to change theaters and perform at the Ziegfeld. Noguchi had planned to project film of actual snow and rain on a backdrop, but the Ziegfeld had no camera equipment. "I had to dash out for some stock snow and project it with a lantern slide."[6] As Cunningham observed, "Noguchi knew how to find ways to bring what he wanted about."[7]

One of the theater projects that meant the most to Noguchi in 1947 and early 1948 was his collaboration with George Balanchine and Igor Stravinsky on the ballet *Orpheus*. He designed the costumes, props, and set, which consisted of mounds shaped like the cones of sand in Zen gardens, pale roundish rocks that levitated, and a few flat bell shapes. The Orpheus myth had great appeal to Noguchi: "Never was I more personally involved in creation than with this piece which is the story of the artist. I interpreted *Orpheus* as the story of the artist blinded by his vision (the mask). Even inanimate objects move at his touch—as do the rocks, at the pluck of his lyre. To find his bride or to seek his dream or to fulfill his mission, he is drawn by the spirit of darkness to the netherworld. He descends in gloom as glowing rocks, like astral bodies, levitate . . ."[8] Likewise, a few years later Noguchi would see the rocks in his Chase Manhattan Bank water garden as seeming to levitate.

While *Cronos*, *The Gunas*, and *Avatar* (all 1947) continued the interlocking slab sculpture mode, that same year he also produced a number

Bird's Nest, 1947.
Wood dowels
and plastic,
16¾ × 18 × 13 in.

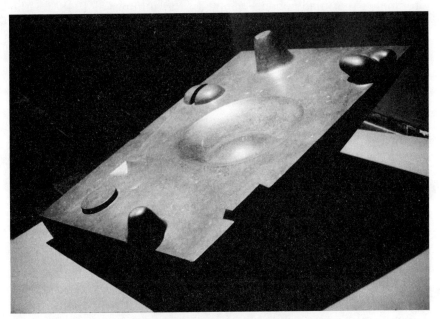

Night Land, 1947. York fossil marble, 22 × 47 × 37½ in. (Courtesy of the Nelson-Atkins Museum of Art, Kansas City; gift of the Hall Family Foundation)

of openwork wall pieces such as *Bird's Nest* and *Rice Fields with Insects*, made of wooden dowels that go every which way. Precedents for this new kind of sculpture can be seen in Medea's fragile wire dress in *Cave of the Heart* and the structure made of wooden rods that served as a prop in *The Seasons*. He also made sculptures that he called landscape tables. *Night Land* harks back to Giacometti's *No More Play* (1931–32), a square of marble with round holes scooped out of its surface that resembles a game board. *Night Land*'s luminous dark marble surface, with its circular hollow and mound and its emergent shapes suggesting gestation, brings to mind the barren dream landscapes of Surrealism. Tilted and seeming to float just above the floor, the sculpture pulls the viewer into a dark landscape of the mind.

In 1947 Noguchi did some design work as well. He made a sculptured ceiling for the Time and Life building's reception room, as well as a ceiling for the American Stove Company in St. Louis. Both had biomorphic, recessed shapes lit, like his Lunars, from within. "At some point," Noguchi said, "architecture becomes sculpture, and sculpture becomes architecture; at some point they meet."[9] He hoped that the integration of sculpture and architecture would create functional environments that made people happy. In the summer of 1948, for the stairwell on the promenade deck of the SS *Argentina*, Noguchi created *Lunar Voyage*, a wall of molded magnesite with electric lights inserted into its crevices. "My idea was to create a completely artificial environment inside, the interstices from which light would emanate, so that one would, in a sense, be inside a sculpture." It was an impulse that he would return to in his later work.

In March 1947 Noguchi took part in an exhibition called *Blood-flames*, organized by the Surrealist critic and poet Nicolas Calas for the Hugo Gallery at 26 East Fifty-seventh Street. Exhibitors included Gorky, Wilfredo Lam, Matta, Hare, Helen Phillips, Gerome Kamrowski, and Jeanne Reynal. The architect Frederick Kiesler created an appropriately surreal setting and provided "boomerang frames" to support the paintings. Calas's catalogue essays on the various artists were abstruse but insightful. The section on Noguchi said his work was so "dictated by the desires of the unconscious" that it evoked fecundity, "sex and fear," and that Noguchi was "a jeweler turned magician . . . sometimes the earth itself, with its erosions and fissures, is transformed into a pillow for our dreams."[10]

That March a reporter for the *Nippon Times* came to interview Noguchi at his MacDougal Alley studio. Legend has it that Noguchi learned from this reporter that his father was still alive. In fact Noguchi had been in touch with his father's family as early as March 1946. Four decades later Noguchi recalled the reporter's visit: "I said the war was because the Japanese people did not have a voice and that they did not have individual rights . . ."[11] He also told the *Nippon Times* that the creative efforts of individuals and the fostering of handicraft would be Japan's salvation.

On May 6, 1947, Yone wrote to Noguchi that he had been at the United Press Office in Tokyo and a Mr. Hobright had shown him the article:

> I know you are doing a very distinguished work of which I feel so applaud. Oh if your mother is living today and sees you of today! . . . I lost almost everything from books and moments [*sic*] to things of daily necessity . . . But I say this not for your sympathy. War is terrible particularly when we lost it. Inflation, inflation—we do not know how it goes up. Though we have no decent clothes to wear, we can not buy them because we have to pay an impossibly fabulous prise [*sic*] for them . . . if you come to Japan again you will see her certainly in a different aspact [*sic*]. I am getting old and feel sad and awful with what happened in Japan. But I have no complaining about it.[12]

Noguchi took his father's despair to mean that Yone regretted his former support for military aggression. On May 15 Noguchi wrote his father back, saying, about the *Nippon Times* piece, "I hope you agree that individual creativity should be fostered in these totalitarian times . . . I should so much like to help in bringing back the dignity of individual labor in the Orient."[13] Once he had located his family, he sent them care packages. In late June, the bed-ridden Yone, who was dying of cancer but did not know it, wrote to Noguchi that his letter had made him weep with joy: "I could not speak for some moment . . . Your [*sic*] very kind to send me a living necessaries which I need very badly. I can not say what I want because whatever you sent me is all welcome."[14] A few weeks after Yone's June letter, Noguchi's seventy-two-year-old father died.

•

Thoughts of transience and mortality, perhaps prompted by his father's death, are emblematic in Noguchi's 1947 design for a sculpture that may have been intended as a memorial for his father as well as a memorial for mankind. *Sculpture to Be Seen from Mars* was to have been a ten-mile-long earthwork in the shape of a highly schematic, yet poignant, human face—the face of everyman looking up at the universe. Noguchi's idea was that it should be built "in some desert, some unwanted area."[15] The pyramid that stood for the nose was to have been a mile high. The model was, Noguchi said, "a flight of the imagination. Made of sand on a board about one foot square and photographed."[16] Noguchi thought of the immense face as someday becoming a vestige of an extinct civilization, proof to inhabitants of Mars that humanity had once lived on earth. Horrified by the bombings of Hiroshima

Sculpture to Be Seen from Mars, 1947. Model in sand, 1 in. square. Destroyed

and Nagasaki, he often spoke of his fear of atomic annihilation. Whether it honors his father or the extinction of human life or both, and even though it is recalled only in a photograph of a model formed out of sand, *Sculpture to Be Seen from Mars* stuns the heart with its pathos.

27

IMPASSE

In 1948 Noguchi felt himself to be at a creative impasse. Though he usually kept his doubts to himself, his friend Dore Ashton recalled that "despite his worldly success, and the high artistic echelons into which he had moved, there was always a lingering doubt, rarely articulated."[1] There are only a few sculptures from 1948. An exquisite one is *The Field*, a small wall piece consisting of a redwood slab cut with slots through which poke marble sprouts—a clear allusion to fertility. The contrast between the perfectly smooth white marble and the rough-hewn surface of the redwood is dramatic, recalling the difference between youth and age.

During this "stuck" time Noguchi worked on lamp designs for Knoll Associates, as well as a free-form sofa with metal legs and a bench to go with it. He also designed tables with biomorphic tops—one for the country house of William A. M. Burden, whose bust he had carved in 1940. Burden's thirteen-foot-long white beechwood dining table had one metal leg and two free-form legs that looked like drooping breasts. For a house in Chappaqua, New York, he made a light fixture and a dark, marble-topped coffee table. The fee for both was $1,600.

Perhaps because he had lost his momentum for sculptural invention in 1948 and 1949, Noguchi did considerable thinking and writing about art, much of which focused on the function of art and the artist's place in society. In March 1949, *Art News* published his long essay "Meanings in Modern Sculpture," in which he posited that the current fascination with individual psychology meant that art no longer served shared values such as those imposed by church or state.[2] But he noted, "If religion dies as dogma, it is reborn as a direct personal expression in the arts . . . [in] the almost religious quality of ecstasy and anguish to be found emerging here and there in so-called abstract art." He appears to have been thinking of the New York School painters, who were just then eliminating recognizable mythic subject matter and moving into an Abstract Expressionist mode. Noting that "all sculptors are optimists," Noguchi expressed his faith in "sculpture's growing reintegration with society," and its return to the role of "the great mythmaker of human environment." The artist's job was to give humanity a sense of order and meaning and to assuage the anxiety of the postwar years. His brilliant articulation of that anxiety must have rung true for many people in the late 1940s: "Our existence is precarious, we do not believe in the permanence of things. The whole man has been replaced by the fragmented self; our anguish is that of Buchenwald and impending cataclysms." The artist must send truth's "light into the darkness of men's hearts."

In his *College Art Journal* article published that fall, Noguchi expressed his wish that art move beyond the sphere of the valuable, collectible object exhibited in an art gallery or museum. Art, he said, should play a role in people's lives, and it should break down the categories of art, architecture, and design: "By sculpture we mean those plastic and spatial relations which define a moment of personal experience and illuminate the environment of our aspirations . . . a reintegration of art toward some purposeful social end is indicated in order to enlarge the present outlet permitted by our limiting categories of architects, painters, sculptors, and landscapists."[3] Such an integration of art and society could be found, he said, in ancient temple sculpture which expressed communal values. But two world wars and industrialization had created a "moral crisis for which there is no succor for the spirit." Artists, he said, must create "order out of chaos, a myth out of the world, a sense of belonging out of our loneliness." Both essays reveal Noguchi's pervasive feelings of meaninglessness and disconnection. Blocked in his art, he needed a new direction.

Adding to Noguchi's unhappiness was the suicide of Arshile Gorky in July 1948. Gorky had achieved a measure of critical success after being taken on by the Julien Levy Gallery in 1945, putting behind him the two disasters that befell him in 1946: cancer and the studio fire. Feeling that time might be short, Gorky worked harder than ever in the summer of 1947. He was like a phoenix, friends said. But he exhausted himself, painting day and night, and by the fall he too was at an artistic impasse. His depression was black. His marriage faltered. In June 1948 Gorky discovered that Agnes had had an affair with his close friend Matta. He was convinced that she would leave him. When his neck was broken in a car accident and his right arm was temporarily paralyzed, he feared he would not be able to paint again. In mid-July, frightened that Gorky might harm her or her children, Agnes took their two daughters and went to Virginia to stay with her parents.

The day after Agnes left, Noguchi was awakened by Gorky's voice calling from his MacDougal Alley studio's garden gate: "Isamu! Isamu! Isamu!" Half awake, Noguchi thought he was dreaming, but "the calling came again like a song."[4] Noguchi went to open the gate and found Gorky in tears. He was holding a papier-mâché bird that he had intended to give to a friend, but he'd gone to the friend's house and, according to Gorky, the friend would not open the door. "Nobody loves me," he told Noguchi. "He felt that people who had pretended to be his friends were not his friends. He felt that he had been completely abandoned, betrayed by his friends, his wife, this one and the other, that people were laughing at him and they had no further use for him because he had this operation."[5] Perhaps Noguchi projected his own feeling of having been taken up by society but never really belonging to it. "I thought he had come to me as a fellow immigrant out of his past."[6]

Apparently Gorky returned to Noguchi's home the next evening and stood at the gate wailing and gesticulating as if he were drunk. Noguchi pretended he wasn't home and for a long time listened to Gorky's voice.[7] When it stopped, Noguchi thought that Gorky had gone to spend the night at Jeanne Reynal's, but in the morning he discovered the painter asleep on his doorstep. When Noguchi finally let him in, Gorky was "gaunt and pale," still wearing the orthopedic collar to support his broken neck. In each hand he held an old rag doll that his daughters had left behind. "This is all I have left," Gorky said. "Noguchi, I am done."[8] Noguchi took Gorky into his studio and they talked for a long while. Gorky had asked various friends to drive him to his Sherman, Connecticut, home. Now he asked Noguchi for a ride. "He looked and sounded so distraught that I was afraid to take him up. I tried to talk him out of it, to calm him down, but he was insistent."[9]

Finally Noguchi was persuaded that the only thing that might console Gorky was to be back in the country. Noguchi waited in the car while Gorky made a quick visit to his doctor. When Gorky returned he was distressed. "They want to do a lobotomy on me!" he told Noguchi. "Well, maybe I am a little cuckoo."[10] Noguchi was worried about driving Gorky without anyone else in the car, so he asked their mutual friend the Cuban-born Surrealist painter Wilfredo Lam to join them. After arriving at Gorky's home in Connecticut, they walked in an orchard, which seemed to restore Gorky's sanity. "There was almost a note of joy as Arshile walked tall among the apple trees," Noguchi recalled.[11] They rang up Gorky's friend Saul Schary, who lived nearby, and asked him to come over. While waiting for Schary, Lam took photographs of Gorky sitting in the grass. He was naked to the waist, but wore his leather neck brace. His eyes were closed as he leaned back in the sun. Noguchi suggested that Gorky call Agnes. He was hopeful that she would come back to Gorky. "So he called her," Noguchi said, "and he turned around and said 'No good, no good.'"[12]

After Schary arrived, the four men went into Gorky's studio. As they looked at his paintings, Gorky seemed to cheer up. His neighbor, the painter Peter Blum, joined them. Since Gorky was now in the company of two neighbors, Noguchi and Lam felt that it was safe to return to the city. The next day Schary visited Gorky again and Gorky told him he had nothing to live for. The following morning Schary returned because he had forgotten his glasses. This time Gorky said his life was over. Schary tried to give Gorky encouragement, but the painter was not in a mood to be bucked up and he asked Schary to leave. Alone again, he called Agnes and told her he was going to kill himself and liberate her. He then went through the woods to a small shed and hanged himself, leaving a note: "Good-bye My Loveds."

Gorky's funeral in the Sherman graveyard was attended by Noguchi, Jeanne Reynal, the Lams, the Calders, the Blums, and Julien Levy and his wife. Gorky's three sisters and their husbands were there, too. Noguchi was surprised to discover that Gorky was Armenian and that his father had only recently died. It began to rain and the mourners drifted away. Noguchi wrote in his autobiography:

> The suicide of Arshile Gorky . . . moved me deeply. I blamed it largely on his wishful involvement with the snobbish world. He

had finally broken into the sacred circle through the intercession of André Breton. I had introduced them. This had nothing to do with his genius; he had already freed his art by his discovery of nature, the beauty of the Virginia countryside, and through his happy family life; but it was Breton who opened the gates to his recognition. His creativity rose with his confidence. But when cancer undermined him, did he not feel doubly betrayed? By expectations to which he was now unequal, by friends and family to whom he felt he could only be a hero? . . . What was the purpose of all this striving? How superficial and cruel the recognition! I have thought of each day since as an undeserved gift. Somehow, I have sought to express myself more fully, to make contact with a larger world, more free and more kindly than the one that killed my friend.[13]

In March 1949, thanks to the intercession of Willem de Kooning, who had exhibited there the year before, the Charles Egan Gallery at 63 East Fifty-seventh Street gave Noguchi his first one-man show since 1935. Egan, the gallery's director, was handsome and personable. Artists liked him because he had a passion for contemporary art and he loved to talk about it. For all his charisma, Charles Egan was a poor salesman and fiscally irresponsible. A heavy drinker, he was often absent from the gallery during working hours. If an artwork sold he was likely to forget to inform—and pay—the artist. When he opened his gallery Egan had no money, so his artist friends helped him fix up the small, top-floor space. Noguchi did the lighting, for which he was paid seven dollars.[14] Noguchi recalled that "Charles Egan was a man who ran his gallery for artists, with no tinge of commerce. My past resentment of galleries and even critics had subsided, having proved to my own satisfaction that I could get along without them for fourteen years. There comes a time, however, when one wants to present one's work to the appraisal of fellow artists."[15]

Noguchi's Egan exhibition included *Avatar, The Gunas, Hanging Man, Night Land, Plus Equals Minus, Cronos,* and a number of open-work rod pieces and smaller works. The prices ranged from $200 to $4,000. Critical response was generally favorable except for a *New York Times* reviewer who was bewildered: "Noguchi's originality is not to be questioned—he is rather bafflingly original . . . Bone-like objects, sex symbolism and pointed objects are repeated in this echoing primitivism . . . Whatever they may mean to the sculptor, it is far from clear that they encompass anything like universal communication."[16] *Art Digest* expressed amazement at the variety of Noguchi's output and commended his "soaring imagination," his "skill and inventiveness," and his work's "elegance and beauty."[17] The *Nation* columnist Clement Greenberg said that Noguchi's "ability to achieve miniature grace on a large scale" was suspect. He disapproved of what he saw as Noguchi's limited vocabulary of biomorphic forms derived from Miró and Arp, and in general he felt that Noguchi's work lacked strength, profundity, and originality. He summed up with backhanded praise: "Few living artists, here or abroad, are capable of an equal felicity of effect, and given the ends he sets himself, he sometimes comes close to perfection. But these ends are not high enough, they are set within the reach of taste but require too little exertion on the part of talent; Noguchi reaches them by what seems too often a display merely of facility— a facility few can match, but facility none the less."[18] His reaction to Noguchi's sculpture would typify the reactions of many future viewers who missed in Noguchi's work the thrust and counterthrust, the physical directness that had begun to seem characteristically American. Compared to the work of his "action painter" colleagues in the New York School, Pollock, de Kooning, and Franz Kline, Noguchi's sculptures lack the muscular pushiness and the idea that a gesture or a mark is propelled by immediate powerful emotion. He shared the angst of the New York School, but his was an angst turned in on itself. Noguchi's carvings do not reach out to grab the viewer. To unlock their secrets, the viewer has to move toward them. Though reviews were mixed, the show marked the end of what Noguchi felt was an impasse. "The winds of the imagination by now blew on me with force from the East."[19]

28

BOLLINGEN TRAVELS

If the nuclear threat, revulsion with the art world, postexhibition blues, Gorky's suicide, and creative doldrums all made a change imperative, Noguchi's immediate impulse was to follow Tara Pandit to India. And so, he said, "I devised a plan of action."[1] In November 1947, one month after Tara left New York, Noguchi discussed the possibility of a travel grant with Hugh Chisholm, assistant editor for the publications of the Bollingen Foundation. Early in 1948 Noguchi submitted his travel grant proposal. On March 30, 1949, four days after his Egan exhibition closed, the Bollingen Foundation granted him a fellowship to travel to Asia to research a book on the "environment of leisure, its meaning, its use, and its relationship to society."[2] It was to begin that July and would last for eighteen months. In his autobiography he recalled: "After the elation and effort that go with preparing an exhibition, comes a depression . . . I was determined to get away from everything."[3] Noguchi had a habit of leaving places and modes of working just when he was earning praise and position in the art world. Perhaps recognition made him feel fraudulent. Also, if his work was going well, he did not want to repeat himself. He had a horror of producing "Noguchis" for collectors to buy. "It has often been pointed out to me that when I have achieved a certain success of style, then I abandon it. There is no doubt a distrust on my part for style and for the success that accrues from it."[4]

Noguchi's writings of the late 1940s are, as we have seen, full of existential angst. He spoke of the void, of chaos, and of loss of meaning.

The Cold War, heightened by Russia's acquisition of nuclear capability, made him, like many Americans, fearful. To find strength Noguchi needed to search for a way to renew the meaning of sculpture. "If I could just tap the continuity of the past, if I could just find for myself an equilibrium, a basic fundament on which to build sculpture."[5] He had never lost what he called an "incipient sort of social consciousness." He wanted to make sculpture that went beyond aesthetics and personal feeling and that was part of lived experience, part of space, something that "related to people's ceremonial view of life."[6] This, he explained, was why he planned to study leisure and not call it art.

On May 12, 1949, Noguchi took off for his beloved Paris. This time, he said, he'd come to Paris "with a commission to write a book for which I had no talent, on a subject I knew nothing about."[7] He spent four weeks seeing old friends and making excursions to Chartres, to Vézelay, and to the Dordogne to see the cave paintings at Lascaux and Les Eyzies-de-Tayac. He also went to Britanny, where he saw the megaliths at Carnac and the island of Gavrinis's megalithic carvings and its cairn, a mound formed by a mass of stones. He tried to look at art without preconception: "I was merely observing for myself and experiencing the real thing in situ; because we see these things in books, but I wanted to actually see it, and in a sense be a part of it."[8]

Noguchi's notes, photographs, and his twenty-three-page recollection of his travels give a picture of a voyager hungry for understanding of foreign ways, indifferent to discomfort, and almost ecstatic in his response to the sites he visited. Noguchi immersed himself in each new culture as he sought answers to how sculpture in the past had had a ceremonial function and expressed shared values. Although he met many people, travel for him was a solitary thing, a process of "inward seeking with distance and silence alone."[9]

In Paris Noguchi visited Brancusi, who he felt had become embittered, perhaps, Noguchi thought, because he had been too isolated during the war. Brancusi told Noguchi that no one understood his sculpture except for a few Americans such as Sturgis Ingersoll and Walter Arensberg.[10] Noguchi would never lose his reverence for Brancusi. In 1981 he made the pilgrimage to Tirgu Jiu in Romania to see the three-part sculptural ensemble Brancusi had made in 1937. "His whole life was based on love," Noguchi said of his teacher. "He was a man who loved humanity, but then he became very bitter. He became bitter because he loved humanity."[11] Noguchi also went to see Le Corbusier and Léger, both of whom he'd met in the early 1940s in the United States. On June 10 Noguchi arrived in Rome and promptly went to the American Academy, where he found his old friend the painter Philip Guston struggling with the elimination of recognizable imagery in favor of abstract, atmospheric fields of exquisitely tender strokes of color. Guston, Noguchi recalled, "would excitedly describe his steps of enlightenment—a peeling down to essences of sensitivity, not revolution but enlightenment."[12] Noguchi wondered what it was that impelled the development of Abstract Expressionism among his painter friends. Was it, he asked, "something in the air that stirred creativity, a potent elixir—that led to new art . . ."

In Italy Noguchi studied the great monuments of sculpture and architecture, looking always for the connection between art and life. The Piazza du Duomo in Florence, for example, impressed him as a place where people gathered for leisure and for prayer. "This is a true space of the mind, the consciousness of an opening outward. To heaven or the world beyond."[13] The notes he jotted down on his travels speak of the church as a theater. Architecture was a "theater in which is played the drama of life."[14] In future years he would try to make sculpture that, like an Italian piazza, shaped space in such a way that people could gather to enjoy each other. Besides Rome and Florence, he also visited Siena, Venice, Padua, Vicenza, Bologna, Arrezzo, Assisi, Paestum, Tarquina, Pisa, Lucca, Bergamo, and Pompei. At Paestum the Temple of Poseidon prompted thoughts about the "sacred relation of man to nature—nature is always clean, there is no such thing as a slum in nature, not in houses that are nature born."[15]

From Bergamo he went to Barcelona, where Antonio Gaudi's church of the Sagrada Familia enthralled him. In August he traveled to Greece and Crete. "No happier situation could be imagined whereby to see for the first time the record of classical antiquity. I entered Delphi as a British Officer arrived with his Jeep, we were the lone occupants of a house from where to forage for figs and pomegranates, and to make an omelet. To trace the white marble remnants, imagining their use from scanty information: that I take is what imagination is for."[16] Growing up on Greek myths and creating sets for Martha Graham's myth-inspired dances, Noguchi felt connected to classical culture. He recorded his impressions of architecture, sculpture, and people in lively sketches swiftly penned in ink. After two and a half weeks in Greece he moved on to Egypt, where he visited Cairo, Saqqara, Luxor, and Abydos.

At last Noguchi arrived in India, the country that had been his prime but unreached destination during his Guggenheim years. And now there was an added attraction: Tara. Noguchi did not stay long in Bombay, where the reunion with Tara took place. "To be in India would have been destiny twenty years before," Noguchi wrote in his Bollingen manuscript. "Now this was tinged with a sadness . . . My sadness came with Tara his [Nehru's] niece for whom nationality had become a barrier—as I already knew too well from Japan. Entering Asia, I felt myself an intruder, if I wish to think so, mixed-blood disqualified additionally beyond the question of race."[17]

Through the Indian League of America, Noguchi had also made many Indian friends, among them Gautam Sarabhai, the eldest son of Ambalal Sarabhai, the head of a wealthy milling family in Ahmedabad, a center of the cotton textile industry in western India. After leaving Bombay he went to visit the Sarabhai family, whose home provided him with a luxurious and friendly place to catch his breath between forays to all parts of India. From Ahmedabad he flew to Madras, where he stayed with his friend, the famous dancer and choreographer Uday Shankar (brother of the musician Ravi Shankar), on the outskirts of the city. While Shankar was occupied with his dance school (a school that taught a mixture of traditional Indian and Western dance), Noguchi took walks and delighted in "open fields and people at their daily chores and ablutions. Cows would amble by and crows collected in great numbers." Shankar helped Noguchi prepare for his journey south, providing him with a bedroll inside of which Noguchi was to pack his belongings. The bedroll was necessary for sleeping in third-class train carriages, at train stations, or in primitive hostels called dak bungalows. Shankar also gave Noguchi a Punjab costume, which Noguchi liked because it disguised his foreignness. "I became practically invisible," he recalled.[18] Before he set off, Noguchi experienced what he called "an expression of friendship without barriers." One night, Shankar woke him up and whispered: "You must be lonely, let my wife come to sleep with you."[19] (Shankar's beautiful wife, Amala, was her husband's dance partner and the mother of his young son.)

Noguchi seems to have wanted to devour every inch of India. Between September 15, 1949, and January 11, 1950, when he left for Bali, he visited some fifty places. In December he slowed down and spent two weeks in New Delhi working on a portrait of Nehru. Although he had lost interest in portraiture, he may have wanted to do this portrait because of Nehru's family connection to Tara.

It was probably during one of the posing sessions that Nehru asked Noguchi to think again about what kind of memorial would be appropriate for Gandhi. On January 7, shortly before he left India for Indonesia, Noguchi wrote to Nehru: "Your Excellency, I have been thinking of the Memorial to Gandhi at Raj Ghat, an improved plan for which I wished to present to you in Ceylon. However, realizing how busy you must be I hesitate to encumber your time."[20] He therefore enclosed his plan, which he described as "extremely simple" and intended to be built in stages. The first stage would be to build "a hedge of massive square monoliths about 9 ft. high, placed on the sides of an octagon, like the threads of a spinning-wheel," that tool with which Gandhi and his followers spun yarn in defiance of the British authorities. Carved on the faces of the monoliths would be "the story of India's people, especially the poor, led to freedom through Gandhi's teaching." At a later stage he planned to add two pathways to bisect the octagon and to suggest the spinning wheel's spokes. "Between these would be placed the expanding alignment of sculptures till they merge as a host covering the field." This memorial was to be yet another of Noguchi's unrealized projects.

Noguchi fell in love with India and returned there many times. Much of what he saw would have clear echoes in his later work. The triangular sundials, circular pits, domes and spheres, and spiral stairways, for example, of the eighteenth-century astronomical observatories in Jaipur and Delhi would reappear in Noguchi's sculptured gardens.

In October Noguchi made a ten-day excursion to Ceylon (now Sri Lanka), during which he was entranced by the giant lion paws carved into the base of a cliff. He next traveled to the temple of Mahabalipuram in the state of Tamil Nadu in northeast India, where he was enthralled by sculptures carved directly into and out of granite boulders. They made him see once again "that sculpture is the one art, the one communication which cannot be conveyed as two-dimensional information—as with a photograph. There is a residual experience that cannot be gotten in any other way than through physical experience, whether by sight, touch, contact, distance and the ever changing relationship of volume and space which comes from the continuous change that time gives, the time of day; that movement gives, or that thought begets. How extraordinary to be so immediately confronted in so pure a form [by] all these facets without distractions."[21] The stone carvings at Mahabalipuram and those at other sites that Noguchi saw during his Bollingen travels convinced him that stone was his true medium.

That fall he also visited the Sri Aurobindo Ashram near Pondicherry, a three-story concrete building designed by Antonin Raymond, who would, two years later, commission Noguchi's first garden. Wanting to learn more about "the basis of Indian belief and creativity," he also visited the ashram in Arunachala founded by the famous Indian guru Bhagavan Sri Ramana Maharshi. At both ashrams Noguchi participated in the rituals, prostrating himself when the guru appeared. Traveling with his bedroll, his notebook, and his camera, playing, as he noted, the role of the mendicant, Noguchi took trains all over India: "My greatest delight is to ride the train at night in India. On the hard shelf of a third class coach, listening to the cliciti-clak of the wheels with the wonderful night air blowing through, nothing can compare."[22] His visual voracity kept him on the move, seeking out temples, mosques, stupas, gardens, sculptures of dancing goddesses, Buddhas, and lingams. He journeyed into the jungle kingdom of Vijayanagar, where he found shelter from rain in a "dak bungalow . . . I live on bananas for the three days searching the mysterious remains fast returning to nature."

Noguchi arrived in Bali on January 12 and he remained there and in Southeast Asia (where he began his portrait of Sukarno) until May 2. Bali was, he said, "that land of the imagination where what is real is what is dreamed. Where people all inhabit the same dream, hear the same music from their heart . . . Music and the dance emanate from each village."[23] He settled in a village called Solo and, as he watched children and adults dancing as if in a trance, he made sketches that captured the dancers' movements and that suggest that he too was in a state of transport that allowed him to draw with greater freedom than ever before. Puppet performances also captivated him: "The shadow play starts at two in the morning and lasts until dawn with children in rapt silent attention." From his position in the shadow chamber, Noguchi drew the puppeteer chanting as he manipulated his cutout puppets.

A highlight of his Indonesian travels was his visit to Borobudur, a ninth-century Buddhist monument in central Java. He was over-whelmed by the immense stone structure with six square platforms topped by three circular platforms, in the center of which is a dome. Borobudur's various terraces symbolize Buddhist cosmology; as a visiting pilgrim climbs upward it is as if he were reaching some kind of enlightenment. Noguchi wondered whether the kind of beliefs that went into the creation of such a marvel could still apply in the modern world. "The evidence of the past attests to the place of sculpture in life and in the ritual of communication with spirit, with tranquility."[24]

29

HARBINGER PIGEON

After visiting Thailand and Cambodia, Noguchi arrived in Japan on May 2, 1950, expecting to be viewed as "an embarrassing stranger."[1] During his 1931 visit, Japan's growing nationalism and militarism had made him feel unwelcome. Now his warm welcome came as a surprise. At the airport were three of his half brothers and his stepmother, the woman who, nineteen years earlier, had pressured her husband to try to keep Noguchi from coming to Japan using the family name. Although this time he had planned only a brief stay, he extended it to five months.

Japan in 1950 was still rebuilding from the rubble of bombed-out buildings, and the country had been transformed by the American military occupation. "How great was my delight," Noguchi wrote in his autobiography, "to find it altogether different. War had indeed improved my own relationship to the Japanese people in the most startling manner. Where there had been a certain reserve before, there was now an open friendliness. Indeed, nowhere have I experienced such spontaneous good will expressed between all people as there in Japan in the spring of 1950. My own explanation of this is that the war had leveled the barriers and hope was now everybody's property."[2] In his 1950 report to the Bollingen Foundation, Noguchi wrote that the Japanese, having experienced the horrors of bombing, had "gained a strange peace of mind . . . they are as it were free, free from the responsibility of being powerful. Art is the one way left for expressing their personality, it is a strong tie to the West."[3]

Noguchi's care packages after the war had paved the way for his reunion with his half siblings and his stepmother. He stayed with them in a recently built house on the plot of land at Sakurayamu 42 in the Nakano section of Tokyo, where his father's house had burned down. The day after Noguchi landed at Haneda Airport, the Tokyo newspapers ran stories about the arrival of this avant-garde American. Not only family members had been at Haneda to meet him, but also reporters who wanted to know why he had come to Japan. Noguchi told them that he wanted to meet young Japanese artists and architects.[4]

During the war, Japan had suppressed artistic freedom in favor of nationalistic art, and anything Western and avant-garde had met with disapproval. Noguchi was swamped by artists and artists' groups wanting to learn from him. "I was kind of like the pigeon coming to Noah's Ark."[5]

In "The Artist and Japan," part of his Bollingen report, Noguchi wrote about Japanese artists' hunger for internationalism and their wish to be part of the modern world.[6] Noguchi noted that familiar phenomenon, the urge of the vanquished to imitate the culture of the victors. Contemporary Japanese artists were painting in Matissean colors because they wished to "forget the drab years of war and be again a part of the bright comfortable world outside."

Noguchi's energy galvanized the Japanese art world. To "prime the pump of their renaissance" was, he felt, his duty.[7] His advice to Japanese artists was not to imitate Western modes but to look to their own culture: "If one must rummage around in the past, better to pick the bones of our own dear dead ancestors."[8] The West, he pointed out, was in the process of learning from Japan, especially Japan's handicrafts and architecture, its love of nature, and its gardens.

Noguchi's essay on the artist in Japan reveals that he had once again immersed himself in the Japanese way of seeing. He wrote of the Zen ideals of *wabi* and *sabi*: "The ideal of poverty is expressed in the ceremonial drinking of a cup of tea . . . If the Hindu says AUM the word expressing Zen is Mu (nothingness, or the void). It is differentiated by such conditions as Wabi and Sabi (rust), the worn away and remaining shadow of materiality. In the least is the most."[9] Here he quoted a haiku poem by Bashō: "Sweeping the garden, / The snow is forgotten / By the broom."

Soon after Noguchi arrived in Japan he attended *Rengoten*, a large exhibition of modern artists sponsored by the major Tokyo newspaper

Mainichi shinbun. He despaired at seeing huge Western-style canvases, which could not possibly fit in a traditional Japanese house. "I wondered how they had gotten so separated from the ideas of their past."[10] There was, however, one painting in the show that appealed to him, a modest work depicting the rear end of a cow and painted with a kind of gesso of ground-up seashells and glue. He liked it for its "rather grey and worn (wabi)" quality, and he sought out the artist Sanko Inoue, who had been trained in Western oil painting and was now a fifty-one-year-old impoverished eccentric living in a mountain temple. It must have been during this visit that Sanko Inoue showed Noguchi an ancient Buddhist mirror, which is said to have been the inspiration for the sculpture called *Mu* that Noguchi would make a month later.

Within a week of his arrival, he was asked to deliver a lecture at the *Mainichi shinbun*'s main office. The hall was so packed that some members of the audience had to stand. Noguchi's subject was the theme he had been exploring during his Bollingen travels: "Art and Community." He talked about his travels and his desire to understand the function of sculpture in the past and its relationship to people's beliefs and to leisure. "Architecture and gardens, gardens and sculpture, sculpture and human beings, human beings and social groups— each must be tightly linked to the other. Isn't this where we can find a new ethic for the artist?"[11] Noguchi went on to reiterate that while he recognized that the wartime restrictions on artistic expression now inspired Japanese artists to join currents of Western art, the Japanese should not imitate American culture. This advice did not sit well with everybody in the Japanese art world. There were those who found Noguchi's enthusiasm for ancient Japanese art and architecture to be a form of patronizing exoticism. The Japanese did not want to wallow in nostalgia. The past was tainted by totalitarianism, war, and defeat. Although the Japanese were anxious to know what was happening in America, Paris remained for them the center of artistic culture.

But Noguchi's recommendation that Japanese artists look to their own traditions did not fall entirely on deaf ears. In rejecting what Japan had become in the past fifteen years, some Japanese artists did turn to prehistoric Japanese artifacts from the Jomon period (1400 to 300 B.C.). Noguchi told Paul Cummings: "After the war the Japanese said 'Oh, we are the Jomon people'" . . . They didn't want to be Japanese. They wanted to be sort of pre-Japan."[12]

To serve as his translator and guide, the *Mainichi shinbun* hired

Saburo Hasegawa, a painter who worked in the tradition of Paul Klee. Hasegawa spoke English and French and, since Noguchi's Japanese was inadequate, he became an indispensable companion. Two years younger than Noguchi, Hasegawa was sensitive and gentle, scholarly and spiritual. But he was also sophisticated and amusing. He had graduated from Tokyo Imperial University with a thesis on the great Japanese painter Toyo Sesshu (1420–1506). After visiting the United States in 1929 he spent two years studying painting in Paris, where he exhibited in the Salon d'Automne and took part in Abstraction-Creation, an international organization of abstract artists formed in 1931. After he returned to Japan in 1932 he spread the word about modernism to other Japanese artists and in 1937 he wrote a book on abstract art. During the war, when the government organized Artists for Greater Japan, Hasegawa refused to serve as a war propaganda artist. He was arrested, and finally he retreated to a village on Lake Biwa where he became involved with Zen, Lao-tsu, the tea ceremony, and haiku poetry.[13]

In a 1952 essay about Noguchi, Hasegawa said that their views were often "worlds apart" and that he and Noguchi had "heated debates." "Nevertheless, from the very first day we met, I have been struck by how much alike we think."[14] They talked about modern European art, Japanese contemporary art versus ancient art, Zen, the tea ceremony, Japanese literature, and art's relation to life. Both had a reverence for ancient Japanese culture and both believed in what Hasegawa called "the perfect union of life and art" as exemplified by the tea ceremony, flower arranging, and Japanese gardens and architecture. Both felt art should have a function. Each was pulled between East and West. Hasegawa appreciated a purity and simplicity that he saw in Noguchi, who told him, "These days I am becoming more and more like a child." Hasegawa also detected Noguchi's deep-seated loneliness: "Perhaps more than any other artist Noguchi feels a piercing sense of solitude."[15]

Though he enjoyed it, Noguchi's busy social schedule in Tokyo wore him out. Not long after he arrived in Japan, he was hospitalized for exhaustion. While recovering, he read avidly about the poetry of Bashō, D. T. Suzuki's writings on Zen, and his own father's writings on art and poetry. In addition, he began to read about Japanese culture and architecture in books by Bruno Taut, a German architect and the-

oretical writer who had fled Nazi Germany via Switzerland to Japan in
the mid-1930s. Noguchi came to share Hasegawa's enthusiasm for
Bashō and the painter Buson, as well as for the sixteenth-century tea
ceremony master Sen no Rikyu, and Ryōkan (1758–1831), a Zen poet,
calligrapher, and monk. Hasegawa must have been bemused when
Noguchi told him that "the Dadaist Duchamp is just like Ryōkan."[16]

When he had recovered, Noguchi and Hasegawa made plans to
travel to Kyoto on an overnight train. Just before they left, Noguchi
had a kind of artistic epiphany when Hasegawa showed him his prized
possession, a copy of Sesshu's famous *Four Seasons Scroll*. Hasegawa
cleared out a room in his house, laid down a blanket to protect the
scroll, and then unrolled it. "I cannot express in words how much
Noguchi admired it," Hasegawa recalled.[17] Hasegawa also showed
Noguchi a collection of postcards illustrating prehistoric Japanese figurines, probably of the Jomon culture, in the collection of the National
Museum in Tokyo. Noguchi pronounced these artifacts to be even
better than haniwa. In Hasegawa's memory, Noguchi grabbed his
Japanese paper, ink, and brush and proceeded to draw some of the
figurines. Before retiring for the night, and in spite of his exhaustion,
Noguchi asked to have another look at the Sesshu scroll. "He stared at
it as though punching holes in it with his gaze," Hasegawa recalled.
On his way to bed Noguchi stopped again, his eye caught by some
detail in the scroll. "Wait just a minute," he said, and he was pulled
once more into the ink-brushed landscape with its changing seasons.
With his eyes moving over the scroll, Noguchi kept up a running
commentary about the composition, the brushstrokes, and the scroll's
vitality.

On May 31 Noguchi and Hasegawa, sponsored by the *Mainichi
shinbun*, set out on a journey to see the ancient art of Japan and to "im-
bibe the tranquility of Zen, about which Hasegawa was an expert."[18] In
his memoir Hasegawa wrote: "During our travels Mr. Noguchi sometimes spoke of the true meaning of kan (quietness), hin (austerity), and
mu (nothingness), especially when he wanted to criticize the material-
istic civilization which dominates today's world."[19] When Hasegawa
reminded Noguchi that many Japanese considered his passion for their
ancient traditions to be a form of exoticism, Noguchi would answer
with a smile and say that just as the Japanese are addicted to Western
art, so he must be addicted to Japanese culture.[20] A few years later,

Hasegawa traveled to America and served as a Zen guru in San Francisco until his death, in 1957.

The first thing Noguchi and Hasegawa went to see after arriving in Kyoto was the exquisite seventeenth-century Katsura Detached Palace, a modest but beautifully proportioned house overlooking one of the most brilliantly designed gardens in Japan. Of the villa itself, Noguchi wrote that in its "ideal simplicity" the palace was a revelation that transported him into a "more perfect world."[21] The two artists were ecstatic about the unity of garden and architecture. Noguchi was especially moved by the Katsura stroll garden, which moves the visitor along a path that twists and turns around a pond and past small teahouses in such a way that at each stopping place rocks and plants that were hidden a moment ago come into view. "The two of us were nearly silent," Hasegawa wrote, "watching . . . a 'ballet of emptiness.'"[22]

During his travels, to help remember what he saw and to prepare for the essay on leisure, Noguchi took photographs, took notes, and made drawings and India ink rubbings. He was an almost hyperactive photographer, shooting four rolls of film at the Katsura Detached Palace and its grounds. "His camera always hangs from his shoulder," Hasegawa recalled, "while under his arm he carries a bundle of Japanese paper, a writing brush, India ink, and an inkstone, all wrapped in a large Sarashina scarf."[23]

In Kyoto Noguchi and Hasegawa visited numerous temples and gardens, including the famous Golden Pavilion: "While I was in Japan," Noguchi recalled, "the Golden Pavilion, Kinkakuji burned down, set afire by a fanatical young priest—a double suicide."[24] Other favorite sites in Kyoto were the Zen gardens at Entsuji and Ginkginkakuji (the Silver Pavilion). The former is famous for its use of so-called borrowed scenery, meaning that the garden incorporates a mountain or some aspect of landscape in the distance as part of its total effect. The Silver Pavilion has an extraordinary garden of raked sand from which rises a conical mound of sand. Years later, dry gardens like this one would inspire Noguchi's Beinecke Rare Book and Manuscript Library garden at Yale.

Perhaps the temple precinct that most affected Noguchi's later work was Ryoanji, with its small walled garden in which fifteen perfectly placed rocks suggest islands floating in the sea of pale raked gravel. This type of Zen garden is not for strolling, but for contemplating from the temple veranda above. Here Noguchi admired the way the space was made to feel immense: "In viewing this garden one has the sense of being transported into a vast void, into another dimension of reality—time ceases, and one is lost in reverie, gazing at the rocks that rise, ever in the same but different spot, out of the white mist of gravel . . . One feels that the rocks were not just placed there, that they grow out of the earth (the major portion buried), their weight is connected with the earth—and yet perhaps for this very reason they seem to float like the peaks of mountains. Here is an immaculate universe swept clean . . ."[25] Noguchi would call his Chase Manhattan water garden "my Ryoanji," and, as at Ryoanji, he placed his rocks so that they appeared to float.

When exploring the Buddhist temples of Kyoto, Noguchi and Hasegawa often sought out the company of the priests Hisamatsu Sensei (the Zen philosopher Shin'ichi Hisamatsu) and Daiki Osho at Daitoku-ji, a Zen temple complex founded in the fourteenth century in the northwestern section of Kyoto.[26] At Daitoku-ji Noguchi and Hasegawa participated in the tea ceremony, which involved listening to "innumerable koans," riddles such as "What is the sound of one hand clapping?" "After too much tea at the first two [temples]," Noguchi recalled, "the master of Mushakoji senkei serves us only hot water. Saburo is ecstatic, announces this is the ultimate 'Tea.'"

Noguchi, who had read Kakuzo Okakura's famous *Book of Tea*, published in 1906, came to love the tea ceremony, which satisfied his yearning for an art that incorporated ritual. After one of his journeys with Hasegawa he wrote about opening a teahouse gate made of twigs and passing "into another world, an inner world or world of dreams."[27] The approach to a teahouse, he said, is an important part of the whole experience. The visitor moves through a garden in which stepping-stones are laid out in an irregular manner so that he must be acutely conscious of the measure of each step. Finally, arriving at the teahouse, a simple but elegant structure with asymmetrical windows, the visitor sits outside on a bench. He then bends to enter through a low door, and the tea master serves tea with all the requisite gestures. During the tea ceremony, Noguchi said, "there is confinement, but no sense of confinement—one may, if one wishes, look out upon a desolate wabi garden; there is a feeling of time's having stopped, of an infinity of winds having weathered and left a shell."[28]

Next they traveled to the city of Uji to visit the eleventh-century temple complex called Byodo-in with its famous Phoenix Hall and a three-night fresh tea festival.[29] Moving farther south they visited the great temple complex of Horyuji at Nara. The Golden Hall had burned down during the war, but Noguchi was stunned by the charred ruins. He set about capturing the blackened framework of beams with his camera. Seeing that Hasegawa was pained by the sight of Horyuji's ruined timbers, Noguchi gave his companion a consoling look and asked, "Isn't it more beautiful now?"[30] Hasegawa told Noguchi: "To treasure the beauty of the ruin of Horyuji, you have to love sabi more than I do. I guess that means you are more Japanese than I am."[31] After sitting quietly for a moment, Noguchi, thinking of Arp's quiet and pared-down simplicity, said: "Arp is just as Japanese as anyone in feeling."

30

SHINBANRAISHA

Back in Tokyo, Noguchi received his first design commission in Japan, a faculty reception room in a soon-to-be-built research building at Keio University that had been damaged in the war. The commission came from Yoshiro Taniguchi, the modernist architect in charge of the reconstruction of Keio's campus. Taniguchi's wish was that the artists and architects he hired would create the "seeds of aesthetic consciousness in the school as it emerged from the ashes of war."[1] The new research building should integrate art and architecture, he said, and it should reflect Japan's new openness.[2] Taniguchi recalled being introduced to Noguchi by the university's dean: "When our eyes met and I heard his words my spirit of design felt an immediate empathy with him. The concept of sculpture which he advocated was an all-embracing one which involved the interior, the garden, and the furniture, everything."[3]

As they climbed the hill upon which the university stands, Noguchi told Taniguchi that it was an acropolis.[4] The commission was sealed with a handshake. Shinbanraisha, meaning "New Welcoming Hall," was intended to honor Yone Noguchi, who had taught at Keio for forty years. "I became preoccupied with this as my own act of reconnection to my father and to his people," Noguchi recalled.[5]

Noguchi and Taniguchi each contributed to the other's design: "We worked together in the heat of the summer days, through the nights, deliberating over numerous sketches, plans and drawings," Taniguchi remembered. Noguchi designed the garden and made three sculptures for it, while Taniguchi designed the building: "Our senses of friendship as artists were truly at one."[6] Taniguchi remembered how intense Noguchi was about work. "I, myself, am severe in my work; he was even more so. But we got on very well together and the collaboration progressed pleasantly."[7] Thirteen years later Taniguchi wrote again about his kinship with Noguchi: "Purity is precious both in Zen and poetry. He, as a sculptor, seeks for it and I, as an architect, desire it."[8]

Noguchi did not want Shinbanraisha to be a memorial exalting a hero, but rather a place of relaxation, a place where the wounds of war might heal, and a place to contemplate "the ideals of beauty" expressed in his father's poetry, which, now that he was reconciled with his father, he had come to admire."[9] It was fitting that he should have been chosen to design the Shinbanraisha, Noguchi said, not only because he was his father's son, but also because "I happened to be that combination of viewpoints of East and West embodied in his poetry. I felt that if I could offer a continuation of that bridge which is the common language of art, I will have offered my part to the human outlook that must one day find all people together."[10]

To create this room and its accoutrements, Noguchi traveled each day to the Tsudayama district on the outskirts of Tokyo to work at the Japan Craft Center, also called the Industrial Arts Institute. Directed by the brilliant designer Isamu Kenmochi, this workshop for research in interior design was sponsored by the Ministry of Trade and Industry. While he worked there, Noguchi moved into the home of his friend the Matisse-inspired painter Genichiro Inokuma. Each morning, Noguchi and Inokuma, dressed in blue jeans and carrying tools and sketchbooks, would sally forth from Inokuma's house in the Tokyo suburb of Denenchofu and travel to the craft center. Inokuma remembered Noguchi's energy and his ferocious concentration. Playing host to Noguchi was, he said, "like having a boy who was constantly out of control."[11] Noguchi's American side revealed itself in his impatience. He often lost his temper. "If a taxi stalled, he'd say, 'Never mind, I'll walk'; or when a sales clerk was too slow, he would say 'Forget it! I don't want it any more.'"[12]

Kenmochi's craft center emphasized the design of modern furnishings using native techniques such as bamboo weaving or winding string around a framework. The hope was to produce items that could be mass-produced and exported. Noguchi designed and made chairs,

Noguchi and Isamu Kenmochi, on the Noguchi-designed bamboo and iron chair prototype, at the Japan Craft Center, 1950

stools, benches, and a table, some of them destined for Shinbanraisha. In his Bollingen manuscript he wrote: "As an extra filip [*sic*] I designed at the very end a bamboo and metal easy chair, not for this room but with the idea of showing how Japanese technique and material could be combined with ours and our market."[13] Astonished at Noguchi's creative force, Kenmochi called him a "worker ant" and an "artist demon."[14]

At the craft center, Noguchi also made a full-scale plaster model for a seven-and-a-half-foot-tall sculpture called *Mu*, a Zen term for nothingness or emptiness. It would later be carved in stone and placed in the garden outside of Shinbanraisha. The piece has a voluminous C shape set on top of a sturdy column. The C could be seen as an abstraction of a thumb and index finger nearly touching to form a circle—a well-known hand position (*mudra*) in Yoga meditation. In many depictions of Buddha his hands are in this *gyan mudra*; it is known as the Seal of Knowledge and is thought to encourage wisdom. But the C shape is also familiar from numerous Surrealist or

Surrealist-inspired paintings and sculptures in which the C often
has a vaguely uterine connotation, especially when there is a seed or
embryonic form placed in the cavity. In *Mu* the C encompasses a pregnant void.

For the job of building *Mu* Noguchi had the help of a twenty-six-
year-old sculptor (now also known as a kite maker) named Tsutomu
Hiroi, who was then a teacher in the sculpture department of the Tokyo School of Fine Arts, and who, in the first half of the 1950s, often
served as his assistant. Noguchi remembered his first meeting with
Hiroi: "Shortly after my arrival [in Japan], . . . a young man came to
call on me in Nakano bearing a small clay Buddhist stupa, a symbol of
Japan's past. Hiroi Tsutomu seemed to be seeking a way into the world
outside the confines that the war had forced on Japan . . . I remember
I declined the gift of the stupa, thinking it too expensive, and not realizing, having just arrived in Japan after twenty years, that one does not
refuse such gifts."[15]

At Kenmochi's craft center, Noguchi made several sketches and
clay models for *Mu*. Hiroi remembers that Noguchi, concerned about
how *Mu* and the sculpture garden would look from inside the faculty
reception room, kept checking his small models' relationship to the
architectural model of Shinbanraisha.[16] He was not satisfied until he
saw the antique hand mirror at Inoue Sanko's home, and, Hiroi recalls,
"The model for *Mu* was completed immediately after this visit." "There
is nothing in a mirror but different images are reflected there depending on the person who looks in it," Noguchi told Hiroi. He must have
been thinking of a Zen observation, promulgated by Suzuki, that a mirror reflects the image of whatever is set before it without itself being
altered. This Noguchi saw as analogous to *Mu* and to the Zen concept
of no-mind.[17] What could be seen through *Mu*'s round opening would
change according to the viewer's position, the time of day, and the
season, Noguchi noted, but the opening itself would remain constant
and was "nothing" or "nothingness."

When Noguchi was finally satisfied with one of his clay models, he
asked Hiroi to enlarge it to two meters. Hiroi recalled that at first the
model they made looked like a giant papier-mâché cactus.[18] The next
step was to mix twenty-three bags of plaster with water, which Noguchi, Hiroi, Inokuma, and Inokuma's wife, Fumiko, applied to *Mu*'s
scaffolding. Using a saw blade wrapped in a folded towel, they scraped

Noguchi working on the plaster original of *Mu*, 1950. Ht. 7 ft. *Mu* was later carved in sandstone and placed in the garden of Keio University, Tokyo.

the wet plaster sideways to give it shape. A photograph shows Noguchi naked to the waist as he scrapes down the sculpture's side in the stifling August heat. Although the top of his head is bald, his forty-five-year-old torso looks as strong and lithe as that of a young man. According to Hiroi, the plaster application was a wild scene. Noguchi worked with such ferocity that he did not notice that he was splattering plaster all over the place. "By the time it was completed, all the people and the room itself were covered in white."[19]

When the full-scale plaster model was finished, it was too large to go through the door of Kenmochi's workshop. Noguchi seemed indifferent to the problem. Kenmochi was indulgent. He felt that Noguchi's total focus on his art was a kind of egotism necessary for artistic genius. He therefore allowed the windows to be broken and *Mu* was liberated. After Noguchi had returned to New York, Hiroi worked with a stonemason to make the sandstone version of *Mu* that is now in Keio's hilltop garden.

31

MITSUKOSHI EXHIBITION

While he was working at Kenmochi's design workshop, Noguchi received an invitation from the Federation of Japanese Artists to hold an exhibition of his photographs of sculptures at the branch of the Mitsukoshi Department Store in Tokyo's Nihonbashi district. Because Noguchi felt that photographs were a poor way of showing sculpture, he set about making new pieces instead. While working in terra-cotta at the ceramic center of Seto, he refused to see any visitors.[1] Within a short time he had produced some twenty stoneware pieces that, like the clay sculptures he had made in Kyoto in 1931, mix Western modernism with Japanese iron-age primitivism. Most of the Seto works were made from unglazed slabs and coils of clay and put together in a lighthearted and often humorous manner. He had, he said, returned to "basic materials, to basic thoughts."[2] For all their improvisatory look, many pieces were in fact developed from drawings. At Seto, Noguchi told the curator and writer Paul Cummings, "I merely continued in what I had been doing—well, it was twenty years before . . . And even today when I go to Japan I continue where I left off."[3]

Noguchi's Mitsukoshi exhibition, whose installation was designed by Taniguchi, opened on August 18, 1950. Included in the show were ceramic sculptures, some of the furniture that he had made at Kenmochi's craft center, and the plans and model for Shinbanraisha that he and Taniguchi had worked on together. There were also clay vases. Since Noguchi shared the Japanese view that there is no division between art and craft, the vases can be seen as sculptures. The exhibition's

Love of Two Boards, 1950. Seto stoneware, 10¹/₈ × 10¹/₈ × 5¹/₂ in.

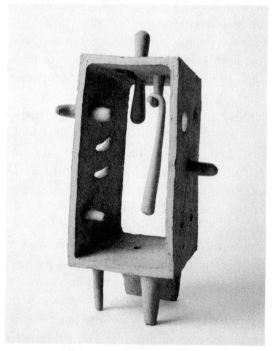

The Policeman, 1950. Seto red stoneware, 13³/₈ × 8³/₄ × 5¹/₈ in.

walls were hung with photographs of sculptures he had made in America. Noguchi's *Wakai Hito* (Youth), a Miróesque figure in the mode of the interlocking slab sculptures of the 1940s and destined for the garden at Shinbanraisha, was prominently displayed, as was the plaster model for *Mu*, which, when it arrived at the Mitsukoshi department store, would not fit in the elevator and had to be cut in half and glued back together. Noguchi recalled that *Mu* "provoked innumerable wisecracks and cartoons."[4]

Several of the ceramic sculptures in the show were formed by a slab of clay enclosing a void and supported on short clay legs. These hollow sculptures seem to turn the Zen concept of nothingness—of no-mind—into absurd-looking creatures. To create limbs or accoutrements, Noguchi rolled clay between his palms and attached the resulting wormlike forms to the body of his sculpture. This kind of primitivism appears to have been inspired by prehistoric Japanese figurines of the Jomon and Yayoi periods.

Bell Child, 1950. Seto stoneware, ht. 5½ in.

Two of Noguchi's Seto sculptures represent children. *Bell Child's* features—just holes for eyes and mouth—were probably inspired by a haniwa in the Tokyo National Museum.[5] Noguchi's enthusiasm for haniwa had not diminished since he first discovered them in 1931. Indeed, while he was preparing his exhibition he purchased two haniwa from an exhibition at the Mitsukoshi Department Store, and the haniwa's hollow cylindrical forms lie behind several of his Seto sculptures. With its outstretched arms and spread-eagle legs sprouting out of its bell-shaped body, *Bell Child* looks helpless. Perhaps Noguchi was thinking about Hiroshima. In his Bollingen manuscript he wrote that when he knew he was going to have a show, he felt he "must do something with Hiroshima in mind. From this came two bell towers."[6] *Bell Tower for Hiroshima*, a study for a seventy-foot-high bell tower that Noguchi envisioned for the Hiroshima Peace Park then being designed by Kenzo Tange, was one of the largest pieces in his show. It consisted of ceramic bells attached to a framework made of thin wooden dowels that was intended to look fragile—Noguchi shared the Japanese fixation on transience. The ceramic bells, which Noguchi envisioned coming from all over the world, do not, in the study, resemble bells. Pinioned or dangling, they look vestigial, like something that has been alive but is now desiccated, a bit like withered oak leaves still attached to branches in late autumn. Perched at the very top of the tallest dowel is a new moon—presumably an image of hope.

"When the show opened," Noguchi recalled, "I wrote with chalk on a black board 'Kane ga naru' the bells will toll from a poem by my father."[7] In white chalk he also drew a huge bell resembling the bells in Shinto shrines and Buddhist temples and recalling also the ancient bronze dotaku bells from the Yayoi period (c. 300 B.C. to A.D. 300). Flames leaping from the bell's silhouette and the wavering line at its base suggest that it is sinking into the sea. On the side of the bell he wrote in Japanese script some lines from a poem his father wrote shortly before he died: "The bell rings, / The Bell rings, / This is a warning! / When this warning rings / Everyone is sleeping / You too are sleeping."[8] For one line in this poem Yone borrowed from John Donne's Meditation 17—"and therefore never send to know for whom the bell tolls; it tolls for thee." Noguchi's proposed bell tower was never built, but it did catch the attention of the Shinzo Hamai, the mayor of Hiroshima, who invited Noguchi to design two bridge railings for the

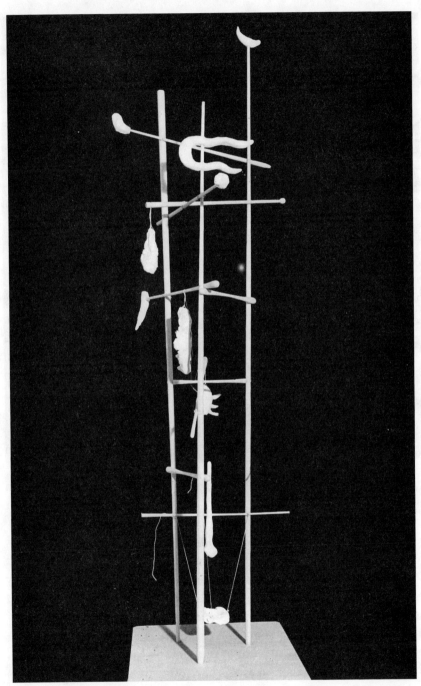

Bell Tower for Hiroshima, 1950. White terra-cotta in wood frame, ht. 40 in. (proposed ht. 70 ft.)

Noguchi sitting in front of his drawing of a bell inscribed with his father's poem, at his Mitsukoshi exhibition, 1950

Hiroshima Peace Park, a project that Noguchi worked on when he returned to Japan the following summer.

The *Mainichi shinbun* said that Noguchi's show had "such enormous vigor and talent and perspective that it is hard to believe that one artist could have produced it in a month's time."[9] The art journal *Atorie* detected the pull of East and West: "In an era when even exhibitions of Japanese paintings imitate the West, this exhibition conveys the feeling of something Japanese-like, even though the sensibility is not Japanese."[10]

During the month before his show, Noguchi divided his time between Kenmochi's craft center, the Seto pottery center, and Keio, where he worked with Taniguchi to prepare his exhibition and on plans for Shinbanraisha. When Shinbanraisha was completed after Noguchi returned to Japan in 1951, it had three levels, the lowest a pavement of stones for walking, the second a wooden floor intended for both walking and sitting, and the third a tatami-covered surface for sitting. There was also latticework seating.[11]

A central feature of Shinbanraisha's design is a circular fireplace, five feet in diameter and raised on stones arranged like slices of a pie. According to Taniguchi, the fireplace was inspired by the hearths sunk into the floors of traditional Japanese homes. Flanking the fireplace are two enormous concrete columns, one supporting the ceiling, the other serving as a chimney. Suspended between the columns and above the fireplace is a sheet metal canopy whose crisp lines bring to mind the folds in origami, a skill Noguchi had learned as a child. Taken as a whole, the faculty room's atmosphere is sober, calming, slightly reverential.

Noguchi also designed the garden outside of Shinbanraisha, the first instance in which he was able to combine inside and outside, and indeed, his first commissioned garden. It was a narrow space with a raised area of gravel laid out in a biomorphic shape that predicts the layout of his UNESCO garden in Paris. Noguchi made three sculptures for it: *Wakai Hito, Mu,* and *Gakusei* (meaning "student"), a fifteen-foot-high openwork structure of iron rods that Noguchi said was his "dedication to aspiring youth."[12] The sandstone *Mu,* the most original of the three, was set on a hill with a view to the west so that at a certain moment the broken circle framed the setting sun. This effect, Noguchi said, made *Mu* "an ishidoro [lantern] of celestial illumination."[13]

When Noguchi flew to New York via Los Angeles on September 5, 1950, he planned to return to Japan as soon as possible. His new-found feeling of connection with Japan, the warmth with which he had been received, and the prospect of major collaborative projects in Tokyo and Hiroshima, made it hard to leave, but his money was running out. Japan had changed him, and he had changed Japan. As Kenzo Tange noted: "His stay in Japan coming as it did in the artistically barren years following the war, was a charmed and stimulating breeze to all of us trying to establish a new creative life in Japan.

Here in Japan, as usually seemed to be his case, he completed a metamorphosis . . . he entered the world of Zen. He could picture the true essence of Japan better than a born Japanese growing to maturity at home. What he perceived rather belonged to the world than to Japan, and he had made it his own."[14]

32

YOSHIKO YAMAGUCHI

Upon his return to New York in September 1950, Noguchi moved into the Great Northern Hotel at 118 West Fifty-seventh Street. Having been away for a year and four months, he felt like a stranger. "New York was totally unreal. I lived only with thoughts of how to get back again to Japan. The book for the Bollingen Foundation was a box of notes and photographs. I felt inadequate to bring order into the manuscript. How can one write with wisdom unless ones [sic] own problems are solved?"[1]

He applied for an extension of his fellowship and "rather forlornly" began visiting galleries to see what he had missed.[2] He discovered that in the last two years, his friends in the New York School had moved from Surrealist-inspired semiabstraction to abstraction in which the mythic imagery was banished, but continued to pervade the paintings' atmosphere as an aura of primal feeling. Even though he always prided himself on not being part of any group, Noguchi felt left out. His contemporaries were having gallery exhibitions and gaining critical renown. He must have had a twinge of envy when he learned that Jackson Pollock, de Kooning, and Gorky had represented the United States at the 1950 Venice Biennale. "I was the absent one."[3] Noguchi told Paul Cummings that whenever he returned to New York from Japan he felt "at a loss" and "a little bit removed. I don't like it . . . I have to be in contact . . . in Japan the contact is not with people but with the earth."[4]

Noguchi saw that the sculptors of his generation, people like David Smith, Seymour Lipton, and David Hare, were all creating sculptures in welded metal. Their work expressed passions that were urgent and sometimes agonistic. By contrast, Noguchi wanted to create sculptures that were about being part of the natural world. He told Katharine Kuh: "I don't think it is so necessary to be concerned with oneself. If you are continually polishing up your signature, it ends by being about all you do . . . In a sense I feel the more one loses oneself, the more one *is* oneself."[5]

In spite of feeling out of step with his colleagues, Noguchi did receive a fair amount of attention in the early 1950s. In January 1951 the Museum of Modern Art opened a show called *Abstract Painting and Sculpture in America* curated by Andrew Carnduff Ritchie, which included works from the early part of the twentieth century up to the present. The contemporary artists were the Abstract Expressionist painters Pollock, de Kooning, Mark Rothko, Motherwell, and Kline. Among sculptors, besides Noguchi, were Lipton, Ibram Lassaw, Herbert Ferber, Calder, Smith, Richard Lippold, Theodore Roszak, José de Rivera, and Peter Grippe. Everyone except Noguchi worked mainly in metal. In November 1950 his article "Notes by an Artist on His Recent Work in Japan" was published in *Arts and Architecture*. Five months later *Interiors* magazine ran a piece on Noguchi's exhibition and projects in Japan.[6] In 1952 *Harper's Bazaar* published Noguchi's article on Kabuki theater.[7] And even better than the press recognition, Noguchi was approached by Antonin Raymond to do a garden for *Reader's Digest's* new headquarters in Tokyo.

Antonin Raymond was the designer of the Sri Aurobindo ashram in Pondicherry, India, which Noguchi had visited during his Bollingen travels. No doubt he and Noguchi had met at the time of Noguchi's Mitsukoshi show. On October 25, 1950, Raymond wrote saying that he needed Noguchi's help. He told Noguchi that in his New York office there was a site plan and a survey that Noguchi could use to make a model for the garden. "I so need somebody to help me think and design," Raymond wrote. "I have to make decisions altogether too quickly, without feeling it out . . ."[8]

On November 22 Raymond wrote to Lila Acheson Wallace, *Reader's Digest's* cofounder, telling her that Noguchi was "a real artist, a rare soul" and that he wanted to help him. He enclosed a copy of this letter of recommendation in a letter to Noguchi that once again begged him to come to Japan. The budget for the garden was only 2,500,000 yen, he warned. "I had to make the situation clear to you, no matter how discouraging. I want so badly to have you here—I have two or three jobs ready for you. One exterior sculpture for Nippon Gakki on the Ginza, another for a large fish refrigerating plant in Tsukiji etc. I know that I could never hope to make the Reader's Digest site anywhere near as interesting alone, without you, as with you. You should be here now, blooming, there is so much to do, instead of vegetating in N.Y."[9] A letter of agreement dated January 30, 1951, stated that Noguchi was to be paid $1,500 plus airfare.

The modest offer came just at the right moment for Noguchi. Not only was this the perfect opportunity to learn more about gardens, but also he had fallen in love with a Japanese actress named Yoshiko Yamaguchi, whom he had met on November 13, 1950, at the opening of an exhibition of kimonos at the Brooklyn Museum.[10] Yamaguchi arrived looking resplendent in a lavish kimono and three days later Noguchi's friends Ayako and Eitaro Ishigaki invited Noguchi and Yamaguchi for dinner. When Ayako Ishigaki told her husband about her idea for this dinner, Eitaro approved. "Isamu likes glamour girls," he said, "and there is a lot that Yoshiko could learn from Isamu."[11] In a clever maneuver, Noguchi arrived at the dinner early with a stack of Japanese magazines full of articles about his work. When Yamaguchi arrived— this time wearing a high-collar, Chinese-style, figure-clinging, floral-patterned dress—the Ishigakis were busy looking at the magazines, which she undoubtedly couldn't miss. Fame was a necessary point in Noguchi's favor: he was sixteen years older than Yamaguchi.

Nevertheless, Ayako spotted an electric charge between her two guests. "Sparks as bright as fireworks seemed to fly from the moment they looked at each other—Yoshiko with her big black eyes and Isamu with his severe gaze."[12] Perhaps Noguchi and Yamaguchi's rapport had something to do with their recognition of each other's underlying sadness. In spite of being blessed with beauty, talent, and success, both felt pulled between different cultures, he with his East-West conflict and she with a tension between her Asian upbringing and her acclimation to Western ways. Neither felt at home in their native country. Yamaguchi had spent her childhood in China and felt it was her real home. She knew she did not look particularly Japanese.[13] "I was spiritually the child of mixed Chinese and Japanese blood," she said, "and [Noguchi] was the actual child of mixed Japanese and American blood."[14]

Years later Yamaguchi would remember that what drew her to Nogu-chi at that first dinner was the sympathy she felt in his voice when he said, "You must have had a hard time during the war between Japan and China."[15] "My heart pounded," Yamaguchi recalled. "Why did this person know how I was completely torn between my motherland Japan, and China where I grew up? 'I was troubled during the war between the U.S. and Japan as well,' the person with gray-blue eyes said."[16]

The war had indeed made trouble for Yamaguchi. The first child of Japanese parents, she was born in 1920 in Manchuria, which, when she was twelve, became a puppet state of Japan. Her father was em-ployed by the South Manchuria Railway Company and taught Manda-rin Chinese to railway employees. Yamaguchi went to a Japanese school until second grade and then to a Chinese school. When she was thirteen her father gave her as an adopted daughter to a pro-Japanese Chinese general who was also president of the Bank of Mukden, a city in Manchuria now called Shenyang. The so-called adoption was a cus-tomary way to seal a bond of friendship. In 1934 Yamaguchi was ad-opted by another of her father's friends, who gave her the name Li Xiang-lan (pronounced "Rikoran" in Japanese) and who sent her to a missionary girls' school. Wearing a Japanese kimono, she made her debut at age thirteen at the Yamato Hotel in Mukden. Her repertoire was mixed: Japanese songs as well as Schubert's "Serenade" and Beethoven's "Ich liebe dich." After she graduated she became a popu-lar actress and singer. Working for a film company backed by the Japa-nese government, she was usually cast as a Chinese beauty enamored of a Japanese soldier or sailor. Her Japanese identity was kept secret. By the war's end Yamaguchi had been in some seventeen films, most of them pro-Japanese propaganda in support of goodwill between Ja-pan and Manchuria, and, in the large scheme of things, in support of Japanese imperialism.

When the war was over Yamaguchi was arrested as a traitor by the Chinese authorities and threatened with execution by a local military council. After she proved her Japanese nationality, she was acquitted and ordered to leave Manchuria. In March 1946 she returned to Ja-pan, took back her Japanese name, and gradually rebuilt her acting career. By 1950 she was a major film star. That year she played a Japa-nese comfort woman in *Escape at Dawn* and costarred with Toshiro

Mifune in Akira Kurosawa's *Scandal*. Also in 1950 the record in which she sang "Fragrance of the Night" was a hit in Japan. In April 1950 she went to Hollywood, where she took the name Shirley Yamaguchi and where, she told *Time* magazine, she wanted "to learn to kiss Hollywood style."[17] In addition to singing engagements in various cities, she was asked to star in King Vidor's film *Japanese War Bride*. In New York she made a splash with the actor Yul Brynner, dancing at nightclubs and enjoying a celebrity-studded social life.

Soon after their first dinner at the Ishigakis', Noguchi and Yamaguchi began to see each other every evening. "We walked together looking at many of his sculptures that decorated gardens in New York. I was astonished by his stage sets when I saw Martha Graham . . . This was the entrance to the world of Isamu . . . Alone, he challenged various contradictions between the East and the West and tried to push himself to the limit."[18] On their third date he asked Yamaguchi to marry him. She was surprised at the speed with which people did things in America.[19] "When he proposed to me I wanted to continue dating," she wrote in her autobiography. "So I had him wait for one year." Later, they agreed to base their relationship on several conditions: neither of them should interfere with the other's career and if their relationship had a negative effect on their work they would separate. Work often kept them apart. Sometimes this made their reunions all the more romantic, sometimes it created tensions.

In early March 1951 Yamaguchi left for Hollywood, where she signed her contract with Twentieth Century Fox, and then flew on to Honolulu en route to Japan. On his way to Japan Noguchi stopped in Honolulu too, and he and Yamaguchi spent twelve days at the Royal Hawaiian Hotel on Waikiki Beach. In late March he flew to Tokyo. Yamaguchi stayed behind for a singing engagement and joined Noguchi in Tokyo on April 21.

Noguchi was full of enthusiasm for the garden he was designing for *Reader's Digest*, and pleased with his fee. He was also happy when, after the first phase of his Bollingen grant expired on December 21, the fellowship was extended for another six months.

During her first weeks back in Japan Yamaguchi plunged into singing engagements. A coloratura soprano with a bell-like voice, she had been trained as a girl by an Italian opera singer. She was also busy with record contracts and with negotiations for various Japanese film projects. On May 28 she returned to Hollywood to start work on *Japanese War Bride* while Noguchi and Hiroi stayed in Tokyo to work on the Reader's Digest garden.

The area allotted for Noguchi's Reader's Digest garden was a little over an acre. He gave the space definition by creating earth mounds and a serpentine water channel shape that wound its way to several elliptical pools. The garden was conceived in the tradition of a Japanese stroll garden: as the visitor moved through it, it offered changing views. Rocks excavated from the site were placed with Zenlike care, as were dwarf bamboo, fruit trees, and large shade trees. At the end of the water channel, and rising from a rectangular pool, was a fifteen-foot-high fountain constructed of welded steel. The fountain's openwork structure of five vertical elements connected by circles and arcs was not unlike his *Bell Tower for Hiroshima* and was similar also to his iron sculpture called *Gakusei* at Keio. For the garden as well, Noguchi made two four-foot-high semiabstract granite figures of a man and a woman. Influenced by Brancusi's *The Kiss*, these figures are modeled on *kokeshi*, the traditional Japanese wooden dolls with large round heads and cylindrical bodies. The female is shaped like a vessel and has slightly swelling breasts and belly. Her oval head has Asian features. The male's head has round Western eyes. To indicate that they are a couple, Noguchi gouged channels to represent fingers and arms locked in an embrace. The *kokeshi* could stand for Noguchi and Yamaguchi or perhaps for the meeting of East and West. *Reader's Digest* rejected the doll figures and the pair is now in the Kamakura Museum of Modern Art.

"To do a garden in Japan is to bring coal to Newcastle," Noguchi remarked, but the project allowed him to combine his knowledge of modernism with Japanese tradition.[20] "Here was an opportunity to learn from the world's most skilled gardeners, the common uekiya of Japan. Through working with them in mud, I learned the rudiments of stone placing—using the stones we could find on the site. There is to each stone a live and a dead side. They are placed according to rules of Shin, Gyo, and So; that is, the formal (Shin), the informal (So), and in-between (Gyo)."[21] In his Bollingen manuscript he wrote: "I remember my contact with the earth when digging up five round stones. I experienced my first, almost ritual improvisation of placing them upon the earth with an exactitude that astonished me."[22]

In June 1951, a few weeks before he finished his work on the garden, Kenzo Tange invited Noguchi to come to Hiroshima. Noguchi was drawn to Hiroshima: "I wished somehow to add my own gesture of expiation. The result was an invitation to submit designs for two bridges spanning the approach to 'Peace Park.'"[23]

On his way, Noguchi stopped in Gifu, a city known for its cormorant fishing festival as well as for the fabrication of paper lanterns. He came for the festival, but Gifu's mayor wanted Noguchi to revitalize the city's paper lantern industry and to create designs that could be exported to the West. Noguchi was introduced to Tameshiro Ozeki, head of a family firm that had been making lanterns since 1891. After touring Ozeki Jishichi Shoten (now called Ozeki & Co., Ltd.), he decided to commit his paper lantern–designing efforts to this firm, with which he continued to collaborate for the rest of his life. Ozeki's son Hidetaro, who runs the firm today, remembers the intensity with which Noguchi looked for the right lantern shapes. During his first visit, Noguchi was riveted by watching lanterns being made. Thin bamboo strips are wound around a wooden mold to create a spiral scaffolding onto which mulberry bark paper is glued. When the glue is dry, the mold is taken apart and removed. Noguchi was entranced with the mulberry bark paper, which looks delicate but is strong. Paper lanterns, he said, "appeal to the particular love of the Japanese for things ephemeral, like the cherry blossoms, like life."[24] In October he designed fifteen new lanterns, eliminating the traditional bent wood rims and designing various wire frameworks to hold the lanterns open and to make it possible to light them with electric bulbs instead of candles. "Presently this became like a cause with me—a new shape, merely, was not enough; it obviously had to be fitted into today's new ways and uses."[25]

On a late June afternoon, accompanied by Hiroi, who would assist him with the bridge rail project, Noguchi stepped down from the train at Hiroshima station. Reporters were on hand to greet him and the city had arranged for a bus to take him, Hiroi, Kenzo Tange, city officials, and members of the press to the site where the bomb had fallen. Photographers caught Noguchi's look of horror held in check by disciplined reserve when he saw the destruction. Rising above the rubble at the

Noguchi in Hiroshima with Kenzo Tange, Tsutomu Hiroi, and, far right, Noguchi's half brother Michio, 1951

blast center was the skeleton of a grand domed building that had housed the city's Chamber of Commerce. Camera in hand, Noguchi moved through the devastated terrain. Hiroshima was, he recalled, "still empty of anything but the remains of destruction made even more poignant by the cleaned streets and an order which had been carried out leaving destruction on display, a catalogue waiting for the future."[26] The two bridges that needed railings were, he said, "still intact as to structure but with nothing above, nor railing. It is proposed that I might do these."

In August Noguchi flew to Los Angeles to be with Yamaguchi as she worked on *Japanese War Bride*. The final approval for the bridge railings commission came just as he was about to leave Japan, and he designed one of the railings on the flight to Los Angeles. In Los Angeles Noguchi played second fiddle to Yamaguchi, but he did enjoy the glamour, which he also courted. He took her, for example, to a dinner party at Charlie Chaplin's house in Beverly Hills, which impressed Yamaguchi very much. Noguchi managed to continue work on the Hiroshima bridge railings with his drawings spread out on Yamaguchi's

Noguchi's bridge railing for Hiroshima, *Tsukuru* (To build), 1952

Twentieth Century Fox dressing table. The monumental finials at the ends of the cement railings symbolized life and death. One, thrusting upward and topped by a half-sphere with its face reaching up to the sun, was originally called "To Live." The half-sphere may relate to Japan's national symbol, the rising sun. The other, shaped like the ribs of a boat, was to have been called "To Die." Later he changed the names to *Tsukuru* (To build) and *Yuku* (To depart). "The one that looks like a skeletal boat," Noguchi said, "derives from the idea of the Egyptian boats for the dead—for departing, as we all must."[27]

At summer's end Noguchi and Yamaguchi moved on to New York, where they both met with critic Aline B. Louchheim, who was writing a piece on Noguchi for *The New York Times.* Noting Noguchi's pleasure in working on public projects in Japan, Louchheim observed: "The sculptor has broken from the imprisonment of a solitary studio. His new place of work is the world."[28] Noguchi once wrote that during this eight-month sojourn in Manhattan, he was "filling in the time while Yoshiko worked."[29] In fact he was working on two projects.

One was a playground for the United Nations Headquarters in Manhattan, a commission that had come from his friend Audrey Hess, wife of the critic Thomas B. Hess, who had written such a positive and insightful article about Noguchi for *Art News* in 1946. The other project was an interior plaza or sculpture garden on the ground floor of the dazzling new Lever House, a glass-fronted office building on Park Avenue designed by Gordon Bunshaft, chief architect at Skidmore, Owings and Merrill.

Audrey Hess had approached Noguchi about the playground commission before he left for Japan to work on the Reader's Digest garden. By June 1951 Noguchi, still in Tokyo, was working on his concept for the playground and was conferring by mail with architect Julian Whittlesey, with whom he was collaborating. On August 7, back in the United States, Noguchi met with the project's sponsors, including Audrey Hess, Mrs. John D. Rockefeller, and Mrs. David Levy (Hess's aunt). The sponsoring group raised $75,000 to pay for a 100-by-140-foot playground to be built northeast of the UN building.

Noguchi designed a play landscape with a grotto, a jungle gym, a multitiered structure for climbing and sliding, a wading pool, swings, and triangular hills in bright colors. There were tunnels and winding paths and round hollows filled with sand. As always, there were mounds. Both the UN's architect, Wallace K. Harrison, and the UN plan director Glenn Bennett were enthusiastic, but Robert Moses, the man who had thwarted Noguchi's *Play Mountain*, was not impressed: "If they want to build it, it's theirs, but I'm not interested in that sort of playground," he said. "If they want us to operate it, it's got to be on our plans. We know what works."[30] Noguchi heard later that Moses had threatened not to put safety railings along the East River if the playground was built.[31] Not surprisingly, the UN succumbed to Moses's pressure and agreed to build instead a conventional playground of the type that Moses approved.

The rejected playground became a cause célèbre in art circles. When in mid-April the Museum of Modern Art exhibited the plaster model together with some of Whittlesey's drawings, it described the UN playground as "the most creative and imaginative play area yet devised."[32] In a short piece about it in the April issue of *Art News*, Thomas Hess extolled the playground's beauty and its integration of modern art and daily life. "Perhaps this is why it was venomously attacked ('a hillside rabbit warren') by the Cheops of toll bridges."[33] This Cheops, he noted, had "no legal or moral right to dictate the UN's aesthetics." According to Hess, plans were under way to find an alternate site for the playground. Noguchi left for Japan in early May, leaving Whittlesey to deal with the project's collapse.

During the fall and winter of 1951, Lever House, Manhattan's first major building to use a glass curtain wall, was still under construction on Park Avenue at Fifty-fourth Street, but Noguchi was able to work there on his model for the building's plaza, which he said was to be an "oasis of art."[34] The Lever House commission was the beginning of a long and fruitful collaboration with Gordon Bunshaft, who played a leading role in the transformation of European modernist architecture from its utopian beginnings to its function as an expression of corporate pride.[35] Born to Russian Jewish immigrant parents in 1909, Bunshaft graduated from MIT with a master's degree in architecture, and in 1937 joined Skidmore, Owings and Merrill. He was taciturn, no-nonsense, and sometimes gruff. Most of the time he and Noguchi got on well—but both were famous for their lack of patience and their total focus on work. In 1968, having completed six projects with Bunshaft, Noguchi wrote: "The architect with whom I have worked most is Gordon Bunshaft . . . It is due to his interest that projects were initiated, his persistence that saw them realized, his determination that squeezed out whatever was in me. I am beholden to him for every collaborative architectural commission I have been able to execute in the United States (with the exception of the Associated Press Relief and the ceiling and waterfall of 666 Fifth Avenue)."[36]

One reason that the two men worked so well together was that Bunshaft recognized and respected the role of the artist in relation to architecture. Of the Lever House project, Bunshaft said, "We hoped to have sculpture integrated with the total design, including landscape, and Noguchi was the only sculptor that I knew of in the world who had the requisite knowledge of architecture, of plant material and of space design."[37]

Inspired by the white sand gardens of Kyoto, Noguchi planned to cover the Lever House plaza with white marble "from which would rise sculptures with small risings and apertures in the marble for planting."[38] The plaster model that he made during his stay in New York had a small version of *Mu* in one corner, and, rising from a circular reflecting pool, three columnar sculptures—abstractions of a man, woman, and child.

On October 16, while the Lever House project was in the stage of receiving quotes for the various elements, Noguchi and Yamaguchi announced their engagement. They then flew via London to Paris, where Noguchi introduced Yamaguchi to Brancusi. Brancusi gave her an appraising gaze and led her to a revolving table upon which stood his polished bronze *Leda* covered with a cloth. He pulled off the cloth and set the table turning so that *Leda* was bathed in fluctuating light. Yamaguchi recalled that she was so taken by the sculpture's beauty that she wept for the happiness of being alive.[39] From Paris Noguchi and Yamaguchi drove to Italy, the next leg of their planned month of traveling in Europe and in India. They reached New Delhi in November. Noguchi wanted to share his passion for India with his fiancée, but Yamaguchi was horrified by the poverty and filth. They visited Nehru in order for Noguchi to show him his plans for the Gandhi memorial that they had discussed two years before.

On November 16 Noguchi flew to Tokyo from Manila and Yamaguchi went to Hong Kong to negotiate a possible role in a Chinese film. When he arrived at Haneda Airport, both his and Yamaguchi's families, plus the press and some of Yamaguchi's friends and business associates, were there to meet the newly engaged couple. A group of chorus girls from the Nichigeki gave Noguchi a bouquet, but the welcomers were disappointed that Yamaguchi was not there. She arrived in Tokyo the following day, and reporters noted that she was wearing a Noguchi-designed kimono made of navy blue fabric covered with *x*'s and *o*'s—hugs and kisses. Their wedding was planned for mid-December. Yamaguchi wrote in her autobiography that she and Noguchi had agreed to have homes both in the United States and in Japan.[40] This way they could be together as much as possible, but they could also pursue their respective careers.

In late November Noguchi traveled to Hiroshima with Kenzo Tange to see how the construction of the bridge railings was going. Noguchi, Tange, and Hiroshima's mayor discussed the possibility of Noguchi designing a memorial to those killed in the bombing. The structure was to hold an underground tablet upon which the names of the 110,000 victims of the American bomb would be recorded. Tange and the mayor saw no problem in having an American design the memorial. It was, after all, meant to have meaning for all mankind, not just for the people of Hiroshima. Noguchi agreed to do it free of charge as an "expiation of our mutual guilt."

Noguchi worked out his model in Tange's Tokyo University office and described his cenotaph design as "a cave beneath the earth (to which we all return). It was to be a place of solace to the bereaved—suggestive still further of the womb of generations still unborn who would in time replace the dead. Above ground was to be the symbol for all to see and remember . . . a mass of black granite, glowing at the base from a light beyond and below."[41] What Noguchi envisioned aboveground was a heavy, bell-shaped granite arch with its ample legs growing wider toward the bottom and continuing below ground level. Between these legs, in an underground room, the names of the dead would be placed in a granite box cantilevered out from the wall. In comparing the part beneath the earth to a womb, he acknowledged the relationship of his memorial to a female figure with two great

Noguchi's model for his *Memorial to the Dead*, Hiroshima, 1952. Plaster. Lost

protective thighs. Thus, as with many of Noguchi's sculptures, the theme is, in part, fertility. Noguchi also associated the granite arch that loomed above the underground cavern with the shape of the atomic blast. And it probably alluded also to John Donne's tolling bell. Another connection was with haniwa, whose cylindrical forms are echoed in the massive granite thighs and which were likewise associated with death. Noguchi saw the arch as an "ominous weight."

In the following month Noguchi worked on his model for the cenotaph with the fervor of someone driven, perhaps not only by a sense of complicity, but also by the demons of his childhood, his conflicts about East versus West, father and mother. Somehow his idea of who he was seemed to ride on the creation of this emblematic monument. It was as if the Hiroshima memorial rooted Noguchi himself in the Japanese earth, the "protective abode" that he had always looked for.

According to what Noguchi wrote for Bollingen, he was in Hiroshima working on the memorial when the date for his wedding was set. "I was informed of my imminent marriage to Yoshiko. Surprised but not displeased, I rushed back to Tokyo to the congratulations and the preparations of an event for which I was totally unqualified."[42]

Noguchi and Yamaguchi were married on the morning of December 15, 1951, at the Meiji Shrine. There were no guests at the Shinto ceremony. One can imagine the couple walking along the broad gravel path that curves through an evergreen forest, passes under torii (gate structures), finally arriving at a huge courtyard. From the shrine they proceeded to the home of the painter Ryuzaburo Umehara, who served as the nakodo, or go-between. Here they exchanged wedding cups of sake. In the evening there was a party at the Hanya En, a traditional Japanese restaurant in a beautiful garden. When the couple arrived, they were met at the Hanya En gate by crowds of reporters, photographers, and curiosity seekers. Among the forty-odd guests were the filmmaker Akira Kurosawa and his lead male actor Toshiro Mifune, opposite whom Yamaguchi had played in Kurosawa's Scandal. Also present was Nagamasa Kawakita, president of Towa Film Company and the man who had intervened with the Chinese authorities in 1945 when Yamaguchi was threatened with execution as a war criminal.

The bridal couple made their way through the throngs of reporters and into the restaurant, where they kneeled in front of a gilt-covered folding screen. Noguchi wore traditional formal Japanese attire, a dark kimono with pantaloons and a tunic. Yamaguchi wore a Noguchi-designed white silk kimono with an obi in a checkerboard pattern. Both carried folded fans and both wore Japanese sandals and *tabi* socks. Before the banquet began, the imperial Gagaku musicians played their ancient music. The newlyweds moved among the guests, welcoming them with a few words. The banquet was eaten on low lacquer trays, with the guests seated Japanese-style on the floor. Noguchi must have wanted to cement their union with an American marriage, for three days later they were married again at the American embassy in Tokyo. Even his wedding was a cross between East and West.

33

KITA KAMAKURA

Shortly before they married, Noguchi and Yamaguchi, together with Tsutomu Hiroi, his wife (who was Yamaguchi's sister), Noguchi's half brother Michio, and various friends, went to Kita Kamakura, a village just north of Kamakura to look for a place for the future newly-weds to live. Some members of the party rode in Noguchi's wine-colored Plymouth sedan, recently acquired from a former American occupation officer. As they approached, Noguchi admired the narrow, winding road with banks so steep it was like a tunnel. They were headed for "World of Dreams" (Mukyo), the home of the renowned potter Kitaoji Rosanjin. Noguchi had visited Rosanjin several times in 1950. "I looked him up," Noguchi said, "after following the trail of his pottery as I came across it in famous restaurants."[1]

Noguchi recalled that in his search for a new home he "remembered the lovely small valley of rice fields between hills and a cluster of old thatched-roof houses near Kita Kamakura."[2] Some of Rosanjin's buildings were for storage, some for workshops, some for Rosanjin's gigantic kiln. Two buildings were used to display his pottery collection, which comprised about three thousand objects, many of great rarity. Noguchi remembered that when he and Yamaguchi visited, the cherry trees were blooming. A photograph shows Noguchi and Yamaguchi in Rosanjin's ceramics storage room. She looks exquisitely feminine. With her perfectly shaped oval face, full lips, and large eyes under high arched eyebrows, she seems an Asian version of Elizabeth Taylor. She is dressed in one of the modified kimonos that Noguchi designed for her and that were much more form-fitting than traditional kimonos. Noguchi eliminated the triple fold around the waist and equipped Yamaguchi's kimonos with zippers or hooks, so that they were easy to put on and take off. In the photograph Yamaguchi examines a circular slab of ceramic upon which she has inscribed an optimistic Chinese character. Noguchi stands close to her and looks down at the piece she is holding. He inscribed his slab with a serpent made with a stroke of dark glaze, apparently an abstract version of the same auspicious message conveyed in Yamaguchi's inscription.

At lunch Noguchi expressed his admiration for Rosanjin's home. Perhaps he mentioned that he would like to find a similar place. Rosanjin, not habitually an affable man, made an extraordinarily generous offer: "Come live here. Live in that house over there, which I put up for myself to look at."[3] The house Rosanjin offered was a two-hundred-year-old farmhouse that Rosanjin had had taken apart and moved to the side of a hill across a narrow valley from his own dwelling. "Live in it as long as you like," he said.[4]

Rosanjin, a huge man by Japanese standards, brimmed with intelligence and humor, but he was also famous for his imperious manner, his caustic tongue, and his short temper. Yamaguchi remembered that no housekeeper lasted in his employ for more than a week. "When he comes out from his bath, they have to serve chilled beer and refreshments just seven seconds after him drying his body. If it lags a few seconds he would scold them. However, to me, he was very different. He was very kind and attentive."[5] With Noguchi, perhaps because he thought Noguchi's sculpture was "more beautiful than Picasso's," and because he knew that he was admired in return, Rosanjin was always agreeable.[6] "I was proud and flattered beyond words," Noguchi said, "by his kind invitation that we use his ancient farm house."[7]

Soon after Noguchi and Yamaguchi moved into Rosanjin's farmhouse, they realized that they needed more space. The house had three small rooms laid out in a row, an outdoor privy, and a separate building for the kitchen. What Noguchi needed most was a studio, and he soon began to build one. "The original house is perched on the edge of rice fields backed up against a hillside where there is no possibility of expansion. I made room for a studio by taking a dump area beyond the bathhouse and excavating into the hill which is here of a kind of hard, earthlike rock."[8] Noguchi planned to spend no more than five hundred dollars for domestic improvements. To keep expenses down, he did much of the work himself, swinging a pickax to open up the cliff. "But beyond the matter of merely achieving space, it ties me further into the soil, and this is my pride and my whimsy."[9] By making a nest, a Japanese-style nest, with his Japanese bride, he was attaching himself to a place. "I was filled with joy and energy."[10] What he wanted, he said, was to build "an oasis for myself and for those close to me."[11]

Photographs of Noguchi and Yamaguchi sitting by the fireplace that he hollowed out of the back wall of his studio, or sitting on the veranda overhanging the rice paddies and cherry trees, make it look as if their life was nothing but love and leisure. Noguchi wrote to Jeanne Reynal: "Just now we are sitting in our little garden, where we have spread mats and cusions [sic] to enjoy the autumn sun. Yoshiko-san is pealing [sic] a persimmon which grows plentifully in the garden. Before us the rice has now been cut and stacked high on poles. We wish you were both here as it is the kind of place where lovers belong."[12]

Noguchi and Yoshiko Yamaguchi on their veranda, Kita Kamakura, 1952

They did have an occasional visitor. A tatami-covered raised area set off from the studio space by a mud wall served as a guest room. On one side of this room Noguchi set a gnarled wooden post upside down, following a Zen idea that a dwelling should not be perfect. Perfection invites bad luck. Among their visitors was the master flower arranger Sofu Teshigahara, who came with a group of friends, and they all danced until the floor caved in.[13]

In his new home, Noguchi arranged a variety of light fixtures, not just Akari, but also a lamp he designed consisting of a bulb with a colander set sideways for a shade, and a lamp created by digging a niche into the earthen back wall, placing a bulb inside, and making a cover out of reed lattice. The farmhouse floors were covered with tatami, thus no shoes were allowed. Besides a straw stool and, for dining, a low table and wooden armrests, there was very little furniture. Noguchi placed his sculptures on earth pedestals he had left during the studio excavation. One sculpture was placed in his tokonoma alcove. "In Japan there is always the Tokonoma, the space for a scroll, a statuette, a vase, a sprig of nature. A beautiful convention[,] it is never forgotten and of great variety—an indulgence of space if you will where there is no space to spare, yet one always has the impression that it gives far more than it takes away."[14]

Noguchi explained to a visiting *New York Times* writer that the Japanese house forced a person to turn inward and to become aware of the inner man rather than focusing on outward vistas.[15] Later that year he wrote about his life in Kita Kamakura: "Should anyone be asked of what is characteristic of my development now I think it is my rediscovery of this intimate nature which I had almost forgotten since childhood. It is anybody's childhood, I suppose, to know nature this way. Yet to know nature again as an adult, to exhaust one's hands in its earth . . . one has to be a potter or a sculptor, and that also in Japan."[16] From Noguchi's point of view, life in Kita Kamakura was idyllic. He and Yamaguchi gardened together and enjoyed the company of various stray Akita dogs. They surely delighted in the ritual of soaking in the large wooden tub that Noguchi had installed in the bathhouse. They also saw quite a bit of Rosanjin, who became for Noguchi a kind of mentor and father figure. When Noguchi and Yamaguchi heard the sound of a wooden clapper coming from Rosanjin's house, they would follow the path through the rice paddy and sit down to yet another extraordinary meal. Rosanjin was friendly to Yamaguchi, but he could be difficult: he

Noguchi and Yamaguchi crossing the rice paddies, Kita Kamakura, 1952

forbade her to hang her laundry where he could see it from his house.
Given the scarcity of flat land around the farmhouse, drying laundry
must have posed a challenge.

Noguchi and Yamaguchi attended Rosanjin's kiln openings—
dramatic events when the kiln was opened after three days of firing.
"There were days that the three of us stayed up all night watching the
kiln," said Yamaguchi.[17] At these openings, Rosanjin's ceramic pieces
were for sale and Yamaguchi often bought some as a way of repaying
Rosanjin for letting them live in the farmhouse free of charge. For
Noguchi part of the thrill was not knowing what firing would do to the
clay's surface or to a glaze. "Baptized by fire," clay pieces transcended the
potter's personality. They became, he said, ancient like Chinese bronzes,
which were "purified of their human scent by super human 'time.'"[18]

The newlyweds' life was full of poetry, but it also involved hard
work. Yamaguchi had a demanding career and could not live the con-
fined life of a Japanese housewife. On many mornings she was picked
up by a limousine and driven over the rough roads to the Toho movie

studio in Tokyo. In December she began work on a film called *Muteki* (Foghorn), and she also worked on several other films in 1952, movies such as *Sword for Hire* and *Woman of Shanghai*. Noguchi worked in his new studio and in Rosanjin's pottery workshop, where he was free to use Rosanjin's various clays. "I made ceramics with Rosanjin using his earth, his 'kam,' and everything else, and he helped me to fire them. He gave me the various glazes and so forth."[19] Toward the end of his Kita Kamakura sojourn, Noguchi said, "The earth of Japan has opened my eyes, as if in discovery of some new horizon."[20] He not only dug his fingers into Rosanjin's clay, he also gathered clay from a nearby stream-bed and prepared it by stepping on it with his bare feet.

In May 1952 Noguchi and Rosanjin traveled to the beautiful town of Imbe in the Okayama Prefecture, a center of the production of Bi-zen pottery. Rosanjin once described Bizen ceramics, which are a rich brown and burnt sienna in color, as having an "unbeautiful beauty." They spent six days at Imbe working in the pottery workshop of Toyo Kaneshige, whose family kiln had been producing Bizen stoneware since the sixteenth century. At the Kaneshige workshop, Noguchi had the help of several assistants who would throw the pots he designed on the wheel. A photograph shows Noguchi sitting cross-legged on a flat pillow, his hands covered with clay as he makes adjustments to a vase set on the wheel. Beside him is a notebook open to a page with many sketches of vessels he planned to make. Kaneshige noted that Noguchi threw himself into work "like seriousness personified."[21]

Noguchi was exacting as he watched over the turning wheel. If the result did not satisfy him he would ask the assistant to redo it again and again. Sometimes he would destroy a piece he didn't like. His method for making ceramic sculptures as opposed to vessels was, Kaneshige wrote, to draw what he wanted to create and to write mea-surements next to the drawing. Then he would make a rough plaster mold and wrap it in clay. After removing the piece from the mold, he would continue to work on it, shaping it with a spatula and cutting it with a knife. "When he trims a flat piece of clay into a shape like a tray," Kaneshige observed, "he cuts so decisively with his knife that it makes your heart skip a beat as you watch. He is extraordinarily skilled with his hands."[22]

Noguchi's ceramic works look spontaneous, but he made them with a deliberation that surprised even Rosanjin. During his stay at Imbe, Noguchi produced fifty-seven pieces, whereas Rosanjin made eight

Noguchi's Bizen stoneware
vase called *Man*, 1952.
21⅞×6½×6 in.

hundred. When Rosanjin and Noguchi returned to Imbe in mid-August
for the kiln opening, Noguchi was not pleased with the dishes he had
made, but he was happy with the abstract sculptures and with the vessels, which he called "sculptures, with flowers."[23] A Bizen stoneware vase
with a rounded middle section was titled *Woman*. A companion piece
was *Man*. Other vases were shaped like a bird or a hand. A dinner plate
titled *Face Dish (Me)* consists of an oval slab with features as arche-
typal as those in *Sculpture to Be Seen from Mars*. The self-portrait is
suspended on a bamboo pole, and Noguchi attached a few dried grasses
to the top of the head, perhaps to indicate the sparseness of his own hair.

　　While living at Kita Kamakura, Noguchi made several trips to Gifu
to work on new Akari designs. Hidetaro Ozeki, who was then a young
man working for his father's firm, would occasionally come to visit
Noguchi at Kita Kamakura, bringing samples of Noguchi's lantern designs. He was struck by Yamaguchi's charm: "Yoshiko was singing a song
while she cleaned the house."[24] When Yamaguchi accompanied Noguchi on one of his Gifu trips, an Ozeki assistant was astonished by how

frequently the couple would retire for lovemaking to the nearby tea-house where they stayed. Noguchi told the assistant that "Yamaguchi was essential to him as an artist."[25] Sex, Noguchi maintained, was a great stimulus to creativity. "Sex is very important to give you a feeling of being alive. There are frequent changes in the history of the human race but one thing that never changes is sex."[26]

"Akari," Noguchi wrote in his autobiography, "was a logical conver-gence of my long interest in light sculptures, *lunars*, and my being in Japan. Paper and bamboo fitted in with my feeling for the quality and sensibility of light. Its very lightness questions materiality . . ."[27] Nogu-chi had been interested in relating light and sculpture since 1928, when he made his neon light sculpture. In 1933 came his illuminated musical weathervane, then the Lunars in the early 1940s, and in 1944 the three-legged cylindrical lamp. For Shinbanraisha, borrowing a tra-ditional Japanese craft called *magemono*, he designed a hanging lamp

Noguchi with
Akari in his
Long Island City
studio, 1960s

formed by bending a thin strip of wood into a circle and adding mulberry paper to its lower surface. Over the years he designed hundreds of Akari, always trying to keep ahead of imitators. One way to foil them was to create asymmetrical lamps. Or he would make the spaces between the bamboo ribs irregular. Sometimes he eliminated the bamboo entirely, forming lamps out of crinkly mulberry paper that gave a lively play of light and shadow, which Noguchi compared to the paper-thin beaten gold of a Minoan mask.[28]

"The name Akari which I coined, means in Japanese light as illumination. It also suggests lightness as opposed to weight . . . Looking more fragile than they are, *akari* seem to float, casting their light as in passing . . . when not in use they fold away in an envelope."[29] Noguchi was proud that he had combined modern function with an old tradition. In addition, his lanterns were useful, affordable art works: "It has been said that to start a home all that is needed is a room, a tatami and AKARI."[30] Besides traveling to Gifu, Bizen, and occasionally to Tokyo, Noguchi also visited Buddhist temples with his friend and former guide Saburo Hasegawa, who was living nearby in Chigasaki and visited often. At some point during his Kita Kamakura idyll, Noguchi and Hasegawa went to meditate at Engaku-ji, the great Zen temple complex in Kamakura that Yone Noguchi had used as a writing retreat. Although Noguchi never became a Zen Buddhist, Zen's approach to life infiltrated his being and his art. In a magazine article about his Hiroshima cenotaph, Noguchi wrote what sounds like a description of meditation: "When you sit in the dim light surrounded by walls, your mind seems to become perfectly clear and to open up. The deep soul of the person who created the closed space awakens us, and the expanding of that person's soul leads us to the unknown horizons of our own soul."[31]

Photographs, Noguchi's words, and even the sculptures he made during this time make Noguchi and Yamaguchi's life at Kita Kamakura look like an extended honeymoon. But there were moments of sadness. Early in March 1952 he received a letter from Hiroshima's Mayor Hamai saying that his design for the Hiroshima cenotaph had been rejected. In their enthusiasm for Noguchi's participation in the Peace Park project, the mayor and Kenzo Tange had not paid the proper respect to the official channel of authority by consulting the Hiroshima Peace Memorial City Construction Committee. Additionally, the com-

mittee's refusal to use Noguchi's design was prompted by the fact that
he was an American. The abstractness of Noguchi's design was also
cited as a factor in the decision. Noguchi believed that the memorial
should transcend nationality: "Hiroshima exists not just for Japan, it
exists for the world," he told a reporter for the *Mainichi shinbun* on
April 8, 1952.[32] He decided to go to Hiroshima with Yamaguchi to see
if the rejection could be reversed. The press made hay with the controversy. Noguchi called the rejection "my one most disagreable experience
in Japan."[33] In the end, the committee insisted that Tange design the
cenotaph, and Tange had to come up with a design in a week's time to
be ready for the anniversary of the bombing. Tange kept Noguchi's idea
of an arch shape, but his design lacked the power and drama of Noguchi's. Noguchi's emotional attachment to his cenotaph was such that
in later years he persisted in trying to get it built either in Washington,
D.C., or near the United Nations headquarters in New York.

Although Noguchi and Yamaguchi were very much in love, there
were problems. The way they lived was Noguchi's choice: "I was placed
in a different world that I did not know at all," wrote Yamaguchi, "and
I tried to absorb everything about it."[34] Both were fiercely intense
and stubborn. And there were cultural disparities. From her point of
view, Noguchi was very much an American. "When we lived together
there was a distinct difference between East and West, a big culture
gap . . . little differences on the surface made a crack in our feelings
and that crack grew."[35] Noguchi did not speak much Japanese and Yamaguchi spoke little English. "It was," she said, "difficult to give nuances
of meaning. Noguchi was very strict with himself, with his friends,
and of course with his wife." Noguchi insisted that they wear kimonos
and he forbade Yamaguchi to cut her hair. "When we lived together in
Rosanjin's farmhouse even the shoes that we wore had to be in accord
with the tone of the house. The shoes were Zori, sandals made of
wood and straw. They were very rough and they didn't fit my feet. My
skin peeled off and I bled when I wore them but he did not allow me
to wear any other shoes."[36] Once when Yamaguchi came home from
working in Tokyo wearing a pair of pink plastic sandals, Noguchi flew
into a rage. "What is this?" he cried, and, Yamaguchi recalled, "without
listening to my explanation, he threw my sandals away in the rice field.
Art and life—he did not tolerate anything that did not match with his
aesthetic . . . It was hard for me to become a work of Isamu."[37] Noguchi

was always telling the Japanese not to imitate Western culture. And here was his wife wearing plastic sandals—the epitome of tacky American commercialism. According to Yamaguchi's brother-in-law, Hiroi, the episode of the plastic sandals was the crack that eventually split Noguchi and Yamaguchi apart.[38]

Yamaguchi was made uncomfortable by other cultural differences as well. She said that when she brought home friends from her filmmaking world, Noguchi grew silent and did not hide his boredom. "When we went to a friend's house and I gave a gift to the host and I said this is from us he would deny it."[39] The conflicts grew increasingly painful. Yamaguchi greatly admired Noguchi's dedication to his work. She saw him as a world-famous artist. By contrast, she was doing something commercial; in spite of her own fame, she felt inferior to him. These tensions could sometimes be smoothed away by lovemaking and by all the things that they did share—intelligence and a great curiosity about life. Certainly there were many moments of joy. Yamaguchi remembered their life as a sort of Shangri-la. But the greatest disappointment was perhaps two miscarriages during this time. Yamaguchi came to realize that she would never be able to bear a child.

With Yamaguchi's help, Noguchi put together an exhibition of his work that opened on September 23, 1952, at the new Museum of Modern Art in Kamakura. It included 120 works, all of which were ceramics except one called *The Ceremony*, which was in cast iron. Noguchi also showed some of his recent Akari, which according to Hidetaro Ozeki "were not an immediate hit."[40]

In the catalogue the ceramic pieces were divided into categories: Bizen-style, Seto-style, Shigaraki-style, Karatsu-style, and Kasama-style, the variety indicating Rosanjin's generosity in letting Noguchi use his clays and glazes. The catalogue had essays by Noguchi, Rosanjin, and Hasegawa.[41] There was also a brief introduction by the museum's Administrative Committee, which advised viewers that to appreciate Noguchi's works they should "suspend all reason and preconceptions and instead approach them straightforwardly as explorations of form." Hasegawa's essay spoke of Noguchi's simplicity and Rosanjin observed that people in Japan did not have the educational background to understand Noguchi's work, which he described as having "a rigorous freedom," a "playfulness of imagination," and "nobility, grace, beautiful line, and vitality." Rosanjin made a curious remark about Noguchi's sculptures: "Though I don't know why, his works never show forceful-ness. And such an arrogant pretentiousness is unknown to him." Here Rosanjin seems to have put his finger on the difference between Nogu-chi and the American sculptors associated with Abstract Expressionism. There is urgency in both Noguchi's and his contemporaries' works, but unlike the sculptors of the New York School, Noguchi pulled his urgency inward until it became a kind of quietude.

Noguchi's catalogue essay is an eloquent statement of his sculp-tural credo. Sculpture, he said, must be experienced physically in space by an ambulatory spectator. It should make "the air breathe" and should provide "a fence against the dark."[42] Sculptures should have "the patina of time" or should even be "beyond time . . . time had bereft them of all weight, the materiality transformed into spirit." If this sounds pon-tificating, it was a style in which many 1950s writers indulged. In gen-eral Noguchi was a clear-thinking writer, but as the years went on, his prose was often tainted with the desire to sound wise and ambiguous like a Buddhist sage.

The sixty sculptures and some fifty-nine vases, dishes, and tea bowls listed in Noguchi's Kamakura exhibition catalogue were made during an eight-month period. This astounding productivity had much to do with his embrace of his Japanese heritage, and his having created a home that not only expressed that embrace, but also gave him a feeling of belonging. Another contributing factor was the freedom and cama-raderie he felt in being able to work with Rosanjin.

Several of Noguchi's ceramic sculptures from these months at Kita Kamakura reveal his joy in matrimony despite its problems. The show's catalogue lists two versions of Yoshiko-san. One is a six-inch-tall, kimono-clad figure with outstretched arms. Her head is separate from her body and she is held up by a dowel so that her feet dangle. Al-though the piece was surely meant to be affectionate, its resemblance to a puppet brings to mind Noguchi's dominating nature, insisting that his wife conform to his Japanese ideal and lifestyle, whereas she might have preferred a less rustic way of life. Another piece called Marriage (but listed in the catalogue as Man and Wife) consists of a male and female formed by rolling out sausage shapes of clay and adding beatific-looking heads on one end and one pair of feet on the other. The couple is covered with a blanket represented by a thin slab of clay. A third sculpture, listed in the catalogue as Nighttime Fragrance and now titled

Yoshiko-san, 1952. Unglazed Karatsu stoneware, 6×6 in.

Marriage, 1952. Unglazed Karatsu
stoneware, 14 in.

Ie Lai Chian, 1952. Shigaraki
stoneware, 17³⁄₈ × 7³⁄₄ × 3¹⁄₂ in.

Ie Lai Chian, refers to Yamaguchi in a more abstract way. The title alludes to the scent of the tuberose flower and comes from his wife's
best-known song. Instead of making a figure to represent Yamaguchi,
Noguchi made what might be seen as an abstract version of her song.
Ten long strips of clay curving upward and seeming to wave in the
wind could stand for the flower's smell wafting in the night air, or they
could be the sound waves of Yamaguchi's singing.

Noguchi's eroticism revealed itself in pieces like *Mother Goddess
No 2*, which looks like an ancient fertility figure and which is simply a
roll of clay with outstretched arms, large breasts, and a small head attached. Perhaps prompted by his and Yamaguchi's wish to have a child,
Noguchi made several of these small, primitivistic fertility figures.
Equally casual in form and sensuous in feeling were the tiny embry-
onic pieces that he called "Beginnings." For his show he hung these
fetishistic objects on three wooden panels. Other sculptures listed in the
catalogue that have titles suggesting his pleasure in conjugal life are
Blanket, Thin Mattress, A Beautiful Woman, and *Home. Curtain of
Dreams* likewise evokes his pleasure in his life at Rosanjin's "World of
Dreams." The "curtain" consists of a wavy slab of Shigari stoneware from

which various protuberances suggest feet and hands belonging to lovers beneath a blanket. *Child* is an even more helpless-looking puppet figure than *Yoshiko-san*. With its swelling breasts and tummy, it may in fact be a woman, perhaps a reference to Yamaguchi's childlessness.

Two of the most intriguing of Noguchi's 1952 sculptures are *Apartment* and *Even the Centipede*. The former is a tall box formed out of clay slabs. Bert Winther-Tamaki has suggested two sources for *Apartment*: Chinese *mingqi*, architectural models inhabited by small figures; and Giacometti's 1930s architectural structures inhabited by animate but abstract forms.[43] Another possible source might be David Smith's 1945 *Home of the Welder*. Noguchi's *Apartment* is, like Smith's *Home*

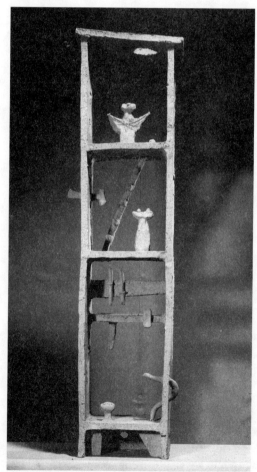

Apartment, 1952. Unglazed Seto red stoneware, 37½×12¼×6¾ in.

of the Welder, about being an artist. On the back of a photograph of *Apartment* Noguchi wrote: "Its secret and real nature is 'The Life of the Artist.'" The dwelling seems to have five floors, four of them inhabited by semiabstract forms. At the top a birdlike figure with outstretched wings looks up toward an opening in the roof, perhaps suggesting the possibility of transcendence through art.

Even the Centipede has eleven ceramic cup shapes attached by hemp cord to a two-by-four. By making the centipede huge and upright, Noguchi suggests the alarm that confrontations with centipedes can cause: "I was living in Japan then and our house there was filled with them. I became rather fond of them; I lost my fear. You know, when

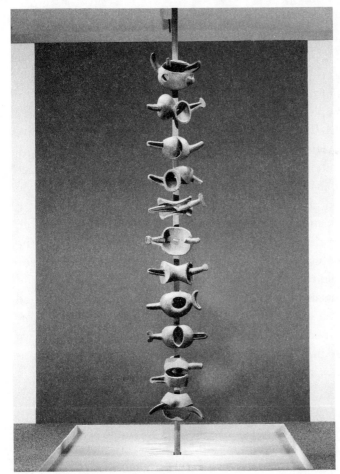

Even the Centipede, 1952. Unglazed Kasama red stoneware, wooden pole, hemp cord, 165⅝ × 18 in.

you kill a centipede, the two halves just walk off. This gave me the idea for a sculpture in sections . . . The work is a shrine to the centipede. Or rather the centipede is now enshrined at the Museum of Modern Art."[44]

Noguchi's year in Kita Kamakura was one of the happiest of his life: "The changing seasons have now made one round—each day a wonder of discovery to me, so intimate is nature here, not only before the eye, it invades ones [sic] being, till the meaning of all its various sights and noises are like a symphony to be heard at all time[s] . . . Whatever quality my work now has is I hope that of nature—that is to say the result of our communion."[45]

Noguchi's Kamakura exhibition closed on October 26 and in December came various reviews, some of which were less than enthusiastic. The climate of opinion about Noguchi, his sculpture, and his role in Japanese culture had changed. He was no longer the pigeon carrying the news about modernism to a Japan hungry to know the culture of the West. In September 1951 the Japanese government agreed on a peace treaty with the United States and forty-seven other nations, which, along with the end of the Occupation, went into effect in April 1952. Japanese intellectuals and leftists were opposed to the peace treaty, in part because it allowed American military bases to remain on Japanese soil even after the Occupation ended. The infatuation with everything American in the immediate postwar years changed into an anti-Americanism that often had a racist tinge. April 28, the day the peace treaty was signed, was called a "Day of National Disgrace." Demonstrators held placards reading GO HOME, YANKEE. Ten thousand protestors chanting antigovernment and anti-American slogans marched to the plaza in front of the Imperial Palace, a place they had been forbidden to gather. The police responded with tear gas and bullets. Two people were killed and roughly two thousand were injured. American-owned automobiles were set on fire and three GIs were thrown into the palace moat.

Given this animosity, it is not surprising that Noguchi's relationship to the Japanese art world was altered. He was no longer the delightful newcomer. Now he was a competitor and Japanese artists were jealous of his success. It was in April, the month that brought the peace treaty and the Occupation's end, that Noguchi's Hiroshima cenotaph was rejected and an article appeared in the newspaper *Tokyo shinbun* excoriating Noguchi's arrogance: "In Isamu Noguchi's blood there is mixed hay which is from overseas . . . Coming to occupied Japan where *Nisei* have clout, he spread the idea in the press that he, of all people, was the most suitable person to make the monument for the slogan 'No More Hiroshima'—thus showing the mixed character of his temperament."[46]

A few reviews were guardedly favorable. Writing about the chorus of negative criticism that Noguchi's show had prompted, Shuzo Takiguchi observed: "Words, words, words—arguments after arguments greet the artist."[47] He went on to note: "There is something about Noguchi that recalls to one's mind a migratory Ulysses, so to speak, that moves from East to West, then from West to East, then back again to West . . . His recent works, in medium and subject-matter, have become Japanese . . . Notwithstanding, there still remains something that prevents us from calling them Japanese—something that requires annotation. In other words, underlying his Japanese works there is the logic, or the illogic of Western construction." Artist and writer Taro Okamoto wrote in the December issue of *Bijutsu techo*: "Isamu Noguchi is a pure-hearted beast, who seizes all kinds of shapes and devours the beauty of each with relish . . . He chews up and swallows traditional Japanese shapes like haniwa, pots, paper lanterns, and the like, and he shapes a new kind of beauty out of them . . . His refined and sophisticated modernist sense is important to Japan where we are inundated with country bumpkins who think they are modern."[48]

On January 18, 1953, Noguchi returned to New York to continue his work on the Lever House project. He also needed to be in Manhattan to prepare for an upcoming exhibition of his recent ceramic work to be held at the Egan Gallery. (After being postponed, this show finally took place at the Stable Gallery in November 1954.) Yamaguchi, busy making a film in Hong Kong, was not able to travel to the United States with Noguchi. She planned to join him after the filming. The Kita Kamakura idyll was over.

34

MY SOLACE HAS ALWAYS BEEN SCULPTURE

Back in Manhattan and temporarily installed in the Great Northern Hotel, Noguchi felt once again like a displaced person. He found a new studio but it took some time before he launched himself into his habitual work mode. A letter of agreement he drew up with Skidmore, Owings and Merrill on February 16, 1953, said he planned to start on the interior garden for Lever House as soon as possible.[1] In his contract he stipulated that during the anticipated four months of design development it was important that "every step of the creative process be related to the actual scale and space. The play of the imagination must be checked with reality, with that which is possible and desirable." His fee was to be ten thousand dollars.[2]

Noguchi envisioned the sculptures he proposed for the Lever House plaza as a "tribute to Brancusi—variations on his theme of Bird and Column."[3] He also noted his debt to ancient Greece and Japan. After making an elaborate model of the ground floor he began to invent the shapes to put into his plaza. "I spared no effort or expense."[4] But he was not happy. In March he wrote to Rosanjin to thank him for the privilege of working beside him and for teaching him and Yamaguchi to "discriminate and savor the quality of real epicurianism . . . Coming back to New York after a year in Yamazaki is a terrible shock. There seems no sense to the mad rush. I am unable to adjust myself to the tempo or the people, and as for the food it is awful. Is it because Yoshiko-san is not here that I feel so homesick for Japan?"[5] He told Rosanjin that because Yamaguchi had not been able to get a visa to come to the

Noguchi's model for his Lever House garden, 1952. Plaster. Unrealized

United States he had postponed his exhibition until fall of the following year. "I am hoping to get Yoshiko's visa soon, but in the meantime I shall be very grateful if you will please look after her and help her."

Yamaguchi's visa problems dragged on. "Gradually I became frantic," Noguchi recalled.[6] When he learned that his wife's visa had been held up because of security issues, he hired a Wall Street lawyer. "Thus started a labyrinthine search into the murky depth of innuendo without substance which lasted into the next spring . . ."[7] Trying to clear Yamaguchi's name, Noguchi traveled back and forth to Washington. "I was told that there were certain questions about her past associations. 'You should know that all artists and scientists are considered subversive until proven otherwise,'" said the State Department official to whom he spoke.

The FBI suspected that Yamaguchi was a Communist spy. A January 1951 army intelligence report said that she had been trained in espionage in China during World War II. "She is alleged to have recently associated with various Chinese, Japanese and Korean Communists."[8] Yamaguchi wondered if the visa denial was prompted by what had happened when she and Noguchi went to the U.S. consulate in Tokyo to formalize their marriage. "A consul general asked me, 'Do you pledge allegiance to the United States of America?' 'No!' I answered reflectively. I struggled between Japan and China. Have one more country to pledge to? No way—it was a 'no' that my subconscious made me say."[9]

Finally, in mid-July 1953, "despairing of any progress" and having finished the final model for Lever House as well as completing the set for Martha Graham's *Voyage*, Noguchi flew to Paris, where he was reunited with Yamaguchi, whom he had not seen for half a year. For several months they traveled in Europe and Asia before returning to Japan in March 1954. On July 30, 1953, Noguchi wrote to Gordon Bunshaft from a place near Versailles where he and Yamaguchi had been living for two weeks. He said they planned to travel to Italy and Spain. "I hope to make a bee line to Carrara, there to make inquiry as to the characteristics of the various marbles [in response] to the weather conditions of New York . . . I dream of the possibility of a freak streak of really white granite somewhere."[10] He suggested that the carving of the sculptural elements of the Lever House plaza might be done in Europe. And, he pointed out, "an investigation of marbles fits in well with my wishing to have a vacation with my wife."

On August 10, after he had visited Carrara and moved on to Florence, Noguchi wrote Bunshaft again, this time enclosing a list of marble prices, and saying that he would investigate marbles in Greece if Bunshaft thought it worthwhile.[11] Bunshaft replied that though everyone was excited about Noguchi's design, it would be best if he returned soon to finalize the cost estimates and secure the Lever House project. "It is sometimes dangerous to let a project like this lag too long," he wrote. This news disturbed Noguchi greatly, as he felt it was his duty not to abandon his wife until her visa issues were resolved, which might take another six weeks. Bunshaft replied with sympathy but once again warned that delay could cause the Lever people to lose interest. "I am telling you this so that you may use your best judgment in deciding when you will return." Despite these warnings, Noguchi and Yamaguchi continued to travel throughout the fall to Egypt, Burma, Thailand, Macao, Cambodia, Indonesia, and Singapore, while Yamaguchi's visa was repeatedly denied with no reason given.

Toward the end of 1953, the couple arrived in Hong Kong, where Yamaguchi was shooting a movie. What should have been a happy time in Noguchi and Yamaguchi's marriage was instead a period of anxiety and frustration. In early January 1954 Noguchi received a letter from his lawyer trying to explain the delay with the visa, but also confirming that a bad year at Lever Brothers had left them reluctant to go through with Noguchi's garden. Though a chance remained that approval from the board of directors in England could push the project forward, the news seemed final. "The Lever Brothers job fell through with a thud," Noguchi recalled. "Did the anguish, under which I had worked, show through, or had they really run out of cash?"[12] Another worry was that the rumors of Yamaguchi being a Communist would hurt his chances of landing commissions for public works. Some relief came in 1954 when his Bollingen grant was renewed for another year.

When Yamaguchi's filming was finished in mid-March, she and Noguchi returned briefly to Rosanjin's farmhouse in Kita Kamakura. While there, Noguchi worked on the arrangements for an exhibition of Rosanjin's ceramics at the Museum of Modern Art in New York. Early that summer he returned to Manhattan to organize his upcoming show at the Stable Gallery. On May 28 Yamaguchi's visa was finally granted and she joined him in June. "When we returned to New York in the summer of 1954," Noguchi recalled, "my immediate concern was to arrange for an exhibition of the ceramics which had remained in storage since I had sent them from Japan. Fortunately the Stable Gallery offered to show them in November . . . My exhibition went well, but I was aware it could not have continuity as I was not able, nor did I want, to continue with the same work."[13] Actually, the reviews of his Stable show were not enthusiastic, and once again Noguchi felt that he was floundering.

His marriage was coming apart as well. In December 1954 Yamaguchi left for Hollywood to work on *House of Bamboo*, a gangster film set in Tokyo about a beautiful young woman who falls in love with an American man whom she initially thinks is a gangster, but who turns out to be her savior. This marked the beginning of a flutter of travel back and forth from Hollywood to Japan. Yamaguchi asked Noguchi to join her, but he did not want to interrupt his work. With two such headstrong people pulling in different directions, tensions mounted.

Following the closing of his Stable show, Noguchi was uncertain what direction to take. "What to do under entirely different conditions becomes a problem: to pick up at some similar point in the past, or go on to what? What necessity forces expression? I remember Marcel Duchamp once said to me 'Don't do anything that pleases you—only do that which you dislike and cannot help but do. This is the way to find yourself. But it is also true that we cannot ever be more than what we are.'"[14] Noguchi knew he had to move forward: "Looking at the evidence of past work, I feel impersonal, vaguely related but somewhat hostile. I have changed in the meantime. It was two years since I had made these ceramics. Had I made more it would have been as an older and different man." Although Noguchi's sculptures are not autobiographical in any obvious way, it is clear that he saw them as intimately related to his life. He once jotted on a sheet of yellow paper: "The chronology of my life and work are intermeshed. I can only continue in the way time's change permits."[15]

Early in 1955 Noguchi received a letter from George Devine, a director with the Shakespeare Memorial Theatre, and from Sir John Gielgud, asking if he would design the sets for their production of *King Lear*. Soon the company asked him to design the costumes as well. Noguchi's response was similar to his reaction to auspicious events in the past: "When in such times of doubt an inquiry comes from out of space, my reaction is, 'Why not?' It is a sign sent by fate."[16] On February 5 Noguchi left for London. Yamaguchi joined him and they spent the next few weeks together in London and Paris.

Noguchi was pleased with his conception for *King Lear*. "To say that such activity is an interruption to my sculpture is only correct if unrealized sculpturally, or merely unrealized, and so a waste of time. *Lear* was neither of these."[17] His sets comprised large geometric panels of color—diamonds, triangles, and rectangular shapes in flat red, blue, yellow, black, white, and gray—that could be moved around the stage by actors. The actors' costumes were a modernist version of Elizabethan attire, highly simplified and a little stiff. The response was, Noguchi said, "an avalanche of abuse from the press."[18] One critic suggested that the horrors of Hiroshima and Nagasaki had propelled Noguchi's imagination to create "colossal chaos." Noguchi wondered: "Had I gone beyond my depth? And yet I had utter confidence that I understood *Lear*—with a fearful joy."[19]

That spring Noguchi returned to New York and designed one of his most exquisite sets, for Martha Graham's *Seraphic Dialogue*, a dance on the theme of Joan of Arc. The set consisted of several sculptures constructed from brass tubes held in suspension by steel cables. For the engineering of this work, Noguchi received technical advice from his friend Edison Avery Price, a lighting engineer who had once dated Noguchi's sister Ailes. The delicate shimmering geometric structures look from a distance as if they were made of wire, and thus recall the wire sculptures by Richard Lippold. Noguchi saw the largest structure as a vision of a cathedral inside of Joan of Arc's head. In its apparent fragility, this abstract cathedral harks back to a collapsible church that Noguchi made for Ruth Page's *The Bells*.

In 1955 various other projects fell through, which he blamed on his personal woes as he and Yamaguchi filed for divorce.[20] It was an amicable separation—both agreeing that their lives had taken them in different directions. From Yamaguchi's point of view, the many months spent apart when her visa was denied had created a rift. Moreover, the marriage had begun to interfere with their work.[21] That spring Yamaguchi was in New York starring in the musical *Shangri-La*, which closed after one month. The following year she married a young Japanese diplomat. Her acting career ended in 1958, but she soon earned fame as the anchorwoman of a television show designed for housewives. As her interests grew more political, she became in 1969 the host of a

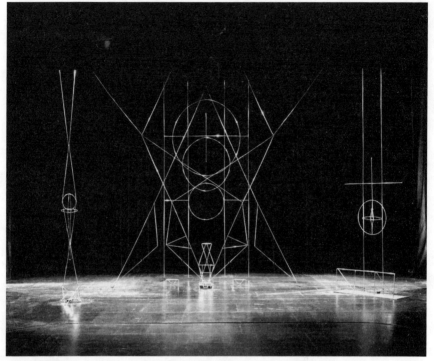

Noguchi's stage set for Martha Graham's *Seraphic Dialogue*, 1955

television program reporting on Palestine and Vietnam. In 1974 she was elected to the House of Councilors (the upper house of the Japanese parliament), serving for three terms (eighteen years), eventually becoming political vice-minister of the Environmental Agency.

Perhaps to salve his sadness over his failed marriage, Noguchi traveled that winter to Japan, Karachi, Pakistan, Kathmandu (Nepal), Calcutta, and Hong Kong. In March 1956 he returned to Japan to work on iron sand castings. He and Yamaguchi met at the inn in Tokyo where Noguchi was staying and divided their collection of Rosanjin's ceramics, a process Noguchi did not necessarily feel was just. Although Yamaguchi had bought the ceramics at kiln openings in order to repay Rosanjin for lending them the farmhouse, he felt that they should be his because he had a much closer relationship with Rosanjin.

"My solace has always been sculpture," Noguchi recalled.[22] So he went to Gifu and made a series of iron and bronze sculptures, inspired by antique Japanese iron pots, a dramatic departure from the ceramics

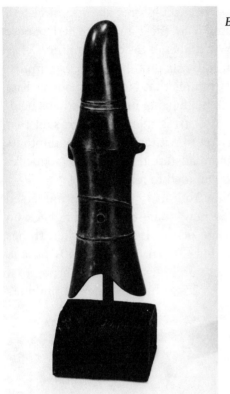

Bell Image, 1956–57. Bronze, ht. 30 in.

The Self, 1956. Iron,
ht. 30 in.

in his Stable Gallery show. But the iron sculptures are not unrelated. *Bell Image*, for example, was inspired by the same ancient Japanese bells that had been the source for a number of his clay sculptures. *The Self*, with its loop of metal embraced by six protuberances, is reminiscent of the miniature clay fertility figures that Noguchi made at Kita Kamakura. The sculpture seems to be hugging itself, or perhaps holding its being together in a time of distress. Noguchi once said that when life became difficult he was apt to withdraw, like a snail into its shell. *The Self* can be seen as a more austere reiteration of Noguchi's 1944–45 *Time Lock*, which clearly alluded to fertility.

When Noguchi returned to New York in June 1956 he immersed himself in various projects—some new, some old. Looking back on this period, he said, "The epic time of the 1950s was when things seemed to happen everywhere at once."[23] In the mid-1950s he collaborated with some young Japanese architects to design a proposal for a monument to commemorate the 2,500th anniversary of Buddha's

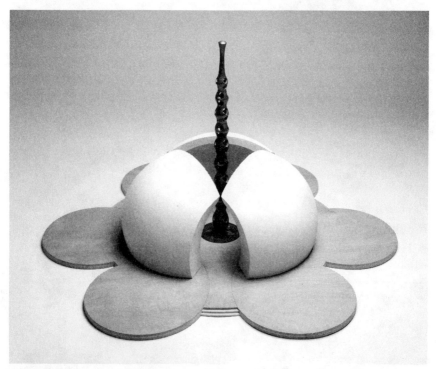

Memorial to Buddha, 1957. Plaster and bronze model, ht. 33 in. Unrealized

entrance into nirvana (in Noguchi's memory it was to commemorate Buddha's birthday).[24] A draft of Noguchi's note submitted with the group's competition entry said that the designers had attempted to present the lotus, the domed stupa, and the ringed spire in modern forms, "making new for us the old, and reminding us that the spirit is (still) paramount."[25] Noguchi's plaster and bronze model and his study drawings show a dome that resembles an eggshell neatly cut into three sections—an abstraction of a lotus flower. In the middle was a spire with nine bulbous sections, in each of which was to be an image of Buddha. The lotus, Noguchi said, alluded to "change and rebirth."[26] His and his collaborators' design won a certificate of commendation, but Nehru and various other government officials felt that most of the proposals were too "grandiose and monumental" and they decided not to build any of the plans submitted.[27]

Another Indian project on Noguchi's mind in 1955 was a sculpture for the new American embassy in New Delhi designed by Edward Durell Stone, an architect with whom Noguchi had collaborated a decade earlier on his unrealized Jefferson Memorial for St. Louis. On April 1, 1955, Noguchi wrote to Stone proposing two large sculptural groupings for the front of Stone's embassy building plus a large circular emblem at the entrance and possibly some sculpture in the interior garden. The studies and scale models would cost $5,000 and the cost of execution, transportation, and erection would be $50,000. On April 21 Stone wrote to Noguchi saying that he'd run into difficulties, but that one piece of sculpture was "in the bag."[28] Negotiations continued for another two years but in the end remained stalled.

Despite what seemed like endless false starts, Noguchi did receive two commissions in October 1955, both of which would be realized. One was from the architectural office of Carson and Lundin for a sculptural wall in the lobby of the new Tishman Building at 666 Fifth Avenue. He was to be paid $2,000 for the preliminary models. If the design was accepted, he would be paid another $3,000 plus $125 per day for any consultations with the firm. Noguchi designed not only a waterfall/wall made of stainless steel fins and contoured glass, but also the floor, which had a geometric pattern reminiscent of the dark bands that edge tatami mats, and the ceiling, which consisted of rows of suspended, curved aluminum louvers coated in white enamel and meant to give the impression of clouds. Between the louvers and behind translucent panels were fluorescent lights. The patterns created by the ceiling louvers and by the waterfall wall fins bring to mind the raked sand patterns in Japanese dry gardens.

The other contract was from Skidmore, Owings and Merrill. Although the Lever House project had not worked out, Noguchi did not hesitate to accept the job: he liked working with Bunshaft. He was asked to create four inner courtyards, an outdoor terrace, and a sculpture for the new Bunshaft-designed headquarters of the Connecticut General Life Insurance Company in Bloomfield, Connecticut, four miles northwest of Hartford. Bunshaft's long, low, open-floored modernist building made of glass and steel was set in a 650-acre office park. Noguchi's interior courtyards meant that most employees would have natural light and a view of open space. As Bunshaft observed, Noguchi's design was made in collaboration with the architecture "so that the

The Family, Connecticut General Life Insurance Company, Bloomfield, Connecticut, 1956–57. Granite

whole thing reads as one total design."[29] Noguchi felt it was his "first perfectly realized garden."[30]

For Connecticut General, Noguchi also created three red granite sculptures, which he said represented a family. The granite required very little carving to suggest a sixteen-foot-high father, a twelve-foot mother, and a six-foot child. Noguchi's family is at once awe-inspiring in its stark primitivism (he saw the three figures as related to Pacific Island totems and to monuments such as Stonehenge) and whimsical in a way that brings to mind the comic imagery of Paul Klee. The rough unpolished surface of the granite is in perfect contrast to Bunshaft's sleek International Style building, and it anticipates Noguchi's late work in which minimal incursions with the chisel allowed stone to speak for itself.

Deciding the location of the three sculptures prompted one of Noguchi and Bunshaft's occasional altercations. The three abstract figures were planned for the terrace, but Bunshaft had misgivings about how they would relate to that space. He therefore arranged for wooden mockups of the figures to be made and had them placed on the terrace to see how they would look. The terrace didn't need sculpture, Bunshaft decided, so they hauled the mockups out to an open space at some distance from the building. "It took all of two hours but it seemed obvious to us that it was the right place to put it. So, in addition to wisdom, there has to be trial and error," Bunshaft recalled.[31] Noguchi wrote in his autobiography: "I chose the site where they are now, away from the buildings, at the last minute after the sculptures were on the way. I do not deny that the results seem to have justified the dispute—which teaches me never to be tied to preconceptions . . ."[32]

35

UNESCO: A SOMEWHAT
JAPANESE GARDEN

In October of 1955 Noguchi was approached by Marcel Breuer, principal architect for the new UNESCO Secretariat Building on the Place de Fontenoy in Paris, about designing a garden for the Delegates' Patio, a small, roughly triangular space between one arm of the Y-shaped concrete Secretariat Building, then under construction, and a cube-shaped office building.[1] Noguchi was always amused that the rationale for offering him the job was that, as the commissioners put it, "from the artistic point of view you are Japanese," and UNESCO wanted an Asian contribution.[2] He was in august company: the other artists invited to contribute were Picasso, Matisse, Miró, Calder, and Henry Moore. The fee was $5,000, but rumor had it that Picasso was paid double. For the next few years, until the new headquarters were inaugurated in 1958, UNESCO was Noguchi's chief focus.

When in 1956 Noguchi went to inspect the Delegates' Patio, he noticed a large sunken space adjacent to it, and he immediately decided that it should become a green garden to offset the pale travertine surfaces of the patio. Calder had originally been assigned this space, but Noguchi made such a good case for putting a garden there that he was given the job.[3] Legend has it that Calder told Noguchi that he would "probably cover the base with powdered sugar and call it Mount Fuji."[4]

Noguchi decided to unite the patio and the garden with a slanting walkway, which he likened to a *hanimichi*, the ramp by which Kabuki actors enter and exit the stage. He also saw the walkway as a veranda, the place where in a Japanese temple you can sit and view the garden

UNESCO garden, with ramp and watercourse leading from the Peace Stone and the Delegates' Patio to lower garden, Paris, 1956–58

below. A visitor descending the walkway is accompanied by the flow of water through a stepped watercourse on one side. The source of this water is a monumental stele or fountain stone on the patio level. Water runs down the stele's face (which is incised with an ideogram for peace), collects in a pool, flows into a trench on one side of the walkway, and empties into a large pool in the lower garden.

For the Delegates' Patio Noguchi designed concrete and stone stools that, in their simplicity, were an homage to the stools Brancusi designed for his 1938 *Table of Silence* at Tirgu-jui in Romania. To define and enliven the patio's space he placed tall semirectangular stones here and there.

By contrast, the lower garden, the so-called Japanese Garden, reveals Noguchi's predilection for biomorphic shapes. Looking down at the garden from above, the shapes of water, grass, gravel, and stone make a patchwork of curving forms whose definition over the years has softened with the growth of numerous trees. In the center of the lower garden, reached by stepping-stones and a bridge, is a raised paved area, which Noguchi said was a kind of piazza to echo the Delegates' Patio. "One arrives on it and departs from it again—with time barriers of stepping stones between—it is a land of voyage, the place for dancing and music . . ."[5]

The lower garden also has a Japanese-style "sacred mountain" (*horai*), upon which Noguchi placed large upright natural rocks and evergreen trees. As the visitor moves along the lower garden's gravel paths, "the vista constantly changes and everything being relative, things suddenly loom up in scale as others diminish. The real purpose of the garden may be the contemplation of the relative in space, time, and life."[6]

The UNESCO project, which Noguchi called "a great job" and "a great lesson," was a major turning point in his career.[7] It drew him closer to Japan and convinced him that his future lay in working with space and stone. About this garden he wrote in his autobiography: "Nothing could have been more opportune or rewarding in showing me the way I must go: toward a deeper knowledge through experience of what makes a garden, above all the relation between sculpture and space which I conceived as a possible solution to the dilemma of sculpture, as it suggested a fresh approach to sculpture as an organic component of our environment."[8]

He realized that he needed to punctuate his garden with stones and to enrich its texture with trees, but the UNESCO garden budget did not include funds for rocks or trees. Noguchi therefore thought of asking the Japanese government for help. UNESCO did not want to approach the Japanese directly, and so Noguchi wrote to Ambassador Toru Hagiwara in Switzerland (who controlled the Japanese contribution to UNESCO), suggesting that the government might assist with the project.[9] Six days later, on January 15, 1957, Hagiwara replied to Noguchi: "I am strongly recommending my government to take up part of your plan as its donation to UNESCO."[10]

Once he felt sure of support from Japan, Noguchi's plans for his lower garden changed to make it more Japanese. He wanted to import stones directly from Japan.[11] Later that month Noguchi was advised to travel to Japan and present his case to government authorities. But Noguchi could not afford to pay for the trip himself and still had no guarantee that he would be paid any fee for the project at all. In February, Noguchi received word that the Committee of Artistic Advisers to UNESCO had reserved $35,000 for the garden and patio plus the agreed-upon $5,000 honorarium for Noguchi. UNESCO could not, however, pay for Noguchi's trip to Japan. With at least some guaranteed funds, Noguchi decided to pay for the trip himself.

On March 9, 1957, while he was briefly in Bombay but on his way to Japan, Noguchi wrote to Ambassador Farugaki, who was posted in Paris, and gave him a summary of the purposes of his UNESCO garden and patio. He said that the Delegates' Patio would be a sort of outside room where the delegates could retire for informal conversation after meetings. He hoped that the space would "evoke a timeless quality, beyond time and beyond passions," thus bringing calm to the delegates so that they could make wiser decisions.[12] The green garden would provide a view for those seated in the patio and would follow the Japanese idea of nature distilled for contemplation.

Noguchi's persistence was rewarded. With the help of people at the Japanese Foreign Ministry, a Committee to Support the Construction of the UNESCO Garden was formed. The Japanese government together with private citizens raised 2,500,000 yen for the project. That April, when Noguchi traveled to Kyoto to look for stones, he was introduced to Mirei Shigemori, a master garden designer whose extraordinarily imaginative and beautiful gardens, such as the one at the Tofuku-ji Temple in Kyoto, combine traditional and contemporary ideas about shape and space. Noguchi called the sixty-two-year-old Shigemori "a man of tea (reflective tastes)" and "of knowledge." Indeed, in 1938 Shigemori had published the twenty-six-volume *Illustrated Book on the History of the Japanese Garden*. To look for stones, Shigemori took Noguchi to a mountain area on the Inland Sea island of Shikoku. Noguchi followed a layout that he had devised in Kenzo Tange's Tokyo office: "There could be no waste . . . no hauling of stones that were not to be specifically useful."[13] Once he had selected the stones, Noguchi returned to Kyoto while his Japanese helpers transported the stones to Tokushima, where in May Noguchi pared

Mirei Shigemori and Noguchi at Tokushima, Shikoku, examining stones for the
UNESCO garden, spring 1957

his cache of eighty stones down to fifty and set them up according to his plan.

In spring 1957 Noguchi traveled to Japan to organize the crating and shipping of the Japanese gift of stones. At a quarry in Okayama that had the pinkish granite called mannari, he selected the fountain stone to be inscribed with the word "peace." He planned to continue on to Paris to work on the garden, but the arrival of letters from various UNESCO officials informed him that the site was not ready for him to start work. Noguchi should, the officials said, postpone his arrival in Paris until the following spring. Stuck in Japan's summer heat, Noguchi was upset.[14] He wanted to be in France when the stones arrived and also wanted to supervise the masonry, foundation work, pool construction, and grading of his garden. "It is my opinion that this garden design is rooted in just those elements which you say [are] to be undertaken without me," he wrote to Hernan Vieco of the Paris office of Breuer, Nervi and Zehrfuss. "Without my supervision of the foundation construction and the placement of the stones I can have no confidence in what the garden will be like." Another problem was that he had already rented a studio in Paris from Pegeen Guggenheim. Who would pay for that? he asked. Yet another worry was that the works for an exhibition he planned to hold in Paris had already been shipped. And in September the Japanese Ministry of Foreign Affairs was sending an expert gardener to Paris to help with the foundation and setting of the stones and with grading. What, Noguchi asked, would happen to this gardener if Noguchi was not there?

He wrote to Breuer reminding him of the huge effort he had made in Japan to obtain the gift of rocks and to organize the shipping so that they would arrive in France in time for him to start work on the garden that summer. Reiterating an idea he had learned from Shigemori, he said that in Japanese gardens it was the invisible part that gave the garden its quality. Although he affirmed that his plans for the garden were accurate, he worried that many aspects of garden construction were subject to unforeseen factors: a garden, he explained, was a work of art which should allow for improvisation. "While I believed myself to be for one season a citizen of Paris, I find myself again isolated and I do not like this."[15]

The forced delay was not just frustrating but hurtful. On July 4 he wrote to Vieco: "Since I am so obviously not wanted there—three

Miyoko Urushibara and Noguchi, 1957

letters and a cable on the subject—I replied to inquiries as to whether I was available for work in Los Angeles, New York and Brazil in the affirmative . . . As a matter of fact I can not understand why there is all the insistence that I should not come there since I am the only one who pays my fare there—or payed my way here [Japan] or payed all the considerable expense I have gone to. So I am forced to the conclusion that I am considered something of a nuisance."[16] Two weeks later he flew to New York.

He soon learned from Vieco that as long as he paid his own way he could come to Paris and begin work on the garden in September. During the intervening weeks in New York, Noguchi took up residence once again in the Great Northern Hotel. At a fireworks display that summer he met twenty-two-year-old Miyoko Urushibara, a young Japanese woman then studying interior design at Pratt. She was sitting behind him and when the fireworks were over she introduced herself, saying how honored she was to meet him. She was elegant and possessed of a beauty tinged with melancholy. Noguchi was entranced. The following day he took her to see his waterfall wall and cloud ceiling at 666 Fifth Avenue. Soon they were seeing each other daily.

In September, when Noguchi was in Paris starting work on the UNESCO garden, he was beset with bureaucratic difficulties. "By the time winter set in, I had managed to get two rocks placed, and realized that French riggers could handle marble statuary but not rocks on a rough terrain."[17] He continued to blame "French inefficiency" for the garden's slow progress throughout the next year.

On September 25 Noguchi wrote Miyoko the first of many love letters: "I'm walking on air having read your letters . . . I am so glad to know that you also want to be together. I thought I was indulging too much in wishful thinking—but love is so strange & wonderful a thing . . . That two people should both love each other at the same time is of course a miracle!"[18] The next month he asked Miyoko to marry him and she accepted. He was, he said, "about 5 ft off the ground! I suddenly lost at least 10 years—which goes to show how with me everything is a matter of the imagination. I had been feeling blue & sort of sick, but the moment I read your letter everything changed—I was all over the place at once and working like mad; but inside I was calm. Now I am happy. This is what you can do for me, give me courage and confidence—I want to be able to do the same for you . . . we will protect each other! You are the only music in my heart."

Noguchi returned to New York and to Miyoko in late November, having worked out the placement of UNESCO's stones. Again staying at the Great Northern, he went to work on Martha Graham's *Clytemnestra*. For this dance he designed a curtain that he said was the golden cloak of Agamemnon and made various lances and a place for Graham to sit, but at this point she wanted props rather than a stage set. Without full control of the aesthetic, Noguchi began to feel that he was not needed.

Noguchi and Miyoko continued to plan their life together, and at some point she must have joined him in Japan, for a photograph shows them with Masatoshi Izumi, who would years later become Noguchi's assistant. But in 1958 Miyoko broke off their engagement. She had been advised by many friends and by her mother that she should not marry until she finished school, and, although she was an independent-minded woman, she acquiesced. His elation was replaced by sadness. As usual work was the cure.

When Noguchi returned to his UNESCO garden, many annoyances were waiting for him. There were delays because of UNESCO's budget concerns, and Noguchi found working with the Japanese gardeners that Shigemori sent that spring difficult. They were trained as traditional gardeners and they did not approve of Noguchi's borrowing from and then transforming the rules of Japanese garden making. There were frequent arguments; the gardeners returned to Japan a month earlier than planned. Furious with Noguchi, one of them told a friend that what was being created was hardly a garden. In October Shigemori sent Noguchi another gardener with even better credentials. Thirty-year-old Touemon Sano had met Noguchi in 1955 when Sano had been asked by the Kyoto prefectural government to help Noguchi. Sano's family had been designing gardens in and around Kyoto for sixteen generations. When he arrived in Paris with gardening tools, dwarf bamboo, maples, camellias, and seventy cherry tree saplings, Noguchi forgot to meet him at the airport. After a taxi ride, Sano found Noguchi in his apartment taking a nap.

It did not set an encouraging tone for the partnership. Noguchi and Sano shared a small apartment at 1 Villa Seurat overlooking the Seine and Notre Dame. Tensions ran high. Of their routine, Sano recalled:

> As soon as we got down to work, the first argument would be over procedure. How the stones and trees should be arranged were issues we battled over for about an hour every morning. Once we had agreed upon the procedure and begun working, all of a sudden, Isamu's eyes glowed and he became full of spirit. There was no chatting and he wouldn't even answer any questions. While sculpting in stone, he took no notice even if his hands were covered with blood. From time to time, he would hold the bow of his spectacles in his mouth and stare at a single point with his arms folded. Nobody could come close to him at such moments. Yet, once work was over and we returned to our lodging for dinner, his eyes resumed an indescribably gentle look. Those blue eyes were full of tenderness and, sometimes, sadness or amiability.[19]

Like the two Japanese gardeners who had left in a huff, Sano was a traditionalist who disagreed with Noguchi's belief that a garden was a modern sculpture. They fought over everything from the placement of stones to the way water flowed and to the shape of the "Sacred Mountain." Noguchi must have followed Sano's advice about the mountain, because he affirmed that it was the most traditional part of the garden. To Sano, even Noguchi's creative process seemed wrong for a garden. Noguchi insisted on placing rocks according to a plan. Sano belived in a more intuitive approach. "A plan on paper never works," he said.[20]

Noguchi came to understand Sano's point of view: "The Japanese garden is made from a collaboration with nature. Man's hands are hidden by time and by the many effects of nature, moss and so forth, so you are hidden. I don't want to be hidden. I want to show. Therefore I am modern."[21] For all that, Noguchi was sufficiently imbued with the Japanese spirit not to want his personality to be too intrusive. He told Katharine Kuh: "The gardens are related to *objet trouvé* in the sense that there must be nothing ostentatious and self-assertive about them. It would do damage to the spirit of the whole for any element to be willfully apparent."[22] In the fall of 1957 he was quoted in *UNESCO House News* as saying his challenge was to contribute to the new headquarters something that would typify the Japanese spirit.[23] But, even though the spirit of the UNESCO garden came from Japan, the composition was, he said, his own.[24] It had "a personal twist," and thus was not a true Japanese garden but rather a "somewhat Japanese garden."[25] He knew it was flawed, but he loved it in part because working on it had, he said, led him "deeper into Japan and into working with stone."[26]

One of Noguchi and Touemon Sano's biggest battles was over shrubs. Sano followed the traditional idea of hide-and-reveal, by which certain aspects of a stroll garden are hidden and then, as the visitor moves, are revealed. He therefore placed shrubs in such a way that they obscured some of the garden's stones. "What are you doing to my sculptures?" Noguchi shouted, kicking one of the offending shrubs.[27] Another time they fought over the setting of the traditional stone lanterns that had been brought from Japan. Sano wanted them to be seen in light filtered through leaves. Noguchi once again kicked at Sano's plantings. In spite of all these conflicts, the two men remained friends.

When UNESCO's headquarters were inaugurated in November 1958, the only positive review was André Chastel's in *The New York*

Times. Noguchi's garden was "correct to the last detail, a chef d'oeuvre," Chastel wrote.[28] Lewis Mumford disparaged both the buildings and Noguchi's garden, which he compared to "a curio snatched by a tourist on his travels, not an integral part of this complex of UNESCO buildings."[29] The Japanese and French response was that the garden was not sufficiently Japanese. In a November 18 letter to a staff member at *Arts and Architecture*, Noguchi wrote, "The critical Press here has been frightening—least harsh perhaps on the garden but the whole project has been thoroughly damned, which it hardly deserves." He said he was leaving for New York to prepare for a show he hoped to hold that spring. "I'm rather pooped with a vacant feeling—oh for some oxygen!"[30]

36

CHANGED VISIONS

After finishing his work for UNESCO in the fall of 1958, Noguchi returned to New York and to the Great Northern Hotel. As always, he experienced a "mixture of elation and depression. Returning I was always struck by the contrasts of America, Japan, and the rest of the world; the difference is materiality . . . I found myself a stranger."[1]

Although he had made several visits to Manhattan during the two years of work on the UNESCO garden, he felt out of touch with the art world. The Abstract Expressionists were still in ascendency, but in 1958 younger artists such as Jasper Johns and Robert Rauschenberg were moving in the direction of Pop Art. A new generation of artists focused on vernacular America and abjured the Abstract Expressionists' striving for the mythic, the primal, and the sublime. Now art was to be cool.

Uncertain about what to focus on next, Noguchi was "seized by a great fear that I had lost touch with reality."[2] He decided to work with sheet aluminum, which seemed appropriate to "the world of the airplane, of speed."[3] The idea of carving in stone, Noguchi's favorite medium, seemed absurd in New York with its glass-and-steel high-rise buildings. And welding pieces of scrap metal together did not appeal to him. If to Noguchi Japan meant connection to the earth, the United States meant responding to technology, about which he was ambivalent. For the moment, however, he chose to immerse himself in this new medium. He set out to create sculptures out of sheet aluminum that suited Manhattan's new architecture. They are, like the work of many younger artists who emerged in the early 1960s, pristine, handsome, and cool.

Noguchi went to see his friend the lighting engineer and manufacturer Edison Price, who had helped him with *Seraphic Dialogue* in 1955 and who worked with all the major architects, including Bunshaft and Buckminster Fuller. Examining the machine tools and sheet metal in Price's factory, Noguchi was excited by the possibility of using such items to make sculpture. "This would bring me in contact with that industrial apparatus which is the real America."[4] Noguchi asked Price if he could use the space after hours. "After some experiments, I asked the Aluminum Company of America to supply me with the necessary sheet aluminum, and, thus armed, set to work."[5]

The architect Shoji Sadao, who had been Buckminster Fuller's assistant, became at this time and for the rest of Noguchi's life Noguchi's most valued helper. Two years earlier they had both been Fuller's guests at an air show in Philadelphia, where they watched one of Fuller's geodesic domes hauled aloft by a helicopter. When Noguchi and Sadao met again at dinner the following week, Noguchi said he thought they could work together in the future. In 1957 Sadao, then in Japan on a Fulbright fellowship, joined Noguchi and Shigemori on Shikoku to watch the setting up of UNESCO's rocks. When Sadao returned to the United States in 1958, Noguchi recommended him to Edison Price, whose firm Sadao joined. Once Noguchi started making aluminum sculptures, he and Sadao would go to Price's workshop every day after closing and on weekends. Noguchi would bring paper models for the sculptures he had in mind. Sadao would draw the piece on graph paper and size it up. "Noguchi was intent on solving problems," Sadao recalls. "Sometimes he'd get frustrated, but usually he was even-tempered. We would work until eleven or so. Then we'd have a simple meal. Noguchi was a frugal guy. We'd go to Horn & Hardart automat, I think on Third and 42nd Street."[6]

When the union workers came into the shop in the morning and saw Noguchi's sculptures, they were amazed at the kind of folds he had been able to make. "By way of self-imposed limitation I insisted on deriving each sculpture from a single sheet of metal—a unity—I thought—was achieved thereby."[7] By folding and puncturing the aluminum he created a sense of depth and volume. The method had much in common with his slotted slab sculptures of the 1940s and

Noguchi in Edison Price's workshop, 1958

with origami. It was as though Noguchi had chosen to explore a mode opposite to that of the gravity-bound rocks half buried in the earth in Zen gardens. Using paper models meant that the sculptures retained a feeling of weightlessness. Noguchi liked to quote the sixteenth-century tea master Sen no Rikyu, saying that in the tea ceremony heavy utensils should be handled as if they were light and light ones as if they were heavy.[8] The apparent lightness of the aluminum sculptures is enhanced by their reflectivity. In this they recall Manhattan's new office buildings with their gleaming glass curtain facades.

Even though Noguchi chose aluminum as a material because he wanted to make sculpture that related to modern urban life, his themes often came from Japanese tradition. One of the strongest aluminum pieces is called Noh Musicians. Another is called Sesshu, after the great fifteenth-century Japanese painter, a reproduction of whose work Noguchi had admired at the home of Hasegawa in 1950. But the aluminum sculptures were also inspired by Picasso's synthetic cubism. Noh Musicians is clearly an homage to Picasso's Three Musicians of 1921, and shares with the Picasso a combination of wit and mystery. The face of the musician on the left is suggested by cutting and folding back the sheet metal so that the light that comes through perforations suggests features. Indeed, many of the aluminum sculptures have a figurative reference. Sesshu, for example, could be an embracing couple.

Looking back on the aluminum sculptures a decade later, Noguchi wrote in his autobiography: "What I wanted was a timely and weightless way of expression . . ."[9] With this group of sculptures Noguchi was, he said, accepting "the present world and its materials as it is, without trying to disguise it. I haven't made it go through an apparent disaster. So much work today has a disaster quality. My work is a kind of nude and frank art, even if it's not always optimistic."[10] At the end of his life Noguchi saw his exploration of metal sculpture as a sidetrack. The aluminum sculptures were, he said, an attempt "to rejoin the modern world, while my main attention was still fixed on finding something beyond."[11]

Noguchi had planned to exhibit the aluminum sculptures at Eleanor Ward's Stable Gallery in 1959. But when Ward saw them she was not impressed. In spite of the fact that various American sculptors were turning to similar materials, Ward said, "You can't make sculpture out of aluminum."[12] She told Noguchi that the pieces looked too commercial and that they would hurt his reputation.

Noh Musicians, 1958. Aluminum and paint, 70¼×39×7¾ in.

Noguchi and Ward decided that instead of the aluminum sculptures he would show the cast iron sculptures that he had made in Japan as well as a group of marble sculptures that he would carve especially for the exhibition. Starting in 1957 he had begun to stop in Greece on his way to and from Japan. "There I found a worker who could block out simple forms in Penteli marble which I could work on later in New York. To have stone cut to approximate dimensions at the source of supply has great advantages. Faults are easily detected, suitability is established, and unwanted pieces discarded prior to shipment."[13] Edison Price gave Noguchi the use of a small room at his factory where Noguchi could use Price's pneumatic tools to carve his marble sculptures. Once again Noguchi demonstrated his propensity for abrupt change in direction. "How quickly do I adapt myself to changed visions. This was

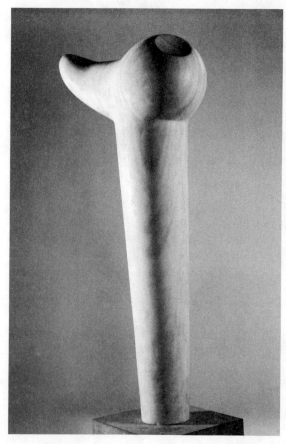

Bird B, 1952–58.
Greek marble,
51½×22¾×13¼ in.

the totally sensuous realm of tactile values. Nothing to do with mindful decisions. I worked in a fury in a cloud of dust and chips, in complete immersion, oblivious to everything but my own confrontation with marble."[14]

From this "cloud" came fourteen sculptures, including *Woman and Child, Recurrent Bird, Bird B,* and *Integral. Woman and Child* is quite recognizable as a Japanese woman wearing an obi and carrying her child tightly swaddled on her back. *Recurrent Bird* consists of a squarish softly curved slab of marble set upright with a protruding hollow cylinder that could be either a bird's beady eye or a beak uttering a song. The stunningly simple *Integral,* an early example of Noguchi's preference not to intrude much on the natural stone, is a fifty-inch-high white marble stele with angular incisions and soft indentations

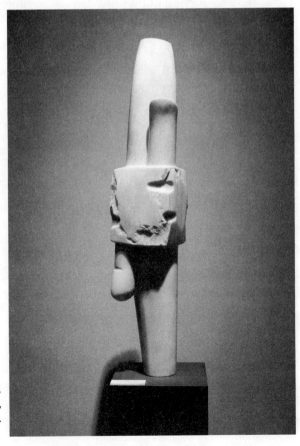

Woman with Child,
1958. Greek marble,
43×9×9¼ in.

that look as if the marble had been worn away by the sea. In several works Noguchi joined his love of Greek sculpture, especially Cycladic, with his devotion to Brancusi. *Idlewild*, or *Bird*, is a tall marble piece that soars like Brancusi's *Bird in Space* and has a swelling chest to put forth its song. It was planned to be a thirty-foot-high sculpture for the International Arrivals Building at Idlewild Airport (later JFK), but the New York Port Authority rejected it. "The exhibition," Noguchi avowed, "was in the nature of a homage to Brancusi, and recapitulated sculptural values I associated with him. Whether it was a victory or defeat, I could not say. I was conscious of having been denied modernity. But then it was also my own volition, and my love and understanding of what was basic to sculpture that led me to do what I did."[15]

The exhibition, which opened at the Stable Gallery in April, received lukewarm reviews. Emily Genauer wrote in *The New York Times* that Noguchi had told her that the sculptures were not abstractions. "They have to do with concepts of peace, stillness, arrival, departure, continuity," she wrote, no doubt paraphrasing what Noguchi

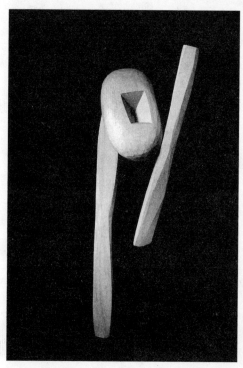

The Cry, 1959. Balsa wood, 86¼×30×20 in. (Courtesy of the Solomon R. Guggenheim Foundation / Art Resource, N.Y.)

had told her. "They are beautiful in surface, most subtly modeled for all their forthrightness of shape."[16] *Art News*'s critic, the painter Fairfield Porter, noted Noguchi's restraint about projecting personal feeling. "Instead of imposing himself, he is a medium for transmitting general identities."[17] In general, to a New York art world focused on the brazen emergence of Pop Art, sculpting in stone seemed old-fashioned.

Noguchi's investigation of lightness in his aluminum sculptures prompted him to work with balsa wood as well. *The Cry* (1959) is made of three carved pieces of balsa, a tall beam for the body, a rough-cut oval that suggests a head, and, attached to it, a long limb set at a dramatic angle. The "head" has a gouged-out hollow—a place for the cry to burst forth. The attached limb of balsa suggests an ear-piercing wail or perhaps a flailing arm. To emphasize its weightlessness, Noguchi raised the sculpture up off the ground on a small steel pole. For the next three years Noguchi continued to explore these balsa wood carvings, producing somber sculptures like *Mortality* in 1959, and *Solitude*, *Victim*, *Soliloquy*, and *Shodo Flowing*, all of which he cast in bronze

Mortality, 1959 (cast 1973).
Balsa wood, 75×20×18 in.

in 1962. In many of these works dangling wooden beams suggest downheartedness. Years later Noguchi said of *Mortality*: "The mortal remains of skin and bone, the tears of things."[18] The sculpture consists of a central upright support surrounded by five long shafts that hang from a lintel to which they were originally attached by twine. One can imagine a doleful clacking together as they swing. Indeed, *Mortality* may have been inspired by old chimes made of dangling sections of metal pipe. *Victim*, Noguchi's largest balsa wood sculpture, suggests a human figure broken in war. "Tragedy," Noguchi wrote of this piece, "is implied by the tension of weight, the tangle of limbs."[19]

When in 1962 he decided to have his balsa pieces cast in bronze, his rationale was that he was interested in making something that was both heavy and light: "Now I wanted the tension of levitation but not weightlessness as such; on the contrary, I wished to stress weight in the elements composing the sculptures, so that their weight would enhance the effect of floating in a gravitational field. It is weight that gives meaning to weightlessness."[20] In the bronze version of *Mortality* the pendant elements look even more dragged down toward the earth. Of this piece he said: "Hanging weight is where bronze functions. Our pendulous and precarious existence is shaped by gravity."[21]

37

PRISCILLA

In July 1959 Noguchi traveled to Italy, where he planned to meet with John Becker, the man who in 1930 had purchased a group of his Paris art school drawings and exhibited them in 1931. Becker had been chosen by Pantheon Books to ghostwrite Noguchi's autobiography. It was in Rome that Noguchi first made contact with Priscilla Morgan, a highly intelligent and charming woman who was to become a central part of his life. A successful agent in charge of television and film rights at William Morris, she was also the American representative at the Spoleto summer arts festival, which had brought her to Rome that summer.

When Priscilla's long friendship with Noguchi began, he was fifty-four and she was thirty-nine. Noguchi left a note at her hotel saying that he wanted her to dine with him three days hence. "Noguchi asked me to leave a note for him at the hotel desk and he would pass by and pick it up at 5:30 a.m. At 5:30 in the morning he called from downstairs. He said he could not read my handwriting: 'Are you going to meet me or not?' he asked."[1]

Born in 1919 in Poughkeepsie, New York, Priscilla was educated at Vassar College, after which she worked in radio and, during World War II, joined the WAVES—the naval corps of Women Accepted for Voluntary Emergency Service. In 1943, working in Washington interviewing returning sailors for the Navy, she met her first husband. After an amicable divorce, she signed on with the prominent Liebling-Wood agency. Television was just becoming a household fixture and her job

Noguchi and Priscilla Morgan, 1967

was to develop a television department. Soon she had her own agency, which the powerful William Morris agency bought in 1955. Noting the brilliance with which she brought people together in such a way that new ideas and artworks emerged, her friend the artist Christo called Priscilla "the great connector."[2] The film director Arthur Penn pointed out that Priscilla had had the insight to bring him together with Warren Beatty, who, a few years later, would star in Penn's *Bonnie and Clyde*. Buckminster Fuller inscribed a book he gave her with the accolade: "The twentieth century's last half's greatest and most affective [*sic*] shepherdess of many of life's most significant creative regenerations."

Priscilla's social circle expanded through her three-year love affair with the affable and cosmopolitan René Bouché, a painter and fashion illustrator. Bouché introduced Priscilla to the artists of the New York School—Willem de Kooning, Mark Rothko, Barnett Newman, and Jack Tworkov—as well as to Richard Lindner, Saul Steinberg, Alexander Calder, and Janice Biala. These new friends gave Priscilla a deep appreciation of the visual arts. She also met people who belonged to an international world of culture—the fashion designer Elsa Schiaparelli, the stage designer and painter Eugene Berman, and the composer Alexei Haieff.

It was in Rome in 1958 that Priscilla met the composer Gian Carlo Menotti, who had just founded the Festival of Two Worlds, an international summer arts festival in Spoleto. Priscilla was so impressed with what he was doing that she left her job at William Morris to become the Spoleto festival's American representative and later associate director. With her infectious enthusiasm and intense commitment to her work, she was able to persuade people like Ezra Pound, Buckminster Fuller, de Kooning, David Smith, and the not-yet-famous composer Philip Glass to come to work at Spoleto. Her firm but genteel insistence usually persuaded people to do what she wanted, and instead of feeling pushed around, she made them feel flattered. Most of the artists that Priscilla engaged became lifelong friends.

A day or so after her exchange of notes with Noguchi, Priscilla called him in Paris to say that she would arrive on July 13 at 5:30 in the afternoon. "Noguchi was waiting for me on the doorstep of the Hotel Vendôme. We went to dinner at Chez Allard at 41 Rue St. André des Arts and after dinner we went to the penthouse apartment overlooking

Ezra Pound, Buckminster Fuller, and Noguchi in Spoleto, 1971

the Seine that had been loaned to him by Alice de Lamar." When they arrived, Noguchi's Japanese friends Mami and Hisao Domoto, both painters living in Paris, were already there. During the evening Priscilla began to suspect that there was something more than friendship between Noguchi and Mami Domoto. "I felt the shadow of another woman was there." But she sensed that the relationship was over.

Noguchi had a bathtub filled with champagne—he had mixed up the date and he thought it was already July 14, Bastille Day. Since Bastille Day wasn't until the next day, Noguchi invited everyone to come back. As Priscilla recalls: "We danced in the streets for several days . . . He was spellbinding to me . . . We had an immediate kinship."

As the years went on Noguchi and Priscilla developed a deep friendship, a partnership that, in its loyalty and mutual understanding, was a kind of marriage, though neither of them wanted an actual marriage. "I was not possessive or clinging," said Priscilla. "I knew he had to have other women. Usually they were Japanese and usually they were married. As long as I knew that I was number one, that was OK with me."

An undated note from Priscilla to Noguchi quotes an Emily Dickinson love poem, which she said expressed what she wanted to say. It begins, "I have no life but this," and ends, "Except through this extent / The Realm of you."[3] Other letters hint at his evasiveness, his need to be free. One note quoted Noguchi telling her that the reason he and Martha Graham got along so well was that they left each other alone. Leaving Noguchi alone was a struggle for Priscilla, a struggle that, with her intelligence and her strong instinct for emotional survival, she mastered most of the time. "We had a close relationship, one of love and great mutual respect. He counted on me. I represented family to him. Noguchi could lose faith in himself very easily. His spirits could go very low very fast. This created a strong bond between us, because I am of a hopeful, cheerful nature."

With her enormous energy, her savoir faire, and her organizational skills, Priscilla was an invaluable help to Noguchi. "I took care of everything that he would want taken care of. I ran everything." She cooked for him, arranged to have his studio cleaned, cared for him when he was sick, gave dinner parties for him to meet potential patrons, helped him with business matters, mediated when Noguchi became testy in contract negotiations, and even picked him up at the airport—in New York City, a true sign of love. "All the energy I had been putting into my writers and actor clients went into Isamu. I tried to make everything smooth for him so that he could go right ahead and do his work."

Not long after their wild Paris encounter, Noguchi and Priscilla saw each other again in New York. He invited her out to a Japanese restaurant and tried to teach her to wield chopsticks. "I was very nervous," she recalls. "He was elegant and flirtatious. He was a seducer and a charmer. I loved watching his . . . brain working." The next day Priscilla invited Noguchi to supper and cooked a steak. "When I asked him, 'Do you carve?' he said, 'Don't you think that's rather insulting?'"

Noguchi's friend Katharine Kuh once described his personality as nomadic, quizzical, and remote, and it was this elusiveness that was a draw for Priscilla. Just as Noguchi felt safer with married women with whom commitment was out of the question, some part of Priscilla enjoyed the excitement of never being able to hold onto Noguchi. Being his companion for the next three decades required a continuous effort of courtship at which she was adept.

Although Noguchi occasionally stayed at Priscilla's garden apartment at 45 East Sixty-first Street, she found him a sublet studio in Sherwood Studios on the southeast corner of Fifty-seventh Street and Sixth Avenue, a building with high ceilings and huge windows that he had lived in earlier in his life. Most evenings Noguchi would turn up at Priscilla's and she would cook for him. He also came to many of her dinner parties. He had, Priscilla notes, a weakness for WASPs and for celebrities, but he was, as Yamaguchi had observed, mercilessly rude if people bored him. He was often irritated by Priscilla's more high-toned social gatherings, feeling perhaps that he, as a bohemian artist, should not indulge in such fancy fare. "I'd put on dinners with important and rich people—ambassadors, social people. Alice [Tully] let me give dinners at her apartment in Hampshire House on Central Park South so that I could raise money for Spoleto." On one such occasion Noguchi picked up Priscilla at Sixty-first Street and together they walked across the southeast corner of Central Park. As they drew near Hampshire House Noguchi became agitated. "I don't know why I'm coming here," he said. "You just want me to meet a rich lady." But when Alice Tully, a woman of great dignity, came to the door, Noguchi was captivated. During dinner Priscilla noticed that Noguchi and Alice were holding hands.

Noguchi did not stay long at Sherwood Studios. He needed more space for the kind of sculptures he wanted to make, so he bought an old carriage house with a back garden in the West Village. "We went to look at it the day he bought it," Priscilla recalls. "Afterward we went to the O. Henry bar [Pete's Tavern] and he had a stiff drink. I talked him out of it." Noguchi realized that the house needed too much work, so he sold it and in 1961 bought a factory building in Long Island City.

The creation of a studio/dwelling at 33-38 Tenth Street in Long Island City, Queens, became for Noguchi a central preoccupation in the early 1960s. To turn the factory into a studio with living quarters he had the help of Yukio Madokoro, a skilled carpenter from Japan, and of a young sculptor named Nobu Shiraishi. "The three of us started in the dead of winter to build within the anonymous space my own environment, free of whatever there was outside."[4] With cement block walls they divided the eighty-by-forty-foot area into three sections: a place to work, a place for storage, and a place to live. Downstairs there was a living room and kitchen with Noguchi-designed tables and a simple foam rubber sofa with bolsters. In the bathroom he installed a traditional Japanese wooden tub. A flight of stairs led to a bedroom that Noguchi arranged in Japanese style with *shoji* screens (fitted with fiberglass instead of paper) and a low bed. At the foot of the stairs was a *tsukubai*, or stone basin, for washing hands, and, level with the floor, a flat stone carved to look like the sole of a foot. This was the designated spot where guests took off their shoes and put on Japanese sandals before mounting the stairs. Noguchi's new space was, he said, "a workshop with living quarter . . . not exactly a home."

In the summer of 1959 Noguchi was asked to design a sculptured entrance plaza for Bunshaft's new First National Bank building in Fort Worth, Texas. In a draft letter of agreement Noguchi said the project would cost between $50,000 and $75,000. His pay would amount to $45,000 plus expenses. Clearly, his fees were increasing: this was nine times as much as he was paid for his UNESCO garden. Early in December Noguchi traveled to Fort Worth to explain his model. Pending budget issues, his proposal was approved and in mid-February 1960 a final agreement was signed.

In the middle of April Noguchi took off for Japan. He stayed at his favorite Tokyo inn (*ryokan*) at 4 Enokizaka, in the Akasaka-Minatoku district. On April 27 he wrote to Bunshaft that he had made a trip to the mountainous area north of Tokyo, where he had found granite suitable for the Fort Worth sculpture. "Coming upon it as if guided by fate I have become so enthusiastic about using it that nothing else will do."[5] The problem, he said, was that the stone was in an inaccessible place in a mountain. "However the granite is IT, so after discussions with representatives of the various types of labor to be employed I have instructed them to proceed with clearing and road building preparatory to getting it out." Noguchi noted that given the October deadline, he would have to work "full speed ahead," his favorite tempo. "Tomorrow I start the enlarged and detailed studies for the refinement of proportions." He sent Bunshaft several samples of stone, including the amazing greenish granite he had just found in the mountains. A few weeks later he wrote Bunshaft that he was carving the granite and expected to return to New York at the end of June.[6] By October he had carved, crated, and shipped the sculptures to Texas. Noguchi left Japan on October 29 and after traveling in India and Europe, he arrived in New York in mid-November. December 29 found him in Fort Worth supervising the installation of the entrance plaza's pair of sculptures.

The "Texas Sculpture," as this project has come to be known, comprises two monumental pieces carved out of the rough gray-green granite he had taken so much trouble to extract. Like primitive totems, they stand guard over the bank's brick-lined entrance plaza. Noguchi saw them as a kind of gateway and as "an energy symbol (money is energy)."[7] Although they are abstract, they allude to the human figure. The front one appears to be reaching upward as if in triumph. The one closer to the bank building reaches straight out as if commanding us to stop. Parts of each sculpture are fluted. Other parts are left rough. Noguchi animated the sculptures by carving a circle in the top part

"Texas Sculpture," First National Bank, Fort Worth, Texas, 1960–61. Tsukuba granite, two elements, ht. 18 ft.

of the up-reaching totem and a square hole in the top part of the out-reaching one. These indentations serve as primitivistic features. The stark, uningratiating stone guardians have a certain macho grace, especially if viewed from an angle at which their projecting elements—their reaching arms—visually join to make one large cactuslike shape, the cactus suggesting Texan values of toughness and endurance.

"1960 was my year of great beginnings," Noguchi said in 1980.[8] Perhaps as a result of the public attention that came with his participation at the Paris UNESCO headquarters, he was, in the early 1960s, swamped with commissions. While at work on the Fort Worth plaza he was approached by Bunshaft about designing a sunken garden for Yale University's Beinecke Rare Book and Manuscript Library. Bunshaft had also talked to him about creating a sunken garden to go in front of his new Chase Manhattan Bank building in downtown Manhattan. The possibility of a sculpture garden in Jerusalem was also under discussion, and in 1961 he completed a fountain for the John Hancock Insurance Company in New Orleans and began designing a playground for Riverside Park in Manhattan, a long collaboration with the architect Louis I. Kahn. The following year he was asked to design two courtyards and a terrace for the IBM Corporation in Armonk, New York. Beyond these commissions, he created sets for Martha Graham's *Acrobats of God* and *Alcestis* (both in 1960) and *Phaedra* (1962). He also invented new Akari lamps and other furnishings, and he worked on his autobiography, sending John Becker tapes of himself reminiscing as well as written notes about his life and work. He traveled often, staying for extended periods in Japan, as well as in Italy, starting in 1962, when he was granted a fellowship at the American Academy in Rome.

After Eleanor Ward refused to show his aluminum sculptures in 1959, Noguchi remained determined to exhibit this body of work. New York's prestigious Knoedler Gallery offered to show them in spring 1961. To get his sculptures ready Noguchi decided to take them to Troy, Ohio, to have them anodized. When Priscilla heard about his plan she said, "If you are driving West, I'm going with you." Noguchi tried to dissuade her but Priscilla could think of nothing better than to accompany the man she loved on a road trip, and eventually persuaded him. Noguchi wrapped his aluminum sculptures carefully and packed them into a rented truck. Priscilla remembers he wore a beret and drove too fast on the Pennsylvania Turnpike. He was not a good driver. A trooper stopped them, but he turned out to be a Nisei, so after a bit of conversation he let Noguchi off with a warning. The next fracas happened when they arrived at the motel where they would spend the night and Noguchi, forgetting that he was driving a truck, drove right into the building's overhang. Priscilla played peacemaker with the angry motel owner.

At the factory in Troy, Priscilla was impressed with the way Noguchi interacted with the workmen: "He knew just how to talk with them. We spent two or three days at the anodizing place, where they made the fronts for cars and refrigerators. Then we drove back." On the return they stopped at Priscilla's Bucks County farm. Because of the truck's height, they could not cross any of Pennsylvania's covered bridges, and the trip took longer than expected. Noguchi was tired and irritable so Priscilla called ahead and asked her housekeeper to put a delicious dinner in the refrigerator and to chill some good wine. But Noguchi was in such a sour mood that when they arrived he went straight to bed.

Despite his effort, the Knoedler Gallery backed out of showing the aluminum sculptures at the last minute. In a rage, he called Priscilla, who set Noguchi up with the codirector of the Cordier-Warren Gallery, Arne Ekstrom, who agreed to give Noguchi an exhibition in mid-May. "Together with fifteen large aluminum sculptures, I included three of balsa wood, and called the exhibition 'Weightlessness' in memory of its initial motivation over three years earlier."[9] In the catalogue, Noguchi said that after using earth and heavy rocks in his UNESCO garden he had a craving for the weightless.[10] Of his move away from the earth-bound, he said: "It's like the continual play in our consciousness—we have the anti-gravitational desire to go to the moon, and yet we want at the same time to stay put . . . Aluminum is a material that has no reputation of age . . . You can gunk it up to look like molten metal but I liked the idea of aluminum as aluminum. I've tried to treat it with respect, as though it were a semi-precious metal."

The Cordier-Warren show sold well, but reviews were mixed. Some critics found the aluminum sculptures cold. In *The New York Times* Stuart Preston commended the "lively and graceful visual experience" that the show offered, but he said, "Anti-humanism triumphs in these semi-geometrical variations on invented shape . . . These new pieces lack the communication with his poetic and mystical searchings elsewhere. In that sense they are less profound."[11] Likewise, Emily Genauer in the *Herald Tribune* found Noguchi's aluminum sculpture "purely formal," "over-stylized," and "unconcerned with any idea or emotion beyond that of weightlessness itself."[12] On a second visit to the gallery she still found the idea of weightlessness "pointless," but she called Noguchi "one of the most gifted and creative sculptors presently working anywhere." In *Art News* Lawrence Campbell described the aluminum sculptures as "lean as harpoons." Volume, he said, emerged from the aluminum sheet "like a dancer in reply to a curtain call."[13] This recognition that the sculptures activated and made tactile the air around them must have pleased Noguchi: finally he was being recognized as a sculptor of space.

38

WORKING WITH NOGUCHI

Installed in his new Long Island City studio in the early 1960s, Noguchi was fired by the idea of creating sculptures that would be "a vital function of our environment." For Yale's Beinecke Library, a rectangular structure with a grid of gray granite framing translucent white marble panels, he proposed a sunken white marble garden with, instead of plants, three marble shapes—a ring, a pyramid, and a cube balanced on one point. The garden feels cerebral, detached from the world, thus suitable to the library site. Its sunken space is framed above by a band of pale granite and below by glass walls that allow library users to look out onto it. Although at first glance the garden's three shapes look precise and geometric, their proportions are slightly off, in keeping with Noguchi's Zen-inspired predilection for asymmetry. He wanted what he called "a non-Euclidian garden concept." Thus, for example, the circle's vertical axis tilts and the hole that gives it a doughnut shape is off center. The pyramid's sides are unequal and the cube is not quite a cube. Noguchi wanted the three shapes to reverberate with energy, to "call to each other."[1] "And pretty soon, there's a kind of hum because of this vibration that is occurring between objects and between the spaces and presently there is a kind of magnetic gyration into which you are then caught."

Beinecke's seemingly pure shapes have a source in the astronomical gardens he had admired in India and in Zen gardens with their white sand cones emerging from a sea of raked white sand. The pattern of curved and straight lines formed by the cracks between the floor's marble sections likewise looks back to raked sand. Inspiration came also from paving patterns Noguchi had seen in Italy. "You can notice," Noguchi said, "that the lines on the marble ground give a kind of perspective, in a sense like the *Frontier* stage set. It opens up. I have often used the ground artificially—that is to say, I think of the ground not just as ground but as a kind of geometry of ground."[2] His garden was an imaginary landscape, "nowhere, yet somehow familiar. Its size is fictive, of infinite space or cloistered containment."[3]

Noguchi waxed poetic about the meaning of the three marble shapes. The pyramid, he said, suggests the earth, the past, and infinity. The cube "signifies chance, like the rolling of dice . . . the cube on its point may be said to contain features of both earthly square and solar radiance." The circle is the sun. "The symbolism of the sun may be interpreted in many ways; it is the coiled magnet, the circle of ever-accelerating force. As energy, it is the source of all life, the life of everyman—expended in so brief a time . . . Looked at in other ways: the circle is zero, the decimal zero, or the zero of nothingness from

Garden for Beinecke Rare Book and Manuscript Library, Yale, 1960–64. Imperial Danby marble (© Ezra Stoller / Esto)

which we come, to which we return. The hole is the abyss, the mirror, or the question mark."[4]

For the Beinecke job Noguchi had the help of a young Texan sculptor named Gene Owens, then head of the art department at Texas Wesleyan College. They had met in 1961 when Noguchi was in Fort Worth working on his sculpture for the First National City Bank building plaza. In August 1962 Owens went to New York to meet with Noguchi, and in the next years he worked with him on six different occasions. The letters Owens wrote to his wife, Loretta, while he was in New York are almost like a diary.[5] The first, written just after he arrived in Manhattan, said that Noguchi's Italian bronzes were about to arrive and would need work. In the meantime he and Noguchi were casting some bronzes at the Modern Foundry and working on the bases for sculptures. Noguchi, he said, would then need help on the Yale job as well as on the playground for Riverside Park. In what is probably his second letter (the letters are often undated), he told his wife that Noguchi had said he enjoyed having him there as a stimulus to work. "I am an audience to him, he said, and you must work for your audience. He said he would slow down once I left but he was going to get the most out of me while I was here. I believe him. But I don't mind it. I wouldn't like it otherwise really . . ."

What must be Owens's third letter, written around March 18, reveals some of the difficulty he experienced in working for Noguchi. "Today went fine I guess, but I am about to go mad . . . Talk about spic and span, boy!" It appears that Noguchi was almost fetishistic about keeping his studio in order. "The chisels were lined up on the shelf," Owens recalls.[6] Once I picked up one of them to use and Noguchi grabbed it. 'Brancusi gave me that one,' he said." During the day, as Noguchi and Owens moved from one sculpture in progress to the next, Noguchi insisted that the tools used on the sculpture they had just set aside be put away, even if they might return to that piece later. Gene reported to Loretta: "A germ hasn't got a chance in that place."

To prepare for a visit from Gordon Bunshaft, Owens made a cast of a small model for Beinecke. In a letter postmarked March 19 Owens told Loretta about a battle that ensued when Bunshaft told Noguchi that he should give Beinecke's sun disk a more elaborate, more baroque shape, and Noguchi refused: "I saw and heard him tangle with an architect from Skidmore Owings and Merrill. Boy it was like a lion

Noguchi and Gene Owens in Noguchi's Long Island City studio, 1960s

and a tiger fighting. The architect told him not to talk to him like he was something from Greenwich. He said one of [Noguchi's] little models looked like a Lifesaver. Isamu gave him hell. They would settle down and then go at it again. There was no place for the sensitive artist in that little transaction. It would have crushed me but not Isamu. He knows he is right."

Noguchi and Owens frequently dined with Priscilla. The first time that Owens met her she gave him the impression of being "obviously very wealthy and important politically." Over the years he came to recognize the strength and complexity of her bond with Noguchi: "Their relationship was strange. I don't know why she put up with it. It was obvious they liked each other. He didn't love her. He thought the world of her. I don't think that he ever had a relationship with a woman as close as his relation to Priscilla . . . Every time I went up there Priscilla was doing something for Noguchi which he wasn't capable of doing for himself."

During his first dinner at Priscilla's, the assembled company talked about collecting and Noguchi said that he didn't see why anyone would want to collect. The idea of possessions appalled him. "You see,"

Noguchi told Owens, "this is why I like to do architectural things; because they are not in anyone's possession really. They belong to the whole public." At this point in their friendship, Owens's impression of Noguchi was that he was "quite a complicated person in a nice way and I want to understand him more. I think there is more wisdom than one is aware of right off. He is certainly a businessman. 60% or more of his day is taken up with letter writing, clients, telephones (he lives on the phone—both phoning and being phoned). Every night is used to politic—but his politicking is a form or serves as his amusement."

At times Owens grew frustrated with Noguchi's stubbornness and his ineptitude with certain technical problems like fabricating a small tool to screw a piece of threaded brass into a recessed area—a task that would have taken Owens ten minutes alone but resulted in days of toil under Noguchi's worried watch. When Noguchi could not solve a problem he would distract himself by making phone calls. "He is the only sculptor I know that builds things with a telephone: *Sculpture By Noguchi*, built with a telephone . . . He has to completely dominate any one around him. I rather suspect that is my purpose." Sometimes the two men would jump into Noguchi's car and seek help from some technically savvy person like Edison Price. In the afternoons, the two would rest and have tea. "At this time Isamu would become very meditative for about ten minutes then pick up the phone and take care of several business calls. Then we would sit and talk and have tea." Often they listened to music.[7]

Noguchi's habit of second-guessing was another irritant. Owens would be drilling a hole and Noguchi would keep interfering and then try to do it himself, do it wrong, and then when Owens pointed out the right way to do it, Noguchi would do it that way and then say that it was his idea. "The point is he personally is never wrong. He has all the confidence in the world." For all his criticisms, Owens admired and loved Noguchi rather as a son loves a difficult father: "He is strong as a horse, stubborn as a mule and has the energy of a 10 year old. He is as good a businessman as you'll find. The best politician I have ever seen and a damned good sculptor."

Owens's next stint with Noguchi was in August 1963, after Noguchi returned from working on commissions in Italy, Israel, and Paris. Again, he found Noguchi almost unbearably stubborn. On August 30 Owens and Noguchi drove up to the IBM site in Armonk, taking with them the model for two terraces that Noguchi had designed. In the next few days they planned to install the stones for the Chase Manhattan Bank's water garden. Owens wrote:

> I swear I don't know if I can take another minute of Mr. Noguchi. Today I started on the plaster for the molds. We had discussed doing them earlier and I had suggested making it in several pieces and then making a mother mold to hold the pieces in place. He said that wouldn't be necessary and was very adamant about it. Well I let it go but this morning he said as though we had never had a previous conversation that it would be best to make a shell to hold the pieces together. After I got the two pieces made and a mother mold to hold them in place he looked at it and said it needed handles. I put the handles on which added about 100# to the weight. He then thought that the middle needed strengthening. He was still uncertain as to it being strong enough when I assured him that he could drive his car over it he seemed satisfied but then when we went to move it it was tremendously heavy and he bitched and complained about it being so heavy he kept saying, 'Oh that's way too heavy. You shouldn't have made it so heavy.' Everybody but that egotistical bastard is wrong.

In the following days Owens and Noguchi put in long hours, working straight through the Labor Day weekend with Owens making molds according to Noguchi's instructions, instructions that Owens often knew were wrong.

Toward the end of his stay in New York, Owens, worn out from hard work, wrote Loretta that he had no news, just "bitching about Isamu and his ego. But really he goes out of his way to get along with me . . ." Owens and Noguchi continued to work together from time to time and they kept in touch over the years. On a trip to New York in February 1965 Owens went out to the Long Island City studio and when he rang the bell he heard a commotion on the other side of the door. Noguchi opened it and said, "I've hurt my foot." While going to the door he had stumbled over an unfinished stone sculpture and broken his fibia at the ankle. Owens drove Noguchi to a doctor. As there was no nurse, the doctor told Owens, "You pull on the foot while I hold the leg." When

Owens heard the bone snap into place he almost passed out, but Noguchi laughed. The doctor put Noguchi's leg in a cast and for the rest of his time in New York Owens became Noguchi's "nurse, chauffeur, assistant, and constant companion."[8] In the evenings Noguchi introduced him to artists, including Claes Oldenburg, George Segal, Ad Reinhardt, Ibram Lassaw, Herbert Ferber, Frederick Kiesler, and Louise Nevelson.

Perhaps it was during this visit that Owens and Noguchi went to a gallery and saw one of Andy Warhol's 1962 paintings of multiple Coke bottles. "Then suddenly Isamu said, 'Gene, we have got to go to the Metropolitan Museum. There's something I want you to see.' The piece in question was a Buddhist shrine made of stone. The inside was lined with hundreds of little Buddhas seated in a meditating position. 'Oh, I see,' I said. 'The Buddhas are like the Coke bottles in Warhol's Coke bottle painting.' Isamu grinned. 'What do you suppose Andy was praying to?' Isamu asked."[9]

39

LEVITATING ROCKS, WINGS OF PRAYER

Gordon Bunshaft's sleek new Chase Manhattan Bank headquarters in Manhattan's financial district was completed in 1961, and in that year Noguchi was commissioned to do a sunken garden in the two-and-a-half-acre plaza in front of it. To contrast with Bunshaft's sixty-story glass-and-aluminum tower, he designed a circular water garden set in a glass-walled well sixteen feet below the plaza's level. Like the Beinecke garden, it is thus visible both from the level of the plaza and from the offices below. Also like Beinecke's garden, it followed the tradition of Zen gardens that were to be contemplated, not entered.

Noguchi said that the patterning of the paving stones that line the pool's floor was inspired by the stylized sea waves in Chinese art. When the pool is drained in the winter, the patterns, which form concentric circles around the seven basalt rocks, resemble the raked sand of Zen gardens. The undulations on the pool's floor were, Noguchi said, like "the wild and surging shell of the sea, and rising out of or floating on it would be the elemental rocks."[1] The pool could also become a fountain with water bubbling or spouting upward.

Some of the seven rocks were pulled out of the bottom of the Uji River near Kyoto and from the banks of the Kamogawa. With their intricate crevices eroded over centuries by the flow of water, they look like philosopher's stones, which ancient Chinese scholars kept in their studies to stimulate meditation. Noguchi called the Chase garden "my Ryoanji." As in that Zen garden, Chase's rocks are like islands in.

Water garden for Chase Manhattan Bank Plaza, New York, 1961–64

But, he explained, this was not really a Japanese garden, because he had used the rocks as elements of a composition, and, unlike the rocks in a Zen garden, which appear embedded in the earth, several of Chase's rocks are poised on top of the ground. "The rocks I found in Japan for this garden contain a levitating as well as a gravitating quality. Some of them will seem to soar, others remain close to the earth."[2] As he watched the rocks being hoisted into place Noguchi described them as seeming to "take off for outer space."[3] "I'm thinking of calling the sculpture 'Exploding Universe.' We live in an expanding universe; we're going to the moon. I've built a moonscape."[4]

While working on the Chase garden from 1961 to 1964, Noguchi had all kinds of ideas about how to enhance its beauty. "We may have some water lilies. I want to drain the place in winter and put in some small trees, maybe. We might have other plantings in the spring and fall. It ought to change with the seasons."[5] Noguchi arranged for carp to swim in his water garden, but the coins that people threw into the pool soon killed them. At the inaugural party on May 6, 1964, the goldfish were still alive and they were mentioned in the speeches, but, as Noguchi wryly noted, his name was not. The speakers were Mayor Robert F. Wagner, Jr.; George Champion, chairman of the bank's board of directors; and David Rockefeller, the bank's president. At lunchtime a huge crowd gathered on the plaza to enjoy band music, tumblers, clowns, and free food and drink. *The New York Times* reported that 20,000 bags of popcorn and 30,000 cups of soda were consumed. The decorations, consisting of 2,000 potted plants that had been destined for a hospital, were carted off by celebrants as souvenirs. The way the Chase Manhattan garden connected to people's lives pleased Noguchi: "Sculpture has been taken off the pedestal—the most artificial restriction ever invented for it."[6]

Noguchi had expected that he would contribute a sculpture to the plaza as well as the water garden. Instead, Bunshaft asked Giacometti to make an enlargement of his *City Square*. Giacometti's response was "*Non, c'est impossible,*" and he died in January 1966 before he could come up with another plan.[7] Noguchi learned that Calder was also being considered for the job. Noguchi wanted to at least be in the running, so he agreed to make ten studies without pay. When they were finished, he invited David Rockefeller and Chase executive John B. McCoy to come to see them. He was, Priscilla recalled, so nervous that his hands shook. When the bankers arrived he argued that since he had been asked to plan the plaza, he should do the sculpture for it, but Rockefeller and McCoy were not convinced. In the end, the bank and Skidmore, Owings and Merrill followed the suggestion of Alfred H. Barr, Jr., director of collections at the Museum of Modern Art, and asked the French painter and sculptor Jean Dubuffet to make a sculpture. Dubuffet's huge and rather silly *Group of Four Trees* was installed in 1972. "The rejection had a profound effect on Noguchi," recalled Priscilla. "When people treated him badly his spirits would fall very low. It was a mixture of rage and sadness."

Late in 1959, when the impresario, songwriter, and Broadway producer Billy Rose approached Noguchi about creating a sculpture garden beside the new National Museum being built in Jerusalem, Noguchi initially turned him down. "I was very hesitant to do anything with Billy because he was a very amusing character, but very unpredictable, and I wasn't about to get abandoned in Israel."[8] But Rose refused to take no for an answer. He told Noguchi that a man who had voluntarily incarcerated himself in a War Relocation Camp could not refuse such a challenge. Noguchi accepted the job because he felt that Jerusalem was "an emotion shared by all of us."[9] "My going to Israel was in a way like going home and seeing people like myself who craved for some reason or other a particular spot on earth to call their own . . . The Jew has always appealed to me as being the endless, continuously expatriated person who really did not belong anywhere. That is the way the artist feels."[10]

By the time the Billy Rose Sculpture Garden was finished in 1965, it was one of the accomplishments of which Noguchi was most proud. At five acres, it was larger than any garden he had designed so far. The idea for a sculpture garden in Jerusalem came about at a party in 1959 when Nahum Goldmann, president of both the World Jewish Congress and the World Zionist Organization, asked Billy Rose to consider donating his collection of some fifty sculptures to the National Museum of Israel. As Rose told the story, he asked Goldmann, "Where will you put it?" and Goldmann replied, "On a hill in the Valley of the Cross in Jerusalem." "You've got yourself a deal," said Rose. "And for good measure I'll build you the garden in which to set up the collection."[11]

In Billy Rose Noguchi met his match in ambition, egotism, and willfulness. Short and plump but with a wonderfully animated face,

Rose was passionate, ebullient, and quick-witted. Their relationship was tumultuous, but they respected each other's intelligence and strength. Noguchi once told a friend, "Billy is shorter than me even in elevator shoes, but he thinks he's bigger."[12] In 1960 Noguchi and Rose traveled to Jerusalem: "January saw us in Israel looking at a rock-strewn hillside where I was told to create a five-acre garden—a challenge indeed!"[13] Noguchi soon left Jerusalem for Haifa to work on a model in the office of the National Museum's designers, Alfred Mansfield and Dora Gad. "Working together and alone, I devised a model showing five curved retaining walls some thirty feet high and over one hundred feet long . . . By curving them both in plan and elevation, and by placing them at different levels, I hoped to create an undulating and walkable landscape, something memorable born out of the adversity of the terrain." Later that year, in an article that he contributed to *Arts and Architecture*, Noguchi wrote that the earth cupped by the retaining walls would be "like great wings" or "like vast ship prows."[14] There would, he said, be no roads or paths, "only free areas of gravel and planting."

Noguchi sits at the construction site of the Billy Rose Sculpture Garden, National Museum, Jerusalem, c. 1965.

The placement of the sculptures themselves would define the space. Once again he wished to create a place for "quiet and contemplation."

When in January Noguchi received a contract drawn up by the America-Israel Cultural Foundation he was wary. Realizing that Billy Rose was more than his equal in powers of negotiation, he went over each of the numbered paragraphs, jotting his reactions in the margins.[15] In answer to a draft of the contract sent to him the following month he wrote: "Responsibility for artistic approval should rest with sculptor and architect mutually and exclusively. Chief architect [Alfred Mansfield] to have final decision." Clearly Noguchi foresaw that Rose would be an interfering patron. He even questioned the name "Billy Rose Sculpture Garden." Why should it bear the patron's name? Years later he told an interviewer that he had demanded a large sum of money for the job "because, I didn't trust him one little bit."[16]

Elaine Rosenfeld, then a thirty-one-year-old employee of the America-Israel Cultural Foundation, managed, with her humor and unflappable charm, to keep the peace between Noguchi and Billy Rose—some of the time. Teddy Kollek, mayor of Jerusalem, called them "two little dictators."[17] If Noguchi was thwarted he would threaten to quit. "I'm going back to New York!" he would shout. One of the scuffles that Noguchi had to deal with was the architect and sculptor Frederick Kiesler's objection to the encroachment of Noguchi's garden upon the area reserved for the Shrine of the Book, a round building with a breast-shaped roof that Kiesler had designed to house the Dead Sea Scrolls. In October 1962 Noguchi altered his design to satisfy Kiesler. "And as with obstruction in general I have used it as a challenge to improve."[18] Most of the obstructions were created by Billy Rose. He and Noguchi argued over things like using basalt on the entrance walls—Rose insisted it would cost too much. Another area of contention was Noguchi's feeling that the museum and the sculpture garden should be integrated and Rose's insistence that they should be separate. In the end, near the museum, Noguchi designed a more structured area with freestanding walls of various geometric shapes in which to place smaller sculptures so that they would not be lost in the garden's sweep of space. Yet another conflict was Noguchi's wish for large concrete plinths, which would not only shape space, but also could serve as bases for sculpture or as benches for foot-weary museum visitors. Rose thought they would cost too much. In the end, the con-

crete bases were poured. They battled as well over Noguchi's wanting
to plant olive trees and Rose's opinion that trees were superfluous.

Although he had an appointment with Rose the next day, in order
to get his thoughts onto paper Noguchi wrote to him on August 8,
1963. The reason for his letter was, he said, "what I fear is a break in
confidence that developed in Israel—where I came to feel that you
thought I was not sufficiently appreciative of the ultimate purpose of
the garden, which is to show sculpture to its best advantage, and that
I was trying to impose elements which were irrelevant, if not a hindrance to its proper viewing."[19] Noguchi wanted, he said, "to enhance
sculptures . . . if the garden is to be a great garden, as it has a good
chance of being, then we must take great care not to willfully make
decisions which we (or others) will later recognize as superficial. According to Katsinzakis* it is God that cries out, not us, in wanting a
thing to happen; and we are but the instrument of his fulfillment." He
went on to explain that sculptures alone could not give the garden
enough spatial definition and that "intermediary elements"—large, flat
bases or plinths, trees, and rocks—were needed to reduce its vast scale.
Without these intermediary elements the sculptures would be like
"lonely sentinels."

Noguchi and Rose had another contretemps as well. Rose was
furious that on December 1, 1964, Noguchi had gone to Israel without his authorization, and he did not want to pay for Noguchi's air-
fare. Because Noguchi had made this trip, he would not have another
trip to Jerusalem financed by Rose until the garden's opening. In a
letter to Hillel Fefferman, the project's principal contractor, Noguchi
expressed his worry that no matter how detailed his instructions and
no matter how clear his blueprints, he needed to be on site to make
decisions.[20]

Having to relinquish so much control infuriated Noguchi. In his
autobiography he blamed the garden's slow progress on Rose's med-
dling: "With all these delays, it was only completed in time for the
opening of the museum in May 1965, after a final desperate five weeks
of activity."[21] Even after the inauguration Noguchi continued to work on
the garden because many details still needed to be resolved. On May 28
he wrote to Teddy Kollek: "As you know, I did my best to have my ideas

* Nikos Kazantzakis, Greek writer, philosopher, and author of *Zorba the Greek*.

prevail against every kind of obstruction. I even got the big bases built and the logic of things finally convinced Billy that Olive trees and rocks were necessary, as well as natural (which he had previously insisted was just my whim)."[22]

The conflict between Noguchi and Rose reignited in June when Rose wrote to Noguchi that he had been overpaid by three thousand dollars. Later that year Noguchi gave Elaine Rosenfeld a cartoonlike drawing inscribed with the words "Souvenir of a struggle." The drawing showed a bird's-eye view of the sculpture garden with two miniature stick figures, one labeled BILLY wielding a stick and the other—Noguchi—running for his life. Rosenfeld, who adored both men, insists that the energy expended in their endless wrangling resulted in a better garden.

Rose died of pneumonia eight months after the garden was finished, but Noguchi's battle did not end there. Rose's foundation refused to pay him for the last five weeks of his work and Noguchi had to hire lawyers to sort this out. He demanded that his name be removed from the north end of the north pavilion, where it had been put without his permission. He had intended, he said, to have his name carved in concrete someplace in the garden, but Rose had forbidden it.[23] Noguchi wrote two essays about the Billy Rose Sculpture Garden. The first, written in the autumn of 1964 when the garden was still in process, began:

> Neva Shaanan—"tranquil habitation" the hill is called. The name is from the Bible. To be asked to make a garden here, near the valley of the Cross, was like entering into the timeless world of antiquity . . . I saw the whole hill as a sort of new Acropolis: the Israel Museum, the Shrine of the Book, together with the adjoining Hebrew University and Knesset. These manifest the spirit of the times as well as the veneration of the State of Israel, for the safekeeping and propagation of that which it values. I wished to make a garden which would be meaningful in this context—both meaningful and memorable . . . Inside the garden the landscape surges and touches the horizon. I wished to retain this dialogue of earth and sky, with no symmetry other than that given by the walls, without any arbitrary paths to break the swell of the earth.[24]

Noguchi's second article, published in *The Jerusalem Post* at the time when the garden opened and in *Arts and Architecture* four months later, was titled "A Garden That Is a Sculpture."[25] He wrote that the garden had meaning even without the addition of the sculptures for which it was intended and that the garden belonged to everybody, not just to Israelis: "We are all Israelis who come here and walk its slopes."

Noguchi had every reason to feel that this garden was one of his most successful works, and he never lost his emotional tie to it. After the garden sustained minimal damage from bombing during the Arab-Israeli War of 1967, he came to make repairs as soon as a cease-fire was called. He visited the garden every few years to consult on changes and on the placement of new sculptures. Looking back two decades later, he reflected with pride, "When I did that garden, many, many people in Israel said I had given them Israel; given Israel a quality . . . a quality of a meaning and continuity."[26]

40

TOWARD AN AUTOBIOGRAPHY

In the summer of 1962, Noguchi was invited to be artist in residence at the American Academy in Rome, where he settled into the life of an expat artist—long walks, good food, forays to Spoleto, where he could stay in Priscilla's apartment overlooking the Duomo. Through Priscilla he met the sculptor Dimitri Hadzi, who admired his work and who introduced him to the foundry he favored. Noguchi was fond of Hadzi, but he liked to tease: "Dimitri, for God's sake! You're a Greek! You've got to carve!" This in spite of the fact that that summer he, like Hadzi, was working in bronze. Hadzi enjoyed the older man's intelligence, but he saw his selfish side: "Isamu Noguchi was a genius at knowing how to use people," he said.[1]

Noguchi's preoccupation with lightness and gravity continued in Rome, where he had his balsa wood sculptures cast in bronze. Venturing into this fine arts material caused him considerable chagrin. Bronze casting went against the "carve direct" imperative instilled in him by Brancusi. He admitted that, aside from his interest in weight and weightlessness, he had another motive for using bronze: his balsa wood pieces did not sell. A sculpture cast in bronze, on the other hand, was "shippable, durable and eminently classifiable as art (saleable). O, painful knowledge! I must reconcile myself to the realities of the art world."[2]

While at the academy, Noguchi began to make sculptures using the floor as a base. He saw the floor as a place or plane that was part of the sculpture as the earth is part of a garden. He had always felt that pedestals removed sculptures from the onlooker. Moreover, he shared

This Earth, This Passage, 1962. Bronze, 4⁷/₈×43³/₄×41¹/₄ in.

the Japanese feeling of respect for the floor not just as something to walk on, but also as a place to sit or to lie down. "Ultimately, the floor as a metaphor for earth is the base beyond all others . . . The floor is our platform of humanity, as the Japanese well know."³

To make *This Earth, This Passage*, he used his feet to model a ring of clay placed on the floor. *Lessons of Musokokushi*, another work in this gravity-bound, primitivistic mode, consists of five rough-textured elements that Noguchi likened to "rocks in some hidden garden in Japan. I was thinking of Muso Kokushi, the legendary master of Zen whose stone arrangements are the most esteemed."⁴ The sensuous contact of clay with the soles of his feet must have felt to Noguchi like some ancient ritual—perhaps stomping on grapes to make wine. It gave him something that he had always longed for—a way of connecting to primal matter, the incontrovertible reality of earth. There was, in addition, the link with his memories of kneading clay with his feet at Kita Kamakura. Making mud-pie-like floor sculptures was perhaps also a way of expiating his guilt over using bronze. Beyond that, the clunky amorphous shapes he created could have been a reaction to the classicism of so much sculpture and architecture that he saw in Rome, or possibly they were a response to critics who found his work too skillful and too elegant. In two other floor pieces from his Roman summer— *Seen and Unseen,* the title taken from one of his father's poems, and *Garden Elements*—volumes resting on the floor bring to mind the half-buried rocks in Zen gardens, which in turn allude to islands emerging from the sea. The more geometric and angular sections of *Floor Frame* look as though they continue beneath the plane of the floor so that in the viewer's imagination the two parts merge into one. In Japan, Noguchi said, rocks planted in the earth "suggest a protuberance from the primordial mass below." The elements of a garden are, in the viewer's imagination, joined beneath the earth. "We are made aware of this 'floating world' through consciousness of sheer invisible mass."[5]

After his summer in Rome, Noguchi began to spend about a month a year working on marble sculptures at Henraux, a company that owned several marble quarries in the area of Querceta, near Pietra Santa and not far from Lucca. The town of Pietra Santa was full of sculptors from all parts of the world who came there to work with stonecutters and bronze-casting foundries. While Noguchi was working on his UNESCO garden, Henry Moore had introduced him to Erminio Cidonio, president of Henraux, which owned the mountain called Altissimo, where Michelangelo had found his marble. Cidonio's goal was to bring modern sculptors such as Jean Arp and Marino Marini to work at Henraux. Noguchi came to love this area, the people he worked with, the machine tools that were available, and the mountain itself. He felt that Michelangelo's spirit permeated the countryside. "How exceptional it is to find a firm dedicated to promoting the modern use of marble."[6]

Noguchi returned to New York in September 1962 to continue his work on his various projects with Bunshaft. He also wanted to move ahead on his autobiography. For this, once again Priscilla Morgan came to the rescue. She recalls that back in September 1959, when Noguchi and Shoji Sadao were helping Fuller set up his exhibition titled *Three Structures by Buckminster Fuller* in the Museum of Modern Art's sculpture garden, Noguchi asked her if she would read the manuscript that John Becker had ghostwritten. Priscilla obliged and decided the manuscript was terrible. "I knew that Isamu was a good writer, because he had given me a book to read in which he'd written the introduction. I told Noguchi, 'I think you should be writing your own autobiography.'" Never one to waste time, Noguchi's response was, "Well, come with me to my publisher on Monday morning." When they met with Pantheon's publishers, Kurt and Helen Wolff, Noguchi urged Priscilla to "tell them what you think." She explained that Noguchi was "a great writer" who should be writing his own book. According to Priscilla, "the Wolffs said they had thought so all along."[7]

From the book's inception in 1959, the collaboration between Becker and Noguchi was fraught. Though Becker professed to be writing in a style suited to Noguchi, the sculptor found little of his own voice reflected in Becker's drafts. Unsurprisingly, Noguchi proved difficult to work with as well. He felt that Becker had misinterpreted his words in the notes and tape recordings that he had provided. Loath to give up control, he sent Becker continuous criticisms and revisions. It was probably in late January 1960 that Becker, tired of the difficult collaboration, told Noguchi to clear any future changes with Pantheon, because "changes will have to be specific and clear and consistent or we'll never get this finished."

Later that year, with the help of an editor recommended by Pantheon, Noguchi rewrote the book as his "own personal story." The book should no longer be considered a collaboration, he told Wolff, and he suggested that a new contract be drawn up giving Becker a smaller percentage of money than originally agreed. He said that he planned to acknowledge Becker's contribution in a foreword. The proposal enraged Becker, who refused to have his name associated with the project and warned that if the text were to be published using one line written by him, he would take legal action.

Priscilla coached Noguchi through months of negotiations with Becker, which led nowhere. Both men refused to back down—Noguchi claiming he had been gravely misunderstood and Becker refusing to be associated with a book he hadn't written. The stalemate eventually led Pantheon's copublisher, the London firm of Percy Lund Humphries, to back out, saying that they sympathized with Becker and would only publish the book that he had written, because publishing Noguchi's revised version would lead to litigation. Pantheon likewise withdrew from the project. The Wolffs were old friends of Becker's, and on March 7, 1960, Helen Wolff wrote to Gerald Gross, an editor in Pantheon's New York office, that "Noguchi's rather ruthless self-assertion brought out Becker's self-assertion, and Pantheon is caught in the squeeze."[8]

Noguchi was shocked when he heard that Lund Humphries was abandoning the book. He wrote to them on April 7, 1960, saying that they were denying him his "basic human right . . . the book is written in the first person and I cannot be made to say things which I do not think and in a way I do not say them." Three days later he wrote to Becker that there had been a mutual misunderstanding of what collaboration meant.[9] He reiterated that he would be happy to collaborate as long as he had the final say about the text. But, he said, given Becker's insistence that his text be published unchanged, his only alternative was to write his own book, deleting Becker's material. Becker should, he said, be compensated for his time and expenses and should have a share of Noguchi's royalties. The next day, April 11, having finished two sets for Martha Graham, Noguchi left for Japan.

In June Priscilla wrote to Noguchi that she had still not heard from Becker. Her hope was to get the rights back and perhaps to find a new writer who would put the text in the third person. She and her lawyer, Robert Montgomery, were talking to possible publishers. Even as she gave Noguchi encouragement, her own mood was sad: "Where," she asked, "are all the simple lovely truths that mean so much and from which all stems. But dearest Isamu, somewhere still you stand as such an extraordinary truth to me."

In the summer of 1962 Priscilla went to London to talk with Thames and Hudson about the possibility of publishing Noguchi's autobiography. Their response was that the text needed shaping and editing and they wanted to find a European copublisher. With this in mind, in late August she went to Amsterdam to meet with the publisher Andreas Landshoff, whose reaction was positive. After several more meetings, she learned that Becker was not eager to continue work on the book. She told Noguchi that she would write Becker "to keep the relationship warm until all is accomplished." Priscilla's four-page single-spaced letter updated Becker on where the book project stood. She said that she hoped that they could "bury the past and start afresh," using the work that both he and Noguchi had done. She said she would "be the go-between and devote my constant time and attention to the interests of a good book." On November 10 she reported to Noguchi that Becker had called and was "warm and cordial" and "pro-Noguchi." Her feeling was that Becker's ego had been injured and that he needed praise (something she was skilled at giving). She ended her letter with "I do love you, Isamu." Two months later he wrote to her: "God Bless you for all your wonderfulness."[10] In the end she persuaded Becker to let Noguchi write his own book.

41

A PRIMER OF SHAPES
AND FUNCTIONS

During the years in which he was battling with John Becker, Noguchi was occupied with several major projects alongside the Chase Manhattan Bank water garden, the Beinecke garden, and the Billy Rose Sculpture Garden. A commission for two interior courtyards and a terrace for the new Bunshaft-designed headquarters of IBM at Armonk, New York, showed Noguchi in a scientific mood. Past and future, science and nature, the earth and the cosmos were his themes. For the courtyard standing for the past and nature, Noguchi combined trees, rocks, and water flowing over stone into a pool. For the north courtyard, where the theme was science and mankind's future, he designed a marble-faced sundial on which he carved figures that represent IBM's business and scientific contributions, a low granite pyramid symbolizing atomic power, and a black dome inscribed with diagrams of "nuclear formations, star galaxies and computer circuitry."[1] A shallow red pool reflected "universes yet to be explored," and a bronze sculpture of two interlocking helixes represented "the code of life."[2]

The project that engaged Noguchi most profoundly had to do with play. In October 1960 Audrey Hess, who a decade earlier had invited Noguchi to design the United Nations playground, asked Noguchi if he would be willing to design a playground for Riverside Park in Manhattan. The playground was to be a memorial for Hess's late aunt, the philanthropist Mrs. Adele Rosenwald Levy, who had helped to found and then headed the Citizens' Committee for Children of New York. This would be Noguchi's fifth project centered on children's play. Part of Noguchi's fascination with playgrounds came from his childhood memory of a forbidding playground on a hill in Japan. He also suggested that his interest in playgrounds came from his "very isolated childhood." A playground was, he said, a place where a child could feel he belonged.[3] For all his cosmopolitan sophistication, Noguchi felt that if an artist stopped being a child, if he lost the child's sense of wonder, he would stop being an artist.[4] He kept a child's tactile relation to the physical world, and he thought of the playground elements as sculptures whose meaning was enhanced by physical contact with the child's body. Noguchi also had a child's ability to reinvent scale—for example, by imagining immense spaces in small areas. Some of the less positive traits of children stayed with him as well: he was prone to tantrums over little things that did not go his way and he was allergic to rejection. Writing about playgrounds in his autobiography, Noguchi suggested that to make a playground he had to think like a child: "I like to think of playgrounds as a primer of shapes and functions; simple, mysterious, and evocative: thus educational. The child's world would be a beginning world, fresh and clear."[5]

When Audrey Hess wrote to Noguchi on October 21, 1960, about the possibility of another playground, Noguchi was hesitant. Four previous playground designs had never been built. "I wasn't going to be bitten again. But upon her insistence, I thought if I had a good architect with me, it might be okay. So I suggested Louis Kahn."[6] In July 1961 Noguchi and Kahn visited the approximately four-and-a-half-acre site overlooking the Hudson River between 101st and 104th Streets. They agreed that they would make a sculptured playground, one that would fit gracefully into the slope of the land.

By August 22 they were able to show sketches to Helen M. Harris, director of United Neighborhood Houses, one of several organizations that supported the project. Helen Harris wrote to Noguchi and Kahn the following day saying that they would be paid ten thousand dollars between them to produce a preliminary plan and a model for the playground. These would then be shown to Newbold Morris, Mayor Wagner, and the fund-raising arm of the Committee for Riverside Park Project (for which Audrey Hess served as chairman). Louis Kahn wrote back accepting the conditions and adding that "I am convinced that he [Noguchi] and I will influence each other in a good way."[7] A few days later Noguchi wrote to Kahn from Tokyo, saying that in his view their

Noguchi and Louis I.
Kahn discussing plans
for a Riverside Park
playground, 1961

chief areas of collaboration were the nursery building and the music
shell. He presumed that his responsibility was "more the form" and
Kahn's "more the structure," and that he would be responsible for "the
general play landscape."

For the next four years Noguchi and Kahn worked together, in-
venting five different designs as they tried to accommodate recom-
mendations and objections from the city Parks Department and other
organizations.[8] They planned a highly unconventional playground, one
which included a cup-shaped nursery building, a fountain and wading
pool, a play mountain with steps, a giant slide built into mounded-up
earth, a large sandbox, a band shell for music and puppet shows, and a
number of play objects made of colored concrete. Their models resemble tabletop landscapes: mounds that look as if the earth had erupted
into small volcanoes contrast with triangles and flights of steps that
seem to unite all the parts together. When the proposal for the second
version was presented to the Parks Department on January 12, 1962,
the reaction was critical. Newbold Morris, New York City's Commissioner of Parks, felt that the project was too expensive, "too grandiose,"

and useful "primarily to one comparatively small group in a local community." Noguchi and Kahn had, he said, "permitted their talented imaginations to soar with the result that we were presented with the design for an unjustifiable architectural monument." It was honest feedback, but in the following months assurance from Mayor Wagner—who was enthusiastic about the project—that the cost of the project would be shared by the Adele Levy Memorial Committee convinced Morris to make more budget concessions.

By September 1962 Noguchi and Kahn had established a service contract with the Parks Department with preliminary plans due in April 1963 and final construction plans due by November 1, 1963. When Gene Owens, who had been helping Noguchi with the Beinecke Library garden, was about to return to Texas in September 1963, Noguchi asked him if he could stay to work on a new Riverside Park playground model to show to Audrey Hess, who, Owens's letters reveal, had been unimpressed with an earlier model. "He is giving me complete control of it . . . I could turn cartwheels." During the five years of designing and redesigning the playground, Noguchi was constantly packing a new model into his Volkswagen hatchback and driving it to Philadelphia to show it to Kahn, then returning to his Long Island City studio to make more changes.

In December Noguchi and Kahn came up with a third plan that further reduced the size of their playground, which now included three mounds: a conical play mountain with a slide and pool, an amphitheater, and a pyramid with tunnels to crawl through. As published in the March 1964 issue of *Progressive Architecture*, the plans look like some ancient archaeological site—a mixture of Oaxaca's Monte Albán, Egypt's Giza, and Peru's Machu Picchu. The fourth version modified the amphitheater, and a fifth scheme further simplified the design. Final cost estimates made in 1966 were based on a sixth version that they came up with late in 1964. Toward the end of their work on the playground Noguchi became unhappy because the architecture dominated the play area.[9] On June 21, 1966, he wrote to Gene Owens: "I'm fed up myself—mostly because I feel the design has become unbalanced by Kahn's changing the scale of his fenestration and introducing a huge wall and architectural element while I was last in Japan. Seems there is nothing I can do about it because that's the way it went to bid. So I say shit!!"[10]

On October 2, 1963, the press reported that opponents of the

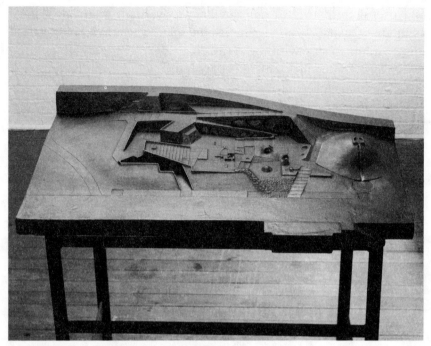

Final model for Riverside Park playground, 1964

playground had picketed the homes of Audrey Hess and her aunt, Marion Rosenwald Ascoli (Mrs. Max Ascoli), both of whom were financial backers. The opponents, who organized themselves into a group called the Riverside Parks and Playgrounds Committee, felt the area of the park chosen for the playground should remain in its natural state. They were horrified by what they assumed would be huge concrete structures intruding on parkland. At one meeting Kahn explained that the playground, with its grass-covered nursery building wedged into the hill and invisible from Riverside Drive, was not being imposed upon the park; rather, "it was inspired by the contours of the land. It is a play of contours in which there is lodged a building."[11] Proponents of the playground set up a table on Broadway manned by volunteers giving out information about the playground. A sound truck toured the neighborhood informing residents about what an asset the playground would be.

Early in February 1964 Noguchi and Kahn presented their plan to the neighborhood residents at a community meeting at PS 145 on West

105th Street. Mrs. Ascoli, Noguchi, and Kahn addressed an audience of three or four hundred people. Other speakers included Newbold Morris and Edward R. Dudley, president of the borough of Manhattan. After the speeches, when the meeting was opened to questions from the floor, the opposition was vocal. But to Noguchi and Kahn the playground was "a fanciful wonderland of mountains and lakes and trees."[12] Noguchi told a reporter: "Playgrounds haven't changed since the invention of the swing and the sandbox. This one will free the child's imagination to create his own games . . ." Kahn added, "We're really boys ourselves. I mean we both still read 'Knights of the Roundtable.'"[13] Finally, after another year of negotiations and redesigns to accommodate size and cost considerations, Mayor Wagner signed the contract for the playground's construction at a City Hall ceremony on December 29, 1965.

Just before the signing, the parks commissioner–designate, Thomas P. F. Hoving, tried to obtain a court order to postpone the signing and to block the project. But the signing took place and Mayor Wagner and Newbold Morris announced that construction would begin immediately. Early in January Noguchi met with Hoving and followed up with a letter saying that he and Kahn wanted to improve rather than impair the character of the park, and that they both knew "the sculptural art of how to make buildings disappear." In a congested city like New York, parks were needed to "alleviate the turmoil in the streets." The word "playground," he said, might be a misnomer. "Play Entry" or "Play Center" might be more appropriate.

There were court hearings, construction was put on hold, and the battle of those for and against the playground continued. On May 31 the newly elected mayor, John V. Lindsay, wrote to the Adele R. Levy Park Committee saying that although he and Hoving disagreed with the location of the playground on park land, the project had already been moved so far through the pipeline that the new administration would allow it to be built and the city would readvertise for bids. But, he demurred, construction could not begin until all the legal issues had been resolved.

Toward the end of September the Adele R. Levy Park Committee learned that another $73,665 was needed before the city could enter into contract with builders. The committee was willing to come up with the additional money, but two days later it was informed by the Parks Department that the city needed an additional contribution of $140,000.

The committee decided that under the present administration the playground could not be built. Audrey Hess broke the news of the project's collapse to Noguchi on October 20: "I am sorrier than you will ever know that we were unable to achieve our objectives in Riverside Park and feel that the City of New York has lost a unique, magnificent opportunity." Hoving apparently called Noguchi and asked him to come to the Parks Department in order to tell him in person that the project was dead. He explained that he had been forced to honor a campaign promise made by Lindsay. Noguchi believed that the opposition to the Riverside Park playground had been motivated by privileged local residents' fear that the playground would draw an "invasion of their quiet park by rowdy Negroes and Puerto Ricans from the slums a few blocks east."[14]

Noguchi's anger at the rejection was acute. When in March 1967 Jean Lipman, editor of *Art in America*, wrote to him that they were doing a special fall issue on playgrounds and would like to include the Riverside Park project, Noguchi agreed to have the playground included when he learned that it would be featured. Jay Jacobs wrote a short essay that included three illustrations of the proposed Riverside Park playground.[15] He observed that, whereas in Japan Noguchi had recently finished a playground called Kodo No Kuni, in his own country Noguchi as a playground designer was "a prophet without honor."

In an essay on the Noguchi-Kahn collaboration, Noguchi's friend the architect Arata Isozaki noted, "That sparks flew between them should be expected."[16] Isozaki quoted Kahn's sanguine view of the collaboration: "I did not speak in terms of architecture. He did not speak in terms of sculpture. Both of us felt the building as contours; not one contour but an interplay of contours so folding and harboring as to make, by such a desire, no claim to architecture, no claim to sculpture." In his autobiography Noguchi had an equally rosy take on their work together: "There could not have been a more devoted and interested collaborator than Louis I. Kahn. A philosopher among architects, I came to feel that each meeting was an enrichment and education for me, and that I should not mind how long it took or how many models I had to make . . ."[17]

Noguchi's fondness and respect for Kahn never abated. In 1974, seven years after the architect died, he offered to make a sculpture in Kahn's memory as a gift to the Kahn-designed Kimbell Art Museum

Constellation for Louis Kahn, 1982. Basalt, four elements, 100×100 ft. (Courtesy of the Kimbell Art Museum, Fort Worth, Texas. Photograph by Veronique Ha-Van)

in Fort Worth, Texas. In a large, enclosed courtyard behind the barrel-vaulted museum, Noguchi created *Constellation for Louis Kahn,* a Ryoanji-like rock garden consisting of four boulders—one upright, one horizontal, and two roughly cubic. The way the stones sit far apart in the grass conveys a mood of loneliness. But the installation of this constellation was anything but bleak. David Hickey, the art editor for the *Fort Worth Star-Telegram,* watched the octogenarian Noguchi, "wound tight as a steel spring, supervising the flying of the last and largest piece of basalt, poised in an almost prayer-like attitude of complete attention—watching the heavy stone, strapped to the crane-hook, come floating toward him out of the sky."[18]

42

THE WHEAT ITSELF

During the five-year period in which Noguchi worked on the River-side Park playground and other large public projects, he also made individual sculptures, and he designed his last two sets for Martha Graham (*Circe*, 1963, and *Cortege of Eagles*, 1966). As always, he traveled a lot, mostly to Japan, Jerusalem, and Italy. In 1965 and 1966, hoping to design a memorial to Jawaharlal Nehru, who had died in 1964, he went to India. He had learned that a forest to honor Nehru was planned for the treeless banks of the Jumna River, and he wanted to make a white, marble, flower-shaped (or possibly circular) platform on a slight rise in the midst of the trees. He explained his concept to Nehru's daughter Indira Gandhi, who in January had become India's prime minister. As with his Gandhi memorial, nothing came of it.

Noguchi exhibited at the Cordier & Ekstrom Gallery at 978 Madison Avenue in 1963 and 1965. The 1963 show included a group of the bronze casts of balsa wood sculptures plus some bronze casts from the clay pieces he had molded with his bare feet on the floor of his studio in Rome. Since for Noguchi sculpture was giving form to space, he cared about how his sculptures were displayed. Gene Owens, who helped install the exhibition, recalled: "I was struck by the way Noguchi tried to control every detail of the show . . . Hours were spent adjusting the lights; we changed the size of bulbs; we substituted spots for floods, moved them here and there until the shadows were just right, only to scrap everything and start over. We moved and shifted pieces until the gallery director, Arne Ekstrom, fled." Noguchi would have liked to change the floor coverings, maybe even repaint the gallery. The bases for the sculptures were a particular concern. A base, Noguchi said, "tends to remove sculpture from man's own proportion and contact. It supplies a fictional horizon. This is the chief reason why I have attempted an integration of sculpture and base; bases that bite into the sculpture, sculpture that rises from the earth."[1] "As we were leaving the Gallery rather late one evening," wrote Owens, "I began to tease Noguchi. I said the elevator, which opened into the gallery was unappealing. The carpet needed to match that in the gallery . . . The game went on until all of New York was made over to fit the show."[2]

On April 2, 1963, the day of Noguchi's opening, Gene Owens wrote to Loretta that Noguchi had met with various newspaper critics at the gallery that morning. "It was a blow to his ego." The critics did not like the work. Visiting the show a few days later, Owens learned more about the machinations of the New York art world. "There was this very continental rich couple in the gallery fixing to buy one of Noguchi's pieces," he told Loretta. "They were undecided but Ekstrom and Noguchi handled them beautifully . . . made it appear that throngs of people were wanting to buy it. They mentioned one name in particular who was a big shot at the Museum of Modern Art. After the people left Noguchi kept quiet about the business end as usual but Ekstrom blabbed on. Evidently he didn't know that I knew what he was talking about but I did." Owens was shocked that museum curators and directors served as advisers to collectors and took 10 percent of the purchase price. The morning when Noguchi and Owens dismantled Noguchi's show, from which only four or five works had been sold, Noguchi was, Owens said, exhausted and "in a foul mood. He tangled in a very loud way with the movers and he and I almost came to blows a couple of times as did he and Ekstrom. The world revolves around Noguchi so he thinks . . . Noguchi ruined the base on one of his sculptures this morning and he tried to blame it on everyone within earshot. Ekstrom calmly asked him with a deadpan expression who was responsible; Noguchi hesitated a moment and said, 'I am god damn it.' Ekstrom without changing his expression, said 'Oh I see,' and walked away very continentally . . ." Owens surmised that Noguchi's sour mood was caused by worry: "I rather suspect it was his love life but he has so many things going it could be anything." When they returned to the studio there were tulips on the table. "Flowers appear mysteriously every so often," he noted. They were probably from Priscilla.

Noguchi's spring 1965 exhibition at Cordier & Ekstrom was his first showing of stone sculpture since the Stable exhibition. Among the sculptures carved in Japan were two versions of *Variations on a Millstone* (one in marble and one in granite), *Black Sun*, and two cube-shaped sculptures. All of these were derived from the Beinecke garden sculptures, and all were imbued with his unfolding passion for Japanese stone. *Jomon* (1963), a primitivistic fertility figure, was made out of the pinkish mannari granite that Noguchi had discovered in Okayama while looking for stone for his UNESCO garden. His growing interest in the roughness of broken stone appeared in *The Mountain*, a sensuous, two-lobed hillock made of red Persian travertine. After giving this sculpture its shape he covered its surface with small indentations made by the chisel.

Noguchi's interest in suspension manifested itself again in the *Gift* from 1964, which comprised twelve abutted sections cut from one chunk of black African marble whose centers he drilled so that the sections could be wired together and then suspended across two brick-shaped pieces of marble. "They exemplify my continuing preoccupation with balanced stress . . . ," he explained, "[the] visual anguish of the crushing weight of stone on the thin edge of gravity."[3] *Gift* is one of the first examples of Noguchi's creating a sculpture by joining pieces of stone with wire or a rod strung through their core, a technique he called "post-tensioning" and that he would use in the late 1960s and early 1970s to make sculptures that combined different colors and textures of marble or granite. "I am an inveterate experimenter," Noguchi wrote in 1987. "My whole involvement with stone might be said to be facets of one search, a mad chase within a single medium to find and overcome its further frontiers of possibility, which continually recede. A case in point is *Gift*."[4]

When Vivien Raynor reviewed Noguchi's 1965 show at Cordier & Ekstrom in *Arts*, she admired the work but with a caveat: "The viewer may be repelled by the apparent lack of warmth in his work, and could question how much of the perfection is produced by the machine, how much by the sculptor."[5] It is curious that she was put off by the machine precision of Noguchi's sculpture in this moment when Minimalism and Pop Art devalued art that showed the touch of the artist's

Gift, 1964. African marble, 11⅝×38⅝×12⅝ in.

hand. In spite of her ambivalence, she concluded, "This is really good stuff." Indeed, for all the perfection of some of his surfaces, and in spite of the fact that Noguchi sometimes made a small model and had assistants using machine tools block out a sculpture on a larger scale, he finished the work himself. Remembering this exhibition in his autobiography, Noguchi said that what he had wanted to do was to treat stone as if it were a "newly discovered medium . . . The execution[s] of all of these were an intimate involvement between myself, the selection of stone, the definition of what to do, and the employment of tools and willing collaborators, wherever I might be. My manner of work is extremely varied. The best is to find a stone and work directly into it."[6]

In the second half of the 1960s Noguchi had four exhibitions, three at Cordier & Ekstrom (1967, 1968, and 1969) and one in 1968 at the Whitney Museum of American Art. The 1967 Cordier & Ekstrom show of twenty small-scale stone sculptures received a glowing review in

The New York Times from Hilton Kramer, who extolled Noguchi's technical mastery and his work's "gemlike strength." The stone pieces were, Kramer said, "pure in feeling, unassertive in their imagery, yet marvelously decisive in the boundaries they observe. This is sculpture that seems to generate an atmosphere of enviable calm."[7] Allergic to trendiness, Kramer admired Noguchi's adherence to an older tradition of beauty and his "unblushing disregard for the esthetic ideologues of the moment." The following spring Ekstrom showed Noguchi's Chinese ink brush drawings from 1930, and in December he presented *Shapes of Light*, a show of Noguchi's new Akari designs offered as sculptural multiples in signed editions of ten. Noguchi concluded the text he wrote for the exhibition's press release by saying: "I believe in the possibilities of art designed for multiple production (not reproduction). Art is art whatever it is called."[8]

Akari was the perfect expression of Noguchi's idea that art could be a useful part of daily life. Starting in 1953 his Akari had been selling at Bonniers, a modern furnishings store on Madison Avenue, and, starting in 1954, they were distributed in Europe through Wohnbedarf AG in Zurich. His constant redesigning made it difficult for stores to sell Akari. He made his lanterns asymmetrical, thus almost impossible to copy, and he sometimes eliminated the bamboo ribs. The *Shapes of Light* exhibition prompted a *New York Times* critic to say that although Akari had been original when he first invented them, they were now a "cliché of modern design."[9] Yet Noguchi, the reviewer said, had rescued them from the banality of the many imitations, and his new lantern designs were "extremely beautiful . . . subtle and elegant."

After the Akari exhibition, Noguchi came to feel that the popularity of his paper lanterns was diminishing his reputation as a sculptor. He decided to cancel an exhibition of Akari planned for spring 1969 at Bloomingdale's department store; however, Priscilla, who with Shoji Sadao was in charge of Akari Associates, which handled Akari's merchandising, must have prevailed, for Noguchi's Bloomingdale's Akari show opened in April 1970. Priscilla told Noguchi that Bloomingdale's was "great," for it was reordering Akari and building a permanent Akari exhibit.

In discussing Akari with Noguchi, Priscilla always tried to be upbeat, even as the financial downturn of the early 1970s began to hurt sales. "There is a new world coming up in the 70's," she wrote, "and Akari is part of what it is."[10] Nonetheless, Noguchi was irked about losing money. In 1971 he told Priscilla that he was not prepared to subsidize Akari Associates, and he suggested that Bonniers could work directly with Ozeki. "As you know," Noguchi's letter went on, "I am always the pessimist and you the optimist . . . Perhaps you will write me that everything is really rosy, big department store sales which will make a loss in selling to Bonniers mean nothing. I hope so . . . I myself am in one of my periods of deep depression. Well cheer up. Things have got to get better." When Bonniers decided to phase out Akari, Noguchi was hurt and angry. "It was too hard for him," Priscilla recalls. "Bonniers' rejection was like stabbing his child. He wanted to give up." Noguchi's emotional attachment to Akari had, according to legend, something to do with his childhood memory of his father placing a light on the far side of a paper *shoji* screen when Noguchi didn't want to go to bed unless he could see the moon. Bruce Altshuler, former director of the Noguchi Museum, suggested that Noguchi's tie to Akari might be that he was trying to "heal psychic wounds" by connecting with "the land of the father who had spurned him."[11]

In a January 1968 lecture at the Detroit Institute of Arts, Noguchi once again defended the artistic value of his lantern and furniture designs: "I see no difference in designing a piece of furniture or a piece of sculpture. Each is as valid. But if you think making money taints art, I make more on my sculpture than on my furniture designs."[12] His defensiveness about his involvement with commercial design was prompted in part by the many people in the art world who began to see him as a designer and not as an artist. A Detroit newspaper reporter who heard Noguchi's lecture said that Noguchi was not a polished lecturer: at one point he announced to his audience, "Bad luck for you if you expected a good speaker." But, the reporter said, Noguchi's "fine brain and human warmth" made up for his long pauses, frequent "a-a-a-a's," and unfinished sentences.

Noguchi's first full-scale retrospective in the United States opened at the Whitney Museum on April 17, 1968, and closed two months later. Curated by John Gordon in consultation with Noguchi, it included sixty-eight sculptures ranging in date from 1928 to 1968, eight objects from his dance sets, and four photographs of his UNESCO, Beinecke, Chase Manhattan, and Billy Rose gardens. All but two of the recent sculptures were carved in stone. A number of the sculptures in the show—for example, *To Darkness, Red Untitled,* and *Hakuin* (all 1965–66), and *Euripedes, The Roar,* and *Green Essence* (all 1966)—further demonstrate Noguchi's interest in the contrast between rough and polished stone. Of *Green Essence* Noguchi said: "This is an early precursor of much of my later work where I attempt to respect nature, adding only my own rawness."[13] In some sculptures such as *The Sun* (1966), he used his chisel to pit part of the surface and he polished the remainder. Other pieces, like *Eros* (1966) and *Sky Frame* (1966), both carved out of pink marble, were highly polished all over. Also included in the Whitney show were sculptures that combined metal and stone and in which the base was part of the sculpture. *Fudo* (1966–67), for example, has a pink mannari granite shape slotted over a stainless steel support. *Fudo's* mix of Japanese stone carved in Japan and steel fabricated in New York reminded Noguchi of his own mixed culture. But, he said, "the conception is as indivisible as I am."[14]

Perhaps the most magnificent of the sculptures in the Whitney show were *Euripedes* and *The Roar,* two monumental works carved from Altissimo marble at Henraux in 1966. *Euripedes* is composed of two parts, both hollowed out to create a feeling of mass without weight. He said that the carving of this sculpture was a challenge "to understand the stone and discover its being . . . to thus eat the stone and know its flavor. *Euripedes* must have been the first of my large efforts in this direction."[15] Indeed, at eighty-two and a half inches high it predicts the great dolmenlike basalt sculptures of Noguchi's last years. It also harks back to the rough and smooth fountain stone at UNESCO headquarters. Noguchi remembered that when he carved *The Roar* he had not wanted to use an already quarried stone. He preferred, he said, "to go up to Altissimo, where Michelangelo had gotten his marble, to find something suitable. This shattered rock was carried down to Querceta, where I then proceeded to meet its challenge."[16] The drill marks, evidence of the wresting of the stone from the mountain, are still there, and much of the sculpture's shape was given by the shattering. Noguchi left part of the stone rough and part he made smooth so that the sculpture seems to belong as much to the mountain as to art. Its form is heroic, its gesture human. *The Roar* inspires awe—a feeling of

The Roar, 1966. White Arni marble, 51⅞×91×24⅛ in.

primal connection that one might have upon hearing a full-throated lion roar. The sculpture's forward thrust is full of animal energy combined with elegiac grace. Like many of Noguchi's sculptures, it has an anthropomorphic reference: the thrust of mass into space seems particularly male.

Noguchi told *Newsweek's* art critic David L. Shirey that his Whitney show was only a "partial retrospective since it doesn't include my industrial designs. I consider them art too."[17] While his exhibition was on, Noguchi was interviewed by his friend the Japanese sculptor and critic Tatsuo Kondo, who was then living in New York and who occasionally served as Noguchi's assistant.[18] Noguchi spoke freely to Kondo about his recent work and his artistic development. "Stone is used simply as stone in recent work," he said. He took himself to task for the perfection of some of his works. Finish, he told Kondo, was not important. "Simply I keep working on it unconsciously. It may be a bad habit . . . it is not my intention to make them neat. Simply I cannot stop myself until I keep on working up to a certain point."

He told Kondo that while his work was diverse, "you will find that there is only one person. I feel that one can see my point [of view] in this exhibition. It is a merit that I am not dependent on style . . . I believe that each work is complete in itself. I don't think it is necessary that one work is related to the other. Rather, I want to start anew on each work. If he is really creative whatever he may do, the finished work would appear newly born with no past nor life history in front of it . . . well, one cannot go so far. But I believe that one should strive toward it."

In speaking about his relation to his contemporaries, Noguchi always called himself a loner: "I am not very community-minded," he told Kondo. His main problem, he said years later, was that since childhood there was a "lack of communication, a lack of real intimacy between myself and my surroundings."[19] Because of his mixed blood, he said, "I am always nowhere."[20] "I tend to do something opposite to what others are doing . . . Well, I am always escaping."[21] Even as Noguchi held himself aloof from people, he said that he wanted his art to "participate in society." He differentiated his art from that of his Expressionist colleagues. He said he aimed for meaning that went beyond his own emotions. He wanted, he said, to help people, not just to satisfy his own ego. Artists should "use their ego to achieve something [more] important than ego . . . I wish that everyone becomes [an] artist and becomes free."

In his *New York Times* review of the Whitney exhibition, Hilton Kramer was both praising and belittling. On the positive side he wrote, "Noguchi must be considered one of the most important of those modern sculptors who have upheld the purity of carving as the essential task of their art."[22] He spoke of Noguchi's "superlative craft . . . grace and tact . . . amazing subtleties . . . and brilliant simplicities." In his opinion Noguchi's sculptures of the last decade were his best. But in the end Kramer felt "depressed" by the show because he felt that its beauty and refinement "generate so little power." Noguchi's Japanese reticence and lack of aggression was a point against him. So was the fact that Noguchi was working within traditions that had "outworn their relevance to contemporary experience." And he had not supplied the "modernist adventure . . . with an impetus and an achievement capable of extending it into the future." Kramer perhaps did not understand that a part of Noguchi sympathized with Japanese and Chinese tradition, which did not emphasize originality, but rather revered exquisite work in the style of an earlier master. In *Newsweek* David Shirey gave Noguchi a full page with many quotes from their interview: "I'm the fusion of two worlds, the east and the west," Noguchi told Shirey, "and yet I hope I reflect more than both . . . My Japanese background gave me a sensibility for the simple. It taught me how to do more with less and how to become aware of nature in all its details. Wheat, for example, when processed, doesn't resemble the grain. If you want to taste wheat, you don't eat bread. My sculpture is the wheat itself."[23]

43

RED CUBE, BLACK SUN

The spring of 1968 was full of excitement for Noguchi. Not only did his Whitney show open, but also his huge *Red Cube* was installed in front of the new Bunshaft-designed Marine Midland Bank Building at 140 Broadway in lower Manhattan. Noguchi was also involved with various large-scale commissions, such as the U.S. Pavilion for Expo 70, the world's fair slated for Osaka, Japan. In addition his autobiography, *A Sculptor's World*, was finally published in New York and London. Katharine Kuh wrote that the book was "moving and taut," and, like Noguchi himself, "wise, discreet, and elusive."[1] Indeed, what Kuh said about the autobiography could also be said about Noguchi's sculpture: "Noguchi's book is written with cool restraint—not an extra word, not a personal flourish mars its limpid rhythms. Yet on every page an almost unbearable loneliness traces the artist's troubled search for his roots . . . Noguchi rarely insists; he simply clues us in . . ." Of Noguchi's work, this most perceptive and sympathetic critic said that although he explored human themes, his sculpture remained "inscrutably objective . . . He is never an overtly autobiographical artist. Even in the autobiography itself he remains aloof, a remote figure who reveals himself only between the lines—but effectively and affectingly."

In the last week of March 1968 Noguchi's *Red Cube* was unveiled. Set in a one-acre plaza, it is sixteen feet on each side and, like the marble cube in the Beinecke garden, it is balanced on one point. Unlike the Beinecke cube, it looks like a giant toy. Noguchi saw his cube as an "extension of the building."[2] Indeed, the grid of Marine Mid-

Red Cube, Marine Midland Bank building, New York, 1968. Steel and paint, ht. 24 ft.

land's glass curtain facade is the perfect foil for the precariously poised cube. The *New York Times* architecture critic Ada Louise Huxtable admired the way Noguchi's cube related to the site, which she said was a "demonstration of New York at its physical best."[3] In *The Sunday Times* (London) John Russell called *Red Cube* "Equilibrium made visible."[4] According to the *Marine Midland Grace Bulletin* the public reaction to the cube ranged from praise to bewilderment to derision. People would go up to the cube and poke their heads into the circular hollow that pierces the cube. Workmen installing the cube were so harassed by questions from passersby that they posted a sign reading PLEASE DON'T ASK US—WE DON'T KNOW."[5]

Red Cube was the product of a great deal of deliberation between Noguchi and Bunshaft, who had secured the commission with its $25,000 fee for Noguchi. There were the usual testy moments, but both men kept their tempers in check. Noguchi once complained (probably not specifically about Bunshaft) that "a lot of architects think they themselves are the sculptors; they don't want another sculptor around."[6] For his part, Bunshaft said that Noguchi understood architecture in a way that most sculptors did not. "He knows it all and probably thinks he can be an architect."[7] Working with Bunshaft, Noguchi claimed that he felt free to do what he wanted. Sometimes, however, his freedom was reined in. His first idea for Marine Midland Bank Plaza was a large Stonehenge-type rock that would have cost $90,000. The project was then temporarily suspended, but Noguchi was persistent: "I felt that it might be nice to put something there. So I called and told them that I would make it cheap in iron."[8] Noguchi made a model of Bunshaft's building and then placed in front of it various small models for painted steel sculptures that could be inexpensively manufactured. Every time he came up with a model that Bunshaft approved, Bunshaft would show it to one of the builders, Harry B. Helmsley, who would reject it. This happened five times before Bunshaft and Helmsley finally agreed on the cube standing on one corner. Helmsley recalled: "Once I saw that, everyone agreed."[9]

A decade later Bunshaft recollected the genesis of *Red Cube*: "I said, god, maybe we ought to have some bright abstract metal forms. So he [Noguchi] went away and came back with little cut-out metal things and plunked them around, about five or six bright red ones. But they were all [planned to be] 10 or 12 feet high and looked like nothing. He had one little cube and put it on edge. I turned to one of our people and said, 'Maybe that cube 16 by 16 feet.' It looked marvelous in scale."[10] *Red Cube* energizes the space around it and the building behind it in a way that relates to the then-current trend of Minimalism. But, as Noguchi pointed out, the idea of making a geometric structure was nothing new, and in 1960, before the development of Minimalism, he had already made a cube for the Beinecke garden at Yale.

In July 1967 Noguchi received a letter from Charles E. Noel of the USIA asking him if he would like to make a proposal for a competition for the design of the U.S. Pavilion at the world's fair to be held in Osaka, Japan, in 1970. The plan he came up with, seen in a plaster model at the Noguchi Museum, looks more like a playground than a pavilion. On September 19, when the competing designs were presented at the USIA offices in Washington, D.C., Noguchi gave an oral presentation called "The World and Its Dream—A treatise on the Moon as a symbol of our changing aspirations, and on Nature as a new awareness through Science." He said his plan would include a "world mound," a tetrahedral space frame of dark glass to indicate mankind's "control of nature's structuring"; and an aluminum arm "like an aeroplane wing, our true flying carpet." There were to be floating objects (using helium and compressed air). "The roof covering half the interior of the World Mound is pneumatic and blue, with membrane divisions so disposed as to allow rain drainage down holes."[11] It is easy to imagine the USIA being stymied by Noguchi's futuristic vision.

Each contestant was given forty-five minutes to present his plan—half an hour for the artist to explain his model and fifteen minutes for questions and answers. Noguchi found this experience demeaning and four days later he wrote to Jack Masey, director of planning and design for the U.S. exhibition at Osaka, saying that during the question-and-answer period he was asked one sarcastic question about the underground architecture, after which the panel members "marched out leaving us sitting there . . . I was really shocked at the air of complete disinterest."[12] Years later Noguchi recognized that the rejection was partly his own fault: "My entry, made with the assistance of Shoji Sadao, was, of course, not that of architecture."[13]

Noguchi's disappointment was assuaged when in July 1968 he

received a telegram from his old friend and collaborator Kenzo Tange, who was in charge of the master plan for Expo 70: "Do you interested to design series of fountains central like of Expo 70."[14] By December Noguchi was under contract to create Expo's nine fountains, which were to be placed in three artificial lakes. He would be paid about twelve thousand dollars. His plans were ready in January 1970. The fountains' shapes were simple and geometric, but their function was complex. There was, for example, a perforated cube that poured water downward. There was also a fountain made up of two rotating intersecting disks, each with a hole in the middle and each spraying water outward. Two submarine fountains emerged and disappeared. Another fountain consisted of five twelve-meter-high columns, from each of which water spiraled out. To Noguchi the action of the water was more important than the shapes from which the water spouted. "I approached the work as something to challenge the commonly held idea of fountains as water spurting upward. My fountains jetted down one hundred

Noguchi with his Expo 70 fountains, 1970

feet, rotated, sprayed, and swirled water, disappeared and reappeared as mist."[15] To cope with the technology and to execute Noguchi's designs, Tange organized a group of fountain makers from five different firms. Looking back, Noguchi saw his fountains as "the dream of technology in the service of art."[16]

Early in the summer of 1968 Noguchi was at Henraux carving marble. From there he flew to London for the July 9 opening of his exhibition at Gimpel Fils at 30 Davies Street, just off Grosvenor Square. He told the London *Times* reporter about Henraux: "It's a sort of elderly sculptors' paradise. Young ones go there too, like me."[17] By the end of the 1960s, although he continued to visit Querceta, a beautiful old town beneath high mountains and near the Ligurian Sea, for the rest of his life, Noguchi found himself more eager to sculpt in Japan than in Italy. He had made, he said, a "transition from marble to hard stone . . . My Italian period lasted until early 1970, when Erminio Cidonio died. By then I had somehow established a place of work on the island of Shikoku on the Inland Sea."[18] On the last page of his autobiography Noguchi wrote: "Why do I continuously go back to Japan, except to renew my contact with the earth? There still remains unbroken the familiarity with earthly materials and the skill of Japanese hands . . . I go there like a beggar or a thief, seeking the last warmth of the earth."[19]

Over the years Noguchi became increasingly attracted to the challenge of carving granite and basalt, which were plentiful in Japan. Sculpting hard stones was "an antidote to impermanence." Stones took their places on the earth in a way that Noguchi, the inveterate traveler, could not. "I find myself a wanderer in a world rapidly growing smaller. Artist, American citizen, world citizen, belonging anywhere but nowhere."[20] Wrestling with such tough partners as granite and basalt must have counteracted what he called "that resonant void, within us and without."

Noguchi had first visited Shikoku when he was looking for stones for UNESCO. At that time Masanori Kaneko, governor of Kagawa Prefecture, welcomed him and helped him in his search. Kaneko, who no doubt knew what Noguchi had done for lantern making in Gifu, was hoping that Noguchi would revitalize the stonecutting industry in the villages of Aji and Mure, both on the outskirts of Takamatsu City.

At the time of his first visit, Noguchi had been busy with other projects and was not yet ready to create a studio in Japan. Instead, it was the sculptor Masayuki Nagare who set up a studio on Shikoku and helped to train local stoneworkers. In the late 1960s Noguchi returned to Shikoku in a search for good stonecutters. He revisited Kaneko, who put him in touch with the architect Tadashi Yamamoto, section chief of the prefectural architectural office. Kaneko asked Yamamoto to find a stonecutter for Noguchi, and Yamamoto took Noguchi to see young Masatoshi Izumi, whose family owned the Izumiya stone company, which, like the majority of the other stoneworking establishments in the vicinity, produced mostly gravestones and lanterns.

Izumi, who had just opened his own stone workshop, recalls that he had previously seen few foreigners and he was "overwhelmed by Noguchi's charismatic atmosphere . . . Noguchi's gaze was intense. He seemed to see into people."[21] Noguchi was not immediately convinced that Izumi was up to the job, so he put him to a test. From his pocket he took three small plaster models for millstonelike sculptures, similar to the sun sculpture in the Beinecke garden. "By the time I come back again please enlarge these," he said.[22] Izumi was astonished at the models Noguchi gave him to enlarge, which looked "very simple." He proceeded to carve the disks out of the famous local Aji granite as well as out of Sanukite. When Noguchi returned to Shikoku a year later, he was impressed. Masatoshi Izumi would, starting in 1968, be central to Noguchi's life and work. Before long Noguchi would establish his own studio on the Izumi family's property in Mure, and it was here, with Izumi's help, that he would carve most of his future works, one of the greatest of which was indeed the Seattle Art Museum's *Black Sun*. "In 1968 I was commissioned by the National Foundation on the Arts to do *Black Sun* for the city of Seattle, which I decided to carve out of black Brazilian granite. This is how I came to establish myself in Shikoku."[23] At nine feet tall, *Black Sun* was the biggest carving Noguchi had ever done. It closely resembles a smaller *Black Sun* that he had carved in granite in 1960–63, and which in turn was a descendant of the Beinecke sun.

The project was initiated in 1967 when the National Foundation on the Arts and the Humanities, chaired by Roger L. Stevens, chose Seattle as one of three American cities to receive a major public sculpture and Noguchi was chosen to produce it. A grant of $45,000 was to be matched by local patrons and by the Seattle Foundation. In late spring 1967 Noguchi was in Seattle to discuss the project with Dr. Richard E. Fuller, president and director of the Seattle Art Museum. Back in Japan in late June, he tried to calculate what *Black Sun* would cost. He wrote to Fuller that if *Black Sun* had a nine-foot diameter it would cost $80,000. A diameter of seven feet nine inches would cost $65,000.[24] On July 21 Richard Fuller wrote to Noguchi that Roger Stevens and others had looked at the mockups of the two sizes and everyone preferred the nine-foot size.[25] Four days later Noguchi wrote to Tadashi Yamamoto, who now functioned as his paid intermediary in the government office of Kaneko, that he was shipping a plaster model to be enlarged three and a half times. He asked Yamamoto to order the granite for *Black Sun* from Brazil and to decide whether Izumi or a stonecutter named Okada should be employed: "I myself prefer Izumi if he can handle so large a job."[26] Kaneko and Yamamoto chose Izumi. On November 2 Noguchi wrote Richard Fuller that when the ten-by-ten-foot block of granite arrived in Japan it would be set up on a site on the bay at Aji. "Since I cannot return here until next May, because of my Whitney Museum Show in April, I have asked that they proceed with the roughing out of the block without me."[27] A mid-January handwritten note from Yamamoto to Noguchi announced: "Arrived! The Black Granite Stone from the Brazil in the 13th of January. Mr Izumi sterted [sic] the carving of Black Sun. We whant [sic] See you March or April."[28]

As Noguchi had instructed, the stonecutters set up a workshop on the beach. At thirty tons, the block of granite was too heavy to move any farther. "We didn't have an appropriate crane to lift it off the boat," Izumi recalls, "so we had to bring one from the port. I did some carving on the beach to make the stone lighter. Seventy percent was cut off the block and then we transported it to my studio." Izumi began by chiseling small holes in the granite and then cracking open the surface by inserting an iron bar into the holes. The process of roughing it out, transforming the stone from a square to a circle, took eight months. Noguchi, who came to Japan when it was still being trimmed, wrote to Gene Owens on May 30, 1968: "I've been at it, the big stone, which takes shape on some earth fill in the bay of the village of Aji on the island of Shikoku in the inland seas."[29] Shikoku was, he said, "indescribably beautiful at this time of year—or any time still, for it is not spoiled. The houses are as they always have been."

Black Sun, 1969. Brazilian granite, 9 ft. (diameter)×30 in. (Courtesy of the Seattle Art Museum. Photograph by Frank Denman)

Every few months Noguchi came to Japan to supervise the carving and to do some himself. After it had been pared down and moved to Izumi's workshop at Mure, the search for its final shape began. Yamamoto's brother-in-law, a priest named Taiko Okada, watched Noguchi at work: "Noguchi's attention span was long and deep. He just focused on what he was doing. He forgot about his surroundings. When he started to carve his personality became different . . . Whenever I saw *Black Sun* I'd tell them it was finished, but Noguchi would feel it and recarve it, so every time I went to see it, it was different."[30]

Working with Noguchi was not always easy for the Shikoku stoneworkers. As Okada recalled:

> He was charming, yes, but strict. One person described him as a "typhoon." . . . He would get angry all of a sudden, then he'd be pleased and happy, then upset again. He would tell a worker to cut here or chisel there and then he would go into his house. When he came back out he would get angry and say he had not told the worker to do whatever he had done . . . Sometimes the stonecutters wouldn't talk to Noguchi for a few days . . . In the end the workers learned a lot and they understood what Noguchi wanted before he said it.

Aware of the high tension inside the circular stone wall he had built to create an outdoor workshop in Mure, Noguchi said it was like being in "hell's boiling point," especially in summer. The stoneworkers were amazed to watch Noguchi carve. His face was so close to the stone that they were afraid that he would be hurt by flying chips. When chips did fly into his eyes he ignored them. The workers tried to minimize the chip-flying: "So we cut softly," Izumi recalls, "but Noguchi did not like this. 'Cut harder!' he said."

Noguchi's procedure was first to draw on the stone with chalk, and then, when he was more certain of what he wanted, he drew with red ink called bengara. He started work early and usually put in a twelve-hour day. After lunch he would go indoors, lie down on the tatami mat and sleep, listen to music, or read. Or he would think about new ideas for work.

When Noguchi felt the shape was right, *Black Sun* was hand-polished with whetstones. Izumi's wife, Harumi, together with six other women and two men, spent four months polishing the granite circle. Gradually it became a smooth and luminous black. Watching one of the women hard at work, Noguchi told her: "You are polishing your soul."[31] When Noguchi went to Shikoku in January 1969 to see *Black Sun*, he wrote to Ibsen Nelson, Chairman of Seattle's Municipal Art Commission, "It's very beautiful, with a superb finish."[32]

In March *Black Sun* was shipped to Seattle. Noguchi received his final payment of twenty thousand dollars in May. The dedication ceremony was planned for September. The piece was perfectly sited, Noguchi felt, in Volunteer Park, across from the entrance to the Seattle Art Museum and with the Puget Sound as a backdrop. Noguchi saw *Black Sun* and the Beinecke Library's white marble sun as complementary and he liked the idea that they were situated on America's opposite coasts. At the unveiling, as Richard Fuller pulled the string and the cloth fell away from the undulating wheel of black stone, Noguchi was full of smiles. "It is appropriate," Noguchi said, "that it should be put in front of the Seattle Art Museum which is a great Oriental museum. It's as if something from inside had been rolled out."[33]

Black Sun is indeed full of movement. As the light changes, the granite's cavities and protrusions make the ring appear to roll, giving the sculpture a quality of instantaneity even as it seems to contain an everlasting stillness. What Noguchi said of his contemporaneous black steel *Skyviewing Sculpture* could as well have been said of *Black Sun*: "I thought of a luminous object as a source of delight in itself—like fire it attracts and protects us from the beasts of the night."[34]

44

THE STONE CIRCLE

For the rest of Noguchi's life, Masatoshi Izumi would be like an extra pair of arms and hands. He was an extra pair of eyes as well, for he seemed to understand what Noguchi had in mind, and he carved Noguchi's stones with patience even when Noguchi was agitated. Completely devoted, Izumi made Noguchi's life in Japan function smoothly just as Priscilla took care of the details in New York. Izumi hired and supervised the assistant stonecutters. He helped Noguchi select rocks on stone-fishing expeditions. He took him to different quarries. He ordered stone from various sources and made sure that it was delivered to Mure. When sculptures were finished he often arranged for their shipping. Izumi and Noguchi also enjoyed moments of leisure. Izumi would organize lunches at local noodle shops, and he and Noguchi and sometimes Okada would dine together. Izumi also accompanied Noguchi on swims. He would take Noguchi to new spots and they would swim far out into the sea. In the evenings he would arrange for Noguchi's dinner. His wife, Harumi, or a housekeeper would cook and Izumi and Noguchi usually ate together.

Stone fishing was the highlight of Noguchi's life on Shikoku. Izumi was amazed at Noguchi's avidity when they visited quarries or searched the land for rock. "We went to Shodoshima Island, to Okayama, and to Sweden, where the quarry was a deeply dug out place like a black cave. Noguchi was always very excited. He had the instinct of an animal about finding a good place to find stone."[1] Once Noguchi told Izumi that he wanted to look for stones on the small island of Okinoshima off

Noguchi working in the stone circle at Mure, Shikoku, with Masatoshi Izumi, 1970

the southwest tip of Shikoku. They traveled to Kochi and from there took an afternoon boat to Okinoshima. Since there was no hotel room available, they stayed in a fisherman's house, where they shared a fish for supper. Since the island had no roads, the following morning they rented two boats, one large and one small, to search the coast for stone. Because of a recent typhoon the waves were nineteen feet high. "Noguchi and I left the bigger boat and took the smaller one in order to get close to the coast. When we were about twenty feet from the rocky shore, the boatman said 'we cannot get closer in the boat.' So Noguchi and I swam toward the coast. Noguchi was a very good swimmer, but I was not. I wondered if I would get home alive. When we reached the shore we could not hold on because there was slippery moss on the rocks." Finally the two men gave up trying to get a purchase on the rock and they swam against the waves back to the boat. When Izumi heaved himself into the boat Noguchi was already safely aboard.

On their quarry visits, Noguchi's hunger for stone was sometimes in conflict with his fear of spending money. He would order a large number of stones and later, full of buyer's remorse, he would cancel part of the order. Realizing that it would be hard to replace the canceled stones and that Noguchi would eventually find a use for them, Izumi would telephone the quarry and restore the full order. "Noguchi hated to waste money," Izumi says. "He would want three or four stones, but I would go and buy a boatful of stones—seventy of them. Noguchi was amazed." Acting as Noguchi's patron, Izumi's family's stone company paid for the stones. "The stones were for the sake of Noguchi's work," Izumi says, and Noguchi's work was the most important thing in Izumi's life.

Noguchi had a genius for attracting people like Izumi, Priscilla, and Shoji Sadao, who could make his life run smoothly. Harumi and Masatoshi Izumi soon became his surrogate family. Noguchi was also close to the Ukita family, who owned the mannari granite quarry and stoneyard in Okayama Prefecture, where Noguchi had first gone in search of granite for UNESCO's fountain stone. Takashi Ukita, who runs the company now and whose grandfather ran it when Noguchi first came there, recalled that Noguchi was like a gentle grandfather: "But once he started working his eye became so sharp and strict that a small child could not talk to him. The atmosphere was tense. When he confronted a stone he did not draw on it immediately. He'd draw in chalk for a few

days, then he would not start carving until he had a plan."[2] When Takashi's older sister came to the worksite to tell Noguchi that lunch was
ready, she would not say a word. Noguchi would ignore her until he felt
ready to break for lunch. "You are very patient," he would say.

Every day Takashi Ukita's mother, instructed by her father-in-law,
cooked different Japanese delicacies for Noguchi, who would always
protest. "Just a rice bowl is enough. Today you don't need to work so
hard." Takashi was astonished to see how clean this man's plate was
after eating. Mrs. Ukita also escorted Noguchi to local places of interest. She took him, for example, to a large Japanese-style garden in
Okayama and pointed out to him a mannari stone monument, which
had been broken because it was too large to move. The pieces had been
reassembled into a huge, dolmenlike stele with the cracks still visible.
The technique, Mrs. Ukita explained to Noguchi, is called *wari mo-
doshi*, which, loosely translated, means "cut and put back together." In
the late 1950s, using this technique, Noguchi made a sculpture for the
Ukita family, and, starting in 1968, he made a number of sculptures,
such as *This Place* and *Another Land*, that are assembled out of the
split pieces of a single stone. The play between the lines formed by
the cracks and the stone's undulations and texture is always exquisite.

When Takashi Ukita was old enough, he and Noguchi would go
swimming. "Noguchi loved to swim. He'd swim way out. It scared us.
He liked to swim in several different places on the same day. He didn't
even dry himself. He just got into the car to go to the next swimming
place." Once Takashi and Noguchi were swimming far from shore and
Takashi said they should swim back, but Noguchi, ever intrepid, said,
"I never think about returning."

Starting in 1969 Noguchi made a home and studio on the island of
Shikoku, spending half a year there, usually three months in the fall
and three months in the spring. Out of fitted rocks he built the stone
circle work space. Gradually the circle was populated by Noguchi's
stone sculptures, each one quiet and still but emitting a mysterious
energy. Since Noguchi was reluctant to part with his best works, the
circle became not just a workplace, but a kind of outdoor museum.

No matter how perfect the working conditions, Noguchi grew restless if he stayed in one place for too long. During Katharine Kuh's
1960 interview she asked whether he wanted to go back to Japan, and
Noguchi had said: "Of course I want to, but I would get lonely there. I

would miss certain kinds of communication—the contact with other artists' thinking which encourages me to follow the sequence of my own thoughts."[3] When Kuh visited Mure in 1973 she noticed that Noguchi "seemed to relax, expand, and belong there, to relinquish the tensions that usually drove him." Still, she recognized Noguchi's feeling of never being at home anywhere.[4] Noguchi told her: "When I'm in Japan, I think I should be in the United States, and when I'm there I want to be back in Japan."[5] But by this time, Kuh observed, Japan appeared to exert "the stronger pull."

Before he had a dwelling on the site, Noguchi would stay in a hotel in Takamatsu, and Izumi would pick him up in the morning and take him to Mure. In 1970 he finally had a residence built at the bottom of a steep hill and just across the road from the stone circle. His architect friend Tadashi Yamamoto had been told by Governor Kaneko to look for a place for Noguchi to live close to Izumi's stonecutting workshop. Yamamoto found an eighteenth-century house that had probably belonged to a merchant or a tradesman, but that had the nobility of a samurai house. It was due to be demolished. "So I had the idea to move it and reassemble it here," Yamamoto recalled.[6]

Izumi and a master carpenter named Shinkichi Dei went to see the house. "It was spooky," says Izumi. "It leaked and the framework for the shoji screens was broken." But Shinkichi Dei judged the beams and posts and some of the plaster walls to be in good shape. Noguchi was less enthusiastic. He did not want to live in a ghost house, he said. In spite of Noguchi's reluctance, Yamamoto decided to take it apart and rebuild it on Izumi's land. "Gradually," Izumi recalls, "Noguchi began to like the house." Shinkichi Dei was hired to rebuild the house according to Noguchi's taste. The walls and partitions were either *shoji* screens or adobe walls composed of earth, oil, and straw. Following Japanese tradition, the layout allowed for a flow between inside and outside. Noguchi could sit on a tatami mat and gaze out at his garden through open *shoji*. With his respect for Japanese tradition, Noguchi used no glass windows, only paper shoji. But he insisted that the house should be light inside. Also he wanted certain modern conveniences. To heat the house hot water pipes were installed beneath the gray stone floor of the front room. On cold nights additional heat came from a brazier. Noguchi kept a television and a record player hidden behind wall panels on the first floor. The slightly raised living room

Noguchi's house in
Mure, Shikoku

was covered with tatami and partitioned off by *shoji*. Whenever Noguchi arrived on Shikoku, he would put down his suitcase and lie down
on the tatami mat. "This is what I need," he would say.[7]

All the rooms were spare—Noguchi was allergic to the idea of dec-
oration and most objects were kept out of sight. Furnishings consisted
of old chests, baskets, and straw stools. Noguchi's Akari perched where
needed or hung from the ceiling, as did a Balinese percussion instrument that looked like a primitive xylophone. Here and there Noguchi's
sculptures emanated their quiet energy. *Wave in Space*, a slab of black
granite whose surface swells like a wave, graced the floor of the front
room. Increasingly after Noguchi set up his Shikoku studio, he made
low-lying sculptures that were a continuation of the landscape/table
sculptures that began with *This Tortured Earth*. The rounded top of
Wave in Space is polished and shiny. Below, where the wave moves up
out of the surrounding water, the stone is pitted. In this respect *Wave*

in Space is like an expanded version of *Origin* (1968), carved from the same black African granite, but *Origin's* roundness is more visceral and makes one think of tumescence and birth, whereas *Wave in Space* evokes the movement of water.

In the back of Noguchi's Mure house a veranda overlooks a small, very private bamboo grove. Here Noguchi placed *Ground Wind,* which he carved in 1969, a dark stone that snakes about twelve feet across the earth. Inspired perhaps by the sections in a stalk of bamboo, its length is made of several sections. Noguchi left *Ground Wind* in Mure: "I thought it too Japanese to come here [New York]. It looks perfect where it is. So I made *Ground Wind # 2*—an abstraction, where the other is more real."[8] A photograph shows Noguchi dressed in a kimono and kneeling in his back garden beside *Another Place* (1968), a roughly square black granite slab broken and reassembled. Eventually weeds grew in the sculpture's cracks and Noguchi, who cared very much about how his sculptures were maintained, moved it to his Long Island City studio.

Noguchi's house had a kitchen in a new addition and a bathroom with a traditional Japanese tub. Leading from the entryway to the second floor is a steep stairway enclosed by vertical wooden railings. The railings on the second floor landing allowed Noguchi to see who was coming before the arriving person could see him. "As a rule, Isamu didn't like guests," Yamamoto recalled.[9] Noguchi's bedroom on the second floor has a tatami-covered, raised platform enclosed by a *shoji* screen. Here at bedtime he would roll out his futon. Next to the bedroom Noguchi's study is furnished with Western appurtenances such as bookshelves, a desk, and two chairs.

At Mure, as in Kita Kamakura, Noguchi allowed his Japanese side to flourish. After his evening soak in his Japanese tub he donned a *yukata* (cotton kimono). Seated on a pillow on the floor, he ate Japanese food. "A Japanese would never live this way," he said. "I can do it because I am not Japanese."[10] Noguchi's lifelong struggle to resolve the East-West conflict energized not only the creation of a perfect place at Mure, but also the sculptures that he produced there.

Noguchi shaped his Mure compound as a work of art. It was the haven that he had always sought—a place where most of what he looked at and touched was of his own choosing. Dore Ashton wrote, "His life's work, as he often said in later years, was about creating an 'oasis.'"[11] His art, he told Ashton, was not about making objects but about creating spaces and forms connected with life. "I wanted to reach what may be defined as a way of life, a space of life, or even a ghetto closed and defended from the world." Closed and defended—very much like Noguchi himself. In spite of his urbanity and charm, Noguchi, fearful of chaos and emptiness, increasingly anxious about the passage of time, pursued his search for identity by making art and by creating a home. He told Dore Ashton's husband, Matti Megged, in 1985: "I think that artists are always making a place of security for themselves, you know. Their studio becomes their home, their museum."[12] But even with his beautiful Shikoku oasis, Noguchi could never settle down. "No matter how comfortable I am I simply can not stay in one place for a long time."[13]

Over the years Noguchi added to his compound two large antique storage houses, or *kura*, that had the robust simplicity and perfect proportions of Greek temples. The inside walls of white adobe mixed with straw supported a wooden latticework. Round posts set on round stone bases held up splendid crossbeams and a tiled roof. One *kura* became Noguchi's studio for when he wanted to work indoors. The other, a former sake warehouse, served as a repository for finished sculptures.

Photographs of Noguchi at Mure tend to show him either confronting a rock or sitting looking contemplative. He also liked to have fun. Besides lunches and dinners with friends, there were visits to nearby temples and shrines. He tried never to miss traditional festivals such as the three-day Obon, a Buddhist celebration to honor the spirits of ancestors. Houses are cleaned, offerings to the dead are made, and lanterns are lit and carried to graves. Sometimes lanterns with candles inside are floated down a river to send off ancestors' spirits. Noguchi would join in the *Bon-Odori* folk dance and dance in the street for hours. Often after attending Obon he would visit Taiko Okada at his Buddhist temple in Sanuki city near Takamatsu. Okada remembers walking with Noguchi in the nearby cemetery and Noguchi's surprise seeing the bamboo frame of a lantern that had lost its paper. Among the graves, Noguchi noticed broken statues of Jizo, a beloved bodhisattva devoted to the protection of travelers, pregnant women, and children, including dead children. Noguchi picked up one of the broken heads and took it with him.

In the graveyard Noguchi also asked to see the tomb of a legendary pearl diver named Ama, who, according to Okada's telling of the story, had retrieved a pearl from a dragon king who had stolen it and taken it to his underwater home. Pursued by the dragon, the diver cut open her breast and put the pearl inside. She managed to swim to the surface with the pearl, but she died of her wound. It was a story Noguchi spoke of often, and in 1982 he made a sculpture called *The Mermaid's Grave*.

Okada, who frequently talked about religion with Noguchi, thought that Noguchi was very much involved with Buddhism. (Noguchi once said that the closest he came to religion was Shinto—he loved the way Shinto imbued nature with spiritual value, the idea that trees and rocks were the abode of deities.) "Noguchi believed in the mystic power of the mountain," Okada says.[14] On one occasion Okada told Noguchi that it was arrogant to break and make art out of the ancient boulders that he had had transported to his stone circle. Okada's reproof embarrassed Okada's brother-in-law, Yamamoto, and Governor Kaneko. But Noguchi told Okada: "I agree with you."[15]

45

TO INTRUDE ON NATURE'S WAY

Noguchi's late basalt and granite monoliths stand like ancient markers of the time's passage. They could be seen as concretizations of mindfulness. We look at them and they seem to look back and take our measure. "I think of them as emanations, as potential of the earth," Noguchi said.[1]

Perhaps these solemn stones have their origin in *Euripedes* from 1966, where Noguchi took a chunk of marble whose surface was rough and cut it only slightly in order to "understand its being." Poised between being a rock and being a sculpture, *Deepening Knowledge* (1969) was one of the first of Noguchi's large upright basalt sculptures in which his intervention was minimal and in which he gave the stone its particular character by hollowing out and polishing only certain parts so that those parts turn dark gray and shiny in contrast to the matte velvety ochre-brown of the stone's untouched surface. Of this sculpture, Noguchi wrote: "I had come to think that the deeper meaning of sculpture had to be sought in the working of hard stone. Through this might be revealed its quality of enduring. The evidence of geologic time was its link to our world's creation."[2] Like *Sculpture to Be Seen from Mars*, these late works serve as testimonials to some future form of life that human beings once inhabited the earth. Talking with Katharine Kuh during her 1973 visit to Mure, Noguchi called basalt and granite "rocky rocks—male rocks, not pliable or feminine. They are terrific challenges."[3] Kuh felt that in Mure, Noguchi's work had "resolved itself." Many people would agree that these late raw stones are Noguchi's finest sculptures. Kuh observed that they are "inscrutably quiet," and "never contrived, never strained." Watching the ferocious focus with which Noguchi approached basalt boulders in the stone circle, she thought that he was "literally pitting himself against the hard stone." Perhaps as he approached his eighth decade, battling with obdurate mineral was a way of defying time. He was proud of the strength of his slender, well-formed body, and determined never to let its physical energy diminish. Cutting into stone, Noguchi could resist age and escape anomie. The process made him feel connected with the earth and this link was perhaps more important to him than his bond with human beings. He never completely trusted people. His deepest engagement was with everlasting stone.

Working in stone was, Noguchi said, a dialogue between himself and the "primary matter of the universe." His friend the architect Arata Isozaki remembered Noguchi muttering as he walked among his late stone sculptures at Mure: "When I face natural stones, they start talking to me. Once I hear their voices, I give them just a bit of a hand. Recently I don't have to carve or polish that much."[4] Isozaki compared Noguchi's approach to stone to that of a twelfth-century Japanese writer about garden design who had said, "Erect a stone the way it wants." But Noguchi also liked to dominate the stone. The dialogue with stone was, he said, a confrontation. "It's like a wild horse . . . I would like to attack it to make it mine. Before I was more subject to the quality of the stone. Now I do not do what the stone tells me. Instead of it telling me, I tell the stone."[5] But of course he listened to the stone before imposing his will upon it.

Noguchi's sculptural process could be swift. Sometimes it went on for years. In 1957, after splitting a large block of Kurama granite, he found he was not sure how to continue, so he left it unfinished. When he broke the stone in two it seemed "an act of blasphemy."[6] Nine years later he returned to it and called it *Myo*. "Eventually I was able to make it mine, a 'sculpture' of my time and forever."[7] Standing sixty-five inches high, *Myo* is both rugged and magisterial. It has a subtle anthropomorphism and, with its inward-hugging energy, can be seen as two bodies kissing.

Noguchi saw uncertainty as part of his creative process: "There are long periods when I don't know what I'm doing. But then it goes clickity-clack down the tracks . . . I've been looking at certain stones I have,

Myo, 1957–66. Kurama granite, 65 × 35 × 15½ in.

pondering what to do with them—especially one heavy one. It has completely baffled me. I'm in a state of not knowing which way I'm going. But I value these times also, these incubation periods. It's very important to be quite empty sometimes. If you're always producing, you're like a machine. It's when you don't know, that you find something new."[8] In speaking of his creative process, he emphasized intuition. As with Abstract Expressionism, much of his work's meaning came through the process of its making. "Many ideas come to my mind while I am working . . . It is not easy for me to develop an idea while I am not actually working."[9] Instinct, surprise, and mistakes were all an important part of his invention. "I think of myself as being led by unexpected forces. If it isn't a surprise there is something wrong . . . Sometimes I don't even know what I'm doing . . . It is approaching the Zen term *Satori*. You become aware . . . I discover art. I don't create it."[10] Another time he described his creative process this way: "One imagines possibilities; much later one begins to know what to make of them . . . In working stone, the primary gesture, the original discovery, the first revelation, can never be repeated or imitated. It is the stroke that breaks and is immutable . . . There is a sequence to stone working. First, the rear half is removed with drill holes and wedges. Afterward comes the carving, splitting with the 'genno,' the sledge hammer used for knocking off large hunks . . . no second thoughts are possible."[11]

Splitting stone was both an act of violence and an act of love. That it was an intrusion he acknowledged when he titled a 1971 sculpture *To Intrude on Nature's Way*. In trying to define the differences between his and Brancusi's work, Noguchi said: "You might say that when Brancusi took a bronze casting and started filing, he eventually got to the inside. I go about it in a different way: I actually split it. I break it. I cut. I go to the jugular. Then I come out again, and it all becomes one."[12] In describing how he made *Brilliance* in 1983, Noguchi explained: "I attack the stone with violence. Is this to tame it or to awaken myself? . . . Destruction is then the road to creation."[13] For Noguchi anger, despair, and conflict propelled his creative process. "I sometimes think that my particular advantage, whatever it is, has been this factor of disturbance and conflict, that I live between two worlds and that I am constantly having conflicts of East and West, past and present."[14] But Noguchi also saw carving stone as an "act of reconciliation . . . The work and nature eventually settle down again in harmony."[15]

Besides the basalt dolmens, several other types of sculpture occupied Noguchi in the first half of the 1970s. He continued to make landscape sculptures in which rounded forms, resembling mountains or breasts, seem to grow from the surface of the rock. His theme was emergence. He also kept on creating sculptures in which a stone was broken and then put back together. In the early 1970s he also explored the joining of different-colored stones to form precise polished shapes, quite different from his rough, boulderlike sculptures. Using the "post-tensioning" technique he adapted from Buckminster Fuller, he united sections of differently colored marble by running a stainless steel wire through a channel in each section's core and then tightening the ends of the wire to give the sculpture its "compressive strength."[16] "Post-tensioning of discrete elements," he said, "became an obsession in the conception as well as in the rationale of structure and execution."[17] Because Noguchi began making these two-toned sculptures in 1968 in Querceta, many people thought that they were influenced by the patterns of different-colored marbles seen in Tuscan churches. Noguchi denied the connection. He said that he was interested in the "structuring of stone," not in the decorative effects of contrasting color.[18] One of his most beautiful post-tensioned sculptures is the nearly six-foot *Sun at Noon* (1969), in which two different colors of orangey-red marble were assembled to form a ring. Because of the color contrast, the ring seems to pulsate and radiate heat. According to Noguchi, this sculpture's astonishing energy comes from "the inherent tensile unity of shape." It is also the conflict between the unity of the circular form and the separateness of the marble segments in contrasting colors that gives this sculpture its tension. One feels the circle's compressed segments might burst apart at any moment.

Several of these two-colored, post-tensioned marble sculptures have a humorous and lighthearted eroticism. *Ding Dong Bat* (1968), for example, is clearly phallic, and the two versions of *She* (1970–71) are clearly vulvar. Copulation is suggested in *To Love*, of the same date, but with Noguchi sexual reference is always discreet, witty, and gentle. He took the idea of sexual pleasure and distilled it to a pure essence. It's as though he were creating an abstract version of the calm yet ecstatic images of sexual union seen in Indian art. Of *To Love*, perhaps

Sun at Noon, 1969.
French red marble and
Spanish Alicante marble,
61 × 61 × 8¼ in.

his most graphic image of sexual intercourse, Noguchi wrote, "A hier-
atic depiction of the act of love—motionless."[19] Several of Noguchi's
carvings are emphatically priapic. Noguchi's friend Anne d'Harnoncourt
remembered taking Noguchi in 1980 to see an exhibition of Indian
sculpture titled *Manifestations of Shiva* at the Philadelphia Museum of
Art, where she was director. In one of the rooms, numerous lingams
stood on a low table. "Noguchi was fascinated by the show . . . when
we got to the last gallery with the lingams, he said, 'Oh my God! I have
to go home! I have to go back to the studio.'"[20]

In 1970 Noguchi began to create open-form, gatelike sculptures
that could be seen as elongated and gently squared-off versions of his
ring or sun sculptures. The difference is that in the gate sculptures,
the empty space inside the framing stone is as expressive as the stone
shape itself. Several works in this new sculptural group are called
Void—a concept with which Noguchi was familiar not only through
his knowledge of Buddhism, but also from his familiarity with existen-

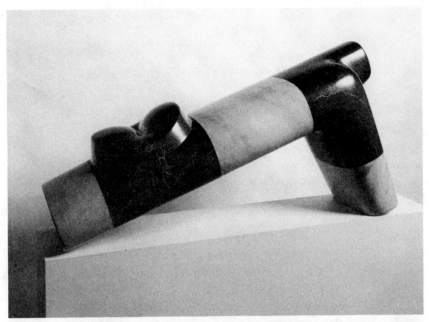

She, 1970–71. Austrian black Porticoi marble and Portuguese rose Aurora marble, 24 × 14¾ × 51 in.

To Love, 1970–71. Austrian black Porticoi marble and Portuguese rose Aurora marble, 14⅞ × 11⅛ × 22⅜ in.

Noguchi with *Energy Void*, in the stone circle at Mure, Shikoku, 1971. Black Swedish granite, ht. 10 ft.

tialism, so popular in the 1950s. His 1950 *Mu* and several of his clay sculptures made in Japan also approached the theme of emptiness, perhaps even referring to the Buddhist concept of no-mind, which I take to mean emptying the mind so that it is more receptive to enlightenment. Noguchi's sculptures on the theme of the void may also refer to the nothingness of death or to the endless space of the universe. Of this new form Noguchi wrote: "I have carried the concept of the void like a weight on my shoulders . . . It is like some inevitable question that I cannot answer."[21] The void sculptures, while peaceful, are like portals to nonbeing. Perhaps the idea of emptiness offered Noguchi the possibility of clarity and calm. The gatelike sculptures also recall torii—the gateways that lead up to Shinto shrines. Passage through a Noguchi gate could be a form of purification on the threshold of a more spiritual world. Indeed, the twelve-foot-high *Energy Void* in Noguchi's museum in Mure is also known as the *Gate of Heaven*. When the painter Sam Francis visited Noguchi at Mure, he dreamed about Noguchi's monumental gate as a gate to paradise, and when he told Noguchi about his dream, Noguchi did not correct him.[22] *Energy Void* was originally commissioned for Pepsico's sculpture garden, but when it was finished, Noguchi thought it was possibly the best sculpture he had ever made; always loath to sell the sculptures that he liked most, he decided to make another version for Pepsico.[23] He never told Pepsico that theirs was the second *Energy Void*.

When Noguchi was working in Japan or Italy, Priscilla Morgan took care of his affairs in New York. She sorted and forwarded his mail. She reorganized his filing system, and, with his accountant Bernie Bergstein, dealt with his bills. She made sure that his studio was clean, his plants were watered, his alarm system was working, his car was functioning. She took potential patrons to see his sculptures, either at the warehouse where some of his work was stored or at his studio. Storage, transportation, and insurance issues were in her hands. She also handled a number of loans and sales. She had frequent exchanges with dealers who might be interested in showing Noguchi's work. She gave the sculptor astute advice about how to deal with commissions—she was a far more diplomatic negotiator than he. She helped him strategize his finances. Most important, she provided him with a social context. Priscilla gave frequent dinner parties—and she did this with great sophistication. Beyond the delicious food and stimulating talk, these dinners put Noguchi in contact with people who might further his career. She was, in fact, the perfect artist's wife.

At Henraux during the summer of 1972, Noguchi was stricken with back pain. In New York that September he underwent spinal surgery. Priscilla recalls that when they arrived at the hospital they were met at the entrance by an African-American nurse with a wheelchair. Noguchi turned to Priscilla and said, "I've always wondered what kind of angel would welcome me to heaven." Back in Japan in October, Noguchi wrote to Priscilla: "I can not begin to tell you how grateful I am for all the attention you gave me in my illness. 'A friend in need' as they say."[24] Nine days later Noguchi wrote Priscilla from Shikoku: "My memories of my last trying times is brightened by all the real kindness you gave me. How I can ever be worthy I don't know."

Half a year later, Noguchi's spinal problems persisted. According to Priscilla, he tended to revere doctors and took their advice seriously, but he was not pleased with his medical treatment during the autumn of 1973 in New York. He complained to Priscilla that his doctor was always away when he needed him, and when he had an appointment the doctor kept him waiting for two hours, only to be told that his ailment was "nothing." Priscilla wrote to Noguchi's doctor on November 12 asking him to be patient and kind when Noguchi came to see him. Noguchi, she told the doctor, was in "one of his despondent moments." He had no energy, she said, and he "feels he is lost." What Priscilla described was surely one of Noguchi's episodes of depression.

The tone of Noguchi's letters to Priscilla is that of someone writing to a good old friend or perhaps to a wife of many years. When Priscilla hadn't written for a while, Noguchi's letters to her sound uneasy. In spite of his attachment—or because of it—he liked to keep her at arm's length. With the possible exceptions of Frida Kahlo, Ann Matta Clark, and Tara Pandit—none of whom was completely available to him—Noguchi never really gave himself to anyone. If he felt that someone was trying to possess or control him, he became skittish, rude, and mean. He once told Shoji Sadao, "I'm nice to women who are bad for me and bad to women who are good for me."[25]

An expert seducer, Noguchi had a steady stream of beautiful young women moving in and out of his life. Most of the time Priscilla was not jealous, or she was too disciplined to show it. Though one young Japanese woman named Nobu irritated Priscilla with her kittenish flirting. "I'd be cooking in the kitchen and Nobu would be giving Noguchi a massage. Isamu loved it. It was like being a king with a court." One time they were all together in Venice riding in a gondola. "I had differed with Noguchi about something and he got mad and argued back. Nobu took his side. I told her, 'If you keep this up I just might push you into the water.' Noguchi enjoyed this kind of attention."

Noguchi would introduce his girlfriends to Priscilla in part so that they would realize that he already had a permanent partner. As Shoji Sadao recalls, Noguchi was adept at carrying on several relationships at once. "He was very secretive. He was a loner. He compartmentalized, kept different parts of his life separate. All his girlfriends have fond memories of him." About Noguchi's philandering, Priscilla says: "He'd make love and leave them. A couple of times I'd say, 'That's it,' and end it. It was sometimes very trying and hard. I could spot when another woman came into his life. He'd lead women on and then they would get possessive. Although I was not possessive or clinging, it was hard because I was not married. He preferred married women because no commitment was possible. He had to be free. He needed space. I understood that and that is the reason I lasted so long."

Nonetheless, Priscilla did not hesitate to tell Noguchi how much she loved him. On New Year's Eve 1960, for example, she wrote: "Dearest Isamu. How grateful I am for you, my love is with you tonight and always. So hope all is well. Once again I miss you beyond words Priscilla." It was probably on February 29, 1968, that she wrote: "But it is Leap Year and I will hold my breath and say that I love you deeply. Did it ever occur to you that I might have been born just for you?" On his birthday that year she wrote, but did not send, a note saying: "If you would marry me you'd feel younger every year. Happy birthday— Priscilla." She closed a letter dated January 17, 1971, with: "Isamu, I miss you and love you so much. Please don't settle for just Japan. You belong to the world and are so valuable and important at this most extraordinary time. Come back soon."

Noguchi's letters to Priscilla from the year after they met come the closest to being intimate and sometimes even romantic: "But you are like a fountain of enthusiasm—I would soon become so dependent that I would dry up without its constant flow." A postcard written on a flight to Honolulu en route to Japan and postmarked August 15, 1960, said: "A perfect trip & perfect beginning, with you looking so lovely— Thank you—bless you—Love Isamu." Except to sign off, Noguchi rarely used the word "love," but it is clear that he did love Priscilla. Sometimes his attachment seemed that of an adolescent boy fighting to be free of dependency on his mother. On social occasions he would often disparage her, especially if she was the hostess. He would needle and tease, and at times Priscilla would just go into another room and wait until his storm was over. Arnold Glimcher, Noguchi's good friend and dealer starting in 1975, does not think that Noguchi was just teasing. "He had a mean streak," Glimcher recalls. "Perhaps it was because of his dual culture, the conflict between east and west. It was embarrassing for guests when he turned on Priscilla. I don't know how she put up with it."[26]

Priscilla was strong enough not to be overly hurt by Noguchi's nastiness. At least she did not let her hurt feelings show. "He liked to put me on," she says. "He was always testing me to find flaws." At the bottom she felt loved and she believes that Noguchi was secretly proud of her. He liked, for example, her long WASP lineage. Uncertain of his own pedigree, it comforted him to be lionized by people who felt secure about class. And, when they first met, he was impressed by her high-powered job at William Morris (which she gave up in order to devote herself to Spoleto and Noguchi). He surely loved Priscilla's great sense of style: she dressed simply but beautifully. Her apartment was exquisitely appointed, and when she set a table everything on it was aesthetically pleasing, especially the flowers.

Priscilla became a master at dismissing Noguchi's insistence on detachment. He acted aloof when she visited him in Japan and she knew he had other girlfriends there. Despite her insistence that this "didn't bother me," in Priscilla's archive are handwritten drafts of two notes to Noguchi written in the summer of 1971 at a moment when he must have been pulling away. One of them had to do with his behavior or attitude when he would join her in Spoleto. She said that in the "compressed atmosphere" of Spoleto and in the company of people like Buckminster Fuller and Ezra Pound, she, too, needed to keep face.

> I know you need many people in your life but surely you can visit me for a few days a year in Spoleto—or devote time to me with other people around. If not I don't think we have much of a real friendship in the large sense & I think my judgment about loving you must not have been very good. I know a letter like this irritates you but then it is not very easy for me to write. Spoleto is an atmosphere in which I have worked very hard for <u>many</u> years. No one assumes you and I are getting married—which you seem to worry so much about—which seems foolish to me in 1971 what anyone thinks <u>about that</u> (at our ages except always the principals [sic] involved) but people do know that I don't view you as just a casual or very good friend. Of course people know I love you very much—but my god, how many people can claim to be so loved in this seemingly loveless world.

She ended this letter (which she may never have sent) saying: "Communication is always so difficult—strange I so seldom really say what I really feel to you." The second note told Noguchi that she loved and admired him "in the most beautiful sense," and that she only wanted to contribute to his "happiness and peace of mind." She begged him to "try to feel some joy in our knowing each other. It has been a long time and I couldn't bear to live without your friendship."

"Handling Noguchi" Priscilla says, "was like taming a lion. The minute I saw his eyelids partly close I would change the subject and avoid his anger attack." She loved his wit, his "purity," and the "deep sadness about him. He had a lonesome quality, which was very appealing to me." Noguchi's sense of not belonging and of being ostracized because of his mixed heritage appealed to her nurturing instinct. More than once, Manhattan doormen directed him to the servants' entrance. "Once we came home and Isamu said, 'I'm nothing. I don't belong any place.' He was flat against the wall, very disturbed by the attitude of prejudice . . . he was full of self-doubt. This was part of our bond. I believed in him . . . I smothered him with love. He needed unconditional nonstop love."

In 1980 Noguchi and Priscilla had a fight bitter enough to keep them apart for half a year. Priscilla remembers it as the most painful time of her life. It happened during a period when Noguchi was working hard to get ready for his *Sculpture of Spaces* show at the Whitney Museum. Just before the show opened, the two were at dinner together and she suggested that he was not paying enough to the people running Akari Associates. Noguchi blew up and dropped her at home. "Two days later the exhibition opened at the Whitney. Laurance Rockefeller gave a party after the opening and Isamu wouldn't even look at me." They didn't speak until Noguchi finally called to apologize.

In November 1970 and in May 1972 Noguchi exhibited at the Cordier & Ekstrom Gallery. The 1970 show, featuring his post-tensioned marble sculptures made in Italy, received good reviews. *Arts* magazine said, "His figures are highly refined abstractions synthesizing aspects of man and nature that are universal and timeless. A haunting, Oriental mysticism exists simultaneously with mathematically calculated forms, marking Noguchi as one of the most original contributors to modern sculpture."[27] John Canaday wrote in *The New York Times* that the sculptures "inspire an awareness of forces allied with nature, which, as the structure of the world, has always been at the core of Noguchi's art."[28] For the 1972 show Ekstrom suggested showing a number of replicas of the same sculpture. The interlocking slab sculpture called *Strange Bird* (1945) was chosen; the show included six bronze and two aluminum versions. This time Canaday wrote that Noguchi was an artist upon whom "all the superlatives have already been applied, and are still deserved."[29]

In spite of the critical success, Noguchi was unhappy with being handled by Arne Ekstrom. According to Varujan Boghosian, a fellow sculptor in the Cordier & Ekstrom stable, Noguchi was dissatisfied especially because Ekstrom had definite ideas about how his gallery space should be used, and, like Noguchi, wanted control. Noguchi would complain that it was Ekstrom's show, not his.[30] He was feeling negative about art dealers in general and he doubted the value of gallery exhibitions. His disgruntlement was, no doubt, exacerbated by back problems and depression. Moreover, his work was not selling well. Neither were his Akari. In this unhappy state of mind he wrote to Anne Rotzler of Gimpel Hanover Gallery in Zurich, Switzerland, on December 16, 1971. He sent her photographs of some works that she might consider putting in a show. Noguchi told Rotzler that he wanted to get the sculptures that he had shown at Ekstrom "away from this country where nothing has happened, even after the prices were lowered by one-third."[31] In a subsequent letter to Rotzler he ventured that perhaps a museum would be a better venue for his work than a gallery and that a dealer could function as an intermediary. He was beginning to think about creating an exhibition space in Long Island City, a notion that would in the mid-1980s bear fruit in the Isamu Noguchi Garden Museum.

In 1972 Noguchi exhibited his post-tensioned marble sculptures at Gimpel Fils at 30 Davies Street in London. In May of the following year the Minami Gallery in Tokyo gave him a show—his first in Japan in eleven years. "In exhibiting again in Japan," Noguchi wrote in the exhibition's catalogue, "I am reminded of how time and places here have formed me, and of my own roots here in childhood."[32] He said that Japan had enabled him to transform reality with his imagination: "It is in this sense that I may be said to have Japan within me." As always he was preoccupied with time's passing: "We are no longer so sure that time flows in one direction only . . . My aim has been to seek this common denominator which transcends race and finally time—the shallow linear time that is synonymous with progress and the new as an end in itself. To me a work of art escapes time when it remains fresh and new and retains forever a wonder."

Noguchi continued to receive inquiries for major sculptural projects. Some never came to fruition, others, thanks to his perseverance, did. Among those that did were *Intetra*, a mist fountain for the Society of Four Arts in Palm Beach, Florida; an aluminum sculpture titled *Shinto* for the Bank of Tokyo's Manhattan branch; *Playscapes*, a playground for Piedmont Park in Atlanta; and *Landscape of Time*, a grouping of rocks for the General Services Administration in Seattle, which a congressman compared to five $100,000 "pet rocks."[33] Perhaps the most successful project of this period was the group of fountains for the new Supreme Court building in Tokyo. Installed in a double inner courtyard between the courtroom and the judges' meeting room are six black granite *tsukubai*, which Noguchi called "overflowing wells." The mood is meditative, almost sacramental. Water emerging from the top of these squarish chunks of granite creates a surface that shines like a mirror, and mirrors, being associated with Japan's mythic origins, had great significance in Japanese culture. The water then flows gently down over the partly rough and partly smooth sides of the stone and into a basin. The ground of one of the courtyards is paved with stone. In the other court the *tsukubai* are set in a bed of white sea pebbles. At one point Noguchi wanted to call these "Illuminating Wells." Since the public does not have access to them, the almost inaudible sound of flowing water, the dark luminosity of wet granite, and the stillness of the stone itself are designed to give spiritual uplift to those in the legal profession. He hoped that his fountains would communicate ideas of "purity and balance" and would prompt insights about justice being done.[34]

On May 10, 1975, Noguchi's exhibition titled *Steel Sculptures* opened at the Pace Gallery at 32 East Fifty-seventh Street in Manhattan. For over a year Noguchi had been corresponding with Arnold B. Glimcher, the gallery's founder and chairman, about his wish to find an outlet for Akari. Glimcher wrote to Noguchi on April 1, 1974, saying that he hoped Noguchi would think positively about joining Pace. "You already know how much we care about your work and want to show it. There is no obstacle too great (taking out windows, knocking down walls) for us to overcome in providing the best environment for your works."[35] Glimcher told Noguchi that he felt a special affinity for Noguchi's stainless steel sculptures and he wanted to purchase some of them immediately. "Isamu, please believe me that it is only our conviction that you are one of the great artists of the Twentieth Century that keeps us trying to convince you of our merit to show your works."

Steel Sculptures included fifteen pieces, some polished and some sandblasted. Reprises of the aluminum sculptures Noguchi made in 1959, the steel pieces were, as Bryan Robertson's catalogue essay pointed out, developed from models consisting of a single sheet of paper cut, folded, and slit. The sculptures' "loaded silence" and "energetic repose" were qualities that could describe most of Noguchi's work.[36] The exhibition was well received. John Russell wrote in *The New York Times* that it was "the major exhibition of New York on 57th Street." Noguchi, he said, "comes up with echoes and ambiguities that keep us by turns amused, stirred, provoked and faintly disconcerted."[37] Hilton Kramer, also in the *Times*, wrote: "No artist of our time has brought a greater sense of delicacy to his sculptural task—or a greater sense of refinement, both sensuous and spiritual in its effect on the viewer—than Isamu Noguchi."[38]

The guest list for the Pace show's opening, which Priscilla surely had a hand in, reads like a who's who of the Manhattan art world. It included everyone from Arthur Penn to Willem de Kooning, from Saul Steinberg to the critic Barbara Rose, from I. M. Pei to Jerome Robbins. New York's wealthy and well connected were included as well, among them Ann Rockefeller Costa, Mary T. Rockefeller, Mary McFadden, Ambassador and Mrs. Angier Biddle Duke, Alice Tully, Louis Auchincloss, Dorothy Norman, Patrick Lannan, and Christophe de Menil. Others whose lives had touched Noguchi's over the years were Ann Alpert (Ann Matta Clark), John Lennon, and Yoko Ono.

From the first half of the 1970s come a number of rounded granite sculptures, many of which have a partially pitted surface that catches light with a soft dazzle. Arne Glimcher, who once watched Noguchi draw the lines where he wanted a stone to be cut, was surprised that Noguchi also made marks where he wanted the chisel to pit. All of these rounded, pitted, granite sculptures are a continuation of Nogu-

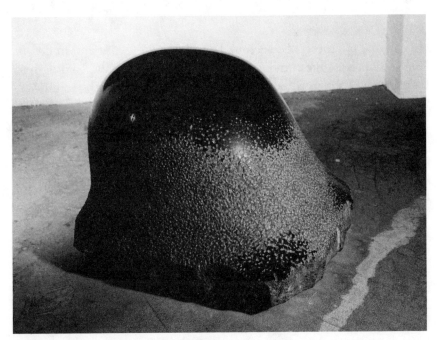

Origin, 1968. African granite, 23 × 30 × 32 in.

Double Red Mountain, 1969. Persian travertine, 11½×40×30¼ in.

chi's theme of emergence seen in *The Mountain* (1964) and in *Origin* (1968), which is like a mountain or an island or a baby coming into being. One of the most beautiful of the pitted pieces is the red travertine *Double Red Mountain* (1969), a pair of hills rising from a smooth, forty-inch-long rectangular ground. The hills' lower halves are rough and their summits are highly polished. Although the sculpture brings to mind the steep reddish slopes of New Mexico, the mountains are also like breasts—once again Noguchi merged landscape and the human body. In his museum's catalogue Noguchi wrote that *Double Red Mountain* was, like his other landscape tables, "a landscape of the mind."[39]

Young Mountain (1970) and *Emergent* (1971) are cut in sections and put back together so that the pitted surface is also articulated by fine cracks. Some of Noguchi's partly pitted and partly polished granite sculptures are recognizably anthropomorphic. *Feminine* (1970) and *Uruguayan* (1974) both suggest pregnant women's torsos. *Seeking* (1974) brings to mind a male torso moving forward on a Greek pediment.

Childhood (1970) and *Emanation* (1971) appear to be abstractions of a human head.

Compared to the refinement and tactile allure of the partly pitted granite pieces, Noguchi's basalt sculptures during these years are raw. *To Intrude on Nature's Way* (1971) stands like an ancient grave marker. Noguchi wrote that because it was partly carved, it differed from the artfully placed stones in Japanese gardens, which are left in their natural state. "But," he said, "I am also a sculptor of the West. I place my mark and do not hide. The crosscurrents eddy around me. In *To Intrude on Nature's Way*, the contradictions between the Eastern and Western approaches are resolved with a minimum of contrivance."[40] *The Inner Stone* (1973) is a chunk of basalt with several cuts in its surface. Only these cut areas are polished. Noguchi credited the availability of a power tool with this sculpture's conception: "Sometimes a new tool, with familiarity of use, will suddenly take hold, and the artist then serves its direction unerringly in the stone's transformation, when the core bit becomes a carving tool."[41]

In these years, in part because his back hurt, Noguchi made groups of smaller sculptures out of pieces of stone left over from the stonecutting process. He took, for example, two cylindrical pieces of granite that had been removed with the core bit from *The Inner Stone* and with them created *Core Piece # 1* and *Core Piece # 2* (both 1974). About his creative process in carving these, he wrote: "The making of sculpture becomes a ritual when the sculptor becomes as one with it and the parts fall into its whole as if in a trance. The residue returns to the earth, or on occasion reappears clothed in new identity."[42] In *End Pieces* (1974), Noguchi took four discarded slabs of Swedish granite that had been removed from a block of stone and created a hollow boxlike form. "There is mystery to a cube," he wrote, "especially a black cube—when does it become a sculpture?"[43]

46

A PLACE FOR PEOPLE TO GO

While at Henraux in the summer of 1971, Noguchi received a call asking him to participate in a competition for a fountain for Detroit's Civic Center Plaza, an eight-acre area overlooking the Detroit River. The late Anna Thomson Dodge (widow of the automotive pioneer Horace Dodge) had made a generous bequest—$2 million—for building a fountain that was to be a memorial for her husband and son. As Noguchi told the Walker Art Center director, Martin Friedman, "To spend $2,000,000 on a fountain isn't easy . . . and, besides, I wasn't interested in making the type which the donor had specified, such as the Barcelona Fountain with a lot of jets going up all over the place in a circular area. I wanted to make a new fountain, a fountain which represents our times and our relationship to outer space."[1]

Mrs. Dodge's will had given Detroit a September 1 deadline and time had nearly run out. Not wanting to forgo the money, the city hastily organized the competition. The eleven-member Horace E. Dodge Fountain Selection Committee's hope was that the fountain and plaza would help revitalize Detroit's derelict downtown, which in recent years had been the site of protests and riots. Noguchi's plan was selected before the deadline. A letter of agreement between the city of Detroit and Noguchi dated August 16, 1971, indicates that in mid-June the city's Common Council had authorized disbursements from Mrs. Dodge's bequest so that Noguchi could be paid twenty thousand dollars to come up with a fountain design, including sketches, written material, cost estimates, and renderings.

Six days before the deadline, Noguchi submitted his proposal to the fountain selection committee. His submission included diagrams of basic types of water effects. He turned up the heat on the rhetoric of persuasion:

> The great fountain, projected as the most magnificent of modern times, rises from the plateau of primal space. It is an engine for water, plainly associating the spectacle to its sources of energy—the engine—so closely a part of Detroit. It recalls and commemorates the dream that has produced the automobile, the airplane and now the rocket. The fountain rises 18 feet into the air, hovering in a cloud of water, incandescent at night.
> The fountain will be an engineering feat in metals.[2]

An early drawing of Noguchi's fountain shows a bridgelike structure that is clearly based on Japanese ceremonial gates. In the center of this long elevated structure Noguchi planned to have a steel ring thirty feet in diameter spouting water up and down and supported on hefty granite piers. Below the fountain, a circular granite basin would spout water upward, interacting with the ring's downward flow. The surrounding area was to be lined with paving blocks set in sand. Given the "many imponderables," Noguchi said, it was difficult to be certain about cost. But he gave an estimate of $400,000.

Two days before a probate court deadline for satisfying the execution of the Dodge will, Noguchi's design was chosen. But a court battle ensued because Mrs. Dodge's architect grandson, who had submitted his own design to the competition, maintained that Noguchi's fountain was not in the place his grandmother had stipulated, which was "at the foot of Woodward." The following July the court ruled that the fountain's proposed site, now relocated closer to Woodward Avenue, did not contradict Mrs. Dodge's wishes.

As with several other projects, Noguchi, having won the competition, enlarged the scope of his work by asking to design not just the fountain but the entire plaza. Robert Hastings, chairman of the fountain selection committee, and also head of the architectural firm that had done the initial design of the plaza, accepted Noguchi's request. Over the next eight years Noguchi became passionately engaged with Detroit's Civic Plaza, for which he designed not only a fountain but also a twisting pylon. He was eager to make a "gateway to the city," a

Horace E. Dodge Fountain, Detroit, 1972–79. Stainless steel, ht. 24 ft.

place where people from all walks of life could connect. The plaza, he hoped, would revitalize downtown Detroit, calm political tensions, and perhaps even reverse the flight to the suburbs. This would not, he said, be just a beautiful sculpture, it would be useful. The need he felt to make something that would become part of people's lives arose, he thought, from his need for belonging. "If through art the world can be made more friendly, more accessible to people, more understandable, more meaningful, then even art has some reason."[3]

The Dodge Fountain required elaborate engineering, which Noguchi's partner Shoji Sadao and various consulting engineers worked out.[4] Noguchi himself liked to solve technical problems and his attention to detail was extraordinary. He would make site visits and take note of everything that was not as it should be—things like the exhaust and fresh air intake stacks, the lighting, the placement of feeder pipes, the position of fog nozzles, the spacing of jets, the height of jetting water. He even invented his own hydraulic nozzle, which produced a cylindrical column of water hollow at its center.

In March 1973 Noguchi presented to the Common Council a revised design for a "cloud-creating" computer-operated fountain, which he said would evoke "a bird rising" as well as "an airplane and jet propulsion."[5] He also presented a plan plus scale model for the plaza with its stainless steel pylon, which made a quarter turn as it moved upward. The plaza would serve Detroit's public by offering a range of activities, including an amphitheater that could be converted into an ice skating rink. There were various pyramids to hide mechanicals and to serve as seating areas. On the day following the presentation the *Detroit Free Press* reported: "Pixyish Japanese-American sculptor Isamu Noguchi, his eyes gleaming as he moved his shiny aluminum pointer from model to diagram to architect's drawing and back again, told Detroit's Common Council Friday what the new $18 million riverfront plaza will look like."[6] It would, Noguchi promised, be "different and better than" New York's Rockefeller Center or Lincoln Center. "It will be a people's park, not a monument." The fountain, which was now to be all stainless steel and twenty-four feet high instead of eighteen feet as originally planned, would have eighty different water and light patterns.

Noguchi kept changing his mind about certain aspects of the design. He had to convey these changes to Sadao, who had to communicate them to the consulting engineers, who were not always pleased at the change orders. On September 16, 1973, he wrote to Priscilla, "So I keep writing to Shoji and he tries to placate feelings all around and diplomatically translate my diatribes into acceptably polite and reasonable requests. Its [sic] probably just as well that I am far away."[7] Noguchi's irascible mood had also to do with his not being able to work on his own sculpture, which, he told Priscilla, was "utterly displaced and I'm distressed that I can not seem to get going." Work on the Detroit plaza did not go smoothly. By the time the project was completed, for all his pride in it, Noguchi had some sour feelings about his years of struggle—delays, lawsuits, the city government's inefficiency, arguments, cost-increasing changes, and mistakes. At one point, for example, when they tested the fountain the force of the water was so strong that a large chunk of the granite basin blew out. Noguchi's relationship with Coleman Young, Detroit's first African-American mayor, had testy moments. Soon after Mayor Young was elected, Noguchi recalled, "He saw what we were doing; our models, our plans and so forth. The first thing he said was, 'Well where's the ethnic festival?'

You see, the ethnic festival was something that had been going on for years along the river."[8] In fact, Noguchi had not planned for an underground space large enough to accommodate the festival, but without hesitating he told Mayor Young that the ethnic festival would be downstairs. He now went back to the drafting board and designed a two-acre area beneath the plaza. The mayor's question, Noguchi said, expanded the underground space from a skating rink and amphitheater to a covered performance area, gallery, restaurant, and room for twenty-six kiosks.

With Mayor Young presiding, the twisted pylon was dedicated on August 28, 1974. "This distinctive landmark," Young declared, "is a big step in developing an outstanding people-oriented, riverfront-downtown area."[9] Noguchi said that the pylon with its quarter turn signified the "spiral of life, the double helix on which all life is based."[10] "It was nothing I did. It was done by nature originally."[11]

Construction of the Dodge Fountain began in 1975 and it was dedicated on July 24, 1976. The fountain's ring, twenty-six feet in diameter and often described as a doughnut, is held aloft by two splayed cylindrical legs that can be seen as a high-tech revisiting of the idea of the female giving birth seen in Noguchi's 1952 memorial to the dead of Hiroshima. The water from the circle jetting downward between heavy thighs might allude to water breaking. A *Detroit Free Press* writer took note of the primal associations in Noguchi's fountain and pylon: "The pylon is the energized phallus," she suggested. "The fountain is a receptacle, the . . . legs shape the delta, with the same kind of sensuality that characterized prehistoric fertility goddesses."[12] Likewise, the *Detroit News* critic noted that the fountain's cylinder and ring shapes were the "timeless forms of birth and regeneration," all appropriate symbols of Detroit's rebirth.[13]

Noguchi's Philip A. Hart Plaza was dedicated on April 20, 1979. Thousands of people gathered, many toting picnic bags. The fountain went through its repertoire of effects and sunshine created rainbows in the upward-spurting spume. The dedication by Mayor Young and Noguchi was preceded by a jazz band concert, a mime-troop performance, and the twenty-six-member Baptist Church choir all dressed in mustard-yellow robes singing "I Love This Place" as the crowd swayed and clapped. Then came speeches. "You now see before your eyes, beneath the shadow of the Renaissance Center, the new Detroit," pro-

Pylon for Philip A. Hart Plaza, Detroit, 1974. Stainless steel, ht. 120 ft.

claimed Mayor Young as the crowd in the five-hundred-seat amphitheater clapped and whistled. "This is a marvelous people place." Noguchi smiled and waved his arms. When it was his turn to talk he said: "This enormous beautiful spot didn't look like much when it was a parking lot. But it's turned out better than ever I could have imagined." He said he had nothing to add to what had already been said: "I've spoken through the fountain."[14]

For all the euphoria on the day of the plaza's dedication, there were, for Noguchi, things that rankled. The trees, bushes, and grass he had planned had not yet been planted. Many technical problems had not been solved. The day before the dedication, at a City Council award presentation ceremony at which he was the honored guest, Noguchi saw fit to complain about the "unconscionable" maintenance of his fountain. The water had been left on during the winter and the pipes froze.[15] He urged the council to hire permanent maintenance.

Noguchi's public criticism didn't sit well with Mayor Young, who responded that dedicated and permanent maintenance wasn't in the budget. Nonetheless, when the two of them left the award presentation Young had his arm over Noguchi's shoulders.[16] Within a week of Noguchi's departure from Detroit, the planting had begun and the fountain was working, but not at its full capacity. The fountain continued to be plagued with technical problems in the years to come, and in 1987 the Detroit Renaissance Foundation raised $800,000 to renovate it.

In spite of the frustrations involved, Noguchi was proud of his work in Detroit. It was his most ambitious project so far, and since many of his plans for public spaces had fallen through, its completion meant a great deal to him. He felt that the fountain and plaza had done much to revitalize downtown Detroit. But he was also worn down by the project. In an interview with *The Detroit News* a few days before the April 20 dedication, he expressed a desire to return to private sculpture: "I will concentrate on just my own work. That way, if I just stop moving around, I could probably find a much happier life. I crave a sense of place." Yet Noguchi's unstoppable creative energy kept him crisscrossing the globe. "I have an unfinished road to walk," he told an interviewer in 1985. "By the time I approach something, I'm off on another mile."[17]

For all his desire to focus on carving stone, even before the Detroit plaza's dedication, Noguchi was considering a number of public com-

Heaven, interior garden at the Sogetsu Flower-Arranging School, Tokyo, 1977–78. Granite

missions. *Kukaniloko* (1977) was a proposal (unrealized) to protect the sacred Hawaiian "birth rocks" from the encroachment of pineapple crops. In 1978 he began to design the Lillie and Hugh Roy Cullen Sculpture Garden for the Houston Museum of Fine Arts, and in 1979 he began to think about Bayfront Park in Miami. There was also an unrealized sculpture garden for the Tennessee Williams Fine Arts Center in Key West.

One of the most successful of these commissions, an interior garden for the display of flowers at Tokyo's Sogetsu Flower-Arranging School, was called *Tengoku,* or *Heaven.* Noguchi's old friend Sofu Teshigahara, the avant-garde flower arranger and painter who was master of the school, asked him to design the lobby of the newly built, eight-story, glass-skinned school building designed by Kenzo Tange. Tange had already designed the lobby, but Teshigahara was not satisfied with Tange's solution, so he told Tange that he would like to ask Noguchi to redesign it. Tange's response was measured and calm: "Is that so? I understand."[18]

On October 13, 1975, Noguchi wrote to Tange that he had sent a model of his lobby to Izumi, who would carve it out of stone. The space was peculiar because the upper balconies of a theater on the floor below projected into the lobby in a stepped sequence, or, as Noguchi put it, "like a ziggurat."[19] Noguchi's solution was to design what he described as "a stepped hill of stone, a place for people to go."[20] He compared the space he created at Sogetsu to a giant tokonoma, which he said was "the most sacred spot in a Japanese house . . . It's heaven, and what I've done there [at Sogetsu] is heaven, you see."[21] The result was a wonderfully alive, many-tiered mountain made of pale granite blocks interspersed with the occasional rough-hewn boulder. The whole space is united by the subtle downward flow of water from a basin on the upper terrace. The stream first drips into a stone *tsukubai* (basin), and then continues downward, sometimes disappearing and reappearing. Although the total volume of *Heaven*'s space is small, it feels as majestic as a mountain, and, because of the skillfully arranged lighting with skylights on the ceiling, you feel, looking upward, as if you were being led into the firmament. Outside the building is a thirty-foot-high, slightly twisted, black granite pylon, which Noguchi compared to the ritual post that sets off a tokonoma in traditional Japanese houses.

Yet another brilliant commission from the second half of the 1970s was for a sculpture for Storm King Art Center, a sculpture park in Mountainville, New York. Here Noguchi created a grouping of pale granite rocks that is one of his greatest and most loved sculptures. Designed to be climbed upon, *Momo Taro* is warm and welcoming in its embrace, more accessible than most of Noguchi's works, but no less mysterious.

According to Peter Stern, president of the Storm King Art Center, when he visited Noguchi to discuss the project, Noguchi marched him through a studio full of metal sculptures. Stern told Noguchi that he wanted a sculpture made of stone. Noguchi gave Stern a noncommittal look and asked, "What drawings do you need?" Stern said, "None."[22] This pleased Noguchi, who explained that he didn't want to make a

Momo Taro, Storm King Art Center, Mountainville, New York, 1977–78. Granite, nine elements

careful model for his sculpture because "anything precise restricts you." Noguchi asked Stern where in the park his sculpture would be placed. Stern said, "Anywhere you like." Noguchi, who tended to choose prominent sites, picked a grassy knoll close to the administration building overlooking the vast rolling park. Noguchi asked if he could make the hill bigger and alter its profile. Starting in 1933 with his giant earthwork *Monument to the Plow*, Noguchi had had an urge to sculpt the earth. This too was agreeable to Stern, and backhoes soon appeared to do the job.

On June 13, 1977, Noguchi wrote to Stern that he would proceed with the project and outlined a verbal agreement. He said he planned to look for suitable stones that summer in Japan, and he would be "listening to what they say." Noguchi had hoped to use pink mannari granite, but it was too expensive, so he settled upon granite from the island of Shodoshima. Years later he told the story of finding *Momo Taro*'s stone: "It was the night time when I climbed the mountain on the island of Shodoshima, where Izumi had spotted a huge stone. Too big to handle, it was broken in two to get it to my studio. Is it from these stones that my concept came, or is it not more correct to say that it derived equally from the hill at Storm King?"[23]

The title *Momo Taro* comes from a popular Japanese folk tale that Noguchi's mother had often recounted to him. A childless couple discovered a giant peach floating down a stream. When they picked it out of the water a miraculous child emerged. He grew up to slay the local dragon.[24]

Noguchi saw that the two pieces of the split boulder resembled a peach cut in half with the pit removed. Since he identified Momotaro as the child of the sun god, the round, split-open boulder could also stand for the sun. To complicate matters further, in Noguchi's mind his sculpture had to do with the Japanese creation myth.[25] The upturned stone on the left was, Noguchi said, not only the sun but also "a mirror, a reflection."[26] The split rock's cavity opening up toward the sky might also have suggested to Noguchi a womb for light. He told Dore Ashton that *Momo Taro* was "a place to go . . . a metaphor for man as an end and a beginning . . . a mirror to the passage of the sun."[27] Perhaps the boulder's two halves with their round cavities refer to procreation, while the seven flatter, more rectangular stones lying close by refer to life's end.

The way *Momo Taro* hugs the grassy hilltop makes it seem as if it were embracing the world. "I'm very much attached now to closeness to earth, sinking into it," wrote Noguchi.[28] But he also felt that the sculpture was playful. When in October 1988 Noguchi visited the site, he said, "I want children around that sculpture. It's made for children."[29] *Momo Taro* is perhaps the most engaging play object that Noguchi ever made. It brings out the child in every visitor. During Noguchi's October visit, a little girl crawled out of the hollow of the peach, held out her hand to Noguchi, and asked him to join her in the peach's cavity. He went in and when he emerged his face was wet with tears.

47

IMAGINARY LANDSCAPES

In April 1978 a major traveling exhibition titled *Noguchi's Imaginary Landscapes* opened at the Walker Art Center in Minneapolis. The museum's director, Martin Friedman, and Noguchi had been talking about mounting an exhibition for some fifteen years. In 1975 Friedman wrote to Noguchi that he wanted to do an exhibition based on Noguchi's theater designs and possibly also a group of related sculptures. Later he decided the show should focus on Noguchi as a sculptor of space and should include Noguchi's gardens and plazas.

At first Noguchi was enthusiastic, but his enthusiasm soured in mid-1978. As with his conflicted relationship with Arne Ekstrom, he wanted to control what was to be in the exhibition. Friedman, however, a highly professional and intelligent director, was no pushover. He knew that his job was to curate the show according to his own vision. After what must have been a tense meeting, Noguchi wrote to Friedman: "Your way of taking charge left me with grave doubts which I am afraid I expressed badly."[1] Noguchi objected to Friedman's selection of sculptures, which seemed to him "a sampling," tacked on and unrelated to the "subject of environment as a 'synergetic' enterprise." Even though Friedman's original idea had been to focus on Noguchi's theater designs, and these certainly qualified as the sculpting of space, Noguchi was upset that Friedman wanted to devote an entire room to his sets for Martha Graham: "I don't want the show to be overwhelmed by Martha any more than having it distracted by a minor sculpture display." Noguchi suggested that Friedman should show Akari and possibly some tabletop sculptures in one of the galleries. If, as Friedman had warned him, the participating museums were only interested in the show as Friedman had conceived it, then, said Noguchi, it would be best to forget about moving it to other venues and instead have a smaller show just at the Walker.

Martin Friedman stood his ground. He wrote Noguchi a long, fair, but tough-minded reply saying that as curator, he had ultimate responsibility for the exhibition's theme and content, and that Noguchi had known from the beginning the environmental concept behind his choices. Moreover, he pointed out that the show's funding had been based on his original proposal for an exhibition of Noguchi's "sculpture, architecture and theater sets."[2] Akari were not included. Friedman's aim, he said, was to "reveal the great formal and humanistic consistency" in Noguchi's work. He told Noguchi that he wanted an immediate resolution to their disagreements. Unless the show remained what he and Noguchi had agreed it should be during their last meeting, the Walker Art Center would cancel it. He gave Noguchi four days to make up his mind.

Priscilla and Shoji Sadao were the peacemakers. Priscilla cooked Noguchi a dinner and invited Shoji and Noguchi's accountant, Bernie Bergstein, to join. "Toward the end of dinner I said, 'I have something to tell you. Martin Friedman told me he is not going to have the show and he means it. I hope you will let Martin do it.'"[3] Noguchi and Friedman patched things up and, as Friedman recalls, they had a lasting friendship.

Noguchi could not attend the April opening of his Walker Art Center exhibition. He was immobilized by his worsening back problems, for which he would have a second surgery in May. Two months later he wrote to Fanny Rumely: "I work too hard and as a result I was felled by a nerve condition last March and have been undergoing various treatments until I was finally operated on twice. And now I'm on the way to recovery and a new lease on life which doctors guarantee will be good for another twenty-five years—so I may last a while longer who knows?"[4] According to Friedman, once he was able to travel, Noguchi did see his show, and he thought that the installation was superb.[5]

Noguchi's Imaginary Landscapes surveyed forty years of work and filled four galleries—one devoted to individual sculptures, another to stage sets, a third to architectural projects, and a fourth to unexecuted public commissions. There was also a performance space designed by Noguchi, a kind of indoor garden called "Variable Landscapes," consisting of a group of movable sculptures made of wood, canvas, and bamboo. Friedman wrote an excellent catalogue. To show the underlying unity of all of Noguchi's work he included a section called "Noguchi's Formal Vocabulary," which revealed the sculptor's preference for certain shapes—columns, twisting pylons, pyramids and triangles, interlocking elements, cubes, circles, spheres, and emerging earth forms.

The critical response was mostly positive. By now, Noguchi was generally described as the grand old man of American sculpture. In *The New York Times* Hilton Kramer pointed out that Noguchi's career was "probably the most varied and far-reaching" of any in the history of American sculpture.[6] The "socially-minded" Noguchi had, he said, expanded the idea of sculpture into public life, while at the same time he produced, with "exquisite invention," numerous small-scale art objects that were "some of the simplest and most beautiful sculpture of the modern age." The stone sculptures had a depth of meaning that "recalls us to elementary experience." Their effect was to clear the viewer's mind and to induce "a more contemplative attitude toward experience . . . they beckon us into a kind of paradise of the spirit where we are made to feel reborn . . . Who else among us," Kramer asked, "has even attempted a rapprochement between art and life on this scale?"

Allan Temko's two reviews for the *San Francisco Chronicle* and the *San Francisco Sunday Examiner & Chronicle* described the great range of Noguchi's art as a result of his "several distinct selves, all exquisitely refined," but related only by their "sense of restless search." He saw Noguchi as a poet who had drawn from nature "hitherto unrealized truths," but whose work was "ultimately remote and strange."[7] Of the public works he wrote: "No contemporary sculpture is nobler than Noguchi's visions of vast monuments and ideal parks."

Noguchi, who had always felt misunderstood and unappreciated by critics, must have been gratified by this outpouring of praise. As the show traveled from city to city, most reviewers said that it was the best proof that Noguchi was one of the great sculptors of the twentieth century.

A major commission that came Noguchi's way in the second half of the 1970s was the Lillie and Hugh Roy Cullen Sculpture Garden in

front of the Mies van der Rohe–designed Brown Pavilion of the Houston Museum of Fine Arts. Another was the Japanese American Cultural and Community Center's plaza in Los Angeles, which Noguchi
started working on in 1979. In addition, a public square and large
granite sculpture for Bologna was begun in 1979, and in that same
year he was commissioned to build his monument to Benjamin
Franklin in Philadelphia, a sculpture he had conceived nearly half a
century earlier. Plans to design Miami's Bayfront Park, his biggest
project to date, were also getting under way.

What Noguchi had in mind for the sculpture garden in Houston
was a stroll garden with red carnelian granite walkways winding between mounded earth forms and freestanding concrete walls in various geometric shapes—rather like those he had designed for display of
the smaller sculptures in the Billy Rose Sculpture Garden. In 1983
Noguchi told a Houston journalist: "I have tried to provide a great variety of areas, with different kinds of enclosures. These will provide, I
hope, a continuous experience, so that we always see something new—as
in life."[8] Two years later he again spoke of his love of surprise and of
making the space look larger than it actually was, as in enclosed Zen
gardens. The garden, he said, "should serve as a place for meditation, a
moment of relaxation or an evening's formal event. Yet, I hope with the
winding paths, trees and grass, it will always look fresh—for timelessness is nature left alone."[9]

The first proposal Noguchi submitted showed the Houston garden
surrounded by a sixteen-foot-high wall, but a number of neighborhood
civic groups and some local architects objected because the wall would
have cut the garden off from the city. Noguchi went back to the drawing board and designed a wall of varying heights. As time went by, irritated by the endless bureaucratic hurdles, Noguchi began to feel that
the garden was a waste of his time and that he should "stick to sculpture however humble, and save one's soul and tranquility."[10]

In 1982 the museum's new director, Peter Marzio, tried to resolve
the various issues that were holding up the garden, and he wrote to
Shoji Sadao in April 1983 listing suggestions for changes that would
make the garden acceptable to the sculpture garden committee. A
week later, hurt and indignant, Noguchi wrote back: "Obviously your
committee is accustomed to dealing with architects and those involved
with service. I happen to be an artist as you know, unaccustomed to

such treatment and cannot comply with your committee's ideas as they occur to them . . . as I say, I am happy to be a sculptor but I cannot go beyond my artistic judgment to please the many desires your committee members think up. I am terribly sorry if my self-respect might stand in the way of the garden's realization, a garden for which I had great expectations."[11]

Sixteen days before the garden's opening on April 5, 1986, Noguchi, with his fierce eye for detail and for felicities of proportion, stood in the middle of Bissonet Street, which borders one side of the garden, and stared at the earth mounded up against the outside of the garden's enclosing wall. Passing cars honked and came to a stop. Finally Noguchi made his decision. He walked up to the garden wall and drew a chalk line to show how high the earth should be. All morning Noguchi continued this process. Onlookers were astonished to see the spry but wizened eighty-one-year-old man leaping over the wall, jumping up on garden benches to get a better view, and dashing from place to place while small bulldozers shaped the earth according to his will. Peter Marzio marveled: "His eye, his intuition, is almost never wrong."[12]

The $3.2 million garden was inaugurated with much fanfare. Among the 6,500 visitors was Noguchi's friend the avant-garde composer John Cage, who took the occasion to premiere several pieces, including *Garden of Sounds* and *Ryoanji*, in which six musicians were dispersed in the crowd. A smiling Noguchi turned to Cage and quipped: "This garden can be destroyed by sculpture. Do you think it can be destroyed by music, too?"[13] Vice President George Bush made a speech. Noguchi and the museum's chairman of the board, Isaac Arnold, Jr., did the formal ribbon cutting. Unlike the inauguration of the Chase Manhattan Bank's water garden, at which Noguchi's name was not mentioned, Noguchi was the center of attention and given a standing ovation. Asked what most pleased him about the Houston garden, Noguchi said that he liked the way the garden's contradictions had been resolved. The space, for example, was enclosed by walls, yet it was open. He hoped that this openness would break down the barriers between visitors and sculpture.[14] "As I walked through today, I find the changing relations of the spaces exactly as I had hoped . . . I think there is a kind of conversation going on, a very quiet conversation between walls and spaces, people and sculptures. The walls are sculptures as far as I am concerned. They form a geometry of playfulness in a sense."[15]

Late in December 1978 Noguchi was asked if he would make a sculpture for the new Japanese American Cultural and Community Center (JACCC) in the Little Tokyo section of Los Angeles. The JACCC had planned a rather narrow, hemmed-in plaza. As he often did, Noguchi looked at the proposed site and came up with a much-expanded plan. At a meeting with the City Redevelopment Agency, he examined the model for the JACCC complex, removed the model for a future gym, and moved the theater to where the gym was supposed to be. This left room for him to design an entire one-acre plaza. Noguchi's contract set his fee for the JACCC plaza at $100,000 for the plaza plus $200,000 for the sculpture. Like a European piazza, the plaza should, he said, be a "gathering place for all people . . . a place for celebration, meditation."[16] He designed a red-brick, multi-level space with a round, black-granite fountain built into a raised square of brick and numerous raised and sunken geometric shapes. At the highest level sat two huge slightly carved basalt boulders from

To the Issei, Japanese American Cultural and Community Center Plaza, Los Angeles, 1980–83. Basalt, two elements, l.d. 120 in.

Shikoku, one erect, the other recumbent. He titled the sculpture *To the Issei* to honor the first-generation Japanese who came to America starting in the late nineteenth century. Noguchi told the journalist Tim Fukai that the two rocks were part of "the ecological continuance of the world" and an "antidote to impermanence."[17] The JACCC plaza and the sculpture were dedicated on July 26, 1983, with a lively ceremony presided over by Mayor Tom Bradley, including a drum performance by the Kinara Taiko group, Obon dancing performed by a Japanese dance group, and a Shinto purification rite and blessing performed by a Shinto priest in traditional costume. Looking over his plaza, Noguchi told JACCC gallery director Miles Kubo, "The children will know how to use it."[18]

While Noguchi was preparing for *Imaginary Landscapes* to be presented at the Philadelphia Museum of Art in 1979, he remembered that he had done a proposal for a Benjamin Franklin memorial forty-six years ago. He scratched his head and said, "I remember this drawing. Let's put it in the show."[19] Anne d'Harnoncourt, then director of the Philadelphia Museum, agreed. Working with Noguchi on the show was, she said, "a total thrill for me. I was very lucky. First of all I was a woman. And he was a flirt. Also I was my father's daughter.* Noguchi loved my father."[20]

When Noguchi's show was in the planning stage, a trustee of the Fairmount Park Art Association (FPAA) saw Noguchi's Benjamin Franklin drawing and thought the monument might be an appropriate way to celebrate Philadelphia's 1982 tricentennial. The FPAA asked Noguchi if he would like to build his *Memorial to Ben Franklin*, and he was delighted. Noguchi's monument is an explicit reference to perhaps Franklin's most famous experiment: flying a kite during an electrical storm. The 1933 plan incorporated the kite at the top, a bolt of lightning in the middle, and beneath the bolt the key with which Franklin elucidated his theory of electricity. At the base were four high-tension insulators. All of this was set precariously on top of a tall steel openwork structure held up by guy wires and inspired by the radio transmitting towers then being built in the United States. Another

---

* Anne's father, René d'Harnoncourt, was a well-known art patron and former director of the Museum of Modern Art.

source for this tall metal structure might be Buckminster Fuller's pencil studies for *Dymaxion 20-Worker-Shelter for Russian Cooperative Mobile Farming* (c. 1932), which also shows an openwork pylon steadied by guy wires.

Noguchi recalled that the idea for his Benjamin Franklin sculpture had occurred to him after he returned to the United States from Japan in 1931. "After coming back to America I felt—patriotic is not the word—but it was a feeling of belonging here."[21] As with his *Monument to the Plow* of the same date, he chose an American theme to celebrate and identify with the country of his birth. Noguchi's enthusiasm for American ingenuity gave him a feeling of kinship with Franklin. "I'm very independent, and I think that's what I like about Benjamin Franklin. He thought for himself. He didn't wait for other people to tell him what to do. He was a great inspiration for a young man wanting to get out into the world."[22] When Noguchi presented his new model to Philadelphia's Art Commission, he explained his work: "The kite is an expression of America. It is nothing but it trapped the energy. It has contact with the deepest forces of nature, but it is also linked to the ground—an expression of intelligence and practicality—and that joining, too, is very American."[23]

The model Noguchi presented in 1982 differed from his original conception in various ways. Now the key was held thirty-three feet off the ground by four painted steel legs. Above it was the forty-six-foot-high stainless steel bolt, and above that was a seventeen-foot-high tubular openwork steel structure (a vestigial version of the steel structure at the base of the 1933 proposal). Resting on top of the openwork structure was the stainless steel kite. As in the earlier plan, the sculpture was held up by guy cables, which, Noguchi told Penny Bach, then project director of the FPAA, were "the eternal connection between the earth and the sky."[24]

Noguchi returned to Philadelphia in early spring 1983 to look for a suitable site for his Franklin monument. Ted Newbold, head of the FPAA, in whose car Noguchi, Penny Bach, and Anne d'Harnoncourt rode during this search, recalled thinking that Noguchi would pick a place in Fairmount Park, but when they entered the park Noguchi said nothing. He just kept craning his neck, searching for a better location. Next they went to look at the sculpture garden at Penn's Landing on the Delaware River, near the Benjamin Franklin Bridge. Noguchi re-

Bolt of Lightning . . . Memorial to Ben Franklin, Philadelphia, 1984. Stainless steel, ht. 101½ ft.

jected this possibility—he never liked the idea of plunking one of his sculptures down in an already existing sculpture garden. As Newbold turned down Vine Street, Noguchi suddenly said, "Stop the car!" He then dashed across several lanes of traffic, terrifying his fellow passengers. "He flew out of the car and jumped up and down. He knew this place was right," Bach recalled. The spot he chose was Monument Plaza at the base of the Benjamin Franklin Bridge on the Philadelphia side.

The Franklin monument was not finished for Philadelphia's tricentennial. As usual with Noguchi's public works, various problems and legal delays slowed its progress. "It took a raft of lawyers and the FPAA, the city, and the Delaware River Port Authority to draw up the legal agreements," Penny Bach explained.[25] As Noguchi kept revising his monument, it grew from sixty to over one hundred feet; the increased height was made possible thanks to the engineering genius of Paul Weidlinger, who had worked with Noguchi on other projects such as the twisted pylon in Detroit's Civic Plaza. Weidlinger took Noguchi's model, measured it, entered the coordinates into a computer, and then generated drawings. He analyzed how the asymmetrical monument could withstand the force of gravity and discovered that the shape that Noguchi had planned made it nearly impossible to engineer. "The sculpture is mad. I would not have done it for anybody I didn't like a lot."[26] At one point Weidlinger decreased the degree of the lightning bolt's "zigzag," which made the sculpture taller. Noguchi trusted Weidlinger, but, Penny Bach observed, he was not happy with the less pronounced angularity of the bolt, and he went back to his original plan. When the engineering studies were finished and Noguchi saw how the kite structure would look, he told Weidlinger, "I'd like to tilt it." Weidlinger agreed.

By 1982 the cost of Noguchi's bolt had risen to $750,000, almost twice the original estimate. When in that year the Delaware River Port Authority, which owned the site and operated the bridge, heard how much the sculpture would cost to maintain, they balked. Just to light the monument with forty 1,100-watt bulbs would cost $5,168 a year for electricity and $14,000 for the bulbs. The wattage and number of lights was reduced, bringing the annual lighting expense to $3,000. The city agreed to foot the bill.

The contract to build Noguchi's bolt went to Crescent Iron Works.

The framework of stainless steel piping, reminiscent of structures made by his lifelong friend Buckminster Fuller, was a challenge for Crescent. Joseph Milani, president of the firm, was impressed by the clarity of Noguchi's plans and the ease with which Noguchi worked with the craftsmen: "He is a very practical person," Milani said, "one of the most practical men I've ever encountered. He knows exactly what he wants."[27] Noguchi and the Crescent workers treated each other with mutual respect: "They did not feel that he was the prince and they were the servants," says Penny Bach.

Memorial to Ben Franklin took a year and a half to fabricate. In the third week of June 1983, it was transported in sections to the bridge site. Noguchi, wearing a hard hat, was there to greet it and to help with its erection. A crowd of about fifty artists, reporters, and passersby gathered to watch cranes lift the pieces high enough for workers on a scaffold to ease them into their correct positions. All this time Noguchi moved from one vantage point to another, watching silently and taking photographs.

"Isamu Noguchi was as full of bounce as a jack-in-the-box," wrote the *Philadelphia Inquirer* staff writer Edgar Williams. "He double-times up the steps of the monument plaza . . . and he was smiling. 'Two more days,' he said, 'and it all comes together; after all these years it's going up.'"[28] When Williams asked Noguchi what he planned to do next, Noguchi said: "Oh, I have a few things planned. Enough to keep me busy until my 100th birthday or thereabout."

The sculpture, which Noguchi titled *Bolt of Lightning . . . Memorial to Ben Franklin*, was dedicated on the night of September 18, 1984, in a ceremony attended by several hundred people. Philadelphia's mayor, W. Wilson Goode, told Noguchi, "You are indeed a genius in our time." Penny Bach remembers the inauguration as being both "fantastic and funny." Speakers on the bunting-festooned podium had to stretch out their speeches because it took a while to get the lights to function. When the sculpture was finally lit, a policeman exclaimed, "Beautiful! I hope people don't drive into it."[29]

Although the crowd was delighted, critics were not so generous. One writer, Edward J. Sozanski of *The Philadelphia Inquirer*, said *Bolt* was like a hood ornament. Monument Plaza, he said, "swallows Noguchi's stainless steel monolith like a canapé."[30] Another *Philadelphia Inquirer* article said the sculpture's top "is an open throating of tubes, clutching the outline of a kite with the grace of an over-extended gullet."[31] Thomas Hine, the *Inquirer's* architectural critic, noted that for motorists crossing the bridge, *Bolt* was just a sliver of silver "out-dazzled by a parade of billboards." Indeed, as you drive over the bridge *Bolt* appears only for an instant. But then, lightning is equally evanescent, and *Bolt of Lightning* has the flash of an idea that lights up the mind and then vanishes.

48

CALIFORNIA SCENARIO

Noguchi was a genius at shaping water in relation to stone to create a feeling of both instantaneity and timelessness. The water flowing down the UNESCO garden's steps is an early example. His 1984 water garden for the Domon Ken Museum in Sakata, Japan, is another. The sparest of Noguchi's gardens, it consists of rock, water, and a clump of bamboo. A sloped area, partly enclosed by architect Yoshio Taniguchi's museum building, is shaped by broad granite steps over which water cascades into a pool below. Noguchi stood a single basalt rock on the third step from the top. In a more literal explanation than was usually his wont, he said that the flowing water symbolized the passing of time and that the rock was the photographer Domon Ken, standing in the middle of the flow.

Perhaps Noguchi's most beautiful use of water is in the garden he created in the early 1980s in Costa Mesa, California. The garden was jointly commissioned in 1980 by the Prudential Insurance Company of America and Henry Segerstrom, an Orange County art patron and developer of the South Coast Plaza Town Center, a business and cultural complex situated not far off the San Diego Freeway. The site Segerstrom had in mind was a 1.6-acre space squeezed between two fifteen-story glass-facade office buildings and a forty-foot-high parking garage. Late in 1979 Segerstrom flew to New York. As planned, he arrived at Noguchi's Long Island City studio at 9:00 a.m. He rang the bell and told the voice that answered that he had come to see Noguchi. The voice, which turned out to be that of Shoji Sadao, said that Noguchi

was home in his Manhattan apartment with a cold. Segerstrom persisted: "Well, I've come from California and I have a flight leaving this
afternoon." Sadao invited Segerstrom to come inside out of the freez-
ing cold. Moved by the beauty of the sculptures he saw, Segerstrom
begged Sadao to call Noguchi to ask if he could come to show him the
site plans for the possible garden commission. At Noguchi's 333 East
Sixty-ninth Street apartment, Noguchi and Segerstrom looked at the
plans for the Costa Mesa site. "He said he didn't like it," Segerstrom
recalled, "and objected to the presence of so many cars. Why didn't
people walk, as they do in New York, he wanted to know. I tried to
point out the virtues of the project, but he was not receptive and his
cold seemed to give him a more negative attitude."[1]

Segerstrom returned to Orange County disappointed but not de-
feated. He wrote Noguchi a flattering letter, further expressing his
"dream" of bringing Noguchi's art to the plaza.[2] A month and a half
later, Tamara Thomas, a Los Angeles art consultant, wrote to Noguchi
telling him what an "ideal client" Segerstrom would be. She did not
exaggerate. When Noguchi finally capitulated, he got on better with
Segerstrom than with any other patron. There was a deep bond of
sympathy between the two men, and the garden that resulted from
this connection was all the more perfect because of it. Thomas told
Noguchi that Segerstrom had envisioned "a very soft green landscape
area" at his Costa Mesa site and she was astonished at Segerstrom's
willingness to accept Noguchi's "bare plaza" concept.[3] Noguchi wrote
back on January 25, 1980: "I am indeed intrigued with your client" and
his "ambition to go beyond what has been done before."

Later that year Noguchi went to see the site in Costa Mesa. He
looked askance at the undistinguished corporate buildings and a garage flanking the space allotted for the garden, but his respect for
Segerstrom and his desire to do something in his native state persuaded him not to turn the project down. "I said I wouldn't do just a
sculpture; the area needed more than that. Mr. Segerstrom agreed,
but he didn't know what he was getting into. I made a plan for the garden as a sort of menu. I wanted to do it all, but I didn't expect him to
buy it all. One does not expect that much support."[4]

In mid-February Tamara Thomas wrote to Noguchi that she and
Segerstrom understood Noguchi's desire only to take on projects that
gave him the possibility of "exploration and growth."[5] It was, she said,

this attitude that made Segerstrom want to work with him. On March 28 Segerstrom wrote to Thomas: "Noguchi has agreed!" He said he wanted Noguchi to create a sculpture as well as the courtyard. "I would like to have in our project not only the expression of Noguchi's mind but also of his hand."[6]

On July 18 Tamara Thomas sent Noguchi a letter of agreement that included the sculpture, which at that point was to be called *Origin Stone*. Noguchi was to be paid $250,000, fifty thousand more than he was paid for JACCC's *To the Issei*. His prices were going up concomitant with his increasing fame. He told the *Los Angeles Times* art critic Suzanne Muchnic: "I decided if I was going to do the project, I wanted to do something for all California—its water, desert, power and agriculture. I wanted to get down to the essence of these elements and effect a congealing of things, which is the way of sculpture. I wanted to show the process by which water comes from a source and ends up as energy and to address the problem of industrial incursion . . . California as the original paradise has been transformed . . . Maybe we destroy natural charm when we impose ourselves. This garden is a sort of soliloquy on why the situation is the way it is."[7]

When the Two Town Center building that flanks the garden was still under construction Noguchi visited the site again. Seeing earth being moved must have whetted his appetite for rocks. On August 1, 1980, he wrote to an official at the Joshua Tree National Park asking if he could remove five rocks from the park and place them in his garden.[8] His request was denied. It was against National Park Service policy to remove rocks. So Segerstrom chartered an airplane and he and Noguchi, together with Segerstrom's son Toren and the project's consulting landscape architect, Kenneth Kammeyer, flew all over California looking for stones. They finally found the right ones in Yucca Valley near Joshua Tree National Park and in Arizona.

On Noguchi's next trip to Costa Mesa, when Segerstrom picked him up at the airport and told him that he had arranged for him to make his presentation to a group of architects and construction people working on Two Town Center, Noguchi said, "No Henry. I want you to see it first. I want you to see it alone."[9] So they drove to Noguchi's hotel, where the sculptor opened a suitcase and pulled out an approximately twenty-by-twenty-inch board upon which he had drawn the elements he planned to include in the garden. He placed several small models in their locations on the board. "Now this is an abstract representation of the geology and geography of the State of California," he said.[10] He then described how each element would work with the others. "Isamu, what do you call this?" Segerstrom asked. *California Scenario*, said Noguchi. He chose the word "scenario" to allude to Southern California's film industry. Segerstrom told Noguchi that his design was "absolutely perfect." Noguchi, Segerstrom realized, "had a singular ability to translate the scope of a universe the size of the State of California into symbolic elements that could be placed in a small-scale area. So the die was cast. There was no redesign."

In November 1980 Segerstrom, his wife, Renée, and Toren visited Noguchi on Shikoku. There they saw the fifteen large pitted granite boulders that were cut on their inner sides so that they would fit together to make the sculpture destined for *California Scenario*— a sculpture whose name had now changed from *Origin Stone* to *The Source of Life*. The Segerstroms watched as the stonecutters put the boulders together and then took them apart again for remitering to get a better fit.

Early in 1981, using a crane, Noguchi, together with two master stonecutters from Japan and the staff of Kammeyer's firm, assembled the twenty-eight-ton, ten-foot-high sculpture over the course of two weeks. He now named the piece *The Spirit of the Lima Bean* in honor of the Segerstrom family, which had been the nation's largest independent producers of lima beans until the mid-1960s, when they converted their land to commercial and residential development. "At first," Segerstrom recalled, "I thought he was teasing me . . . I think he changed the name out of respect for our friendship and our ability to work together."[11] Noguchi said that *The Spirit of the Lima Bean* "gives continuity to the history of the spot, its previous use, a sense of time and place."[12]

As the garden progressed, Segerstrom talked through many aspects of the design with Noguchi, to whom he always deferred. He allowed Noguchi to make some expensive changes in the plantings and in the way the water in the stream flowed. He even helped to move the project along when Noguchi was elsewhere. Looking back two years after the project was completed, Noguchi said, "A rare individual who abetted all this with warm personal involvement was Henry Segerstrom, and I am grateful."[13]

California Scenario consists of six elements that refer to California's environment plus *The Spirit of the Lima Bean*. The elements are (1) Forest Walk, a grove of redwoods beside a horseshoe-shaped white granite path; (2) Energy Fountain, a cone faced with granite and topped by a stainless steel cylinder from which water spurts upward to suggest California's dynamism; (3) Land Use, a coffinlike block of white granite set on an eight-foot-high knoll covered with honeysuckle—this might refer to the misuse of land because of industrial development, but in a letter Noguchi put a more positive spin on it: "Memory recognizes 'Land Use,' a passage of life and a testament to those who made America";[14] (4) Water Source, a tall, triangular form made of sandstone with water flowing down a channel cut into its face and into a meandering stream; (5) Desert Land, a circular mound covered with sand-colored pebbles and planted with native Californian cacti and other desert plants; and (6) Water Use, a polished white granite pyramid into the base of which the meandering stream disappears.[15]

In creating a garden full of symbols, Noguchi was following Japanese tradition. The six elements in *California Scenario* were, Noguchi said, meant to create a tranquil setting that was an abstract evocation of California. The peacefulness is there—spare, quiet, and Zenlike. But so is a vitality that comes from the perfection of each element's placement and from the way one element relates to the next, either by contrast (organic versus geometric, hard versus soft, dark versus light, wet versus dry) or by the overall harmony of all the different materials. Noguchi preferred, he said, to work not with a single thing but with relationships between things, because they "gather energy between them and talk to each other."[16]

California Scenario has the exquisite simplicity of the Beinecke garden, but, for all its precision and restraint, it is much more human. As in a Japanese stroll garden, the visitor's movements are carefully orchestrated. We are gently led across the sandstone terracing, stopping at one element and then the next, all of them enlivened by the sparkle and gurgle of water. Embedded deep into the sandstone terracing, the rocks—some vertical, some recumbent—speak quietly to the geometric shapes nearby, creating a dialogue between nature and human intelligence. What is astounding is the way this small courtyard enclosed by glass-walled office buildings and the white plastered walls of the garage is made to feel limitless. It is a beautiful example of the

California Scenario, Costa Mesa, California, 1980–82

artist's childlike ability to imagine vastness within tiny places and to encapsulate eternities of time within an instant. The viewer, too, can imaginatively transform the space, so that, for example, the triangle out of which water emerges is like a distant mountain and the meandering stream seems to be a wide river cutting through a canyon. The white pyramid into which the stream disappears could be as big as a pyramid in Egypt. The enclosed space pulls us into the poetry of Noguchi's symbolic world. It may be an oasis of peace, but it also emanates a mood of loneliness that underlies much of Noguchi's best work.

As always, Noguchi was extraordinarily scrupulous, even obsessive, in his attention to detail. His letters to Kammeyer and to Segerstrom discuss everything from the joints in the sandstone paving to the number of barrel cacti, to the design of the trash baskets and cigarette stands. "As with everything else," he told them, "my conscience won't let me abandon responsibility even down to this latest stub disposal."[17] At one point he wrote to Segerstrom that he was not satisfied with the way the water flowed in the stream. He recommended removing the jets from the stream and replacing them with a four-inch feeder line that would wind its way under the sandstone paver ledges. He wanted "babbling effects" in certain parts of the stream; these, he said, could be created by invisible three-inch-high dams. Another time he wrote that an additional filtration tank was necessary to produce a surge of water out of the base of Water Source.

Noguchi also paid close attention to his compensation. He tended to overreach when it came to what he should be paid—possibly this had to do with his general feeling that his sculpture was underappreciated. His propensity to ask for more money than stipulated in his contracts can perhaps be understood if one remembers the poverty Noguchi had endured in his youth. On December 8, 1981, he sent Segerstrom a bill asking for $130,000 more than was agreed upon in his original contract. His justification was that extra work was needed for all the garden's elements, as well as for his designs for benches, stone tables, light source stones, garbage receptacles, and cigarette stands. Segerstrom's response was sympathetic, but he explained that there was no further money to be had. Part of the funding had been provided by the Prudential Insurance Company, which was unwilling to pay anything more.

Noguchi wrote back to Segerstrom on April 2, 1982, that when he had signed the contract he had already done his overall design for *California Scenario*, and that he signed it in spite of the fact that it seemed unfair to him because it tied him to the realization of every detail. He did this, he said, because "I was interested in leaving in California something significantly beautiful which I knew could not be done except with the equal interest which I perceived to be yours . . . But how is one to decide what is fair? After all this is my profession and means of sustenance. I may be blamed for having enticed you. What is the role or process of art if not continuous development and refinement from vague beginnings to the clarity of its final exposition? Nothing may be known in advance nor can contracts be defined ahead in legal terms without getting in return the kind of response that is seen everywhere in architecture, design, or the art[s] which are minion[s] to the commercial world."[18] Years after the garden was finished, the money issue still rankled. When Segerstrom wrote to Noguchi in 1986 about making a film about *California Scenario*, Noguchi replied that he would collaborate with the filmmaking if Segerstrom could convince Prudential to pay the bill for the extra work.

California Scenario was inaugurated in mid-May 1982, and Segerstrom managed to persuade Noguchi to stay for half of the four-day celebration. Suzanne Muchnic's story on the opening in the *Los Angeles Times* said that there was "enough pomp circumstance, food and drink to daunt serious socialites."[19] The celebration was justified, she said, for *California Scenario* was, to her mind, "the most ambitious, absorbing and successful outdoor sculpture in the area." Allan Temko wrote that Noguchi's garden was "one of the 20th century's supreme environmental designs . . . [an] oasis of high philosophic splendor."[20] *Artforum* called Noguchi's garden a "stately oasis with its quiet assertion of human values."[21] Many of those closest to Noguchi say that he considered *California Scenario* to be the best garden he had designed. Other times Noguchi said that it tied as favorite with the Billy Rose Sculpture Garden. Much of the pleasure he took in this project had to do with the gentlemanly, extraordinarily supportive patron who helped him at every turn. In his museum's catalogue Noguchi wrote that in creating his garden he and Segerstrom had "a true confluence of interest [which] is evident in its resolution. Would it have been the same working for an insurance company?"[22]

49

BAYFRONT PARK

By contrast with the smoothness with which *California Scenario* came into being, the redesign of Miami's Bayfront Park involved many years of conflict, frustration, and disappointment. It was perhaps Noguchi's least successful project, and it remained unfinished at his death. There are various accounts of how the idea of inviting Noguchi to design the park came about. In the autumn of 1978 a young woman named Kitty Roedel, then director of marketing for Miami's Downtown Development Authority, attended a conference in Denver and happened to see a magazine article about *Noguchi's Imaginary Landscapes*, then on view at the Denver Art Museum. Roedel was so impressed that she skipped the conference and went to see the exhibition. "When I got to the bronze model for Noguchi's playground for Riverside Park, a voice came into me saying, 'Isamu Noguchi can redo Bayside Park.' I returned to Miami and I nudged everybody to death."[1]

Roedel talked to influential Miamians, among them Florence Bassett Knoll, an interior designer who had worked with Noguchi on his Connecticut General project, and she asked a museum director friend to write to Noguchi to see if he would be interested in coming to Miami to discuss the project. "Noguchi came and we showed him the park," Roedel recalls.[2] He called the twenty-eight-acre Bayfront Park his "largest space sculpture," and said it would "cap an effort of fifty-three years to actually make *Play Mountain*."[3] Noguchi had a twinkle in his eye when he told a reporter that he hoped to get this new version of *Play Mountain* built before Robert Moses died. "I'd like him to take a good look."

Bayfront Park, created in 1924 from landfill and set between Biscayne Boulevard and Biscayne Bay, had once been a splendid green
space with broad walkways lined with royal palms. Now, after years of
neglect, it had become a hangout for derelicts drinking alcohol from
bottles hidden in paper bags. At night, when downtown Miami office
towers emptied out, the deserted park was a dangerous place to go.
Efforts to improve and enlarge the park began in 1969 when Miami
passed a "Parks for People" bond issue, which made it financially possible for the city to acquire portions of bay frontage still held in private
hands. Legal and financial issues held things up. A decade later the
Downtown Development Authority and the city of Miami were determined to fulfill the 1969 bond issue's commitment to redevelop Bayfront Park. Maurice Ferré, Miami's mayor, was enthusiastic, and he,
too, takes credit for the idea of having Noguchi renovate Bayfront
Park. He invited Noguchi to visit with Sadao and arranged for them to
travel to Bayfront Park on Florence Knoll's yacht. Noguchi was entranced
by Miami's relation to water and to islands. "The bay there is a tremendous opening, like a huge window, that kind of space and opening interests me. On the one side you have the big buildings and the Boulevard
and on the other side is ocean, the Atlantic Ocean, and off and beyond
is Europe."[4]

According to Noguchi, when he first visited Miami it was to discuss the possibility of making a sculpture for Bayfront Park. As was his
habit, he enlarged the scope of the commission. Seeing how decrepit
the park looked, he said, "Your park is terrible. What you need is a new
park."[5]

Noguchi's commission to redesign Bayfront Park came through
early in 1980. The hope was that the park would, like Detroit's Civic
Plaza, revitalize the city's downtown.[6] When Noguchi brought his preliminary design to Miami in June, he proposed that the main branch
of the Miami-Dade County Library, which was in the park, should be
demolished because it cut off the view of the bay from Flagler Street.
He also proposed that the park should be isolated from the traffic on
Biscayne Boulevard by creating a thirteen-foot-high berm, which
would have bleachers for watching the Orange Bowl Parade. He
wanted a large fountain where seawater would tumble over a mound of
rocks. "The Sea Fountain will feature a turbulence of water that will
splash over the sides of the fountain in a violent way, like sea waves,

Bayfront Park with Sea Fountain, Miami, 1980–88. 28 acres

and hit upon the lava stones."[7] As in several other such jobs, he included an amphitheater. The initial response was positive. "What you have come up with here," said Mayor Ferré, "could become a focal point for the whole downtown."[8]

In July Noguchi returned to Miami to present a revised design and a budget to the city commissioners. In response to criticisms from various officials, he had eliminated the berm with its bleachers (which the commissioners had said would obstruct the view of the park and bay). He also flattened out the amphitheater, turning it into a very shallow bowl partly sunken into the ground. At the presentation Mayor Ferré said, "This project is the right project, at the right time, in the right place." Ferré then turned the podium over to Noguchi, who, dressed in a dapper seersucker suit, presented his balsa wood and clay model. Bayfront, Noguchi said, would be green and full of trees. It would give a "sense of peace and calm," and it would help to regenerate the city. He envisioned it as "a park for people. Not an escape from the City but a place to go to, a place of congregation," like a cathedral, or a front parlor, or an American village green, or a Spanish plaza.[9]

The city commissioners endorsed Noguchi's preliminary design. The plan was then submitted to the planning advisory board for further study. In a few months Noguchi was to present a final design and a contract was to be drawn up. In a long exchange of letters concerning his much-revised contract, Noguchi vented his ire about the city's "lack of firm direction."[10] Early in 1981, furious that his amphitheater had been given a different axis, he wrote to Ferré: "The problem which must be faced is that an artist simply cannot abdicate his responsibility . . . Change in all its permutations is equally the artist's art." He suggested that if Miami could not cope with such a "recalcitrant" artist, he could withdraw from the project and let the architectural consultants take over. This hurdle must have been surmounted, but the issues of money and artistic control still had to be worked out. Kitty Roedel recalls Noguchi's dissatisfaction with the many contracts sent to him: "He would get weird about money. But he was not stingy as a person."[11] Noguchi finally accepted a simple letter of agreement drawn up in 1982. He would be paid $130,000.

Over the next few years Bayfront Park went through many changes. Eventually it was to include, besides the amphitheater and the seawater fountain, a bay walk, a rock garden, a ninety-foot-high light tower for laser shows, and a white marble spiral slide called *Slide Mantra* (shown at the 1986 Venice Biennale). Most of the south end of the park was not finished when Noguchi died in December 1988.

Progress on the park was halting. There were numerous stumbling blocks: lack of funds, the controversy over the tearing down of the library, the disagreement about the construction of an underground parking lot, to name a few. Cantankerous commissioners demanded constant revisions. The seemingly endless holdups meant that Noguchi had to travel to Miami some fifty or sixty times in the last decade of his life. Kitty Roedel recalls: "The Park was a twelve-year and thirty million dollar headache. They weren't ready. The commissioners were a bunch of hayseeds. The Parks Department hated us. People said they did not like Noguchi because he was Japanese and we fought a war with Japan. The local architects and designers were mad that we gave the work to Noguchi. Mayor Ferré was very good. He was an intelligent, sophisticated guy, a strong and popular mayor. I formed a committee to create a buffer so that Noguchi would not be harassed by all of this."[12]

A city news bulletin for May 1984 announced that the City Commission had approved the park development plan and that phase one, the creation of the bay walk, the large seawater fountain, and three new piers, should begin construction in the fall. The ground-breaking did not take place until August 1985. In 1986 Kitty Roedel asked Noguchi whether during the seven or eight years that they had been working on the park he'd ever doubted that his plan would be realized. Noguchi answered: "I never doubt that anything that is good [will] be realized, you see. Especially if I make it . . . Since you only have one life to lead why start doubting?"[13] Roedel noted that Noguchi had, during a recent walk through the park construction site, told her that this project was possibly the most significant of his entire career, "significant for me but probably significant for the wide application it has to cities and to people's leisure time." When Roedel asked him whether he would undertake other large-scale projects, he said: "No. This will be my last. I should know better than to do this anymore."

Roedel and Noguchi became close collaborators and intimate friends. Most of the time they were harmonious, but as Roedel recalls: "Noguchi had a temper. He'd get mad at me. We had lots of fights. But we were glued at the hip."[14] Roedel adored Noguchi and he loved women, especially women who could help him achieve his goals. Indeed, at one point in their long friendship they were close enough to plan a European trip together.

During his last trip to Miami, in November 1988, he battled over an underground garage that he felt would mar his design. He was so angry with the way the city commissioners interfered with his design that he threatened to quit. Another conflict was over his memorial to the *Challenger* space shuttle, which had exploded in 1986 killing seven astronauts. For the *Challenger Memorial* Noguchi designed a twisting one-hundred-foot openwork pylon made out of numerous sections of steel pipe painted white. The construction was inspired by Buckminster Fuller as well as by Vladimir Tatlin's design for *Monument to the Third International*. Once again, the double helix in the pylon's torque represented the DNA chain and was, Noguchi said, both "a symbol of aspiration cut short" and "a symbol for the continuance of life."[15]

In early November the new mayor, Xavier Suárez, was ready to

Challenger Memorial, Bayfront Park, Miami, 1988. Steel and paint, ht. 100 ft.

scrap the *Challenger* project for lack of funds and also because of his disagreement with Noguchi over an expensive forty-foot wall with which Noguchi wanted to surround the memorial.[16] Finally Noguchi and Suárez came to a compromise: the pylon would be built without the wall and Noguchi and Suárez would meet in January to decide whether the wall was necessary. Noguchi died before that meeting could take place. In early February 1989, when the *Challenger Memorial* was dedicated, Suárez told *The Miami Herald*, "Maybe Noguchi inspired me from above, but I now think it needs a wall. I think Noguchi might have had a point."[17]

For all the problems, during Noguchi's November visit, he and Assistant Mayor Rosario Kennedy took a walk through the park and, Kennedy recalls, "he loved what he saw."[18] Noguchi's appetite for making gardens and parks never abated. By making them he could transcend the personal and go beyond time. "When you do a park or a garden, you in a sense circumvent time. It's a kind of fortuitous gift above the head of the critics. It's like playing God."[19] With a chuckle, he elaborated: "It's an extension of God's purpose, you see. I'm not playing God. I'm his assistant."

Bayfront Park remained unfinished when he died the following month. In spite of the various improvements that Noguchi was able to achieve, the park did not fulfill the hopes he expressed when he called it a "metaphor for the world of children" that could serve as "a wedge of art into the heart of a new world."[20]

50

ALL THINGS WORTHWHILE
MUST END AS GIFTS

While Noguchi was enduring the trials of creating Bayfront Park, he was also engaged in projects that gave him enormous satisfaction. One of these was a garden on the hill behind his house in Mure. When he began this two-year project in 1983 he wrote: "I approach my 79th birthday this month with growing awareness. I celebrate it by building a garden in my place of refuge in Shikoku. It is a gift to the future, and to the people who harbored my mother and gave me my years of childhood. How true it is that all things worthwhile must end as gifts. What other reason is there for art?"[1]

With the help of Masatoshi Izumi, he shaped the hill and gave his garden a rhythm and unity by making a circuitous path to the summit. Along the path the visitor passes carefully placed boulders and a few Noguchi sculptures. The hill's steepness was a challenge: "I've got these steps, and the way the steps are arranged in very odd patterns makes it interesting. You feel like you're being held from slipping away by a group of large rocks." While he was building the garden, there were, he said, "about 14 typhoons, one after the other," and his work kept being washed out. "As fast as I would build it up the water would come and ruin it. It was kind of nature testing me and challenging me to come up with a better answer. It seems to be stabilized for once. I am astonished. I'm really astonished."[2] What stabilized it was a riverbed of rocks that he constructed to guide the water downhill. Wanting as usual to sculpt more space than he was given, Noguchi followed the Japanese concept of borrowed landscape, in which elements of nature outside of a garden are seen as part of the garden. He encompassed the surrounding mountains, Yakuri and Yashima, as part of his sculpture.[3] The Inland Sea, visible from the top of the hill, even the sky, belonged to his garden, too. "I love working large," he said. "I would like to sculpt the world itself if I had time."[4]

Another project of great emotional importance was the creation of his museum in Long Island City, Queens—a magnificent gift to the people of New York. Since 1961 Noguchi had enjoyed the remoteness of his studio in this bleak industrial area full of warehouses and small factories. For several years he had had his eye on a two-story brick building, an abandoned photoengraving plant, across the street from his studio. In the mid-1970s he bought it. In 1980 he purchased an adjacent gas station and, after removing the structure, built a cinder-block extension to the brick building. Starting in 1981, with Shoji Sadao, he began to transform this structure into a museum. Noguchi spent some three million dollars on the project. The New York City Department of Cultural Affairs contributed fifty thousand dollars.

Part of the land became an 8,500-square-foot walled sculpture garden where he intermingled his works with a mixture of Japanese and American plantings: katsura trees, Japanese black pine, weeping cherry, golden bamboo, Korean boxwood, magnolia, ailanthus, abelia, and juniper. He covered most of the ground with small stones—he had an aversion to grass and felt that stones were a better setting for sculpture. With its relaxed pathway curving past perfectly placed sculptures, its wooden benches, and its stone *tsukubai* fountain, the garden is yet another Noguchi oasis.

Noguchi insisted that he did not build his museum out of vanity. He "did it out of despair."[5] Mindful of how his sculpture would be displayed and conserved in the future, Noguchi had approached both the Metropolitan and the Whitney museums, but they could not accommodate all his work. He did not want his art to be deaccessioned or stuck away in some museum basement. Moreover, he knew that many of his sculptures were so heavy that they might crush a museum's floor. But there were some aspects of a museum that he longed for: "A museum is, I suppose, a repository against time . . . there is a semblance of eternity, a sense of permanence that is implied by a museum, and a removal from time's passage."[6] Ever self-reliant, he decided to create a museum himself. He had seen that Brancusi's Paris studio had been turned into a museum. Why not follow his mentor's example?

In a brochure that used to be given to museum visitors, Noguchi wrote: "I define the reason for the Isamu Noguchi Museum as a desire to show the totality of my work as an evolving relationship significant to our time . . . The Museum shows in particular my own part in the widening ideas of environment starting in 1933; my experimental approach to structure and the theater during the 1940s; and my search for a sculpture outside the confines of the studio since then." He went on to say that his exploration of stone, which he called the "matrix of sculpture," was exhibited along with its opposite—his work in paper and his fascination with light. "This is called a garden museum as a metaphor for the world, and how an artist attempted to influence its becoming."[7]

In his museum's excellent catalogue, with its many reproductions accompanied by Noguchi's brief notes, he offered another purpose for his museum: "This museum and catalogue attempt to define my role as a crossing where inward and outward meet, East and West."[8]

The Isamu Noguchi Garden Museum, beloved by many New Yorkers as a place where one can be transported to a more serene and unencumbered world, is an artwork in itself. Its 11,000 square feet of indoor gallery space house more than 250 of Noguchi's works created over a period of sixty years. The space is divided into fourteen areas, beginning with a large, rather severe room that is only partially enclosed by high cinder-block walls. Here Noguchi placed his most recent sculptures, the imposing basalt and granite monoliths that he carved—or rather barely carved—on Shikoku. By transforming rock in only the most minimal way, Noguchi was able to create a perfect melding of nature and art. Some of these sculptures are anthropomorphic, especially the erect ones like *Break Through Capestrano* (1982). *Venus* (1980) suggests a kneeling female. All of them occupy space with quiet force. Like African or Easter Island effigies, they give off an aura of magic and they seem to have withstood vast swaths of time.

In his preface to his museum's catalogue, Noguchi wrote, "To counter the passing, I would seek the enduring. From the depth of time-consuming hardness to find the lasting and essential . . ."[9] Stone, he once noted, was said to be "the affection of old men."[10] He called stone

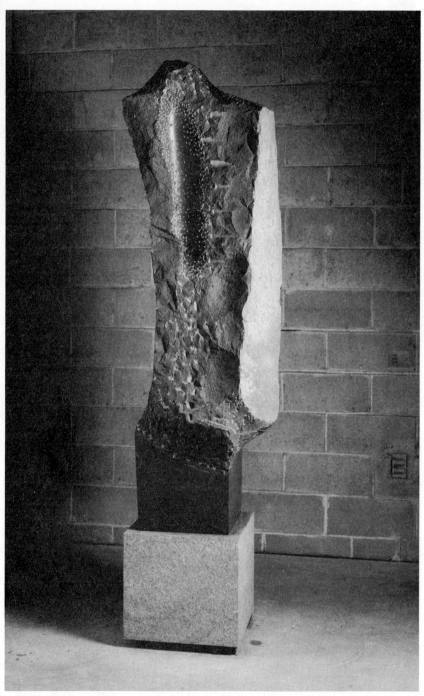

Age, 1981. Basalt, 78⅜ × 24½ × 21¼ in.

"our fundament . . . stone is the direct link to the heart of the matter—a molecular link."[11] By 1987, when his museum's catalogue was published, the eighty-three-year-old Noguchi was beginning to feel his age. Stone was a comfort. It was, he said, "the earth itself, even as it changed with weather and time, it remained as a marker . . . forever in the now."[12] One of the most somber basalt sculptures in the museum's grouping of late works is *Age* (1981), which suggests an aging body seen from the back and indented with the marks of time's passage. One side of this "torso" is cut off and has turned the mustard brown of the inner stone. Here Noguchi could have been referring to the lost past, to memory, to the return to earth, or he might simply have wanted the contrast of dark gray and warm tan. He wrote of *Age*: "A gift comes from the past, the residue of what we have already done. The unwanted part. Then one day there is revealed to us another potential which we are now ready for, to find from our own past the needed confidence: out of violence comes a calm."[13]

The galleries on the museum's second floor are full of light from huge windows. The sculptures here are arranged more or less chronologically. Noguchi gave special attention to his sets for Martha Graham, his furniture designs, and his unrealized projects. Always he insisted on the underlying continuity of all his work: "The areas are all different aspects of the same thing."[14] To his mind, there was no progress in art history or in his own development. An artist simply did the best he could at any given moment. Also, his definition of art was broad. In his view gardens, theater sets, furniture, and playgrounds were all sculpture. His museum's catalogue ends with the sentence: "Call it sculpture when it moves you so."[15]

By the time the museum opened in 1985 Noguchi was generally considered the greatest living American sculptor, maybe even the world's greatest. His chief American competitors, Calder and David Smith, were dead. So were Picasso, Matisse, and Henry Moore. Yet Noguchi continued to think of himself as an outsider. Late in life he told an interviewer: "I think you'll be interested in the museum . . . as an example of one artist who couldn't make it into the social world of art. A lone wolf."[16] For all his renown, and for all the brute strength of his late stone sculptures, there were many people who continued to think that his work was too elegant or even slick. Some observers saw him as more of a designer than an artist, ignoring the fact that Noguchi,

Venus, 1980. Manazuru stone, 94⅛ × 31¼ × 18⅞ in.

following Japanese tradition, saw no division between art and design. The incredible variety of his work, the way he changed course once he had invented a way of making sculpture that satisfied him, meant that for many viewers Noguchi had no signature style. He was hard to pigeonhole, and that was the way he liked it. He distrusted style—perhaps all the more so because critics sometimes found his work too stylish. An artist, he said, must keep freeing himself from the past, his own past and that of history.[17] If he felt his work was settling into a style, for him it "lost its keen edge of originality. That's why I'm always off on my own investigations. In a way I'm an eternal novice."[18]

Although Noguchi was even more suspicious of art dealers than he was of museums, he had numerous exhibitions in the 1980s. Being revered and sought after made him uncomfortable. He told Newsday's Amei Wallach: "When people say you are a great master, or a master, I feel, 'Oh my God, I'm really in a rut!'"[19] He told another writer that he continued to have exhibitions because that way at least people said, "okay, he's an artist." But, he admitted, "I'm always trying to get away. I'm suspicious of other people—and of myself. And so I always feel, 'You're not where you're supposed to be.'"[20]

In 1980, concurrent with the Whitney's version of the Imaginary Landscapes show, the Pace Gallery and the André Emmerich Gallery gave Noguchi a seventy-fifth-birthday exhibition. Pace showed recent small sculptures in granite and basalt and Emmerich showed sculptures from the 1960s and 1970s, including a group of granite landscape tables. The critical response was positive. Time magazine's brilliant art critic Robert Hughes declared, "Isamu Noguchi is the pre-eminent American sculptor."[21] Hughes admired Noguchi's "subtle, precise and informal" touch, his refinement, clarity, and intensity. Noguchi's art had, he said, "a power to rid the mind of its daily rubbish" and to induce a meditative calm. Yet Hughes also saw a fiercely concentrated emotion contained in Noguchi's simple and apparently calm stone shapes. Noguchi, Hughes said, "is entitled to be seen . . . as one of the very few surviving masters of the modernist tradition: the chief living heir, not only to his teacher Brancusi, but also to the classical Japanese feeling for material and nature." The art historian Sam Hunter, who had published a monograph on Noguchi in 1978, wrote an essay for the birthday show's catalogue in which he called Noguchi "one of the most arresting and paradoxical yet consistent artistic personalities of our time."[22]

Noguchi's numerous exhibitions in the 1980s confirmed his position as the grand old man of American sculpture. In May 1988 Pace presented *Bronze and Iron Sculpture*, Noguchi's last exhibition before his death. In her perceptive and sympathetic catalogue essay, Dore Ashton noted that "the spirit of inquiry, un-assuaged to this day is, I think, the prime motor of Noguchi's imagination."[23] Noguchi agreed. In a 1986 interview he had said: "I'm constantly on the search and finding from the stone itself new possibilities . . ."[24]

During the late 1970s and 1980s Noguchi received many awards. He most often responded to such tokens of respect by scoffing. To him, the word "distinguished" was derogatory. Yet he longed for recognition. In 1977 he won the Skowhegan Award. In 1982 he traveled to the MacDowell Colony in New Hampshire to receive the Edward MacDowell medal for outstanding lifelong contribution to the arts. In

Noguchi and Martha Graham at a dinner at which Noguchi was presented with a Skowhegan Award, 1977

1984 he won the New York State Governor's Art Award as well as the Japanese-American Citizens League Biennial Award. The following year the Municipal Art Society gave him the President's Medal of Honor, and in 1986 he was a recipient of the Kyoto Prize from the In-amori Foundation, which included about $300,000. When he heard about the latter he was in Pietra Santa. "Kyoto Prize?" he said. "What's that?" Even when his friend the sculptor Kan Yasuda explained that it was a huge honor, Noguchi was dismissive: "What do I have to do to get it? Are they going to take my picture with someone?"[25] Nonetheless, Noguchi was surely happy that the country of his father was finally recognizing him. He even hosted a dinner at an expensive restaurant afterward, to the surprise of many of his friends—Noguchi was famous for not picking up the bill.

In 1987 Noguchi was awarded the National Medal of Arts by President Ronald Reagan. According to what he told Katharine Kuh, he at first refused to accept the prize. "The reason I did that," Noguchi explained, "was because I didn't like his policy of turning over everything to business."[26] In fact, Noguchi was pleased: the medal honored him as an American. His back was painful at the time, so Priscilla, who accompanied him to Washington, where they stayed at the Hay Adams Hotel, arranged for them to travel in a Lincoln limousine in which Noguchi could stretch out in the back.[27] Reagan was reported to have said that Noguchi's work was "a fusion of East and West, at once static and moving, solid and space defining, old and new."[28] In 1988 New York's Sculpture Center gave Noguchi the award for Distinction in Sculpture and, in the same year, came an honor that proved to him that the quality of his work was recognized by the country that had ostracized him as a half-breed. He was granted the Third Order of the Sacred Treasure by the Japanese government.

But the honor that gave Noguchi the most satisfaction was being chosen by Henry Geldzahler in 1986 to represent the United States at the forty-second Venice Biennale, the most venerable and, at that time, the most important of all the international art expositions. At first he refused the offer, citing the Japanese internment camps as a difficult part of American history to overlook. But upon further consideration, he realized that the invitation validated an aspect of his nationality in a way he had always wanted. "I was now a bona fide American, recognized as such."[29] Also his feeling of being undervalued as an artist and

Priscilla Morgan, Noguchi, Elaine Weitzen, and an unidentified woman at an award dinner at the Sculpture Center, New York, 1988

out of touch with the art world must have been placated. But no amount of attention was enough. He once told Paul Cummings, "I have always had a sort of out-of-the-running kind of feeling. I still do."[30]

Henry Geldzahler's choice of Noguchi was a surprise to many people, but the decisions of this charming, quirky, and brilliant gadfly and art guru were often unpredictable. Always so up-to-date on the latest thing in the New York art scene, Geldzahler was known for his early support for Pop Art and for the younger artists who emerged in the 1970s, such as Julian Schnabel, Jean-Michel Basquiat, and Kenny Scharf. Explaining why he chose Noguchi, Geldzahler said that Noguchi's "magisterial" work was not well known in Europe. Moreover, he suggested that Noguchi's calm and meditative sculpture could be an antidote to the image that Europeans had of American culture as aggressive and uncouth—the land, as Geldzahler put it, of "Reagan and Rambo."[31]

Noguchi titled his Venice show *Isamu Noguchi: What Is Sculpture?*

A few months before the opening he told Kitty Roedel that his exhibition would be "an exposition of my particular interests which are very extensive, very wide. It goes all the way from stone to paper."[32] He chose to devote two of the American pavilion's five gallery spaces to Akari. The other three rooms and the courtyard between the pavilion's two wings displayed sculptures. In one room was a recent steel sculpture, a tetrahelix, which, as Noguchi said in the exhibition catalogue, referred to DNA. Another gallery showed five rough stones called *Beginnings*, which Noguchi saw as "deviations from the stone gardens of Japan."[33] In a third gallery he placed *Ends*, a six-foot-square hollow black cube made of six rough-cut granite slabs that were end pieces sliced off while creating other sculptures. The cube is mute and inert as a grave, yet, because the dark and invisible emptiness within is part of the sculpture, it has a powerful presence. Noguchi wrote that the cube was "the end, the final realization of man, different from the rest of nature. It is the realization of death and that man is here only temporarily and must establish his mark in the cube."[34] The show also included sculptures from earlier decades, some of them models cast in bronze for unrealized projects such as *Play Mountain* and the Riverside Park playground.

The two rooms of Akari were something that Noguchi insisted upon even though many friends—including Priscilla Morgan, Arne Glimcher, and the sculptor Mark di Suvero, Noguchi's friend and neighbor in Long Island City—advised him against it. "He wanted to thumb his nose at the Biennale," said Glimcher, "because he felt that he should have had the honor years before."[35] Di Suvero had warned Noguchi that if he showed so many Akari he would not win the grand prize for best artist. But Akari were, Noguchi said, "the one thing that I've done out of pure love, nothing to do with commerce."[36] Although he was happy to be honored as an American, he rather perversely put together an exhibition that stressed his Japanese side: "I deliberately went out of my way to be more Japanese than necessary, because it's an American pavilion. I put in these Akari—obviously Japanese."[37] Indeed Noguchi's friend the art critic Tadayasu Sakai, who was then director of the Kamakura Museum of Modern Art, remembers Noguchi visiting the Japanese pavilion, for which Sakai served as commissioner, and saying that his own work was far more Japanese than the work by Japanese artists displayed there.[38] He wanted his Biennale show to demonstrate his way of thinking in opposites: light/dark, heavy/light, stone/

paper, old/new, East/West, and so on. The huge round Akari that occupied a square room in the American pavilion could not have been more opposite from the heavy black cube called *Ends*.

Slide Mantra, a ten-foot-high, cylindrical, white-marble slide/sculpture, similar to a slide Noguchi had designed in 1966 for his Riverside Park playground, was the hit of the show. He told Roedel that *Slide Mantra* was to be "a space that you can slide down, a space that confines you, and a space that opens up."[39] To Gene Owens he described the slide as a birth experience: "The hole, the passage, the containment creates the vortex from which we are ejected. Renaissance."[40] Interviewed during the Venice Biennale, he said, "I call it *Slide Mantra*, why? Because first of all I got that idea probably unconsciously from

Slide Mantra, in the courtyard of the American pavilion, Venice Biennale, 1986. Marble, ht. 10 ft. Now in Bayfront Park, Miami

the truncated cylinder from India."[41] Noguchi had often drawn on his memories of the eighteenth-century astronomical observatories at New Delhi and Jaipur that he had first seen in 1950 on his Bollingen travels. The structures at these observatories include many different geometric shapes, one of which is a cylinder enclosing a winding stairwell.

The idea to create *Slide Mantra* came when he visited Venice in 1985 to check out the spaces available in the American pavilion. The courtyard, he decided, needed a white marble slide. He went to Querceta and, with the help of his favorite carver, Giorgio Angeli, with whom he had worked for many years, and assisted also by the young Japanese sculptor Kan Yasuda, he proceeded to carve the slide out of white marble from Altissimo. Yasuda recalls that Noguchi was under time pressure to get the slide ready for the Biennale's June opening, and he turned up in Querceta with a model made out of a paper tube and measuring only about two inches high. "This is the model," he announced, full of excitement. "I thought of this twenty-five years ago. Wouldn't it be nice to make a large version of this?"[42] Giorgio Angeli, Yasuda, and Noguchi went to Venice to inspect the American pavilion's courtyard. Yasuda recalled: "We spent days studying the balance between the space in which the sculpture was to be installed and the work itself, finding the best route for transporting the sculpture along the canals, booking a traghetto (tugboat), contemplating the form and weight of the sculpture, and measuring places here and there in Venice with a tape measure."[43] Back in Querceta, they made a large plaster model. Angeli's assistants brought sixty tons of Carrara marble down from the mountain quarry. A few months later the slide had been given its basic shape and Noguchi was able to try it out in order to find the right pitch. "Isamu slid down it again and again," Yasuda recalled. "He found it so speedy that it would be dangerous for children. Therefore, he would carve it a little more and try it again. This process was repeated over and over again. At one point he said, looking like a mischievous child, 'Art is something to be felt through a child's buttocks.'" The clothes designer Issey Miyake, who had met Noguchi in 1979 at the International Design Conference in Aspen, Colorado, observed Noguchi testing his slide as well. After Miyake visited Noguchi in Mure in the summer of 1980 and Noguchi picked him up at the airport and took him straight to the Inland Sea for a swim, the two men became, as Miyake put it, "heart-to-heart friends." Watching children enjoying his slide, Noguchi murmured to Miyake, "If they keep climbing up and sliding down over and over again, they should be able to understand a little bit about what sculpture is all about from their buttocks."[44]

At the Biennale the public was invited to enter the cylindrical enclosure, to climb the winding stairs within, and, having reached the top, to sit down and slide to the bottom, where a bed of wood chips would soften the landing. Noguchi explained: "Up steps through a hole we slide down a double helix . . . I wished to show my long held belief that play could lead to a new appreciation of sculpture."[45] When the Venice Biennale closed, *Slide Mantra* was shipped to Bayfront Park, where, except when children take possession of it, it seems a little forlorn.

The response to Noguchi's Venice Biennale show was mixed. Europeans found the diversity of the work puzzling, and they felt that the Akari were craft or design products, not art. John Russell Taylor, writing in *The Times* (London), said that Noguchi's show posed the question: "How little can you get away with and still be called sculpture?"[46] He admired *Slide Mantra*, but the rest of the show gave him the "impression of having wandered unawares into a Conran lighting showroom."

When someone in Venice asked Noguchi what he planned to do next, he said he would spend a little time in Pietra Santa "just to relax a bit from this ordeal."[47] His days at the Biennale had been pressured. Having to play social lion at lunches and dinners given in his honor always irked him. And the certainty that because of his insistence on showing Akari he would not win the grand prize must have saddened him a little. After Pietra Santa, he told his interlocutor, his plans were uncertain: "I have no idea. I have no idea," he said. But he added, "I know very well if I go back to Japan and am confronted with a stone, it'll talk to me somehow. I'll hit it on its head. I'll do something. I'll do anything to make it say something to me."

51

KYOKO

In the days leading up to the Biennale's opening, Noguchi lunched every day with his entourage, which included Shoji Sadao and his wife, Tsuneko; Priscilla Morgan; Glimcher and his wife; and a young Japanese couple, Kyoko and Junichi Kawamura, both of whom had become central to Noguchi's life in the last few years. Every night there was an elegant social gathering, one of which, hosted by Glimcher's Pace Gallery, was a dinner for two hundred people at the "Antique Garden" of the Cipriani Hotel. "It was on the ground floor, right on the water," Glimcher recalls. "There were paper lanterns. It was beautiful and Noguchi had a good time."[1] Glimcher was surprised that when Noguchi and his group of friends walked around Venice, Noguchi would walk ahead with beautiful Kyoko Kawamura while her husband, Junichi; the Sadaos; the Glimchers; and Priscilla would trail behind. If Priscilla minded, she was too proud to let on.

The night before the opening, Noguchi was guest of honor at a party cohosted by the Peggy Guggenheim Museum and the American consul general in Venice. An artist friend hurrying to get to the party on time ran into Noguchi with the Kawamuras going fast in the opposite direction.[2] Noguchi, it seems, did not want to be feted. The Grand Prize had not yet been announced, but since it was generally known that he was not going to win, he probably felt some chagrin. On the other hand he may have fled from social contact because, as Izumi recalls, two of his front teeth had just broken. His health had not been good in the last year, and he was feeling old and restless, as if time were running out. Kan Yasuda recalls that at a seated dinner party for four hundred people at the American pavilion, Noguchi stood at the podium when it was time for him to say a few words and, after noting that the goal of the Venice Biennale was collaboration between artists of different ethnicities, said, "I am half Japanese, you know."[3] Then he left the stage. Noguchi left Venice for Pietra Santa early in the morning on June 29, the Biennale's opening day. He was accompanied by Yasuda and his wife; Izumi and his wife, Harumi; and the Kawamuras.

Noguchi had met Junichi Kawamura in 1975 when Junichi was a young architect in Kenzo Tange's office and was involved with the Sogetsu Kaikan project, then in its early stages. Impressed by Noguchi's brilliance and his deep understanding of architecture, and enchanted by Noguchi as a man as well as an artist, Junichi made him a sort of mentor. "Noguchi's eyes were beautiful," he recalls. "He looked young and energetic, although he was seventy. He was energetic in relation to women, too."[4]

Junichi wanted Kyoko to meet Noguchi, so in January 1978, after the Sogetsu job was finished, they traveled to Shikoku. When they arrived in Mure, Noguchi led them into the stone circle, where his immense black granite *Energy Void* dominated the space. Kyoko, a professional koto (Japanese zither) player, had studied Japanese music at Tokyo National University of Fine Arts and Music, but she knew almost nothing about contemporary art. She was, she says, "shocked and impressed" by the loop of stone. "I had never seen this type of sculpture before. Noguchi told me he thought it was one of his best." Kyoko's fresh and untutored response to his work must have pleased Noguchi. He sat in the void of *Energy Void* and had his picture taken. He and his two young guests so enjoyed their lunch together that the couple stayed on for dinner.

Although Kyoko spoke little English and Noguchi's Japanese was not fluent, she felt a kinship with him when she discovered his love of music. After dinner, having learned that she was a koto player, Noguchi put on some of the records of indigenous music that he had collected over the years. One of the records was a koto recording by Kyoko's former teacher. "When I first met Noguchi I felt he was a foreigner, but then his favorite music was the same as mine. He played Indian music and Indonesian gamelan music." When Noguchi put on African drum music and started to dance, Kyoko and Junichi joined him. He was not, Kyoko recalls, adept at social dancing, but he was good at improvising.

This lively and warm encounter with two such admiring young people must have been welcome. At the time of their visit, Noguchi was still saddened by the suicide of his lover Ayako Wakita, the wife of his former assistant Ajiro Wakita, a young abstract painter. The Wakitas had been living in New York when, unhappy in her marriage and disappointed by Noguchi's lack of commitment, Ayako left both men, returned to Japan, and hanged herself.

Noguchi and the Kawamuras remained good friends for the next five years. Then, in 1982, Kyoko and Noguchi began a love affair that lasted until his death, six years later. Noguchi was touched when, at the November 1982 opening of his Akari show at Osaka's Kasahara Gallery, Kyoko presented him with a bouquet of cosmos flowers. Drawn to her warmth, her beauty, and her youth, he invited her to come with him to the opening of an Arshile Gorky exhibition at Tokyo's Seibu Museum of Art. The following month Noguchi sent Kyoko a plan he had drawn for landscaping the area around his Mure home, together with a note that said, "As you can see there will be a stage where you will play the koto and sing. I can almost hear you!" He sent warm regards to Junichi and closed with "To you I send love."[5]

Kyoko began to visit Noguchi's compound in Mure and she often accompanied him on his travels. In Mure, when she came out to the stone circle to watch Noguchi work, instead of treating her like an unwanted distraction as he was wont to do with other visitors, he would greet her with a gentle smile. By nature a quiet person, Kyoko was happy to observe and not talk. "Izumi told me it was a sacred space," she recalls. Indeed, at the end of the workday Izumi would have his assistants scatter salt on the stone circle's ground to purify it. While Noguchi was working, Kyoko would stay in the house playing the koto that Noguchi had given her so that he could enjoy her music. The sound of her playing seemed to give him a measure of calm. "When I stopped playing he would come and say, "'Why did you stop?'" One of the sculptures that Noguchi was working on in the early 1980s was *Kyoko-san*, which at five feet two is approximately the height of Kyoko. It is clearly a female form—a curved cut defines buttocks. There is also the hint of a breast, and the sculpture's spritely movement suggests a kimono-clad woman dancing.

Kyoko-san, 1984. Adesite, ht. 64 in.

In September 1983 Kyoko accompanied Noguchi to the city of Sakata to attend the opening of the Domon Ken Museum. They also visited his beloved Kyoto, where he took her to see all the temples and gardens that had had such an impact on his vision. In summer 1984 in Pietra Santa he spent the day working on marble sculptures assisted by Giorgio Angeli, who invited them to dinner almost every night. In mid-July they went to Forte di Marmi, a beach resort not far from Pietra Santa. Here Kyoko took a photograph of Noguchi wearing a European-style, rather minimal black knit bathing suit that showed off his trim physique. In the photograph Noguchi lounges in a beach chair clearly enjoying the feeling of sun soaking into his body and relishing, too, the adulatory gaze of his young lover. As always, he wears a hat to protect his bald head. After this moment of leisure they toured Italy, visiting Florence, Bologna, and Venice. Then, following a brief stay in New York, Noguchi returned to Mure to work and to be with Kyoko.

That fall Kyoko and Junichi attended Noguchi's eightieth birthday party at Sogetsu Kaikan, cohosted by several of Noguchi's good friends including Kenzo Tange, Hiroshi Teshigahara, Yoshio Taniguchi, and Issey Miyake. Among the guests were many who had furthered Noguchi's career in Japan. From New York came Shoji Sadao and Priscilla Morgan. Noguchi welcomed the guests and, acting bewildered, said, "Do I have so many friends?" which made everyone laugh.[6] It had taken a long time, but Noguchi was surely gratified finally to be loved and honored in his father's country. His recent stone sculptures, among them *Kyoko-san*, were displayed in Sogetsu Kaikan's stone garden that Noguchi had called *Heaven*. The show received favorable press. The *Asahi shinbun* said that the works revealed the character of the stone itself as well as expressing the "sheer will power of the still-youthful Noguchi."[7] At an after-party gathering Noguchi took off the elegant jacket that was a gift from Issey Miyake and danced with Kyoko, honoring her by making their relationship public.

Noguchi and Kyoko Kawamura dancing at Noguchi's eightieth birthday party, Tokyo, 1984

Noguchi's friends and associates describe Kyoko as petite, unassertive, sweet, and lovely to look at. Maurice Ferré, who visited Kyoto
with Noguchi and Kyoko, said: "Noguchi invited a gorgeous Japanese
lady to spend that weekend. Kyoko was a wonderful woman—beautiful,
expressive, intelligent. She was quiet and did not participate in conversations."[8] Kyoko was emphatically feminine. As apparently behooved a
Japanese woman, her behavior was deferential. She was always looking
after Noguchi's comforts, massaging his back when it hurt, giving him
affection when he felt down. Most people saw Noguchi and Kyoko's
relationship as more physical than intellectual. In terms of intellect,
Priscilla was a more vigorous partner. But Noguchi enjoyed a real intimacy with Kyoko and he trusted her enough to tell her about his childhood. She recalls that there were tears in his eyes when he talked about
his mother reading him Greek myths.

Junichi did not appear to mind his wife's attachment to Noguchi.
He and Kyoko seemed to have agreed to give each other a great deal of
freedom. In addition, Noguchi was highly supportive of Junichi's career, often steering work his way. The three of them frequently traveled together. According to Bonnie Rychlak, Noguchi's assistant at the
Noguchi Museum, "It was a ménage à trois." Noguchi loved the adula-
tion and affection that both spouses gave him. Being with Kyoko assuaged his loneliness and his despair at the acceleration of time's passage.
She made him feel vital, handsome, and successful.

At Noguchi's eightieth birthday party, the art dealer Ryunosuke
Kasahara asked Kyoko to persuade Noguchi to let him mount an exhibition of recent stone sculptures in his Osaka gallery. "When I first
met him I thought Noguchi was like a Zen Buddhist monk or priest,"
Kasahara recalls.[9] Noguchi, however, was difficult: "He was a very
strict man with a short temper, but he had a gentle aspect as well. He
did not trust people. Unlike Henry Moore, Noguchi was selfish, sometimes very cold, sometimes warm, like fire or ice. On that first visit
Noguchi told me in a harsh voice, 'I do not like gallery owners,' and I
thought, 'This is a unique and interesting man.' I had to approach Noguchi many times before his attitude changed. On the fifteenth approach I saw a sculpture called *Childhood* made of aji stone and I
asked to buy it. Noguchi said, 'It's expensive.'" Kasahara bought the
sculpture, which infuriated Masatoshi Izumi because Noguchi was famous for not wanting to part with his stone sculptures.

On February 9, 1985, Noguchi attended the opening of his *Space of Akari and Stone* exhibition, designed by Arata Isozaki and installed by Tokyo's Seibu Museum, after which he and Kyoko traveled to the Barrier Islands off the coast of Indonesia, where they swam and enjoyed the long white sand beach. "He was a good swimmer," Kyoko recalls. "The waves were very high, and I could not get back to shore. Noguchi swam out and pulled me to shore." From Indonesia they traveled in March to India, a country that Noguchi loved and wanted Kyoko to know. Part of his reason for going to India had been to give his friend Prime Minister Indira Gandhi advice about how to revive Indian folk art and to promote its export. Although she had been assassinated four months prior to their arrival, Noguchi was welcomed as a guest of the government. The trip to India was not a success. Kyoko recalls that Noguchi came down with a cold and became so ill he had to be hospitalized. Kyoko arranged Japanese meals for him and to comfort him she sang Japanese lullabies. As soon as he was strong enough to travel Noguchi and Kyoko returned to Japan, and from there Noguchi went on to New York.

Around this time Noguchi told Kyoko that he felt he was weakening. He still suffered from back problems. He had had an enlarged prostate (in the 1960s he had a prostate operation). His teeth kept breaking for no apparent reason, and he had had cataract surgery on both eyes. In a diary entry from fall 1986 Kyoko wrote that Noguchi seemed "driven as though he had to hurry because he had no time left."[10] Arata Isozaki noted Noguchi's being always "on the run . . . Perhaps it is that Isamu is continually gauging the amount of work he still had to do."[11]

In April 1987 in Honolulu his back was so painful that he was hospitalized. Painkillers, shiatsu sessions, and ten days of rest enabled him to walk again. He returned to Japan and began to see an acupuncturist in Otsu, near Kyoto. In New York in the summer of 1987 he was again immobilized with pain. A Japanese acupuncturist gave him some relief and he took up a regimen of physical therapy to strengthen his spine. Late in September he was once again hard at work in his Mure stone circle.

Four days before Christmas 1987 Noguchi and Kyoko flew to Los Angeles on their way to Santa Fe to spend the holiday with Ailes. Wanting to show Kyoko all of his best works while he was still strong enough to travel, he took her to *California Scenario*.[12] In Santa Fe Noguchi and Ailes sat before a fire and shared memories of their mother. On New Year's Eve in Manhattan, Noguchi, Kyoko, and Junichi went to a party given by I. M. Pei and watched fireworks from his balcony. A day or so later Junichi and Kyoko took Hiroyuki Hattori, the young president of a high-tech firm in the city of Sapporo, Japan, out to Long Island City to talk to Noguchi about a park that they hoped Noguchi would create in Sapporo. As they toured the museum, Noguchi stopped to look at some of the bronze models for his unrealized projects such as *Play Mountain* and *Monument to the Plow*. "My best things have never been built," he observed.[13] Even in his last years Noguchi kept hoping to find a place to build *Play Mountain* and his *Memorial to the Dead of Hiroshima*.

In March 1988 Noguchi, Kyoko, and Junichi went to Sapporo (on Japan's northern island of Hokkaido), where Hattori and the mayor guided them around the outskirts of the city to look at possible sites for the future park. First they went to a piece of land where a new university of the arts would be built. They had lunch in a forest, Kyoko recalls, but Noguchi showed his disinterest in this site by asking in the middle of lunch, "Until when do we have to be here?" The place had many trees, Noguchi pointed out, and it did not need to be improved with art. Next they went to the Sapporo Art Park. Noguchi was disgusted: "It's like a graveyard of sculptures," he said. Finally they went to Sapporo's municipal dump, a vast open space at Moerenuma. It was surrounded on three sides by a loop in the Toyohira River, and it had a broad hill where garbage had been piled. Noguchi was immediately taken with it and wanted to turn the whole 400-acre space into one large sculpture—the biggest of his entire career.

Having made a model for the park in Junichi's Tokyo office, he returned to Sapporo a few weeks later. He went there again in the third week of May, and he made a final trip to Sapporo on October 18. His plan for the park included all kinds of imaginatively designed play equipment, a slide in the shape of Mount Fuji, a glass pyramid inspired by the one I. M. Pei had built at the Louvre, a pyramidal hill tall enough for skiing, a stage, a fountain, a swimming pool, a grassy mound surmounted by an open pyramid made of stainless steel columns, and facilities for various sports. What must have made Noguchi happiest was that he would finally build his *Play Mountain*, and, at thirty meters high, it would be even bigger than his rejected design from 1933.

Moerenuma Park, Sapporo, Japan, a posthumously completed project

That July Noguchi took Kyoko to Paris for five days. They visited Monet's home and garden at Giverny. He also took her to the Musée d'Orsay to see his favorite painting, Henri Rousseau's *The Snake Charmer*, which she found menacing. From Paris they went to Pietra Santa, after which they stopped in Rome before moving on to Greece in August, where they stayed on the island of Paros in a small hotel near the summer home of Noguchi's Philadelphia friend, Penny Bach. When Bach took her guests to Paros's famous marble quarries she was struck by Noguchi's avidity. "Isamu practically ran into the depth of the quarry. It's below ground and therefore scary. He wanted to go down into the depth, but I said we should do it another day accompanied by some experienced friends."[14] With the potter Stelios Ghikas they descended the deep shafts of the ancient marble quarries at Marothi, where Noguchi found a translucent chunk of Parian marble that he wanted to take home with him.[15] It was too heavy to carry, and in any case Bach told him it was illegal to remove any marble from the quarry. Noguchi was tenacious: he planned to ask the film star Melina Mercouri, who was then cultural minister of Greece, to let him have the rock.

Bach also took Noguchi and Kyoko to her favorite beach at Kolymbithres (meaning "baptismal basins"). To avoid crowds they went early in the morning. "It was primeval," Bach says. The water was turquoise and the beach with its golden sand was flanked by beautiful stone formations. "We swam and rested on rocks. I was lying fairly nude on a rock and Noguchi took all of these pictures of me."[16] Noguchi was happy: "A person should bathe here before he dies," he said.

Noguchi told Bach that he wanted to go to Delos, a Cycladic island with extraordinary archaeological sites, and the legendary birthplace of Artemis and Apollo. Bach made arrangements for the trip by boat. "The wind came up the day before," she recalls. "Noguchi was not feeling well and he said he didn't want to go. I was surprised: Isamu and I were both experience junkies. I'd never known him not to want to do something." Before Noguchi and Kyoko left for a speaking engagement in Delphi, he told Bach that her house needed an Akari lamp. "I said, 'I guess I do.' He sent me six Akari lamps, one for every room in the house."

After participating in a conference in Delphi about the state of art (August 19 to 21), Noguchi and Kyoko flew to Japan, where, on August 26, during a long interview with Kazue Kobata (intended as an aid to his future biographer), Noguchi said, "[I'm] trying to figure out how many sculptures I can make." In late September he was back in Paris for the rededication of his UNESCO garden. He was delighted with how much the trees had grown in thirty years. Time's passage was clearly on his mind when he told a Japanese journalist: "Nowadays everything in the world has become too 'instant.' People are interested only in the newest things in culture, and they chase one thing after another. That is very dangerous."[17] In his last years Noguchi often spoke disparagingly about the state of the world, and especially about the state of the art world, which he saw as overly commercial and obsessed with novelty. "I think a terrible thing is happening to the arts. There is a kind of proliferation, an enormous irresponsibility . . . I have totally given up the idea of doing sculpture. The idea of doing art as such is sort of ruined by the art business . . . It is not merely the increase of people but the increase of things, ideas and trends. It is all the fault of advertising, the fault of education, the desire for money and success. All that has been rolling into this enormous garbage heap which is going to flatten us all."[18]

In 1988 Noguchi was even more restless than usual. It was a restlessness that could only be assuaged by work—especially by the carving of hard stone that, being timeless, allowed him to venture outside of time. He crisscrossed the world, moving from New York to Miami to Japan to Italy, as well as to many other cities. "I have always been a wanderer. I have never been able to be a practicing artist in the sense of production and a gallery and applause and success."[19] But he was certainly successful. In October he was in New York to accept the Order of the Sacred Treasury at the Japanese consulate. A pendant of gold rays hanging from a ribbon was hung around his neck. A newspaper report quoted Noguchi in a sanguine mood: "I think that the world is in a state of transfiguration and that America and Japan play a leading role . . . and it is my tremendous good fortune that I find myself at that particular point where I might be of some influence."[20]

52

NO BEGINNINGS, NO ENDINGS

A November 17, 1988, photograph of Noguchi celebrating his eighty-fourth birthday on Shikoku shows a wizened yet vital man holding a carving knife with which he is about to cut two birthday cakes. At the party Noguchi showed his assembled guests his new model for Moerenuma Park, and Issey Miyake showed a video of his fall collection of clothes full of pleats that, like the ribs of Akari, gave life to light. From Miyake and Noguchi's point of view, the clothes were works of art in themselves. On this birthday Kyoko remembers Noguchi gazing at the autumn-flowering persimmon tree in the garden behind his house and saying, "Will I see the persimmon flower next year?"[1]

When Kasahara visited Mure in Noguchi's last years, Noguchi seemed, he said, "to be looking for a way to return to his origin . . . One evening just before dinner, when he recited his father's poem 'The Inland Sea,' he was about to burst into tears, so he sat down not wanting to show his tears."[2] During the day Kasahara watched Noguchi at work in the stone circle. "He was banging the stone with his chisel, but he was old, so he just put a mark on the stone and asked the stonecutter to work on it. He tried to carve but he was not strong enough." One evening the cook brought out a seabream that was still alive for Noguchi and Kasahara's inspection. "This live fish made a sound on the cutting board," Kasahara recalls. "When Noguchi heard it he exclaimed, 'Oh, that's wonderful! That kind of liveliness can come to us after we eat this fish.'"

Two days after his birthday Noguchi and Kyoko traveled to Kyoto to

stay at Yamakiku, Noguchi's favorite *ryokan*, run by Kinuko Ishihara.
His back continued to give him trouble so he went to nearby Otsu to
see his acupuncturist. "It seemed to help him," Ishihara recalls. "In the
evenings he asked me to put down only one futon in his room instead
of two because he wanted a hard bed for his back."[3] Yamakiku was not
an especially luxurious *ryokan*, but it was very exclusive—guests had
to be recommended by other guests, and it only had three rooms. "He
treated my *ryokan* as if it were his house," says Ishihara. "He felt relaxed and cozy there. Our neighbor had a huge garden and Noguchi
loved to sit and look at the garden. The *ryokan* was near the zoo and
Noguchi liked hearing the animals' cries. When he arrived he'd say,
'I'm home!' He would go straight to his room and read a book. He spent
a lot of time reading in his room. When he left he'd say, 'I'm going.' He'd
come on short notice. If the *ryokan* was full he'd get angry because he
assumed that it was like his own house."

Noguchi's relationship with Kyoko was romantic, but also conve-
nient and comfortable. She not only looked after him, she also helped
to take care of Akari sales in Japan. He sometimes looked after her,
too. "One day Isamu told me that he wanted to give me something. I

Noguchi working in the stone circle, Mure, Shikoku, late 1980s

said no, so he paid for his dentist to fix my teeth." He asked her to marry him but she refused. She already had a husband of whom she was fond. Noguchi asked, "Why don't you leave him?" With Junichi, Kyoko had an affluent, easygoing, and full life. Moreover, she did not want to separate in part because of the negative feelings about divorce in Japan. She recalls that in his last years Noguchi was contemplating making a more permanent home in Japan. No doubt he would have shared that home with Kyoko and Junichi. "He wanted to be near the sea and he wanted it to be warm. He liked Kyoto, but it was cold in winter. He thought of the Izu peninsula [on the Pacific coast] or Chigasaki."

Soon after his eighty-fourth birthday Noguchi and Kyoko went to Osaka, from where he would fly to New York in time for Thanksgiving. In Osaka they met with the architect Tadao Ando and Ryunosuke Kasahara to discuss Noguchi's upcoming show of bronze sculptures. Noguchi was not happy with one possible venue for his exhibition, so they went to see a recently completed space, designed by Ando. "It was an annex, a space on top of a building of about ninety-nine square meters," says Kasahara.[4] Noguchi decided this was where he wanted his sculpture to be shown. That evening Noguchi and Kyoko went to a Bunraku (puppet) show, a traditional form of theater that Noguchi had always enjoyed. When the play was over he and Kyoko went backstage to meet the narrator, a well-known performer who was about to retire. Perhaps because of the actor's age, Noguchi, feeling old himself, was moved by the encounter. The next day Noguchi flew to New York. Kyoko planned to join him on December 17.

Noguchi had Thanksgiving dinner at Priscilla's apartment. With Shoji and Tsuneko Sadao there, it was very much a family group. From New York Noguchi flew to Italy, where he spent his days in Pietra Santa working single-mindedly on six marble sculptures. He came down with a cold, in spite of which, from early in the morning until night, he kept working outside in the rain.[5] When he arrived back in New York on December 12 he took to his bed. He was scheduled to go to a meeting of his foundation's board of directors the day after he arrived. Priscilla, hearing his hoarse voice, advised him to skip the meeting. She would go and later would fill him in on what was accomplished. When Priscilla arrived at Noguchi's Sixty-ninth Street apartment, she found him feverish and lacking an appetite. She squeezed fresh orange juice for

Noguchi celebrating his last birthday, Mure, Shikoku, November 1988

him. The next night Noguchi was no better, so Priscilla decided to stay at his apartment to look after him as she had done after his various back operations. On December 16 Noguchi's doctor made a house call, diagnosed pneumonia, and arranged for an ambulance to take Noguchi to New York University Medical Center. Noguchi dressed carefully, so carefully that Priscilla asked him why he wanted to look so elegant if he was only going to the hospital. Noguchi said that she would not understand, meaning that with her patrician appearance she would always be treated with deference, whereas he, a mixed-breed, needed to dress like a gentleman. On their way to the hospital he told Priscilla that he didn't think that he would leave the hospital alive. Perhaps he was thinking of his mother, who had been hospitalized in mid-December and died of pneumonia two and a half weeks later. Noguchi once told Kitty Roedel that he did not want to die the way his mother had.

According to hospital records Noguchi was admitted on December 17. "He called me from the hospital," Kyoko recalls. "He asked me to come to New York. I had the key to his apartment. We planned to go to Mexico together—while he was in Pietra Santa he had read a thick guidebook about Mexico to prepare for our trip. He told me he would die if he stayed in that hospital. He wanted to move to another hospital. I wanted to go to New York, but Shoji Sadao said, 'Don't come. If you tried to care for him Priscilla would be offended.'"

Over the next few days none of the drugs that the doctors prescribed helped; Noguchi's condition worsened. Priscilla watched over him and kept all other visitors away, even his sister Ailes, who flew in from Santa Fe. Priscilla thought that if he saw Ailes he would think he was going to die. The one person Priscilla did allow at Noguchi's bedside was Arne Glimcher. Glimcher gave Noguchi a momentary lift by talking about his next Pace Gallery exhibition. "When I visited, Noguchi had been in intensive care but he was now back in his room. I told him that he looked much better. His doctor and Priscilla thought he was better. But Noguchi said something strange to me. He said that his mother had died in the hospital of pneumonia and he was going to die of pneumonia at the age of eighty-four."[6]

Noguchi became more and more withdrawn. When Priscilla read *The New York Times* to him he was no longer interested. At three in the morning of December 24 he had a heart attack and was moved back into the intensive care unit. An oxygen mask was put over his nose and mouth. Unable to talk, he communicated by writing notes. One of the notes said, "Am I finished with pneumonia? What date?"[7] Another almost illegible note, written perhaps around December 27, asked, "Is Sunday New Year Maybe 4th for Kyoko? Ask Jack What is today. When can I eat." The word "eat" was so shakily written that he wrote it a second time in larger letters. After wearing the oxygen mask for three days, Noguchi tried to take it off. He tried to remove the intravenous needle from his arm as well, so the doctors ordered his hands and feet tied to the bed. At 1:32 in the morning of December 30 Noguchi died, according to the hospital, of heart failure.

When Kyoko arrived in New York she was not allowed to see Noguchi's body. She was told that it was already far away. Noguchi was cremated and half of his ashes were placed in a corner of his museum's garden. The other half was taken to Mure. Thus, even in death he was divided between East and West. His funeral and burial services were private. On February 7 there was an afternoon memorial service at the Noguchi Museum attended by some four hundred people. Kyoko played the koto and sang. There was music by another of Noguchi's friends, and speeches by Shoji Sadao and Anne d'Harnoncourt, among others. At a gathering at Priscilla's after the memorial the guests were shocked when Junichi said how proud he was to have shared his wife with Noguchi.

A few months later there were two other memorial services. Following Japanese custom, the one in the Mure stone circle took place one hundred days after Noguchi's death. After the service, Noguchi's ashes were carried to the top of his garden and placed inside a large upright oval boulder of pinkish mannari granite, which, years before, Noguchi had found in Okayama and had transported to Mure. Admiring the boulder after it was installed in the stone circle, he had asked Izumi, "Would it be okay for me to be inside this stone?"[8] Izumi told Noguchi that it was too early for him to die. In 1985 Noguchi drew a line with red bengara around the stone's girth. "By the time Noguchi died the line had faded away," says Izumi, "but we could just see where it was and we cut the stone in half and I carved out a hollow for his ashes." The ashes were placed in the cavity, and the two halves of the egg-

Noguchi's grave on top of the hill garden behind his house at Mure, Shikoku

shaped rock were put back together. Poised on a mound at the hill's summit, the rock has a wide view of nearby mountains and, in the distance, the Inland Sea, whose islands had given Noguchi such a wealth of stone and inspiration.

A week after the Mure memorial the Segerstroms arranged a memorial at *California Scenario*. There was a koto player dressed in a kimono, and a traditional tea ceremony performed by a woman from the Orange County chapter of a tea ceremony school. One hundred and fifty people were offered bowls of bitter green tea and a brunch of fruit, sushi, frittata, and sweets. Shoji Sadao spoke of the relationship between the Eastern and Western ceremonies: "There's a kind of symmetry to it and almost a mystical thing about it," he said. Toren Segerstrom spoke of Noguchi as a brilliant artist who believed in the power of gardens. "To say you love someone sometimes is not enough. To say 'Thank you' to someone for showing you a different way of looking at the world is sometimes not enough. To create a new garden, no matter how big or small, is to say, 'Thank you, Isamu Noguchi.'"[9]

Noguchi was mourned by friends, coworkers, and lovers. Even though he was cool, secretive, and very much a loner, people who knew him were saddened. Priscilla devoted her life to his legacy, working hard to make the Noguchi Museum the wondrous place it is. When she spoke about Noguchi there was a passion in her voice that made it clear he was alive in her thoughts. Just as she was once the perfect artist's wife, she was now the artist's dedicated widow. Shoji Sadao has worked hard to finish projects that were not completed before Noguchi's death. He oversaw, for example, the completion of *Time and Space*, a monumental sculpture at the Takamatsu airport, which, like Noguchi's homage to the lima bean at *California Scenario*, looks like a cluster of elephantine boulders. The most important unfinished project that Sadao shepherded to completion was *Moerenuma Park*, which opened in July 2005. Kyoko Kawamura treasures Noguchi's memory and speaks wistfully about his death. Although her marriage seems happy and stable and her career flourishes, with regard to Noguchi she still seems bereft.

The art world bemoaned the loss of Noguchi as the grand old man of twentieth-century sculpture. His obituaries were full of accolades. Allen Wardwell, then the director of the Noguchi Museum, told the press: "America has lost its greatest living sculptor. Of course he was much more than a sculptor—he was a designer of spaces, stage sets, gardens, fountains and the decorative arts. He was a great thinker and visionary."[10] Martin Friedman called Noguchi "a paramount and essential figure in the evolution of 20th-century sculpture."[11] Anne d'Harnoncourt said, "He never lost his extraordinary youthful sense of invention and enthusiasm. The creation of his museum spaces in Long Island City was an extraordinary gesture, beautifully carried out. He did it with great grace . . . He was a wonderful free spirit."[12] Art historian Albert Elsen, who has written so authoritatively about modern sculpture, wrote in *Art Journal* that Noguchi's Dodge Fountain in Detroit was "one of the greatest fountains ever designed."[13] In *The New Yorker* Calvin Tomkins called Noguchi "the most significant public artist of his time."[14] The sculptor Joel Shapiro posed the question: "There is David Smith and Noguchi and who else in this country?"[15] Tadao Ando wrote that Noguchi was "the last master since Henry Moore . . . Words cannot describe my anguish at his passing."[16]

Ninety-four-year-old Martha Graham had seen Noguchi not long before he died. When she learned of his death, she said: "So much of my life has been bound artistically with Isamu Noguchi. I feel the world has lost an artist who, like a shaman, has translated myths of all our lives into living memory. The works he created for my ballets brought to me a new vision, a new world of space and the utilization of space. Isamu, as I do, always looked forward and not to the past."[17]

Noguchi looked both ways. For him time flowed both forward and backward. He longed to return to origins. "I wanted to see the horizon again as in the beginning of things."[18] But time's passage never stopped bothering him. "I still don't seem to have come to terms with time," Noguchi said in 1964.[19] In his autobiography he wrote: "And if I sometimes built pieces that appeared to have some abiding worth, they, too, were like spirit money, signs to ward off the disaster of time."[20] His anxiety about life's brevity drove his creative process, as did his unease with the pull of East and West. He needed to encompass time within his sculpture, either by concretizing it in stone or by making gardens in which the ambulatory viewer moved through time. He wanted to transcend time by creating something beautiful and enduring, but he also wanted to go with time's flow, allowing his work to change over the years and to return to the earth, which, as he so often said, we all must. To challenge time and to acquiesce to time, stone was his chosen weapon. "Stone breathes with nature's time cycle. It doesn't resist entropy, but is within it. It begins before you and continues through you and goes on. Working with stone is not resisting time, but touching it."[21] In his mind his stone sculptures were just temporary incursions into a process of change that would go on forever: "All I do is provide an invasion of a different time element into the time of nature."[22]

Walking in his museum's garden with Dore Ashton, Noguchi once mused: "I have come to no conclusions, no beginnings, no endings."[23] He maintained this open-ended stance, partly because he was so full of wonder. "I'm still making discoveries, I'm still finding new ground. That is to say, once ground is found, there's any amount of it left to find. You go from one place to another, but the earth is round and infinite. It's a continuous discovery."[24] "Awareness" was a word that Noguchi used often. When asked if there was anything for which he wanted to be remembered, he answered: "If I could have contributed something to an awareness of living, and awareness of this changing and this continuity."[25] Sometimes when he spoke of awareness, he waxed mystical and otherworldly. Art, he said, comes "from the awakening person. Awakening is what you might call the spiritual. It is a linkage to something flowing very rapidly through the air. I can put my finger on it and plug in."[26] Another time he said: "The whole world is art . . . If one is really awake, he will see that the whole world is a symphony."[27] He called sculpture a process of "opening *awareness* . . . Art is quite invisible and weightless; it hovers over the surface. Appearing anywhere, oblivious of time, we know it when we hear it, see it, clear as recognition."[28] Speaking of this awakened state with Martin Friedman, Noguchi said: "If you allow yourself to be—or imagine yourself to be—part of all phenomena, then you are able to be anywhere, and the artist is merely the shaman who is able to contact all these other phenomena. Therefore, you are really free and you really don't belong anywhere."[29] In the mid-1980s he set forth his concept of awareness in *The Awakening*, a tall basalt sculpture that stands motionless but alert, its smooth skin marked by just a few cuts of the chisel. With its silence and mystery this stone awakening is indeed shamanlike. It listens.

To the end of his life Noguchi kept talking about not belonging. In 1988 he told a Japanese interviewer: "You might say, in some way, that I'm an expatriate wherever I am, either in America or in [Japan]; that

I'm, after all, half-breed there or half-breed here."[30] Julien Levy noted that Noguchi as an outsider became extra vigilant, "landing always like a cat on his feet."[31] For Noguchi his sense of homelessness was an impetus: "My longing for affiliation has been the source of my creativity."[32] Noguchi, the nomad, sought and found, by making sculpture, a way to embed himself in the earth, in nature, in the world. "We are," he said, "a landscape of all we know."[33]

NOTES

ABBREVIATIONS

Ashton Dore Ashton. *Noguchi East and West*. New York, 1992.

BM Isamu Noguchi. Bollingen Manuscript, a twenty-three-page unpublished text about his travels, written years later. NA.

Cummings interviews Paul Cummings. Interviews with Isamu Noguchi. November and December 1973. Archives of American Art, Smithsonian Institution. Also NA.

Duus Masayo Duus. *The Life of Isamu Noguchi: Journey without Borders*. Princeton, NJ: Princeton University Press, 2004.

Essays and Conversations Isamu Noguchi. *Essays and Conversations*. Edited by Diane Apostolos-Cappadona and Bruce Altshuler. New York: Abrams, 1994.

Hakutani Yoshinobu Hakutani, ed. *Selected English Writings of Yone Noguchi: An East-West Literary Assimilation*. Volume 2. Cranbury, NJ: Prose, 1992.

Mus. Cat. *The Isamu Noguchi Garden Museum*. Museum catalogue. New York, 1987.

IN Isamu Noguchi.

KK Katharine Kuh. "An Interview with Isamu Noguchi." *Horizon* 2, no. 4 (March 1960): 104–12 (reprinted in *Essays and Conversations*, 130–35).

Kobata interview Kazue Kobata. Interview with Isamu Noguchi. Tape transcript, 1988. NA.

LG Leonie Gilmour.

LG to CB Leonie Gilmour, letter to Catherine Bunnell. NA.

LL Lilly Library, Indiana University, Bloomington, Indiana.

NA Archives of the Isamu Noguchi Garden Museum, New York.

Sc W Isamu Noguchi. *Isamu Noguchi: A Sculptor's World*. New York: Harper and Row, 1968.

YN Letters   Yone Noguchi. *Collected English Letters*. Introduction by
              Ikuko Atsumi. Tokyo: Yone Noguchi Society, 1975.
YN to LG   Yone Noguchi, letter to Leonie Gilmour. In YN Letters.

INTRODUCTION

1. Sc W, 161.
2. Isamu Noguchi, "The Road I Have Walked," text of Noguchi's speech in commemoration of the Kyoto Award, in *Play Mountain: Isamu Noguchi and Louis Kahn* (Tokyo: Watarium and Isamu Noguchi Foundation, 1996).
3. John Gruen, "The Artist Speaks: Isamu Noguchi," *Art in America* 56 (March–April 1968): 29.
4. Austin Faricy, "Rocks, Not Plants Dominate Noguchi's Sculptured Garden," *The Saturday Star-Bulletin* (Honolulu), August 2, 1958, NA.
5. Isamu Noguchi, "Ishi: Pari no 'Nihon no niwa' o tsukuru," *Geijutsu shincho*, July 1957, 153–57, translated in Duus, 277.
6. Mus. Cat., 26.
7. Sandra Earley, *The Sunday Post* (Bridgeport, CT), September 15, 1985, clipping, NA.
8. *Essays and Conversations*, 61.

1. PARENTS

1. LG to CB, April 27, 1915.
2. KK, 104–12.
3. Michael Brenson, "Isamu Noguchi, the Sculptor, Dies at 84," *New York Times*, December 31, 1988.
4. Jean Clareboudt, "Isamu Noguchi: Precurseur," *Artpress* 137 (June 1984): 26–29, clipping, NA. Translation by author.
5. KK, 104–12.
6. Kobata interview, 26 and 45.
7. *Essays and Conversations*, 131.
8. Sc W, 11.
9. Cummings interviews, 3.
10. Duus, 21.
11. Kobata interview, 2.
12. LG to CB, April 25, 1900.
13. YN to LG, February 4, 1901.
14. Ibid., February 21, 1901.
15. LG, letter to Frank Putnam, April 3, 1906, NA.
16. Duus, 11.
17. Hakutani, 212.
18. Ibid., 213.
19. Duus, 13.
20. Hakutani, 234.
21. Ibid., 233.
22. Ibid., 219.
23. Ibid.
24. Yone Noguchi, *Seen and Unseen, or Monologue of a Homeless Snail* (San Francisco:

Gelett Burgess and Porter Garnett, Bohemian Press, 1897), and *The Voice of the Valley* (San Francisco: Doxy Press, 1897).

25. Hakutani, 223.
26. Ibid., 222.
27. YN Letters, 10.
28. Kosen M. Takahashi, letter to Blanche Partington, March 24, 1899, in YN Letters, 34–35.
29. YN Letters, 38–39.
30. Ibid., 44.
31. See Roger Austin, *Genteel Pagan: The Double Life of Charles Warren Stoddard*, ed. John W. Crowley (Amherst: University of Massachusetts Press, 1991).
32. Yone Noguchi, letter to Charles Stoddard, July 3, 1900, in YN Letters, 46.
33. *Genteel Pagan*, 142.
34. YN Letters, 48.
35. Ibid., 96–97.
36. Ibid., 56.
37. Ibid., 58.
38. Ibid., 66.
39. Ibid., 85.
40. Ibid., 94.
41. Ibid., 136.
42. Ibid., 141.
43. Ibid., 190.
44. Duus, 37.
45. Yone Noguchi, *Dual Citizen* (1921), reprinted in Duus, 37.

2. DEAR BABY

1. LG to CB, October 30, 1904.
2. LG, letter to Ailes Gilmour, n.d., NA.
3. *Los Angeles Herald*, "Yone Noguchi's Babe Pride of Hospital," November 27, 1904, clipping, NA.
4. Ibid.
5. Duus, 36.
6. Kobata interview, 90.
7. LG to CB, January 1, 1905.
8. YN Letters, 191.
9. Ethel Armes, letter to Charles Stoddard, n.d., 1905, Bancroft Library, University of California, Berkeley.
10. YN Letters, 192.
11. LG to CB, October 4, 1905.
12. Duus, 36.
13. LG to CB, January 20, 1906.
14. LG, letter to YN, February 24, 1906, in YN Letters, 196–97.
15. Ibid.
16. LG, letter to Frank Putnam, March 14, 1906, NA.
17. LG, letter to Frank Putnam, May 27, 1906, NA.
18. LG, letter to Charles Stoddard, December 6, 1906, NA.

19. Duus, 50.
20. Ibid., 45–46.
21. LG, letter to Frank Putnam, January 23, 1907, NA.

3. TOKYO

1. Duus, 46.
2. Hakutani, 264–70. Quotes from Yone Noguchi's narrative about Isamu's early days in Tokyo are in Hakutani, 264–70.
3. Ibid.
4. IN, notes for a planned autobiography, NA.
5. LG, letter to Frank Putnam, n.d., probably May 1907, NA.
6. Kobata interview, 3.
7. Sc W, 11.
8. Ibid.
9. Hakutani, 264–70.
10. Ibid.
11. Kobata interview, 4.
12. Yonejiro Noguchi, *Kamakura* (Japan: Valley Press, 1910).
13. YN Letters, 204–5.
14. LG to CB, July 1907.
15. LG, letter to Frank Putnam, February 26, 1908, NA.
16. LG to CB, March 13, 1908.
17. Ibid., April 4, 1908.
18. Yone Noguchi, letter to Charles Stoddard, July 26, 1908, in YN Letters, 206.
19. Sc W, 11.
20. LG to CB, June 13, 1909.
21. Duus, 57.
22. Leonie called it the "Kotojoganko (girl's school) Hiranuma."
23. LG to CB, November 3, 1910.
24. Ibid., December 23, 1910.
25. Sc W, 11.
26. KK, 106.
27. Kobata interview, 8–9.
28. Cummings interviews, 1.
29. LG to CB, May 3, 1911.
30. Duus, 63.
31. Kobata interview, 11.

4. CHIGASAKI

1. LG, letter to Ailes Gilmour, n.d., probably 1928, NA.
2. Sc W, 11.
3. LG to CB, January 15, 1912.
4. Sc W, 12.
5. KK, 106.
6. Sc W, 12.
7. Kobata interview, 12.

8. Ibid.
9. *Sc W*, 12.
10. Kobata interview, 36.
11. Duus, 65.
12. Kobata interview, 36.
13. Duus, 65–66.
14. Matsuo Miyake, letter to LG, September 28, 1905, NA.
15. Ibid., November 1907, NA.
16. Ibid., February 1910, NA.
17. Ibid., October 1910, NA.
18. LG to CB, 1912.
19. Kobata interview, 9–10.
20. Ibid.
21. LG to CB, January 1913.
22. Ibid., March 7, 1913.
23. YN Letters, 213.
24. Kobata interview, 110.
25. Blake Green, "A Rootless Artist Comes Home Again," *San Francisco Chronicle*, May 5, 1982, clipping, NA.
26. *Sc W*, 14.
27. YN Letters, 215.

5. ST. JOSEPH COLLEGE

1. Kobata interview, 17.
2. LG to CB, September 23, 1913.
3. Hakutani, 62 and 67.
4. Kobata interview, 14.
5. Ibid.
6. *Sc W*, 11–12.
7. Kobata interview, 11.
8. LG to CB, March 1, 1914.
9. Ibid., May 6, 1914.
10. Ibid., August 23, 1914.
11. Kobata interview, 12.
12. Duus, 71. The information about Noguchi's summer friendships comes from Duus, 70–72.
13. LG to CB, November 5, 1914.
14. Ibid.
15. Ibid., April 27, 1915.
16. IN and Ailes Gilmour, videotaped conversation by Jody Spinden, quoted in Duus, 71.
17. LG to CB, August 29, 1915.
18. *Sc W*, 12. It is possible that Noguchi was remembering his work the previous year with the carpenters who built the Chigasaki house.
19. Roberta Brandes Gratz, "Sculptor to the World," *New York Post*, April 9, 1968.
20. IN, introduction to *Spectacular Heroes of Japan*, exhibition catalogue (New York: Japan Society, 1985), 13.

21. Kobata interview, 15.
22. LG to CB, February 24, 1916.
23. Ibid., n.d., 1916.
24. Ibid., July 31, 1916.
25. Duus, 72.
26. LG to CB, August 29, 1916.
27. Ibid., January 23, 1917.
28. Sc W, 13.
29. Kobata interview, 19–20.
30. Ibid.
31. Ibid.
32. "The Daniel Boone Idea in Education," Scientific American 109, no. 19 (November 8, 1916): 361–62.
33. Ibid.
34. LG, letter to the Superintendent of the Interlaken School, April 5, 1918, Rumely Mss., Manuscripts Department, LL.
35. Sc W, 13.
36. Kobata interview, 31.
37. Sc W, 13.
38. Mary Cooke, "Isamu Noguchi: Torn between East and West," The Honolulu Advertiser, April 6, 1973, NA.
39. Kobata interview, 37.
40. Duus, 80–81.
41. Kobata interview, 31.

6. INTERLAKEN

1. Sc W, 14.
2. Kobata interview, 35.
3. Sc W, 14.
4. KK, 109.
5. C. A. Lewis, letter to Edward A. Rumely, July 25, 1918, LL.
6. Thomas B. Hess, "Isamu Noguchi: '46," Art News 45 (September 1946): 38.
7. Kobata interview, 39.
8. Duus, 84.
9. Kobata interview, 22.
10. Ibid., 43.
11. LG, letter to Miss Rumely, September 14, 1918, LL.
12. Sc W, 14.
13. Kobata interview, 22 and 33.
14. Sc W, 14.
15. LG, letter to Superintendant, Interlaken School, October 5, 1918, LL.
16. Ibid., October 14, 1918, LL.
17. Kobata interview, 33.
18. Sc W, 14.
19. Kobata interview, 32.
20. Ibid., 110.
21. Ibid., 41.

7. LA PORTE

1. Sc W, 14.
2. Ashton, 31.
3. IN, letter to Mary Rumely Munn, February 16, 1988, LL.
4. Edward A. Rumely, letter to IN, September 15, 1919. Rumely's letters to Noguchi are in LL.
5. IN, letter to Edward A. Rumely, n.d. IN's letters to Edward A. Rumely are in LL.
6. Kobata interview, 41.
7. Ibid., 40.
8. Calvin Tomkins, "The Art World: Rocks," The New Yorker, March 24, 1980, 76.
9. YN to LG, September 9, 1919. The lower half of this torn letter is in the NA.
10. Fanny Rumely, letter to Edward A. Rumely, n.d., 1920, LL.
11. IN, letter to Edward A. Rumely, 1920 or '21.
12. La Porte High School Yearbook (1922), quoted in Duus, 95.
13. The La Porte Herald, December 31, 1988, clipping, NA.
14. R. K. McLean, M.D., letter to Henry Segerstrom, January 15, 1988, NA.
15. Sc W, 14.
16. Kobata interview, 46.
17. In Noguchi's memory, that summer Borglum was busy making a huge sculptural memorial for Newark, New Jersey, with "more than forty figures, over life-size, including some horses." Although Borglum later did do several sculptures for Newark, Noguchi must have been referring to the Confederate Memorial.
18. Kobata interview, 46.
19. Cummings interviews, 6.
20. Sc W, 14–15.
21. Bonnie Rychlak and Ian Buruma, Noguchi and the Figure, exhibition catalogue (Mexico City: MARCA, 1999), 36.
22. Julien Levy, "Isamu Noguchi," Creative Art 12, no. 1 (January 1933): 29–35.
23. Duus, 97.

8. I BECAME A SCULPTOR

1. Edward A. Rumely, letter to Columbia University, fall 1922, NA.
2. Sc W, 15.
3. Hideo Noguchi's renown came from his culturing of the spirochete bacterium Treponema pallidum, which causes syphilis, and then developing a skin test for the diagnosis of syphilis. Later his research to find a vaccine for yellow fever took him to Africa, where he died of the fever in 1928.
4. Kobata interview, 47.
5. Ibid., 80.
6. KK, 107.
7. Kobata interview, 45.
8. IN, letter to Edward A. Rumely, September 6, 1923.
9. Sc W, 15.
10. Kobata interview, 30–31.
11. LG to CB, March 27, 1927.
12. Kobata interview, 58.

13. Bonnie Rychlak, *The Full Figure and Portraiture, 1926–1941,* exhibition brochure (New York: Noguchi Museum, 2008), n.p.
14. Cummings interviews, 9.
15. IN, "The Road I Have Walked," 98.
16. *Sc W,* 15.
17. Cummings interviews, 9.
18. IN, notes for a planned autobiography, NA. Curiously, Arshile Gorky, who became a close friend of Noguchi's in the early 1930s, changed his name from the Armenian Vosdanig Adoian to the Russian-sounding Arshile Gorky about the same time. He surely felt that an artist would have greater success as a Russian than as an Armenian.
19. IN, letter to Edward A. Rumely, March 26, 1924.
20. Ibid., n.d.
21. Ibid., March 20, 1924.
22. Fanny Scott Rumely, memoir of Edward A. Rumely, manuscript, LL.
23. Edward A. Rumely, letter to IN, June 2, 1924.
24. Edward A. Rumely, letter to IN, n.d.
25. Sam Hunter, *Isamu Noguchi* (New York: Abbeville, 1978), 32.
26. Isabel Rumely, letter to IN, September 20, 1965, LL.
27. Mary Relief Rumely, letter to IN, March 1, 1970, LL.
28. Hunter, *Isamu Noguchi,* 32.
29. Cummings interviews, 9.
30. Quoted in Duus, 102–3.
31. Cummings interviews, 10.
32. Ibid.
33. Ibid., 9.
34. Duus, 100.
35. Cummings interviews, 10.
36. IN, statement about *Undine,* February 25, 1927, LL.
37. Cummings interviews, 10.
38. Ibid., 9
39. *Sc W,* 16.
40. Ibid. Noguchi meant Stieglitz's Intimate Gallery—Stieglitz did not open An American Place until 1929. Noguchi also remembered seeing in a gallery on Sixth Street an exhibition of John Quinn's collection, which included a Brancusi sculpture that Quinn had bought at the Armory Show in 1913. Cummings interviews, 11.
41. Ibid.
42. Cummings interviews, 11–12.
43. J. B. Neumann, handwritten manuscript, n.d., Museum of Modern Art, IN, Artist's File.
44. Herbert Seligman, *Alfred Stieglitz Talking* (New Haven, CT: Yale University Press, 1966), 62–63.
45. Kobata interview, 73.
46. *Sc W,* 12.
47. Edward A. Rumely, letter to Henry Allen Moe, January 15, 1927, NA.
48. IN, Guggenheim Proposal, 1926, reprinted in *Sc W,* 16–17, and in *Essays and Conversations,* 16–17.
49. LG to CB, March 27, 1927.

50. LG, letter to IN, March 21, 1927, NA. All the letters from LG to IN quoted hence-forth are in NA.
51. LG to CB, March 27, 1927.
52. Ibid.
53. When Hamnett lived in Paris, she, Brancusi, and the British sculptor Jacob Epstein had made a daily pilgrimage to the Paris cemetery where Oscar Wilde was buried and where Epstein had placed a grave monument that he had sculpted—a figure with an erect penis. Every day the cemetery's caretakers covered the offending member with a cloth. Epstein and Hamnett's daily mission was to remove the cloth. IN, "Brzeska and the Grave of Pound," *Geijutsu-Shincho*, November 19, 1978, un-published translation in NA.
54. IN, letter to Edward A. Rumely, Easter Sunday, 1927.

9. I WILL RIVAL THE IMMORTALS

1. IN, "The Road I Have Walked," 99.
2. IN, letter to Edward A. Rumely, April 6, 1927.
3. Cummings interviews, 12.
4. In the mid-1920s Rumely became involved with vitamins and health; he established the Vitamin Food Company, which made Vegex.
5. IN, letter to Edward A. Rumely, July 10, 1927.
6. Edward A. Rumely, letter to IN, March 31, 1927.
7. IN, letter to Edward A. Rumely, n.d., c. April 1927.
8. Cummings interviews, 13.
9. Kobata interview, 14.
10. *Sc W*, 18.
11. IN, letter to LG, November 8, 1927, NA.
12. IN, letter to Edward A. Rumely, n.d.
13. Quoted in Duus, 118–19.
14. IN, letter to Andrée Ruellen, November 30, 1927, John W. Taylor and Andrée Ruel-len Papers, Archives of American Art, Smithsonian Institution.
15. Duus, 118–19.
16. Ibid., 120.
17. IN, "Noguchi on Brancusi," in *Essays and Conversations*, 110.
18. Kobata interview, 63.
19. KK, 108.
20. Carola Giedion-Welcker, *Constantin Brancusi*, trans. Maria Jolas and Anne Leroy (New York: George Braziller, 1959), 220.
21. Paul Richard, "Master of Space: Isamu Noguchi, Dean of American Sculptors," *The Washington Post*, June 7, 1980, 5.
22. IN, "Noguchi on Brancusi," 112.
23. Quoted in Hilton Kramer, "Noguchi Show at Whitney Branch: Silly Catalogue, Splendid Exhibition," *The New York Observer*, November 20, 1989, 21.
24. Ashton, 242.
25. IN, "Noguchi on Brancusi," 111.
26. Liviu Floda, "An Interview with Isamu Noguchi on Brancusi," *Journal of the Ameri-can Romanian Academy of Arts and Sciences* 8–9 (1986): 272–73, clipping, NA.
27. Ibid.

28. Kobata interview, 12.
29. Quoted in Bert Winther-Tamaki, "The Ceramic Art of Isamu Noguchi: A Close Embrace of the Earth," in *Isamu Noguchi and Modern Japanese Ceramics: A Close Embrace of the Earth*, exhibition catalogue (Washington, D.C.: Arthur M. Sackler Gallery, Smithsonian Institution, in association with University of California Press, 2003), 4.
30. Anna C. Chave, "Brancusi and Noguchi," *Isamu Noguchi: Sculptural Design* (Weil am Rhein, Germany: Vitra Design Museum, 2001), 40.
31. KK, 106.
32. Floda, "Interview with Isamu Noguchi on Brancusi," 271.
33. IN, "Noguchi on Brancusi," 111.
34. Ibid.
35. IN, letter to LG, c. September 1927.
36. LG, letters to IN, May 4, August 3, and October 30, 1927.
37. Sc W, 16.
38. Kobata interview, 84.
39. KK, 108.
40. Ibid.
41. Sc W, 18.
42. Quoted in Chave, "Brancusi and Noguchi," 34.
43. IN, "Noguchi on Brancusi," 114.
44. Floda, "Interview with Isamu Noguchi on Brancusi," 273.
45. IN, letter to Henry Allen Moe, September 15, 1927, NA.

10. OUT FROM THE SHADOW OF A BIG TREE

1. IN, letter to Edward A. Rumely, November 30, 1927.
2. Ibid., December 31, 1927.
3. IN, Guggenheim report, December 15, 1927, LL.
4. Sc W, 18.
5. Noguchi certainly knew Stuart Davis: he had sculpted a head of Davis's wife in 1926 and Davis was Ruellen's Paris neighbor.
6. Cummings interviews, 16.
7. Ibid.
8. Kobata interview, 63.
9. Ibid.
10. IN, letter to Henry Allen Moe, January 12, 1928, LL.
11. IN, letter to Edward A. Rumely, January 12, 1928.
12. Sc W, 18.
13. Kobata interview, 64.
14. IN, "The Road I Have Walked," 99.
15. Sc W, 18.
16. Cummings interviews, 14.
17. IN, "On the Structure and Carving of Bronze Plate," in *Isamu Noguchi: The Bronzes, 1987–1988*, exhibition catalogue (Osaka: Kasahara Gallery, 1989).
18. Sc W, 18.
19. Ibid.
20. Ibid.
21. IN, letter to Edward A. Rumely, January 28, 1929.

22. Sc W, 18–19.
23. Cummings interviews, 64.

11. HEAD BUSTER
1. Sc W, 17.
2. Ruth Green Harris, "Paintings and Sculpture Shown in Paris," The New York Times, March 31, 1929, clipping, NA.
3. Cummings interviews, 16–17.
4. Kobata interview, 83.
5. Sc W, 19.
6. Mary Gabriel, "Isamu Noguchi's Long Goodbye," Museum and Arts Washington (March/April 1989): 60, NA.
7. IN, "The Road I Have Walked," 99.
8. IN, notes for a planned autobiography, NA.
9. Katharine Kuh, interview with IN, transcript, 261, Archives of American Art, Smithsonian Institution, Washington, D.C.
10. IN, letter to President Sukarno, September 18, 1951, NA.
11. Nancy Grove, Isamu Noguchi: Portrait Sculpture, exhibition catalogue (New York: Whitney Museum of American Art, 1989), n.p.
12. Amy Wolf, On Becoming an Artist: Isamu Noguchi and His Contemporaries, 1922–1960, exhibition catalogue (New York: Noguchi Museum, 2010), 42.
13. IN, "George Gershwin," in Essays and Conversations, 22–23.
14. Diana Tittle, "Heiress in Exile," Cleveland, June 1977, 86, NA.
15. Benjamin Forgey, "Noguchi, Honing his Craft," The Washington Post, April 15, 1989, 1 and 6.
16. Kay Murphy Halle, letter to IN, September 28, 1966, NA.
17. Levy, "Isamu Noguchi," 32–33.
18. Cummings interviews, 18.
19. Buckminster Fuller, "What I Am Trying to Do," note to IN, May 1, 1967, NA.
20. IN, "The Road I Have Walked," 99.
21. IN, "Buckminster Fuller," in Essays and Conversations, 117.
22. Ibid., 116.
23. Buckminster Fuller, typescript of article on IN, 21, NA, reprinted in Sc W, 8.
24. Kobata interview, 68.
25. KK, 108.
26. "The Dymaxion American," Time, January 10, 1964, 49.
27. IN, letter to Jacques Barzun, January 12, 1978, NA.
28. Buckminster Fuller, Foreword, Sc W, 7.
29. Buckminster Fuller, "Isamu Noguchi," The Palette, Magazine of the Connecticut Arts Association (Winter 1960): 5.
30. Martha Graham, Blood Memory (New York: Doubleday, 1991), 218–19.
31. IN, "The Road I Have Walked," 99.
32. IN, "Tribute to Martha Graham," in Essays and Conversations, 120.
33. Edward Alden Jewell, review of Noguchi's Marie Sterner exhibition, The New York Times, 1930, clipping, NA.
34. Jerome Klein, review of Noguchi's Marie Sterner exhibition, The Chicago Evening Post, February 11, 1930, clipping, NA.

35. The Harvard Society for Contemporary Art was founded in 1928 by three Harvard classmates, Lincoln Kirstein (whose portrait Noguchi had sculpted in 1929 and who later was a founder with George Balanchine of the New York City Ballet), Edward Warburg (who was a founder and board member of the Museum of Modern Art), and John Walker (who later became director of the National Gallery in Washington, D.C.).
36. *The Chicago Evening Post*, April 8, 1930, clipping, NA.
37. *Sc W*, 19.
38. IN, letter to Edward A. Rumely, March 30, 1930.

12. TO FIND NATURE'S REASONS

1. Edward A. Rumely, telegram to IN, April 15, 1930, NA.
2. Buckminster Fuller, telegram to IN, April 15, 1930, NA.
3. Buckminster Fuller, letter to IN, April 17, 1930, NA.
4. *Sc W*, 19.
5. LG, letter to IN, May 6, 1930.
6. LG, letter to IN, June 14, 1930.
7. Edward Alden Jewell, exhibition review, *The New York Times*, March 8, 1931, clipping, NA.
8. *Sc W*, 19.
9. Ibid.
10. Ibid., 19–20. Yone Noguchi had written to Leonie and she had forwarded to her son the request that he not travel to Japan using the name Noguchi.
11. Kobata interview, 64–65.
12. Ibid.
13. IN, letter to Ailes Gilmour, n.d., NA.
14. IN, letter to LG, July 30, 1930, NA.
15. LG, letter to IN, October 24, 1930.
16. IN, letter to LG and Ailes Gilmour, November 21, 1930, NA.
17. *Sc W*, 20. Dore Ashton noted that if Noguchi became friends with Marshal Chang Hsueh-liang he most likely remained politically disengaged while in China, for Chang was vehemently anti-Japanese and wished to expel the Japanese from China. Ashton quoted Edgar Snow's *Red Star Over China*: "Chang Hsueh-liang, as everyone knows, was until 1931 the popular, gambling, generous, modern-minded, golf-playing, dope using paradoxical warlord—dictator of the 30,000,000 people of Manchuria." Ashton, 14. Noguchi recalled that though Japan did not attack China until the following year, the Chinese were already deeply wary of Japanese aggression.
18. Cummings interviews, 19.
19. Mus. Cat., 234.
20. *Sc W*, 20.
21. Kobata interview, 73.
22. *Sc W*, 20.
23. Ibid.
24. Katharine Kuh, interview with IN, transcript, 71, Archives of American Art, Smithsonian Institution, Washington, D.C.
25. Jack Foster, "Japanese-American Artist Fears for Old Peiping," *New York World-Telegram*, December 3, 1937, clipping, NA.

26. *Sc W*, 20.
27. IN, letter to Ailes Gilmour, December 28, 1930, NA.

13. A CLOSE EMBRACE OF THE EARTH
 1. Wolf, *On Becoming an Artist*, 44.
 2. IN, postcard to Ailes Gilmour, January 1931, NA.
 3. IN, letter to LG, January 28, 1931, NA.
 4. IN, "The Road I Have Walked," 100.
 5. Quoted in Duus, 130.
 6. Unidentified clipping, n.d., NA.
 7. Translated from article in *Mainichi shinbun*, January 29, 1931, quoted in Duus, 130.
 8. Ibid.
 9. *Sc W*, 20.
10. Ibid.
11. Ibid.
12. Kobata interview, 88.
13. Ibid.
14. IN, "Theatre of Heroes and Phantoms," *Harper's Bazaar*, June 1952, NA.
15. Rhony Alhalel, "Conversation with Isamu Noguchi," *Kyoto Journal* (Spring 1989): 36.
16. Mus. Cat., 238.
17. Cummings interviews, 21.
18. *Sc W*, 20.
19. Hakone Conference transcript, 1984, quoted in Ashton, 37.
20. Ashton, 37.
21. Kobata interview, 72.
22. Alhalel, "Conversation with Isamu Noguchi," 36; *Sc W*, 21.
23. Ashton, 42.
24. BM, 15.
25. *Sc W*, 20.
26. Levy, "Isamu Noguchi," 34.
27. IN, letter to LG, June 1, 1931, NA.
28. Ibid., July 24, 1931, NA.
29. IN, letter to Yone Noguchi, November 1931, NA.
30. IN, letter to Ailes Gilmour, September 24, 1931, NA.
31. Kobata interview, 92.

14. LONELY TRAVELER, SOCIAL LION
 1. *Sc W*, 21.
 2. IN, letter to Yone Noguchi, November 1, 1931, NA.
 3. In July a piece Leonie wrote was accepted by a journal called *Asia*. It included photographs of Japanese garden stones, the type of stones that would in time be inspirational for Noguchi.
 4. *Art News*, December 17, 1932, clipping, NA.
 5. Bonnie Rychlak, *The Full Figure and Portraiture, 1926–1941*, exhibition brochure (New York: Noguchi Museum, 2008–09), n.p.
 6. Kay Halle, letter to IN, April 1, 1965, NA.

7. IN, interviewed by the author, Long Island City, NY, April 1977.
8. John Goldsmith Phillips, in *The Metropolitan Museum of Art Bulletin* 29, no. 11 (November 1934): 195–97.
9. Rose Mary Fisk, "Two Artists as Revealed by Drawings," *The Chicago Evening Post*, February 23, 1932, clipping, NA.
10. Henry McBride, "Noguchi in Sculpture and Drawing," *The Sun* (New York), February 20, 1932, clipping, NA.
11. *The New Yorker*, February 27, 1932, clipping, NA.
12. *The New York Times*, March 8, 1932, clipping, NA.
13. Inez Cunningham, review of Noguchi's exhibition, *The Chicago Evening Post*, March 8, 1932, clipping, NA.
14. Ruth Page, interview transcript, New York Public Library for the Performing Arts, Lincoln Center.
15. *Sc W*, 21.
16. Karen's Column, "Bronze Bust Subject of Whopping Tale," *The Washington Times*, June 1, 1989, clipping, NA.
17. IN, "Buckminster Fuller: A Reminiscence of Four Decades," *Architectural Forum* 136 (January–February 1972): 59 (reprinted in *Essays and Conversations*, 118–19). In 1930 Fuller had taken over a magazine called *T-Square* and changed its name to *Shelter*. He brought it out sporadically for two years. In November 1932 Fuller reproduced Noguchi's extraordinary new sculpture, *Miss Expanding Universe*, on *Shelter's* cover, and to this issue Noguchi contributed an article titled "Shelters of the Orient," which drew parallels between traditional Asian buildings and modern Western architecture and compared Japanese houses to Fuller's Dymaxion House.
18. Levy, "Isamu Noguchi," 35.
19. Ibid., 29–30.
20. *Time*, December 18, 1932, clipping, NA.
21. Edward Alden Jewell, exhibition review, *The New York Times*, December 17, 1932, clipping, NA.
22. Henry McBride, exhibition review, *The Sun* (New York), December 1932, quoted in unidentified magazine, clipping, NA.
23. John Gruen, "The Artist Speaks: Isamu Noguchi," 58–62.

15. TOWARD A SCULPTURE OF SPACE

1. *Sc W*, 21.
2. Cummings interviews, 23.
3. *Sc W*, 21.
4. IN, "The Sculpture of Spaces," in *Isamu Noguchi: The Sculpture of Spaces*, exhibition catalogue (New York: Whitney Museum of American Art, 1980), 13.
5. IN, quoted in the catalogue for his exhibition at the Marie Harriman Gallery (New York, 1935).
6. Cummings interviews, 22.
7. IN, "The Sculpture of Spaces," 13.
8. Cummings interviews, 22.
9. "Playgrounds Are No Game," *New York Post*, February 9, 1980, clipping, NA.
10. IN, note in Marie Harriman Gallery exhibition catalogue.
11. *Sc W*, 22.

12. Ibid., 21.

13. Quoted in Amei Wallach, "Hanging Out with Bucky, Thinking Big," *The New York Times*, May 21, 2006, 35. Between 1933 and 1935 Fuller produced three Dymaxion Cars. The first was shown to the public with much fanfare in 1933. When the U.S. automobile industry refused to let Fuller's new car enter their annual exhibition in Manhattan, Fuller attracted attention by driving this car around the block outside the showroom. Fuller's hopes to find a manufacturer for his car were dashed when it was rear-ended and it rolled over in a race in Chicago, killing the driver. Although the accident was not caused by the car's novel design, prospective investors vanished.

14. Sydney Burney was a British art and antiquities dealer who, in 1933, mounted an exhibition of African art that posited the idea that this art was of equal value to the art of Western cultures.

15. IN, letter to LG, July 9, 1933, NA.

16. Ibid., July 25, 1933, NA.

17. Julien Levy, *Memoir of an Art Gallery* (New York: Putnam, 1977), 144–45.

18. IN, letter to LG, August 17, 1933, NA.

19. IN, letter to LG, September 3, 1933, NA.

20. IN, notes for a planned autobiography, NA.

21. Ibid.

22. IN, in Hiro Narita's film *Isamu Noguchi: Stones and Paper*, 1997.

16. ART WITH A SOCIAL PURPOSE

1. PWAP New York Office, report on IN, February 28, 1934, quoted in Duus, 149.

2. Nancy Grove, *Isamu Noguchi Portraits,* exhibition catalogue (Washington, D.C.: National Portrait Gallery, 1989), 14.

3. IN, note on project for Ely Jacques Kahn, 1934, NA.

4. Cummings interviews, 23.

5. "Playgrounds Are No Game," *New York Post*, February 9, 1980.

6. IN, "The Sculpture of Spaces," 13.

7. In 1934 and 1935 Averell Harriman was administrator for the National Recovery Administration.

8. The models for public projects exhibited at Marie Harriman's gallery included his memorial to Carl Mackley, *Monument to Ben Franklin, Play Mountain*, and *Monument to the Plow*. Among the portrait sculptures were *Clare Boothe Brokaw, Mrs. Carlos Davila, Lilian Palmedo, Immo Gulden, A. Conger Goodyear*, and *Audrey McMahon*, the latter soon to be head of the New York office of the Federal Art Project of the WPA.

9. *The New York Times*, February 8, 1935, clipping, NA.

10. Edward Alden Jewell, "Noguchi Sculpture in Metal Exhibited," *The New York Times*, January 31, 1935, clipping, NA.

11. Edward Alden Jewell, *The New York Times*, February 3, 1935, clipping, NA.

12. *Sc W*, 22–23.

13. Ibid.

14. Margaret Rose Vendryes, "Hanging on Their Words," in *Race Consciousness: African-American Studies for the New Century* (New York: New York University Press, 1997), 156–59.

15. Ibid.

16. Martha Graham, "From Collaboration, a Strange Beauty Emerged," *The New York Times*, January 8, 1989.
17. *Sc W*, 23.
18. Ashton, 54.
19. *Sc W*, 125.
20. Ibid., 123.
21. Robert Tracy, interview with IN, reprinted in *Essays and Conversations*, 80.
22. *Sc W*, 123.
23. Cummings interviews, 27.
24. *Sc W*, 23.

17. MEXICO

1. Cummings interviews, 27.
2. *Sc W*, 23.
3. Siqueiros, in turn, may have been influenced by Noguchi's Abelardo Rodríguez mural when he did his cement relief mural at the Universidad Nacional Autónoma de Mexico in 1952–56. Oles, "Noguchi in Mexico," 30.
4. IN, "What's the Matter with Sculpture?" *Art Front* 19, nos. 9–10 (1936): 13–14, reprinted in *Essays and Conversations*, 18–19.
5. Kobata interview, 61.
6. Amy Wolf, *On Becoming an Artist: Isamu Noguchi and His Contemporaries, 1922–1960*, exhibition catalogue (New York: Noguchi Museum, 2010), 71.
7. IN, interviewed by the author, Long Island City, NY, April 1977.
8. Ibid. The blue house was Kahlo's childhood home (now the Frida Kahlo Museum). Rivera had purchased it from Kahlo's father to help with the family's finances. After Kahlo and Rivera divorced and remarried in 1939–40, they made the blue house their home.
9. Ibid.
10. IN, letter to Frida Kahlo, n.d. Noguchi's letters to Kahlo are in the Frida Kahlo Museum archive, Mexico City.
11. *Sc W*, 24.
12. IN, letter to Frida Kahlo, n.d.
13. IN, interviewed by the author.

18. NEW YORK, 1936–39

1. *Sc W*, 24.
2. Ibid.
3. IN, quoted in the catalogue for his exhibition at the Marie Harriman Gallery, New York, 1935.
4. *Sc W*, 24. The Radio Nurse was produced with technological advice from Commander E. F. McDonald, Jr., president of Zenith, who aimed "to create a device which will be simple, beautiful and at the same time distinctively different from any inter-communicating set or radio now in use." McDonald wanted to be able to hear if his young daughter was crying in her stateroom on his yacht.
5. Ibid., 26.
6. IN, interviewed by Tatsuo Kondo, April 22, 1981. Mr. Kondo kindly played the tape for me on October 23, 2009, and Takako Shimizu was good enough to give an immediate translation.

7. *Sc W*, 30.
8. Cummings interviews, 75.
9. Cummings interviews, 36.
10. *Sc W*, 24.
11. Cummings interviews, 29.
12. Ibid.
13. Michael Taylor, "Gorky and Surrealism," in *Arshile Gorky: A Retrospective*, exhibition catalogue (New Haven, CT: Yale University Press, in association with the Philadelphia Museum of Art, 2010), 99.
14. Cummings interviews, 29.
15. Kobata interview, 55.
16. Jack Foster, "Japanese-American Artist Fears for Old Peiping," *New York World-Telegram*, December 3, 1937, clipping, NA.
17. *The New York Times*, December 12, 1937.
18. Noguchi also wrote an English translation of the inscription for Mr. Li. It reads slightly differently: "From great China we once learned the art of life. Now with Western tools, apt pupils, we torture the earth that gave so much. But China's future is in her children who[,] growing into manhood in times like these[,] gain character to love justice and resist tyrany [*sic*]." Quoted in Robert J. Maeda, "Note: Isamu Noguchi and the Peking Drawing of 1930," *American Art*, National Museum of American Art, Smithsonian Institution (Spring 1999): 86–87. I have taken the information about the inscription from Maeda's well-researched discoveries. Noguchi stamped this translation with his seal and signed his name.
19. YN Letters, 226–27.
20. *Sc W*, 24.
21. IN, letter to Walter Teague, May 18, 1939, NA.
22. Cummings interviews, 28.
23. *Sc W*, 24.
24. *The New York Times*, October 10, 1938, clipping, NA.
25. Rockefeller Center press release, "The Facts and Highlights on Associated Press Rockefeller Center Plaque," NA.
26. *Sc W*, 24.
27. Unidentified newspaper, clipping, n.d., NA.
28. *New York Herald Tribune*, May 2, 1940, clipping, NA.
29. Ibid.
30. *Schenectady Union-Star* (NY), May 3, 1940, clipping, NA.
31. IN, "Noguchi on Brancusi," 113–14.
32. *The Honolulu Advertiser*, May 14, 1940, clipping, NA.
33. Unidentified newspaper, May 13, 1940, clipping, NA.
34. Reprint of article in *Architectural Forum*, October 1940, NA.
35. *Sc W*, 25.

19. CALIFORNIA

1. Cummings interviews, 30.
2. IN, interviewed by Karlen Mooradian, in Mooradian, *The Many Worlds of Arshile Gorky* (Chicago: Gilgamesh Press, 1980), 181.
3. Agnes Gorky Fielding, interviews with the author, 2000–2002. Unless otherwise noted, all quotes from Agnes Gorky Fielding come from these interviews.

4. Ibid.
5. Agnes Magruder, letter to Esther Magruder, July 1941, Agnes Gorky Fielding's personal archive.
6. Katharine Kuh, interviewed by Avis Berman, 1982–83, Archives of American Art, Smithsonian Institution; and Katharine Kuh, *My Love Affair with Modern Art: Behind the Scenes with a Legendary Curator*, edited by Avis Berman (New York: Arcade Publishing, 2006), 206.
7. Hess, "Isamu Noguchi," 48.
8. *Sc W*, 25.
9. Ibid.
10. Mary V. Dearborn, *Mistress of Modernism: The Life of Peggy Guggenheim* (Boston: Houghton Mifflin, 2004), 183.
11. *Sc W*, 25.
12. Radio script of program presented by the Anti-Axis Committee over KFWB, January 17, 1942, NA.
13. Kobata interview, 94.
14. Cummings interviews, 40.
15. "Statement of Policy and Aims," Nisei Writers and Artists for Democracy, NA.
16. *Sc W*, 25.
17. Kobata interview, 94.
18. Ibid., 98.
19. On March 20 the American Civil Liberties Union wrote to President Roosevelt that the evacuation was a violation of civil rights and was detrimental to democracy. The order to evacuate was, the letter said, questionable "on the constitutional grounds of depriving American Citizens of their liberty and use of the property without due process of law." A copy of this letter is in the NA.
20. A copy of this circular is in the NA.
21. Kobata interview, 98.
22. Cummings interviews, 40.
23. *Sc W*, 25.

20. POSTON

1. Quoted in Robert J. Maeda, "Isamu Noguchi: 5-7-A, Poston, Arizona," *Amerasia Journal* 20, no. 2 (1994): 66–67.
2. Cummings interviews, 41.
3. *Sc W*, 25.
4. Kobata interview, 58.
5. Circular of Information for Enlistees and Their Family, NA. Poston had 72,000 acres, 41,000 of them suitable for agriculture.
6. Pamphlet, September 1942, NA.
7. Poston Information Bulletin, NA.
8. IN, draft of an article for *Reader's Digest*, 1942, NA.
9. IN, unsigned memorandum, n.d., NA.
10. Quoted in Maeda, "Isamu Noguchi: 5-7-A, Poston, Arizona," 67.
11. IN, draft of article for *Reader's Digest*.
12. *Sc W*, 25.
13. IN, draft of article for *Reader's Digest*.

14. Theodore H. Haas, memorandum, July 17, 1942, NA.

15. Cummings interviews, 42.

16. *Sc W*, 25.

17. Kobata interview, 99.

18. *Sc W*, 25.

19. Duus, 172.

20. Maeda, "Isamu Noguchi: A Defining Moment in My Life," *Amerasia Journal* 20, no. 2 (1994), 57.

21. IN, letter to Man Ray, May 30, 1942, NA.

22. Robert J. Maeda, "Isamu Noguchi: 5-7-A, Poston, Arizona," 70–71.

23. Bert Winther, "Isamu Noguchi: Conflicts of Japanese Culture in the Early Post War Years," Ph.D. dissertation, NYU, UMI, Ann Arbor, Michigan, 1992, 61.

24. Alfred Frankenstein, *San Francisco Chronicle*, July 12, 1942, clipping, NA.

25. The July 1942 letter from the Farm Security Administration to IN is in the NA.

26. IN, draft of article for *Reader's Digest*, 3.

27. Maeda, "Isamu Noguchi: 5-7-A, Poston, Arizona," 68.

28. Duus, 172.

29. Kobata interview, 58.

30. Duus, 173–74. Even before he entered Poston, Noguchi had been at pains to explain these last two visits. Among his papers is a long typed letter dated March 27, 1942, from Noguchi to a Mr. Adamic, explaining the purposes of his trips to Carmel and Santa Barbara. IN, letter to Mr. Adamic, March 27, 1942, NA.

31. IN, letter to Ailes Gilmour, November 9, 1942, NA.

32. Kobata interview, 109.

33. Cummings interviews, 42.

34. Ibid.

35. *Sc W*, 26.

36. IN, "Trouble among Japanese Americans," *The New Republic* 108, no. 5, February 1, 1943, 142–43.

37. In January 1945 Noguchi received an undated letter from the office of the Western Defense Command in San Francisco saying that because of military necessity, he was prohibited from entering the West Coast defense zone. He was told that he could request a hearing about this exclusion. On January 30 Noguchi asked for a hearing. It is possible that his exclusion was prompted by his answers to certain loyalty questions on a five-page application for a permit to leave Poston. He had not answered the question "Have you forsworn any and all allegiance which you may knowingly or unknowingly have held to the Emperor of Japan?" And when asked, "If not, do you now repudiate such allegiances?" he had circled "no." After his hearing the Western Defense Command wrote Noguchi on February 27 saying that he was now "authorized to travel and reside within certain military areas heretofore prohibited to persons of Japanese ancestry."

21. MACDOUGAL ALLEY

1. Avis Berman, "MacDougal Alley: New York's Art Alley de Luxe," *Architectural Digest*, November 1990, 192.

2. *Sc W*, 26.

3. Mus. Cat., 238.

4. *Sc W*, 26.
5. Cummings interviews, 40–46.
6. *Sc W*, 26.
7. Mus. Cat., 240.
8. Ibid., 152.
9. Cummings interviews, 48.
10. Mus. Cat., 18 and 242.
11. *Sc W*, 27.
12. Ibid.
13. Jeanne Reynal, letter to Agnes Gorky, December 1, 1944, Archives of American Art.

22. LETTERS TO ANN
1. IN, letter to Ann Matta Clark, March 14, 1945, Centre Canadien d'Architecture, Montréal. I am grateful to Giovanna Carnevale for her research in the Gordon Matta-Clark Archive, which contains Noguchi's letters to Ann Matta Clark. Her letters to Noguchi are in NA.
2. Anaïs Nin, *The Diary of Anaïs Nin*, vol. 4, 1944–47 (New York: Harcourt Brace Jovanovich, 1971), 103 and 99–100.
3. Malitte Matta, interviewed by the author, Paris, June 23, 2008. An undated note from Ann to Noguchi thanks him for a gift of money. In his will Noguchi left her $10,000.

23. NOGUCHI AND MARTHA GRAHAM, PASSIONATE COLLABORATORS
1. Kazuyuki Nimura et al., interview with IN, in "Isamu Noguchi on Gardens, Sculpture and Architecture," translated by the Noguchi Museum, *Hirobu* 228 (April 1983): 47–50.
2. *Sc W*, 125.
3. Graham, *Blood Memory*, 223.
4. *Sc W*, 29.
5. IN, notes for a planned autobiography, NA.
6. Agnes de Mille, *Martha: The Life and Work of Martha Graham* (New York: Random House, 1956), 211.
7. *Sc W*, 125.
8. Ibid., 126.
9. Ibid.
10. Martin L. Friedman, *Noguchi's Imaginary Landscapes*, exhibition catalogue (Minneapolis: Walker Art Center, 1978), 30.
11. *Sc W*, 122.
12. Graham, *Blood Memory*, 218–19.
13. Ibid.
14. "Noguchi: The Sculptor Acclaimed for Stage Settings and Designs for Ballet," in *Art Voices from Around the World*, December 1962, 20, NA.
15. *Sc W*, 29.
16. Quoted in Harold C. Schonberg, "Isamu Noguchi, Throwback," *The New York Times Magazine*, April 14, 1968, 29.
17. Ashton, 56.

18. *Sc W*, 123.
19. Friedman, *Imaginary Landscapes*, 23.
20. Malitte Matta, interviewed by the author.
21. Friedman, *Imaginary Landscapes*, 29.
22. Robert Tracy, *Goddess: Martha Graham's Dancers Remember* (New York: Limelight Editions, 1997), 274.
23. Graham, *Blood Memory*, 232.
24. IN, "Tribute to Martha Graham," in *Essays and Conversations*, 122.

24. THE ROCK AND THE SPACE BETWEEN

1. *Sc W*, 28.
2. IN, "On the Structure and Carving of Bronze Plate."
3. KK, 108.
4. *Essays and Conversations*, 35.
5. KK, 108.
6. Margaret Sheffield, "Perfecting the Imperfect: Noguchi's Personal Style," *Artforum* 18, no. 8 (April 1980): 69–70.
7. Valerie J. Fletcher, "Isamu Noguchi: Master Sculptor," in *Isamu Noguchi: Master Sculptor*, exhibition catalogue (New York: Whitney Museum of American Art, 2005), 89.
8. KK, 108.
9. Reproduced in Hess, "Isamu Noguchi," 35.
10. KK, 108.
11. Thomas B. Hess, "The Whitney Draws Slowly to the Left," *Art News* 45, no. 1 (March 1946): 62.
12. IN, statement in *Fourteen Americans*, exhibition catalogue (New York: Museum of Modern Art, 1946), reprinted in *Essays and Conversations*, 24.
13. Hess, "Isamu Noguchi," 48–49.
14. Ibid., 34.
15. Ibid., 49.
16. Quoted in Michel Gill, "Stones and Paper: The Work of Isamu Noguchi," *Humanities* 18, no. 3 (May–June 1997): 18.
17. Joe Gibbs, "Fourteen Americans at the Modern," *Art Digest* 20 (September 1946): 30.
18. Japanese-American Sculptor Shows Weird New Works," *Life*, November 11, 1946, 12–13, 15.

25. TARA

1. Duus, 189.
2. IN and Nayantara Pandit, postcards to Frida Kahlo, NA.
3. Nayantara Pandit, letters to IN, NA.
4. Duus, 201.

26. 1946–48

1. *Essays and Conversations*, 85.
2. *Sc W*, 130.

3. Merce Cunningham, interviewed by the author, New York City, February 13, 2007.
4. *Sc W*, 130.
5. David Vaughan, "Merce Cunningham's *The Seasons*," *Dance Chronicle* 18, no. 2 (1995): 314.
6. Ibid., 316.
7. Merce Cunningham, interviewed by the author.
8. *Sc W*, 131.
9. Unidentified newspaper, n.d., clipping, NA.
10. Nicolas Calas, essay in *Bloodflames*, exhibition catalogue (New York: Hugo Gallery, 1947), n.p.
11. Kobata interview, 54.
12. YN, letter to IN, May 6, 1947, NA.
13. IN, letter to Yone Noguchi, May 15, 1947, NA.
14. Duus, 207.
15. Friedman, *Imaginary Landscapes*, 45.
16. Mus. Cat., 152.

27. IMPASSE

1. Ashton, 79.
2. IN, "Meanings in Modern Sculpture," *Art News* 48, no. 3 (March 1948): 12–15, 55–56, reprinted in *Essays and Conversations*, 33–36.
3. IN, "Contemporary Documents: Towards a Reintegration of the Arts," *College Art Journal* 9 (1949): 59–60, reprinted in *Essays and Conversations*, 27–28.
4. Gaston de Havenon, "Reminiscence of Gorky," handwritten manuscript in the collection of the Archives of American Art, New York. For the story of Gorky's suicide see Hayden Herrera, *Arshile Gorky: His Life and Work* (New York: Farrar, Straus and Giroux, 2004), 605.
5. IN, interviewed by Karlen Mooradian, 1966, tape recording, Eastern Diocese of the Armenian Church of America, New York.
6. *Sc W*, 30.
7. Katharine Kuh, interviewed by Matthew Spender, in Spender, *From a High Place* (New York: Knopf, 1999), 368.
8. *Sc W*, 30.
9. Diane Rosenberg Karp, "Arshile Gorky: The Language of Art," Ph.D. dissertation, University of Pennsylvania, 1982, 37.
10. Mooradian interview.
11. *Sc W*, 30.
12. Mooradian interview.
13. *Sc W*, 30.
14. Mark Stevens and Annalyn Swan, *De Kooning: An American Master* (New York: Knopf, 2004), 221–25.
15. *Sc W*, 29.
16. *The New York Times*, March 6, 1949, clipping, NA.
17. Judith Kaye Reed, review of Noguchi's show at the Charles Egan Gallery, *Art Digest* (March 1949), 12, clipping, NA.
18. Clement Greenberg, "Art," *The Nation*, March 19, 1949, 341.
19. *Sc W*, 29.

28. BOLLINGEN TRAVELS

1. Cummings interviews, 46.
2. The Bollingen Foundation, which took its name from Bollingen Tower, Carl Jung's country home in the Swiss town of Bollingen, had been set up in 1945 to support scholarly study and intercultural activities. The foundation's ideology was imbued with Jungian thought, and its initial purpose was to disseminate Jung's work. Until 1968, when it became inactive and was subsumed into the Andrew W. Mellon Foundation, the Bollingen Foundation granted over 300 fellowships and published some 250 books by writers such as Joseph Campbell, D. T. Suzuki (*Zen and Japanese Culture*), and Alan W. Watts (*The Way of Zen*).
3. *Sc W*, 29–30.
4. Ibid., 29.
5. Michael Brenson, "Noguchi Gets MacDowell Medal for a Life's Work," *New York Times*, July 19, 1982.
6. Cummings interviews, 46.
7. BM, 17.
8. Cummings interviews, 55.
9. BM, 1.
10. Ibid., 2.
11. IN, "Noguchi on Brancusi," 113–14.
12. BM, 3.
13. Ibid.
14. IN, Bollingen notes, n.d., NA.
15. Ibid.
16. BM, 5.
17. Ibid., 7.
18. Ibid., 8.
19. Ibid.
20. IN, letter to Jawaharlal Nehru, January 7, 1950, NA.
21. BM, 9.
22. Ibid., 11.
23. Ibid., 13.
24. *Sc W*, 31.

29. HARBINGER PIGEON

1. BM, 15.
2. *Sc W*, 31.
3. IN, "The Artist and Japan: A Report of 1950," unpublished manuscript of his report to the Bollingen Foundation, 3, NA.
4. Duus, 208.
5. Cummings interviews, 60.
6. IN, "The Artist and Japan," 1.
7. IN, "Notes by the Artist on His Recent Work in Japan," *Arts and Architecture* 67, no. 11 (November 1950): 24–27.
8. IN, "The Artist and Japan," 2.
9. Ibid.
10. Ibid., 3.

11. IN, "Geijutsu to shudan shakai—Art and Community," *Bijutsu techo* 31 (July 1950): 3–5, quoted in Duus, 209. According to Noguchi's friend the sculptor Tsutomu Hiroi, who was in the audience and met Noguchi the following day, the painter Takeo Terada served as translator. Hiroi recalls that after the lecture he asked Terada to write a letter of introduction for him to meet Noguchi. "So I made an appointment to meet Noguchi at his family's new built house." Tsutomu Hiroi, interviewed by the author, Tokyo, October 24, 2009.
12. Cummings interviews, 48.
13. Ashton, 91.
14. Saburo Hasegawa, "My Time with Isamu Noguchi," *Geijutsu-Shincho*, typed translation, NA.
15. Saburo Hasegawa, "The Isamu Noguchi Exhibition," in the exhibition catalogue for Noguchi's 1952 show at the Kamakura Museum of Modern Art, unpublished translation, NA.
16. Hasegawa, "My Time with Isamu Noguchi," n.p.
17. Ibid.
18. Sc W, 31.
19. Hasegawa, "My Time with Isamu Noguchi."
20. Saburo Hasegawa, quoted in article in *The New York Times*, n.d., clipping, NA.
21. IN, "The Artist and Japan," 4.
22. Saburo Hasegawa, *Roh* (Sha San Sei: Japan, 1951).
23. Hasegawa, "My Time with Isamu Noguchi."
24. IN, "The Artist and Japan," 4.
25. IN, unpublished text, NA, quoted in Ashton, 111.
26. BM, 16.
27. Ashton, 107.
28. Ibid., 109.
29. BM, 16.
30. Ashton, 102.
31. Ibid.

30. SHINBANRAISHA

1. Yoshiro Taniguchi, "A Meeting to Isamu Noguchi," in *Isamu Noguchi Sculptures,* exhibition catalogue (Tokyo: Minami Gallery, 1973).
2. Ibid.
3. Ibid.
4. Ashton, 126.
5. Sc W, 31.
6. *Shinbanraisha/A Cultural Memory*, exhibition brochure (New York: Noguchi Museum, 2006), n.p.
7. Taniguchi, "A Meeting to Isamu Noguchi."
8. Ibid.
9. IN and Yoshiro Taniguchi, "The Faculty Retreat of Keio University," clipping of article in an unidentified Japanese magazine, February 1952, NA.
10. Ibid.
11. Ashton, 96.
12. Priscilla Morgan, interviewed by the author, New York City, May 23, 2006.

13. BM, 17.
14. Duus, 216.
15. IN, preface to a book on Tsutomu Hiroi, carbon copy of manuscript, NA.
16. Tsutomu Hiroi, "A Masterwork United to the Cosmos," in *Isamu Noguchi, Human Aspect as a Contemporary: 54 Witnesses in Japan and America* (Shikoku Shimbun, Japan: 2002), 48.
17. Winther-Tamaki, "The Ceramic Art," 23.
18. Hiroi, "A Masterwork United to the Cosmos," 48.
19. Ibid., 49.

31. MITSUKOSHI EXHIBITION

1. The Oriental Decorative Ceramic Sculpture Research Institute was recommended to Noguchi by the Japanese painter Tamiji Kitagawa (1894–1989), whom he had met in Mexico in 1936. Since Kitagawa had family connections at Seto, he made the arrangements for Noguchi to work there.
2. IN, "Notes by the Artist on His Recent Work in Japan," *Arts and Architecture* 67, no. 11 (November 1950): 26–27.
3. Cummings interviews, 60.
4. Sc W, 31–32.
5. Winther-Tamaki, "The Ceramic Art," 26.
6. BM, 17.
7. Ibid.
8. Quoted in Winther-Tamaki, "The Ceramic Art," 26.
9. *Mainichi shinbun*, September 12, 1950, quoted in Duus, 217.
10. Sadao Wada, "Isamu Noguchi no koto," *Atorie* 28 (November 1950): 46–51, quoted in Duus, 218–19.
11. In 2006 Shinbanraisha was reinstalled upstairs. In spite of efforts made to keep the same atmosphere, it was a site-specific sculpture planned to be integrated with Noguchi's garden design. Noguchi's concept is thus very much changed.
12. IN and Taniguchi, "The Faculty Retreat."
13. Ibid.
14. Kenzo Tange, "A True Man of the World," in *Isamu Noguchi*, exhibition catalogue (Tokyo: Minami Gallery, 1973), n.p.

32. YOSHIKO YAMAGUCHI

1. Sc W, 32.
2. BM, 18.
3. Cummings interviews, 55.
4. Ibid., 60.
5. KK, 112.
6. A. D., "Noguchi: Traveling Sculptor Pauses in Japan," *Interiors*, March 1951, 140–45, clipping, NA.
7. IN, "Theater of Heroes and Phantoms," *Harper's Bazaar*, June 1952, clipping, NA.
8. Antonin Raymond, letter to IN, October 25, 1950, NA.
9. Antonin Raymond, letter to IN, November 22, 1950, NA.
10. The kimono show at the Brooklyn Museum was designed by Noguchi's friend Chiyo

Tanaka, to whom Noguchi had given advice about how to make traditional Japanese clothing function better in a Western milieu. Noguchi had also been instrumental in securing this venue for the show by recommending Tanaka's work to his sister Ailes' husband, Herbert Joseph Spinden, curator of American Indian and Primitive Art at the Brooklyn Museum.

11. Duus, 224.
12. Ibid.
13. Ian Buruma, "Haunted Heroine," *Interview*, September 1989, 124–27.
14. Winther-Tamaki, "The Ceramic Art," 32.
15. Yoshiko Yamaguchi, *Ri Koran: Watashi no Hansei* (Half My Life as Ri Koran), quoted in "History of Hiroshima: 1945–1995," part 2, p. 3, www.hiroshimapeacemedia.jp /mediacenter. (Bert Winther-Tamaki put the quote this way: "You must have suffered during the war . . . I too suffered during the war between America and Japan." "The Ceramic Art," 32.)
16. Shirley Yamaguchi, *War, Peace, and Songs*, English translation in NA. I am grateful to Jenny Dixon for sending me this translation.
17. "Isamu-san and Shirley Too," *Time*, November 3, 1952, 76.
18. Yamaguchi, *War, Peace, and Songs*.
19. "Isamu-san and Shirley Too," 76.
20. Aline B. Louchheim, "Noguchi and Sculpture Gardens," *The New York Times*, September 30, 1951.
21. *Sc W*, 163.
22. BM, 18.
23. *Sc W*, 32.
24. IN, "Japanese Akari Lamps," in *Essays and Conversations*, 102.
25. Ibid., 103.
26. Louchheim, "Noguchi and Sculpture Gardens."
27. BM, 19.
28. Louchheim, "Noguchi and Sculpture Gardens."
29. BM, 20.
30. *New York Journal American*, October 7, 1951, clipping, NA; and Aline B. Louchheim, "UN Turns Down Funds For 'Super' Playground," *The New York Times*, October 8, 1951.
31. BM, 21.
32. Louchheim, "Noguchi and Sculpture Gardens."
33. Thomas B. Hess, "The Rejected Playground," *Art News*, April 1952.
34. *Sc W*, 33.
35. Paul Goldberger, "Gordon Bunshaft, Architect, dies at 81," *The New York Times*, August 8, 1990; and Paul Goldberger, "Gordon Bunshaft: A Man Who Died Before His Time," *The New York Times*, August 19, 1990.
36. *Sc W*, 172.
37. Friedman, *Imaginary Landscapes*, 47.
38. *Sc W*, 164.
39. Duus, 232.
40. Yoshiko Yamaguchi with Sakuya Fujiwara, *Looking Back on My Days as Ri Koran (Li Xianglan)* (1987). I am grateful to Katsumi Yokobori of the Japan Foundation for giving me an oral translation of the section of the book dealing with Noguchi.

41. *Sc W*, 164.
42. BM, 21.

33. KITA KAMAKURA

1. *Sc W*, 32. In Hiroi's recollection, Noguchi became aware of Rosanjin's pottery when he, Hiroi, and Tange stopped at a restaurant in Nagoya on their way to Hiroshima. Noguchi had admired the dishes and had asked the waitress who made them. When he learned that it was Rosanjin, he decided that he must meet him. Tsutomu Hiroi, interviewed by the author, Tokyo, October 24, 2009.
2. *Sc W*, 32.
3. IN, "The Road I Have Walked," 102.
4. *Sc W*, 32.
5. Yamaguchi, *War, Peace, and Songs*.
6. Duus, 246.
7. BM, 22.
8. IN, "Projects in Japan," *Arts and Architecture* (October 1952): 24–26, excerpt reprinted in *Essays and Conversations*, 96–98.
9. *Essays and Conversations*, 96.
10. *Sc W*, 33.
11. IN, "Entre Oriente y Occidente," *Sumario*, April 1994, 22, NA. Translation by the author.
12. IN, letter to Jeanne Reynal, autumn 1951, Archives of American Art, reprinted in Duus, 259.
13. IN, "On the Artist Teshigahara Sofu," typed manuscript, October 17, 1977, NA.
14. BM, 3.
15. Betty Pepis, "Artist at Home," *The New York Times Magazine*, August 31, 1952, 26.
16. IN, Shuzo Takiguchi, and Saburo Hasegawa, *Noguchi* (Tokyo: Bijutsu Shuppan-sha, 1953), n.p.
17. Yamaguchi, *War, Peace, and Songs*.
18. Winther-Tamaki, "The Ceramic Art," 36.
19. IN, "The Road I Have Walked," 102.
20. IN, untitled essay in the exhibition catalogue for Noguchi's 1952 show at the Kamakura Museum of Modern Art, n.p., reprinted in *Essays and Conversations*, 37–38.
21. Duus, 248.
22. Ibid.
23. IN, Takiguchi, and Hasegawa, *Noguchi*, n.p.
24. Hidetaro Ozeki, interviewed by the author, Gifu, Japan, October 29, 2009.
25. Ian Buruma, "Back to the Future," *The New Yorker*, March 4, 1999, 32.
26. Ian Buruma, "Between Two Worlds," *The New York Review of Books* 52, no. 10, June 9, 2005.
27. *Sc W*, 33.
28. IN, "On Washi," in Sukey Hughes, *Washi: The World of Japanese Paper* (Tokyo and New York: Kodansha, 1978), 26.
29. Tomotsu Ogata, "Isamu Noguchi: The Wandering Artist," *Japan Illustrated* (Summer 1974).
30. IN, "The Meaning of Akari," in *Space of Akari and Stone* (San Francisco: Chronicle

Books, 1986), English translation of 1985 exhibition catalogue published by Seibu Museum of Art, Tokyo.

31. Duus, 254.
32. Ibid., 255.
33. IN, letter to John Collier, February 4, 1953, NA.
34. Yamaguchi, *War, Peace, and Songs.*
35. Yamaguchi with Fujiwara, *Looking Back on My Days.*
36. Ibid.
37. Yamaguchi, *War, Peace, and Songs.*
38. Tsutomu Hiroi, interviewed by the author.
39. Yamaguchi, *War and Peace Songs.*
40. Hidetaro Ozeki, interviewed by the author.
41. Translations of the catalogue essays are in NA.
42. IN, "Essay for Museum of Modern Art, Kamakura," in *Essays and Conversations,* 37–38.
43. Winther-Tamaki, "The Ceramic Art," 63.
44. KK, 109.
45. IN, Takiguchi, and Hasegawa, *Noguchi,* n.p.
46. Bert Winther-Tamaki, "The Rejection of Isamu Noguchi's Hiroshima Cenotaph: A Japanese American Artist in Occupied Japan," *Art Journal* (Winter 1994): 26.
47. Shuzo Takiguchi, "A Strange Journey," *Mizue* 568 (December 1952): 20–31, quoted in Bert Winther-Tamaki, *Art in the Encounter of Nations: Japanese and American Artists in the Early Postwar Years* (Honolulu: University of Hawaii Press, 2001), 137.
48. Duus, 250–51; and Taro Okamoto, "The Work of Isamu Noguchi," *Bijutsu techo* 63 (December 1952), quoted in *Akari Light Sculpture by Isamu Noguchi,* exhibition catalogue (Tokyo: National Museum of Modern Art, 2003).

34. MY SOLACE HAS ALWAYS BEEN SCULPTURE

1. IN, letter to Messrs. Skidmore, Owings and Merrill, February 16, 1953, NA.
2. Various drafts of Noguchi's contract with Skidmore, Owings and Merrill are in NA.
3. IN, note in exhibition brochure, Stable Gallery, New York, April 29–May 30, 1958.
4. BM, 53–54.
5. Duus, 259.
6. BM, 54.
7. Ibid.
8. Duus, 263.
9. Yamaguchi, *War, Peace, and Songs.*
10. IN, letter to Gordon Bunshaft, July 30, 1953, NA. The correspondence between Noguchi and Gordon Bunshaft is in NA.
11. IN, letter to Gordon Bunshaft, August 10, 1953.
12. *Sc W,* 34.
13. Ibid.
14. Ibid.
15. The paper is in NA.
16. *Sc W,* 34.
17. Ibid.

18. Ibid., 131.
19. Ibid.
20. Ibid., 35.
21. Yamaguchi, *War, Peace, and Songs.*
22. *Sc W*, 35.
23. Mus. Cat., 160.
24. The competition, sponsored by the Lalit Kala Akadami in New Delhi, elicited 127 entries from around the world.
25. IN, handwritten draft of his note accompanying a proposal for a monument to honor Buddha, 1956, NA.
26. *Sc W*, 168.
27. Indira Gandhi, letter to IN, NA.
28. Edward Durell Stone, letter to IN, April 21, 1955, NA.
29. Oral history of Gordon Bunshaft, interview by Betty J. Blum (compiled under the auspices of the Chicago Architects Oral History Project, Department of Architecture, Art Institute of Chicago), 175.
30. Ibid.
31. Friedman, *Imaginary Landscapes,* 61.
32. *Sc W*, 165. When Connecticut General's building and gardens opened in 1957 they drew much attention in magazines such as *Time, Life, Fortune,* and even *The Saturday Evening Post.* Three years later Noguchi and Skidmore, Owings and Merrill were awarded a gold medal in landscape architecture for this project.

35. UNESCO: A SOMEWHAT JAPANESE GARDEN

1. The other two architects involved in the project were the Italian Pier Luigi Nervi and the Parisian Bernard Zehrfuss. The former is thought to have concerned himself mainly with the engineering aspect of the project, and the latter played the role of executive architect. Marc Treib, *Noguchi in Paris: The Unesco Garden* (San Francisco: William Stout, 2003), 133.
2. Michel-Louis Conil, "Le Jardin de Noguchi," *Information and Documents* 110 (October 1959): 18–20.
3. *Sc W*, 166.
4. Treib, *Noguchi in Paris,* 134.
5. IN, "Garden of Peace: Unesco Gardens in Paris," in *Essays and Conversations,* 61.
6. KK, 111.
7. *Sc W*, 165.
8. Ibid., 165–66.
9. IN, letter to Toru Hagiwara, January 9, 1957, NA. Noguchi's correspondence with Hagiwara and other officials about the UNESCO garden is in NA.
10. Toru Hagiwara, letter to IN, January 15, 1957.
11. IN, letter to Michel Dard, January 8, 1957.
12. IN, letter to Ambassador Farugaki, March 9, 1957.
13. *Sc W*, 166.
14. The first of these letters telling Noguchi not to come to Paris came in May. Hernan Vieco of the Paris office of Breuer, Nervi and Zehrfuss wrote telling him to postpone his arrival for two months. Noguchi wrote back that Vieco's letter had arrived too late and that he had planned to start work on the garden that summer. He said that he had "done the impossible" to get the stones shipped and that they would arrive in

Marseille on July 21. He planned to come to Paris on July 3, in time to cope with the stones' arrival. He received several more letters and cables, all asking him to postpone. Noguchi persisted in his plan. On June 15 he wrote Vieco again, saying that the stones had been shipped and that he would arrive in Paris on July 3. On June 25 the acting secretary of the Committee of Artistic Advisers wrote him that Breuer was "strongly in favor of your delaying your arrival in Paris until March 1958. He thinks that it would be a great mistake to have you start on your project before the masonry, foundation works, the pond and rough grading of the garden and patio are ready for you and the construction of the third building sufficiently advanced so as not to hinder your work." Noguchi replied on July 1 that he was perplexed: "What can I do until then, and what is to become of the garden?" He said that one of his problems with postponing was financial, "in that I had determined to invest this year with no pay commensurate to what I have been spending toward the realization of an ideal."

15. IN, letter to Marcel Breuer, July 2, 1957, NA.
16. IN, letter to Hernan Vieco, July 4, 1957.
17. Sc W, 166–67.
18. Duus, 281. The letters from Noguchi to Miyoko Urushihara are quoted in Duus, 281–82.
19. Touemon Sano, "A Work Reflecting the History of Our Friendship," in Isamu Noguchi, Human Aspect, 68–69.
20. Ashton, 147.
21. Alhalel, "Conversation with Isamu Noguchi," 35.
22. KK, 11.
23. IN, in UNESCO House News 22, October 18, 1957, 5, NA.
24. IN, essay on his UNESCO garden in Essays and Conversations, 61–62.
25. IN, "The Sculpture of Spaces," 21.
26. Sc W, 165–66.
27. Ashton, 147.
28. André Chastel, "Paris Unesco Building Stirs Controversy," The New York Times, January 4, 1959.
29. Treib, Noguchi in Paris, 122–23.
30. IN, letter to John Entenza, November 18, 1958, NA.

36. CHANGED VISIONS

1. Sc W, 35.
2. Mus. Cat., 11.
3. Sc W, 35.
4. Ibid.
5. Ibid., 36.
6. Shoji Sadao, interviewed by the author, Long Island City, NY, March 2007. All quotes from Sadao come from this interview.
7. Sc W, 36.
8. Ibid., 37.
9. Ibid., 36.
10. "Floating," Newsweek 57, no. 21, May 22, 1961, NA.
11. IN, "On the Structure and Carving of Bronze Plate."
12. Shoji Sadao, interviewed by the author.
13. Sc W, 35.

14. Ibid., 36.
15. Ibid.
16. Emily Genauer, "Japan, Mexico and Far North Provide Week's New Exhibits," *The New York Times*, June 1959, clipping, NA.
17. Fairfield Porter, review, *Art News* 58, no. 4 (Summer 1959).
18. Mus. Cat., 90.
19. Ibid., 88.
20. *Sc W*, 37.
21. Mus. Cat., 90.

37. PRISCILLA

1. Priscilla Morgan, interviewed by the author, New York City, May 23, 2006. Unless otherwise noted, all quotes from Priscilla Morgan come from this and several subsequent interviews with Priscilla Morgan.
2. Jean Nathan, "The Miracle Worker," *Vogue*, December 2007, 236.
3. Priscilla Morgan's letters to Noguchi and his letters to her are in Priscilla Morgan's personal archive.
4. *Sc W*, 37.
5. IN, letter to Gordon Bunschaft, April 27, 1960, NA.
6. Ibid., May 26, 1960, NA.
7. *Sc W*, 169.
8. IN, "The Sculpture of Spaces," 21.
9. *Sc W*, 37.
10. Quoted in E.G. (Emily Genauer), "Noguchi's 'Weightlessness,'" *New York Herald Tribune*, May 21, 1961.
11. Stuart Preston, *The New York Times*, May 21, 1961, clipping, NA.
12. Emily Genauer, "Noguchi's 'Weightlessness,'" *Herald Tribune*, May 21, 1961.
13. Lawrence Campbell, "Reviews and Previews," *Art News* 60, no. 4 (Summer 1961).

38. WORKING WITH NOGUCHI

1. Friedman, *Imaginary Landscapes*, 65.
2. IN, "The Road I Have Walked," 102.
3. *Sc W*, 170–71.
4. Mus. Cat., 164.
5. Gene Owens's letters are in his personal archive. I am grateful to him for sending me copies of these letters and other documents, such as his diary notes from the months he worked with IN and other texts.
6. Gene Owens, telephone interviews with the author, May 17, 2009, and July 18, 2009.
7. Owens, handwritten manuscript.
8. Owens, letter to the author, n.d.
9. Owens, handwritten manuscript.

39. LEVITATING ROCKS, WINGS OF PRAYER

1. *Sc W*, 171.
2. John Gruen, "Japanese Garden for Wall Street," *The New York Times*, September 13, 1963.

3. *Sc W*, 171.
4. "Total Sculpture," *New York*, December 14, 1963, clipping, NA.
5. Ibid.
6. Ibid.
7. Harriet Senie, "Urban Sculpture: Cultural Tokens or Ornaments to Life?" *Art News* 78, no. 7 (September 1979): 108–14.
8. Friedman, *Imaginary Landscapes*, 67.
9. *Sc W*, 174.
10. Friedman, *Imaginary Landscapes*, 67.
11. Unidentified newspaper, n.d., clipping, NA.
12. Elaine Rosenfeld Weitzen, interviewed by the author, New York City, June 16, 2009.
13. *Sc W*, 172–73.
14. IN, "Sculpture Garden of the New National Museum in Jerusalem," *Arts and Architecture* 77, no. 10 (October 1960): 22.
15. Draft of contract for Billy Rose Sculpture Garden, NA.
16. Charlotte Zwerin, *Isamu Noguchi: The Sculpture of Spaces*, documentary film, 1999.
17. Duus, 304.
18. IN, letter to Ralph I. Goldman, October 1962, NA.
19. IN, letter to Billy Rose, August 8, 1963, NA.
20. IN, letter to Hillel Fefferman, December 6, 1964, NA.
21. *Sc W*, 173.
22. IN, letter to Teddy Kollek, May 28, 1965, NA.
23. IN, letter to Karl Katz, August 9, 1965, NA.
24. IN, "A Sculpture Garden in Jerusalem," in *Essays and Conversations*, 68–69.
25. IN, "A Garden That Is a Sculpture," in *Essays and Conversations*, 70–71.
26. IN, "The Road I Have Walked," 103–04.

40. TOWARD AN AUTOBIOGRAPHY

1. Dimitri Hadzi, interviewed by the author, Wellfleet, MA, summer 2003, and New York City, January 2004.
2. *Sc W*, 38.
3. Mus. Cat., 122.
4. Ibid., 88.
5. *Sc W*, 40.
6. Ibid., 38.
7. Indeed, a January 22, 1958, letter from Kurt Wolff to Peter Gregory of the London publishing house Percy Lund Humphries said: "Personally, I had always hoped that Noguchi himself would do the text." Diane Adler, typed summary of the exchanges among Noguchi, John Becker, and Pantheon Books in regard to the Noguchi autobiography, February 1962, NA.
8. Helen Wolff, letter to Gerald Gross, March 7, 1960. See also Diane Adler, typed summary.
9. IN, letter to John Becker, April 10, 1960, NA. The NA has several drafts of this letter, including a copy of the typed final draft. A handwritten draft with many passages crossed out has a more extensive defense of his role in the dispute.
10. IN, letter to Priscilla Morgan, January 24, 1963.

41. A PRIMER OF SHAPES AND FUNCTIONS

1. "Gardens at Corporate Headquarters Symbolize Man's Past and Future," *IBM News* 1, no. 18, September 25, 1964, NA.
2. *Sc W,* 172.
3. Jerry Tallmer, "Playgrounds Are No Game," *New York Post,* February 9, 1980, NA.
4. *Sc W,* 161.
5. Ibid.
6. Ibid.
7. Correspondence and documents about the Riverside Park playground are in NA.
8. IN, "The Sculpture of Spaces," 18.
9. "More distressing to me," Noguchi wrote, "was my belated realization that the architect must above all, be primarily responsible to the architecture. Its scale is often as not in contradistinction to its surroundings. A playground, however, is necessarily scaled to the use of children. There is a limit to its adaptability to changes in architectural scale. While I marshaled my plans to cope with an ever more formidable fenestration, in the end I could not help feeling that while I might agree with the resolution as architecture, the playground itself, because of its limited space, had become visually inadequate . . . Our playground took too long." IN, quoted in ibid., 43.
10. Noguchi's letters to Gene Owens are in Owens's personal archive.
11. Joseph Lelyveld, "Model Play Area For Park Shown," *The New York Times,* February 5, 1964.
12. Ibid.
13. Ibid.
14. *Sc W,* 178.
15. Jay Jacobs, "Prophet without Honor," *Art in America* 55, no. 6 (November–December 1967): 44–45.
16. Arata Isozaki, "Sparks of Creation," in *Play Mountain,* 43 and 58.
17. *Sc W,* 178.
18. David Hickey, "Work of Noguchi," *Fort Worth Star-Telegram,* August 5, 1983.

42. THE WHEAT ITSELF

1. *Sc W,* 39.
2. Gene Owens, "The Garden of Older Gods," in *Retrospective: Gene Owens,* exhibition catalogue (Fort Worth: Texas Christian University, 1991).
3. *Sc W,* 36.
4. Mus. Cat., 254.
5. Vivien Raynor, exhibition review, *Arts* 39, no. 9 (May–June 1965).
6. *Sc W,* 39.
7. Hilton Kramer, exhibition review, *The New York Times,* April 8, 1967.
8. IN, note in exhibition press release for *Shapes of Light,* December 1968–January 1969, NA.
9. *The New York Times,* December 7, 1968, clipping, NA.
10. Priscilla Morgan, letter to IN, January 17, 1971.
11. Bruce Altshuler, "The Akari Light Sculpture of Isamu Noguchi," 4, Noguchi Museum Web site, Research and Resources.
12. Carolyn Hall, "Noguchi Discusses Sculpture, Design," unidentified Detroit newspaper, n.d., clipping, NA.

13. Mus. Cat., 98.
14. Ibid., 116.
15. Ibid., 58.
16. Ibid., 60.
17. David L. Shirey, "Art," *Newsweek*, April 29, 1968, clipping, NA.
18. Tatsuo Kondo, "A Conversation with Isamu Noguchi," *Geijitsu Shincho*, July 19, 1968, 15–20, translated for the Noguchi Foundation, NA.
19. Kobata interview, 23.
20. *Osaka naimichi*, November 20, 1984, quoted in Duus, 359.
21. Kondo interview, 2.
22. Hilton Kramer, "Isamu Noguchi: A Selective Anthology," *The New York Times*, April 21, 1968.
23. Shirey, "Art."

43. RED CUBE, BLACK SUN

1. Katharine Kuh, "April Belonged to Noguchi," *The Saturday Review*, June 1, 1968, clipping, NA.
2. IN, "The Cube," typed text, NA.
3. Ada Louise Huxtable, "Sometimes We Do it Right," *The New York Times*, March 31, 1968.
4. John Russell, *The Sunday Times* (London), April 28, 1968.
5. "The Public Reacts to Noguchi's 'Cube,'" *Marine Midland Grace Bulletin*, April 1968, 16, clipping, NA.
6. Senie, "Urban Sculpture," 108.
7. Ibid., 111.
8. Ibid., 3.
9. Ibid., 111.
10. Katharine Chafee, "Noguchi the Artist as Poet," *The Straight Creek Journal*, October 26, 1978, 15.
11. IN, draft of presentation to USIA, 1967, NA.
12. IN, letter to Jack Masey, September 23, 1967, NA.
13. Mus. Cat., 174.
14. Kenzo Tange, telegram to IN, July, 1968, NA.
15. Mus. Cat., 174.
16. IN, "The Sculpture of Spaces," 25.
17. *The Times* (London), July 9, 1968, clipping, NA.
18. Mus. Cat., 55
19. *Sc W*, 40.
20. Ibid., 39.
21. Masatoshi Izumi, interviewed by the author, Mure, Japan, October 31, 2009. All quotes from Izumi, unless otherwise noted, come from this interview.
22. Duus, 314.
23. Mus. Cat., 19.
24. IN, letter to Richard E. Fuller, June 26, 1967, NA.
25. Richard E. Fuller, letter to IN, July 21, 1967, NA.
26. IN, letter to Tadashi Yamamoto, July 25, 1967, NA.
27. IN, letter to Richard E. Fuller, November 2, 1967, NA.

28. Tadashi Yamamoto, letter to IN, January 15, 1968, NA.
29. IN, letter to Gene Owens, May 30, 1968, Gene Owens's personal archive.
30. Taiko Okada, interviewed by the author, Takamatsu, Shikoku, Japan, October 30, 2009.
31. Masatoshi Izumi, interviewed by the author.
32. IN, letter to Ibsen Nelson, February 7, 1969, NA.
33. Unidentified clipping, n.d., probably September 1969, NA.
34. Noguchi's comment is part of a collage on the subject of his *Skyviewing Sculpture* in NA.

44. THE STONE CIRCLE

1. Masatoshi Izumi, interviewed by the author.
2. Takashi Ukita, interviewed by the author, Okayama, Japan, October 2009. All quotes from Takashi Ukita come from this interview.
3. KK, 111.
4. Katharine Kuh, *My Love Affair with Modern Art*, 204 and 208–9.
5. Ibid., 206.
6. Tadashi Yamamoto, interviewed by Ohtaka, typed transcript, NA.
7. Masatoshi Izumi, interviewed by the author.
8. Mus. Cat., 80.
9. Yamamoto, interviewed by Ohtaka.
10. Benjamin Forgey, "Noguchi at Shikoku," *Landscape Architecture* 80, no. 4 (April 1990): 58.
11. Ashton, 16.
12. Ibid., 17.
13. Duus, 324.
14. Taiko Okada, interviewed by the author.
15. Ibid.

45. TO INTRUDE ON NATURE'S WAY

1. Amei Wallach, "The Poet of Space," *Newsday* (Long Island, NY), January 2, 1989.
2. Mus. Cat., 20.
3. Katharine Kuh, "Noguchi in Japan," *World*, March 3, 1973, 61.
4. Arata Isozaki, "Listening to the Intent of Nature," in *Isamu Noguchi, Human Aspect*, 30–31.
5. Takashi Oka, tape-recorded interviews with IN, November 14 and 15, 1986. I am grateful to Jenny Dixon for providing me with the recording.
6. Margaret Sheffield, "Perfecting the Imperfect," 70.
7. Ibid., 12.
8. Elizabeth Pond, "Isamu Noguchi," interview with IN, part II, *The Christian Science Monitor*, August 24, 1973, NA.
9. *Osaka naimichi*, November 20, 1984, quoted in Duus, 359.
10. Oka, interviews with IN.
11. Mus. Cat., 40.
12. Quoted in *Isamu Noguchi: Beginnings and Ends*, exhibition catalogue (New York: Pace Wildenstein Gallery, 1994). This passage was adapted from a June 1986 interview with Noguchi at the Venice Biennale, unpublished transcript in NA.

13. Mus. Cat., 28.
14. Alhalel, "Conversation with Isamu Noguchi."
15. Sheffield, "Perfecting the Imperfect," 69.
16. Mus. Cat., 100.
17. Ibid., 64.
18. Ibid., 97.
19. Ibid., 140.
20. Anne d'Harnoncourt, interviewed by the author, Philadelphia, February 13, 2008.
21. Mus. Cat., 64.
22. Ashton, 258.
23. Arnold Glimcher, interviewed by the author, New York City, March 20, 2013.
24. IN, letter to Priscilla Morgan, October 21, 1972.
25. Shoji Sadao, interviewed by the author.
26. Glimcher, interviewed by the author.
27. *Arts* (December/January 1970–71), clipping, NA.
28. John Canaday, "Art: Recent Sculptures by Noguchi," *The New York Times*, November 14, 1970, clipping, NA.
29. John Canaday, exhibition review, *The New York Times*, May 20, 1972.
30. Varujan Boghosian, interviewed by the author, June 12, 2012.
31. IN, letter to Anne Rotzler, December 16, 1971, NA.
32. Typed manuscript for Noguchi's Minami Gallery exhibition catalogue, dated February 20, 1973, NA.
33. Linda LaMarre, "He Sculpts the Landscape," *The Detroit News Magazine*, April 15, 1979, 32.
34. Mus. Cat., 52.
35. Noguchi's correspondence with the Pace Gallery is in NA.
36. Bryan Robertson, *Noguchi's Stainless Steel Sculpture*, exhibition catalogue (New York: Pace Gallery, 1985).
37. John Russell, review of Noguchi's exhibition at Pace, *The New York Times*, June 15, 1975, clipping, NA.
38. Hilton Kramer, review of Noguchi's exhibition at Pace, *The New York Times*, May 17, 1975, clipping, NA.
39. Mus. Cat., 126.
40. Ibid., 68.
41. Ibid., 82.
42. Ibid., 124.
43. Ibid., 42.

46. A PLACE FOR PEOPLE TO GO

1. Friedman, *Imaginary Landscapes*, 80.
2. IN, proposal sent to the Horace E. Dodge Fountain Selection Committee, August 1971, NA.
3. IN, "The Road I Have Walked," 103.
4. Beamer/Wilkinson & Associates, an electrical and mechanical engineering firm based in Oakland, California, was intimately involved in the Detroit project. Others who assisted with the technological aspects were Louis W. Klei of the Department of Public Works of the City Engineers Office, and Paul Weidlinger, a good friend of

Noguchi's and a prominent structural engineer. In addition, Robert Hastings's architectural firm, Smith, Hinchman & Grylls Associates, served as structural, mechanical, and electrical consultants.

5. Smith, Hinchman & Grylls Associates Inc., *News*, March 30, 1973, NA. Noguchi was not just waxing poetic when he spoke of the relationship of his fountain to airplanes. In a 1971 letter to Sadao he wrote, "it occurred to me that the structure was very similar to that of the aeroplane wing in its relation to the fuselage."

6. Peter Benjamin, "River Plaza to Be Park—Not Monument," *Detroit Free Press*, March 31, 1973, NA.

7. IN, letter to Priscilla Morgan, September 16, 1973.

8. Martin Friedman, *Imaginary Landscapes*, 80.

9. Robert S. Wisler, "Mystery Tower Is Dedicated," *The Detroit News*, August 29, 1974.

10. Ibid.

11. *Detroit Free Press*, August 29, 1974, clipping, NA.

12. Marsha Miro, "What Noguchi's Genius Has Brought to Detroit," *Detroit Free Press*, April 29, 1979.

13. Joy Hakanson Colby, "Hart Plaza: Noguchi's Finest Hour," *The Detroit News*, April 15, 1979.

14. Luis M. Heldman, "Nice Day, Hidden Dirt and Fountain," *Detroit Free Press*, April 21, 1979.

15. Ibid.

16. Ibid.

17. Sandra Earley, "Noguchi," *The Miami Herald*, August 11, 1985.

18. Duus, 330.

19. Ashton, 212.

20. IN, preface, *The Sculpture of Spaces*.

21. Friedman, *Imaginary Landscapes*, 85.

22. Bruce W. Bassett, *Sculptors at Storm King: Seven Modern Masters*, 2000.

23. Mus. Cat., 204.

24. There are two versions of how the Storm King sculpture got its title. In one version the idea of calling it *Momo Taro* came up when Noguchi was carving the round cavity on one of the faces of the split boulder. "When the hole was carved, everyone said, 'Oh, that's Momotaro.'" The other version maintains that even before the stone was split there was a hollow cavity inside the granite boulder, and when, upon splitting the boulder, the stonecutters discovered it, they exclaimed, "Momotaro!"

25. In Shinto mythology, the sun goddess Amaterasu fled into a cave because her younger brother, god of the seas, was wreaking havoc on earth. Her absence caused darkness to fall on Japan. To lure her out, the gods hung a mirror on a tree outside her cave. Amaterasu emerged and sunlight was restored. She bequeathed the mirror to her descendant Ninigi, and this sacred mirror, part of the imperial regalia, is stored in the Ise shrine, which is dedicated to Amaterasu.

26. Bruce W. Bassett, *Isamu Noguchi*, documentary film, 1980.

27. Ashton, 278.

28. Elizabeth Pond, "Isamu Noguchi," interview with IN, part I, *The Christian Science Monitor*, August 23, 1973, NA.

29. Bruce W. Bassett, *Sculptors at Storm King: Seven Modern Masters Reveal Their Creative Adventure*, documentary film, October 1988.

47. IMAGINARY LANDSCAPES

1. IN, letter to Martin Friedman, May 17, 1977, NA.
2. Martin Friedman, letter to IN, May 20, 1977, NA.
3. Priscilla Morgan, interviewed by the author, New York City, April 17, 2008.
4. IN, letter to Fanny Rumely, August 8, 1978, LL.
5. Martin Friedman, interviewed by the author, New York, January 16, 2008.
6. Hilton Kramer, "The Purist of Living Sculptors," *The New York Times*, May 21, 1978, 33.
7. Allan Temko, exhibition reviews in the *San Francisco Chronicle*, August 8, 1979, and in the *San Francisco Sunday Examiner & Chronicle*, August 12, 1979.
8. Ann Holmes, "Noguchi Designs Planned MFA Garden," *Houston Chronicle*, September 30, 1983.
9. Carol J. Everingam, "A Place for Sculpture," *The Houston Post*, April 20, 1985, 26.
10. IN, letter to J. Patrick Lannan, January 6, 1977, NA.
11. IN, letter to Peter Marzio, April 25, 1983, NA.
12. Susan Chadwick, "Lillie and Hugh Roy Cullen Sculpture Garden," *The Houston Post*, March 30, 1986.
13. Quoted in "Sketchbook," *Art and Antiques* (Summer 1986), clipping, NA.
14. Teresa Byrne-Dodge, "A Geometry of Playfulness: The Cullen Sculpture garden at Houston's Museum of Fine Arts," *Southern Accents*, October 1986, 112, NA.
15. Interview with IN, January 3, 1986, press material for the April 6, 1986, opening of Noguchi's Houston garden, NA.
16. William Wilson, "Noguchi Comes Home," *Los Angeles Times*, May 8, 1979.
17. Tim Fukai, "Sculptor Isamu Noguchi Comes Home to Little Tokyo," August 24, 1983, unidentified newspaper, clipping, NA.
18. Miles Kubo, "Noguchi Sculpture Highlights JACCC Plaza," clipping, NA.
19. Penny Balkin Bach, interviewed by the author, Philadelphia, February 14, 2008. Noguchi's memory of the Benjamin Franklin memorial's inclusion in the Philadelphia show is slightly different. In 1987 he wrote that the model, rather than the drawing, was in the show. (He remembered wrong.) He said that a reporter discovered a 1934 clipping showing the design and that this caught the eye of the FPAA and led to the commission. Mus. Cat., 144.
20. Anne d'Harnoncourt, interviewed by the author.
21. Douglas C. McGill, "A Sculpture by Noguchi Dedicated in Philadelphia," *The New York Times*, September 19, 1984.
22. Ibid.
23. Thomas Hine, "A Flashy Birthday Gift to Philadelphia," *The Philadelphia Inquirer*, March 10, 1982, Section B, 1 and 4, NA.
24. Penny Balkin Bach, interviewed by the author.
25. Quoted in *The New York Times*, September 16, 1984, clipping, NA.
26. Thomas Hine, "A Pipe Dream Coming True," *The Philadelphia Inquirer*, September 22, 1983.
27. Thomas Hine, "A Pipe Dream Come True," *The Philadelphia Inquirer*, September 22, 1983.
28. Edgar Williams, "Ben's Bolt," *The Philadelphia Inquirer*, June 22, 1984.
29. Ibid.
30. Edward J. Sozanski, review in *The Philadelphia Inquirer*, July 15, 1984.
31. *The Philadelphia Inquirer*, July 1984, clipping, NA.

48. *CALIFORNIA SCENARIO*

1. Cathy Curtis, interview with Henry Segerstrom, "Sculptor's Spirit Lives in Garden," *Los Angeles Times*, January 15, 1989.
2. Henry Segerstrom, letter to IN, December 3, 1979, NA.
3. Tamara Thomas, letter to IN, January 17, 1980, NA. Tamara Thomas's letters to IN and his letters to her are in NA.
4. Suzanne Muchnic, "Noguchi's Garden: An Earth-Moving Project," *Los Angeles Times*, May 17, 1982.
5. Tamara Thomas, letter to IN, February 3, 1980.
6. Henry Segerstrom, letter to Tamara Thomas, March 28, 1980, NA.
7. Muchnic, "Noguchi's Garden."
8. IN, letter to Rick Anderson, August 1, 1980, NA.
9. Cathy Curtis, "Sculptor's Spirit Lives in Garden."
10. Photocopy of South Coast Plaza project data, Two Town Center, NA.
11. Photocopy of a South Coast Plaza publication, 135, NA.
12. Ibid.
13. IN, letter to Paul J. Ruffing, July 23, 1984, NA.
14. Ibid.
15. *California Scenario*'s elements are described in a brochure in NA.
16. Friedman, *Imaginary Landscapes*, 55.
17. IN, letter to Kenneth Kammeyer, October 18, 1981, NA.
18. IN, letter to Henry Segerstrom, April 2, 1982, NA.
19. Muchnic, "Noguchi's Garden."
20. Allan Temko, "Noguchi's California Parable," *San Francisco Review of Books*, September 26, 1982, 12.
21. Peter Clothier, "Costa Mesa, Isamu Noguchi, South Coast Town Center," *Artforum* (April 1982), NA.
22. Mus. Cat., 182.

49. BAYFRONT PARK

1. Kitty Roedel, telephone interview with the author, June 3, 2009. Noguchi confirmed that his involvement with Bayfront Park came about because Kitty Roedel had seen *Imaginary Landscapes* and had asked him to come to Miami. In Noguchi's memory it was his 1933 *Play Mountain* that attracted her eye. Mus. Cat., 190.
2. Roedel, interview with the author.
3. LaMarre, "He Sculpts the Landscape," 32.
4. Kitty Roedel, "The City Slant Interviews: Isamu Noguchi," *The City Slant*, Spring 1986, 7.
5. Earley, "Noguchi."
6. Jon Nordheimer, "Miami's Bayfront Park Is Focus of New Design for Downtown," *The New York Times*, n.d., clipping, NA.
7. Ronn Ronck, "Isamu Noguchi," *The Honolulu Advertiser*, n.d., clipping, NA.
8. Eric Rieder, "Unveiled for Park," *The Miami Herald*, June 17, 1980.
9. Beth Dunlop, "City Escapes," *The Miami Herald*, June 15, 1980.
10. IN, letter to Maurice Ferré, December 10, 1981, NA. Unless otherwise noted, all documents concerning Bayfront Park are in NA.
11. Roedel, interview with the author.

12. Ibid.
13. Transcript of Kitty Roedel's interview with IN, n.p., NA.
14. Roedel, interview with the author.
15. Louise Thomson, "Challenger Memorial Up in Air," *Miami Today,* January 7, 1988; and Patrick May, "Sculpture May Rise for Astronauts," *The Miami Herald,* January 7, 1988.
16. Bill Gjebre, "Challenger Memorial Fund Raising Promised," *The Miami News,* March 25, 1988.
17. Ronnie Ramor, "Suárez: Noguchi's Wall Idea Not So Bad," *The Miami Herald,* February 3, 1989.
18. Rosario Kennedy, telephone interview with the author, June 2009.
19. Earley, "Noguchi."
20. IN, statement written for the Miami Downtown Development Authority, August 9, 1984, NA.

50. ALL THINGS WORTHWHILE MUST END AS GIFTS

1. IN, note in *Hot Dipped Sculptures,* exhibition catalogue (Osaka: Kasahara Gallery, 1983).
2. IN, letter to Kitty Roedel, September 2, 1988, NA.
3. Mus. Cat., 188.
4. Alex Kerr, "Isamu Noguchi's Playground," in *Play Mountain,* 134.
5. Roedel, interview with IN, n.p.
6. Mus. Cat., 55.
7. IN, Isamu Noguchi Garden Museum brochure, NA.
8. Mus. Cat., 12.
9. Ibid.
10. Ibid., 19.
11. John Gruen, "The Artist Speaks," 29.
12. IN, "The Sculpture of Spaces," 18.
13. Mus. Cat., 24.
14. IN, "Dialogue: Isamu Noguchi," reprinted in *Essays and Conversations.*
15. Mus. Cat., 285.
16. Kobata interview, 56.
17. Roedel, interview with IN, n.p.
18. Michael McClure, "Noguchi Notes," in *Isamu Noguchi,* exhibition catalogue (Osaka: Kasahara Gallery, 1983).
19. Amei Wallach, "A One-Man Show Place," *Newsday,* February 19, 1985.
20. Jesse Kornbluth, "Noguchi Does It His Way," *New York Magazine,* May 20, 1985, 78.
21. Robert Hughes, "Sense and Sensibility in Stone," *Time,* March 17, 1980, 84.
22. Sam Hunter, "Isamu Noguchi," in *Isamu Noguchi: 75th Birthday Exhibition,* exhibition catalogue (New York: Pace Gallery and Andre Emmerich Gallery, 1980).
23. Dore Ashton, *Isamu Noguchi: Bronze and Iron Sculpture,* exhibition catalogue (New York: Pace Gallery, 1988).
24. Interview with IN at the Venice Biennale, 1986, unpublished transcript, NA.
25. Duus, 372.
26. Kobata interview, 65.
27. Shoji Sadao, interviewed by the author.
28. Unidentified newspaper, n.d., clipping, NA.
29. Kobata interview, 63.

30. Cummings interviews, 45.
31. Mary Anne Staniszewski, "Art, Inc: Behind the Biennale," *Manhattan Inc*, July 1986, 126.
32. Roedel, interview with IN, n.p.
33. IN, quoted in *Beginnings and Ends*; and IN, interview at the Venice Biennale.
34. IN, essay, exhibition catalogue, Venice Biennale, 1986.
35. Arnold Glimcher, interviewed by the author.
36. Kobata interview, 65.
37. Ibid.
38. "Art and National Identity: A Critic's Symposium," *Art in America* (September 1991), 83.
39. Roedel, interview with IN, n.p.
40. IN, letter to Gene Owens, April 22, 1986, Gene Owens's personal archive.
41. IN, interview at the Venice Biennale.
42. Kan Yasuda, "Soliloquy on the Essence of Art," in *Isamu Noguchi, Human Aspect*, 100.
43. Ibid., 100–101.
44. Issey Miyake, "Message Beyond Space-Time," in *Isamu Noguchi, Human Aspect*, 145.
45. IN, statement about *Slide Mantra* prepared for Miami officials in charge of Bayfront Park, NA.
46. John Russell Taylor, *The Times* (London), July 1, 1986, clipping, NA.
47. IN, interview at the Venice Biennale.

51. KYOKO

1. Arnold Glimcher, interviewed by the author.
2. Duus, 371.
3. Kan Yasuda, interviewed by the author, Tokyo, October 22, 2008.
4. Kyoko and Junichi Kawamura, interviewed by the author, Tokyo, October 22 and November 8, 2009.
5. IN, letter to Kyoko Kawamura, December 20, 1982, Kyoko Kawamura's personal archive. I am grateful to Kyoko Kawamura for sending me the plans and the note.
6. Kan Yasuda, interviewed by the author.
7. Duus, 344.
8. Maurice Ferré, telephone interview with the author, June 2009.
9. Ryunosuke Kasahara, interviewed by the author, Kyoto, November 6, 2009.
10. Duus, 375.
11. Arata Isozaki, "To Envision a Living Space: The Isamu Noguchi Exhibition Installation," 1984, NA.
12. Duus, 376.
13. Kyoko and Junichi Kawamura, interviewed by the author. Noguchi had said the same thing to Paul Cummings in 1973 (Cummings interviews, 71).
14. Penny Balkin Bach, interviewed by the author.
15. Penny Balkin Bach, "Cultural Konversations from the Kastro," *Art Journal* (October/December 1994), clipping, NA.
16. Penny Balkin Bach, interviewed by the author.
17. Duus, 383.
18. Alhalel, "Conversation with Isamu Noguchi."
19. Earley, "Noguchi."
20. Richard C. Dillard, article in *Economic World*, October 1988, clipping, NA.

52. NO BEGINNINGS, NO ENDINGS

1. Kyoko Kawamura, interviewed by the author, Tokyo, October 22 and November 8, 2009. All quotes from Kawamura are from these interviews.
2. Ryunosuke Kasahara, interviewed by the author.
3. Kinuko Ishihara, interviewed by the author, Kyoto, November 6, 2009.
4. Ryunosuke Kasahara, interviewed by the author.
5. Kan Yasuda, interviewed by the author.
6. Arnold Glimcher, interviewed by the author.
7. The notes that IN wrote in the hospital are in Priscilla Morgan's personal archive.
8. Masatoshi Izumi, interviewed by the author.
9. Laura J. Tuchman, "Sculptor Isamu Noguchi Remembered," *Orange County Register,* April 17, 1989, clipping, NA.
10. Obituary, *St. Paul Pioneer Press,* AP dispatch, n.d., clipping, NA.
11. Michael Brenson, "Isamu Noguchi, the Sculptor, Dies at 84," *The New York Times,* December 31, 1988.
12. Ibid.
13. Albert Elsen, *Art Journal* (December 1989–February 1990): 293, clipping, NA.
14. Calvin Tomkins, *The New Yorker,* March 9, 1990, 62, clipping, NA.
15. Michael Brenson, "Isamu Noguchi, the Sculptor, Dies at 84."
16. Tadao Ando, note in *Isamu Noguchi: The Bronzes, 1987–1988,* exhibition catalogue (Osaka: Kasahara Gallery, 1989).
17. Brenson, "Isamu Noguchi, the Sculptor, Dies at 84."
18. IN, "The Sculpture of Spaces," 24.
19. IN, letter to Julian Mack, February 14, 1964, NA.
20. *Sc W,* 28.
21. Michael Brenson, "Noguchi Holds Time in His Hands," *The New York Times,* July 20, 1982.
22. Edward M. Gomez, "The Passing of a Purist: Isamu Noguchi, 1904–1988," *Time,* January 16, 1988, 37.
23. Dore Ashton, "Noguchi," in *Isamu Noguchi: New Sculpture,* exhibition catalogue (New York: Pace Gallery, 1983), 5.
24. Milton Esterow and Sylvia Hochfield, interview with IN, "The Courage to Desecrate Emptiness," *Art News* 85, no. 3 (March 1986): 103.
25. Michael Brenson, "Noguchi Holds Time in His Hands," *The New York Times,* July 20, 1982, clipping, NA.
26. Roger Lipsey, *An Art of Our Own: The Spiritual in Twentieth Century Art* (Boston: Shambhala, 1988), 355.
27. Robert Tracy, "Artist's Dialogue: Isamu Noguchi," 72.
28. IN, note in *Sculpture by Isamu Noguchi,* exhibition catalogue (Tokyo: Minami Gallery, 1973).
29. Friedman, *Imaginary Landscapes,* 7.
30. Kobata interview, 35.
31. Levy, "Isamu Noguchi," 30.
32. *Osaka mainichi,* quoted in Duus, 359.
33. Mus. Cat., 126.

ACKNOWLEDGMENTS

The kind cooperation of many people made this biography of Isamu Noguchi possible. I am especially grateful for all the help and encouragement I received from the staff of the Isamu Noguchi Foundation and Garden Museum, New York. Jenny Dixon, with her wish to make this book as complete and accurate as possible, was a huge support. Amy Hau, whose knowledge of Noguchi is vast, provided me with box after box of archival documents. I am greatly indebted to Amy for her help. Heidi B. Coleman was unflagging in the process of finding photographs with which to illustrate this book, for which I am enormously grateful. Bonnie Rychlak shared her memories of and insights into Noguchi with me. I thank her for her generosity.

The person to whom I owe an immense debt of gratitude is the late Priscilla Morgan. She took a passionate interest in the progress of my book, cheering me on over the years. The numerous interviews I conducted with her gave me not only information about Noguchi's life but also an understanding of his person. In addition, she gave me access to her personal archive of letters to and from Noguchi.

Shoji and Tsuneko Sadao were wonderfully supportive of the project. In interviews Shoji provided me with much information, and he also helped me to make contact with people who knew Noguchi in Japan. I am deeply appreciative of the help of both Shoji and Tsuneko.

Shoji encouraged me to apply to the Japan Foundation for their Invitation Program for Cultural Leaders. I give thanks to the Japan Foundation for making it possible for me to travel to Japan to interview people who knew Noguchi; to see Noguchi's works in Japan; to visit his studio and home in Mure, Shikoku; and also to gain some understanding of Japanese culture and history. In the foundation's New York office, Mari Imaizumi was unstinting with her help. The foundation made interview appointments for me in Japan and provided me with translators to help with those interviews. I could not have written this book had I not spent three extraordinary weeks in Japan. Among the people who assisted with my work there were Katsumi Yokobori, Takako Shimizu, Ichiko Ono, and Sumiyo Terai.

Numerous people gave freely of their time and recollections in interviews in Japan, the United States, and France. In Japan I am most grateful to Tsutomu Hiroi, Kyoko and Junichi Kawamura, Kan Yasuda, Tatsuo Kondo, Yoshio Taniguchi, Shinichi Okada, Hidetaro Ozeki, Ryunosuke Kasahara, Takashi Ukita, Kinuko Ishihara, Masatoshi Izumi, Harumi Izumi, Taiko Okada, and Shinkichi Idei.

In the United States I thank all the inteviewees whose memories helped me to build a picture of Noguchi. Besides Priscilla Morgan and Shoji Sadao in New York, Gene Owens in Texas was extraordinarily generous in sharing his memories of working with Noguchi and in sending me copies of numerous documents in his personal archive. Others without whose help this book could not have been written are Martin Friedman, Arnold Glimcher, Thomas Messer, Diane Botnick, Luchita Mullican, Elaine Weitzen, Kitty Roedel, Maurice Ferré, Rosario Kennedy, Nancy Herstand, Elise Grinstein, Stan Taeger, Isaac Shapiro, Merce Cunningham, Martin Margulies, Anne d'Harnoncourt, Toshiko Takaezu, Florence Knoll Bassett, Penny Bach, Jonathan Marvel, Peter Stern, Bobbie Oliver, Mary Frank, Russell and Julie Patterson, Michael Blackwood, Michael Brenson, Noriko Prince, Nizette Brennan, Walter Dusenberry, Alexandra Snyder, Li-Lan, Rachel Horowitz, Dimitri Hadzi, Agnes Gorky Fielding, and Varujan Boghosian. In San Juan, Puerto Rico, Lucilla Fuller Marvel was generous with her recollections, and in Paris, Malitte Matta offered excellent insights.

I am thankful to the Canadian Centre for Architecture in Montreal for giving me access to their archive of correspondence between Noguchi and Ann Matta Clark, and I am deeply grateful to Giovanna Carnevale, who did research in this archive and made copies of letters for me.

I am grateful to the owners of Noguchi's works for the privilege of reproducing photographs of their sculptures in my book. In particular, the Isamu Noguchi Foundation and Garden Museum has been marvelously generous in providing me with image files of Noguchi's works and in giving me permission to illustrate them in this biography.

A special note of appreciation goes to my editors, Ileene Smith and John Knight. They have worked brilliantly and hard to shape my manuscript into a book. The copy editor, Walter Havighurst, did a heroic job of tidying text and catching errors. Jonathan Lippincott designed the book with a sure sense of scale and placement. Finally, and most important, I wish to thank my husband, Desmond Heath, for his amazing support during the years in which I was researching and writing Noguchi's biography.

INDEX

Page numbers in *italics* refer to illustrations.

ILLUSTRATION CREDITS

Berenice Abbott: page 143
Rhont Alhalel: page 502
Shigeo Anzai: pages 389, 485, 505
Henry Buhl: page 483
Rudy Burckhardt: page 221
Arnold Eagle: page 214
Eliot Elisofon: pages 188, 227
Green Area Department, City of Sapporo: page 496
Bill Jacobson: page 343 (Mortality)
F. S. Lincoln: pages 106, 131, 133
Barbara Morgan: page 145
Kevin Noble: pages 96, 102 (Marion Greenwood), 190 (both images), 191, 192, 194, 197, 225, 237 (Bird's Nest), 270 (both images), 316, 319, 321, 373, 393, 422, 423 (both images), 433 (both images), 477, 479, 491
Michio Noguchi: pages 341 (Woman and Child), 397, 400, 409, 413, 419, 424, 444, 464
Stephanie Rancou: page 481
Ezra Stoller: page 357
Atelier Stone: pages 93, 95, 97
Soichi Sunami: page 240
Martha Swope: page 359
William Taylor: pages 193, 382
Charles Uht: page 311
Vytas Valaitis: pages ii–iii
Kozo Watabiki: pages 469, 472